Sara McLanahan

Family in Transition

Family in Transition

**Rethinking Marriage,
Sexuality,
Child Rearing,
and Family Organization**

Fourth Edition

Arlene S. Skolnick
Jerome H. Skolnick
University of California, Berkeley

Little, Brown and Company
Boston   Toronto

Library of Congress Cataloging in Publication Data
Main entry under title:

Family in transition.

    1. Family—Addresses, essays, lectures.
I. Skolnick, Arlene S., 1933–   . II. Skolnick,
Jerome H.
HQ518.F336   1983   306.8′5   82-14914
ISBN 0-316-79706-5

Library of Congress Catalog Card Number 82-14914

ISBN 0-316-79706-5

9 8 7 6 5 4 3 2 1

MU

Published simultaneously in Canada
by Little, Brown & Company (Canada) Limited

Printed in the United States of America

Produced by Ron Newcomer & Associates

Cover Photo Credits:

Front Cover: (top) Alen MacWeeney/Archive Pictures Inc.;
   (middle) Helen Nestor; *(bottom)* Dick Schwartz/Office of Human
   Development Services/Department of Health & Human Services

Back Cover: Stephen Spielman

For the fourth time, for Michael and Alexander

Preface to the Fourth Edition

Family life in America has been "in transition" since we began to work on the first edition of this book, over a decade ago. In looking over the three earlier editions, we have been struck not only by how much families themselves have changed, but how different was the climate of opinion about the family each time we set about doing a new revision. We have tried to describe these differences in the introduction.

In this fourth edition, nearly half the articles are new. We have been torn between keeping old favorites and making room for new writing, which continues to grow in quantity and quality. We are pleased to be reprinting selections from two major recent books on family—Andrew Cherlin's *Marriage, Divorce, Remarriage*, a study of recent demographic trends in family life, and *Middletown Families*, in which Theodore Caplow and colleagues report on how the family has fared in the community studied over 50 years ago by Helen and Robert Lynd. There is a new section on relationships, reflecting the various forms intimacy is taking these days, as well as the theoretical interests of researchers trying to understand the nature of close bonds. There is also a new section on public policy and the family. Other new topics include the impact of changing death rates on family life, the effects of unemployment, and that menacing and embarrassing by-product of sexual revolution—herpes.

By now we have had so many conversations with colleagues that it is hard to know how to single them out. We are grateful to the students and teachers who have used this book and helped shape its contents with their comments and assessments of articles which appeared in the last editions. As always, the Center for the Study of Law and Society and its staff—headed by Rod Watanabe—have provided able and critical assistance. We are especially grateful to Christina Miller, who guided the manuscript through various phases of completion, and are also grateful to our research assistant, Merry Kassoy, who located materials that were difficult to find.

Arlene Skolnick
Jerome H. Skolnick
Berkeley, California
September, 1982

Contents

the possibility of pleasures long denied, for others it has created new problems.

Family in Transition

Introduction:
Family in Transition

As the 1980s began, the conservative columnist Paul Weyrich predicted that the family would be to the coming decade what the Vietnam War was to the 1960s. "Family" had become a fighting word, linked to some of the most explosive issues in American politics: abortion, school busing, the Equal Rights Amendment, censorship, school prayer, the rights of homosexuals. "The family" has been an important theme in the past two presidential elections. A White House Conference on Families, promised by Jimmy Carter in the campaign of 1976, took years to arrange and eventually turned into a battleground between opposing groups. Each defended its own definition of the family and its own view of the most important problems facing the family.

The political uproar followed more than a decade of dramatic changes. The leading statistical indicators of family life provide the most clear-cut evidence of recent shifts (Weed, 1981). Divorce has risen to record levels; if current rates persist, almost half of all marriages will end in divorce. Marriage rates have declined to the lowest level since 1940; in 1980 a fifth of all women between the ages of twenty-five and thirty had still never married. Single-parent families increased by more than three quarters during the 1970s, while married-couple families with children actually declined in number.

Birth rates also declined. Despite the fact that the women born during the post–World War II baby boom are now starting to have babies, there is little likelihood that we will see a new baby boom. During the 1970s, the number of women in the labor force, including married women with children under eighteen, increased and reached what Jessie Bernard (1975) has called a "tipping point." This is the moment that a formerly "normal" pattern of behavior—in this case being a full-time housewife—becomes the choice of a minority. Premarital sex also passed a tipping point in the 1970s; by 1980, few brides were virgins, and sex became, for most Americans, a normal part of male-female relationships.

The number of unmarried couples living together has also risen. In 1980 the number of such couples counted by the Census Bureau had reached 1,560,000—three times the number in 1970. Although the proportion of unmarried adults in such arrangements is small, the younger generation is

1

approaching the level of Sweden, where 12 percent of all couples live together informally (Trost, 1976). Attitudes toward unmarried cohabitation have changed also. No longer considered living in sin or confined to the very poor, it has become a socially acceptable way of life in middle-class circles, especially among educated and professional persons.

The rise of the single-person household marks another significant departure from the past, when the unattached individual was likely to live with relatives or with an unrelated family. In 1980 about 23 percent of American households contained only one person. This population consists mainly of two age groups: young people who have not yet married and the formerly married, mostly older people who have lost a spouse. Not only are unattached individuals more likely to live in nonfamily households, but there has been marked increase in the population of young singles. Whether these young men and women will marry later or never remains to be seen.

In addition to census data, a variety of surveys also indicates important changes in attitudes. The avant-garde ideas of the 1960s concerning such matters as premarital sexuality, women's equality, and the value of self-realization have spread to the mainstream of the American population. For example, between 1964 and 1974, surveys of women's attitudes revealed a consistent trend away from tradition and toward greater similarity between men's and women's roles inside and outside the home (Mason, Czajka, & Aiker, 1976). In 1957, four fifths of the respondents in one national survey thought that a man or woman who did not want to marry was sick, immoral, and selfish. By 1976, only one fourth of respondents thought that choice was bad. Two thirds were neutral, and one seventh viewed the choice as good (*ISR Newsletter*, 1979). A major study of changes in American attitudes over two decades reveals a profound change in how people think about family life, work, and themselves (Veroff, Douvan, & Kulka, 1981). Summing up many complex findings, the authors conclude that America has undergone a "psychological revolution" in the past twenty years. Twenty years ago, people defined their satisfactions and problems—and indeed, themselves—in terms of how well they lived up to traditional work and family roles. Today, people have become more introspective, more attentive to inner experience. Fulfillment now means finding intimacy, meaning, and self-definition, rather than the satisfactory performance of traditional roles.

All of these changes, occurring in a relatively short time, have given rise to fears about the future of the family. Anyone who watches television, reads newspapers, *Time*, or *Newsweek* will learn, again and again, that the family is "breaking down," "falling apart," "declining," "disintegrating," "disappearing," "besieged," or at the very least, "in trouble." In part, these anxieties about the family account for much of the appeal of the so-called Moral Majority and the New Right. There is a great nostalgia for the good old days before the advent of working women, high divorce rates and the "me generation."

Meanwhile, during the same years in which the family has been emerging as an object of public anxiety and debate, a large number of scholars have been quietly turning out a torrent of research on the family, past and present. Once something of a scholarly backwater in the field of sociology, the study of the family has recently excited the interest of scholars in a range of disciplines—history, demography, economics, law, psychology, and psychiatry. As a result of this new interest and new methods, the field of family studies is flourishing and providing us with more information about family life than has ever before been available. Ironically, much of the new scholarship is at odds with the public perception that the family is in crisis, as well as with the nostalgic notion that in the past, families were strong and stable.

Because of the shifts in public beliefs about the family, as well as the new family scholarship, this fourth edition of *Family in Transition* is in many ways different from the first. In the first edition of this book, we had to argue strenuously that the middle-class family patterns of the 1950s and early 1960s did not represent a model of the family in all times and places. Strange as it now seems, most family sociologists tended to dismiss any signs of change in the family as illusions or misconceptions. They also discounted the possibility that there could be serious changes in family roles, expectations, and behavior.

When we put together the first edition of this book over twelve years ago, the changes that are now commonplace were just beginning to be felt. The youth movements of the 1960s and the emerging women's movement were challenging many of the assumptions on which conventional marriage and family patterns had been based. The mass media were regularly presenting stories that also challenged in one way or another traditional views on sex, marriage, and family. For example, people were becoming aware of "the population explosion" and of the desirability of "zero population growth." There was a growing realization that the ideal three-, four-, or five-child family of the fifties might not be very good for the country as a whole, nor for every couple. Meanwhile, Hollywood movies were presenting a new and cynical view of marriage. It was almost taken for granted that marriages were unhappy, particularly if the spouses were middle class, middle aged, or affluent. Most dramatically, many people were openly defying conventional standards of behavior. Thus, college girls were beginning to live openly with young men, unwed movie actresses were publicizing rather than hiding their pregnancies, and homosexuals were beginning openly to protest persecution and discrimination.

It seemed as if something was happening to family life in America, even if there were no sharp changes in the major statistical indicators of family life, or in sexual behavior, or in the division of labor between husbands and wives. People seemed to be looking at sex, marriage, parenthood, and family life in new ways, even if behavior on a mass scale was not changing very noticeably.

Thus, we argued that significant social and cultural change could happen even without massive changes in overt behavior patterns. We quoted the observation of John Gagnon and William Simon (1970) that the moment of change may be when new forms of behavior seem plausible. For example, even though there was no evidence that the size of the homosexual population had grown, homosexuality had become a more plausible form of behavior. That is, knowing someone was a homosexual did not automatically mean that he or she was to be defined as a moral pariah. In the same way, whether or not there had been great changes in rates of premarital sex or unwed motherhood, the fact that people could now be open about such behavior and go on in normal ways with the rest of their lives seemed highly significant.

In putting together the readings for that first edition of *Family in Transition*, we found relatively little awareness that changes in sexuality, marriage, and parenthood were happening. More importantly, as we have seen, the professional literature seemed to deny that change was possible in family structure, the relations between the sexes, and parenthood. The following were thought to be here to stay: The conventional nuclear family, the male as the sole breadwinner, the dependent housewife, and premarital virginity.

Most social scientists shared a particular set of assumptions about the nature of the family and its relation to society: human beings were equipped with a fixed set of psychological needs and tendencies, which were expressed in the family. An extreme version of this view was the statement by an anthropologist that the nuclear family (mother, father, and children) "is a biological phenomenon . . . as rooted in organs and physiological structures as insect societies" (La Barre, 1954, p. 104). Another major assumption was that family stability was the basis of social order. Any changes in the basic structure of the family roles or in childrearing were assumed to be unworkable, if not unthinkable.

The family in modern society was portrayed as a streamlined, more highly evolved version of a universal family. The traditional or preindustrial family was a workplace, a school, a hospital. According to Talcott Parsons and his followers (1951, 1954), the modern family underwent structural differentiation or specialization. It transferred work and educational roles to other agencies and specialized in childrearing and emotional support. No less important for having relinquished certain tasks, the modern family was now the only part of society to carry out such functions.

These ideas about the family have lost their credibility. As Glenn Elder (1978) recently observed, the study of the family and its relation to social change during the postwar era was "shaped more by simplistic abstract theory and ideological preferences" than by the detailed study of the realities of family life in particular times, places, and circumstances.

The family theories of the postwar era were descriptively correct insofar as they portrayed the ideal middle-class family patterns of a particular society at a particular historical period. But they went astray in elevating the status quo to the level of a timeless necessity. In addition, the theories could not embrace variations in family lives or stylistic change. Such family life-styles as, for example, that of the working mother or the single-parent family, could be seen only as deviant. Similarly, social change in family life on a large scale, as in the rise of women's employment or of divorce, could be interpreted only as social disorder and the disintegration of the social system.

Still another flaw in the dominant sociological view was its neglect of major internal strains within the family, even when it was presumably functioning as it was supposed to do. Paradoxically, these strains were vividly described by the very theorists who idealized the role of the family in modern society. Parsons, for example, noted that when home no longer functioned as an economic unit, women, children, and old people were placed in an ambiguous position. They became dependent on the male breadwinner and were cut off from society's major source of achievement and status.

Parsons saw women's roles as particularly difficult; being a housewife was not a real occupation. It was vaguely defined, highly demanding, yet not considered real work in a society that measures achievement by the size of one's paycheck. The combination of existing strains and the demystifying effects of the challenges to the family status quo seem to have provided, as Judith Blake (1978, p.11) points out, a classic set of conditions for social change.

A Time of Troubles

The recent changes in the family would have been unsettling even if other social conditions had remained stable. But everything else was also changing quickly. Despite assassinations and turmoil in the streets, the sixties were an optimistic period. Both the dissident movements and the establishment agreed that progress was possible, that problems could be solved, and that today's children would live in a better world. Both sides believed in limitless economic growth.

No one foresaw that the late 1970s would dramatically reverse this optimism and the social and economic conditions that had sustained it. The seventies were a time of deepening malaise. Rather than hearing of limitless abundance and an end to scarcity and poverty, we heard of lowered expectations, survival, and lifeboat ethics. For the first time in history, Americans had to confront the possibility that their children and children's children might not lead better lives.

This malaise, arising from sources outside the family, seems to be mingling in strange ways with the attitudinal and behavioral changes of recent years. There is some evidence that people are turning inward toward home, family, and private life. People who think of themselves as critics of society no longer necessarily assume that they must also be critics of the family or of monogamy.

In fact, one of the surprising themes of this historical moment is the cele-bration of family in the name of social criticism. A new domesticity of the left has emerged on the intellectual scene. For some, the defense of the fam-ily is a new way of fighting an old enemy—corporate capitalism. For others, marching under the banner of the family seems to be a means of advancing social policies that can no longer be justified in the name of the poor. Ken-neth Keniston and the Carnegie Council on Children, for example, in their report *All Our Children* (1977) reflect this familistic trend. Their liberal pol-icy analysis would increase government spending for families. Meanwhile, conservatives fall back on the family as a way of reducing the state's budget-ary problems: if families would take care of the very young, the very old, the sick, and the mentally ill, there would be less need for day care, hospitals, Social Security, and public resources and agencies.

Some radical attacks on the modern world and its ways seem consonant with traditional conservative arguments. Historian Christopher Lasch (1978) argues that while the family once provided a haven of love and decency in a heartless world, it no longer does so. The family has been invaded by outside forces—advertising, the media, experts, and family professionals—and stripped of its functions and authority. Corporate capitalism, with its need for limitless consumption, has created a "culture of narcissism," in which nobody cares about anybody else.

While Lasch laments the passing of the strong, authoritarian father, Alice Rossi (1978) denounces the intrusion of technological society into the natural biological processes of motherhood. In a startling reversal of her earlier fem-inist writings, Rossi revives the idea of biologically based maternal instincts.

All of this ferment has made our task here more complicated. In the past we had to argue against the overly optimistic assumptions of the 1950s view that all was for the best in the best of all possible family and social worlds. Now it is necessary to deal with pessimism of the 1980s. In its most extreme form, this pessimism turns the notion of progress upside down and replaces it with a fierce nostalgia. The past is portrayed as a time of strong and stable families, while the present is interpreted as a nightmarish wasteland with hardly a single redeeming virtue. Reality of course lies somewhere in be-tween; change does not always mean progress, but it does not always mean social disorganization either.

The State of the Contemporary Family

What sense *can* be made of the current changes in family life? The various statistics we quoted earlier can be and are being interpreted to show that the family is either thriving or falling apart. Falling birthrates can be taken to mean that people are too selfish to want to have any or many children. Or they can mean that people are no longer having children by accident, without thought, or because of social pressure, but because they truly want children. High divorce rates can signify that marriage is an institution on the rocks or is considered so important that people will no longer put up with the kinds of dissatisfactions and empty-shell marriages previous generations tolerated. High rates of remarriage could mean that people are giving up not on marriage but on unsatisfactory relationships. Or they can be thought to mean that the strain of living in a capitalistic society drives people into marriage but makes marriage difficult to sustain. Is the rise in illegitimacy a sign of moral breakdown? Or does it simply reflect a different, more enlightened set of moral norms, reflecting a society no longer eager to punish unmarried mothers or to damage a child's life chances because of the circumstances of its birth?

Part of the confusion surrounding the current status of the family arises from the fact that the family is an inherently problematic area of study; there are few if any self-evident facts, even statistical ones. Take, for example, the recent trends in family life we mentioned earlier—rising divorce rates and declining marriage and birth rates. Such statistics are often cited as evidence that the family is indeed falling apart. But the meaning of such statistics is far from clear.

Researchers have found that when the statistics of family life are plotted for the entire twentieth century, or back into the nineteenth century, a surprising finding emerges: today's young people—with their low marriage, high divorce, and low fertility rates—appear to be behaving in ways consistent with long-term historical trends (Cherlin, 1981; Masnick & Bane, 1980). The recent changes in family life only appear deviant when compared to what people were doing in the 1940s and 1950s. The now middle-aged adults who married young, moved to the suburbs, and had three, four, or more children, were the generation that departed from twentieth-century trends. As one study put it, "Had the 1940s and 1950s not happened, today's young adults would appear to be behaving normally" (Masnick & Bane, 1980, p. 2).

Thus, the meaning of change in a particular indicator of family life depends on the time frame it is placed in. If we look at trends over too short a period of time—say ten or twenty years—we may think we are seeing a marked change, when, in fact, an older pattern may be reemerging. For some issues, even discerning what the trends are can be a problem. Whether or not we conclude that there is an "epidemic" of teenage pregnancy depends on how we define adolescence and what measure of illegitimacy we use. Contrary to the popular notion of skyrocketing teenage pregnancy, teenaged childbearing has actually been on the decline during the past decade (Furstenberg et al., 1981). It is possible for the *ratio* of illegitimate births to all births to go up at the same time as there are declines in the *absolute* number of such births and in the likelihood that an individual will bear an illegitimate child. This is not to say that concern about teenage pregnancy is unwarranted, but the reality is much more complex than the simple and scary notion of an "epidemic" implies.

Given the complexities of interpreting data on the family, it is little wonder that, as Joseph Featherstone observed (1979, p. 37), the family is a "great intellectual Rorschach blot." One's conclusions about the current state of the family often derive from deeper values and assumptions one holds in the first place about the definition and role of the family in society. We noted earlier that the family theories of the postwar era were largely discredited within sociology itself (Blake, 1978; Elder, 1978). Yet many of the assumptions of those theories continue to influence discussions of the family in both popular and scholarly writings. Let us look in more detail at these persistent assumptions.

1: The Assumption of the Universal Nuclear Family

To say that the family is the same everywhere is in some sense true. But the differences are more interesting, just as a portrait of an individual is interesting because of the person's uniqueness rather than because faces usually have eyes, ears, and a mouth. Families possess even more dissimilar traits than do faces. They vary in organization, membership, life cycles, emotional environments, ideologies, social and kin networks, and economic and other functions. Although anthropologists have tried to come up with a single definition of family that would hold across time and place, they generally have concluded that doing so is not useful (Geertz, 1965; Stephens, 1963).

The idea of the universal nuclear family is based on biology: A woman and a man must unite sexually to produce a child. But no social kinship ties or living arrangements flow inevitably from biological union. Indeed, the definition of marriage is not the same across cultures. Although some cultures have weddings and notions of monogamy and permanence, many cultures lack one or more of these attributes. In some cultures, the majority of people mate and have children without legal marriage and often without living together. In other societies, husbands, wives, and children do not live together under the same roof.

In our own society, the assumption of universality has usually defined what is normal and natural both for research and therapy and has subtly influenced our thinking to regard deviations from the nuclear family as sick or perverse or immoral. As Suzanne Keller (1971) points out:

> The fallacy of universality has done students of behavior a great disservice. By leading us to seek and hence to find a single pattern, it has blinded us to historical precedents for multiple legitimate family arrangements.

An example of this disservice is the treatment of illegitimacy. For decades the so-called principle of legitimacy, set forth by Malinowski (1930), was taken as evidence for the universality of the nuclear family. The principle stated that in every society a child must have a socially recognized father to give the child a status in the community. Malinowski's principle naturally leads to the assumption that illegitimacy is a sign of social breakdown.

Although the principle has been usually treated by social scientists as if it were a natural law, in fact it is based on certain prior assumptions about society (Goode, 1960; Blake, 1978). Chiefly, it assumes that children inherit their status from their father or from family origin rather than achieve it themselves. The traditional societies that anthropologists study are of course societies that do ascribe status in this way. Modern, democratic societies, such as the United States, are based, in theory at least, on achievement; a child's future is not supposed to be determined solely by who its father happens to be. The Malinowski principle, however compelling in understanding traditional societies, hence has decreasing relevance for modern ones. Current legal changes that blur the distinction between legitimate and illegitimate births may be seen as a way of bringing social practice in line with national ideals.

2. The Assumption of Family Harmony

Every marriage, as Jessie Bernard (1973) has pointed out, contains two marriages: the husband's and the wife's. Similarly, every family contains as many families as family members. Family members with differing perspectives may find themselves in conflict, occasionally in bitter conflict. Outside intervention is sometimes necessary to protect the weaker from the stronger. Those who romanticize the family as a haven of nurture are curiously silent on the problem of child abuse or other kinds of family violence.

To question the idea of the happy family is not to say that love and joy are not found in family life or that many people do not find their deepest satisfactions in their families. Rather, the happy family assumption omits important, if unpleasant, aspects of family life. Western society has not always assumed such a sentimental model of the family. From the Bible to the fairy tale, from Sophocles to Shakespeare to Eugene O'Neill to the soap opera, there is a tragic tradition portraying the family as a high-voltage emotional setting, charged with love and hate, tenderness and spite, even incest and murder.

There is also a low comedy tradition. George Orwell once pointed out that the world of henpecked husbands and tyrannical mothers-in-law is as much a part of the Western cultural heritage as Greek drama. Although the comic tradition tends to portray men's discontents rather than women's, it scarcely views the family as a setting for ideal happiness.

Nor have social theorists always portrayed the family as harmoniously fulfilling the needs of its members and society. Around the turn of the century, the founders of sociology took for granted that conflict was a basic part of social life and that individuals, classes, and social institutions would struggle to promote their own interests and values. Freud and Simmel were among the leading conflict theorists of the family. They argued that intimate relations inevitably involve antagonism as well as love. This mixture of strong positive and negative feelings sets close relationships apart from less intimate ones.

In recent years, family scholars in a number of areas have been reviving these older ideas about the family. Some scholars have even been studying such family violence as child abuse and wife beating to understand better the realistic strains of family life. Long-known facts about family violence have not until recently been incorporated into a general analysis of the family. More policemen are killed and injured dealing with family fights than in dealing with any other kind of situation; of all the relationships between murderers and their victims, the family relationship is most common (Steinmetz and Straus, 1974). Recent studies of family violence reveal that it is much more widespread than had been assumed, cannot easily be attributed to mental illness, and is not confined to the lower classes. Family violence seems to be a product of psychological tensions and external stresses that can affect all families at all social levels.

The study of family interaction has also undermined the traditional image of the happy, harmonious family. About two decades ago, researchers and therapists began to bring mental patients and their families together to watch how they behaved with one another. Was there something about family interaction that could explain the behavior of disturbed offspring? Oddly, whole family groups had not been systematically studied before.

At first, the family interactions were interpreted as pathogenic: a parent expressing affection in words but showing nonverbal hostility, alliances being made between different family members, families having secrets, one family member being singled out as a scapegoat to be blamed for the family's troubles, parents caring for children only as reflections of themselves, parents making belittling and sarcastic statements to children. As more and more families began to be studied, such patterns were found in many families, not just in those families with a schizophrenic child. As comparisons were made, it became harder to perceive differences between normal families and those with mentally ill offspring. Although family processes discovered by this line of research did not teach us much about the causes of mental illness, they made an important discovery about family life: so-called normal families can often be, in the words of one study, "difficult environments for interaction."

3. The Assumption of Parental Determinism

Throughout American history, the family has been seen as the basis of social order and stability. Through reproduction and socialization, the family presumably guarantees the continuation of society through time. Traditionally, theories of socialization have taken either of two perspectives. In the first—social molding—the child is likened to a blank slate or lump of clay, waiting to be shaped by the environment. In the second—animal taming—the infant is a wild beast, whose antisocial instincts need to be tamed by parents.

Despite their differences, both views of socialization have much in common. Both consider children as passive objects and assign an all-powerful, Pygmalion-like role to parents. Both view the child's later life as a reenactment of early experience. Both view conformity to social norms as the outcome of successful socialization. Both tend to blame deviance of any kind (mental illness, crime, drug use) on the family. Finally, both share a view of socialization as a precarious enterprise, with failure and unhappiness the likely result of any parental mistake.

Although the belief that early family experience is the most powerful influence in a child's life is widely shared by social scientists and the public, it is not well supported by evidence and theory. There are serious flaws in two of its underlying assumptions: the assumption of the passive child and the assumption that parents independently exert influence in a virtual vacuum.

The model of the passive child is no longer tenable. Recent empirical work in human development shows that children come into the world with unique temperamental and other characteristics, and children shape parents as much as parents shape children. Further, thanks to the monumental work of Piaget in intellectual development and of Chomsky in language development, we know that the child's mind is not an empty vessel or a blank state to be filled by parental instruction. Children are active agents in the construction of knowledge about the world. Even behavioristic, stimulus-response psychologists recognize the importance of the child's own activity in the learning process.

The assumption of parental determinism is also not well founded. Parents are not simply independent agents who train children free of outside influence. An employed parent may behave quite differently than an unemployed one. Parents indirectly communicate to their children what to worry about—job loss, prejudice, and discrimination. The stresses or supports parents find in the neighborhood, the workplace, the economy, and the political climate all influence childrearing.

Children also learn from the world around them. The parental determinism model has encouraged the peculiar belief that children know nothing about the world except what parents teach. Poor black children therefore are said to do badly in school because their parents fail to use the right techniques. It is easier to blame the parents than to change the neighborhood, the school, or the economy or to assume that ghetto children's correct perception of their life chances has something to do with school performance.

Finally, other kinds of research show that early experience is not the all-powerful, irreversible kind of influence it has been thought to be. An unfortunate childhood does not necessarily lead to a despairing adulthood. Nor does a happy childhood guarantee a similarly sunny adulthood (McFarlane, 1964).

4. The Assumption of a Stable, Harmonious Past

Laments about the current decay of the family imply some earlier era when the family was more stable and harmonious than it is now. But unless we can agree what earlier time should be chosen as a baseline and what characteristics of the family should be selected for, it makes little sense to speak of family decline. Historians have not, in fact, located a golden age of the family gleaming at us from the depths of history (Demos, 1975).

Recent historical studies of family life also cast doubt on the reality of family tranquility. Historians have found that premarital sexuality, illegitimacy, generational conflict, and even infanticide can best be studied as a part of family life itself rather than as separate categories of deviation.

The division of families into a normal type and a pathological type is simply not borne out by historical evidence. For example, William Kessen (1965), in his history of the field of child study, observes:

> Perhaps the most persistent single note in the history of the child is the reluctance of mothers to suckle their babies. The running war between the mother, who does not want to nurse, and the philosopher-psychologists, who insist she must, stretches over two thousand years (pp. 1–2).

The most shocking finding of the new historical studies is the prevalence of infanticide throughout European history. Infanticide has long been attributed to primitive peoples or assumed to be the desperate act of an unwed mother. It now appears that infanticide provided a major means of population control in all societies lacking reliable contraception, Europe included, and that it was practiced by families on legitimate children. Historians now believe that rises and falls in recorded birthrates may actually reflect variations in infanticide rates (Shorter, 1973).

David Hunt's (1970) study of childrearing practices in early modern France found what would be considered by today's standards widespread mistreatment of children or, as he puts it, a "breakdown in parental care," although his study was limited to upper-class families. Rather than being an instinctive trait, having tender feelings toward infants—the sense that a baby is a precious individual—seems to emerge only when infants have a decent chance of surviving and adults experience enough security to avoid feeling that children are competing with them in a struggle for survival. Throughout many centuries of European history, both of these conditions were lacking. In the allocation of scarce resources, European society, as one historian put it, preferred adults to children (Trexler, 1973, p. 110).

Even during more recent and prosperous historical times, the nostalgic image of a more stable and placid family turns out to be a myth. Death and birth, essentially uncontrollable and unpredictable, hovered constantly over every household only about seventy years ago. It is hard to comprehend how profoundly family life has been affected by the reduction in mortality and spread of contraception during the past six or seven decades. Although infant and child mortality rates had begun to decline a century earlier, the average family could not assume it would see all its infants survive to middle or old age. Death struck most often at children. But adults with an average life expectancy of about fifty years (Ridley, 1972) would often die in the prime of their productive years. The widow and widower with young children were more familiar figures on the social landscape than the divorced person is today.

To put it another way, it has been only during the twentieth century that a majority of people could expect to live out a normal family cycle: leaving home, marrying, having children, and surviving to age fifty with one's spouse still alive. Before 1900, only 40 percent of the female population experienced this life cycle. The majority either died before they got married, never married, died before childbirth, or were widowed while their children were still young (Uhlenberg, 1974).

Contrary to the myth of the three-generation family in past time, grandparents are also a twentieth-century phenomenon (Hareven, 1978). In the past, when people lived shorter lives, they married later. The lives of parents and children thus had fewer years in which to overlap. As a result of these trends, there is for the first time in history a significant number of families with four generations alive at the same time.

A Heritage of Family Crisis

Our ancestors not only experienced family instability, they worried about the shakiness of the family as an institution. The idea that the family is falling apart is not really new. In fact, if we use a deep enough historical perspective, we see that the postwar era with its optimistic view of family life was the exception rather than the rule in American life. It was part of what one historian calls "the long amnesia" (Filene, 1975): the decades between the 1920s and the 1960s during which concerns were muted about family crises, women's roles, childrearing, and declining morals, which had so agitated earlier generations. Anxiety about the family is an American tradition. Some historians trace it to the 1820s and the beginning of industrialism. Others would date the sense of crisis even earlier, from the time the first settlers set foot on American soil. Immigration, the frontier, geographic and social mobility—the basic ingredients of the American experience—were all disruptive of parental authority and familial bonds.

Although concern about the family may have begun earlier, anxiety increased during the second quarter of the nineteenth century, and discussions took on an entirely new tone. There began to be a widespread sense of alarm about the decline of the family and of parental authority. A new self-consciousness about family life emerged; writings about the family dealt anxiously with the proper methods of childrearing and with women's special roles.

In contrast to earlier periods, people began to experience a split between public and private life: the world outside the home came to be seen as cold, ugly, and threatening, while the home became a cozy retreat. The home was idealized as a place of perfect love and harmony, while at the same time it was blamed as the cause of juvenile delinquency, crime, and mental illness. These conflicting themes have a decidedly contemporary ring.

The Rise of the Modern Family

These anxieties about the family that began in the 1820s were in response to the changed circumstances brought about by modernization, a shorthand way of referring to the massive growth of industrial capitalism that occurred in the nineteenth century. Modernization created dilemmas for family life that have not been resolved to this day. Although the changes and dilemmas to be discussed in the following paragraphs exist to some extent in all urbanized, advanced technological societies (i.e., in the Soviet Union and Eastern Europe as well as the United States), they may be found in their purest and most acute form under advanced capitalism, particularly in America.

Modernization implies not merely economic or technological change but also profound social and psychological change. It affects all aspects of life: the physical environment, the types of communities people live in, the way they view the world, the way they organize their daily lives, the meaning of work, the emotional quality of family relationships, plus the most private aspects of individual experience.

It is, of course, a great oversimplification to talk about the effects of modernization on what is known as the family. Living in an industrial economy has had a different impact on people in different social classes and ethnic groups. Poor and working-class families were and still are confronted with survival issues: the need for steady incomes, decent housing, and health care, the tensions that result from not being sure basic needs will be met. In order to ensure survival and because their values tend to be familistic rather than individualistic, working-class, immigrant, and poor families have usually depended on strong networks of kin and kinlike friendships. Middle-class, affluent families, freed from worries about basic subsistence, confront in more acute ways the social and psychological dilemmas brought on by modernization. They more often fit the model of the inwardly turned, emotionally intense, relatively isolated nuclear family.

Since the nineteenth century, when the effects of industrialism and urbanization began really to be felt, scholars have debated the impact of industrialization on the family. Many scholars and laymen were convinced that the family had outlived its usefulness. For the first time in history, men and women could find work and satisfy basic needs outside the bonds of blood or marriage. They felt, therefore, that the family would disintegrate.

The functional sociologists of the postwar era scoffed at predictions of family disintegration. As we saw earlier, they judged it to be more important than ever. The family nurtured and raised children and provided refuge for adults from the impersonality and competition of public and industrial life.

It now appears that both views were right and wrong. Those who thought that life in a mass society would undermine family life were correct. But they were wrong in assuming that most people would want to spend their lives as isolated individuals. Those who argued that the conditions of urban-industrial society create exceptional needs for nurturant, intimate relationships were also correct. But they never understood that those same conditions would make it hard for the family to fulfill such needs. Family ties have become more intense than they were in the past, and yet at the same time they have become more fragile.

Although most Western Europeans never lived in large extended-family households (Laslett and Wall, 1972), kinship ties exerted much stronger constraints over the individual before the modern era. Work and marriage were not matters of individual choice. A person's economic and marital destiny was determined by hereditary status, tradition, and economic necessity. Continuity of marriages and conformity to prescribed behavior, both within the family and outside it, were enforced by severe economic, familial, and community sanctions.

Another extremely important aspect of family life in past times was its embeddedness in the community. The home was not set off as a private place, a refuge to make up for deprivations in the world of work. There was no world of work outside the home; family members were fellow workers. Nor did the world outside one's front door consist of strangers or half-strangers, as neighbors often are today. Rather, most people lived in a community of people known since childhood and with whom one would expect to have dealings for the rest of one's life. These outsiders could enter the household freely and were entitled, and even obligated, to intervene if relations between parents and children and husbands and wives were not as they should be. The most vivid example of community control over family life in preindustrial times was the practice known as *charivari:* community festivals in which people who violated family norms would be mocked and shamed (Shorter, 1975).

Modernization involves political as well as economic and social change. In English and American history, striking parallels exist between political ideals and the family, with the family being seen as a small version of the state—a little commonwealth. When the divine right of kings prevailed, the family ideal was likewise hierarchy and authority, with children and wives owing unquestioning obedience. When ideas about democracy and individual rights challenged the rule of kings, family ideologies also became more democratic (Stone, 1977). An ideology of liberation still accompanies replacement of the traditional pattern of work and family by the modern one. Modernization promises freedom of opportunity to find work that suits one's talents, freedom to marry for love and dissolve the marriage if it fails to provide happiness, and greater equality in in the family between husband and wife and between parents and children (Goode, 1963).

In addition to promoting an ideology of individualism, modern technological societies change the inner experience of the self. The person living in an unchanging, traditional social world does not have to construct an identity to discover who he or she really is. "I am the son of this man, I came from that village, I work at that trade" would be enough to tell a man who he was.

There is still another source of the modern preoccupation with self. Much of daily life in modern society is spent in such roles as student, worker, customer, client. People begin to experience themselves as replaceable role players (Berger, Berger, & Kellner, 1973; Davis, 1973). As we become aware of a discrepancy between the role we are playing and our real and whole selves, we come to have a need for a private world, a set of relationships in which we can express those aspects of ourselves that must be repressed in role demands of work and public behavior. Individualization and intimacy are, as Howard Gadlin (1977) puts it, "the Siamese twins of modernization."

Although the need for intimacy increases, the very conditions creating that need make it more difficult to satisfy. For example, affluence may buy privacy, but, like King Midas' touch, family privacy is a drama that turns up unexpected costs when fulfilled. The family's "major burden," writes Napier (1972), "is its rootlessness, its aloneness with its tasks. Parents are somewhere else; the business you can't trust; the neighbors you never see; and friends are a help, when you see them, but never enough. Sometimes, late at night, the parent wakes up and on a sea of silence hears the ship creak, feels it drift, fragile and solitary, with its cargo of lives" (p. 540).

Family privacy needs illustrate only one example of how contradictory cultural instructions clash in the modern family. There is also the contradiction between a newer morality of enjoyment and self-fulfillment and an older morality of duty, responsibility, work, and self-denial. Fun morality is expressed by the advertising industry, credit cards, the buy-now-pay-later philosophy. The new morality can reunite families in activities that everyone can enjoy, but it also pulls family members apart in its emphasis on individual pursuit of enjoyment. Also, fun morality imposes a paradoxical demand: in the past, one could live up to demands of marriage and parenthood by doing one's duty. Today duty is not enough; we are also obliged to enjoy family life

(Wolfenstein, 1954). As a result, pleasurable activities, including sex itself, become matters for evaluation and therefore of discontent.

Ironically, then, many of the difficulties besetting family life today are the consequences of some very positive changes: the decline of infant mortality and death rates in general, the fact that people are living longer, the use of birth control, the spread of mass education, and the increasing control of the individual over basic life decisions (whether to marry, when to marry, whom to marry, whether or not to have children, and how many to have).

This very voluntariness can be disturbing. Freedom in modern family life is bought at the price of fragility and instability. Now the whole structure of family life comes to rest on a tenuous basis: the mutual feelings of two individuals. As Georg Simmel (1950, pp. 118–144) has shown, the couple or dyad is not only the most intimate of social relationships, it is also the most unstable. In traditional family systems, the inevitable tensions of marriage are contained by kin and community pressures, as well as by low expectations concerning the romance or happiness to be found in marriage.

Demographic and economic change has had a profound effect on women's roles. When death rates fall, as they do with modernization, women no longer have to have five or seven or nine children to make sure that two or three will survive to adulthood. Women today are living longer and having fewer children. After having children, the average woman can look forward to three or four decades without maternal responsibilities. Since traditional assumptions about women are based on the notion that women are constantly involved with pregnancy, childrearing, and related domestic concerns, the current ferment about women's roles may be seen as a way of bringing cultural attitudes in line with existing social realities.

As people live longer, they can stay married longer. Actually, the biggest change in twentieth-century marriage is not the proportion of marriages disrupted through divorce, but the potential length of marriage and the number of years spent without children in the home. Census data suggest that the statistically average couple marrying now will spend only 18 percent of their married lives raising young children, compared with 54 percent a century ago (Bane, 1976). As a result, marriage is becoming less of a union between parents raising a brood of children and more of a personal relationship between two people.

To sum it up then, a knowledge of family history reveals that the solution to contemporary problems will not be found in some lost golden age. Families have always struggled with outside circumstances and inner conflict. Our current troubles inside and outside the family are genuine, but we should never forget that many of the most vexing issues confronting us as men and women, parents and children, derive from the very benefits of modernization—benefits too easily taken for granted or forgotten in the lately fashionable denunciation of modern times. There was no problem of the aged in the past, because most people never aged; they died before they got old. Nor was adolescence a difficult stage of the life cycle when children worked and education was a privilege of the rich. And when most people were hungry illiterates, only aristocrats could worry about sexual satisfaction and self-fulfillment.

However grim the present moment may appear, there is no point in giving in to the lure of nostalgia. There is no golden age of the family to long for, nor even some past pattern of behavior and belief that would guarantee us harmony and stability if only we had the will to return to it. Family life is bound up with the social, economic, and ideological circumstances of particular times and places. We are no longer peasants, Puritans, pioneers, or even suburbanites circa 1955. We face conditions unknown to our ancestors, and we must find new ways to cope with them.

References

Bane, M. J. 1976. *Here to Stay*. New York: Basic Books.

Berger, P., Berger, B. and Kellner, H. 1973. *The Homeless Mind: Modernization and Consciousness*. New York: Random House.

Bernard, J. 1973. *The Future of Marriage*. New York: Bantam.

Bernard, J. 1975. "Adolescence and Socialization for Motherhood." In Dragastin, S. E. and G. H. Elder, *Adolescence in the Life Cycle*. New York: Wiley, pp. 227–252.

Blake, J. 1978. "Structural Differentiation and the Family: A Quiet Revolution." Presentation at American Sociology Association, San Francisco.

Cherlin, A. J. 1981. *Marriage, Divorce, Remarriage*. Cambridge: Harvard University Press.

Davis, M. S. 1973. *Intimate Relations*. New York: The Free Press.

Demos, J. 1975. "Myths and Realities in the History of American Family Life," in H. Grunebaum and J. Christ (eds.). *Contemporary Marriage: Structure, Dynamics and Therapy*. Boston: Little, Brown and Company.

Elder, G. 1978. "Approaches to Social Change and the Family." In *Turning Points*, edited by J. Demos and S. S. Boocock, pp. 1–38. Supplement to *American Journal of Sociology*, vol. 84, p. S34.

Featherstone, J. 1979. Family Matters. *Harvard Educational Review*, 49, No.1, pp. 20–52.

Filene, P. 1975. *Him, Her, Self: Sex Roles in Modern America*. New York: Mentor.

Furstenberg, F. F., Jr., Lincoln, R. and Menken, J. 1981. *Teenage Sexuality, Pregnancy and Childbearing*. Philadelphia: University of Pennsylvania Press.

Gadlin, H. 1977. "Private Lives and Public Order." In *Close Relationships: Perspectives in the Meaning of Intimacy*. Amherst: University of Massachusetts Press, pp. 73–86.

Gagnon, J. H. and Simon, W. 1970. *The Sexual Scene*. Chicago: Transaction.

Geertz, G. 1965. "The Impact of the Concept of Culture on the Concept of Man." In *New Views of the Nature of Man*, edited by J. R. Platt, pp. 93–118. Chicago: University of Chicago Press.

Goode, W. J. 1960. "A Deviant Case: Illegitimacy in the Caribbean." *American Sociological Review*, vol. 25, pp. 21–30.

Goode, W. J. 1963. *World Revolution and Family Patterns*. New York: The Free Press.

Hareven, T. K. 1978. "Family Time and Historical Time." In *The Family*, edited by A. S. Rassi, J. Kagan, and T. K. Hareven. New York: W. W. Norton and Company, pp. 57–70. (Reprint of *Daedalus*. Spring 1977.)

Hunt, D. 1970. *Parents and Children in History: The Psychology of Family Life in Early Modern France*. New York: Basic Books.

ISR Newsletter. 1979. Institute for Social Research. The University of Michigan. Winter.

Keller, S. 1971. "Does the Family Have a Future?" *Journal of Comparative Studies*, Spring, 1971.

Keniston, K. 1977. *All Our Children: The American Family Under Pressure.* New York: Harcourt Brace Jovanovich.

Kessen, E. W. 1965. *The Child.* New York: John Wiley.

LaBarre, W. 1954. *The Human Animal.* Chicago: University of Chicago Press.

Lasch, C. 1978. *Haven in a Heartless World.* New York: Basic Books.

Laslett, P., and Wall, R. (eds.). 1972. *Household and Family in Past Time.* Cambridge: Cambridge University Press.

Macfarlane, J. W. 1964. "Perspectives on Personality Consistency and Change from the Guidance Study." *Vita Humana,* vol. 7, pp. 115–126.

Malinowski, B. 1930. "Parenthood, the Basis of the Social Order." In *The New Generation,* Calverton and Schmalhousen, New York: Macauley Company, pp. 113–168.

Masnick, G. and Bane, M. J. 1980. *The Nation's Families: 1960–1990.* Boston: Auburn House.

Mason, K. O., Czajka, J., and Aiker, S. 1976. "Change in U.S. Women's Sex Role Attitudes, 1964–1974." *American Sociological Review,* 41, pp. 573–596.

Napier, A. 1972. Introduction to section four in *The Book of Family Therapy,* edited by A. Farber, M. Mendelsohn, and A. Napier. New York: Science House.

Parsons, T. 1951. The Social System. Glencoe, Ill.: Free Press.

Parsons, T. 1954. The Kinship System of the Contemporary United States. In *Essays in Sociological Theory.* Glencoe, Ill. Free Press.

Rossi, A. S. 1978. "A Biosocial Perspective on Parenting." In *The Family,* edited by A. S. Rossi, J. Kagan, and T. K. Hareven. New York: W. W. Norton and Company. (Reprint of *Daedalus,* Spring 1977.)

Ridley, J. C. 1972. "The Effects of Population Change on the Roles and Status of Women." In *Toward a Sociology of Women,* edited by S. Safilios-Rothschild. Lexington, Mass.: Xerox College Publishing, pp. 372–386.

Shorter, E. 1973. "Infanticide in the Past." *History of Childhood Quarterly,* Summer, pp. 178–180.

Shorter, E. 1975. *The Making of the Modern Family.* New York: Basic Books.

Simmel, G. 1950. *The Sociology of George Simmel,* edited by K. Wolff. New York: Free Press.

Steinmetz, D., and Straus, M. A. (eds.) 1974. *Violence in the Family.* New York: Dodd, Mead Co.

Stephens, W. N. 1963. *The Family in Cross-Cultural Perspective.* New York: World.

Stone, L. 1977. *The Family, Sex and Marriage in England, 1500–1800.* New York: Harper and Row.

Trost, J. 1976. "Married and Unmarried Cohabitation: The Case of Sweden with Some Comparison." In *Beyond the Nuclear Family Model,* edited by L. Lenew-Obew. Beverly Hills: California Sage.

Trexler, R. C. 1973. "Infanticide in Florence: New Sources and First Results." *History of Childhood Quarterly,* Summer, pp. 98–116.

Uhlenberg, P. 1974. "Cohort Variations in Family Life Cycle Experiences of U.S. Females." *Journal of Marriage and the Family,* pp. 284–292.

Veroff, J., Douvan, E., Kulka, R. A. 1981. *The Inner American: A Self-Portrait from 1957 to 1976.* New York: Basic Books.

Weed, J. A. 1981. *Status of Families.* Unpublished manuscript. Bureau of the Census, Population Division. September.

Wolfenstein, M. 1954. "Fun Morality: An Analysis of Recent American Child Training Literature." In *Childhood in Contemporary Cultures,* edited by M. Mead and M. Wolfenstein. Chicago: University of Chicago Press, pp. 168–178.

1

The Changing Family

Introduction

Chapter 1   Family Origins and History

Kathleen Gough
The Origin of the Family

William J. Goode
World Revolution and Family Patterns

Barbara Laslett
Family Membership, Past and Present

Tamara K. Hareven
American Families in Transition: Historical Perspectives on Change

Peter Uhlenberg
Death and the Family

Chapter 2   The Current Debate

Christopher Lasch
The Family as a Haven in a Heartless World

Mary Jo Bane
Here to Stay: Parents and Children

Andrew Cherlin
The Trends: Marriage, Divorce, Remarriage

Suzanne Keller
Does the Family Have a Future?

Introduction

The study of the family does not fit neatly within the boundaries of any single scholarly field; genetics, physiology, archeology, history, anthropology, sociology, and psychology all touch upon it. Religious and ethical authorities claim a stake in the family. Also, troubled individuals and families generate therapeutic demands on family scholarship. In short, the study of the family is interdisciplinary, controversial, and necessary for the formulation of social policy and practices. Interdisciplinary subjects demand competence in more than one field. At a time when competent scholars find it difficult to master even one corner of a field—say the terminology of kinship, or the history of feminism, or the physiology of sexual arousal—intellectual demands on students of the family become vast. Although writers on the family confront many issues, their professional competence is usually limited. Thus a biologist may cite articles in psychology to support a position, without comprehending the tentativeness with which psychologists regard the researcher and his work. Similarly, a psychologist or sociologist may draw upon controversial biological studies. Professional competence means more than the ability to read technical journals; it includes informal knowledge—being "tuned in" to verbal understandings and evaluations of research validity. Usually a major theory or line of research is viewed more critically in its own field than outsiders realize.

Interdisciplinary subjects present other characteristic problems. Each discipline has its own assumptions and views of the world, which may not directly transfer into another field. For example, some biologists and physically oriented anthropologists analyze human affairs in terms of individual motives and instincts; for them, society is a shadowy presence, serving mainly as the setting for biologically motivated individual action. Many sociologists and cultural anthropologists, in contrast, perceive the individual as an actor playing a role written by culture and society; according to this view, the individual has no wholly autonomous thoughts and impulses. An important school of psychologists sees people neither as passive recipients of social pressures nor as creatures driven by powerful lusts, but as information processors trying to make sense of their environment. There is no easy way to reconcile such perspectives. Scientific paradigms—characteristic ways of looking at the world —determine not only what answers will be found, but what questions will be asked. This fact has perhaps created special confusion in the study of the family.

"We speak of families," R. D. Laing has observed, "as though we know what families are. We identify, as families, networks of people who live together over time, who have ties of marriage or kinship to one another" (Laing 1971, p. 3). Yet as Laing observes further, the more one studies the emotional dynamics of groups presently called "families," the less clear it becomes how these differ from groups not designated "families." Further, contemporary family patterns and emotional dynamics may not appear in other places and times.

As an object of study, the family is thus plagued with a unique set of problems. There is the assumption that family life, so familiar a part of everyday experience, is easily understood. But familiarity may breed a sense of destiny—what we experience is transformed into the "natural":

> One difficulty in the psychological sciences lies in the familiarity of the phenomena with which they deal. A certain intellectual effort is required to see how such phenomena can pose serious problems or call for intricate explanatory theories. One is inclined to take them for granted as necessary or somehow "natural." (Chomsky 1968, p.21)

Only in the past decade or so have family scholars come to recognize how problematic a subject "the family" is and how hard it is to answer basic questions: Is there a definition of family that can apply to all places and times? What is the relationship between the family as an abstraction and particular families with their own idiosyncrasies and differences from each other? What "test" can we apply to distinguish between a family and a group that is not a family?

The selections in part 1 discuss both the concept of the family and the development of the family from prehistoric times through the contemporary United States. As one reads the selections, one observes the enormous variation that is possible in family structure and family organization through time and its accompanying economic and social conditions. Moreover, a careful examination of every family system reveals deeply embedded notions of propriety, health, legality, sex, and age role assignments. Only one thing seems constant through time and place with respect to relations among men, women, and children—everyone feels strongly about these. Moreover, prevailing family forms and norms tend to be idealized as the right and proper ones. Perhaps that is because, although the family is scarcely the building block of society claimed by early functional sociologists, it is without doubt the institution possessing the most emotional significance in society. If you believe in a woman's right to medical abortion, or if you don't, and if you have an egalitarian or subordinate vision of the roles of men, women, and children, you probably feel strongly about these—even more strongly than you feel about inflation and unemployment. The family grabs us where we live. Not only do we become excited about it, but is seems more than any other institution to generate controversy and moral indignation.

References

Chomsky, N. 1968. *Language and Mind.* New York: Harcourt, Brace and World.
Laing, R. D. 1971. *The Politics of the Family.* New York: Random House.

Chapter 1

Family Origins and History

The Origin of the Family

Kathleen Gough

The trouble with the origin of the family is that no one really knows. Since Engels wrote *The Origin of the Family, Private Property and the State* in 1884, a great deal of new evidence has come in. Yet the gaps are still enormous. It is not known *when* the family originated, although it was probably between 2 million and 100,000 years ago. It is not known whether it developed once or in separate times and places. It is not known whether some kind of embryonic family came before, with, or after the origin of language. Since language is the accepted criterion of humanness, this means that we do not even know whether our ancestors acquired the basics of family life before or after they were human. The chances are that language and the family developed together over a long period, but the evidence is sketchy.

Although the origin of the family is speculative, it is better to speculate with than without evidence. The evidence comes from three sources. One is the social and physical lives of nonhuman primates—especially the New and Old World monkeys and, still more, the great apes, humanity's closest relatives. The second source is the tools and home lives of hunters and gatherers of wild provender who have been studied in modern times.

Each of these sources is imperfect: monkeys and apes, because they are *not* prehuman ancestors, although they are our cousins; fossil hominids, because they left so little vestige of their social life; hunters and gatherers, because none of them has, in historic times, possessed a technology and society as primitive as those of early humans. All show the results of long endeavor in specialized, marginal environments. But together, these sources give valuable clues.

From *Journal of Marriage and the Family* (November 1971), pp. 760–770, Copyrighted 1971 by the National Council on Family Relations. Reprinted by permission.

Defining the Family

To discuss the origin of something we must first decide what it is. I shall define the family as "a married couple or other group of adult kinsfolk who cooperate economically and in the upbringing of children, and all or most of whom share a common dwelling."

This includes all forms of kin-based household. Some are extended families containing three generations of married brothers or sisters. Some are "grand-families" descended from a single pair of grandparents. Some are matrilineage households, in which brothers and sisters share a house with the sisters' children, and men merely visit their wives in other homes. Some are compound families, in which one man has several wives, or one woman, several husbands. Others are nuclear families composed of a father, mother, and children.

Some kind of family exists in all known human societies, although it is not found in every segment or class of all stratified, state societies. Greek and American slaves, for example, were prevented from forming legal families, and their social families were often disrupted by sale, forced labor, or sexual exploitation. Even so, the family was an ideal which all classes and most people attained when they could.

The family implies several other universals. (1) Rules forbid sexual relations and marriage between close relatives. Which relatives are forbidden varies, but all societies forbid mother-son mating, and most, father-daughter and brother-sister. Some societies allow sex relations but forbid marriage between certain degrees of kin. (2) The men and women of a family cooperate through a division of labor based on gender. Again, the sexual division of labor varies in rigidity and in the tasks performed. But in no human society to date is it wholly absent. Child care, household tasks, and crafts closely connected with the household tend to be done by women; war, hunting, and government, by men. (3) Marriage exists as a socially recognized, durable, although not necessarily lifelong relationship between individual men and women. From it springs social fatherhood, some kind of special bond between a man and the child of his wife, whether or not they are his own children physiologically. Even in polyandrous societies, where women have several husbands, or in matrilineal societies, where group membership and property pass through women, each child has one or more designated "fathers" with whom he has a special social, and often religious, relationship. This bond of *social* fatherhood is recognized among people who do not know about the male role in procreation or where, for various reasons, it is not clear who the physiological father of a particular infant is. Social fatherhood seems to come from the division and interdependence of male and female tasks, especially in relation to children, rather than directly from physiological fatherhood, although in most societies, the social father of a child is usually presumed to be its physiological father as well. Contrary to the beliefs of some feminists, however, I think that in no human society do men, as a whole category, have *only* the role of insemination and *no* other social or economic role in relation to women and children. (4) Men in general have higher status and authority over the women of their families, although older women may have influence, even some authority, over junior men. The omnipresence of male authority, too, goes contrary to the belief of some feminists that in "matriarchal" societies, women were either completely equal to or had paramount authority over men, either in the home or in society at large.

It is true that in some matrilineal societies, such as the Hopi of Arizona or the Ashanti of Ghana, men exert little authority over their wives. In some, such as the Nayars of South India or the Minangkabau of Sumatra, men may even live separately from their wives and children, that is, in different families. In such societies, however, the fact is that women and children fall under greater or lesser authority from the women's kinsmen—their eldest brothers, mothers' brothers, or even their grown-up sons.

In matrilineal societies, where property, rank, office, and group membership are inherited through the female line, it is true that women tend to have greater independence than in patrilineal societies. This is especially so in matrilineal tribal societies where residence is matrilocal—that is, men come to live in the homes or villages of their wives. Even so, in all matrilineal societies for which adequate descriptions are available, the ultimate headship of households, lineages, and local groups is usually with men. (See Schneider and Gough, 1961, for common and variant features of matrilineal systems.)

There is in fact no true "matriarchal," as distinct from "matrilineal," society in existence or known from literature, and the chances are there never has been.* This does not mean that women and men have never had relations that were dignified and creative for both sexes, appropriate to the knowledge, skills, and technology of their times. Nor does it mean that the sexes cannot be equal in the future or that the sexual division of labor cannot be abolished. I believe that it can and must be. But it is not necessary to believe myths of a feminist Golden Age in order to plan for parity in the future.

Primate Societies

Within the primate order, humans are most closely related to the anthropoid apes (the African chimpanzee and gorilla and the Southeast Asian orang-utan and gibbon), and of these, to the chimpanzee and the gorilla. More distantly related are the Old, and then the New, World monkeys, and finally, the lemurs, tarsiers, and tree shrews.

All primates share characteristics without which the family could not have

*The Iroquois are often quoted as a "matriarchal" society, but in fact Morgan himself refers to "the absence of equality between the sexes" and notes that women were subordinate to men, ate after men, and that women (not men) were publicly whipped as punishment for adultery. Warleaders, tribal chiefs, and *sachems* (heads of matrilineal lineages) were men. Women did, however, have a large say in the government of the long-house or home of the matrilocal extended family, and women figured as tribal counsellors and religious officials, as well as in arranging marriages. (Lewis H. Morgan: The League of the *Ho-de-ne Sau-nee or Iroquois,* Human Relations Area Files, 1954) developed. The young are born relatively helpless. They suckle for several months or years and need prolonged care afterwards. Childhood is longer, the closer the species is to humans. Most monkeys reach puberty at about four to five and mature socially between about five and ten. Chimpanzees, by contrast, suckle for up to three years. Females reach puberty at seven to ten; males enter mature social and sexual relations as late as thirteen. The long childhood and maternal care produce close relations between children of the same mother who play together and help tend their juniors until they grow up.

Monkeys and apes, like humans, mate in all months of the year instead of in a rutting season. Unlike humans, however, female apes experience unusually strong sexual desire for a few days shortly before and during ovulation (the oestrus period) and have intensive sexual relations at that time. The males are attracted to the females by their scent or by brightly colored swellings in the sexual region. Oestrus mating appears to be especially pronounced in primate species more remote from humans. The apes and some monkeys carry on less intensive, month-round sexuality in addition to oestrus mating, approaching human patterns more closely. In humans, sexual desires and relations are regulated less by hormonal changes and more by mental images, emotions, cultural rules, and individual preferences.

Year-round (if not always month-round) sexuality means that males and females socialize more continuously among primates than among most other mammals. All primates form bands or troops composed of both sexes plus children. The numbers and proportions of the sexes vary, and in some species an individual, a mother with her young, or a subsidiary troop of male juveniles may travel temporarily alone. But in general, males and females socialize continually through mutual grooming* and playing as well as through frequent sex relations. Keeping close to the females, primate males play with their children and tend to protect both females and young from predators. A "division of labor" based on gender is thus already found in primate society between a female role of prolonged child care and a male role of defense. Males may also carry or take care of children briefly, and nonnursing females may fight. But a kind of generalized "fatherliness" appears in the protective role of adult males towards young, even in species where the sexes do not form long-term individual attachments.

Sexual Bonds Among Primates

Some nonhuman primates do have enduring sexual bonds and restrictions, superficially similar to those in some human societies. Among gibbons a single male and female live together with their young. The male drives off other males and the female, other females. When a juvenile reaches puberty it is thought to leave or be expelled by the parent of the same sex, and he eventually finds a mate elsewhere. Similar *de facto,* rudimentary "incest prohibitions" may

---

*Combing the hair and removing parasites with hands or teeth.

have been passed on to humans from their prehuman ancestors and later codified and elaborated through language, moral custom, and law. Whether this is so may become clearer when we know more about the mating patterns of the other great apes, especially of our closest relatives, the chimpanzees. Present evidence suggests that male chimpanzees do not mate with their mothers.

Orang-utans live in small, tree-dwelling groups like gibbons, but their forms are less regular. One or two mothers may wander alone with their young, mating at intervals with a male; or a male-female pair or several juvenile males may travel together.

Among mountain gorillas of Uganda, South Indian langurs, and hamadryas baboons of Ethiopia, a single, fully mature male mates with several females, especially in their oestrus periods. If younger adult males are present, the females may have occasional relations with them if the leader is tired or not looking.

Among East and South African baboons, rhesus macaques, and South American woolly monkeys, the troop is bigger, numbering up to two hundred. It contains a number of adult males and a much larger number of females. The males are strictly ranked in terms of dominance based on both physical strength and intelligence. The more dominant males copulate intensively with the females during the latter's oestrus periods. Toward the end of oestrus a female may briefly attach herself to a single dominant male. At other times she may have relations with any male of higher or lower rank provided that those of higher rank permit it.

Among some baboons and macaques the young males travel on the outskirts of the group and have little access to females. Some macaques expel from the troop a proportion of the young males, who then form "bachelor troops." Bachelors may later form new troops with young females.

Other primates are more thoroughly promiscuous, or rather indiscriminate, in mating. Chimpanzees and also South American howler monkeys live in loosely structured groups, again (as in most monkey and ape societies) with a preponderance of females. The mother-child unit is the only stable group. The sexes copulate almost at random and most intensively and indiscriminately during oestrus.

A number of well-known anthropologists have argued that various attitudes and customs often found in human societies are instinctual rather than culturally learned and come from our primate heritage. They include hierarchies of ranking among men, male political power over women, and the greater tendency of men to form friendships with one another, as opposed to women's tendencies to cling to a man. (See, for example, Morris, 1967; Fox, 1967).

I cannot accept these conclusions and think that they stem from the male chauvinism of our own society. A "scientific" argument which states that all such features of female inferiority are instinctive is obviously a powerful weapon in maintaining the traditional family with male dominance. But in fact, these features are *not* universal among nonhuman primates, including some of those most closely related to humans. Chimpanzees have a low degree of male dominance and male hierarchy and are sexually virtually indiscriminate. Gibbons have a kind of fidelity for both sexes and almost no male dominance or hierarchy. Howler monkeys are sexually indiscriminate and lack male hierarchies or dominance.

The fact is that among nonhuman primates male dominance and male hierarchies seem to be adaptations to particular environments, some of which did become genetically established through natural selection. Among humans, however, these features are present in variable degrees and are almost certainly learned, not inherited at all. Among nonhuman primates there are fairly general differences between those that live mainly in trees and those that live largely on the ground. The tree dwellers (for example gibbons, orang-utans, South American howler, and woolly monkeys) tend to have to defend themselves less against predators than do the ground dwellers (such as baboons, macaques, or gorillas). Where defense is important, males are much larger and stronger than females, exert dominance over females, and are strictly hierarchized and organized in relation to one another. Where defense is less important there is much less sexual dimorphism (difference in size between male and female), less or no male dominance, a less pronounced male hierarchy, and greater sexual indiscriminacy.

Comparatively speaking, humans have a rather small degree of sexual dimorphism, similar to chimpanzees. Chimpanzees live much in trees but also partly on the ground, in forest or semiforest habitats. They build individual nests to sleep in, sometimes on the ground but usually in trees. They flee into trees from danger. Chimpanzees go mainly on all fours, but sometimes on two feet, and can use and make simple tools. Males are dominant, but not very dominant, over females. The rank hierarchy among males is unstable, and males often move between groups, which vary in size from two to fifty individuals. Food is vegetarian, supplemented with worms, grubs, or occasional small animals. A mother and her young form the only stable unit. Sexual relations are largely indiscriminate, but nearby males defend young animals from danger. The chances are that our prehuman ancestors had a similar social life. Morgan and Engels were probably right in concluding that we came from a state of "original promiscuity" before we were fully human.

Human Evolution

Judging from the fossil record, apes ancestral to humans, gorillas, and chimpanzees roamed widely in Asia, Europe, and Africa some 12 to 28 million years ago. Toward the end of that period (the Miocene) one appears in North India and East Africa, Ramapithecus, who may be ancestral both to later hominids and to modern humans. His species were small like gibbons, walked upright on two feet, had human rather than ape cornerteeth, and therefore probably used hands rather than teeth to tear their food. From that time evolution toward humanness must have proceeded through various phases until the emergence of modern homo sapiens, about 70,000 years ago.

In the Miocene period before Ramapithecus appeared, there were several time spans in which, over large areas, the climate became dryer and subtropical forests dwindled or disappeared. A standard reconstruction of events, which I accept, is that groups of apes, probably in Africa, had to come down from the trees and adapt to terrestrial life. Through natural selection, probably over millions of years, they developed specialized feet for walking. Thus freed, the hands came to be used not only (as among apes) for grasping and tearing, but for regular carrying of objects such as weapons (which had hitherto been sporadic) or of infants (which had hitherto clung to their mothers' body hair).

The spread of indigestible grasses on the open savannahs may have encouraged, if it did not compel, the early ground dwellers to become active hunters rather than simply to forage for small, sick, or dead animals that came their way. Collective hunting and tool use involved group cooperation and helped foster the growth of language out of the call systems of apes. Language meant the use of symbols to refer to events not present. It allowed greatly increased foresight, memory, planning, and division of tasks—in short, the capacity for human thought.

With the change to hunting, group territories became much larger. Apes range only a few thousand feet daily; hunters, several miles. But because their infants were helpless, nursing women could hunt only small game close to home. This then produced the sexual division of labor on which the human family has since been founded. Women elaborated upon ape methods of child care and greatly expanded foraging, which in most areas remained the primary and most stable source of food. Men improved upon ape methods of fighting off other animals and of group protection in general. They adapted these methods to hunting, using weapons which for millennia remained the same for the chase as for human warfare.

Out of the sexual division of labor came, for the first time, home life as well as group cooperation. Female apes nest with and provide foraged food for their infants. But adult apes do not cooperate in food getting or nest building. They build new nests each night wherever they may happen to be. With the development of a hunting-gathering complex, it became necessary to have a G.H.Q., or home. Men could bring meat to this place for several days' supply. Women and children could meet men there after the day's hunting and could bring their vegetable produce for general consumption. Men, women, and children could build joint shelters, butcher meat, and treat skins for clothing.

Later, fire came into use for protection against wild animals, for lighting, and eventually for cooking. The hearth then provided the focus and symbol of home. With the development of cookery, some humans—chiefly women and perhaps some children and old men—came to spend more time preparing nutrition so that all people need spend less time in chewing and tearing their food. Meals—already less frequent because of the change to a carnivorous diet

—now became brief, periodic events instead of the long feeding sessions of apes.

The change to humanness brought two bodily changes that affected birth and child care. These were head size and width of the pelvis. Walking upright produced a narrower pelvis to hold the guts in position. Yet as language developed, brains and hence heads grew much bigger relative to body size. To compensate, humans are born at an earlier stage of growth than apes. They are helpless longer and require longer and more total care. This in turn caused early women to concentrate more on child care and less on defense than do female apes.

Language made possible not only a division and cooperation in labor but also all forms of tradition, rules, morality, and cultural learning. Rules banning sex relations among close kinfolk must have come very early. Precisely how or why they developed is unknown, but they had at least two useful functions. They helped to preserve order in the family as a cooperative unit by outlawing competition for mates. They also created bonds *between* families, or even between separate bands, and so provided a basis for wider cooperation in the struggle for livelihood and the expansion of knowledge.

It is not clear when all these changes took place. Climatic change with increased drought began regionally up to 28 million years ago. The divergence between prehuman and gorilla-chimpanzee stems had occurred in both Africa and India at least 12 million years ago. The prehuman stem led to the Australopithecenes of East and South Africa, about 1,750,000 years ago. These were pygmylike, two-footed, upright hominids with larger than ape brains, who made tools and probably hunted in savannah regions. It is unlikely that they knew the use of fire.

The first known use of fire is that of cave-dwelling hominids (Sinanthropus, a branch of the Pithecanthropines) at Choukoutien near Peking, some half a million years ago during the second ice age. Fire was used regularly in hearths, suggesting cookery, by the time of the Acheulean and Mousterian cultures of Neanderthal man in Europe, Africa, and Asia before, during, and after the third ice age, some 150,000 to 100,000 years ago. These people, too, were often cave dwellers and buried their dead ceremonially in caves. Cave dwelling by night as well as by day was probably, in fact, not safe for humans until fire came into use to drive away predators.

Most anthropologists conclude that home life, the family and language had developed by the time of Neanderthal man, who was closely similar and may have been ancestral to modern homo sapiens. At least two anthropologists, however, believe that the Australopithecenes already had language nearly 2 million years ago, while another thinks that language and incest prohibitions did not evolve until the time of homo sapiens some 70,000 to 50,000 years ago. (For the former view, see Hockett and Ascher, 1968; for the latter, Livingstone, 1969). I am myself inclined to think that family life built around tool use, the use of language, cookery, and a sexual division of labor must have been established sometime between about 500,000 and 200,000 years ago.

Hunters and Gatherers

Most of the hunting and gathering societies studied in the eighteenth to twentieth centuries had technologies similar to those that were widespread in the Mesolithic period, which occurred about 15,000 to 10,000 years ago, after the ice ages ended but before cultivation was invented and animals domesticated.

Modern hunters live in marginal forest, mountain, arctic, or desert environments where cultivation is impracticable. Although by no means "primeval," the hunters of recent times do offer clues to the types of family found during that 99 percent of human history before the agricultural revolution. They include the Eskimo, many Canadian and South American Indian groups, the forest BaMbuti (Pygmies) and the desert Bushmen of Southern Africa, the Kadar of South India, the Veddah of Ceylon, and the Andaman Islanders of the Indian Ocean. About 175 hunting and gathering cultures in Oceania, Asia, Africa, and America have been described in fair detail.

In spite of their varied environments, hunters share certain features of social life. They live in bands of about 20 to 200 people, the majority of bands having fewer than 50. Bands are divided into families, which may forage alone in some seasons. Hunters have simple but ingenious technologies. Bows and arrows, spears, needles, skin clothing, and temporary leaf or wood shelters are common. Most hunters do some fishing. The band forages and hunts in a large territory and usually moves camp often.

Social life is egalitarian. There is of course no state no organized government. Apart from religious shamans or magicians, the division of labor is based only on sex and age. Resources are owned communally; tools and personal possessions are freely exchanged. Everyone works who can. Band leadership goes to whichever man has the intelligence, courage, and foresight to command the respect of his fellows. Intelligent older women are also looked up to.

The household is the main unit of economic cooperation, with the men, women, and children dividing the labor and pooling their produce. In 97 percent of the 175 societies classified by G. P. Murdock, hunting is confined to men; in the other 3 percent it is chiefly a male pursuit. Gathering of wild plants, fruits, and nuts is women's work. In 60 percent of societies, only women gather, while in another 32 percent gathering is mainly feminine. Fishing is solely or mainly men's work in 93 percent of the hunting societies where it occurs.

For the rest, men monopolize fighting, although interband warfare is rare. Women tend children and shelters and usually do most of the cooking, processing, and storage of food. Women tend, also, to be foremost in the early household crafts such as basketry, leather work, the making of skin or bark clothing, and, in the more advanced hunting societies, pottery. (Considering that women probably *invented* all of these crafts, in addition to cookery, food storage, and preservation, agriculture, spinning, weaving, and perhaps even house construction, it is clear that women played quite as important roles as men in early cultural development.) Building dwellings and making tools and ornaments are variously divided between the sexes, while boat building is largely done by men. Girls help the women, and boys play at hunting or hunt small game until they reach puberty, when both take on the roles of adults. Where the environment makes it desirable, the men of a whole band or of some smaller cluster of households cooperate in hunting or fishing and divide their spoils. Women of nearby families often go gathering together.

Family composition varies among hunters as it does in other kinds of societies. About half or more of known hunting societies have nuclear families (father, mother, and children), with polygynous households (a man, two or more wives, and children) as occasional variants. Clearly, nuclear families are the most common among hunters, although hunters have a slightly higher proportion of polygynous families than do nonhunting societies.

About a third of hunting societies contain some stem-family households— that is, older parents live in together with one married child and grandchildren, while the other married children live in independent dwellings. A still smaller proportion live in large extended families containing several married brothers (or several married sisters), their spouses, and children. (For exact figures, see Murdock, 1957; Coult, 1965; and Murdock, 1967. In the last-named survey, out of 175 hunting societies, 47 percent had nuclear family households, 38 percent had stem families, and 14 percent had extended families.) Hunters have fewer extended and stem families than do nonhunting societies. These larger households become common with the rise of agriculture. They are especially found in large, preindustrial agrarian states such as ancient Greece, Rome, India, the Islamic empires, and China.

Hunting societies also have few households composed of a widow or divorcee and her children. This is understandable, for neither men nor women can survive long without the work and produce of the other sex, and marriage is the way to obtain them. That is why so often young men must show proof of hunting prowess and girls of cooking before they are allowed to marry.

The family, together with territorial grouping, provides the framework of society among hunters. Indeed, as Morgan and Engels clearly saw, kinship and territory are the foundations of all societies before the rise of the state. Not only hunting and gathering bands, but the larger and more complex tribes and chiefdoms of primitive cultivators and herders organize people through descent from common ancestors or through marriage ties between groups. Among hunters, things are simple. There is only the family, and beyond it the band. With the domestication of plants and animals, the economy becomes more productive. More people can live together. Tribes form, containing several thousand people loosely organized into large kin groups such as clans and lineages, each composed of a number of related families. With still further development of the productive forces the society throws up a central political leadership, together with craft specialization and trade, and so the chiefdom emerges. But this, too, is structured through ranked allegiances and marriage ties between kin groups.

Only with the rise of the state does class, independently of kinship, provide the basis for relations of production, distribution, and power. Even then, kin groups remain large in the agrarian state and kinship persists as the prime organizing principle within each class until the rise of capitalism. The reduction in significance of the family that we see today is the outgrowth of a decline in the importance of "familism" relative to other institutions, that began with the rise of the state but became speeded up with the development of capitalism and machine industry. In most modern socialist societies, the family is even less significant as an organizing principle. It is reasonable to suppose that in the future it will become minimal or may disappear, at least as a legally constituted unit for exclusive forms of sexual and economic cooperation and of child care.

Morgan and Engels (1942) thought that from a state of original promiscuity, early humans at first banned sex relations between the generations of parents and children but continued to allow them indiscriminately between brothers, sisters, and all kinds of cousins within the band. They called this the "consanguineal family." They thought that later, all mating within the family or some larger kin group became forbidden, but that there was a stage (the "punaluan") in which a group of sisters or other close kinswomen from one band were married jointly to a group of brothers or other close kinsmen from another. They thought that only later still, and especially with the domestication of plants and animals, did the "pairing family" develop in which each man was married to one or two women individually.

These writers drew their conclusions not from evidence of actual group-marriage among primitive peoples but from the kinship terms found today in certain tribal and chiefly societies. Some of these equate all kin of the same sex in the parents' generation, suggesting brother-sister marriage. Others equate the father's brothers with the father and the mother's sisters with the mother, suggesting the marriage of a group of brothers with a group of sisters.

Modern evidence does not bear out these conclusions about early society. All known hunters and gatherers live in families, not in communal sexual arrangements. Most hunters even live in nuclear families rather than in large extended kin groups. Mating is individualized, although one man may occasionally have two wives, or (very rarely) a woman may have two husbands. Economic life is built primarily around the division of labor and partnership between individual men and women. The hearths, caves, and other remains of Upper Palaeolithic hunters suggest that this was probably an early arrangement. We cannot say that Engels's sequences are completely ruled out for very early hominids—the evidence is simply not available. But it is hard to see what economic arrangements among hunters would give rise to group, rather than individual or pairing marriage arrangements, and this Engels does not explain.

Soviet anthropologists continued to believe in Morgan and Engels's early "stages" longer than did anthropologists in the West. Today, most Russian anthropologists admit the lack of evidence for "consanguineal" and "punaluan" arrangements, but some still believe that a different kind of group marriage intervened between indiscriminate mating and the pairing family. Semyonov, for example, argues that in the stage of group marriage, mating was forbidden within the hunting band, but that the men of two neighboring bands had multiple, visiting sex relations with women of the opposite band (Semyonov, 1967).

While such an arrangement cannot be ruled out, it seems unlikely because many of the customs which Semyonov regards as "survivals" of such group marriage (for example, visiting husbands, matrilineage dwelling groups, widespread clans, multiple spouses for both sexes, men's and women's communal houses, and prohibitions of sexual intercourse inside the huts of the village) are actually found not so much among hunters as among horticultural tribes and even quite complex agricultural states. Whether or not such a stage of group marriage occurred in the earliest societies, there seems little doubt that pairing marriage (involving family households) came about with the development of elaborate methods of hunting, cooking, and the preparation of clothing and shelters—that is, with a fully fledged division of labor.

Even so, there *are* some senses in which mating among hunters has more of a group character than in archaic agrarian states or in capitalist society. Murdock's sample shows that sex relations before marriage are strictly prohibited in only 26 percent of hunting societies. In the rest, marriage is either arranged so early that premarital sex is unlikely, or (more usually) sex relations are permitted more or less freely before marriage.

With marriage, monogamy is the normal *practice* at any given time for most hunters, but it is not the normal *rule*. Only 19 percent in Murdock's survey prohibit plural unions. Where polygyny is found (79 percent) the most common type is for a man to marry two sisters or other closely related women of the same kin group—for example, the daughters of two sisters or of two brothers. When a woman dies it is common for a sister to replace her in the marriage, and when a man dies, for a brother to replace him.

Similarly, many hunting societies hold that the wives of brothers or other close kinsmen are in some senses wives of the group. They can be called on in emergencies or if one of them is ill. Again, many hunting societies have special times for sexual license between men and women of a local group who are not married to each other, such as the "lights out" games of Eskimo sharing a communal snow house. In other situations, an Eskimo wife will spend the night with a chance guest of her husband's. All parties expect this as normal hospitality. Finally, adultery, although often punished, tends to be common in hunting societies, and few if any of them forbid divorce or the remarriage of divorcees and widows.

The reason for all this seems to be that marriage and sexual restrictions are practical arrangements among hunters designed mainly to serve economic and survival needs. In these societies, some kind of rather stable pairing best accomplishes the division of labor and cooperation of men and women and the care of children. Beyond the immediate family, either a larger family group or the whole band has other, less intensive but important kinds of cooperative activities. Therefore, the husbands and wives of individuals within that group can be summoned to stand in for each other if need arises. In the case of Eskimo wife lending, the extreme climate and the need for lone wandering in search of game dictate high standards of hospitality. This evidently becomes extended to sexual sharing.

In the case of sororal polygyny or marriage to the dead wife's sister, it is natural that when two women fill the same role—either together or in sequence —they should be sisters, for sisters are more alike than other women. They are likely to care more for each other's children. The replacement of a dead spouse by a sister or a brother also preserves existing intergroup relations. For the rest, where the economic and survival bonds of marriage are not at stake, people can afford to be freely companionate and tolerant. Hence, premarital sexual freedom, seasonal group license, and a pragmatic approach to adultery.

Marriages among hunters are usually arranged by elders when a young couple are ready for adult responsibilities. But the couple know each other and usually have some choice. If the first marriage does not work, the second mate will almost certainly be self-selected. Both sexual and companionate love between individual men and women are known and are deeply experienced. With comparative freedom of mating, love is less often separated from or opposed to marriage than in archaic states or even than in some modern nations.

The Position of Women

Even in hunting societies it seems that women are always in some sense the "second sex," with greater or less subordination to men. This varies. Eskimo and Australian aboriginal women are far more subordinate than women among the Kadar, the Andamanese, or the Congo Pygmies—all forest people.

I suggest that women have greater power and independence among hunters when they are important food obtainers than when they are mainly processors of meat or other supplies provided by men. The former situation is likelier to exist in societies where hunting is small-scale and intensive than where it is extensive over a large terrain, and in societies where gathering is important by comparison with hunting.

In general in hunting societies, however, women are less subordinated in certain crucial respects than they are in most, if not all, of the archaic states, or even in some capitalist nations. These respects include men's ability to deny women sexuality or to force it upon them, to command or exploit their labor or to control their produce, to control or rob them of their children, to confine them physically and prevent their movement, to use them as objects in male transactions, to cramp their creativeness, or to withhold from them large areas of the society's knowledge and cultural attainments.

Especially lacking in hunting societies is the kind of male possessiveness and exclusiveness regarding women that leads to such situations as savage punishments or death for female adultery, the jealous guarding of female chastity and virginity, the denial of divorce to women, or the ban on a woman's remarriage after her husband's death.

For these reasons, I do not think we can speak, as some writers do, of a class division between men and women in hunting societies. True, men are more mobile than women and they lead in public affairs. But class society requires that one class control the means of production, dictate its use by the other classes, and expropriate the surplus. These conditions do not exist among hunters. Land and other resources are held communally, although women may monopolize certain gathering areas, and men, their hunting grounds. There is rank difference, role difference, and some difference respecting degrees of authority between the sexes, but there is reciprocity rather than domination or exploitation.

As Engels saw, the power of men to exploit women systematically springs from the existence of surplus wealth and, more directly, from the state, social stratification, and the control of property by men. With the rise of the state, because of their monopoly over weapons, and because freedom from child care allows them to enter specialized economic and political roles, some men—especially ruling-class men—acquire power over other men and over women. Almost all men acquire it over women of their own or lower classes, especially within their own kinship groups. These kinds of male power are shadowy among hunters.

To the extent that men *have* power over women in hunting societies, this seems to spring from the male monopoly of heavy weapons, from the particular division of labor between the sexes, or from both. Although men seldom use weapons against women, they *possess* them (or possess superior weapons) in addition to their physical strength. This does give men an ultimate control of force. When old people or babies must be killed to ensure band or family survival, it is usually men who kill them. Infanticide—rather common among hunters, who must limit the mouths to feed—is more often female infanticide than male.

The hunting of men seems more often to require them to organize in groups than does the work of women. Perhaps because of this, about 60 percent of hunting societies have predominantly virilocal residence. That is, men choose which band to live in (often, their fathers'), and women move with their husbands. This gives a man advantages over his wife in terms of familiarity and loyalties, for the wife is often a stranger. Sixteen to 17 percent of hunting societies are, however, uxorilocal, with men moving to the households of their wives, while 15 to 17 percent are bilocal—that is, either sex may move in with the other on marriage.

Probably because of male cooperation in defense and hunting, men are more prominent in band councils and leadership, in medicine and magic, and in public rituals designed to increase game, to ward off sickness, or to initiate boys into manhood. Women do, however, often take part in band councils; they are not excluded from law and government as in many agrarian states. Some women are respected as wise leaders, story tellers, doctors, or magicians or are feared as witches. Women have their own ceremonies of fertility, birth, and healing, from which men are often excluded.

In some societies, although men control the most sacred objects, women are believed to have discovered them. Among the Congo Pygmies, religion centers about a beneficent spirit, the Animal of the Forest. It is represented by wooden trumpets that are owned and played by men. Their possession and use are hidden from the women and they are played at night when hunting is bad, someone falls ill, or death occurs. During the playing men dance in the public campfire, which is sacred and is associated with the forest. Yet the men believe that women originally owned the trumpet and that it was a woman who stole fire from the chimpanzees or from the forest spirit. When a woman has failed to bear children for several years, a special ceremony is held. Women lead in the songs that usually accompany the trumpets, and an old woman kicks apart the campfire. Temporary female dominance seems to be thought necessary to restore fertility.

In some hunting societies women are exchanged between local groups, which are thus knit together through marriages. Sometimes, men of different bands directly exchange their sisters. More often there is a generalized exchange of women between two or more groups or a one-way movement of women within a circle of groups. Sometimes the husband's family pays weapons, tools, or ornaments to the wife's in return for the wife's services and, later, her children.

In such societies, although they may be well treated and their consent sought, women are clearly the moveable partners in an arrangement controlled by men. Male anthropologists have seized on this as evidence of original male dominance and patrilocal residence. Fox and others, for example, have argued that until recently, *all* hunting societies formed outmarrying patrilocal bands, linked together politically by the exchange of women. The fact that fewer than two-thirds of hunting societies are patrilocal today and only 41 percent have band-exogamy is explained in terms of modern conquest, economic change, and depopulation.

I cannot accept this formula. It is true that modern hunting societies have been severely changed, deculturated, and often depopulated by capitalist imperialism. I can see little evidence, however, that the ones that are patrilocal today have undergone less change than those that are not. It is hard to believe that in spite of enormous environmental diversity and the passage of thousands, perhaps millions, of years, hunting societies all had band exogamy with patrilocal residence until they were disturbed by western imperialism. It is more likely that early band societies, like later agricultural tribes, developed variety in family life and the status of women as they spread over the earth.

There is also some likelihood that the earliest hunters had matrilocal rather than patrilocal families. Among apes and monkeys, it is almost always males who leave the troop or are driven out. Females stay closer to their mothers and their original site; males move about, attaching themselves to females where availability and competition permit. Removal of the wife to the husband's home or band may have been a relatively late development in societies where male cooperation in hunting assumed overwhelming importance.* Conversely, after the development of horticulture (which was probably invented and is mainly carried out by women), those tribes in which horticulture predominated over stock raising were most likely to be or to remain matrilocal and to develop matrilineal descent groups with a relatively high status of women. But where extensive hunting of large animals or, later, the herding of large domesticates, predominated, patrilocal residence flourished and women were used to form alliances between male-centered groups. With the invention of metallurgy and of agriculture as distinct from horticulture after 4000 B.C., men came to control agriculture and many crafts, and most of the great agrarian states had patrilocal residence with patriarchal, male-dominant families.

Conclusions

The family is a human institution, not found in its totality in any prehuman species. It required language, planning, cooperation, self-control, foresight, and cultural learning and probably developed along with these.

The family was made desirable by the early human combination of prolonged child care with the need for hunting with weapons over large terrains. The sexual division of labor on which it was based grew out of a rudimentary prehuman division between male defense and female child care. But among humans this sexual division of functions for the first time became crucial for food production and so laid the basis for future economic specialization and cooperation.

Morgan and Engels were probably right in thinking that the human family was preceded by sexual indiscriminacy. They were also right in seeing an egalitarian group quality about early economic and marriage arrangements.

*Upper Palaeolithic hunters produced female figurines that were obvious emblems of fertility. The cult continued through the Mesolithic and into the Neolithic period. Goddesses and spirits of fertility are found in some patrilineal as well as matrilineal societies, but they tend to be more prominent in the latter. It is thus possible that in many areas even late Stone Age hunters had matrilocal residence and perhaps matrilineal descent, and that in some regions this pattern continued through the age of horticulture and even—as in the case of the Nayars of Kerala and the Minangkabau of Sumatra—into the age of plow agriculture, of writing, and of the small-scale state.

They were without evidence, however, in believing that the earliest mating and economic patterns were entirely group relations.

Together with tool use and language, the family was no doubt the most significant invention of the human revolution. All three required reflective thought, which above all accounts for the vast superiority in consciousness that separates humans from apes.

The family provided the framework for all prestate society and the fount of its creativeness. In groping for survival and for knowledge, human beings learned to control their sexual desires and to suppress their individual selfishness, aggression, and competition. The other side of this self-control was increased capacity for love—not only love of a mother for her child, which is seen among apes, but of male for female in enduring relationships and of each sex for ever-widening groups of humans. Civilization would have been impossible without this initial self-control, seen in incest prohibitions and in the generosity and moral orderliness of primitive family life.

From the start, women have been subordinate to men in certain key areas of status, mobility, and public leadership. But before the agricultural revolution, and even for several thousands of years thereafter, the inequality was based chiefly on the unalterable fact of long child care combined with the exigencies of primitive technology. The extent of inequality varied according to the ecology and the resulting sexual division of tasks. But in any case it was largely a matter of survival rather than of man-made cultural impositions. Hence the impressions we receive of dignity, freedom, and mutual respect between men and women in primitive hunting and horticultural societies. This is true whether these societies are patrilocal, bilocal, or matrilocal, although matrilocal societies, with matrilineal inheritance, offer greater freedom to women than do patrilocal and patrilineal societies of the same level of productivity and political development.

A distinct change occurred with the growth of individual and family property in herds, in durable craft objects and trade objects, and in stable, irrigated farmsites or other forms of heritable wealth. This crystallized in the rise of the state, about 4000 B.C. With the growth of class society and of male dominance in the ruling class of the state, women's subordination increased and eventually reached its depths in the patriarchal families of the great agrarian states. Knowledge of how the family arose is interesting to women because it tells us how we differ from prehumans, what our past has been, and what have been the biological and cultural limitations from which we are emerging. It shows us how generations of male scholars have distorted or overinterpreted the evidence to bolster beliefs in the inferiority of women's mental processes—for which there is no foundation in fact. Knowing about early families is also important to correct a reverse bias among some feminist writers, who hold that in "matriarchal" societies women were completely equal with or were even dominant over men. For this, too, there seems to be no basis in evidence.

The past of the family does not limit its future. Although the family probably emerged with humanity, neither the family itself nor particular family forms are genetically determined. The sexual division of labor—until recently, universal—need not, and in my opinion should not, survive in industrial society. Prolonged child care ceases to be a basis for female subordination when artificial birth control, spaced births, small families, patent feeding, and communal nurseries allow it to be shared by men. Automation and cybernation remove most of the heavy work for which women are less well equipped than men. The exploitation of women that came with the rise of the state and of class society will presumably disappear in poststate classless society—for which the technological and scientific basis already exists.

The family was essential to the dawn of civilization, allowing a vast qualitative leap forward in cooperation, purposive knowledge, love, and creativeness. But today, rather than enhancing them, the confinement of women in homes and small families—like their subordination in work—artificially limits these human capacities. It may be that the human gift for personal love will make some form of voluntary, long-term mating and of individual devotion between parents and children continue indefinitely, side by side with public responsibility for domestic tasks and for the care and upbringing of children. There is no need to legislate personal relations out of existence. But neither need we fear a social life in which the family is no more.

References

Coult, Allen D. *Cross Tabulations of Murdock's World Ethnographic Sample.* Columbia: University of Missouri Press, 1965.

Fox, Robin. *Kinship and Marriage.* London: Pelican Books, 1967.

Hockett, Charles F., and Robert Ascher. "The Human Revolution." In *Man in Adaptation: The Biosocial Background,* edited by Yehudi A. Cohen. Chicago: Aldine, 1968.

Livingstone, Frank B. "Genetics, Ecology and the Origin of Incest and Exogamy." *Current Anthropology,* February 1969.

Morris, Desmond. *The Naked Ape.* Jonathan Cape, 1967.

Murdock, G. P. "World Ethnographic Sample." *American Anthropologist,* 1957.

Murdock, G. P. *Ethnographic Atlas.* Pittsburgh: University of Pittsburgh, 1967.

Schneider, David M., and Kathleen Gough. *Matrilineal Kinship.* Berkeley and Los Angeles: University of California Press, 1961.

Semyonov, Y. I. "Group Marriage, Its Nature and Role in the Evolution of Marriage and Family Relations." In *Seventh International Congress of Anthropological and Ethnological Sciences,* Vol. IV. Moscow, 1967.

World Revolution and Family Patterns

William J. Goode

Idealization of the Recent Past: The United States

In order to weigh the extent and type of changes now taking place in family systems in various parts of the world, it is necessary to examine the recent past; otherwise no trends can be seen. We then usually discover only idealized or stereotyped descriptions of family systems of a generation ago. We must correct such stereotypes in order to measure present-day trends.

In another context, I labeled this stereotype of the United States family of the past, when *praised,* "the classical family of Western nostalgia." It is a pretty picture of life down on grandma's farm. There are lots of happy children, and many kinfolk live together in a large rambling house. Everyone works hard. Most of the food to be eaten during the winter is grown, preserved, and stored on the farm. The family members repair their own equipment, and in general the household is economically self-sufficient. The family has many functions; it is the source of economic stability and religious, educational, and vocational training. Father is stern and reserved and has the final decision in all important matters. Life is difficult but harmonious, because everyone knows his task and carries it out. All boys and girls marry, and marry young. Young people, especially the girls, are likely to be virginal at marriage and faithful afterward. Though the parents do not arrange their children's marriages, the elders do have the right to reject a suitor and have a strong hand in the final decision. After marriage, the couple lives harmoniously, either near the boy's parents or with them, for the couple is slated to inherit the farm. No one divorces.

Those who believe we are seeing progress rather than retrogression often accept the same stereotype but describe the past in words of different emotional effect. We have progressed, they say, from the arbitrary power of elders toward personal freedom for the young, from cold marriages based on economic arrangements to unions based on the youngsters' right of choice, from rigidly maintained class barriers between children to an open class system, from the subjugation of the wife to equalitarianism and companionship in marriage, and from the repression of children's emotions to permissiveness.

Like most stereotypes, that of the classical family of Western nostalgia leads us astray. When we penetrate the confusing mists of recent history we find few examples of this "classical" family. Grandma's farm was not economically self-sufficient. Few families stayed together as large aggregations of kinfolk. Most houses were small, not large. We now *see* more large old houses than

From the *Journal of Marriage and the Family* (November 1971), pp. 624–635. Copyright © 1971 by William J. Goode. Reprinted by permission.

small ones; they survived longer because they were likely to have been better constructed. The one-room cabins rotted away. True enough, divorce was rare, but we have no evidence that families were generally happy. Indeed, we find, as in so many other pictures of the glowing past, that in each past generation people write of a period *still* more remote, *their* grandparents, generation, when things really were much better.

If, then, the stereotype of the United States and Western family is partially incorrect, we may suppose stereotypes of other past family systems to be similarly in error. We shall, therefore, describe current changes in family patterns while ascertaining, where possible, what the patterns of the recent past were.

The Conjugal Family as an Ideal Type

As now used by family analysts, the term *conjugal family* is technically an *ideal type;* it also represents an ideal. The concept was not developed from a summary or from the empirical study of actual United States urban family behavior; it is a *theoretical* construction, derived from intuition and observation, in which several crucial variables have been combined to form a hypothetical structural harmony. Such a conceptual structure may be used as a measure and model in examining real time trends or contemporary patterns. In the ensuing discussion, we shall try to separate the fundamental from the more derivative variables in this construction.

As a concept, the conjugal family is also an *ideal* in that when analysts refer to its spread they mean that an increasing number of people view some of its characteristics as *proper* and legitimate, no matter how reality may run counter to the ideal. Thus, although parents in the United States agree that they *should* not play an important role in their children's choice of spouse, they actually do. Relatives *should* not interfere in each other's family affairs, but in a large (if unknown) percentage of cases they do. Since, however, this ideal aspect of the conjugal family is also part of the total reality, significant for changes in family patterns, we shall comment on it later as an ideology.

The most important characteristic of the ideal typical construction of the conjugal family is the relative exclusion of a wide range of affinal and blood relatives from its everyday affairs: There is no great extension of the kin network. Many other traits may be derived theoretically from this one variable. Thus, the couple cannot count on a large number of kinfolk for help, just as these kin cannot call upon the couple for services. Neither couple nor kinfolk have many *rights* with respect to the other, and so the reciprocal *obligations* are few. In turn, by an obvious sociological principle, the couple has few moral controls over their extended kin, and these have few controls over the couple.

The locality of the couple's household will no longer be greatly determined by their kin since kinship ties are weak. The couple will have a "neolocal" residence; that is, they will establish a new household when they marry. This in turn reinforces their relative independence, because it lowers the frequency of social interaction with their kin.

The choice of mate is freer than in other systems, because the bases upon which marriage is built are different: The kin have no strong rights or financial interest in the matter. Adjustment is primarily between husband and wife, not between the incoming spouse and his or her in-law group. The courtship system is therefore ideally based, and, at the final decision stage, empirically as well, on the mutual attraction between the two youngsters.

All courtship systems are market or exchange systems. They differ from one another with respect to who does the buying and selling, which characteristics are more or less valuable in that market, and how open or explicit the bargaining is. In a conjugal family system mutual attraction in both courtship and marriage acquires a higher value. Nevertheless, the elders do not entirely lose control. Youngsters are likely to marry only those with whom they fall in love, and they fall in love only with the people they meet. Thus, the focus of parental controls is on who is allowed to meet whom at parties, in the school and neighborhood, and so on.

When such a system begins to emerge in a society, the age at marriage is likely to change because the goals of marriage change, but whether it will rise or fall cannot be predicted from the characteristics mentioned so far. In a conjugal system, the youngsters must now be old enough to take care of themselves; that is, they must be as old as the economic system forces them to be in order to be independent at marriage. (Alternative solutions also arise: Some middle-class youngsters may marry upon the promise of support from their parents, while they complete their education.) Thus, if the economic system changes its base, for example, from agriculture to industry, the age at marriage may change. The couple decides the number of children they will have on the basis of their own needs, not those of a large kin group; and contraception, abortion, or infanticide may be used to control this number. Whether fertility will be high or low cannot, however, be deduced from these conjugal traits. Under some economic systems, for example, frontier agriculture, the couple may actually need a large number of children.

This system is bilineal or, to use Max Gluckman's term, multilineal: The two kin lines are of nearly equal importance, because neither has great weight. Neolocality and the relative freedom from control by an extended kin network prevent the maintenance or formation of a powerful lineage system, which is necessary if one line is to be dominant over the other.

Since the larger kin group can no longer be counted on for emotional sustenance, and since the marriage is based on mutual attraction, the small marital unit is the main place where the emotional input-output balance of the individual husband and wife is maintained, where their psychic wounds can be salved or healed. At least there is no other place where they can go. Thus, the emotions within this unit are likely to be intense, and the relationship between husband and wife may well be intrinsically unstable, depending as it does on affection. Consequently, the divorce rate is likely to be high. Remarriage is likely because there is no larger kin unit to absorb the children and no unit to prevent the spouses from reentering the free marriage market.

Finally, the couple and children do recognize some extended kin, but the husband recognizes a somewhat different set of kindred than does his wife, since they began in different families. And the children view as important a somewhat different set of kindred than do their parents: The parents look back a generation greater in depth than do the children and perhaps a greater distance outward, because they have had an adult lifetime in which to come to know more kin. That is, each individual takes into account a somewhat different set of kindred, though most of them are the same for all within the same nuclear unit.

The foregoing sketch is an ideal typical construction and thus must be compared with the reality of both behavior *and* ideal in those societies which are thought to have conjugal family patterns. To my knowledge, no such test has been made. Very likely, the *ideals* of a large proportion of United States families fit this construction very well. Some parts of the construction also fit the *behavior* of a considerable but unknown fraction of United States families, for example, the emphasis on emotionality within the family; the free choice of spouse; and neolocality, bilineality, and instability of the individual family. On the other hand, data from both England and the United States indicate that even in lower-class urban families, where the extension of kin ties might be thought to be shorter (following the ideal type), many kin ties are active. . . . No one has measured the intensity and extensiveness of kin ties in a range of societies in order to ascertain how Western family patterns compare in these respects. It is quite possible that those countries thought to be closest to the conjugal pattern do in fact have a less extended kin network.

Nevertheless, the ideal type conflicts sharply with reality *and* theory in one important respect. Theoretical considerations suggest that, without the application of political pressure, the family *cannot* be as limited in its kin network as the ideal typical construction suggests. Both common observation and theory coincide to suggest that (1) grandparent-grandchild ties are still relatively intense and (2) emotional ties among siblings are also strong. Consequently, (3) parents-in-law interact relatively frequently with their children-in-law, and (4) married people have frequent contacts with their brothers- or sisters-in-law. It follows, then, that (5) children maintain contacts, at least during their earlier years, with their uncles and aunts, as well as with their first cousins. Without question, of all types of "visiting" and "social occasions," the most common, even in the urban United States, is "visiting with relatives."

If no active ties are maintained with the categories of kin mentioned above, the family feels that some explanation is called for and pleads some excuse ("They live too far away" or "We've never gotten along well").

In addition, perhaps most families have *some* tie with one or more relatives still further away in the kin network. Those noted above seem to be linked to the nuclear family in an inescapable way; it is difficult to ignore or reject any of them without simultaneously rejecting a fellow member of *one's own* nuclear family. The child cannot ignore his uncle without hurting one of his own parents, and reciprocally. A girl may not neglect her sister-in-law without impairing her relationship with her brother. Of course, brother and sister may combine against their own spouses, and social interaction may continue even under an impaired relationship. Cousins are dragged along by their parents, who are siblings and siblings-in-law to one another. The extension of the family network to this point, then, seems determined by the emotional ties within the nuclear family unit itself. To reduce the unit to the nuclear family would require coercive restriction of these ties between siblings or between parents, as the Chinese commune has attempted to do.

The "Fit" Between the Conjugal Family and the Modern Industrial System

The argument as to whether political and economic variables, or the reverse, generally determine family patterns seems theoretically empty. Rather, we must establish any determinate relations (whichever direction the causal effect) among any particular family variables and the variables of other institutional orders—not a simple task. Even the relation between the conjugal family and industrialization is not yet entirely clear. The common hypothesis—that the conjugal form of the family emerges when a culture is invaded by industrialization and urbanization—is an undeveloped observation which neglects three issues: (1) the theoretical harmony or "fit" between this ideal typical form of the family and industrialization; (2) the empirical harmony or fit between industrialization and any actual system; and (3) the effects upon the family of the modern (or recent past) organizational and industrial system, that is, how the factors in the system influence the family.

At present, only the first of these can be treated adequately. The second has been dealt with primarily by researchers who have analyzed a peasant or primitive culture with reference to the problem of labor supply and who suggest that family systems *other* than the conjugal one do not adequately answer the demands of an expanding industrial system. Malinowski asserted, for example, that although young Trobriander men could earn more by working on plantations than by growing yams, they preferred to grow yams because this activity was defined as required for their family roles. Similarly, a head tax was necessary to force young men to leave their families to work in the South African mines. Men's objections to women's leaving the home for outside jobs have limited the labor supply in various parts of the world, especially in Islamic areas. On the other hand, within conjugal or quasi-conjugal systems such as those in the West, the strains between family patterns and industrial requirements have only rarely been charted empirically.

This last task would require far more ingenious research designs than have been so far utilized. It requires that the exact points of impact between family and industrial organization be located and the degree of impact measured. Succeeding chapters will devote some attention to this problem. Specific decisions or choices need to be analyzed in which both family and industrial variables are involved.

Nevertheless, if we are to achieve a better understanding of world changes in family systems, it may help if we can correct the theoretical analyses of the first problem, the fit between the ideal typical form of the conjugal family and industrialization. It seems possible to do this through some reference to common observations about both United States and European family patterns.

Let us consider first the demands of industrialization, which is the crucial element in the complex types of change now occurring in even remote parts of the world. Although bureaucratization may occur without industrialization (witness China), and so may urbanization (for example, Dahomey, Tokugawa Japan), neither occurs without some rise in a society's technological level, and certainly the modern system of industry never occurs without *both* urbanization and bureaucratization.

The prime social characteristic of modern industrial enterprise is that the individual is ideally given a job on the basis of his ability to fulfill its demands, and that this achievement is evaluated universalistically; the same standards apply *to all who hold the same job.* His link with the job is functionally specific; in other words, the enterprise cannot require behavior of him which is not relevant to getting the job done.

Being achievement-based, an industrial society is necessarily open-class, requiring both geographical and social mobility. Men must be permitted to rise or fall depending on their performance. Moreover, in the industrial system, jobs based on ownership and exploitation of land (and thus on inheritance) become numerically less significant, again permitting considerable geographical mobility to that individuals are free to move about in the labor market. The neolocality of the conjugal system correspondingly frees the individual from ties to the specific geographical location where his parental family lives.

The conjugal family's relationship to class mobility is rather complex. Current formulations, based on ancient wisdom, assert that by limiting the extensiveness of the kin network, the individual is less hampered by his family in rising upward in the job structure. Presumably, this means that he owes less to his kin and so can allocate his resources of money and time solely to further his career; perhaps he may also more freely change his style of life, his mode of dress, and speech, in order to adjust to a new class position without criticism from his kin. On the other hand, an industrial system pays less attention to what the individual does off the job, so that family and job are structurally somewhat more separated than in other systems. Consequently, one might reason that differential social or occupational mobility (as among siblings or cousins) would not affect kin ties. Yet the emotional ties within the conjugal system are intense, compared to other systems, so that even though there are fewer relatives, the weight of kin relationships to be carried upward by the mobile individual might be equivalent to that in a system with more, but less intense, ties.

An alternative view must also be considered. Under some circumstances the kin network actually contributes greatly to the individual's mobility, and "social capillarity" as a process (that is, that individual rises highest who is burdened with least kin) moves fewer people upward than does a well-integrated kin network. A brief theoretical sketch of this alternative view also throws light on the supposed "adjustment" between the needs of the small conjugal family and those of a modern industrial system.

First, in the modern industrial system, the middle and upper strata are by definition more "successful" in the obvious sense that they own it, dominate it, occupy its highest positions, and direct its future. One must concede that they are "well adjusted" to the modern industrial society. Paradoxically, their kin pattern is in fact *less* close to the ideal typical form of the conjugal family than is the family behavior of the lower strata. The upper strata recognize the widest extension of kin, maintain most control to give and receive help from one another.

Consequently, the lower strata's freedom from kin is like their "freedom" to sell their labor in an open market. They are less encumbered by the weight of kin when they are able to move upward, but they also get less help from their kin. Like English peasants, who from the sixteenth to eighteenth centuries were gradually "freed" from the land by the enclosure movement, or nineteenth-century workers, who were "freed" from their tools by the development of machinery, the lower strata have fewer family ties, less family stability, and enjoy less family-based economic and material security. The lower-class family pattern is indeed most "integrated" with the industrial system but mainly in the sense that the individual is forced to enter its labor market with far less family support—his family *does not prevent industry from using him for its own goals.* He may move where the system needs him, hopefully where his best opportunity lies, but he *must* also fit the demands of the system, since no extended kin network will interest itself greatly in his fate. The job demands of the industrial system move the individual about, making it difficult for him to keep his kin ties active; and because his kin are also in the lower strata he has little to lose by relinquishing those ties. In short, lower-strata families are most likely to be "conjugal" and to serve the needs of the industrial system; this system may not, however, serve the needs of that family pattern. This means that when industrialization begins, it is the lower-class family that loses least by participating in it and that lower-class family patterns are the first to change in the society. We might speculatively infer further that *now,* a century after the first great impact of industrialization of the lower-class family in the Western urban world, family patterns of Western middle and upper classes may be changing more rapidly than those of the lower. (Whether rural changes may not be occurring equally rapidly cannot be deduced from these inferences.) However, although this inference may be empirically correct, the available data demand a more cautious inference: Whether or not the middle and upper strata *are* now changing more rapidly in the Western world, they *do* have more resources with which to resist certain of the industrial system's undermining pressures (e.g., capital with which to support their youngsters through a long professional training) and a considerable interest in resisting them because their existing kin network is more active and useful. We would suppose, then, that in an industrializing process both the peasants and primitives are forced to adjust their family patterns to the demands of industrial enterprise more swiftly and see less to lose in the adjustment. By contrast, the middle and upper strata are better able to utilize the new opportunities of industrialization by relinquishing their kin ties more slowly, so that these changes will occur only in a later phase of industrialization, such as the United States is now undergoing.

Continuing now with our analysis of the "fit" of the conjugal family to industrial needs, the more limited conjugal kin network opens mobility channels somewhat by limiting the "closure" of class strata. In general, rigid class boundaries can be maintained partly by the integration of kin bonds against the "outsider" through family controls. When the network of each family is smaller, the families of an upper stratum are less integrated, the web of kin less tightly woven, and entrance into the stratum easier. Since the industrial system requires relatively free mobility, this characteristic of the conjugal pattern fits the needs of that system. This general principle also holds for classical China, where an empirically different system prevailed. A successful family would normally expand over generations but thereby have insufficient resources to maintain so many at a high social rank. That is, the reciprocal exchange necessary for tightness and closure of the kin system could be kept up only by a few individual families in the total network. If all the families in the network shared alike as kinsmen (which did not happen), the entire network would lose social rank. If the few well-to-do families helped their kin only minimally and maintained ties with other upper stratum families, the integration of the stratum was kept intact and the stratification system was not threatened.

The modern technological system is psychologically burdensome on the individual because it demands an unremitting discipline. To the extent that evaluation is based on achievement and universalism, the individual gets little emotional security from his work. Some individuals, of course, obtain considerable pleasure from it, and every study of job satisfaction shows that in positions offering higher prestige and salaries a higher proportion of people are satisfied with their work and would choose that job if they had to do it again. Lower level jobs give little pleasure to most people. However, in higher level professional, managerial, and creative positions the standards of performance are not only high but are often without clearly stated limits. The individual is under considerable pressure to perform better than he is able.

The conjugal family again integrates with such a system by its emphasis on emotionality, especially in the relationship of husband and wife. It has the task of restoring the input-output emotional balance of individualism in such a job structure. This is so even for lower strata jobs where the demands for performance are kept within limits by an understood quota but where, by contrast with upper strata jobs, there is less intrinsic job satisfaction. Of course, the family cannot fully succeed in this task, but at least the technological system has no moral responsibility for it and can generally ignore the problem in its work demands.

Bilateral in pattern, this family system does not maintain a lineage. It does not concentrate family land or wealth in the hands of one son through whom the property would descend, or even in the hands of one sex. Dispersal of inheritance keeps the class system fluid. Daughters as well as sons will share as heirs, and a common legal change in the West is toward equal inheritance by all children (as is already the situation generally in the United States). Relatively equal advantages are given to all the sons, and although even United States families do not invest so heavily in daughters as in sons (more boys than girls complete college), the differences in training the two sexes are much less than in other family systems. Consequently, a greater proportion of all children are given the opportunity to develop their talents to fit the manifold opportunities of a complex technological and bureaucratic structure.

The conjugal system also specifies the status obligations of each member in much less *detail* than does an extended family system, in which entrepreneurial, leadership, or production tasks are assigned by family position. Consequently, wider individual variations in family role performance are permitted, to enable members to fit the range of possible demands by the industrial system as well as by other members of the family.

Since the young adult is ideally expected to make his own choice of spouse and the young couple is expected to be economically independent, the conjugal system, by extending the adolescent phase of development, permits a long period of tutelage. For example, it is expected that the individual should be grown up before marrying. Note, however, that it is not the family itself that gives this extended tutelage, but public, impersonal agencies, such as schools, military units, and corporations, which ideally ignore family origin and measure the individual by his achievement and talent. This pattern permits the individual to obtain a longer period of training, to make a freer choice of his career, and to avoid the economic encumbrance of marriage until he has fitted himself into the industrial system. Thus, the needs of the industrial system are once more served by the conjugal family pattern.

The *different* adjustment of families in *different* classes to the industrial system emphasizes the *independence* of the two sets of variables, the familial and the industrial, as well as the presence of some "disharmonies" between the two. Further points where the two do not adjust fully may be noted here. The modern woman is given little relief from child care, which is typically handed over to one person, the wife, rather than to several women, some of them elders, who are part of the family unit in more extended systems. Adjustments in modes of child care, which seem to accompany industrialization, are in part a result of the decline of a family tradition handed down from older women to the younger. With the weakening of ties with the older generation younger women depend increasingly on the published opinions of experts as a guide for child-rearing practices.

Even the substantial development of labor-saving devices and technology has not lightened labor in the modern United States home, contrary to both advertising in women's magazines and the stereotyped notions of Europeans. Most of these devices merely raise the standards for cleanliness and repairs, and allow the housewife to turn out more "domestic production" each day. Every study of the time allocation of mothers shows that housewives work extremely long hours. For those who have assumed otherwise, let me remind them that the washing machine brings back into the home a job that an earlier generation delegated to lower-class labor or the laundry; that the vacuum cleaner merely raises standards without substantially speeding up work; that the electric sewing machine is exactly analogous to the washing machine. On the other hand, the organized activities of children have become so complex, and the number of objects in the house so numerous, that even the middle-class housewife must spend much of her time in essentially administrative activities when she is not laboring with her hands. Marx, commenting on John Stuart Mill's doubt that mechanical inventions had lightened man's toil, asserted that lightened toil was not the *aim* of the capitalist use (for the modern scene, read "industrial use") of machinery. While one might quarrel with Marx's concept of *deliberate* aim, it remains true that it is difficult to release even well-trained women from their household tasks and especially from their emotional tasks; there is no one to substitute for that labor, unless new agencies such as communal nurseries are created. In addition, since the amount of work is great and there is presumptive equality of husband and wife, the husband generally has to step in to help after work, which in turn diverts some of his energy from his occupation.

Ignoring the question of feasibility of additional time, it also remains true that for women, the roles of wife and mother are their central obligations. For this reason, and because there is no one else who can be given the care of house and children, over the past half-century in the United States, women have not become much more "career-minded" than they were, and polling evidence suggests that a similar conclusion may be applied to Europe. Even though an increasing percentage of women in the United States are in the labor force, as in some countries of Europe, there has been over the past few decades (in the United States) only a very slight increase in the proportion of mothers of small children who are in the labor force, and these are predominantly in the lower income groups, where the economic pressure to work is great. Much of the recent great increase in female participation in the United States labor force has been concentrated in the older age groups. Toward the higher economic strata, generally a lower proportion of women work.

Unlike men, women do not as yet think of job holding as a *career,* as a necessary and intrinsic part of their destiny. From 1910 to 1950 in the United States, while the conjugal family was spreading beyond the city, the proportion of women in the established professions did not change greatly. The number of women physicians increased from 6 percent to 6.1 percent. In dentistry, the proportion decreased slightly. In law, engineering, architecture, and the ministry, the increase was substantial, but in none did the proportion rise above 4.1 percent. In college teaching there was a slight increase, so that women constituted 23.2 percent of the total in 1958, as compared with 19.8 percent in 1899–1900. The proportion of college-educated women who have gone into the established professions has dropped during the past half-century, although of course the percentage of women has increased substantially within a range of technical or semiprofessional jobs in the natural sciences. Clearly, the "needs" of industrialization are not in easy adjustment with the role obligations of women.

Family Membership, Past and Present

Barbara Laslett

Recent sociological discussions of the family have a curiously contradictory character. The growth of a counterculture in the 1960s and early 1970s both rejected and posed alternatives to traditional forms of the family (Skolnick, 1973). Interpreting student and antiwar activism as a failure in the family's ability to provide coherent socialization experience for its children (Flacks, 1971) led people to question the adequacy of family norms and traditional family life. To use Arlene Skolnick's (1973) phrase, the nuclear family was thought to be "alive, but not well." In contrast to this view, other discussions of the contemporary family emphasize its robustness. Mary Jo Bane (1976:xiv), for instance, concluded that the demographic data she analyzed show "surprising evidence of the persistence of commitments to family life . . ."—that the family is "here to stay."

From *Social Problems*, Vol. 25, No. 5 (June 1978), pp. 476–490. Copyright © 1978 by the Society for the Study of Social Problems. Reprinted by permission of the Society and the author.

Marriage and divorce statistics mirror the apparent contradictions exemplified by these views. In the United States, marriage continues to be an exceedingly popular institution. A comparison of marriage rates in twenty-two selected countries (Carter and Glick, 1976:387) shows that in 1965, only Egypt had a higher marriage rate than the United States, while in every year between 1970 and 1974, the United States rate was higher than that of any other country included in their comparison.[1] Of course the high rate of marriage in the United States may well be affected by the fact that Americans also have the highest divorce rate compared to seventeen of these same countries. Although there has been a slight decline in the American remarriage rate since 1974, the divorce rate has been increasing steadily since 1965 (Carter and Glick, 1976:391). Nevertheless, Bane suggests (1976:34) that "it is not marriage itself but the specific marital partner that is rejected."

In addition to marriage and divorce statistics, other aspects of family life have been attracting public and professional interest. Whether the increasing attention to family violence (Steinmetz and Straus, 1975; Gelles, 1974; Steinmetz, 1977) indicates a higher incidence of violence or simply more public discussion of it is difficult to know; in either case, child and wife battering are clear indications of family "troubles." Even the rise in the professions of marriage and family therapy[2] can be interpreted in two ways—as indicating increasing difficulties within the family or of greater efforts to resolve problems. One may therefore ask, why is the contemporary family "not well—but here to stay"?

Several answers have been given to why the family is not well. Skolnick (1973), for instance, suggests that earlier conceptualization tended to sentimentalize the family and its relationships, to view the family in utopian terms, and to ignore the strains and conflicts which daily life involves. Only recently have conceptualizations derived from conflict theory been applied to family dynamics. Other answers have suggested that large-scale political and economic changes have contributed to the difficulties that the modern family now faces (Flacks, 1971; Zaretsky, 1976).

Functional theory, particularly Parsons, has provided one answer to why the family is "here to stay." The argument is familiar and emphasizes an increasing *division of labor* within and between social institutions—structural differentiation—which has characterized the process of historical change. Under these conditions, the family has assumed a more specialized set of functions for the larger society—that of primary socialization agent for children and the stabilization of adult personalities. Thus, "the family has become *a more*

---

[1]The marriage rate has declined somewhat since 1972 but without changing the status of the United States compared to other countries.

[2]In 1960, the membership of the American Association of Marriage and Family Counselors was 237; by 1976 it had risen to 4230. In every year since 1970 (at which time the membership was 973), the percentage annual increase in membership ranged from twenty-four percent to thirty-seven percent. (American Association of Marriage and Family Counselors, personal communication from administrative offices, Claremont, Calif.)

specialized agency than before . . . but (is) not in any general sense less important, because the society is dependent *more* exclusively on it for the performance of *certain* of its vital functions" (Parsons and Bales, 1955:9-10).

Recent statements by social scientists elaborate upon this view of the contemporary family's "socio-emotional specialization." Berger and Kellner (1975), for instance, state that "marriage occupies a privileged status among the significant validating relationships for adults in our society." Providing a very Parsonian explanation for this development, they say

> this character of marriage has its roots in much broader structural configurations of our society. The most important of these, for our purpose, is the crystallization of a so-called private sphere of existence. . . . defined and utilized as the main social area for the individual's self-realization.

Weigert and Hastings (1977) also discuss the significance of the family's specialized role when they say "the basic relationships of the nuclear family . . . are central to the processes of identity formation . . ." And Zaretsky (1976:30) introduces a class dimension into this characterization of the contemporary family when he says

> under capitalism an ethic of personal fulfillment has become the property of the masses of people . . . Much of this search for personal meaning takes place within the family and is no reason for the persistence of the family in spite of the decline of many of its earlier functions.

Noting that in modern society the development of personal identity and the satisfaction of personal needs have become specialized functions of the family leaves two important questions unanswered: 1) how was institutional differentiation at the macro-structural level transformed into individual, emotional, expectations within the family, and 2) can the family, in practice rather than soley in theory, satisfy the demands assigned to it by its functional specialization? The following analysis will address the first of these questions by drawing upon the results of recent research in demographic and family history.[3]

The thesis presented here is that changes in household composition, in the demography of kinship, and in the relationship between the family and other institutions have contributed to the greater emotional significance of the family through their impact on the socialization process. These changes, since the end of the nineteenth century,[4] have caused family membership in the United States to have increased significance for personal identity and emotional gratifi-

---

[3]A more complete formulation, in which macro-economic changes will be more fully discussed, is in preparation as part of the author's study of the family and social change in nineteenth century Los Angeles. For a preliminary statement see B. Laslett, 1978b.

[4]For this discussion, the twentieth century family will be contrasted with the family in earlier historical periods, with full recognition that such a gross dichotomy obscures variation in the rates and timing of the developments important for understanding how historical change has affected the family. See B. Laslett, 1973, for a discussion of why the twentieth century family can legitimately be differentiated from the family in earlier historical periods.

cation. (Aries, 1975, and Shorter, 1975, provide similar arguments about the European family.) In addition, changes in ideology have reinforced the belief that family relationships have become more important for individual development, self-definition, and satisfaction in life.

An analysis which shows *how* family membership has become more significant to individual identity does not, thereby, support a sentimental view, focused only on the positive results of domestic interaction. The intense feelings generated by intimate relationships can be positive or negative, and family relationships may be particularly vulnerable in this respect. In fact, when strong feelings are involved, conflict, abuse, and family dissolution may be more frequent.

Thus, to describe the history of the family's increased importance as a source of personal identity and satisfaction in life is not to say that it successfully satisfies the demands its increasing specialization and importance impose upon it. Several social scientists (Lasch, 1977; Slater, 1970, 1977) have suggested that inherent contradictions within the family make its success unlikely. It is precisely this disparity—between expectations structurally and normatively encouraged and the ability to satisfy them—which is central to understanding the contradictions in contemporary family life.

Family Structure and Socialization

Recent research on the history of the family in Western Europe and North America shows that the membership of most households, both past and present, was—and is—composed primarily of nuclear family members. (See, for instance, Anderson, 1971; Demos, 1970; Greven, 1970; Katz, 1975; P. Laslett, 1972, 1977; Parish and Schwartz, 1972; Blumin, 1975; B. Laslett, 1975, 1977). It is important, however, to distinguish the family, defined in terms of the co-resident domestic group, from the kinship group extending beyond the household.

The most frequently used data for investigating the structure of family life in past times are parish records, and census and other types of nominal listings, which usually report information on the co-resident domestic group. Empirical research findings on kinship ties beyond the household are more difficult to obtain and fewer are available. (For some examples, see Anderson, 1971; Plakans, 1977.) While the use of findings about the organization of the co-resident domestic group to discuss family structure in past times has been defended by some scholars (P. Laslett, 1972), its limitations have been criticized by others (Berkner, 1975). Conclusions based on household-level data clearly provide only partial information, since the residential unit is but one way to define the family. (See Goody, 1972, for a further discussion of this issue.)

Dispute over the proper—and possible—unit of analysis in historical family research contributes to contradictory interpretations about how the family has changed. While, as has been suggested, several social scientists argue that the family has become increasingly important, others take an opposite view. Wells (1971:278) in discussing the effects of demographic change on the life cycle of American families, says that there has been a "relative decrease in the importance of children in the life of twentieth-century families . . ." Kobrin (1976) makes a similar argument in relation to the increased proportion of persons living alone in the twentieth century.

There is reason to question these conclusions, however, since some of the same demographic factors on which they are based have increased the availability of kin with whom contact is both possible and likely to occur—particularly parents and grandparents. Although child-rearing as traditionally defined —the care of pre-adult, resident children—may occupy a smaller proportion of the family life cycle in contemporary America than was true in the past, advances in the technology relevant for contact and communication—such as automobiles, highway systems, telephones—mean that residence may no longer be central to the continuation of relationships among family members.

Given the scarcity of empirical research on the nonresidential family in the past, the following discussion will present the results of two research traditions not usually related to each other. It will first examine findings on the household unit and then the demographic changes which have affected the size and structure of the kinship group. The impact of migration and urbanization on the availability of family members will also be discussed. The relation between these research findings—and their importance for understanding the significance of family membership in contemporary society—will be integrated through a discussion of their possible effects on socialization within the family.

Household Composition

As indicated, the nuclear family was in past times the predominant type of co-residential domestic group. This finding does not imply that all people lived in nuclear families for all of their lives; life cycle variation in the kin composition of the residential family has been found in several historical studies (Goody, 1972; Hareven, 1975; Herlihy, 1972; Berkner, 1972; B. Laslett, 1975). Household structure has also been shown to be related to socio-economic characteristics of the head of the household, demographic factors, ethnicity, land-holding patterns, and inheritance practices (Glasco, 1975; Gutman, 1976; Katz, 1975; Coale et al., 1965; B. Laslett, 1975, 1977; Farber, 1972; Berkner and Mendels, in press; Furstenberg et al., 1975). Despite these sources of variation, there continues to be support for the view that the nuclear family household was, and is, the modal category of the co-resident domestic group in most western societies in both the preindustrial past and under comtemporary forms of social and economic organization.

While predominantly nuclear in its kinship structure, the preindustrial and early industrial household was also likely to include others unrelated to the conjugal family unit. Among such persons were servants, boarders, and lodgers, apprentices, employees, and other people's children.[5] (B. Laslett, 1973; Blumin, 1975; Kobrin, 1976). Modell and Hareven (1973) show that "the proportion of urban households *which at any particular point in time* had boarders or lodgers was between fifteen and twenty percent."[6] Today, on the contrary, non-kin are unlikely to be included among the membership of many households. In 1970, only 3.5% of all households included in the federal census had one or more resident members unrelated to the head (U.S. Bureau of the Census, 1973:246).

One characteristic distinguishing the contemporary household from domestic settings in the past, therefore, is that few now contain nonrelatives. But in nineteenth century America, interaction with non-kin outside the household was likely to be supplemented by contact with resident non-kin. A large proportion of persons interacted with non-kin as part of the daily life within their homes. Although the qualitative character of such contact cannot be known solely from this kind of evidence—the extent to which non-relatives were integrated into the family's life and affairs—non-kin shared the household where many nineteenth century children and adults lived.

Under contemporary conditions, socialization within the household refers primarily to interactions between parents and their children. The psychodynamic structure of this process is, therefore, likely to reflect the personalities and personal histories of individuals linked together by family ties. Thus, identification and role modeling—the processes involved in the psychodynamic structure of personality development—are defined primarily by characteristics of individuals within the nuclear family group and become identified with membership in a specific family unit. There is a strong imprint of family membership.

[5] The periods of service, apprenticeship, and boarding common for young people in the preindustrial Western experience was not usually spent in the homes of kinsmen, although by the beginning of the twentieth century this may have begun to change.

[6] Overall figures may underestimate the proportion of households which included "strangers within the co-resident domestic group, since taking in boarders was related to the family life cycle. Modell and Hareven (1973), for instance, report that among a sample of native, working-class families in the industrial north in 1890, twenty percent of the families with a resident child under five took in boarders if the household head was under twenty-five years of age compared to thirty-five percent of the households with a child of comparable age but when the head was forty-five years of age or older. Berkner (1972) also finds life cycle variation in the presence of residence agricultural workers among eighteenth century peasant households in Austria.

Taking in boarders has usually been associated with urbanization (Modell and Hareven, 1973) and seems to have been higher in urban than rural areas (B. Laslett, 1977b). There is evidence, however, that it occurred in rural communities as well (Blumin, 1975; Roberts, 1904).

This feature of contemporary household composition has relevance for various stages of growth throughout the life cycle, during which themes develop, are enacted, and become identified with a particular family. According to Hess and Handel (1969:18):

> A family theme is a pattern of feelings, motives, fantasies, and conventionalized understanding grouped about some locus of concern which has a particular form in the personalities of the individual members. The pattern comprises some fundamental view of reality and some way or ways of dealing with it. In the family themes are to be found the family's implicit direction, its notion of "who we are."

Development and reiteration of such themes is likely to provide the basis for a more heightened sense of differentiation between family and non-family members in the present than in the past, when households included both kin and non-kin.

In adolescence, the influence of non-kin was likely to continue, but was due as much to the adolescents' moving as to the household composition of their families of origin, for adolescence in earlier times was marked by the removal of young adults from their parents' homes. They left to find work, to become servants and apprentices and, some have argued, to get an education and build character (Morgan, 1944; Demos, 1970; Shorter, 1975). This pattern seems to have occurred in various parts of Western Europe (see, for instance, Anderson, 1971; McBride, 1976; Schofield 1970; Shorter, 1975) and North America (Bloomberg, 1974; Dublin, 1975; Katz, 1975; Little and Laslett, 1977).

Recent historical research shows (Katz, 1975; Bloomberg, 1974; Little and Laslett, 1977) that in the late nineteenth century, at least in the industrializing economies of the new world, adolescents experienced a lengthening period of dependency upon their parents. Prior to that time, many spent their adolescence outside the parental home. Of course visiting home and parents was possible and did take place although how often depended on the terms of the contract governing the life of the servant or apprentice as well as the distance involved. Thus, contact with kin for many adolescents and young adults in the past was more likely to be a special occasion than a daily or weekly occurrence.[7]

These aspects of household composition are likely to have influenced the socialization process of both adults and children in the past, as they do in the present. We can see the significance of these structural changes most clearly in relation to adolescence—a period characterized in contemporary psychological thought (Erikson, 1959) by a search for a separate identity on the part of young adults. The increased identification of the self with a particular family unit, and the greater clarity of boundaries between family and non-family members, may have increased the need to differentiate one's self

---

[7]The implications of these changes in residence for the meaning of adolescence is discussed in Little and Laslett, 1977.

from the family group as part of the transition to adulthood, thereby sharpening parent-child conflict during adolescence.[8] Furthermore, the wish to establish one's own identity is more likely to be experienced by both parents and children as a rejection of and rebellion against the more clearly formulated identity with a particular family. Thus, the search for a separate identity involves questioning parental norms and authority, since it is parents who symbolize in the strongest emotional terms, the norms and authority of the adult world.

Understanding the impact of household composition on socialization within the family should not be limited to the young people involved. Under the conditions of contemporary family living, parents are also more likely than in the past to develop strong identification with their children. Each of the child's developmental stages poses developmental tasks for the parents as well, reawakening themes and conflicts from their own youth and posing the psychological tasks associated with aging. It is not surprising that two contemporary concerns of psycho-dynamic thought center simultaneously on problems of adolescence and "the mid-life crisis." These "crises of growth" reflect the increased intensity of family relationships and the increased importance of family membership for personal identity to which historical changes in household composition have contributed.

Demography and Kinship

Three demographic factors are of particular importance in comparing the size and structure of the kinship group in past and present western societies: mortality, age-at-marriage, and fertility. Although several types of kin will be considered, ascendant kin are most relevant for discussing the availability of persons intentionally likely to assume roles in the socialization process, particularly for children.[9]

Mortality

In the past, people simply did not live long enough to form a sizeable pool of older relatives with whom contact was possible. In 1900, the expectation of life at birth (for the white population) in the United States was 48.2 years for

---

[8]Modell et al. (1976) discuss other structural reasons which would explain the greater conflict associated with adolescence in contemporary society.

[9]Demos (1972:656) points out the potential significance of older siblings in the socialization process of children in the large families found in Plymouth Colony. Shorter (1975:26), however, says that in Europe usually only two or three children were in residence simultaneously. Given the tendency for employment to begin at relatively young ages, it is older siblings who were most likely to have left their parents' homes. The residence patterns of adolescents before the end of the nineteenth century (Bloomberg, 1974; Katz, 1975; Little and Laslett, 1977) suggest that the same may have been true in North America.

males and 51.1 years for females. In 1970, these figures had risen to 68.0 years for males and 75.6 years for females. (U.S. Bureau of the Census, 1975: 56). While some nineteenth century American mortality data is available, questions have been raised about its adequacy (Vinovskis, 1972, 1974); the decline in mortality in the twentieth century, however, when vital registration data have become increasingly available is clearer (see Taeuber and Taeuber, 1958).

Although infant mortality made a major contribution to death rates in earlier times, higher mortality in the past affected adults as well as infants. At age twenty, the expectation of life of white males was 42.4 additional years in 1900 and 50.3 additional years in 1970; the comparable figures for white women are 43.8 and 57.4 additional years, respectively (U.S. Bureau of the Census, 1976:56). One consequence of the changing mortality rates is that "the chances that today's typical bride and groom will both survive the next fifty years (to their golden wedding anniversary) are more than twice as great as were the chances of such survival for their counterparts in 1900–02" (Metropolitan Life, February, 1976). Thus, fewer parents and grandparents were available in earlier historical periods to participate in the socialization of their children and grandchildren.

Differential mortality by sex is also relevant to kin contacts. In twentieth century America, there has been an increasing sex difference in life expectancy. While the length of life (at birth and older ages) of both sexes has increased between 1900 and 1970, the increase for women has been greater than the increase for men, as the expectation of life figures quoted earlier indicate. Findings from contemporary research on the family (Adams, 1968:167) show the importance of parents for continued kin contact among their adult children; when parents are alive, contact is greater than after the parents' deaths. The mother's survival may be particularly important in this respect, since women are more active in maintaining family ties (Adams, 1968:27–28). Since women have greater longevity than men, contacts among related adults may be sustained even longer than would be likely without this pattern of differential life expectancy by sex.[10]

Age-at-Marriage

The median age at first marriage in the United States in 1890 was 26.1 years for men and twenty-two years for women; in 1950 it was 22.8 and 20.3 years (U.S. Bureau of the Census, 1976:19); and in 1974 it was 23.1 and 21.1 years, respectively (U.S. Bureau of the Census, 1974:1). The late nineteenth century figures may well represent the high point of an upward trend, since available data indicate that people married younger in the colonial period. (See Wells,

[10]Linkages along the male line may be stronger when there are economic ties between fathers and their children. The decline in family businesses and self-employment (Blau and Duncan, 1967:41) in the twentieth century would thus lessen the salience of father-adult child contact.

1972 for colonial America, as well as Britain and France at a comparable time period; Farber, 1972; and Sklar, 1974, for late nineteenth and early twentieth century European data.) In the twentieth century, however, compared to the late nineteenth, children are born earlier in their parents' life span and are more likely to survive. Under such circumstances, family members will be available both for more of the individual's life, because of increases in life expectancy of the older generation, and for greater periods of the family life cycle because new families begin at earlier ages.[11]

Fertility

While the pool of potential kin may be affected by declining mortality and age-at-first-marriage, changing fertility rates are also relevant for estimating the size and structure of the kinship group in the present compared to the past. Fertility in the United States has declined (see Coale and Zelnik, 1963; Taeuber and Taeuber, 1957). The question is whether lowered fertility offsets the effects of decreased mortality, so that the number of living relatives per family in the present is no different from in the past.

Historical data to answer this question directly are not available. Goodman, Keyfitz and Pullum (1974), however, provide suggestive material in their estimates of the number of surviving female relatives of different types given the fertility and mortality of the United States in 1967 and Madagascar in 1966, that is, a country with low fertility and low mortality—the modern demographic profile—compared to a society with high fertility and high mortality—the preindustrial patterns.[12] This analysis shows that three factors are relevant for estimating the number of female kin alive under the two demographic regimes: the age of the woman; the distance of the kinship link between a woman and her relative and whether the relative is an ascendant, descendant, or lateral kin. In general, the results show that in societies with low fertility and low mortality, older relatives are more available and younger relatives are less available. Although some lateral relatives would also be less available under western, industrial demographic conditions, the difference is small. The advantage in terms of the size of the kinship pool does not appear to be marked for one type of society compared to another. Gray's (1977) application of the

[11]The impact of age-at-marriage on the size of the kinship group is clearly seen where it has been early, not late, and where high fertility has been encouraged. See Gutman (1976) for a discussion of these factors in relation to the black family.

[12]It could be argued that contemporary Madagascar and preindustrial America are so unalike that the Goodman, Keyfitz, and Pullum (1974) estimates cannot be used even suggestively. There are several reasons to reject this position: 1) The model is purely mathematical and takes account of no other characteristics of Madagascar society except its gross reproduction rate and expectation of life at birth. 2) The demographic rates used to generate the model's estimates for Madagascar are sufficiently close to the pre-industrial American figures to validate their usefulness as suggestive (although certainly not conclusive) indicators.

Goodman, Keyfitz, and Pullum model to 1920, 1930, and 1970 U.S. demographic rates shows, however, that to the extent that there is a difference, more living kin are available to contemporary Americans than was true in earlier periods.

If one differentiates between relatives not in terms of generation but in terms of relational proximity to an individual, another aspect of the kinship structure emerges. The only categories of kin where Goodman, Keyfitz, and Pullum show that the high fertility, high mortality society has a marked advantage over the low fertility, low mortality society is in terms of cousins and granddaughters. Data on social contact between kin in the contemporary United States (Adams, 1968) suggest that interaction is most frequent between closest kin (parents, children and siblings) and falls off sharply as one moves further away from primary bonds. Demos (1970:124) found that the most significant kin connections in Plymouth colony were also those between members of the primary family unit. In the absence of primary family members, however, more distant kin may have been of greater importance (see Greven, 1970). It should be remembered, however, that migration—a significant feature of American life throughout its history—is higher among younger adults. Although proportionately more young adults may have been alive under preindustrial demographic conditions, their availability for purposes of interaction with other family members may not have been as great as numbers alone would suggest.

The demographic factors reviewed have implications for understanding patterns of family interaction and the processes of socialization both within the household and the extended kin group. Glick (1977) says that "the larger the family the larger proportion of time that children are likely to spend interacting with each other, whereas the smaller the family the greater the proportion of time the children are likely to spend interacting with their parents . . ." Thus, changes in mortality, fertility, and age-at-marriage, as well as changes in household composition, are likely to affect the processes of role modeling and identification that occur within the contemporary family. It is likely to increase the impact of parents in the socialization process. Despite the increased proportion of mothers in the labor force, the overwhelming proportion of children are cared for by their own parents or other relatives, rather than by non-relatives (U.S. Bureau of the Census, 1976). Furthermore demographic changes have also resulted in the availability of more ascendant kin, particularly grandparents, uncles, and aunts, who may elaborate the meaning of kinship throughout the individual life cycle. Given the increased importance of family membership established in the early years of the socialization process, for both children and adults, and the means of contact and communication which technological advances have made available, common residence is no longer likely to be as significant a determinant contact as in earlier historical periods.

Urbanization and Migration

Two factors relevant to the distribution of population also affect the availability of kin with whom contact may occur: (1) urbanization and (2) migration. Although rapid urbanization has been a feature in the American experience since the early nineteenth century (Potter, 1974), the twentieth century has witnessed an increasing concentration of population in large urban centers. Kin may be concentrated in areas where fairly frequent contact is easier to make and harder to avoid, because of the expansion of the highway system, the widespread availability of automobiles, air travel, and the telephone.

Migration, a characteristic of American life both in the past and present (Lee, 1964: 127), has often been used to explain the absence of kin contact among mobile populations. The act of migration (particularly overseas migration) reduces the pool of potential kin available both to the migrant and the non-migrant. Furthermore, the process of internal (vs. overseas) migration can also thin the ranks of kin with whom contact is possible. Here again, literacy and the technology of communication are important, for once a relative leaves a community, contact between family members depends on the available modes of communication. But the impact of migration may also depend on whether it occurs early or late in the historical development of an area.

In earlier generations, migrating family members established themselves in places which did not include members of their own kin group. The potential for kin contact was reduced or eliminated because of migration. First generation migrants would be most lacking in ascendant kin since migration typically occurs among the younger categories. (See U.S. Bureau of the Census, 1976:122, for data on foreign immigrants by age between 1820 and 1970.) The likelihood that kin would be found in the place of destination of the next generation of migrants, however, is increased by the simple fact that earlier migration of family members had occurred. Nineteenth as well as twentieth century migrants have been shown to choose their destinations in part because of the presence of kin group members in the new area (Hareven, 1975; McLaughlin, 1971; Hendrix, 1975, 1976). Thus, migration, particularly under modern technological conditions, does not necessarily reduce contact to the degree suggested by earlier authors, although it does, perhaps, render it voluntary (Shorter, 1975).

To summarize, structural factors have created the potential for family membership to become a more salient feature of personal identity in the contemporary period compared to the western, pre-industrial past through its effect on socialization within the household, on the increased number of ascendant kin, and the spatial distribution of the kin group. In addition, developments in the technology of contact and communication and increased literacy make it easier for family members to be in touch with each other whether or not they live close together.

In the earlier period, the co-resident domestic group was less often confined to primary kin group members, while in the present context, more households contain nuclear family members only. Thus, within the home, non-kin are not as likely to diffuse identification with a particular family. Greater numbers of ascendant kin outside the home are available to amplify the identification developed within it.

The Ideology of Family Life

Beliefs about family life in contemporary American society tend to reflect and reinforce the intimacy and intensity which residential and demographic factors make possible. The early Puritan ideology in America emphasized the role of the family as guardian of the public, as well as the private, good. Not only did religion specify the approved relationships between family members —their duties and responsibilities to each other—but it also made it a sacred duty of church members to see that edicts were carried out. It was not sufficient for people to be moral in public—they also had to be moral in private, and religion provided a legitimating ideology for minding other people's family affairs.

In contrast to these beliefs, the idea of the private family and the home as a personal sanctuary grew throughout the nineteenth century. Family life began to be characterized as an oasis, a retreat, a haven from the uncertainties, immoralities, and strains of life in a rapidly changing society (Jeffery, 1972; Sennett, 1970). Elder's (1974) suggestion that "the family as refuge" was one reaction of American families to the Depression of the 1930's indicates that this theme has continued within the twentieth century. Insecurities in public roles and disappointments in the occupational sphere—made all the more painful, perhaps, by a political ideology which emphasizes individual success and advancement—reinforced a belief in the family as the only place where meaningful relationships are possible.

The theme of the family as a retreat can also be found in recent discussions of contemporary non-traditional family forms such as communes and open marriages (Sussman, 1972). These alternative family forms are thought to provide the opportunity for deep and meaningful personal relationships to a greater extent than other types of family living. Thus, the family continues to be seen as a haven from the large society. Sussman (1972:8) says:

> Life is for meaningful relationships on a micro-level where one can control one's own destiny or at least not be subordinated; a level which provides numerous options and optimal freedom for deep relationships.

The ideology of family living, even in its most avant-garde form, continues to emphasize the importance of the family as a refuge from the larger society. This perspective is based on the belief that it is only within the family that a sense of personal control and intimacy can be found (also see, Zaretsky, 1976).

Whether or not this belief and the needs it expresses can actually be satisfied within the family is another issue.

The relationship of the family to other social institutions reinforces the search for meaning within the family. One of the features said to characterize modern industrial societies, compared to those which preceded them historically, is an increase in the importance of achieved versus ascribed attributes. In the life of families in Andover, Mass., in the seventeenth century (Greven, 1970), access to arable land was crucial to the adult life of sons. The father's control over land affected many aspects of the son's adult behavior—including when he could marry. The growth of an occupational system emphasizing an individual's educational achievement, and the increasing availability of public education, have loosened the constraints which past authority patterns and practices were likely to impose (Goode, 1963). Family contacts may therefore be less crucial to achieving one's place in the modern occupational world.

But the very fact that family contacts may no longer play such an important part in placing individuals in their public social roles—thus reducing the instrumental usefulness of kin contacts—may serve to increase their socio-emotional importance. In a society whose ideology values individual achievement and scorns nepotism, family membership may be prized simply because it does not have to be earned. The ascribed character of family membership may be experienced as a positive attribute for the very reason that it can be "taken for granted."

The socialization that occurs within the twentieth century American family is likely to contribute to the "taken for granted" character of family relationships. As the differentiation between the norms, values, and location of the family compared to other institutions has increased, the differences between the family and other areas of social life have sharpened. The contemporary family's private character (B. Laslett, 1973), by providing a "backstage area" (Goffman, 1959) where persons can relax from performing their public roles, contributes to an ideology that defines the family primarily in socio-emotional terms. What is frequently forgotten in these formulations, is that performers not only relax backstage, but they also prepare for—and sometimes rehearse—their public roles. Thus, the potentially contradictory and confusing messages communicated within the domestic setting can create discrepancies between the ideology and actuality of contemporary family life.

Changes in economic organization within the general society may have affected the emotional meaning of family relationships in other ways. In the past, when the family was the unit of production as well as the unit of consumption, work and family roles were intertwined to a greater extent than in the present. The systematic separation of home and work activities which began in nineteenth century America, the decline in proprietorship in the contemporary period, and the increase in the salaried and bureaucratic sector of the economy (Blau and Duncan, 1967) means that fewer family members may be working together than was true in an earlier period. In the past, relations between employers and employees, masters and servants or apprentices, and parents and children shared greater emotional similarity than is true today (see P. Laslett, 1971; Farber, 1972; Douglas, 1921:55). But it is precisely a decline in the intertwining of what we now see as diverse social roles which permits the intensification of the emotional aspects of family relationships.

A similar argument can be made in relation to the family as educator. Before public schooling was widely available, much education occurred in the home (Cremin, 1974). Removing the requirement that parents teach, monitor, and correct their children's intellectual development reduces potential conflict between aspects of their behavior as parents. Today, parents do not have to satisfy the sometimes contrary demands of expecting achievement in the sphere of cognitive development while simultaneously providing socio-emotional resources for their children's psychological development.

This argument is not meant to imply that parents are less concerned about the educational achievement of their children. The opposite may be true. (See LeVine, 1974, for a discussion of how parents' goals for their children affect child-rearing behavior.) Alice Rossi (1968) has suggested that in the absence of clear-cut standards, mothers and fathers often use children's report cards and pediatricians' reports to judge their performance as parents. But the availability of institutions to foster their children's attainment of instrumental skills outside the home permits and encourages a greater concentration on the affective character of the relationships within it.

Structural conditions within the household which contribute to the increased emotional intensity of comtemporary parent-child relations, are reinforced by the relations between the family and other social institutions. Children's educational and occupational attainments are more likely to take on greater psychological meaning—to become reflections or extensions of parents' personal fantasies and ambitions. The possibility of testing these fantasies against reality—or understanding what makes fantasies more or less possible ambitions—is not as available to modern parents who share less of an experiential world with their children than did parents in the pre-industrial period.

Social contact outside the residential unit may help to confirm or diminish the importance of family membership for personal identity. Frequent interaction between extended family members provides a basis for the continuing reaffirmation of the sense of membership generated within the residential family. Many studies since World War II show the importance of contact between kin compared to non-kin in the United States (Axelrod, 1956; Greer, 1956; Bell and Boat, 1957; Sussman and Burchinal, 1962; Lawson, 1974). Thus, the importance of kinship is not only theoretical. It is real, since it appears to provide the most significant basis for interaction when options are available. That this is true even when technology which makes contact easier also makes it a matter of choice (Shorter, 1975), is testimony to the salience of family membership in contemporary America.

Conclusions

The preceding analysis suggests that the significance of family membership has changed in the United States. Changes in household composition and the demography of kinship, in the technology of communication and the spread of literacy, in the ideology of family life and the relationship of the family to other social institutions have affected the process of socialization in ways increasing the family's salience in the formation of personal identity. Earlier fears that urbanization and industrialization would weaken "the bonds of kinship" (Wirth, 1938) have not been bourne out. To the contrary, the historical changes that have been described have resulted in an "intensified . . . weight of meaning attached to the personal relations of the family" (Zaretsky, 1976:66).

But if this has occurred, why are there the family problems and strains noted at the beginning of this paper? Weibert and Hastings (1977) suggest that the contemporary family's "specialized function of affectivity and expressivity for the sustenance of emotionally charged personal identities" also makes it a particularly powerful source of pain and conflict. In addition, the specialized and bureaucratic organization of modern life has made the family one of the few *locations* where the expression of strong feeling is legitimate, thus increasing the likelihood that emotionally charged interactions—both positive and negative—will occur.

Perhaps the most important question to be asked about the modern family is not whether it is "here to stay" but whether it can sustain and satisfy the search for meaning and the weight of expectation that it has come to have. The contradiction implied by saying the contemporary family is "here to stay, but not well" can be understood only when the second question posed at the beginning of this paper has been answered: Does, and can, the family have the resources—both material and emotional—to satisfy the demands which are placed upon it in contemporary American society?

References

Adams, Bert N.
  1968   *Kinship in an Urban Setting.* Chicago: Markham
Anderson, Michael
  1971   *Family Structure in Nineteenth Century Lancashire.* Cambridge: Cambridge University
          Press.
Aries, Philippe
  1975   "La famille." *Encounter* 45(August):7–12.
Axelrod, Morris
  1956   "Urban structure and social participation." *American Sociological Review* 21(February):13–18.
Bane, Mary Jo
  1976   *Here to Stay: American Families in the Twentieth Century.* New York: Basic Books.
Bell, Wendell and Marion D. Boat
  1957   "Urban neighborhood and informal social relations." *American Journal of Sociology*
          62(January):391–398.

Berger, Peter, and Hansfried Kellner
   1975   "Marriage and the construction of reality." Pp. 219–233 in Dennis Brisset and Charles
          Edgley (eds.) *Life As Theatre: A Dramaturgical Sourcebook*. Chicago: Aldine.
Berkner, Lutz K.
   1972   "The stem family and the development cycle of the peasant household: An Eighteenth-
          century Austrian example." *American Historical Review* 77(April):398-418.
   1975   "The use and misuse of census data for the historical analysis of family structure."
          Journal of Interdisciplinary History 6(Spring):721–738.
Berkner, Lutz K., and Franklin F. Mendels
   forth-   "Inheritance systems, family structure and demographic patterns in western Europe
   coming (1700–1900)."Mimeographed.
Blau, Peter M., and O. D. Duncan
   1967   *The American Occupational Structure*. New York: John Wiley.
Bloomberg, Susan
   1974   "The household and the family: The effects of industrialization on skilled workers in
          Newark, 1840–1860." A paper presented at the meetings of the Organization of Ameri-
          can Historians, Denver.
Blumin, Stuart M.
   1975   "Rip Van Winkle's grandchildren: Family and household in the Hudson Valley, 1800–
          1860." *Journal of Urban History* 1(May):293–315.
Carter, Hugh, and Paul C. Glick
   1976   *Marriage and Divorce: A Social and Economic Study,* revised edition. Cambridge,
          Mass.: Harvard University Press.
Coale, Ansley J., and Melvin Zelnik
   1963   *New Estimates of Fertility and Population in the United States.* Princeton, N.J.: Prince-
          ton University Press.
Coale, Ansley J. et al.
   1965   *Aspects of the Analysis of Family Structure.* Princeton, N.J.: Princeton University Press.
Cremin, Lawrence A.
   1974   "The family as educator: Some comments on the recent historiography." *Teachers
          College Record* 76(December):250–265.
Demos, John
   1970   *A Little Commonwealth.* New York: Oxford University Press.
   1972   "Demography and psychology in the historical study of family life: A personal report."
          Pp. 561–570 in Peter Laslett (ed.), *Household and Family in Past Time.* Cambridge:
          Cambridge University Press.
Douglas, Paul H.
   1921   *American Apprenticeship and Industrial Education. Studies in History, Economics and
          Public Law XCI,* New York: Columbia University Press.
Dublin, Thomas
   1975   "Women, work and the family: Women operatives in the Lowell Mills, 1830–1860."
          Feminist Studies 3(Summer):30–39.
Elder, Glen H., Jr.
   1974   *Children of the Great Depression: Social Change in Life Experience.* Chicago: Univer-
          sity of Chicago Press.
Erikson, Erik H.
   1959   "Identity and the life cycle." *Psychological Issues,* 1.
Farber, Bernard
   1972   *Guardians of Virtue: Salem Families in 1800.* New York: Basic Books
Flacks, Richard
   1971   *Youth and Social Change.* Chicago: Markham
Furstenberg, Frank F., Jr., Theodore Hershberg, and John Modell
   1975   "The origins of the female-headed black family: The impact of the urban experience."
          Journal of Interdisciplinary History 6(Autumn):211–233.
Gelles, Richard J.
   1974   The violent home: A study of physical aggression between husbands and wives. Beverly
          Hills, Calif.: Sage Publications.
Glasco, Laurence A.
   1975   "The life cycle and household structure of American ethnic groups: Irish, Germans,

and native-born whites in Buffalo, New York, 1855." *Journal of Urban History* 1(May):399–364.

Glick, Paul C.
1977   "Updating the life cycle of the family." *Journal of Marriage and the Family* 39(February):5–13.

Goode, William J.
1963   *World Revolution and Family Patterns.* New York: Free Press.

Goodman, Leo A., Nathan Keyfitz, and Thomas W. Pullum
1974   "Family formation and the frequency of various kinship relationships." *Theoretical Population Biology* 5(February):1–27.

Goody, Jack
1972   "The evolution of the family." Pp. 103–124 in P. Laslett (ed.), *Household and Family in Past Time.* Cambridge: Cambridge University Press.

Gray, Anke Van Hilst
1977   "Who was really there? An historical look at available kin." An empirical paper presented to the Department of Sociology, University of Southern California.

Greer, Scott
1956   "Urbanism reconsidered." *American Sociological Review* 21(February):22–25.

Greven, Philip
1970   *Four Generations: Population, Land and Family in Colonial Andover, Massachusetts.* New York: Cornell University Press.

Gutman, Herbert G.
1976   *The Black Family in Slavery and Freedom, 1750–1925.* New York: Pantheon.

Hareven, Tamara K.
1975a   "Family time and industrial time: Family and work in a planned corporation town, 1900–1924." *Journal of Urban History* 1(May):365–389.
1975b   "The laborers of Manchester, New Hampshire, 1912–1922: The role of family and ethnicity in adjustment to industrial life." *Labor History* 16(Spring):249–265.

Hendrix, Lewellyn
1975   "Kinship and economic-rational migration: A comparison of micro- and macro-level analyses." *Sociological Quarterly* 16(Autumn):534–543.
1976   "Kinship, social networks, and integration among Ozark residents and out-migrants." *Journal of Marriage and the Family* 38(February):97–104.

Herlihy, David
1972   "Mapping households in medieval Italy." *Catholic Historical Review* 58(April):1–24.

Hess, Robert D., and Gerald Handel
1967   "The family as a psychosocial organization." Pp. 10–29 in Gerald Handel (ed.), *The Psychosocial Interior of the Family: A Source Book for the Study of Whole Families.* Chicago: Aldine.

Jeffrey, Kirk
1972   "The family in utopian retreat from the city: the nineteenth century contribution." *Soundings* 40(Spring):21–41.

Katz, Michael B.
1975   *The People of Hamilton, Canada West.* Cambridge, Mass.: Harvard University Press.

Kobrin, Frances E.
1976   "The fall in household size and the rise of the primary individual in the United States." *Demography* 31(February):127–138.

Lasch, Christopher
1977   *Haven in a Heartless World: The Family Besieged.* New York: Basic Books.

Laslett, Barbara
1973   "The family as a public and private institution: An historical perspective." *Journal of Marriage and the Family* 35(August):480–492.
1975   "Household structure on an American frontier: Los Angeles, California, in 1850." *American Journal of Sociology* 81(July):109–128.
1977   "Social change and the family: Los Angeles, California, 1850–1870." *American Sociological Review* 42(April):269–291.
1978a   "Household structure and the social organization of production: Los Angeles, California, in 1850." A paper to be presented at the IXth World Congress of Sociology, Uppsala, Sweden.

1978b "Strategies for survival: An historical perspective on the family and development." A
       paper to be presented at the IXth World Congress of Sociology, Uppsala, Sweden.
Laslett, Peter
1971   *The World We Have Lost.* Second Edition. London: University Paperbacks.
1972   *Household and Family in Past Time.* (Ed.) Cambridge: Cambridge University Press.
1977   *Family Life and Illicit Love in Earlier Generations.* Cambridge: Cambridge University
       Press.
Lawson, John E., Jr.
1974   *The Impact of the Local Metropolitan Environment on the Patterning of Social Contacts.*
       Ph.D. dissertation, Dept. of Sociology, University of Southern California.
Lee, Everett S.
1964   "Internal migration and population redistribution in the United States." Pp. 123–136
       in Ronald Freedman (ed.), *Population: The Vital Revolution.* Garden City, N.Y.:
       Anchor Books.
LeVine, Robert A.
1974   "Parental goals: A cross-cultural view." *Teachers College Record* 76(December):226–
       239.
Little, Margaret, and Barbara Laslett
1977   "Adolescence in historical perspective: The decline of boarding in 19th century Los
       Angeles." A paper presented at the annual meetings of the American Sociological
       Association, Chicago.
McBride, Theresa M.
1976   *The Domestic Revolution: The Modernization of Household Service in England and
       France, 1820–1920.* New York: Holmes and Meier.
McLaughlin, Virginia Yans
1971   "Working class immigrant families: first generation Italians in Buffalo, New York." A
       paper delivered before the Organization of American Historians, New Orleans.
Metropolitan Life
1976   "Likelihood of a golden wedding anniversary." *Statistical Bulletin,* 57(February):4–7.
Modell, John, and Tamara K. Hareven
1973   "Urbanization and the malleable household: an examination of boarding and lodging
       in American families." *Journal of Marriage and the Family* 35(August):467–479.
Modell, John, Frank Furstenberg, and Theodore Hershberg
1976   "Social change and transitions to adulthood in historical perspective." *Journal of
       Family History* 1(Autumn):7–32.
Morgan, Edmund S.
1944   *The Puritan Family.* New York: Harper.
Parish, William L., and Moshe Schwartz
1972   "Household complexity in nineteenth-century France." *American Sociological Review*
       37(April):154–173.
Parsons, Talcott, and Robert F. Bales
1955   *Family, Socialization and Interaction Process.* Glencoe, Ill.: Free Press.
Plakans, Andrejs
1977   "Identifying kinfold beyond the household." *Journal of Family History* 2(Spring):3–27.
Potter, J.
1974   "Demography: the missing link in American history." A paper presented at the meet-
       ings of the Organization of American Historians, Denver.
Roberts, Peter
1904   *Anthracite Coal Communities.* New York: Macmillan.
Rossi, Alice S.
1968   "Transition to parenthood." *Journal of Marriage and the Family* 30(February):26–39.
Schofield, R. S.
1970   "Age-specific mobility in an eighteenth century rural English parish." *Annales de
       demographie historique:* 261–274.
Shorter, Edward
1975   *The Making of the Modern Family.* New York: Basic Books.
Sennett, Richard
1970   *Families Against the City: Middle Class Homes of Industrial Chicago, 1872–1890.*
       Cambridge, Mass.: Harvard University Press.

Sklar, June L.
　1974　"The role of marriage behaviour in the demographic transition: The case of eastern Europe around 1900." *Population Studies* 28(July):231–248.
Skolnick, Arlene
　1973　*The Intimate Environment: Exploring Marriage and the Family.* Boston: Little, Brown.
Slater, Philip
　1970　*The Pursuit of Loneliness: American Culture at the Breaking Point.* Boston: Beacon Press.
　1977　Footholds: Understanding the Shifting Sexual and Family Tensions in Our Culture. New York: E. P. Dutton.
Steinmetz, Suzanne K.
　1977　*The Cycle of Violence: Assertive, Aggressive and Abusive Family Interaction.* New York: Praeger.
Steinmetz, Suzanne K., and M. A. Straus (eds.)
　1974　*Violence in the Family.* New York: Dodd, Mead & Co.
Sussman, Marvin B. (ed.)
　1972　*Non-Traditional Family Forms in the 1970s.* Minneapolis, Minn.: National Council on Family Relations.
Sussman, Marvin B., and L. G. Burchinal
　1962　"Kin family network: unheralded structure in current conceptualization of family functioning." *Marriage and Family Living* 24.
Taeuber, Conrad, and Irene B. Taeuber
　1958　*The Changing Population of the United States.* New York: Wiley
U.S. Bureau of the Census
　1973　*Census of Population: 1970.* Subject Reports. Final Report PC(2)-4A. Family Composition. Washington, D.C.: U.S. Government Printing Office.
　1974　*Current Population Reports,* Series P–20, No. 271. "Marital Status and Living Arrangements: March 1974." Washington, D.C.: U.S. Government Printing Office.
　1976　*Current Population Reports,* Series P–20, No. 298. "Daytime Care of Children: October 1974 and February 1975." Washington, D.C.: U.S. Government Printing Office.
　1976　*The Statistical History of the United States: From Colonial Times to the Present.* Washington, D.C.: U.S. Government Printing Office.
U.S. Dept. of Health, Education and Welfare
　1975　*Vital Statistics of the United States, 1970.* Vol. 1—Natality. Public Health Service. Rockville, Md.: National Center for Health Statistics.
Vinovskis, Maris A.
　1972　"Mortality rates and trends in Massachusetts before 1860." *Journal of Economic History* 32(March):184–213.
　1974　"The demography of the slave population in antebellum America." *Journal of Interdisciplinary History* 5(Winter):459–467.
Weigert, Andrew J., and Ross Hastings
　1977　"Identity loss, family and social change." *American Journal of Sociology* 82(May):1171–1185.
Wells, Robert
　1971　"Demographic change and the life cycle of American families." *Journal of Interdisciplinary History* 2(Autumn):273–282.
　1972　"Quaker marriage patterns in a Colonial perspective." *William and Mary Quarterly, Third Series* 24(July):415–442.
Wirth, Louis
　1938　"Urbanism as a way of life." *American Journal of Sociology* 44(July):3–24.
Zaretsky, Eli
　1976　*Capitalism, the Family and Personal Life.* New York: Harper & Row.

American Families in Transition: Historical Perspectives on Change

*Tamara K. Hareven**

Introduction: Myths About the Past

The American family has recently been the subject of much concern. Anxiety over its future has escalated over the past decade; the youth movement of the 1960s, and subsequently the women's movement, have brought it under scrutiny and attack. Policy debates over governmental family welfare programs have also directed attention to it. More recently, the emergence of the elderly in American society as a significant group with its own problems has led to a further examination of inadequacies of the family that contribute to the isolation of older people in modern America.

The consequences of all these developments, combined with the impact of increasing divorce rates and declining birth rates and the increase in the proportion of single-parent families, have given rise to the fear that the family might be breaking down or going out of existence. Anxiety over family breakdown is not unique to our times. It appears that since the time of the Founding Fathers every generation has expressed its doubts about the stability and continuity of the family. This very intense concern over the fate of the family both in the past and today points to the crucial place that the family holds in American culture. Yet the question still needs to be asked: Is the family in crisis, or is it simply undergoing some important changes? What can we learn from the past about the transitions the family life is undergoing and the directions in which it is heading?

Through much of American history, the family has been seen as the linchpin of the social order and the basis for stable governance. Even though changes appear more gradually in the family than they do in other institutions, educators, moralists, and social planners frequently express fear of family breakdown under the pressures of social changes. Every generation has thought itself to be witnessing the breakdown of the "traditional" family. In the era of the American Revolution, much anxiety was expressed about the possible disappearance of the American family, and during the Civil War the nation's crisis was projected onto the fate of the family itself. More than any other developments, however, industrialization and urbanization have been viewed as the major threats to traditional family life over the past decade and a half.

From *Normal Family Processes*, Froma Walsh, ed., pp. 446–466. © 1982 The Guilford Press, New York. Reprinted by permission.

*Department of History, Clark University, Worcester, Massachusetts, and Center for Population Studies, Harvard University, Cambridge, Massachusetts.

Family disorganization has been identified as a major characteristic of industrial society and has been associated with the loss of a Utopian preindustrial past. Even the adaptation of functions of and within the family that developed in response to social change were frequently interpreted as manifestations of breakdown.

Perceptions of American family life today are governed by commonly held myths about American family life in the past. Such myths maintain that there once was a golden age of family relations, when three generations lived together happily in the same household. This belief in a lost golden age has led people to depict the present as a period of decline and family breakdown. Nostalgia for a mythical past has resulted in the idealization of such families as the Waltons of TV and the world that supposedly produced them.

In order to come to grips with the problems of the present, it is essential to examine changes in family life over the past two centuries. A historical consideration of the family places some of the changes in their proper context. Looking at developments over time enables us better to assess the uniqueness of present conditions, and it also helps us to distinguish between long-term trends and temporary developments. To what extent are some of these changes part of a continuing historical process, and to what extent are they new departures? Most importantly, a historical consideration enables us to distinguish between passing fads and critical changes, and it can even offer some precedents from the past that could be revived and applied to present conditions.

In the ensuing discussion, I first examine major historical changes in the American family in relation to the current, seemingly "dramatic" transitions. I discuss changes in the following areas: organization of the family and kin; family functions and values; and changes in the life course.

Change and Continuity in Family Structure

Recent research on the family in preindustrial American society has dispelled the myths about the existence of ideal three-generational families in the American past (Demos, 1970; Goode, 1963; Greven, 1970; Laslett, 1965; Laslett & Wall, 1972).[1] There has never been in American society an era when three generations were coresiding in the same household. The "great extended families" that have become part of the folklore of modern industrial society were rarely actually in existence. Households and families were simple in their structure and not drastically different in their organization

---

[1]Historians have frequently confused "family" with "household." This distinction must be made clear, however, if changes in the family are to be put in proper perspective. The "household" is the residential unit, which has also been recorded in the population censuses. The "family" can contain kin living inside the household, as well as relatives outside the household. It is now clear that preindustrial households were not extended. But this does not mean that the family was nuclear and isolated. Although several relatives did not reside in the same household, they were still interactive (see Hareven, 1971, 1974).

from contemporary families. Nuclear households, consisting of parents and their children, were characteristic residential units (although, as will be suggested later, they often contained strangers in addition to nuclear family members). Three generations rarely lived together in the same household. Given the high mortality rate in preindustrial societies, most parents could not have expected to live with their grandchildren (Davis, 1972; Glick, 1947, 1957). (On the changing life cycles of American women in particular, see Uhlenberg, 1969.) It would thus be futile to argue that industrialization destroyed the great extended family of the past, since such a family type rarely existed. And, as will be shown below, the process of industrialization had actually contributed in many ways to strengthening family ties and to increasing the chances of family members to stay together in the same place for longer time periods.

Contrary to popular assumption, preindustrial households were thus not filled by large numbers of extended kin. These households did contain strangers, however, who lived in the home as boarders, lodgers, apprentices, or servants. In this respect, the composition of the household in the preindustrial and early industrial period was significantly different from that in contemporary society. The tendency of families to include strangers in the household was connected with an entirely different concept of family life. In contrast to the current emphasis on the family as a private retreat, the household of the past was the site of a broad array of functions and activities that transcended the more restricted circle of the nuclear family. This fact had especially important implications for the role of women: it meant that women were involved in a variety of domestic management tasks beyond the care of their immediate family members. They took care of apprentices, boarders, and possibly other strangers who were placed with the family because they were delinquent youth, orphaned children, or abandoned old men or women.

The household then, was not the exclusive abode of the nuclear family. It did not include relatives other than nuclear family members, but it did include strangers. The presence of strangers in the household continued in different forms throughout the 19th and into the early 20th century. Although apprentices virtually disappeared from households by the middle of the 19th century, and dependent, delinquent, and sick people were being placed in institutions, the practice of taking strangers into the household persisted— primarily through boarding and lodging. Throughout the 19th and early 20th centuries, about one-fourth to one-third of the population either had lived in someone's household as a boarder or had taken in boarders or lodgers at some point in their lives (Modell & Hareven, 1973). Boarding and lodging fulfilled the function of what Taeuber has referred to as "the social equalization of the family" (1969, p. 5). Young men and women in their late teens and 20s who had left their own parents' households, or who had migrated from other communities, lived as boarders in the households of older people whose own children had left home. This practice thus enabled young people to stay in surrogate family arrangements, while at the same time it provided old people with the opportunity to continue heading their own households without being isolated.

The practice of taking in boarders and lodgers was extremely valuable in providing continuity in urban life and in allowing new migrants and immigrants to adapt to urban living. Its existence suggests the great flexibility in families and households, a flexibility that has been lost over the past half century. Increasing availability in housing and the spread of the values of privacy in family life have led to the phasing out of this practice. The practice has survived to some extent among black families, but it has almost virtually disappeared from the larger society. With its disappearance, the family has lost some of its major sources of resilience and adaptability to urban living. Thus, the most important change in American family life has not been the breakdown of a three-generational family pattern, but, rather, the loss of flexibility in regard to taking strangers into the household.

The practice of boarding and lodging has been replaced since the 1920s by solitary living. The increase in the rates of "primary individual" households, as the Census Bureau refers to the households of individuals residing alone, is a spreading phenomenon. While in the 19th century solitary residence was almost unheard of, now a major portion of the population resides alone. The disquieting aspect of this pattern is in the high percentage of aging widows living alone. Thus, solitary residence for a major portion of the population is not a matter of free choice, but rather an unavoidable and often unbearable arrangement. Again, what has been lost is not a great extended family of the past, but the flexibility of the family that enabled households to expand when necessary and to take people in to live in surrogate family settings rather than in isolation (Kobrin, 1976).

Another pervasive myth about family life in the past has been the assumption that industrialization broke up traditional kinship ties and destroyed organic interdependence between the family and the community. Once again, historical research has shown that industrialization led to the redefinition of the family's roles and functions, but by no means broke up traditional family patterns. In industrial communities, the family continued to function as a work unit. Relatives acted as recruitment, migration, and housing agents for industrial laborers, helping each other to shift from rural to industrial work. Preindustrial family patterns and values were carried over into the industrial system, providing important continuities between rural and urban industrial life (Anderson, 1971; Hareven, 1978, 1982 forthcoming). Rather than being a passive victim, the family was an active agent in the process of industrialization. Families migrated in groups to industrial centers, recruiting workers into the factory system, and often several family members continued to work in the same place. Migration to industrial communities did not break up traditional kinship ties. Rather, families used these ties to facilitate their own transitions into industrial life.

Despite changes wrought under the impact of industrialization, reliance on kin as the most basic resource for assistance persisted. Throughout the 19th and 20th centuries, kin in rural and urban areas continued to engage in mutual assistance and in reciprocal services. Kin performed a crucial role in initiating and organizing migration from rural areas to factory towns locally and from rural communities abroad to American factories. While rural/urban or overseas migration temporarily depleted kinship groups, networks were gradually reconstructed in the new location through chain migration. Thus, although people did not share the same household with relatives outside the nuclear family, they were still enmeshed in close ties with their kin outside the household.

In 19th-century American cities, chain migration facilitated transition and settlement, assured a continuity in kin contacts, and made mutual assistance in personal and family crises an important factor in the adjustment of immigrants to the urban environment. Even in the later part of the last century and in the early parts of this one, workers who migrated from rural areas to cities in most industrializing communities carried major parts of their kinship ties and family traditions into new settings. Young unmarried sons and daughters of working age, or young married couples without their children, tended to migrate first. After they found jobs and housing, they would send for their relations. Chain migration thus helped maintain ties and continuities between family members in their new communities of settlement. In factories or other places of employment, newly arrived workers utilized the good offices of their relatives who were already working in the establishment to facilitate the hiring of their newly arrived kin.

Hiring and placement through kin often continued even in large-scale modern factories. Kinship networks were able to permeate and infiltrate formal, bureaucratized industrial cooperatives and to cluster within them. Even where they worked in different locales, kin made collective decisions about the work careers of their members. Workers migrated in kin groups and carried with them traditional patterns of kin assistance, but adapted these to the requirements of modern industrial organizations. Immigrants successfully adapted their traditional kinship patterns to modern modes of production and the organization of work, which required familiarity with bureaucratic structures and organizations, adherence to modern work schedules, responsiveness to the rhythms of industrial employment, and specialization in technological skill (Anderson, 1971; Hareven, 1978, 1982 forthcoming).

Changing Family Functions and Values

Industrialization, however, did affect major changes in family functions. Through a process of differentiation, the family gradually surrendered functions previously concentrated within it to other social institutions. During the preindustrial period, the family not only reared children, but also served as a workshop, a school, a church, and an asylum. Preindustrial families meshed closely with the community and carried a variety of public responsibilities within the larger society. "Family and community," writes Demos, "private and public life, formed part of the same moral equation. The one supported the other and they became in a sense indistinguishable" (1970, p. 186).

In preindustrial society, most of the work took place in the household. Reproductive roles were therefore congruent with social and economic roles. Children were considered members of the work force and were seen as economic assets. Childhood was a brief preparatory period terminated by apprenticeship and the commencement of work, generally before puberty. Adolescence was virtually unknown as a distinct stage of life. Such a social system encouraged the integration of family members into common economic activities. The segregation along sex and age lines that characterizes middle-class family life in modern society had not yet appeared.

As long as the household functioned as a workshop as well as a family home, there was no clear separation between family life and work life. Even though preindustrial families contained large numbers of children, women invested relatively less time in motherhood than their successors in the 19th century and in our time did and still do. The integration of family and work allowed for an intensive sharing of labor between husbands and wives and between parents and children that would not exist in industrial society.

Even though households were nuclear, family members were not totally isolated from kin who were residing in the neighborhood. Consequently, the tasks of child rearing did not fall exclusively on mothers; other relatives living nearby also participated in this function. As long as the family was a production unit, housework was inseparable from domestic industries or agricultural work, and it was valued, therefore, for its economic contribution. Since children constituted a viable part of the labor force, motherhood, too, was valued for its economic contributions, and not only for its nurturing qualities.

Under the impact of industrialization, many of these functions were transferred to agencies and institutions outside the family. The work place was separated from the home, and functions of social welfare were transferred from the family to asylums and reformatories. "The family has become a *more specialized agency* than before," note Parsons and Bales, "probably more specialized than in any previous known society . . . but not in any general sense less important, because the society is dependent *more* exclusively on it for the performance of *certain* of its vital functions" (1955, pp. 9–10). These vital functions included (and include) childbearing, child rearing, and socialization. The family ceased to be a work unit and limited its economic activities primarily to consumption and child care.

The transformation of the household from a busy work place and social center to a private family abode involved the withdrawal of strangers, such as business associates, partners, journeymen, apprentices, and boarders and lodgers, from the household; it also involved a more rigorous segregation in the tasks and the work responsibilities of different family members. New systemized work schedules led to the segregation of husbands from wives and fathers from children in the course of the work day. In middle-class families, housework lost its economic and productive value. Since it was not paid for, and since it no longer led to the production of visible goods, it had no place in the occupational hierarchy.

Differentiation and specialization in work schedules significantly altered the daily lives of men and women who worked outside the home. Housework, on the other hand, continued to be governed by traditional time schedules, remaining throughout the nineteenth century a nonindustrial occupation. This is another reason (in addition to economic ones) why housework has been devalued in modern society, where achievement is measured not only by products but also by systematic time and production schedules. This may also explain why, since the 19th century, the home economics movement has been so intent on introducing efficient management and industrial time schedules into the home. For several decades, reformers maintained the illusion that if housework were more systematically engineered, it would become more respectable.

In trying to assess the significance of the changes in family life brought about by industrialization, we must recognize the fact that these changes were gradual, and that they varied significantly from class to class as well as among different ethnic groups. While historians have sometimes generalized for an entire society on the basis of middle-class experience, it is now becoming clear that preindustrial family patterns persisted over longer time periods in rural and in urban working-class families. Since the process of industrialization was gradual, domestic industries and a variety of small family enterprises carried over into the industrial system. In New England, for example, during the first half of the 19th century, rural families were sending their daughters to work in factories while the farm continued to be the family's economic base (Dublin, 1979). In most working-class families, work continued to be considered a family enterprise, even if it did not take place in the home. In such families, the work of wives, sons, and daughters was carefully regulated by the collective strategies of the family unit. Many of what we perceive today as individual work careers were actually part of a collective family effort.

Even though the process of industrialization offered women opportunities for independent work outside their homes, women continued to function as an integral part of the productive effort of the family unit, even when they worked in factories. Working women were bound by family obligations and contributed most of their earnings to their parents—a woman's work was considered part of the family's work, not an independent career. Even during periods of large-scale industrial development, families continued to function as collective economic units, in which husbands, wives, and children were all responsible for the well-being of the family unit. This continuity in the function of the family economy as a corporate enterprise is significant for understanding the limited changes in working-class gender roles under the impact of the industrial revolution. Industrialization changed the nature and the pace of the work, but these families survived as collective economic units for a long time to come (Hareven, 1982 forthcoming).

Industrialization, however, had a more dramatic effect on the experience of the middle class. The separation between the home and the work place that followed in the wake of industrialization led to the glorification of the home as a domestic retreat from the outside world. The new ideology of domesticity that developed in the first half of the 19th century relegated women to the home and glorified their domestic role. (On the cult of domesticity, see Jeffrey, 1972; Sennett, 1971; Welter, 1966; Young & Wilmott, 1973.)

These changes were closely connected with the decline in the number of children a woman had and with the new attitudes toward childhood. The discovery of childhood as a distinct stage of life was intimately tied to the emergence of the middle-class family in Europe and in the United States in the early 19th century. Stripped of the multiplicity of functions that had been previously concentrated in the household, these families developed into private, domestic, and child-centered retreats. Children were no longer expected to join the work force until their late teens, a major indication of the growing recognition of childhood as a distinct stage of development. Instead of considering children as potential working members of the family group, parents perceived them as dependent subjects of tender nurture and protection. This was the emergence of the domestic middle-class family as we know it today (Aries, 1962; Bremner, Barnard, Hareven, & Mennel, 1970–1974; Demos, 1970; Greven, 1970; Kett, 1971).

The glorification of motherhood as a full-time career served both to enshrine the family as a domestic retreat from the world of work and to make families child-centered. The gradual separation of the home from the work place that had started with industrialization reached its peak in the designation of the home as a therapeutic refuge from the outside world. As custodians of this retreat, women were expected to have attributes distinctly different from those of the working wife who had been an economic partner in the family. Tenderness, gentleness, affection, sweetness, and a comforting demeanor were all considered ideal characteristics for the domestic wife. Sentiment began to replace instrumental relationship. (On family sentiment, see Aries, 1962, 1981.)

The ideology of domesticity and the new view of childhood combined to revise expectations of parenthood. The roles of husbands and wives became gradually segregated; a clear division of labor replaced the old economic partnership, with the husband now responsible for economic support and the wife's efforts directed toward homemaking and child rearing. With men leaving the home to work elsewhere, time invested in fatherhood occurred primarily during leisure hours. Thus, the separation of husbands from wives and parents from children for major parts of the day came about. The cult of domesticity emerged as a major part of the ideology of family life in American society. One of its central assumptions was the role of women as custodians of the domestic retreat and as full-time mothers. The very notion has dominated perceptions of women's roles in American society until very recently and has shaped the prevailing assumptions governing family life. One of its major consequences was the insistence that women confine their main activities to the domestic sphere, and that women's work in the labor market would be harmful to the family and to society (Lerner, 1969; Scott, 1970; Welter, 1966).

Ironically, this ideology was adopted by middle-class families just at the point in time when rural and immigrant women were recruited into the newly established giant textile centers. Even though the ideology of domesticity originated in urban middle-class families, it emerged as part of the ideology of American family life in the larger society. Second- and third-generation immigrant families embraced this outlook as part of their "Americanization" process. The ideals of urban middle-class life emerged as the ideology of the larger society and subsequently handicapped the role of women as workers outside the home as well.

The impact of the ideology of domesticity became apparent in patterns of women's labor force participation. In the late 19th century, despite the convergence of many factors that could actually have facilitated women's work outside the home, very few women actually took advantage of the opportunity. Demographic changes, combined with technological advances, offered advantageous conditions for the entry of married women into the labor force. By the late 19th century the birth rate had declined, particularly among native-born families. Women had fewer children and at the same time benefited from new labor-saving appliances, which should have freed up their time considerably. Expanded industrial and commercial facilities, made easily accessible by new transportation systems, provided increased employment opportunities for women. But despite all this, 97% of all married women did not assume gainful employment, because ideological barriers placed women's domestic and work roles in conflict (Kenniston & Kenniston, 1964; Smuts, 1959; Sweet, 1973; Tilly & Scott, 1978).

The ideology of domesticity also began to influence working-class and immigrant families during the early part of the 20th century. As immigrants became "Americanized," particularly in the second generation, they internalized the values of domesticity and began to view women's work outside the home as demeaning, as having low status, or as compromising for the husband and dangerous for the children. Consequently, married women entered the labor force only when driven by economic necessity.

It is important to realize, however, that despite its threat in the larger society, and despite its adoption as the dominant ideology in "American culture," a majority of working-class and ethnic families continued to adhere to the earlier way of life; most importantly, they maintained a collective view of the family and its economy. In contrast to the values of individualism that govern much of family life today, the traditional values of family collectivity persisted at this level of American society.

With the growth of industrial child labor in the 19th century, working-class families continued to recognize the economic value of motherhood, as they had in rural society. Segregation along age groups within working-class families was almost nonexistent. Children were socialized for industrial work from an early age and began to contribute to the family's work effort at a lower age than specified by law. They were considered an asset, both for their contribution to the family's economy during their youth and for the prospect of their support during their parents' old age. Parents viewed their efforts in child rearing as investments in future social security.

The relationships between husbands and wives, parents and children, and other kin were based upon reciprocal services, support, and assistance. Such exchange relationships, often defined as "instrumental," were based on the assumption that family members were all engaged in mutual obligations and in reciprocal relationships. Although such obligations were not specifically defined by contract, they rested on the accepted social norms of what family members owed to each other. In the period preceding the welfare state and public assistance, instrumental relationships provided important supports to individuals and families, particularly during critical life situations (Anderson, 1971; Hareven, 1978).

A collective view of familial obligations was the very basis of survival. From such a perspective, marriage and parenthood were not merely love relationships, but partnerships governed by family economic and social needs. In this respect, the experience of 19th-century working-class families and of ethnic families in the more recent past was drastically different from that of middle-class ones, in which sentimentality emerged as the dominant base of family relationships. This is not to argue that husbands and wives in the past did not love each other or that parents harbored no sentiment for their children. It suggests, rather, that sentiment was secondary to family needs and survival strategies. Under such conditions, childbearing and work were not governed by individual decisions. Mate selection and the timing of marriage were regulated in accordance with collective family considerations, rather than directed by strictly individual whim. The transfer of property and work partnerships were important considerations in the selection of partners. At times, such collective family "plans" took priority over individual preferences. Parents tried to delay the marriage of the last child in the household—commonly that of a daughter—in order to secure continued economic support, especially in later life when they were withdrawing from the labor force.

The major historical change in family values has been a change from a collective view of the family to one of individualism and sentiment. These have led to an increasing emphasis on individual priorities and preferences over collective family needs. They have also led to an exaggerated emphasis on emotional nurture, intimacy, and privacy as the major justification for family relations. This shift in values has contributed considerably to the "liberation of individuals," but it has also eroded the resilience of the family and its ability to handle crises. Moreover, it has contributed to a greater separation among family members and especially to the isolation of older people.

Changes in the Life Course

The full impact of changes in family values and functions on the condition of the family today can be best understood in the context of demographic changes affecting the time of life transitions, such as marriage, parenthood, the "empty nest," and widowhood. Since the end of the 19th century, important changes have occurred in the family cycle that have affected age configurations within the family and generational relations (Hareven, 1977).

Beginning in the early 19th century, the American population has experienced a steady decline in the birth rate. Over the 19th and early 20th centuries, the birth rate of the American population went down steadily; it declined from an average of 7.04 children per family in 1800 to 3.56 children per family in 1900. This decline and the subsequent decline since 1900 have had a profound impact on the cycle of family life, especially on the timing of marriage, the birth of the first child and of subsequent children, and the spacing of children. They have also considerably affected the meaning of marriage and of parenthood. In traditional society, little time elapsed between marriage and parenthood, since procreation was the major goal of marriage. In modern society, contraception has permitted a gap between these two stages of the family cycle. Marriage has become recognized as important in its own right, rather than merely as a transition to parenthood (Smith, 1974; Wells, 1971; Yasuba, 1961).

One widely held myth about the past is that the timing of family transitions was once more orderly and stable than it is today. The complexity that governs family life today and the variations in family roles and in transitions into them are frequently contrasted to this more placid past. The historical record, however, frequently reveals precisely the opposite condition: patterns of family timing in the past were often more complex, more diverse, and less orderly than they are today. Voluntary and involuntary demographic changes that have come about since the late 19th century have in fact paradoxically resulted in greater uniformity in the timing of transitions along the life course, despite greater societal complexity. The growing uniformity in timing has been accompanied by a shift from involuntary to voluntary factors affecting the timing of family events. The increase in life expectancy, the decline in fertility, and the earlier marriage age have, for example, greatly increased the chances for temporal overlap in the lives of family members. Families are now able to go through a life course much less subject to sudden change than that experienced by the majority of the population in the 19th century.

The "typical" family cycle of modern American families includes early marriage and early commencement of childbearing, but a small number of children. Families following this type of family cycle experience a compact period of parenthood in the middle years of life; then an extended period encompassing one-third of their adult life, without children; and finally, often, a period of solitary living following the death of a spouse, most frequently that of the husband (Glick, 1955, 1977; Glick & Parke, 1965).

This type of cycle has important implications for the composition of the family and for relationships within it in current society: husbands and wives are spending a relatively longer lifetime together; they invest a shorter segment of their lives in child rearing; and they more commonly survive to grandparenthood. This sequence has been uniform for the majority of the population since the beginning of the 20th century. In contrast to past times, most families see their children through to adulthood with both parents still alive. As Uhlenberg (1974) points out, the normal family cycle for women—a sequence of leaving home, marriage, family formation, child rearing, launching, and survival at age 50 with the first marriage still intact—unless broken by divorce—has not been the dominant pattern of family timing before the early 20th century. Prior to 1900, only about 40% of the female population in the United States experienced this ideal family cycle. The remainder either never married, never reached marriageable age, died before childbirth, or were widowed while their offspring were still young children.

In the 19th century, the combination of a later age at marriage and higher fertility provided little opportunity for a family to experience an "empty nest" stage. Prior to the decline in mortality among the young at the beginning of the 20th century, marriage was frequently broken by the death of a spouse before the end of the child-rearing period. Even when fathers survived the child-rearing years, they rarely lived beyond the marriage of their second child. As a result of higher fertility, children were spread over a wider age range; frequently, the youngest child was just entering school as the oldest was preparing for marriage. The combination of later marriage, higher fertility, and widely spaced childbearing resulted in a different timing of family transitions. Individuals became parents later, but carried child-rearing responsibilities almost until the end of their lives. Consequently, the lives of parents overlapped with those of their children for shorter periods than they do currently.

Under the demographic conditions of the 19th century—higher mortality and higher fertility—functions within the family were less specifically tied to age, and members of different age groups were consequently not so completely segregated by the tasks they were required to fulfill. The spread of children over a larger age spectrum within the family had important implications for family relationships, as well as for their preparations for adult roles. Children were accustomed to growing up with larger numbers of siblings and were exposed to a greater variety of models from which to choose than they would have been in a small nuclear family. Older children often took charge of their younger siblings. Sisters, in particular, carried a major share of the responsibility for raising the youngest siblings, and they frequently acted as surrogate mothers if the mother worked outside the home or had died. The smaller age overlap between children and their parents was also significant: the oldest child was the one most likely to overlap with its father in adulthood, and the youngest child was the least likely to do so.

The oldest child would have been most likely to embark on an independent career before the parents reached old-age dependency; the youngest children were most likely to carry responsibilities for parental support and to overlap in adulthood with a widowed mother. The oldest child had the greatest chance to overlap with grandparents, the youngest child the least. Late-marrying children were most likely to be responsible for the support of a widowed mother, while early-marrying children depended on their parents' household space after marriage. One can better grasp the implications of these differences in age at marriage, number of children, assigned tasks, and generational overlap when one takes into consideration the uncertainties and the economic precariousness that characterized the period. These made the orderly sequence of progression along stages of the family cycle, which sociologists have observed in the contemporary American population, impossible for the 19th-century family.

Another comparison between what is considered the "normal" family cycle today and its many variants in the 19th century reverses one more stereotype about the past—namely, that American society has been experiencing breakdown and diversification in family organization. In reality, the major transitions in family roles have been characterized by greater stability and conformity because of the greater opportunity for generational continuities. The opportunity for a meaningful period of overlap in the lives of grandparents and grandchildren is a 20th-century phenomenon, a surprising fact that runs counter to the popular myth of a family solidarity in the past that was based on three-generational ties.

The relative significance of transition into family roles also differed in the 19th century. In the 19th century, when conception was likely to take place very shortly after marriage, the major transition in a woman's life was represented by marriage itself. But, as the interval between marriage and first pregnancy has increased in modern society, the transition to parenthood has become more significant than the transition to marriage. Family limitation has also had an impact on the timing of marriage. Since marriage no longer inevitably leads to parenthood, postponing marriage is no longer needed to delay it. On the other end of the life course, transitions into the "empty nest" roles are much more critical today than they were in the past, when parental or surrogate-parental roles encompassed practically the entire adult life span. Completion of parental roles today involves changes in residence, changes in work, and, perhaps, eventual removal into institutions or retirement communities (Chudacoff & Hareven, 1978).

The overall historical pattern of family behavior has thus been marked by a shift from involuntary to voluntary forces controlling the timing of family events. It has also been characterized by greater rigidity and uniformity in the timing of the passage from one family role to another. In their comparison of such transitions in 19th-century Philadelphia with those of the present, Modell, Furstenberg, and Hershberg (1976) conclude that transitions into adult roles (departure from the family of origin, marriage, and the establishment of a household) follow a more ordered sequence and are accomplished over a shorter time period in a young person's life today than they were in the 19th century. Such transitions to familial roles also coincide today with transitions into occupational roles: "Transitions are today more contingent, more integrated because they are constrained by a set of formal institutions. 'Timely' action to nineteenth-century families consisted of helpful response in times of trouble; in the twentieth century, timeliness connotes adherence to a schedule" (Modell, Furstenberg, & Hershberg, 1976, p. 30).

The demographic changes that have led to this isolation, continued with the decline in "instrumental" relations in the family discussed earlier, have caused isolation of older people in American society—a problem that is much more severe and immediate than the issue of "family breakdown." While the major historical changes in family functions occurred in the 19th and early 20th centuries, changes in the timing of family transitions are much more strictly 20th-century phenomena and particularly affect the family in our times. Changes in the family cycle, such as the emergence of the "empty nest," extensions of the period of widowhood, and increasing age segregation in the family and the larger society, reflect major discontinuities that have resulted in increasing problems in the middle and later years of life. It is precisely in this area that one needs to be concerned with future changes in the family.

Implications of Change

One of the major causes of the anxiety about the future of the family is rooted not so much in reality as in the tension between the idealized expectation in the culture and the reality itself. Nostalgia for a lost family tradition that in fact never existed has prejudiced our understanding of the conditions of families in contemporary society. Thus, the current anxiety over the fate of the family reflects not merely problems in the family, but a variety of fears about other social problems that are eventually projected onto the family.

The real problems that the American family is facing today are not symptoms of breakdown, as is often suggested. Rather, they reflect the difficulties that the family faces in its adaptation to recent social changes, particularly in the loss of diversity in household membership it had in the past, the reduction of the variety of its functions, and, to some extent, the weakening of its adaptability. The idealization of the family as a refuge from the world and the myth that the work of mothers is harmful have added considerable strain. The continuous emphasis on the family as a universal private retreat and as an emotional haven is misguided in light of the historical experience. In the past, the family fulfilled a broad array of functions, not merely emotional ones. Most of its functions in the past were intertwined with the larger community. Rather than being the custodian of privacy, the family prepared its members for interaction with the larger society. Family relationships were valued not merely for their emotional contents, but for a wide array of services and contributions to the collective family unit. By contrast, one of the major sources of the crisis of nuclear families today is its difficulty in adapting to the emotional functions thrust upon it and to the expectations of romantic love that accompany marriage, precisely because these functions and expectations represent an artificial boundary between individuals and the larger society.

Concentration on the emotional functions of the family has grown at the expense of another of its much-needed roles in industrial society; namely, the preparation of its members for their interaction with bureaucratic institutions. In American society, the education and welfare systems have made dramatic inroads into areas that had previously been the private preserve of the family. At the same time, however, the tendency of the family to shelter its members from other social institutions has weakened its ability to affect the structure of or to influence the programs and legislation that public agencies have directed at the family.

Attitudes towards family life in American society have been governed by the stereotype of the "ideal family," which is based on the middle-class nuclear family. In reality, American society has contained within it great diversities in family types and family behavior that were associated with the recurring entrance of new immigrant groups into American society. Ethnic, racial, cultural, and class differences have also resulted in diversity in family behavior. The tensions between family behavior in the dominant culture and the traditional patterns of the black family and of immigrant families has been a continuing pattern in American life (Hareven & Modell, 1980).

There has been a tendency toward homogenization of American culture, through the absorption of ethnic traditions on the one hand, and immigrant acceptance of the dominant cultural models on the other. Immigrants, primarily in the second generation, adopted "American" family behavior, and this adoption has been reflected in several areas: a decline in fertility, earlier marriage, growing privatization of the family, withdrawal of women and children from the labor force, and changing patterns of consumption and tastes. However, this ongoing process did not result in total assimilation of family ways and traditional customs, because the influx of new immigrants kept introducing new cultural variety. The result has been continuing diversity in family patterns. Contrary to the official creed of the "melting pot," a great many varieties of ethnic family behavior have survived in American society, and new patterns are still being introduced through recent migration. It is therefore unrealistic to talk simply about *the* American family.

For over a century, until very recently, the stereotype of the private nuclear family as the ideal family in American society has been dominant. Alternative forms of family organization, such as those of the black family or of other ethnic families, were misinterpreted as "family disorganization" simply because they did not conform to the official stereotype. But actually, over the past decade, the strength and resilience of ethnic and black family ways has been recognized. These traditional resources of family and kinship among black and ethnic families have been rediscovered as the middle-class nuclear family, besieged by its own isolation, has proven its limitations in coping with stress.

One of the most unique features of American families today is their cultural and ethnic diversity; this diversity, which is in itself a continuation of a historical pattern, is now being valued as a source of strength and continuity, rather than, as in the past, being decried as a manifestation of deviance. One of the challenges today faced by individuals and policy makers is the creative use of these family patterns in coping with contemporary problems.

An understanding of the historical changes over the past century provides a different perspective on family life today. There is no question that American families have been undergoing important transitions over the past century. But the main question is that of whether these changes represent family breakdown and whether they threaten the disappearance of the family. Some of these transitions represent the continuation of a long historical process: the decline in the birth rate, the earlier marriage rate, and changes in the timing of life transitions are all the result of a continuing process of change over the past century and a half. Similarly, the moratorium from adult responsibilities that teenagers now experience and the increasing isolation of older people on the other end of the cycle, are both the results of long-term historical changes.

On the other hand, the increase in divorce rates and the concomitant increase in single-parent households represent a much more dramatic transition in our times. But the rise in divorce as such, which has been often cited as a symptom of family breakdown, should not be necessarily misconstrued. In the 19th century people did not resort to divorce as frequently as they do now, because divorce was considered socially unacceptable. This does not mean, however, that families were living happily and in harmony. A high rate of desertion and separation of couples replaced legal divorce. And incompatible couples who did not resort to divorce or separation lived together as strangers or in deep conflict. Thus, the increase in divorce statistics as such is no proof of family breakdown. In some respects, it is proof that people care enough about the contents and quality of family life and marriage to be willing to dissolve an unsatisfactory marriage (and commonly to replace it with a more successful one).

Much anxiety has also been expressed over the increase in the proportion of couples living together unmarried, over homosexual partners or parents, and over a whole variety of alternative family forms and life styles. What we are witnessing in all these varieties of life styles are not necessarily new inventions. Many different forms have been in existence all along, but they have been less visible. The more recent forms of alternative life styles have now become part of the official fiber of society, because they are now being tolerated much more than in the past. In short, what we are witnessing is not a fragmentation of traditional family patterns, but, rather, the emergence of a pluralism in family ways.

Thus, from a long-range perspective, the greatest concerns over family life in America need not be divorce, the declining birth rate, or alternative life styles. Of much greater concern for the future, and especially for policy, should be the problem of the isolation of the elderly and the inability of families in all ages to cope with inflation and with diminishing resources.

The historical lesson is valuable in demonstrating the extent to which a variety of traditional family ways and continuities with the past are still surviving in American society today. It is particularly helpful in revealing the salient role of surrogate families (taking in boarders and lodgers), as well as in emphasizing the effectiveness of kinship ties in coping with migration, economic insecurity, and personal family crises. The persistence of kinship ties as a major source of support has been a source of resilience and strength in urban neighborhoods. This rediscovery of the strength of kin should not lead us, however, to a new myth of self-reliance. It would be a mistake to assume that the fact that family members are helping each other in times of crisis means that families should be left to take care of their own. The historical experience also suggests the high price that family members had to pay in order to support their kin and help aging parents. The pressures on the nuclear family today, combined with economic and technological stresses, would make it difficult if not impossible for families to sustain continued assistance and support for their kin, especially for aging relatives.

A creative and constructive family policy will have to take into consideration, therefore, both the survival of support networks among kin and the escalating pressures on individuals and families. Such a policy, by necessity, will have to provide public programs and assistance where informal support networks fall short. It will also need to strengthen kinship and neighborhood support networks without bureaucratizing them.

Acknowledgments

An earlier version of this chapter was prepared for the Research Forum on Family Issues, White House Conference on Families, April 1980.

I am grateful to Kathleen Adams for her editorial help.

References

Anderson, M. *Family structure in nineteenth-century Lancashire.* Cambridge, England: Cambridge University Press, 1971.

Aries, P. [*Centuries of childhood*] (R. Baldick, trans.). New York: Knopf, 1962.

Aries, P. [*The hour of our death*](H. Weaver, trans.). New York: Knopf, 1981.

Bremner, R. H., Barnard, J., Hareven, T. K., & Mennel, R. M. (Eds.). *Children and youth in America* (3 vols.). Cambridge: Harvard University Press, 1970–1974.

Chudacoff, H. P., & Hareven, T. K. The later years of life and the family cycle. In T. K. Hareven (Ed.), *Transitions: The family and the life course in historical perspective.* New York: Academic Press, 1978.

Davis, K. The American family in relation to demographic change. In C. F. Westoff & R. Parke, Jr. (Eds.), *Demographic and social aspects of population growth.* Washington, D.C.: U.S. Government Printing Office, 1972.

Demos, J. *A little commonwealth: Family life in Plymouth Colony.* New York: Oxford University Press, 1970.

Dublin, T. *Women at work: The transformation of work and community in Lowell, Massachusetts, 1826–1860.* New York: Columbia University Press, 1979.

Glick, P. C. The family cycle. *American Sociological Review,* 1947, *12,* 164–174.

Glick, P. C. The life cycle of the family. *Marriage and Family Living,* 1955, *18,* 3–9.

Glick, P. C. *American families.* New York: Wiley, 1957.

Glick, P. C. Updating the life cycle of the family. *Journal of Marriage and the Family,* 1977, *39,* 5–13.

Glick, P. C., & Parke, R., Jr. New approaches in studying the life cycle of the family. *Demography,* 1965, *2,* 187–212.

Goode, W. J. *World revolution and family patterns.* New York: Macmillan, Free Press, 1969.

Greven, P. *Four generations: Population, land and family in colonial Andover, Massachusetts.* Ithaca, N.Y.: Cornell University Press, 1970.

Hareven, T. K. The history of the family as an interdisciplinary field. *Journal of Interdisciplinary History,* 1971, *2,* 399–414.

Hareven, T. K. The family as process: The historical study of the family cycle. *Journal of Social History,* 1974, *7,* 322–329.

Hareven, T. K. Family time and historical time. *Daedalus,* Spring 1977, pp. 57–70.

Hareven, T. K. The dynamics of kin in an industrial community. In J. Demos & S. Boocock (Eds.), *Turning points.* Supplement to *American Journal of Sociology,* 1978, *84.*

Hareven, T. K. *Family time and industrial time.* New York: Cambridge University Press, 1982 forthcoming.

Hareven, T. K., & Modell, J. Ethnic families. In S. Thernstrom (Ed.), *Harvard encyclopedia of American ethnic groups.* Cambridge: Harvard University Press, 1980.

Jeffrey, K. The family as Utopian retreat from the city: The nineteenth-century contribution. In S. TeSelle (Ed.), *The family, communes, and Utopian societies.* New York: Harper & Row, 1972.

Kenniston, E., & Kenniston, K. An American anachronism: The image of women and work. *American Scholar,* 1964, *33,* 353–375.

Kett, J. H. Growing up in rural New England, 1800–1840. In T. K. Hareven (Ed.), *Anonymous Americans: Explorations in nineteenth century social history.* Englewood Cliffs, N.J.: Prentice-Hall, 1971.

Kobrin, F. The fall in household size and the rise in the primary individual in the United States. *Demography*, 1976, *13*, 127–138.

Laslett, P. *The world we have lost.* London: Methuen, 1965.

Laslett, P., & Wall, R. (Eds.). *Household and family in past time.* Cambridge, England: Cambridge University Press, 1972.

Lerner, G. The lady and the mill girl. *Mid-Continent American Studies Journal*, 1969, *10*, 5–14.

Modell, J., Furstenberg, F., & Hershberg, T. Social change and transitions to adulthood in historical perspective. *Journal of Family History*, 1976, *1*, 7–32.

Modell, J., & Hareven, T. K. Urbanization and the malleable household: An examination of boarding and lodging in American families. *Journal of Marriage and the Family*, 1973, *35*, 467–478.

Parsons, T., & Bales, R. F. *Family socialization and interaction process.* Glencoe, Ill.: Free Press, 1955.

Scott, A. F. *The Southern lady: From pedestal to politics, 1830–1930.* Chicago: University of Chicago Press, 1970.

Sennett, R. *Families against the city: Middle-class homes of industrial Chicago, 1872–1890.* Cambridge: Harvard University Press, 1971.

Smith, D. S. Family limitation, sexual control, and domestic feminism in Victorian America. In M. S. Hartman & L. Banner (Eds.), *Clio's consciousness raised: New perspectives on the history of women.* New York: Harper & Row, 1974.

Smuts, R. W. *Women and work in America.* New York: Columbia University Press, 1959.

Sweet, J. *Women in the labor force.* New York: Academic Press, 1973.

Taeuber, I. B. Change and transition in family structures. In *The family in transition* (Fogarty International Center Proceedings). Washington, D.C.: U.S. Government Printing Office, 1969.

Tilly, L., & Scott, J. *Women, work, and family.* New York: Holt, Rinehart & Winston, 1978.

Uhlenberg, P. R. A study of cohort life cycles: Cohorts of native-born Massachusetts women, 1830–1920. *Population Studies*, 1969, *23*, 407–420.

Uhlenberg, P. R. Cohort variations in family life cycle experiences of United States females. *Journal of Marriage and the Family*, 1974, *36*, 284–292.

Wells, R. V. Demographic change and the life cycle of American families. *Journal of Interdisciplinary History*, 1971, *2*, 273–282.

Welter, B. The cult of true womanhood, 1820–1860. *American Quarterly*, 1966, *18*, 151–174.

Yasuba, Y. *Birth rates of the white population in the United States, 1800–1860.* Baltimore: Johns Hopkins University Press, 1961

Young, M. D., & Wilmott, P. *The symmetrical family: A study of work and leisure in the London region.* London: Routledge & Kegan Paul, 1973.

Death and the Family

Peter Uhlenberg *

The impact of mortality change upon family structure, although sometimes mentioned, has been seriously neglected in studies of family history. Many of the most significant changes in the American family—the changing status of children, the increasing independence of the nuclear family, the virtual disappearance of orphanages and foundling homes, the rise in societal support of the elderly, the decline in fertility, the rise in divorce—cannot be adequately understood without a clear recognition of the profound changes that have occurred in death rates. And the decline in mortality in this century has been dramatic. At the beginning of this century about 140 infants out of every 1,000 born died in the first year of life; now only 14 out of 1,000 die. In this same period the average life span has increased from less than 50 to 73. The mortality decline in this century is greater than the total mortality decline that occurred during the 250 years preceding 1900.

In searching for the meaning of aggregate statistics on death for individuals and families, we must consider the effects of a death upon the survivors. Habenstein suggests that,

> Each death initiates significant responses from those survivors who in some way have personally or vicariously related to the deceased. Inevitably, the collectivities in which the dead person held membership also react (1968:26).

The family is often the most important group in which an individual has membership and in which close relationships exist, so it is here that we should expect death to have its greatest impact. The loss of a parent, a child, a sibling, or a spouse disrupts established family patterns and requires readjustment. As the experience of losing intimate family members moves from a pervasive aspect of life to a rare event, adjustments in family structure become imperative.

If the mortality decline since 1900 has been so large and if this decline has major repercussions for the family, why has it been neglected in studies of family change?[1] One important reason is the difficulty involved in trying to measure accurately the effects of a mortality change. Suppose, for example,

From *Journal of Family History*, Vol. 5, No. 3 (Fall 1980), pp. 313–320. Copyrighted 1980 by the National Council on Family Relations. Reprinted by permission.

*Peter Uhlenberg was awarded the Ph.D. in demography at the University of California, Berkeley, in 1971. He is now Associate Professor of sociology at the University of North Carolina, where he is engaged in research on the size and composition of successive cohorts entering old age, their socioeconomic-political environment, and the implications of historical change in the way these factors interact to produce changing life experiences.

[1]Several studies have discussed the significance of mortality level for the social structure (Blauner, 1966; Aries, 1962; Habenstein, 1968), but they do not present quantitative information regarding its effect upon the family.

that we want to describe the effect of mortality upon the family position of children at various historical times. If we attempt to specify the situation in its full complexity, we must deal with the age of mothers and fathers at the birth of their children, the birth position of children, and the age-sex configuration of siblings. Furthermore, we must recognize that cohorts of individuals live out their lives in a dynamic environment in which the force of mortality is constantly changing. Even if we could construct a conceptually complex model to elaborate the detailed mortality experiences of individuals, we would not have the necessary statistics to make use of it. Nor can a retrospective survey provide the data we would need, since only survivors to the present could be interviewed.

The purpose of this article is to suggest an alternative approach by constructing relatively simple measures of how different mortality levels affect important aspects of the family. Rather than attempting to summarize the total impact of mortality upon a cohort, the present study develops hypothetical situations to provide insights into the dynamic role of death in family life. The emphasis is upon ways in which mortality impinges upon family structure, and how observed changes in mortality over this century have encouraged change in the American family.

For perspective on historical change in mortality, I will focus upon three dates in the twentieth century: approximately 1900, 1940, and 1980 (actually, 1976). At each date, the role of mortality will be considered from the perspective of individuals at four different locations in the life course. The stages of life are: childhood, young adulthood, middle age, and old age. The calculations use period life tables[2] for each date, which means that the measures do not reflect the actual experience of any cohort. Rather, the picture presented reveals the implications of mortality conditions at specific points in time. In other words, the question asked is how would mortality at the 1900 (or 1940 or 1980) level impinge upon the family experience of individuals?

Childhood

Mortality change has affected the family experience of children in three ways. First, an increasing likelihood that a newborn will survive through childhood may influence the nature of parent-child relations. Second, declining mortality in the middle years of life affects the chances of orphanhood for children. Third, changing adult mortality also alters the prospects for having grandparents alive during childhood.

Parent-Child Relations

There is widespread agreement that mortality levels in a society constrain attitudes and feelings that parents have toward their infant children. As

---

[2]The life tables are for the U.S. white population.

Ariès writes, under conditions of very high infant and childhood mortality "people could not allow themselves to become too attached to something that was regarded as a probable loss" (1962:38; also see Blauner, 1966). As infant mortality has declined, childhood has become a more clearly differentiated stage of life, and families have increasingly focused upon children and emphasized the nurturance of children. Comparing the modern and historical American family, Skolnick concludes,

> What seems to have changed is the psychological quality of the intimate environments of family life.... Within the home the family has become more intense emotionally (1978:115).

Surely other factors in addition to changed mortality encouraged the deepening of emotional bonds between family members. But a look at the extent of changing survival prospects for infants since 1900 points clearly to the critical role that this change played in the increased intimacy of the parent-child relationship.

Several calculations to demonstrate the magnitude of the drop in child deaths since 1900 are presented in Table 1. First, the probability that an individual baby would survive his or her childhood increased from .79 in 1900 to .98 in 1976. The second calculation answers the question, what is the probability that a couple bearing three children would have at least one child die before reaching age 15? The answer is that under 1900 mortality conditions half of the parents would experience the loss of a child; under 1976 conditions only 6 percent would. But the rate of birth as well as death fell over this century. As a result, the probability of an average parent experiencing the death of a child changed even more. Women bearing children around 1900 had, on average, 4.2 children, while projections suggest that women currently bearing children will average about 2.1. Thus the third calculation in Table 1 shows that the probability of a child dying for parents with an average number of children for that period dropped from .62 in 1900 to only .04 in 1976. As the parental experience of having a child die changed from routine to exceptional, the simulus to invest greater emotion and resources has grown.

Orphanhood

The dependency of children upon adults for care and socialization necessitates fully developed social arrangements to deal with orphans in societies with high rates of mortality. Adoption within an extended kinship system and placement of children in orphanages were two mechanisms used to deal with the social problem of orphans in nineteenth-century America. But during the twentieth century orphanhood changes from a common occurrence to a rare event. Consequently, social institutions designed to deal with this problem have virtually disappeared. From the perspective of successive cohorts of children, the change has profoundly altered their experiences in families.

Table 1. Measures of Death to Children in Families: 1900; 1940; 1976.

Year	Probability of surviving from 0 to 15	Probability of 1 or more dying out of 3	Average number of children per mother[a]	Probability of 1 or more dying out of average number of births
1900	.79	.50	4.2	.62
1940	.94	.17	2.8	.16
1976	.98	.06	2.1	.04

[a]For 1900 and 1940 this is the average completed family size for women who were aged 25–29 at these dates. For 1976 the figure is the expected completed family size for women aged 25–29 in 1976.

Sources: U.S. Public Health Service, 1969; NCHS, 1978; Grabill *et al,* 1958; U.S. Bureau of the Census, 1978a.

Table 2 contains data which show the effect of varying mortality levels upon the probability of orphanhood. Since probability of death is related to age, some assumption about the age of men and women at occurrence of parenthood is required. Over this century the median age of women at the birth of their children has ranged from 27.2 to 25.4, and fathers have, on average, been about 3 years older than mothers. Therefore, the choice of a mother aged 27 and a father aged 30 for the calculations in Table 2 is a reasonable approximation to the typical experience over this time interval.[3] From the table we can read the probability of orphanhood for those born under these circumstances.

If mortality levels characteristic of 1900 persisted over time and the probability of death for the father and mother was independent, about 24 percent of the children born would lose at least one parent before reaching age 15; one out of 62 would have both parents die. Under mortality conditions existing in 1976, only 5 percent of all children would see a parent die, while one in 1,800 would lose both parents. So declining mortality has operated to increase greatly the family stability of children.

Of course, increasing divorce has had the counter influence of increasing family disruption for children. At current levels of divorce, about 36 percent of all children will experience a disrupted family (Bumpass, 1978). But the social significance of disruption due to death differs from disruption due to divorce. Current discussions of the effects of family disruption upon children should consider the very high rate of family instability that has been the historical experience of children prior to the modern era of low mortality. Further, those interested in designing social policy for the family would benefit from studying the historical ways of dealing with orphans.

---

[3]Varying the ages of parents at the birth of the child a few years in either direction has negligible effects upon the probability of orphanhood. For example, if the mother was 25 and the father 28, the probability in 1900 would be .23 instead of .24, and the probability in 1976 would be unchanged.

Table 2.   Probabilities of Parents and Siblings Dying Before a Child Reaches
Age 15: 1900; 1940; 1976.[a]

Year	Probability of 1 or more parent dying	Probability of 1 or more of 2 siblings dying	Probability of death to member of nuclear family
1900	.24	.36	.51
1940	.10	.12	.21
1976	.05	.04	.09

[a]See text for specific family context of the child.
Sources: U.S. Public Health Service, 1969; NCHS, 1978.

In addition to the reduced probability of losing a parent during childhood, there has also been a great reduction in the probability of a sibling dying. One good example indicates the magnitude of this change. Consider the situation of a first-born child to a mother aged 27 and a father aged 30, where the parents have two additional children at two-year intervals. That is, the first-born child has siblings born when he or she is two and four. What is the probability that this child will experience the death of a sibling before reaching age 15? Under 1900 mortality conditions the probability is .36, while under 1976 conditions, it is only .04. Combined with the possibility of a parent or sibling dying during childhood, the chances of a child losing someone in the nuclear family before he or she reaches age 15 drops from .51 to .09. Since the average number of siblings for a child born later in this century is much lower than for someone born earlier, the actual experience of encountering the death of an intimate family member has declined even more dramatically than these calculations suggest. Compared to the past, children now are almost entirely shielded from the death of close relatives, except that of elderly grandparents.

Grandparents' Survival

Not only did the mortality decline improve the likelihood that all members of the nuclear family would survive one's childhood, but also it increased the average number of living grandparents. Consider the probability of a child having grandparents alive if he or she is born to a father aged 30 and mother aged 27 and if both parents were similarly born when their fathers and mothers were 30 and 27 respectively. Under 1900 mortality conditions, one-fourth of the children would have all grandparents alive at birth; by 1976 it increased to almost two-thirds (Table 3). The probability of three or more grandparents being alive when the child was age 15 increased from .17 to .55. Thus, mortality change has greatly increased the potential for family interaction across more than two generations. The actual role of grandparents in the lives of children cannot be determined from these simple demographic data. But the increased presence of grandparents suggests that

Table 3.   Distribution of Children by Number of Living Grandparents When Child Is Aged 0 and 15 Under Conditions of 1900, 1940, and 1976.[a]

Year	Number of grandparents alive at age 0				Number of grandparents alive at age 15			
	0–1	2	3	4	0–1	2	3	4
1900	.08	.26	.42	.25	.48	.35	.15	.02
1940	.02	.13	.40	.46	.29	.39	.26	.06
1976	.00	.05	.31	.63	.12	.33	.39	.16

[a]See text for details.
Sources: Same as Table 2.

statements about their declining importance in the lives of children are probably exaggerated or wrong.

Young Adults

The mortality decline since 1900 has greatly altered the prospects that a marriage between young adults will be broken by death before old age. If a man and woman marry when they are aged 25 and 22, the probability that either of them will die within 40 years after their marriage dropped from .67 in 1900 to .36 in 1976. This decline in early widowhood more than offsets the rise in divorce (Table 4), so that the stability of marriages during the child-rearing years has actually increased over this century. When the declining age at completion of childbearing (Glick, 1977) is also considered, the higher probability of both husband and wife surviving to the empty nest stage of life is even more marked.

With current low mortality the prospective view of married life is quite different from what it was in the past. A man and a woman marrying at the average marriage age can anticipate jointly surviving a median of 45 years, i.e., until the husband is 70 years old. The prospect of living with one person over such a long time period, especially when one anticipates significant but unknown social change, may influence one's view of marriage. In particular, it may cause higher uncertainty about whether or not the marriage can survive until broken by death. If a couple enters into marriage accepting the option of divorce as a possibility, the chances of actually ending the marriage with a divorce are probably increased. Further, the period of time in which a divorce can occur has been lengthened. Thus it seems likely that the decreasing likelihood of marital disruption due to death has contributed to the increased rate of divorce in recent years.

Another, and more frequently noted, effect of lowered death rates upon the family behavior of young adults concerns fertility decisions. As shown in Table 1, the experience of having an infant or child die has moved from a common to a very uncommon event for American parents. The great vari-

Table 4.   Probability of Marital Disruption Due to Death or Divorce Within the First 40 Years: 1900; 1940; 1976.

Year	Broken by death[a]	Broken by death or divorce[a]
1900	.67	.71
1940	.50	.63
1976	.36	.60

[a] Assuming husband is 25 and wife is 22 at time of marriage.
Sources: Same as Table 2; plus Preston and McDonald, 1979; Glick, 1977.

ability that existed in 1900 between the number of children ever born and the number who eventually reached adulthood has disappeared. It is now possible for parents to anticipate the survival of all their children through childhood. Thus, the planning of family size has become feasible, and the need to have additional children to protect against possible loss no longer exists. A couple bearing two children can now be almost 95 percent confident that both will reach age 20. Consequently, an interesting effect of lowered mortality is the downward pressure it exerts upon fertility.

Middle Aged

Discussions of the family role of the middle-aged have generally emphasized the changes involved as children leave home and as relationships with adult children are developed. Two ways of viewing the changes that occur when parents no longer have dependent children are noted by Winch (1971). On the positive side:

> With the fulfillment of the parental role and the consequent reduction of responsibilities comes the promise of a more relaxed mode of life and the ultimate leisure of retirement.

While on the negative side:

> The "empty nest" psychology implies that since the parents' job is completed, they are no longer needed. They may look forward to declining strength, declining productivity, declining health, and, usually, in retirement to diminished income.

Both of these views picture the post-parental phase as a period of greatly reduced family responsibility. Clearly the average length of this segment of life has grown as the probability of surviving into old age has increased. But interestingly, the fall in mortality is also altering the nature of the empty nest stage of life. Brody (1978) has nicely captured this change when she writes, "The 'empty nests' of some of the grandparent generation are being refilled with members of the great-grandparent generation."

An increasing number of persons entering the "young-old" stage of life have parents who are still living and who are in need of substantial assistance. Older people are not generally abandoned by their children. Rather, adult children are now, as in the past, the primary care givers to the elderly in American society (Brody, 1978; Sussman, 1976). The big change has not been in norms regarding the responsibility of children to their elderly parents, but in the likelihood of a middle-aged person faced with the actual situation of having parents still alive. A quantitative assessment of the increased presence of parents for the middle-aged is given in Table 5.

The number of parents and parents-in-law still alive for a husband aged 55 and wife aged 52 under mortality conditions prevailing at selected historical periods is shown. The calculations assumed that both husband and wife were born when their fathers were aged 30 and their mothers were aged 27 (which is close to the average age at parenthood over this century). As in the previous calculations, period life tables are used to capture mortality conditions at specific time periods, so the data do not reflect the experiences of actual cohorts. A shift from 1900 mortality conditions to those of 1976 implies an increase in the proportion of middle-aged couples who have living parents from 48 to 86 percent. With 1976 mortality conditions, half of all middle-aged couples would have two or more elderly parents alive.

Old Age

As discussed earlier, marital instability prior to old age has declined over this century. At the same time, the remarriage rate for those with disrupted marriages has increased. Consequently, a much larger proportion of men and women are married and living with a spouse when they arrive at old age, and a slightly higher proportion of the total older population is now married (51 percent in 1900 vs. 52 percent in 1970). But while these data indicate an increased involvement of older persons in nuclear families, it is also true that average number of years that women spend in widowhood has greatly increased. The increased period of widowhood is a result of the much greater improvement in life expectancy for women than for men. The lengthening old-age period of life is increasingly divided into two parts for women: an earlier phase in which they are married and a later phase in which they are widows.

Selected values of life expectancy from life tables for men and women are presented in Table 6. From these values it can be seen that under the given mortality conditions, the average number of years that a typical wife can expect to outlive her husband has increased from 3.8 in 1900 to 9.7 currently. Primarily as a consequence of the increasing survival advantage of females over males, the ratio of widows to widowers over age 65 has grown from 2.2:1 in 1900 to 5.6:1 in 1976. With such a large imbalance, remarriage is clearly an option for very few of the older widows. Therefore, mortality

Table 5.   Distribution of Middle-Aged Couples by Number of Their Parents
Still Alive Under Conditions in 1900, 1940, and 1976.

	Number of parents alive:			
Year	0	1	2+	Total
1900	.52	.38	.10	1.00
1940	.37	.43	.20	1.00
1976	.14	.39	.47	1.00

Source: Same as Table 2.

change has created a major increase in the significance of the final stage of
life for women, a period of widowhood in which few men are around. What
the family experience of the rapidly growing number of older women, whose
children themselves are approaching old age, will be is not entirely clear. In
1976, however, about 70 percent of the widows over age 65 were living either
alone or in institutions (Metropolitan Life, 1977). Thus, a large majority of
older women are now living their last years of life outside of a family context. Of course, this does not mean that they necessarily lack significant kinship links, but it does indicate that their daily life is not enmeshed in a
family.

Conclusion

Declining mortality during the twentieth century has had a major impact
upon the American family. The role of mortality as an independent variable
producing change has been noted in the following areas:

1. Increasing survival prospects for infants has encouraged stronger emotional bonds between parents and children.
2. Decreasing deaths to adults aged 20 to 50 has reduced the proportion of
   children who experience orphanhood.
3. Decreasing mortality has eliminated the experience of a member of the
   nuclear family dying for most children.
4. Increasing survival rates has increased the number of living grandparents
   for children.
5. Decreasing mortality has increased the number of years that marriages
   survive without being disrupted by death. This change has probably contributed to the increase in divorce.
6. Decreasing infant and child deaths has allowed more careful planning of
   family size and has encouraged a reduction in fertility.
7. Increasing survival rates has lengthened the "empty nest" stage of the
   family.
8. Decreasing mortality has increased the number of elderly persons dependent upon their middle-aged children.

Table 6.   Average Years of Life Remaining at Selected Ages for Men and Women in the U.S.: 1900; 1940; 1976.

	Life table values					
Year	(1) $\overset{o}{e}_{22}(F)$	(2) $\overset{o}{e}_{25}(M)$	(3) $(1)-(2)$	(4) $\overset{o}{e}_{62}(F)$	(5) $\overset{o}{e}_{65}(M)$	(6) $(4)-(5)$
1900	42.3	38.5	3.8	14.0	11.5	2.5
1940	49.5	43.3	6.2	15.6	12.1	3.5
1976	56.8	47.1	9.7	20.4	13.7	6.7

Sources: Same as Table 2.

9. Increasing survival advantages for women relative to men has lengthened the period of widowhood at the end of the life course.

Bibliography

Ariès, Phillippe
   1962   Centuries of Childhood: A Social History of Family Life. Robert Baldick, trans. New York: Random House.
Blauner, Robert
   1966   "Death and Social Structure." Psychiatry 29:378–394.
Brody, Elaine M.
   1978   "The Aging of the Family." The Annals 438:13–27.
Bumpass, Larry and Ronald Rindfuss
   1978   "Children's Experience of Marital Disruption." Paper presented at the Annual Meeting of the Population Association of America.
Glick, Paul
   1977   "Marrying, Divorcing, and Living Together in the U.S. Today." Population Bulletin 32.
Grabill, Wilson H., Clyde V. Kiser and Pascal K. Whelpton
   1958   The Fertility of American Women. New York: Wiley.
Habenstein, Robert W.
   1968   "The Social Organization of Death." In David L. Sills, ed. International Encyclopedia of the Social Sciences 4:26–28.
Metropolitan Life
   1977   "Widows in the United States." Statistical Bulletin 58:8–10.
NCHS
   1978   Vital Statistics of the United States, 1976, vol. 2-Section 5. Life Tables. Hyattsville: U.S. Department of HEW.
Preston, Samuel H. and John McDonald
   1979   "The Incidence of Divorce with Cohorts of American Marriages Contracted Since the Civil War." Demography 16:1–25.
Skolnick, Arlene
   1978   The Intimate Environment: Exploring Marriage and the Family. 2nd ed. Boston: Little, Brown and Co.
Sussman, Marvin B.
   1976   "The Family Life of Old People." In Robert H. Binstock and Ethel Shanas, eds., Handbook of Aging and the Social Sciences. New York: Van Nostrand Reinhold.
U.S. Bureau of the Census
   1978a   Current Population Reports, Series P-23, No. 70.
   1978b   Current Population Reports, Series P-23, No. 77.
U.S. Public Health Service
   1969   Vital Statistics of the United States: 1967, Vol. 2, Part A.
Winch, Robert F.
   1971   The Modern Family. 3rd ed. New York: Holt, Rinehart, Winston.

Chapter 2

The Current Debate

The Family as a Haven in a Heartless World

Christopher Lasch

The family in the form familiar to us took shape in the United States and western Europe in the last half of the eighteenth and the first half of the nineteenth centuries, although its antecedents can be traced back to an earlier period. The chief features of the Western family system can be simply, if somewhat schematically, set forth. Compared with practices in most other societies, marriage takes place at a late age, and large numbers of people remain unmarried. As these demographic facts imply, marriages tend to be arranged by the participants instead of by parents and elders; at best the elders have a veto. Young couples are allowed to court with a minimum of interference from adults, on the understanding that their own self-restraint will take the place of adult supervision—an expectation that is not unreasonable considering that courting couples are typically young adults themselves and that young women in particular have been trained from an early age to accept advances from the other sex without compromising their reputation.

At the same time the habits of self-inhibition acquired during courtship are not easily relinquished in marriage, and the Western marriage system therefore gives rise to much sexual tension and maladjustment, which is more keenly felt than it would be elsewhere because marriage is supposed to be based on intimacy and love. The overthrow of arranged marriage was accomplished in the name of romantic love and a new conception of the family as a refuge from the highly competitive and often brutal world of commerce and industry. Husband and wife, according to this ideology, were to find solace and spiritual renewal in each other's company. Especially the woman was expected to serve, in a well-worn ninteenth-century phrase, as an "angel of consolation."

Reprinted by permission of the author and the publisher from *Salmagundi* (Fall 1976), pp. 42–55.

Her mission of mercy extended of course to her children as well, around whom middle-class family life increasingly centered. A new idea of childhood, as Aries has shown, helped to precipitate the new idea of the family. No longer seen simply as a little adult, the child came to be regarded as a person with distinctive attributes of his own, impressionability, vulnerability, and innocence, that required a warm, protected, and prolonged period of nurture. Whereas formerly children had mixed freely in adult society, parents now sought to segregate them from premature contact with servants and other corrupting influences. Educators and moralists began to stress the child's need for play, for love and understanding, and for the gradual, gentle unfolding of his nature. Child-rearing became more demanding as a result, and emotional ties between parents and children were strengthened at the same time that ties to relatives outside the immediate family were greatly weakened. Here was another source of persistent tension in the middle-class family—the emotional overloading of the parent-child connection.

Still another source of tension was the change in the status of women that the new family system required. The bourgeois family simultaneously degraded and exalted women. On the one hand, it deprived women of many of their traditional employments, as the household ceased to be a center of production and devoted itself to childrearing instead. On the other hand, the new demands of childrearing, at a time when so much attention was being given to the special needs of the child, made it necessary to educate women for their domestic duties. Better education was also required if women were to become suitable companions for their husbands. A thoroughgoing reform and extension of women's education was implicit in the new-style domesticity, as Mary Wollstonecraft, the first modern feminist, was one of the first to appreciate when she insisted that if women were to become "affectionate wives and rational mothers," they would have to be trained in something more than "accomplishments" that were designed to make young ladies attractive to prospective suitors. Early republican ideology had as one of its main tenets the proposition that women should become useful rather than ornamental. In the categories immortalized by Jane Austen, women were called on to give up sensibility in favor of sense. Thus bourgeois domesticity gave rise to its antithesis, feminism. The domestication of woman gave rise to a general unrest, encouraging her to entertain aspirations that marriage and the family could not satisfy. These aspirations were one ingredient in the so-called marriage crisis that began to unfold at the end of the nineteenth century.

To summarize, the bourgeois family system, which had its heyday in the nineteenth century and now seems to be slowly crumbling, was founded on what sociologists have called companionate marriage, on the child-centered household, on the emancipation or quasi-emancipation of women, and on the structural isolation of the nuclear family from the kinship system and from society in general. The family found ideological support and justification in the conception of the family as an emotional refuge in a cold and competitive society. Before turning to the late nineteenth-century crisis of the family, we need to examine a little further the last of these social facts—the concept of the family as a haven in a heartless world. This ideal took for granted a radical separation between work and leisure and between public life and private life. The emergence of the nuclear family as the principal form of family life reflected the high value modern society attached to privacy, and the glorification of privacy in turn reflected the devaluation of work. As production became more complex and efficient, work became increasingly specialized, fragmented, and routine. Accordingly work came to be seen as merely a means to an end —for many, the end of sheer physical survival; for others, of a rich and satisfying personal life. No longer regarded as a satisfying occupation in its own right, work had to be redefined as a way of achieving satisfactions or consolations outside work. Production, in this view, is interesting and important only because it enables us to enjoy the delights of consumption. At a deeper level of mystification, social work—the collective self-realization of mankind through its transformation of nature—appears merely as the satisfaction of private wants.

There is an even deeper sense in which work was degraded when it was mechanized and reduced to a routine. The products of human activity, especially the higher products of that activity such as the social order itself, took on the appearance of something external and alien to mankind. No longer recognizably the product of human invention at all, the man-made world appeared as a collection of objects independent of human intervention and control. Having objectified himself in his work, man no longer recognized it as his own. One of the best examples of this externalization of human creativity is the capitalist economy, which was the collective creation of human ingenuity and toil but was described by the classical economists as a machine that ran according to immutable laws of its own, laws analogous to the laws of nature. These principles, even if they had existed in reality instead of merely in the minds of Adam Smith and Ricardo, were inaccessible to everyday observation, and in the lay mind, therefore, the market economy defied not merely human control but human understanding. It appeared as a complex network of abstractions utterly impenetrable and opaque. John Adams once demonstrated his grasp of modern banking and credit by complaining that "every dollar of a bank bill that is issued beyond the quantity of gold and silver in the vaults represents nothing and is therefore a cheat upon somebody." Jefferson and Jackson, as is well known, held the same opinion. If the governing classes labored under such confusion, we can easily imagine the confusion of the ordinary citizen. He lived in a world of abstractions, where the relations between men, as Marx observed, assumed the fantastic shape of relations between things. Thus labor-power became a commodity, measurable in abstract monetary terms, and was bought and sold on the market like any other commodity.

At bottom, the glorification of private life and the family represented the other side of the bourgeois perception of society as something alien, impersonal, remote, and abstract—a world from which pity and tenderness had been effectively banished. Deprivations experienced in the public world had to be compensated in the realm of privacy. Yet the very conditions that gave rise to the need to view privacy and the family as a refuge from the larger world made it more and more difficult for the family to serve in that capacity.

By the end of the nineteenth century American newspapers and magazines were full of speculation about the crisis of marriage and the family. From the 1890s down to the 1930s, discussion of the decline of the family became increasingly intense. Four developments gave rise to a steadily growing alarm: the rising divorce rate, the falling birth rate among "the better sort of people," the changing position of women, and the so-called revolution in morals.

Between 1870 and 1920 the number of divorces increased fifteen times. By 1923, one out of every seven marriages ended in divorce, and there was no reason to think that the trend toward more and more frequent divorce would reverse itself.

Meanwhile "the diminution of the birth rate among the highest races," as Theodore Roosevelt put it in 1897, gave rise to the fear that the highest races would soon be outnumbered by their inferiors, who reproduced, it was thought, with total disregard for their ability to provide for the rising generation. The middle classes, on the other hand, clearly paid too much attention not only to the future but to their own present comfort. In the opinion of conservatives they had grown soft and selfish, especially middle-class women, who preferred the social whirl to the more serious pleasures of motherhood. Brooks Adams, spokesman for crusty upper-class reaction, described the new woman as the "highest product of a civilization that has rotted before it could ripen." Progressives also worried about the declining birth rate, but they blamed it on the high cost of living and rising standards of comfort, which led young men either to avoid marriage or to postpone it as long as possible. Women were not to blame for "race suicide," according to a leading woman's magazine. The "actual cause" was the "cost of living impelling the masses to pauperdom." The American man, with reason, "is afraid of a large family."

The changing status of women was obvious to the most casual observer. More and more women were going to college, joining clubs and organizations of all kinds, and entering the labor force. What explained all this activity and what did it signify for the future of the family? The feminists had a simple answer, at least to the first of these questions: women were merely "following their work out of the home." Industry had "invaded" the family, stripped it of its productive functions. Work formerly carried on in the household could now be carried out more efficiently in the factory. Even recreation and child-rearing were being taken over by outside agencies, the former by the dance-hall and the popular theater, the latter by the school. Women had no choice but to "follow their occupations or starve," emotionally if not in literal fact. Confined to the family, women would become parasites, unproductive "consumers upon the state," as a feminist writer put it in 1910.

Faced with an argument that condemned leisure as a form of parasitism, anti-feminists could have insisted on the positive value of leisure as the precondition of art, learning, and higher forms of thought, arguing that its benefits ought to be extended to the American businessman. But an attack on feminism launched from an essentially aristocratic point of view—an attack that condemned feminism as itself an expression of middle-class moralism and philistinism—hardly recommended itself to those who wished above everything else to preserve the sanctity of the home. American critics of feminism preferred to base their case on the contention that woman's usefulness to society and her own self-fulfilling work lay precisely in her sacred duties as wife and mother. The major premise of feminism—that women should be useful, not ornamental —had to be conceded; even while the conclusions feminists drew from this premise, the conclusions, they would have argued, that followed inevitably, were vigorously repudiated.

For the same reason a total condemnation of the feminist movement had to be avoided. Even the denunciation of "selfishness" was risky. In the mid-nineteenth century, defenders of the home had relied heavily on appeals to woman's duty to sacrifice herself for the good of others; but by 1900 this kind of rhetoric, even when translated into the progressive jargon of "service," had begun to seem decidedly out of date. The view that woman's destiny was to live for others gradually gave way to the view that woman too had a right to self-fulfillment—a right, however, that could best be realized in the home. In a word, the critics of feminism began to argue that motherhood and housewifery were themselves deeply satisfying "careers," which required special training in "homemaking," "domestic science," and "home economics." The invention of such terms expressed an attempt to dignify housework by raising it to the level of a profession. By rationalizing the household and child care, opponents of feminism hoped also to make the family a more effective competitor with the outside agencies that were taking over its functions.

If feminism disturbed the partisans of domesticity with its criticism of the home's inefficiency and its attempt to provide the "restlessness" of modern women with outlets beyond the family, the movement to liberate sexuality from conventional restraints troubled them much more deeply. Feminism at least allied itself with progressivism and with the vision of women's purifying influence over society; indeed the very success with which it identified itself with dominant themes in middle-class culture forced anti-feminists to refrain from attacking it frontally. The "new morality," on the other hand, directly challenged prevailing sexual ethics. It proclaimed the joys of the body, defended divorce and birth control, raised doubts about monogamy, and condemned interference with sexual life on the part of the state or community.

Yet even here the defenders of the family soon learned that unyielding condemnation was by no means the best strategy. In the long run it was no advantage to the family to associate itself with censorship, prudery, and political reaction. Instead of trying to annihilate the new morality, it made more sense to domesticate it—to strip away whatever in the ideology of sexual emancipation was critical of monogamy while celebrating a freer and more enlightened sexuality within marriage. Incidentally this operation provided the housewife with another role to complement her new role of consumer-in-chief—the multifaceted role of sexual partner, companion, playmate, and therapist.

Sex radicals not only called for a revolution in morals, they claimed that such a revolution was already under way. They cited statistical surveys that seemed to show a growing trend toward adultery and premarital sex. Faced with this evidence, the beleaguered champions of marriage executed another strategic retreat. The evidence showed, they argued, that the so-called revolt against marriage was not a revolt against marriage at all, merely an attack on the "sex-monopoly ideal" with which marriage had formerly been rather unnecessarily associated. Since "emphasis on exclusive sex possession" actually had a "destructive effect," it could safely be abandoned. Similarly the "virginity standard"—the requirement that the woman be a virgin at marriage—could be dispensed with. Exclusiveness in sex should be regarded as an ideal to be approximated, not as a standard to be imposed on everyone from without. Each couple should decide for themselves whether they would consider infidelity as evidence of disloyalty.

Another piece of ideological baggage that had to be thrown overboard, according to the emerging body of authoritative opinion on marriage and to spokesmen for arrangements that later came to be known as "open marriage," was the notion that marriage should be free of conflict and tension. Quarrels should be regarded as a normal part of marriage, events that should be taken in stride and even turned to productive purposes. Quarrels might even have a beneficial effect if they were properly "stage-managed" and rounded off with "an artistic consummation."

A fierce attack on romantic love played as important a part in the defense of marriage as in the criticism of marriage. Romantic love, it was thought, set impossibly high standards of devotion and loyalty—standards marriage could no longer meet. By undermining "sober-satisfying everyday life," romance wrought as much havoc as prudery, its twin. In the minds of radicals and conservatives alike, romantic love was associated with illusions, dangerous fantasies, and disease—with consumptive heroines, heroes wasting away with feverish desire, and deathbed farewells; with the overwrought, unhealthy music of Wagner, Strauss, and Puccini. Romantic love threatened both psychic and physical stability. The fashionable talk of marriage as an art conveyed a conception of marriage and the family that drew not so much from esthetics as from science and technology—ultimately from the science of healing. When marriage experts said that marriage was the art of personal "interaction," what they really meant was that marriage, like everything else, rested on proper technique—the technique of stage-managing quarrels, the technique of mutual agreement on how much adultery the marriage could tolerate, the technique of what to do in bed and how to do it. The new sex manuals, which began to proliferate in the twenties and thirties, were merely the most obvious examples of a general attempt to rationalize the life of the emotions in the interest of psychic health. That this attempt entailed a vigorous assault on "illusion" and fantasy is highly significant. It implies a concerted attack on the inner life, which was perceived as a threat to stability, equilibrium, and adjustment to reality. Marriage was to be saved at the expense of private life, which it was simultaneously expected to foster. The therapeutic program eroded the distinction between private life and the marketplace, turning all forms of play, even sex, into work. The experts made it clear that "achievement" of orgasm required not only proper technique but effort, determination, and emotional control.

So far I have spoken of the emergence of the nuclear family and its impact on popular thought, with particular attention to the ways in which the popular mind, led by the guardians of public health and morality, struggled with evidences of the family's growing instability. It remains to be seen how the same questions were dealt with at a more exalted level of thought—sociological theory. The social sciences devoted a great deal of attention to the crisis of marriage and the family. In particular the discipline of sociology, having divorced itself from the evolutionary and historical perspectives that had once dominated it, and having defined its field as the study of contemporary institutions and the social relations to which they gave rise, found it necessary to deal in detail with the contemporary family and what was happening to it. Much of what sociology had to say had already been anticipated in popular debate. Indeed it is clear that the sociology of the family in America arose in part as an answer to popular misgivings about the family. The role of sociology was to soothe those apprehensions with the voice of calm scientific detachment. Taking up certain lines of defense that had been suggested by doctors, social workers, psychotherapists, or scholars writing for a popular audience, sociology restated them in far more elaborate and extensive form, at the same time removing them from the polemical context in which they had originated. Claiming to have no stake in the outcome of investigations into the functions of the family, sociology provided the family with an elaborate ideological defense, which soon found its way back into popular thought and helped to bring about an important revival of domesticity and the domestic virtues in the thirties, forties, and fifties.

In effect, sociology revived the nineteenth-century myth of the family as an oasis and restated it in what looked like scientific form. First it dismissed the evidence of the family's decline by translating it into the language of functional analysis; then it showed that loss of certain functions (notably economic and educational functions) had been compensated by the addition of new ones.

Ernest W. Burgess, founder of a flourishing school of urban sociology at the University of Chicago, was one of the first to propose, in the early twenties, that what the family had lost in economic, protective, educational, religious, and recreational functions, it had made up in "affectional and cultural" functions. According to Burgess, the family had been "reduced" to an affectional group, "united by the interpersonal relations of its members," but the reduction in its size and scope had strengthened, not weakened, the family by enabling it to concentrate on the interplay of "interacting personalities." As the "institutional" functions of the family declined, the "personality" functions, in the words of W. F. Ogburn, took on greater and greater importance.

The rise of functionalism in social science coincided with, and was made possible by, the repudiation of historical approaches. At one time students of the family (and of other institutions as well) had attempted to arrange various institutional forms of the family in an evolutionary sequence or progression. Theoretical arguments about the family usually boiled down to arguments about historical priority. One group of theorists, following Bachofen, Morgan, and Engels, held that marriage had evolved from promiscuity to monogamy and the family from matriarchal to patriarchal forms. Others, like Westermarck, argued that patriarchal monogamy was the original form of the family. By the 1920s, these disputes had begun to seem inconclusive and heavily ideological, with the adherents of the matriarchal theory predicting the imminent demise of the monogamous family and their opponents seeking to demonstrate its permanence and stability. Sociology now rejected more modest historical theories as well—for example, theories that sought to link the decline of the patriarchal, extended family in Europe to changes in social and economic organization. Instead of attempting to explain the family's history, social science now contented itself with analyzing the way it functioned in various cultures. It was not altogether incidental that this functionalist analysis of the family, worked out first by anthropology in company with psychoanalysis and then applied by sociology to the contemporary family, had reassuring implications for the question of the family's future. The great variety of family forms suggested that while the family varied enormously from one culture to the next, in some form it was always found to be indispensable. The family did not evolve or decline, it merely adapted itself to changing conditions. As industry and the state took over the economic, educational, and protective work of the family, society at the same time became more impersonal and bureaucratic, thereby necessitating the creation of an intimate, protected space in which personal relations could continue to thrive. In the words of the urban sociologist Louis Wirth, "the pecuniary nexus which implies the purchasability of services and things has displaced personal relations as the basis of association"—everywhere, that is, except within the family. Joseph Folsom, a specialist in family sociology, noted in 1934 that modern society gave rise to a "generally increased need for intense affection and romance," while at the same time it "increased the difficulty of satisfying this need." As he put it somewhat quaintly, a "cultural lag" had arisen "between the increasing need for love and the practical arrangements to promote it." Ernest R. Mowrer, another family sociologist, argued along similar lines: "One of the most pronounced and striking phases of modern life is the repression of the emotions" —a tendency from which the family alone is exempt. Accordingly the family becomes "all the more important as the setting for emotional expression." In the rest of life, emotions have no place. "A business man is supposed to be cold, unfeeling, and 'hard-boiled.' Exchange . . . is unemotional and objective." The family, on the other hand, satisfies "the desire for response." Pent-up rage as well as pent-up love find expression in domestic life, and although this rage creates tensions in the family it is also a source of its continuing vitality. Familial tension, Mowrer argued, ought to become the primary concern of sociological study, through which it can be understood and therefore kept under control.

By reviving nineteenth-century conceptions of the family in allegedly scientific form, the sociology of the family accomplished something almost brilliant in its way: it stood the evidence of the family's decline on its head. Sociology invoked loss of functions, the drastic shrinkage of the family, and even the rising divorce rate to prove the stability, not the decline, of the family. Academic scholarship demonstrated that it was precisely the loss of its economic and educational importance that permitted the family to discharge its emotional functions more effectively than ever. The "loss of functions," instead of undermining the family, allowed it to come more fully into its own. There was only one trouble with this line of argument—a major one, however, with ramifying theoretical implications. Having abandoned historical analysis, sociology rested its claims to scientific status on a functional analysis of modern society—an analysis, that is, which purported to show how all the pieces fit together to make up a smoothly functioning social order. Yet at the same time it saw the family as in conflict with society—a haven of love in a loveless world. Nor could it argue, except by drastically simplifying the problem, that this conflict was itself functional. The view that family life alone provided people with the emotional resources necessary to live and work in modern society remained convincing only so long as the socializing function of the family was ignored. The family might be a haven for adults, but what about the children whom it had to prepare to live in precisely the cold and ugly world from which the family provided a haven? How could children raised under the regime of love learn to "function" in the marketplace? Far from preparing the young for this ordeal, the family, if it operated as sociology insisted it did operate, could only be said to cripple the young, at the same time that it offered a psychological refuge for the cripples, now grown to maladjusted maturity, that it had itself produced.

For a time, sociology could deal with these problems by ignoring them— that is, by ignoring the family's role in socializing the child. Some writers went so far as to insist that child-rearing had become incidental to marriage. But the rise of the so-called culture-and-personality school in American anthropology soon made this view untenable. The work of Ruth Benedict, Margaret Mead, and others made it clear that in every culture socialization is the main function of the family. A sociology that confined itself to the analysis of marriage could not stand comparison with the theoretical achievements of this new anthropology. The sociology of the family had to provide a theory of socialization or collapse into a rather pretentious form of marital counselling. Specifically it had to explain how an institution organized along very different principles from the rest of society could nevertheless train children to become effective members of society.

This was the problem, in effect, to which Talcott Parsons addressed himself in that part of his general theory which dealt with socialization—in Parsonian terminology, with tension-management and pattern-maintenance. Parsons begins by placing the study of the family in a broader social context—already a considerable advance over the work of his predecessors. According to Parsons, the family's famous loss of functions should be seen as part of the more general process of "structural differentiation"—the basic tendency of modern society. As the social division of labor becomes more and more complex, institutions become more specialized in their functions. To take an obvious example, manufacturing is split up into its various components, each of which is assigned to a special unit in the productive system. Specialization of functions increases efficiency, as is well known. Similarly the family performs its emotional services more efficiently once it is relieved of its other functions, which can be more efficiently carried on in institutions expressly designed for those purposes.

Having established a strong link between the development of the family and other social processes, Parsons now has to consider what other sociologists ignored, the family's role in socializing the child. How does the family, an institution in which social roles are assigned by ascription rather than achievement, train the child to enter a society in which roles are achieved rather than ascribed? The isolation of the family from the rest of the kinship system encourages a high degree of dependency between parents and children, yet at the same time the family has to equip the child to break these ties of dependency and to become an independent, self-reliant participant in the larger world. How does it manage to do both of these things at once, to tie children to their parents and yet to lay the ground work for the severance of those ties?

Briefly, Parsons proposes that the emotional security the family gives to the child in his early years is precisely the psychic foundation of the child's later independence. By providing the child with a great deal of closeness and warmth and then by giving him his head, the isolated nuclear family trains a type of personality ideally equipped to cope with the rigors of the modern world. Permissiveness, which many observers mistake for a collapse or abdication of parental responsibility, is actually a new way of training achievement, according to Parsons. It prepares the child to deal with an unpredictable world in which he will constantly face "unstructured situations." In the face of such contingencies he will have little use for hard-and-fast principles of duty and conduct learned from his parents. What he needs is the ability to take care of himself, to make quick decisions, and to adapt quickly to many types of emergencies. In a slower world, parents could indoctrinate their children with moral precepts adaptable to any foreseeable occasion, but modern parents, according to Parsons, can hope only to provide their young with the inner resources they need to survive on their own. This kind of training requires an intense dependency in early childhood followed by what strikes many foreigners as "incredible leeway" later on. But we should not be deceived by this "leeway." What looks like "abdication" is simply realism.

Youth culture, Parsons argues, is a differentiated part of the socialization system, the function of which is to ease the adolescent's transition from particularism to universality, ascription to achievement. Youth culture provides the adolescent with the emotional security of relationships that are "largely ascriptive" yet take him outside his own family. By providing this kind of "emotional support," the subculture of American adolescents fills an important set of needs, complementing the family on one side and the school on the other. Not only does it take young people out of the family but it helps to select and certify them for their adult roles—for example, by reinforcing appropriate ambitions while discouraging ambitions that are beyond the individual's abilities or his family's means to support.

This summary does not do justice to the elegance of the Parsonian theory of the family. We must press on to a further point: that for its elegance, the Parsonian theory has little capacity to explain empirical events, as any theory must. Far from explaining events, it has been overtaken by them. Writing in 1961, on the eve of an unprecedented upheaval of American youth, Parsons thought young people were becoming less hedonistic and more serious and "progressive," but his theory hardly anticipated the emergence of a youth culture that condemned American society in the most sweeping terms, repudiated the desirability of growing up in the usual way, and sometimes appeared to repudiate the desirability of growing up at all. It would be the height of perversity to interpret the youth culture of the sixties and seventies as a culture that eases the transition from childhood to maturity, when the attainment of adult status and responsibilities is seen by the culture as a betrayal of its ideals, by definition a "sell-out," and therefore becomes in the eyes of young people something to be accepted only with deep feelings of guilt. As for the argument that a heightened dependence in childhood is the basis of increased autonomy in adulthood, it does not explain why, in our society, personal autonomy seems more difficult than ever to achieve or sustain. Nor does it explain why so many signs of a massive cultural and psychological regression should appear just at the historical moment when, according to Parsons, the family has emerged from a period of crisis and has "now begun at least to be stabilized."

It is precisely the instability of the family that most emphatically repudiates the Parsonian theory of it. Youth culture itself has made the family a prime target—not just something to "rebel" against but a corrupt and decadent institution to be overthrown. That the new youth culture represents more than adolescent rebellion is suggested by the way its attack on the family reverberates, appealing to a great variety of other groups—feminists, advocates of the rights of homosexuals, cultural and political reformers of all kinds. Hostility to the family has survived the demise of the political radicalism of the sixties and flourished amid the conservatism of the seventies. Even the pillars of society show no great inclination to defend the family, historically regarded as the basis of their whole way of life. Meanwhile the divorce rate continues to rise, young people avoid or at least postpone marriage, and social life organizes itself around "swinging singles." None of these developments bears out the thesis that "loss of functions" made the family stronger than ever by allowing it to specialize in the work it does best. On the contrary, no other institution seems to work so badly, to judge from the volume of abuse directed against it and the growing wish to experiment with other forms.

Here to Stay: Parents and Children

Mary Jo Bane

Worry about the family is mostly worry about the next generation. Falling birthrates, rising divorce rates, increasing numbers of working mothers, and other indicators of the alleged decline of the family would probably seem much less alarming if adults alone were affected by the making and dissolving of families. People are distressed by these trends not because they signal a decline in the quality and richness of adult lives but because they seem to threaten the next generation. If the trends continue, will there be a next generation? Will it turn out all right? Will it be able to maintain and perhaps even improve the world?

These feelings about the importance of generational continuity lie, I suspect, behind the implicit and explicit comparisons that one generation makes with the generations before it. Modern families and modern methods of child rearing are almost always measured against the families of earlier times. The comparison is usually unfavorable to modern families. In contrast, when mod-

From *Here to Stay: American Families in the Twentieth Century* by Mary Jo Bane. © 1976 by Mary Jo Bane. By permission of Basic Books, Inc., Publishers, New York. Notes omitted. These notes provide detailed documentation of historical and demographic sources and can be found in Bane on pages 159–162.

ern technology and economic institutions are evaluated against earlier times the judgment is far more often made that things are better. In technology, progress is the standard. In social institutions, continuity is the standard, and when change occurs, it is seen as decline rather than advance.

Decline and *advance* are not easily defined terms, of course. What some people see as good child rearing, others may see as stifling repression and yet others as rampant permissiveness. But some agreement probably exists on the basic principles of how a society ought to treat its children: Children should receive secure and continuous care; they should be neither abused nor abandoned. Children should be initiated into adult society with neither undue haste nor unduly long enforced dependency—in other words, allowed to be children and permitted to become adults. Probably most important, Americans believe that children should be wanted both by their parents and by society.

Arguments that modern families are failing their children usually cite rising divorce rates and the rising proportion of mothers working as evidence that children are less well cared for by their parents now than in the past, that their environments are less secure and less affectionate. In addition, statistics on falling birthrates are sometimes used as evidence that modern Americans want and value children less than earlier generations. But data on parental care, family size, and the ties between generations can be used to make a different argument: that discontinuities in parental care are no greater than they were in the past; and that changes in fertility rates may lead to an environment that, according to generally agreed on criteria, is more beneficial for children.

Demographic Facts and the Age Structure of Society

Intergenerational relationships are profoundly influenced by the age structure of society, since that structure determines how many generations are alive at any one time and what proportion of the population has living ancestors or descendants. The age structure can also influence whether a society "feels" mature and stable or young and vibrant. Certain activities or patterns may seem characteristic of a society because they are characteristic of the largest age group in the population.

A combination of birth and death rates creates the age structure of a society. These two rates also determine the rate of growth of the population, which can in turn affect the density and structure of living arrangements. Birth and death rates thus define the demographic context within which the relationships between generations must be worked out. As technology provides the basic facts of economic life, demography defines the basic facts of social life.

Today's great-grandparents were born during a period when the population of America was growing at a rapid rate. The European populations from which the American colonists had come had been relatively stable in size, with death rates balancing birthrates over long-term cycles of prosperity followed by epidemics and famines. In the seventeenth-century, death rates began to fall dramatically and steadily, probably because of general improvements in nutrition and the physical environment. Death rates fell at all ages; not only did mature people live longer, but more infants survived to childhood and more children to maturity. And more women lived to have more children. The result was a rapid population growth that has characterized the United States at least since the U.S. Census began in 1790, and probably much earlier.

Falling death rates, however, have been partially balanced by falling birthrates. In the United States, birthrates have been gradually falling for as long as data have been collected. They probably began to fall about 1800 or possibly earlier, and in the last few years they have fallen below replacement level. If they remain at replacement level, the United States will reach a stable population level about the year 2000. In the United States, therefore, the rate of natural population growth was probably highest in the early and mid-nineteenth century. Around 1800 the population grew at a rate of almost 3 percent per year. By 1880 it was growing at around 2 percent per year and by 1974, at six-tenths of one percent.

A rapidly growing population is different from a stable population in several ways. One is age structure. Demographers find that the average age of populations that are not growing can range from about twenty-seven years when mortality rates are very high (probably characteristic of pre-industrial Europe) to about thirty-eight years when mortality rates are very low (the United States of the future). In contrast, a rapidly growing population is young. The median age of the population of the United States shown in Table 1 illustrates the point.

As population growth has slowed down, the American population has become gradually older. This aging is perhaps the most important difference between the world of our great-grandparents and our own world, and contributes to many of the changes that have taken place in family and intergenerational relationships.

It may seem strange that a population becomes younger as death rates fall. As people live longer should the population not become older? The reason it does not is that in all the societies that demographers have studied, death rates

Table 1. Proportion of American Women Who Are Widows, by Age, 1976

Age Group	% Widows
Under 35	1.0
35–39	1.9
40–44	3.2
45–54	7.2
55–64	19.1
65–74	42.0
75+	69.7

are highest both late in life and early in life. Declines in death rates are usually most dramatic among infants. More infants survive, contributing more children to the population. More women survive to reproductive age and contribute even more children to the population. Thus lower mortality rates result in a younger average age of the population even though average life expectancy at birth rises.

Imagine, for example, a population in which half the babies died at birth and half lived to be 50. The average life expectancy would be 25 years, and the average age of the population would also be 25 years. Now imagine that infant mortality rates fell, so that everyone lived to be 50. The average life expectancy would then be 50. The average age of the population would still be 25, if the population remained stable in size. But if birthrates remained the same as they were when death rates were high, the population would be bound to grow, since more women would live to reproductive age and there would be more babies and children than older people. Thus mortality rates would have produced a younger rather than an older population.

Another interesting characteristic of a rapidly growing population, related to its age structure, is that working-age adults comprise a relatively small proportion of the population. Working-age adults (age 15–64) made up 58 percent of the rapidly growing population of the United States in 1880. In contrast, 68 percent of the population of the United States in 1940 was made up of working-age adults. The nonworkers in a rapidly growing population are almost all children, since the proportion of old people is extremely low. On the other hand, when death rates are low and the population is stable in size, almost half of the nonworkers are over 65.

A third feature of a rapidly growing population is that it must every year induct a relatively large number of young people into adulthood and into the work force. More must start work than retire. This can put a strain on adult society in general and on the economy in particular. If the economy is not growing as rapidly as the population, the problem of what to do with young people can become acute.

Changes in the rate of population growth produce changes in the age structure of a society that are in turn reflected in the problems the society must cope with, the mechanisms it uses to do so, and the general feel of the society. In a rapidly growing population, children and adolescents must be more visible. A young, childlike society may be a more congenial place for children to live. But it may not. Children may be more precious when they are relatively rare. A more mature society may have more physical and emotional resources to give to the care of children. It may display a greater ease in inducting children —since there are fewer of them—into the adult society.

Teenagers may cause major social problems when they make up a disporportionately large segment of the population. When they are fewer, especially when the number entering the labor force equals the number retiring, they can be integrated much more easily. This interpretation might partially explain cycles of concern over youth. It might also partially explain societal attitudes toward children. Dr. Spock, after all, advocated permissive child-rearing in the first edition of his book in 1947, when children were relatively rare. He changed his mind in 1968, for a variety of reasons no doubt. But whether Spock realized it or not, he may simply have been reacting to what must have seemed a veritable surfeit of children. In the coming decades, children and adolescents will make up a small proportion of the population. Through this simple demographic change, they may become less of a problem and more of a precious resource.

Childlessness and Family Size

Declining birthrates not only change the position of children in society as a whole, but they can also affect the status of children in individual families. Low birthrates that occur because fewer women are having children should probably be interpreted differently from rates that are low because many women are having a smaller number of children. High rates of voluntary childlessness in the society might reflect a cleavage in the society. If people who did not have children were different from those who did—if, for example, they were better educated or concentrated in the professional occupations—the potential for social conflict would be great. Public support for children would certainly be hard to master if only low-status (or only high-status) parents had children. At the same time, the family environments of children would not necessarily change much. If fewer women had children but still had large numbers, most children would continue to be brought up in large families.

If, on the other hand, low birthrates occurred because most people continued to have children but had fewer of them, political divisions between the childless and others would be less likely. But an important change would take place in the family environments of children. More children would be brought up in small families. The consequences would more likely be beneficial to both the children and the society.

Decreasing family size rather than increasing childlessness accounts for most of the declining fertility in the United States. The U.S. Census first gathered data on the total number of children women had had over their reproductive years in 1910. The census data is probably accurate for women born as early as 1846 and as late as 1935, since most women now complete their childbearing before age 35. The fertility of women born after 1935 can be predicted from two sources: from Census Bureau questions that ask women how many children they expect to have, and from projections of fertility rates based on the number of children they have had so far. These combined sources provide fairly accurate descriptions of the fertility history of women born since the middle of the nineteenth century.

Between 90 and 95 percent of women marry at one time or another. The proportion has fluctuated over the years, with a slight increase in recent decades in the proportion of women marrying. The proportion of married women who have no children has also fluctuated over the years—first up, then down. The childless proportion rose from about 8.2 percent of married women born 1846–55 to a high of over 20 percent of the married women born between 1901 and 1910. Childlessness then fell to 7.3 percent among married women born 1931–35.

It is hard to say why childlessness rose during the nineteenth century, but it may have to do with the unhealthful conditions facing women in the factories or the economic difficulties experienced especially by the immigrants. One explanation for the high rates of childlessness among married women born around the turn of the century is the economic depression of the 1930s. When unemployment rates are high, birthrates almost always fall. In the 1930s unemployment reached a new high and birthrates a new low.

The decline in childlessness since the 1930s is equally hard to explain. It may have to do with improvements in general health and with new medical treatments for sterility and infertility. Involuntary childlessness may have virtually disappeared. Predictions about the future are thus predictions about voluntary childlessness, which is now possible through the relative ease of birth control and abortion.

Predictions might be based on the characteristics of women who remained childless in the past. Among women born before 1920 who were surveyed by the 1970 census, those who were childless were more likely to be black, to have been born in the Northeast, to have married at older ages, to have gone to college, to have lived in urban areas, and to have been married to professional or white-collar workers rather than farmers or laborers. In general, the childless were better educated and better off. High rates of childlessness among blacks are the exception and may be explained by health conditions.

These correlates suggest that childlessness should have increased over time as more women became better educated and better off. But that is the opposite of what actually happened. The cross-sectional data also suggest that childlessness should decrease during hard times since fewer people are well-off. But this too is precisely the opposite of the historical fact. The economic and demographic correlates of childlessness are, therefore, not very useful bases for making predictions about what will happen.

Some predictions can be made, however, on the basis of what women say about the number of children they expect to have. In 1975 less than 5 percent of wives who were interviewed about family plans expected to remain childless. This proportion was relatively constant throughout the age groups. The proportion of women who expect to remain childless went up slightly from 1967–1974, but then went down again in 1975. Better-educated women and white women are more likely to expect to remain childless, but the difference is not great.

The most interesting thing about these figures on expected childlessness is that they are so low. If as few women remain childless as say they expect to, the childless proportion among women born between 1940 and 1955 will be the lowest ever recorded. Even if the rate of childlessness for all women were equal to the expected rate for college women, childlessness would still be at its lowest recorded level. Under either condition, however, the country is due for some upswing in births, as those who have put off having children is due for some upswing in births, as those who have put off having children begin to have them. One problem with the data is that the Census Bureau interviews only married women about their family plans, not unmarried women who may or may not marry and may or may not expect children in the future. Another is that women who now see themselves as putting off children may later be unable to have them, or decide not to. This problem can be partially corrected by making projections from birthrates by age. One demographic study uses these rates to estimate that 10 percent of women born around 1945 will actually remain childless, rather than the 5 percent who expect to. The Census Bureau made a series of projections from similar data, with similar results. These studies project a slightly higher rate of childlessness than that found among women born during the 1930s, but still lower than that among women born 1901–10. It seems safe to say that the vast majority of American women will continue to have at least one child.

Although there has been no systematic increase over the century in the proportion of women who have no children, there has been a systematic and dramatic decrease in the number of children each mother has. The average married woman in colonial Massachusetts may have had as many as eight children. The average mother born 1846–55 had 5.7 children. The average number of children decreased steadily for sixty years, reaching 2.9 children among women born 1911–15. It then rose for a short period during the postwar baby boom; women born 1931–35 have had an average of 3.4 children per woman with children. It is now once again falling. Yet the proportion of women having no children or having only one child has not increased over the century. The big change has thus been in the proportion of women having very large families, a change which has occurred for all races and education levels. Many fewer women have five or more children; many more women have two or three.

Looking at these numbers from the viewpoint of the children illustrates the change that has taken place over four generations. Statistics about average family size do not accurately reflect the size of the family into which the average child is born. The family of the average child is larger than the average family because more children are born into larger families.

If this sounds like a riddle, imagine ten families distributed as follows:

1-child—4 families
2-child—3 families
3-child—2 families
4-child—1 family

The average family size is $4(1) + 3(2) + 2(3) + 1(4) \div 10 = 2$. But the twenty children are distributed as follows:

>1-child families—4 children
>2-child families—6 children
>3-child families—6 children
>4-child families—4 children

The average child is born into a family of $4(1) + 6(2) + 6(3) + 4(4) = 50 \div 20 = 2.5$ children, and has an average of 1.5 brothers and sisters. When large families are included in the calculations the differences between average family size and the average number of brothers and sisters can be very dramatic.

From the point of view of the child, a better indication of family size than average family size is the average number of brothers and sisters that children of different generations have. The great-grandparents of today's children had on the average six brothers and sisters. Their grandparents had five brothers and sisters. Their parents—depression babies—had on the average three brothers and sisters. Today's children may have as few as two. The low birthrates of the depression occurred partly because of high rates of childlessness and only children. There were, however, many large families. In contrast, the low fertility rates of the early 1970s are the product of low rates of childlessness and only children, accompanied by extremely small numbers of large families. Most children in the 1970s are born into two- or three-child families. If these patterns continue, the average child born in the next decade will have only two brothers and sisters.

Small families mean a quite different life for children. Some of the differences are probably detrimental to children, but, on the whole, small families seem to be beneficial. A number of studies suggest that children from small families do better in school and score better on standardized tests than children from large families. Part of the explanation is that smaller families are usually better off financially. But even when these families are equally well-off, children from large families do not get as much education, as good jobs, or as high earnings as children from small families.

One of the most interesting studies on family size and achievement investigated the reasons for the superior performance of children from small families. The study first looked at the amount of time that parents and other adults spent with children. Middle children in large families received considerably less adult care and attention than children in smaller families or than first and last children in larger families. Parental attention must be shared by more people when the family has more children living at home, a condition that affects middle children in large families more than others.

The study then looked at the effect of family size on achievement. It found that a variable representing the child's share of family time and financial resources had a more important effect on achievement, both educational and occupational, than most other background characteristics.

Children from large families seem to be somewhat slower in physical development than children from small families. Emotional and social differences have not been so clearly documented, although there is some evidence that children from small families are more likely to think well of themselves. On the other hand, cross-cultural studies have shown that children who care for younger children are more nurturing and responsible and less dependent and dominant than others. Because children are more likely to have taken care of younger siblings when they come from larger families, smaller families may produce fewer independent and helpful children. In general, though, the trend toward smaller families among all segments of the population has probably done more to increase and equalize cognitive development and schooling than any other demographic trend.

The data on childlessness and family size, in short, do not suggest a societal abandonment of children. A large increase in childlessness now that involuntary childlessness is almost nonexistent would indicate that a substantial portion of the population wanted no children, but this has not occurred. The vast majority of adults have at least one child. Average family size has decreased, but the decline has taken place mostly in larger families. Family size is converging for the entire population on the two- or three-child ideal. These smaller families seem to be advantageous for children rather than a sign of societal indifference.

Living Arrangements of Children

Another indicator of the place of children in the society is whether parents and children live together. Children who live with their parents are certainly better off than children raised in orphanages. They may or may not be better off than children raised by relatives or foster parents. At any rate, whether or not children live with their parents provides some indication of the strength of ties between parents and children.

Many people assume that the rising divorce rates of the last few decades mean that fewer children now live with their parents. This assumption is not completely accurate. The data suggest that the proportion of children who live with at least one of their parents rather than with relatives, with foster parents, or in institutions has been steadily rising.

The U.S. Census has published information about the living arrangements of people only since 1940. Since then the proportion of children living with at least one of their parents in a separate household has gone steadily up, from about 90 percent in 1940 to almost 95 percent in 1970. The increase seems to have occurred for two reasons. The first reason is that the proportion of children who lost a parent through death and divorce combined fell gradually during the first half of the century and probably fell before that as well. Among children born between 1911 and 1920, about 22 percent lost a parent through death and 5 percent had parents divorce sometime before their eighteenth birthday. Gradually declining death rates meant that fewer children lost parents as the century went on. Smaller families had the same effect, since more children were born to younger parents. The result was that about 20 percent of the children born during the 1940s lost parents through death or divorce. Only for children born around 1960 did rising divorce rates begin to counteract the effects of falling death rates. The proportion of children who experienced a parental disruption fell until then; only recently has disruption increased.

The second reason for the rise in the proportion of children living with at least one parent between 1940 and 1970 is a dramatic increase in the proportion of widowed and divorced women who continued living with their children after their marriage ended. In 1940 only about 44 percent of women with children but without husbands headed their own families. The rest must have sent their children to live with their grandparents or other relatives or to orphanages. By 1970 almost 80 percent of divorced, separated, and widowed women with children headed their own families. Some women, especially the young and unmarried, continue to leave their children with their grandparents. Most, however, now keep the family together. The children may not live with both their parents, but they do live with at least one. In 1975, despite rising divorce rates, only 2.7 percent of children under 14 lived with neither of their parents. The aggregate figures do conceal a racial difference: In the same year, 1975, 7.5 percent of non-white children were living with neither parent, compared with 1.7 percent of white children. But for non-whites as well as whites, the percent living with neither parent has been going down, from 9.8 percent for non-whites in 1968 to the present figure.

Although the proportion of children living with at least one parent has risen, rising divorce rates since 1960 have caused a decrease in the proportion of children under 14 living with both parents. In 1960, 88.5 percent of all children under 14 lived with two natural or adoptive parents; by 1974 the number had fallen to 82.1 percent. This trend is likely to continue. Estimates from death and divorce rates indicate that nearly 40 percent of the children born around 1970 will experience a parental death, divorce, or separation and consequently live in a one-parent family at some point during their first eighteen years. The proportion living with neither parent, however, is likely to remain small.

The effects on children of these changes in living arrangements are not well understood. Hardly anyone argues that the divorce or death of parents is good for children, but the extent of the harm done has not been documented. There is some evidence that children from broken homes do not do as well in school as children from unbroken homes. Much of the disadvantage seems to come, however, from the fact that many one-parent homes are also poor. Moreover, children whose parents divorce are no worse off than children whose homes are unbroken but also unhappy. Although the evidence is scanty, it suggests that most children adjust relatively quickly and well to the disruption and that in the case of divorce the disruption may be better than the alternative of living in a tension-filled home.

No studies have looked at the effects on children of various living arrangements after divorce. This is surprising, given the significant change that has taken place over the last thirty years in what normally happens to children. Probably children who stay with their mothers are better off than children with foster parents or relatives, although individual circumstances can vary widely. Staying with the mother may make the event less disruptive and less distressing; only one parent is lost rather than both. The increased tendency of widowed and divorced mothers to keep their children may, therefore, be good for the children.

The effect of the growing tendency of women with children but without husbands to set up separate households rather than live with relatives or friends is less clear. Since single-parent families seem to live on their own whenever they can afford to, they must see advantages to the arrangement. On the other hand, single parents have the almost impossible reponsibility of supporting and caring for a family alone. The absence of other adults to relieve the pressure must increase the tension and irritability of single parents (unless, of course, the presence of other adults would increase tension and irritability even more). Children in separate households gain the undivided attention of their mothers and often establish extremely close supportive relationships. But they lose the company of other adults and the exposure to a variety of adult personalities and role models that larger households might provide. Separate households are clearly what most single parents want, but it would be interesting to know exactly what they give up in having them.

Child Care Arrangements

Like data on living arrangements, data on child care arrangements are often cited as evidence of the state of parent-child relationships. People often talk as if children are best off when they are taken care of exclusively by their mothers. The rise in the proportion of mothers who hold paid jobs is, therefore, cited periodically as an indicator of the decline of the family. Most concern, of course, is focused on young children; Americans have long believed that older children should go to school and play on their own, not be continually supervised by mother. But even care arrangements for young children involve more than simply care by the mother. Care arrangements have changed over the century, but it is not clear that families and mothers have become less important. Nor is it clear whether the changes are good or bad.

The most important activity of contemporary children up to the age of 14 is watching television. The average preschooler seems to watch television about thirty-three hours per week, one-third of his waking hours. The average sixth-grade child watches about thirty-one hours. Since television sets only became common during the 1950s, the importance of television has clearly been a development of the last quarter century. It represents a tremendous change in how children of all ages are cared for. Television is by far the most important new child care arrangement of this century.

The next most important activity of children's waking hours is going to school. Children now spend an average of about nineteen hours a week in school. A larger proportion of children of all ages go to school now than ever before. They start school earlier and stay in school longer. The most dramatic change of the last ten years has been in the proportion of very young children enrolled in nursery school and kindergarten. In 1965 about 27 percent of all 3- to 5-year-olds were enrolled in school; by 1973, 41 percent of this age group were in school.

Other important changes have occurred in the length of the school year and in average daily attendance. In 1880 the average pupil attended school about eighty days per year. By the 1960s the typical school year was 180 days and the average pupil attended about 164 days. Both these changes mean that children enrolled in school spend more time there. School, therefore has steadily gained in importance as a child care arrangement.

Compared with these two dramatic changes in child care arrangements— the growth of television and school—changes caused by mothers working outside the home appear almost trivial. It is true that the proportion of mothers with paid jobs has risen sharply over the last twenty-five years, particularly among mothers of preschool children. In 1950, 12 percent of married women with children under six were in the labor force; by 1974 the proportion had grown to nearly 40 percent. Many of these working mothers arranged their schedules so that they worked only when their children were in school or when fathers were at home to take care of the children. About 70 percent, however, made other child care arrangements. The most common was to have a relative or sitter come to the home and care for the children. Only about 10 percent of the preschool children of working mothers went to day care centers.

How much of a difference these arrangements make in the lives of children depends on what actually happens to them and who actually spends time with them. There is no evidence as to how much time mothers a century ago spent with their children. Undoubtedly, it was less than contemporary nonworking mothers, since mothers of a century ago had more children and probably also had more time-consuming household tasks.

Contemporary nonworking mothers do not spend a great deal of time exclusively with their children. A national study done in 1965 found that the average nonworking mother spent 1.4 hours per day on child care. A study of 1,300 Syracuse families in 1967–68 showed that the average nonworking mother spent sixty-six minutes a day in physical care of *all* family members and forty-eight minutes in other sorts of care on a typical weekday during the school year. The amount of time varied with the age and number of children.

A small 1973 Boston study, by White and Watts, found that of the time they were observed mothers spent about a third interacting with their children (but one expects that mothers being observed by Harvard psychologists might depart somewhat from their normal routines). The children in the study, age 1 to 3, spent most of their time in solitary playing or simply watching what went on around them.

Working mothers spend less time on child care than nonworking mothers, but the differences in the amount of time mothers spend exclusively with their children are surprisingly small. In the Syracuse study, the correlations between the amount of time women spent on physical care of family members and whether or not they are employed were very small, once family size and children's ages were taken into account. When all family members, not just wives, were looked at, the correlations were even smaller. There is some evidence that working mothers especially in the middle class try to make up for their working by setting aside time for exclusive attention to their children. They probably read more to their children and spend more time in planned activities with them than do nonworking mothers.

There is no evidence that having a working mother per se has harmful effects on children. When a mother works because the father is incapacitated, unemployed, or paid poorly, the family may be poor and disorganized and the children may suffer. In these cases, however, the mother's working is a symptom and not a cause of more general family difficulties. In other cases where mothers work, children are inadequately supervised and may get into trouble. Again, though, the problem is general family difficulty. The Gluecks' study of lower-class boys, often cited as evidence that working mothers raise delinquent children, shows no direct link between the mothers' employment and delinquency. It did find that in lower-class homes children of working mothers were less likely to be adequately supervised, and that there was a tie between lack of supervision and delinquency whether the mothers worked or not. In families where the mother's employment is not a symptom of deeper family trouble, children seem not to turn out any differently from other children.

Parents and Teenagers

For the last century or so, Americans have become attuned to the existence and peculiarities of that stage in life between childhood and adulthood that we call adolescence. Adolescence is apparently a creation of relatively recent times; at least its problems have only recently attracted widespread attention. Certainly, as Margaret Mead showed so well, adolescent difficulties do not occur universally. Whatever the distinctive characteristics of the adolescent personality, however, there have been some noticeable changes over the last century in the living and working arrangements of adolescents. The general trend is to tie adolescent boys to parents for an increasing length of time and to begin to liberate adolescent girls.

In mid-nineteenth-century America, it was common practice for young men, and to a lesser extent young women, to leave their parents' house and live for a few years as a lodger or servant in some other older person's house before marrying and setting up independent households. The best information on family structure in the mid-nineteenth century comes from Michael Katz's study of Hamilton, Ontario. Boarders and lodgers were then an important feature of life. In 1851 more than half of the young men aged around 20 were living as boarders in the household of a family other than their own. But industrialization was accompanied by business cycles and increased schooling, which in turn brought striking changes in the lives of young people. By 1861 only a third of Hamilton's young men were living as boarders. More lived at home and went to school. Nearly a third were neither employed nor in school. The nineteenth-century specter of gangs of young men roaming the city streets must have arisen because gangs of young men were indeed roaming the streets.

In the United States also, many young men of the middle and late nineteenth century lived for a time as boarders. Boarding was a different phenomenon, however, in rural and urban areas. In cities young men typically lived with families but worked elsewhere. Rural youth were more often live-in farm help. By 1970, boarding out had virtually disappeared; less than 2 percent of 15- to 19-year-olds were living as boarders or servants. Instead they were living at home and going to school. The rise in school attendance was dramatic. In 1910, about 30 percent of 16- to 19-year-old boys were in school compared to about 73 percent in 1970. The employment situation for teenagers is still, as it was in mid-nineteenth century Hamilton, dreadful. The young men have not been put to work, but they have been induced to stay in school.

Young women, so often forgotten in historical discussions, are working more and going to school more. Typically, young women lived at home performing domestic tasks until they married. In mid-nineteenth-century Hamilton, for example, about 36 percent of the 18- and 19-year-old women were employed and about 5 percent went to school. Another 5 percent were married. The rest must have been living at home, doing domestic chores or doing nothing. During the growth of schooling in the nineteenth century, girls' attendance rates rose even faster than boys'. In 1970 in the United States, young women were still living at home, but they were going to school rather than helping mother. The vast majority (88.6 percent) of the 16- and 17-year-olds and 41.6 percent of the 18- and 19-year-olds were enrolled in school. Most of the rest were working at paid jobs, and some were raising children.

Among both men and women, there seems to have been a slight increase in the last decade in the proportion who live away from their parents during their late teenage years. Even in 1974, however, this group was a minority. Among 18- and 19-year-old men, about 7 percent were married and living with a wife and only about 6 percent were living on their own. Among 18- and 19-year-old women, 21 percent were married and 9 percent were living on their own.

Virtually all 14- to 17-year-olds lived with their parents. The living arrangements of 20- to 24-year-olds will be examined in Chapter Three.

In short, there has been no significant emancipation of teenagers from their families. In comparison with nineteenth-century teenagers in urban areas, in fact, contemporary teenage boys are much more dependent on their parents for shelter and support. What they do at home is another matter, but they do live there.

Children in the Family and Society

In summary, demographic materials suggest that the decline of the family's role in caring for children is more myth than fact. None of the statistical data suggests that parental watchfulness over children has decreased over the span of three generations; much suggests that it has increased. The most important difference between today's children and children of their great-grandparents' and grandparents' time is that there are proportionately fewer of them. They make up a smaller proportion of society, and there are fewer of them per family. Like children born during the 1930s, but unlike children born during the 1950s, children of the 1970s face a predominantly adult world. If the rate of population growth continues to stabilize, the society of the next decades will be older and the families smaller than any previously found in America.

Parent-child bonds also persist despite changes in patterns of disruption and living arrangements after disruption. The proportion of children who lose a parent by death has gone steadily down over the generations. The proportion who live with a parent after a death or divorce has gone steadily up. Even in recent years when family disruptions have begun to rise again to high levels, almost no children have gone to relatives, foster homes or institutions.

The trend toward more mothers in the paid labor force has probably not materially affected parent-child bonds. Even though more mothers work outside the home and more children go to school earlier and longer, the quantity and quality of actual mother-child interaction has probably not changed much. In short, the major demographic changes affecting parents and children in the course of the century have not much altered the basic picture of children living with and being cared for by their parents. The patterns of structural change so often cited as evidence of family decline do not seem to be weakening the bonds between parents and children.

The Trends: Marriage, Divorce, Remarriage

Andrew Cherlin

We often think of social change in terms of the differences between one generation and the next—between our parents' lives and our own lives or between our own lives and our children's lives. When we look at the trends in marriage, divorce, and remarriage in the United States since World War II, the experiences of two successive generations stand in sharp contrast: the men and women who married and had children in the late 1940s and 1950s, and their sons and daughters, who entered adulthood in the late 1960s and 1970s. Most of the members of the older generation were born in the 1920s and the 1930s, and they grew up during the Great Depression and the war years. This group is relatively small because fewer babies were born during the late 1920s and the hard times of the 1930s. But when they reached adulthood, this generation had a large number of children. About five out of six of the women whose peak childbearing years occurred in the 1950s gave birth to at least two children, and those births were bunched at an earlier time in their lives. The result was a great increase in births between the end of World War II and 1960, an increase which we now call the postwar baby boom. In 1957, at the peak of the boom, 4.3 million babies were born in the United States, compared to 2.4 million in 1937. (By comparison, there were 3.5 million births in 1979.) Thus the relatively small generation of parents in the 1950s gave birth to a much larger generation—the children of the baby boom.

In the 1950s, when the members of the older generation were in their twenties and thirties, the country's marriage rate was high and rising, and its divorce rate was relatively low and stable. But as the younger generation matured, all that changed. The divorce rate began to rise in the early 1960s and doubled between 1966 and 1976. As more and more young people put off marrying, the marriage rate fell, though the number of couples living together without marrying more than doubled in the 1970s. The birth rate fell to an all-time low.

In this chapter I compare the experiences of these two generations as they have married, divorced, and remarried. But we must be careful not to assume that just because the older generation came first, their family patterns were more typical of twentieth-century American family life. Put another way, we shouldn't assume that all the changes since the 1950s were deviations from the usual way of family life in the United States. In fact, I argue that the 1950s were the more unusual time, that the timing of marriage in

Reprinted by permission of the publisher from *Marriage, Divorce, Remarriage* by Andrew Cherlin, Cambridge, Mass.: Harvard University Press. Copyright © 1981 by the President and Fellows of Harvard. Portions of the original have been omitted.

the 1970s was closer to the typical twentieth-century pattern than was the case in the 1950s. The divorce experiences of both generations differed from the long-term trend in divorce. In addition, the rate of childbearing in the 1950s was unusually high by twentieth-century standards. A close look at the historical record, then, suggests that in some ways the 1970s were more consistent with long-term trends in family life than were the 1950s. . . .

Entering Marriage

One hardly needs to have the latest national statistics to know that young adults are not marrying as quickly as they were just ten or twenty years ago. Anyone who knows recent college graduates, for example, realizes that more and more of them are postponing marriage until their mid- or late twenties. Getting married within weeks of graduation—seemingly a symbol of success for many college women in the 1950s and early 1960s—is now much less common. In the past decade there also has been a great increase in the number of young adults who have moved in with someone of the opposite sex without marrying first. Some observers have expressed concern that the later age at marriage and the increase in "cohabitation" or "living together" might indicate a weakening of our system of marriage and family life. Others are more sanguine but believe that these changing patterns of coupling will alter American family life.

Almost every adult in the United States eventually marries, although in some eras people tend to marry earlier than in others. In the postwar period there have been sharp fluctuations in the timing of marriage, with an especially noticeable difference between the 1950s and the 1970s, as can be seen by comparing the lifetime experiences of several cohorts. Figure 1 shows the actual and projected marriage experiences of women born in the periods 1910 to 1914, 1920 to 1924, 1930 to 1934, 1940 to 1944, and 1950 to 1954. The graph displays for each cohort the estimated age at which 25, 50, and 75 percent of those who will ever marry have already done so.

Figure 1 shows that there has been little change in the age by which one-quarter of all those women who will ever marry have done so. The age at which 50 percent have married—the median age of marrying for each cohort—shows more change. It was highest for the oldest cohort, then it declined by about one and one-half years for women born in the 1930s and 1940s, and more recently it has risen again. The figure that shows the most change is the age at which three-fourths have married: it was above twenty-five years for the 1910–1914 cohort, fell below twenty-three for the middle cohorts, and now has risen above twenty-four for the youngest cohort.

This pattern of change suggests that so far in this century a fixed proportion of women in any cohort marry early, regardless of the historical circumstances. Conversely, the variation in the timing of marriage mainly reflects the changing behavior of those women who tend to wait until their early

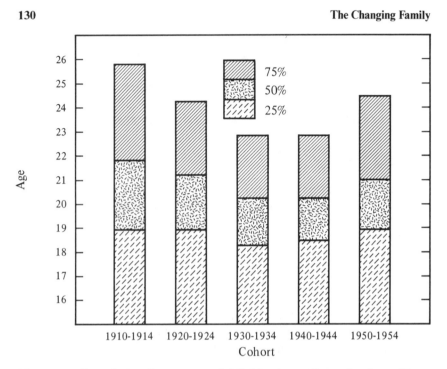

Figure 1   Cumulative Percentage of All Marriages Occurring by a Given Age, for Five Birth Cohorts of Women from 1910 to 1954.

twenties to marry. Among women born in the 1930s and 1940s, those who remained single through their teenage years married relatively quickly when they reached their early twenties. But in the preceding and succeeding cohorts, single women in their twenties took longer to marry. As a result, the spread between the 25 and 75 percent marks decreased from nearly seven years for the 1910 to 1914 cohort to about four years in the middle cohorts, and more recently it has increased to about five and a half years for the 1950 to 1954 cohort.

These changes do not necessarily imply that large numbers of the young women of the early 1980s will remain unmarried throughout their lives. Currently, as Figure 1 suggests, the timing of marriage for young women is becoming increasingly similar to that of cohorts born early in the century, and more than nine out of ten women in these older cohorts married eventually. In fact, more than 90 percent of the members of every birth cohort on record (records extend back to the mid-1800s) have eventually married. . . .

Childbearing

A brief look at trends in childbearing may tell us something about the differences between the parental generation of the 1950s and their children's generation. Most people are familiar with the broad outlines of the postwar trend in childbearing, or fertility, to use the demographer's term for child-bearing: the annual birth rate spurted upward just after the war and then, after a brief respite, increased sharply during the 1950s. It then fell just as sharply in the 1960s and 1970s. We now know that during the 1950s women were having their first child earlier in their lives, and subsequent children were born closer together; after 1960 women had their first child at a later age and spaced subsequent children further apart. These trends in the timing of fertility—the accelerated pace of the 1950s and the postponement of the 1960s and 1970s—amplified the peaks and valleys of the baby boom and bust as measured by annual birth rates. We can obtain a more meaningful picture of the trends by examining the lifetime levels of fertility for different cohorts. The lifetime levels measure changes in the volume of childbearing over time, independent of changes in the timing of births during women's reproductive years.

Figure 2 displays the cohort total fertility rate for single-year birth cohorts of women born between 1891 and 1950, based on data assembled by Nor-man B. Ryder. The cohort total fertility rate is the mean number of children born per woman in a particular cohort. For cohorts of women past their re-productive years, this rate can be calculated from survey or birth registra-tion data; for the more recent cohorts, future levels of fertility must be estimated. As can be seen in Figure 2, the mean number of births per woman born in 1891 was 3.0. This figure, as best we can tell, declined throughout the nineteenth century: it was 4.1 for the 1867 cohort and perhaps 7 or 8 for those born in the early 1800s. The total fertility rate declined to a low of 2.3 for the 1908 cohort—who came of age early in the depression—and then rose precipitously to a high of 3.2 for the 1933 cohort—who came of age in the 1950s—before beginning a steep slide to the estimated level of 1.9 for the 1950 cohort.

The graph demonstrates that trends in lifetime levels of childbearing in this century have followed a single, massive wave pattern that peaked with the cohorts of women who married and began to bear children in the decade following World War II. This great rise in fertility is at variance with the long-term historical decline in childbearing over the past 150 years. To be sure, Figure 2 and our sketchy knowledge of nineteenth-century fertility pat-terns also suggest that the fertility of the cohorts who reached adulthood during the depression was unusually low. And the fertility of the most recent cohorts appears to be at an all-time low, although that seems to be in line with the longer historical decline. The more unusual phenomenon, in a long-term perspective, is the great increase in childbearing among those born dur-ing the 1920s and 1930s. Cohort trends in childbearing, like trends in age at marriage, suggest that the cohorts who grew up during the depression and the war years—not the cohorts who grew up during the postwar years—stand out as more historically distinctive.

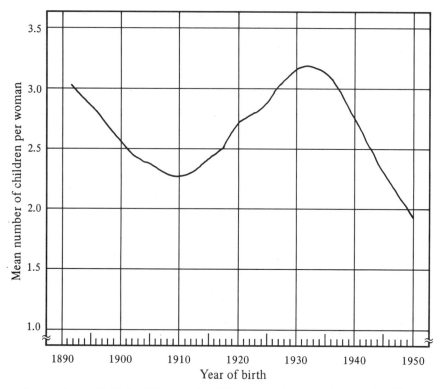

Source: Norman B. Ryder, "Components of Temporal Variations in American Fertility," in Robert W. Hiorns, ed., *Demographic Patterns in Developed Societies* (London: Taylor and Francis, 1980), pp. 15–54.

Figure 2   Cohort Total Fertility Rate for Single-Year Birth Cohorts, 1891 to 1950.

Marital Dissolution

No trend in American family life since World War II has received more attention or caused more concern than the rising rate of divorce. The divorce rate, however, has been rising since at least the middle of the nineteenth century. Figure 3 shows the number of divorces per 1,000 existing marriages (after 1920, per 1,000 married women) in every year between 1860 (the earliest year for which data are available) and 1978. These are annual measures, reflecting the particular social and economic conditions of each year. We can see, for example, that the annual rate of divorce increased temporarily after every major war: there is a slight bulge in the graph following the Civil War, a rise in 1919 and 1920 following World War I, and a large spike in the years immediately after World War II. We can also see how the depression temporarily lowered the divorce rate in the early 1930s: with jobs

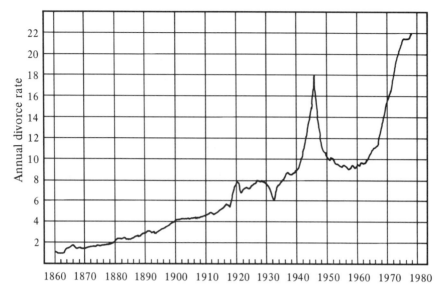

Sources: 1860–1920, Paul H. Jacobson, *American Marriage and Divorce* (New York: Rinehart, 1959), Table 42; 1920–1967, U.S. National Center for Health Statistics, Vital and Health Statistics, series 21, no. 24, *100 Years of Marriage and Divorce Statistics* (1973), Table 4; 1968–1978, U.S. National Center for Health Statistics, Vital Statistics Report, Advance Report, vol. 29, no. 4, supplement, *Final Divorce Statistics 1978*, Table 2.

Figure 3   Annual Divorce Rates, United States. For 1920–1978: Divorces Per 1,000 Married Women Aged 15 and over; for 1860–1920: Divorces Per 1,000 Existing Marriages.

and housing scarce, many couples had to postpone divorcing until they could afford to do so.

Ignoring for the moment the temporary movements induced by war and depression, there is a slow, steady increase in the annual rate of divorce through the end of World War II. Since the war, however, the graph looks somewhat different. In the period from 1950 to about 1962 the annual rates are lower than what we would expect on the basis of the long-term rise. Then starting about 1962, the annual rates rise sharply, so that by the end of the 1970s the rate of divorce is well above what would be predicted from the long-term trend. Thus if we compare the annual rates from the 1950s with those from the 1970s, as many observers have tended to do, we are comparing a period of relatively low rates with a time of very high rates. The result is to make the recent rise loom larger than it would if we took the long-term view.

It is true that the rise in annual divorce rates in the 1960s and 1970s is much steeper and more sustained than any increase in the past century, but to gauge the significance of this recent rise, it is necessary to consider the lifetime divorce experiences of adults, rather than just the annual rates of divorce. In Figure 4 the dotted line is an estimate of the proportion of all marriages begun in every year between 1867 and 1973 which have ended, or will end, in divorce before one of the spouses dies. Following conventional usage among demographers, I refer to all people marrying in a given year as a "marriage cohort." For marriage cohorts after 1910, the lifetime record is incomplete, and I have relied on projections prepared by Samuel H. Preston, John McDonald, and James Weed. Any projection, of course, can be undermined by future events, so the importance of Figure 4 lies more in the general trends it shows than in its precise estimates for recent marriage cohorts. We can see from the dotted line that the proportion of all marriages in a given year that eventually end in divorce has increased at a faster and faster rate since the mid-nineteenth century. Moreover, the increase has been relatively steady, without the large fluctuations which the annual rates show in times of war or depression.

In order to make the underlying long-term trend clearer, the graph also shows the smooth curve that most closely fits the pattern of change in the proportions. People who married in the years when the dotted line is above the smooth curve were more likely to become divorced than the long-term historical trend would lead us to expect; people who married in years when the dotted line is below the smooth curve were less likely to become divorced than would be expected. We can see, for instance, that although the annual divorce rates were temporarily low in the early 1930s, more of the people who married just before or during the depression eventually became divorced than we would expect from the long-term trend. The hardship and distress families suffered when husbands lost their jobs irrevocably damaged some marriages, and many unhappy couples later divorced after economic conditions improved enough to allow them to do so. Conversely, Figure 4 indicates that the lifetime proportions ever divorced for those marrying between the end of the war and the late 1950s probably will not reach the expected levels based on the long-term trend. To be sure, a greater proportion of them will divorce than was the case for previous marriage cohorts, but the increase will be modest by historical standards.

On the other hand, for those who married in the 1960s and early 1970s, the increase may exceed what would be predicted by the long-term trend. Couples who married in 1970, for instance, lived the early years of their marriage during a period of very high annual divorce rates. By 1977, only seven years after they had married, one-quarter of these couples had already divorced. In contrast, it was twenty-five years before one-quarter of those who married in 1950 had divorced. If the annual divorce rates stay the same in the 1980s and 1990s as they were in 1977, 48 percent of those who mar-

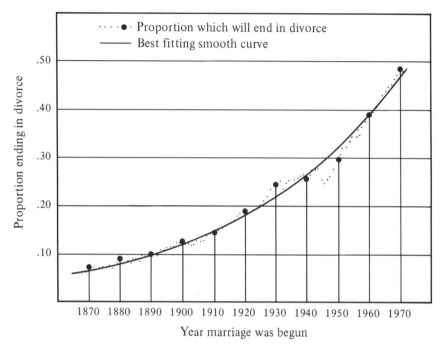

Figure 4   Proportion of Marriages Begun in Each Year that Will End in Divorce, 1867 to 1973.

ried in 1970 will eventually divorce, according to a recent estimate. . . . Scholars disagree on how fast the divorce rate will increase in the near future, but almost no one expects a drop in the annual rates. Barring an unforeseen downturn in divorce in the near future, then, for those marrying in the late 1960s and early 1970s the lifetime proportions ever divorced are likely to be exceptionally high, even compared to the long-term rise in divorce.

In sum, although annual measures of divorce often show large fluctuations from year to year or decade to decade, the lifetime proportions ever divorced for people marrying in a given year have risen in a regular fashion for the past century, with some variations. Those who married during the depression and those who married in the 1960s and early 1970s experienced even higher levels of divorce over their lifetimes than the historical trend would predict. And those who married in the decade or so following the war were the only cohorts in the last hundred years to show a substantial, sustained shortfall in their lifetime levels of divorce. This latter group, of course, includes most of the parents of the baby boom children. Figure 4 suggests that the lifetime level of divorce for the baby boom parents was unusually low; for their children it will be unusually high. . . .

Remarriages have been common in the United States since its beginnings, but until this century almost all remarriages followed widowhood. In the Plymouth Colony about one-third of all men and and one-quarter of all women who lived full lifetimes remarried after the death of a spouse, but there was little divorce. Even as late as the 1920s, brides and grooms who were remarrying were more likely to have been widowed than divorced. Since then, however, the increase in divorce and the decline in mortality have altered the balance: by 1978, 87 percent of all brides who were remarrying were previously divorced, and 13 percent were widowed. For grooms who were remarrying in 1978, 89 percent were divorced. Thus it is only in recent decades that remarriage after divorce has become the predominant form of remarriage. And since the turn of the century, such remarriages have increased as a proportion of all marriages. In 1900 only 3 percent of all brides—including both the single and the previously married—were divorced. In 1930 9 percent of all brides were divorced, and in 1978, 28 percent of all brides were divorced.

Part of this increase in remarriage is caused simply by the greater proportion of divorced people in the general population. In addition, a greater proportion of divorced people remarry each year today than earlier in the century. In 1920 and again in 1940, about 100 out of every 1,000 divorced and widowed women aged fourteen to fifty-four remarried each year, but by the late 1960s the remarriage rate had jumped to more than 150 per 1,000. Although the rate has since dropped to 134 per 1,000 in the period 1975 to 1977, it is still considerably above earlier levels. The recent decline in the annual remarriage rates may mean that fewer divorced people will remarry in the future, but it also may reflect only a postponement of remarriage.

The upshot of all this is that most people who get divorced remarry. About five out of six men and about three out of four women remarry after a divorce, according to the experiences of the older generations alive today. And those who are going to remarry do so soon after their divorce: about half of all remarriages take place within three years after divorce. In addition, the average age at which people remarry appears to have declined somewhat during the century. Women born in 1910 to 1914 who remarried following divorce had a median age of about thirty-five when they remarried; for young adults in the 1970s and early 1980s, that median will probably be about thirty. . . .

An Overview

The indicators I have reviewed show that in attempting to summarize the changes in marriage, divorce, and remarriage since World War II, it is important to choose our frame of reference with care. We often contrast the situation of the 1950s with that of the 1970s, implicitly assuming that the

1950s were representative of family life throughout the first half of the century. Thus we sometimes conclude that the family patterns of the 1970s differ sharply overall from what was experienced in the past. But as I have shown in this chapter, this sweeping conclusion is unwarranted; in many respects it is the 1950s that stand out as more unusual.

Does the Family Have a Future?

Suzanne Keller

Some thirty-five years ago, two venerable students of human behavior engaged in a six-session debate on marriage and the family over the B.B.C. Their names were Bronislaw Malinowski and Robert Briffault, the one a world-famous anthropologist best known for his studies of the Trobriand Islands, the other a social historian devoted to resurrecting the matriarchies of prehistory. Of the two, paradoxically, it was Briffault, the self-trained historian, who turned out to be the cultural relativist, whereas Malinowski, a pioneer in cross-cultural research, exhibited the very ethnocentrism his studies were designed to dispel.

Both men noted that the family was in trouble in their day. Both were distressed by this and sought to discover remedies if not solutions. Despite their common concern, however, they were soon embroiled in vivid and vociferous controversy about the nature of the crisis and its cure (*Marriage: Past and Present,* ed. M. F. Ashley-Montagu, Boston, Porter Sargent, 1956).

Briffault concluded from this reading of the evidence that the family rests on sentiments rooted in culture and social tradition rather than in human nature. Unless one grasps these social and cultural essentials, one cannot hope to understand, much less cure, what ails it. No recourse to natural instinct or to the "dictatorship of tradition or moral coercion" could save the modern family from its destined decline.

Malinowski disagreed. The family, he admitted, might be passing through a grave crisis, but the illness was not fatal. Marriage and the family, "the foundation of human society" and a key source of spiritual and material progress, were here to stay, though not without some needed improvements. Among these were the establishment of a single standard of morality, greater

From the *Journal of Comparative Family Studies* (Spring 1971). Reprinted by permission.

legal and economic equality between husband and wife, and greater freedom in parent-child relations.

The disagreement of these two men stemmed, as it so often does, not from different diagnoses but from different definitions of the phenomenon. Malinowski defined the family as a legal union of one man and one woman, together with their offspring, bound by reciprocal rights and duties and cooperating for the sake of economic and moral survival. Briffault defined the family much more broadly as an association involving economic production and sexual procreation. In his sense, the clan was a family.

The two agreed on only one point: parenthood and, above all, maternity are the pivots in the anatomy of marriage and the family. If these change so must the familial organization that contained them. Thus if one can identify such pivotal changes their difficulties are overcome while ours may be said to be just beginning.

There is good reason to suppose that such changes are now upon us. The malaise of our time reflects not simply a temporary disenchantment with an ancient institution but a profound convulsion of the social order. The family is indeed suffering a sea change.

It is curious to note how much more quickly the popular press, including the so-called women's magazines, have caught on to changing marital, sexual, and parental styles. While many of the experts are still serving up conventional and tradition-bound idols—the hard-working, responsible, breadwinner husband-father; the self-effacing, ministering wife-mother; the grateful, respectful children—these magazines tempt the contemporary reader with less standard and more challenging fare. Whether in New York or in Athens, the newsstands flaunt their provocative titles—"Is This the Last Marrying Generation?", "Alimony for Ex-Husbands," "Why We Don't Want to Have Children," "Are Husbands Superfluous?"—in nonchalant profusion. These and other assaults on our sexual and moral codes in the shape of the new theater, the new woman, the new youth, and TV soap operas akin to a psychiatrist's case files, persuade us that something seems to be afoot in the whole sphere of marriage and family relations which many had thought immune to change. In point of fact the question is not *whether* the family is changing but how and how much; how important are these changes, how permanent, how salutary? The answers depend largely on the way we ask our questions and define our terms.

The family means many things to many people, but in its essence it refers to those socially patterned ideals and practices concerned with biological and cultural survival of the species. When we speak of the family we are using a kind of shorthand, a label for a social invention not very different, in essence, from other social inventions, let us say the corporation or the university, and no more permanent than these. This label designates a particular set of social practices concerned with procreation and child rearing, with the heterosexual partnership that makes this possible and the parent-child relations that make it enduring. As is true of all collective habits, once established, such practices

are exceedingly resistant to change, in part because they evoke strong sentiments and in part because no acceptable alternatives are offered. Since most
individuals are unable to step outside of their cultures, they are unable to note
the arbitrary and variable nature of their conventions. Accordingly, they
ascribe to their folkways and creeds an antiquity, an inevitability, and a universality these do not possess.

The idea that the family is universal is highly misleading despite its popularity. All surviving societies have indeed found ways to stabilize the processes
of reproduction and child care else they would not have survived to tell their
tale. But since they differ greatly in how they arrange these matters (and since
they are willing to engage in hot and cold wars to defend such differences), the
generalization does not help us explain the phenomenon but more nearly
explains it away.

In truth there are as many forms of the family as there are forms of society,
some so different from ours that we consider them unnatural and incomprehensible. There are, for example, societies in which couples do not share a
household and do not have sole responsibility for their offspring; others in
which our domestic unit of husband and wife is divided into two separate units,
a conjugal one of biological parents and a brother-sister unit for economic
sustenance. There are societies in which children virtually rear each other and
societies in which the wise father does not know his own child. All of these
are clearly very different from our twentieth century, industrial-urban conception of the family as a legally united couple, sharing bed and board, jointly
responsible for bearing and rearing their children and formally isolated from
their next of kin in all but a sentimental sense. This product of a long and
complicated evolutionary development from prehistoric times is no simple
replica of the ancient productive and reproductive institutions from which it
derives its name and some of its characteristic features. The contemporary
family really has little in common with its historic Hebrew, Greek, and Roman
ancestors.

The family of these great civilizations of the West was a household community of hundreds, and sometimes thousands, of members (*familia* is the Latin
term for household). Only some of the members were related by blood, and
by far the larger part were servants and slaves, artisans, friends, and distant
relations. In its patriarchal form (again culturally variable), this large community was formally held together by the role of eldest male, who more nearly
resembled the general of an army than a modern husband-father. In its prime,
this household community constituted a miniature society, a decentralized
version of a social organization that had grown too large and unwieldly for
effective management. In this it resembles the giant bureaucracies of our own
day and their proposed decentralization into locally based, locally staffed
subsystems, designed to offset the evils of remote control while nevertheless
maintaining their connection with it. Far from having been universal, this
ancient family type, with its gods and shrines, schools and handicrafts, was not

even widely prevalent within its own social borders. Confined to the landed and propertied upper classes, it remained an unattainable ideal for the bulk of common men who made up the society.

The fallacy of universality has done students of human behavior a great disservice. By leading us to seek and hence to find a single pattern, it has blinded us to historical precedents for multiple legitimate family arrangements. As a result we have been rather impoverished in our speculations and proposals about alternative future arrangements in the family sphere.

A second common fallacy asserts that the family is *the* basic institution of society, hereby revealing a misunderstanding of how a society works. For as a social institution, the family is by definition a specialized element which provides society with certain needed services and depends on it for others. This means that you cannot tamper with a society without expecting the family to be affected in some way and vice versa. In the comtemporary jargon, we are in the presence of a feedback system. Whatever social changes we anticipate, therefore, the family cannot be kept immune from them.

A final fallacy concerns the presumed naturalness of the family in proof of which a motley and ill-assorted grab bag of anecdotal evidence from the animal kingdom is adduced. But careful perusal of ethological accounts suggests that animals vary as greatly as we do, their mating and parental groupings including such novelties as the love death, males who bear children, total and guilt-free "promiscuity," and other "abnormal" features. The range of variation is so wide, in fact, that virtually any human arrangement can be justified by recourse to the habits of some animal species.

In sum, if we wish to understand what is happening to the family—to our family—in our own day, we must examine and observe it in the here and now. In so doing it would be well to keep in mind that the family is an abstraction at best, serving as guide and image of what a particular society considers desirable and appropriate in family relations, not what takes place in actual fact. In reality there are always a number of empirical family types at variance with this, though they usually pay lip service to the overarching cultural ideal.

Challenges to the Contemporary Industrial Family

In the United States, as in other industrial societies, the ideal family consists of a legally constituted husband-wife team, their young, dependent children, living in a household of their own, provided for by the husband's earnings as main breadwinner, and emotionally united by the wife's exclusive concentration on the home. Probably no more than one-third of all families at a particular moment in time, and chiefly in the middle and would-be middle classes, actually live up to this image. The remaining majority all lack one or more of the essential attributes—in lacking a natural parent, or in not being economically self-sufficient, or in having made other necessary modifications.

One contrasting form is the extended family in which the couple share household arrangements and expenses with parents, siblings, or other close relatives. The children are then reared by several generations and have a choice of models on which to pattern their behavior. This type, frequent in working class and immigrant milieus, may be as cohesive and effective as the ideal type; but it lacks the cultural legitimacy and desirability of the latter.

A third family type, prevalent among the poor of all ethnic and racial backgrounds, is the mother-child family. Contrary to our prejudices this need not be a deviant or distorted family form, for it may be the only viable and appropriate one in its particular setting. Its defects may stem more from adverse social judgments than from intrinsic failings. Deficient in cultural resources and status, it may nevertheless provide a humane and spirited setting for its members, particularly if some sense of stability and continuity has been achieved. Less fortunate are the numerous non-families, ex-families, and non-intact families such as the divorced, the widowed, the unmarriageables, and many other fragmented social forms who have no recognized social place. None of these, however, threaten the existing order, since they are seen and see themselves as involuntarily different, imperfect, or unfortunate. As such they do not challenge the ideals of family and marital relations but simply suggest how difficult it is to live up to them. When we talk of family change or decline, however, it is precisely the ideal standards which we have in mind. A challenge to them cannot be met by simple reaffirmations of old truths, disapproval, shock, or ridicule of the challengers, or feigned indifference. Such challenges must be met head on.

Today the family and its social and psychological underpinnings are being fundamentally challenged from at least three sources: (1) from accumulated failures and contradictions in marriage; (2) from pervasive occupational and educational trends including the changing relations between the sexes, the spread of birth control, and the changing nature of work; and (3) from novel developments in biology. Let me briefly examine each.

It is generally agreed that even in its ideal form, the industrial-urban family makes great, some would say excessive, demands on its members. For one thing it rests on the dyadic principle or pair relationship which, as Georg Simmel observed long ago, is inherently tragic and unstable. Whether in chess, tennis, or marriage, two are required to start and continue the game but only one can destroy it. In this instance, moreover, the two are expected to retain their separate identities as male and female and yet be one in flesh and spirit. No wonder that the image of the couple, a major source of fusion and of schism in our society, is highly contradictory according to whether we think of the sexes as locked in love or in combat. Nor do children, the symbols of their union, necessarily unify them. Their own growing pains and cultural demands force them into mutually exclusive socio-sexual identities, thereby increasing the intimate polarity. In fact, children arouse parental ambivalence in a number of ways, not the least of which is that they demand all but give back all too little. And yet their upbringing and sustenance, the moral and emotional climate, as well as the accumulation of economic and educational resources needed for survival, all rest on this small, fragile, essential but very limited unit. Held together by sentimental rather than by corporate bonds, the happiness of the partners is a primary goal, although no one is very sure what happiness means nor how it may be achieved and sustained.

To these potentials for stress and strain must be added the loss of many erstwhile functions to school, state, and society, and with it something of the glamour and challenge of family commitments. Few today expect the family to be employment agency, welfare state, old-age insurance, or school for life. Yet once upon a time, however, with fewer resources, some new burdens have been added stemming from rising standards of child health, education, and welfare. This makes parents even more crucially responsible for the potential fate of their children over whom they have increasingly less exclusive control.

Like most social institutions in the throes of change, moreover, the modern family is also beset by numerous internal contradictions engendered by the conflict between traditional patterns of authority and a new egalitarianism between husbands and wives and parents and children. The equality of the spouses, for example, collides with the continuing greater economic responsibilities, hence authority, of the husband. The voluntary harness of love chafes under the constraint of numerous obligations and duties imposed by marriage; and dominance patterns by sex or age clash with new demands for mutuality, reciprocity, equity, and individualism. These, together with some unavoidable disillusionments and disappointments in marriage, set the stage for the influence of broader and less subjective social trends.

One such trend, demographic in nature but bound to have profound social implications, concerns the lengthened life expectancy and the shortened reproductive span for women. Earlier ages at marriage, fewer children per couple, and closer spacing of children means: the girl who marries at 20 will have all her children by age 26, have all her children in school by her early thirties, have the first child leave home for job, schooling, or marriage in her late thirties, and have all her children out of the home by her early forties. This leaves some thirty to forty years to do with as personal pleasure or social need dictate. The contrast with her grandmother is striking: later marriage and more children spaced farther apart meant all the children in school no earlier than her middle or late thirties and the last to leave home (if he or she ever did) not before her early fifties At which time grandmother was probably a widow and close to the end of her own life span. The empty nest thus not only occurs earlier today, but it lasts longer, affecting not this or that unfortunate individual woman but many, if not most, women. Hence what may in the past have been an individual misfortune has turned into a social emergency of major proportions. More unexpected free time, more time without a socially recognized or appreciated function, more premature retirements surely puts the conventional modern wife, geared to the domestic welfare of husband, home, and children, at a singular disadvantage relative to the never-married career woman. Destined to outlive her husband, stripped of major domestic responsibilities in her prime years, what is she to do with this windfall of extra hours and years? Surely we must expect and prepare for a major cultural shift in the education and upbringing of female children. If women cannot afford to make motherhood and domestic concerns the sole foci of their identities, they must be encouraged, early in life, to prepare themselves for some occupation or profession not as an adjunct or as a last resort in case of economic need but as an equally legitimate pursuit. The child rearing of girls must increasingly be geared to developing a feminine identity that stresses autonomy, non-dependency, and self-assertion in work and in life.

Some adjunct trends are indirectly stimulating just such a reorientation. When women are compelled, as they often are, to earn their own living or to supplement inadequate family resources necessitated by the high emphasis on personal consumption and the high cost of services increasingly deemed essential as national standards rise, conventional work-dependency patterns are shattered. For, since the male breadwinner is already fully occupied, often with two jobs, or if he cannot or will not work, his wife is forced to step in. Thus there is generated internal family pressure—arising from a concern for family welfare but ultimately not confined to it—for wives to bearing gainfully employed outside of the home. And fully three-fourths in the post-childbearing ages already are, albeit under far from ideal conditions. Torn between home and job, between the precepts of early childhood with its promise of permanent security at the side of a strong male and the pressures of a later reality, unaided by a society unaware or indifferent to her problems, the double-duty wife must manage as best she can.

That this need not be so is demonstrated by a number of modern societies whose public policies are far better meshed with changing social realities. Surely one of our more neglected institutions—the single-family household which, despite all the appliances, remains essentially backward and primitive in its conditions of work—will need some revamping and modernizing. More household appliances, more and more attractive alternatives to the individually run household, more nursery schools, and a total overhaul of work schedules not now geared to a woman's life and interests cannot be long in coming. While these will help women in all of their multiple tasks, they may also of course further challenge the presumed joys of exclusive domesticity.

All in all, it would appear that the social importance of the family relative to other significant social arenas will, as Briffault, among others, correctly anticipated, decline. Even today when the family still exerts a strong emotional and sentimental hold, its social weight is not what it once was. All of us ideally are still born in intact families but not all of us need to establish families to survive. Marriage and children continue to be extolled as supreme social and personal goals but they are no longer—especially for men—indispensable for a meaningful existence. As individual self-sufficiency, fed by economic affluence or economic self-restraint, increases, so does one's exemption from unwanted economic as well as kinship responsibilities. Today the important frontiers seem to lie elsewhere, in science, politics, and outer space. This must affect the attractions of family life for both men and women. For men, because they will see less and less reason to assume full economic and social responsibilities for four to five human beings in addition to themselves as it becomes more difficult and less necessary to do so. This, together with the continued decline of patriarchal authority and male dominance—even in the illusory forms in which they have managed to hang on—will remove some of the psychic rewards which prompted many men to marry, while the disappearance of lineage as mainstays of the social and class order will deprive paternity of its social justification. For women, the household may soon prove too small for the scope of their ambitions and power drives. Until recently these were directed first of all to their children, secondarily to their mates. But with the decline of parental control over children, a major erstwhile source of challenge and creativity is removed from the family sphere. This must weaken the motherwife complex, historically sustained by the necessity and exaltation of motherhood and the taboo on illegitimacy.

Above all, the move towards worldwide population and birth control must affect the salience of parenthood for men and women, as a shift of cultural emphasis and individual priorities deflates maternity as woman's chief social purpose and paternity as the prod to male exertions in the world of work. Very soon, I suspect, the cultural presses of the world will slant their messages against the bearing and rearing of children. Maternity, far from being a duty, not even a right, will then become a rare privilege to be granted to a select and qualified few. Perhaps the day is not far off when reproduction will be confined to a fraction of the population, and what was once inescapable necessity may become voluntary, planned choice. Just as agricultural societies in which everyone had to produce food were once superseded by industrial societies in which a scant 6 percent now produce food for all, so one day the few may produce children for the many.

This, along with changing attitudes towards sex, abortion, adoption, illegitimacy, the spread of the pill, better knowledge of human behavior, and a growing scepticism that the family is the only proper crucible for childrearing, creates a powerful recipe for change. Worldwide demands for greater and better opportunities for self-development and a growing awareness that these opportunities are inextricably enhanced or curtailed by the family as a prime determinant of life-chances will play a major role in this change. Equal opportunity, it is now clear, cannot stop at the crib but must start there. "It is idle," commented Dr. Robert S. Morrison, a Cornell biologist, "to talk of a society of equal opportunity as long as that society abandons its newcomers solely to their families for their most impressionable years" (*New York Times,* October 30, 1966). One of the great, still largely unchallenged injustices may well be that one cannot choose one's parents.

The trends that I have sketched would affect marriage, male-female, and parent-child relations even if no other developments were on the horizon. But there are. As yet barely discernible and still far from being applicable to human beings, recent breakthroughs in biology—with their promise of a greatly extended life span, novel modes of reproduction, and dramatic possibilities for genetic intervention—cannot be ignored in a discussion devoted to the future of the family.

Revolution in Biology

If the early part of this century belonged to physics and the middle period to exploratory ventures into outer space, the next few decades belong to biology. The prolongation of life to double or triple its current span seems virtually assured, the extension of female fertility into the sixties is more than a distinct possibility, and novel ways of reproducing the human species have moved from science fiction to the laboratory. The question then arises, What will happen when biological reproduction will not only be inadvisable for the sake of collective well-being but superseded by new forms and eventually by nonhuman forms of reproduction?

A number of already existing possibilities may give us a foretaste of what is to come. For example, the separation of conception from gestation means that motherhood can become specialized, permitting some women to conceive and rear many children and others to bear them without having to provide for them. Frozen sperms banks (of known donors) are envisioned from which prospective mothers could choose the fathers of their children on the basis of particularly admired or desired qualities, thereby advancing an age-old dream of selecting a distinguished paternity for their children based on demonstrated rather than potential male achievement. And it would grant men a sort of immortality to sire offspring long after their biological deaths as well as challenge the implicit equation now made between fathers and husbands. Finally, the as yet remote possibility to reproduce the human species without sexual intercourse, by permanently separating sex from procreation, would permit unmarried women (and men) to have children without being married, reduces a prime motive for marriage and may well dethrone—inconceivable as this may seem—the heterosexual couple. All of these pose questions of legal and social policy to plague the most subtle Solon. Who is the father of a child—the progenitor or the provider where these have become legitimately distinct roles? Who is the mother—the woman who conceives the child or the one who carries it to term? Who will decide on sex ratios once sex determination becomes routine? Along with such challenges and redefinitions of human responsibility, some see the fate of heterosexuality itself to lie in the balance. In part of course this rests on one's assumptions about the nature of sexuality and sexual identity.

Anatomy alone has never been sufficient for the classification of human beings into male and female which each society labors to develop and then calls natural. Anatomy is but one—and by no means always a reliable—identifying characteristic. Despite our beliefs, sex identification, even in the strictest physical sense, is by no means clear-cut. Various endeavors to find foolproof methods of classification—for example, for participation in the Olympics—have been unsuccessful, as at least nine separate and often uncorrelated components of sexual phenotype have been identified. But if we cannot count on absolute physical differentiations between the sexes, we do even less well when it comes to their social and psychological attributes. Several decades of research have shown beyond doubt that most of what we mean by the difference between the sexes is a blend of cultural myth and social necessity, which must be learned, painstakingly and imperfectly, from birth on. Once acquired, sexual identity is not fixed but needs to be reinforced and propped up in a myriad of ways of which we are quite unaware.

In the past this complicated learning process was guided by what we may call the categorical reproductive imperative, which proclaimed procreation as an unquestionable social goal and which steered the procreative and sexual capacities and aspirations of men and women toward appropriate channels virtually from birth on. Many other features strengthened these tendencies—symbolism and sentiment, work patterns and friendships, all kinds of subtle and not so subtle rewards and punishments for being a "real" man, a real woman. But once the reproductive imperative is transformed into a reproductive ban, what will be the rationale for the continuance of the exclusive heterosexual polarity in the future? If we keep in mind that only two out of our forty-six chromosomes are sex-carrying, perhaps these two will disappear as their utility subsides. Even without such dramatic changes, already there is speculation that heterosexuality will become but one among several forms of sexuality, these having previously been suppressed by strong social sanctions against sexual deviation as well as their inability to reproduce themselves in standard fashion. More than three decades ago, Olaf Stapleton, one of the most imaginative science fiction writers of the century, postulated the emergence of at least six subsexes out of the familiar ancient polarity. At about the same time, Margaret Mead, in the brilliant epilogue to her book on sex and temperament (*Sex and Temperament in Three Primitive Societies,* William Morrow and Co., New York, 1935), suggested a reorganization and recategorization of human identity not along but across traditional sex lines so as to produce a better alignment between individual capacity and social necessity. In our time we have witnessed the emergence of UniSex (the term is McLuhan's) and predictions which range from the disappearance of sex to its manifold elaboration.

Some are speculating about a future in which only one of the current sexes will survive, the other having become superfluous or obsolescent. Depending on the taste, temperament—and sex—of the particular writer, women and men have alternately been so honored (or cursed). It is not always easy to tell which aspect of sex—the anatomical, psychological, or cultural—the writer has in mind, but as the following comment suggests, much more than anatomy is at stake.

> Does the man and woman thing have a future? The question may not be hypothetical much longer. Within 10 years . . . we may be able to choose the sex of our offspring; and later to reproduce without mating male and female cells. This means it will someday be possible to have a world with only one sex, woman, and thereby avoid the squabbles, confusions, and headaches that have dogged this whole business of sex down the centuries. A manless world suggests several scientific scenarios. The most pessimistic would have society changing not at all, but continuing on its manly ways of eager acquisition, hot competition, and mindless aggression. In which case, half the women would become "men" and go right on getting ulcers, shouting "charge" and pinning medals on each other. (George B. Leonard, "The Man and Woman Thing," *Look,* December 25, 1968)

Long before the demise of heterosexuality as a mainstay of the social order, however, we will have to come to terms with changing sexual attitudes and mores ushered in by what has been called the sexual revolution. This liberalization, this rejection of old taboos, half-truths, and hypocrisies, also means a crisis of identity as men and women, programmed for more traditional roles, search for the boundaries of their sexual selves in an attempt to establish a territoriality of the soul.

Confusion is hardly, of course, a novel aspect of the human condition. Not knowing where we have come from, why we are here, or where we are headed, it could hardly be otherwise. There have always been dissatisfied men and women rejecting the roles their cultures have assigned them or the responsibilities attached to these. But these are the stuff of poetry and drama, grist for the analyst's couch or the priest's confessional, in other words private torments and agonies kept concealed from an unsympathetic world. It is only when such torments become transmuted into public grievance and so become publicly heard and acknowledged that we can be said to be undergoing profound changes akin to what we are experiencing today.

Returning now to our main question—Does the family have a future?—it should be apparent that I expect some basic and irreversible changes in the decades ahead and the emergence of some novel forms of human togetherness. Note that the current scene does not already offer some provocative variations on ancient themes, but most of these gain little public attention, still less approval, and so they are unable to alter professed beliefs and standards. Moreover, every culture has its own forms of self-justification and self-righteousness; and in our eagerness to affirm the intrinsic superiority of our ways, we neglect to note the magnitude of variations and deviations from the ideals we espouse. What are we to make, for example, of such dubious allegiance to the monogamous ideal as serial marriages or secret adulteries? Or, less morally questionable, what of the quasi-organized part-time family arrangements necessitated by extreme occupational and geographic mobility? Consider for a moment the millions of families of salesmen, pilots, seacaptains, soldiers, sailors and junior executives where the man of the house is not often *in* the house. These absentee husbands—fathers who magically reenter the family circle just long enough to be appreciated, leaving their wives in charge of the homes they pay for and of the children they sired, are surely no more than part-time mates. If we know little about the adjustments they have had to make or their children's responses, this is because they clearly do not fit in with our somewhat outmoded stereotyped notions of what family relations ought to be. Or consider another home-grown example, the institution of governesses and boarding schools to rear upper-class children. Where is the upper-class mother and how does she spend her time between vacations and homecoming weekends? Then there are of course many countries around the world—Israel, Sweden, and socialist countries, some of the African societies—where all or nearly all women, most of them mothers, work outside of the home as a matter of course. And because these societies are free from guilt and ambivalence about the working mother, they have managed to incorporate these realities more gracefully into their scheme of things, developing a number of useful innovations along the way. Thus even in our own day, adaptions and modifications exist and have not destroyed all notions of family loyalty, responsibility, and commitment.

In fact, people may be more ready for change than official pronouncements and expert opinions assume. The spread of contraceptive information and the acceptance of full birth control have been remarkable. The relaxation of many erstwhile taboos has proceeded at breakneck speed, and the use of public forums to discuss such vital but previously forbidden topics as abortion, homosexuality, or illegitimacy is dramatic and startling in a society rooted in Puritanism. A number of studies, moreover, show that the better educated are more open to reexamination and change in all spheres, including the family. Since these groups are on the increase, we may expect greater receptivity to such changes in the future. Even such startling proposed innovations as egg transplants, test-tube babies, and cloning are not rejected out of hand if they would help achieve the family goals most Americans prize. (See "The Second Genesis" by Albert Rosenfeld and the Louis Harris Poll, *Life,* June 1969, pp. 31-46.)

Public response to a changing moral and social climate is of course hard to predict. In particular, as regards family concerns, the reactions of women, so crucially bound up with motherhood and child rearing in their self-definitions, are of especial interest. In this connection one study of more than 15,000 women college students attending four year liberal arts colleges in the United States is relevant for its findings on how such a nationwide sample of young coeds, a group of great future significance, feels about marriage, motherhood, and career. (Charles F. Westoff and Raymond H. Potvin, *College Women and Fertility Values,* Princeton University Press, 1967.) Selecting only those items on which there was wide consensus and omitting details of interest to the specialist, the general pattern of answers was unmistakable. The large majority of these would-be wives and mothers disapproved of large families (three or more children), did not consider children to be the most important reason for marriage, favored birth control and birth planning, and thought it possible for a woman to pursue family and career simultaneously. They split evenly on the matter of whether a woman's main satisfaction should come from family rather can career or community activities, and they were virtually united in thinking that mothers with very young children should not work. The latter strongly identifies them as Americans, I think, where nursery schools and other aids to working mothers—including moral support—are not only lacking but still largely disapproved of.

Thus if we dare to speculate further about the future of the family, we will be on safe ground with the following anticipations: (1) a trend towards greater, legitimate variety in sexual and marital experience; (2) a decrease in the negative emotions—exclusiveness, possessiveness, fear, and jealously—associated with these; (3) greater room for personal choice in the kind, extent, and duration of intimate relationships, which may greatly improve their quality as people will both give and demand more of them; (4) entirely new forms of communal living arrangements in which several couples will share the tasks of child rearing and economic support as well as the pleasures of relaxation; (5) multistage marriages geared to the changing life cycle and the presence or absence of dependent children. Of these proposals, some, such as Margaret Mead's, would have the young and the immature of any age test themselves and their capacities to relate to others in an individual form of marriage which would last only so long as it fulfilled both partners. In contrast to this, older, more experienced, and more mature couples who were ready to take on the burdens of parenthood would make a deeper and longer lasting commitment. Other proposals would reverse this sequence and have couples assume parental commitments when young and, having discharged their debt to society, be then free to explore more personal, individualistic partnerships. Neither of these seems as yet to be particularly appealing to the readers who responded to Mead's proposal as set forth in *Redbook Magazine.* (Margaret Mead, "Marriage in Two Steps," *Redbook Magazine,* July 1966; 'The Life Cycle and Its Variation: The Division of Roles," *Daedalus,* Summer 1967; "A Continuing Dialogue on Marriage: Why Just Living Together Won't Work," *Redbook Magazine* April 1968.)

For the immediate future, it appears that most Americans opt for and anticipate their participation in durable, intimate, heterosexual partnerships as anchors and pivots of their adult lives. They expect these to be freer and more flexible than was true in the past, however, and less bound to duty and involuntary personal restrictions. They cannot imagine and do not wish a life without them.

Speculating for the long-range future, we cannot ignore the potential implications of the emerging cultural taboo on unrestricted reproduction and the shift in public concern away from the family as the central preoccupation of one's life. Hard as it may seem, perhaps some day we will cease to relate to families, just as we no longer relate ourselves to clans, and instead be bound up with some new, as yet unnamed principle of human association. If and when this happens, we may also see a world of Unisex, Multisex, or Nonsex. None of this can happen, however, if we refuse to shed some of our most cherished preconceptions, such as that monogamy is superior to other forms of marriage or that women naturally make the best mothers. Much as we may be convinced of these now, time may reveal them as yet another illusion, another example of made-to-order truths.

Ultimately all social change involves moral doubt and moral reassessment. If we refuse to consider change while there still is time, time will pass us by. Only by examining and taking stock of what is can we hope to affect what will be. This is our chance to invent and thus to humanize the future.

2

Gender and Sex

Introduction

American society has recently experienced both a sexual revolution and a sex-role revolution. The first has liberalized attitudes toward erotic behavior and expression; the second has changed the roles and statuses of women and men in the direction of greater equality. Both revolutions have been brought about by the rapid social changes of recent years, but both revolutions also represent a belated recognition that traditional beliefs and norms did not reflect how people actually behaved and felt.

The conventional idea of sexuality defines sex as a powerful biological drive continually struggling for gratification against restraints imposed by civilization. The notion of sexual instincts also implies a kind of innate knowledge: A person intuitively knows his or her own identity as male or female, he or she knows how to act accordingly, and he or she is attracted to the "proper" sex object—a person of the opposite gender. In other words, the view of sex as biological drive pure and simple implies "that sexuality has a magical ability, possessed by no other capacity, that allows biological drives to be expressed directly in psychological and social behaviors" (Gagnon & Simon, 1970, p. 24).

The whole issue of the relative importance of biological versus psychological and social factors in sexuality and sex differences has been obscured by polemics. On the one hand, there are the strict biological determinists who declare anatomy is destiny. On the other hand, there are those who argue that all aspects of sexuality and sex-role difference are matters of learning and social conditioning.

There are two essential points to be made about the nature-versus-nurture argument. The first is that extreme positions overlook the connection between biology and experience:

> In the theory of psychosexual differentiation, it is now outmoded to oppose or juxtapose nature vs. nurture, the genetic vs. psychological, or the instinctive vs. the environmental, the innate vs. the acquired, the biological vs. the psychological, or the instinctive vs. the learned. Modern genetic theory avoids these antiquated dichotomies. . . . (Money & Ehrhardt, 1972, p. 1)

The second and related point concerns a misconception about how biological forces work. Both biological determinists and their opponents assume that if a biological force exists, it must be overwhelmingly strong. But the most sophisticated evidence concerning both gender development *and* erotic arousal suggests that physiological forces are gentle rather than powerful. Acknowledging the possible effects of prenatal sex hormones on the brains of human infants, Robert Stoller (1972) thus warns against "biologizing":

> While the newborn presents a most malleable central nervous system upon which the environment writes, we cannot say that the central nervous system is neutral or neuter. Rather, we can say that the effects of these biological systems, organized prenatally in a masculine or feminine direction, are almost always . . . too gentle in humans to withstand the more powerful forces in human development, the first and most powerful of which is mothering. . . . (p. 211).

Research into the development of sex differences thus suggests not an opposition between genetics and environment but an interaction. Gender identity as a child and occupation as an adult are primarily the product of social learning rather than of anatomy and physiology.

In terms of scholarship, the main effect thus far of the sex-role and sexual revolutions has been on awareness and consciousness. For example, much social science writing was suddenly revealed to have been based on sexist assumptions. Many sociologists and psychologists took it for granted that women's roles and functions in society reflected universal physiological and temperamental traits. Since in practically every society women were subordinate to men, inequality was interpreted to be an inescapable necessity of organized social life. Such analysis suffers from the same intellectual flaw as the idea that discrimination against nonwhites implies their innate inferiority. All such explanations fail to analyze the social institutions and forces producing and supporting the observed differences. In approaching the study of either the physical or the social relations between the sexes, it is therefore important to understand how traditional stereotypes have influenced both popular and professional conceptions of sexuality and sex differences.

Jessie Bernard's, Joann Vanek's, and Mirra Komarovsky's and William J. Goode's articles on male and female sex roles develop this theme in different ways but generally examine how stereotyping influences and sets limits on male and female socialization. These limits rob both men and women of a broader potential, for example, gentleness for men, achievement for women. Stereotyping thus diminishes the capacity of both women and men to fulfill a broader potential than conventional sex roles dictate.

When we think about the current liberalization of sexual behavior and attitudes in recent times, we tend to think of such striking phenomena as the transformation of men into women and vice versa, group sex, the new openness about homosexuality, and aspects of unconventional or taboo sexuality. Yet equally significant, if not so spectacular, are changes in sexual behavior within marriage. Morton Hunt argues in his selection that "a dramatic and historical change has taken place in the practice of marital coitus in America." If Hunt's data are correct, there has been a great increase in marital eroticism in recent years; married people of all ages are having sex relations more often; they are spending more time in foreplay and intercourse; and they are engaging in formerly taboo activities such as oral sex. Hunt argues that women appear to be equal, rather than reluctant, participants in the increased eroticism. He thus notes that many more women report having regular orgasms than they did in the past, and only a tiny fraction complain that their husbands are too demanding sexually in contrast to the two-thirds majority who made that complaint in the past.

It would be a mistake, however, to think that the sexual revolution has brought nothing but uninhibited joy. It has also produced new problems and anxieties. Lillian Breslow Rubin's selection deals with the difficulties experienced by blue-collar couples trying to cope with the new sexuality. For wives caught between the new standards for sexual performance and their own and their husband's earlier training, having an orgasm can often seem to be just another chore in a life already full of chores. Middle-class women, more comfortable with the idea of sexual experimentation, feel guilty about the hang-ups that may prevent them from acting on their liberated beliefs. For their part, men who encourage their wives to be more erotically active may be turned off if the women become so.

The "herpes syndrome," as reported here by Daniel Laskin, is an even more painful and alarming by-product of the sexual revolution. Because herpes is a highly contagious, recurrent, and incurable disease, fear of contracting it has tempered the enthusiasm for exercising sexual freedom of many otherwise swinging singles—and also marrieds. Those millions who have already fallen victim to the disease are in even worse predicaments—social and psychological as well as physical.

Irony often seems to accompany social movements. In many areas of social life, reformers who intend certain outcomes may unintentionally achieve their opposite. For example, revolutions premised on ideals of social equality may produce authoritarian and repressive governments. Although the movement toward sexual freedom was less organized than most revolutionary movements, its ironies are similar, that is, it may have resulted in more pain and even more sexual repression than anybody could have anticipated in the 1960s when the loose configuration of ideas and advocacy behind the sexual liberation movement began to cohere.

References

Gagnon, J. H., and Simon, W. 1970. *The Sexual Scene*. Chicago: Aldene.

Money, J., and Ehrhardt, A. A. 1972. *Man and Woman, Boy and Girl*. Baltimore: Johns Hopkins Press.

Stoller, R. J. 1972. "The Bedrock of Masculinity and Femininity: Bisexuality." *Archives of General Psychiatry*, 26, pp. 207–212.

Chapter 3

Hers and His

The Good-Provider Role: Its Rise and Fall

Jessie Bernard

Abstract

The general structure of the "traditional" American family, in which the husband-father is the provider and the wife-mother the housewife, began to take shape early in the 19th century. This structure lasted about 150 years, from the 1830s to 1980, when the U.S. Census no longer automatically denominated the male as head of the household. As "providing" became increasingly mediated by cash derived from participation in the labor force or from commercial enterprises, the powers and prerogatives of the provider role augmented, and those of the housewife, who lacked a cash income, declined. Gender identity became associated with work site as well as with work. As affluence spread, the provider role became more and more competitive and escalated into the good-provider role. There were always defectors from the good-provider role, and in recent years expressed dissatisfaction with it increased. As more and more married women entered the labor force and thus assumed a share of the provider role, the powers and prerogatives of the good-provider role became diluted. At the present time a process that Ralph Smith calls "the subtle revolution" is realigning family roles. A host of social-psychological obstacles related to gender identity have to be overcome before a new social-psychological structure can be achieved.

The Lord is my shepherd, I shall not want. He sets a table for me in the very sight of my enemies; my cup runs over (23rd Psalm). And when the

From *American Psychologist*, Vol. 36, No. 1 (January 1981), pp. 1–12. Copyright 1981 by the American Psychological Association. Reprinted by permission of the publisher and author.

Israelites were complaining about how hungry they were on their way from Egypt to Canaan, God told Moses to rest assured: There would be meat for dinner and bread for breakfast the next morning. And, indeed, there were quails that very night, enough to cover the camp, and in the morning the ground was covered with dew that proved to be bread (Exodus 16:12–13). In fact, in this role of good provider, God is sometimes almost synonymous with Providence. Many people like Micawber, still wait for him, or Providence, to provide.

Granted, then, that the first great provider for the human species was God the Father, surely the second great provider for the human species was Mother, the gatherer, planter, and general factotum. Boulding (1976), citing Lee and deVore, tells us that in hunting and gathering societies, males contribute about one fifth of the food of the clan, females the other four fifths (p. 96). She also concludes that by 12,000 B.C. in the early agricultural villages, females provided four fifths of human subsistence (p. 97). Not until large trading towns arose did the female contribution to human subsistence decline to equality with that of the male. And with the beginning of true cities, the provisioning work of women tended to become invisible. Still, in today's world it remains substantial.

Whatever the date of the virtuous woman described in the Old Testament (Proverbs 31:10–27), she was the very model of a good provider. She was, in fact, a highly productive conglomerate. She woke up in the middle of the night to tend to her business; she oversaw a multiple-industry houshold; *her* candles did not go out at night; there was a ready market for the high-quality linen girdles she made and sold to the merchants in town; and she kept track of the real estate market and bought good land when it became available, cultivating vineyards quite profitably. All this time her husband sat at the gates talking with his cronies.

A recent counterpart to the virtuous woman was the busy and industrious shtetl woman:

> The earning of a livelihood is sexless, and the large majority of women . . . participate in some gainful occupation if they do not carry the chief burden of support. The wife of a "perennial student" is very apt to be the sole support of the family. The problem of managing both a business and a home is so common that no one recognizes it as special. . . . To bustle about in search of a livelihood is merely another form of bustling about managing a home; both are aspects of . . . health and livelihood. (Zborowski & Herzog, 1952, p. 131)

In a subsistence economy in which husbands and wives ran farms, shops, or businesses together, a man might be a good, steady worker, but the idea that he was *the* provider would hardly ring true. Even the youth in the folk song who listed all the gifts he would bestow on his love if she would marry him—a golden comb, a paper of pins, and all the rest—was not necessarily promising to be a good provider.

I have not searched the literature to determine when the concept of the good provider entered our thinking. The term *provider* entered the English language in 1532, but was not yet male sex typed, as the older term *purveyor* already was in 1442. Webster's second edition defines the good provider as "one who provides, especially, colloq., one who provides food, clothing, etc. for his family; as, he is a good or an adequate provider." More simply, he could be defined as a man whose wife did not have to enter the labor force. The counterpart to the good provider was the housewife. However the term is defined, the role itself delineated relationships within a marriage and family in a way that added to the legal, religious, and other advantages men had over women.

Thus, under the common law, although the husband was legally head of the household and as such had the responsibility of providing for his wife and children, this provision was often made with help from the wife's personal property and earnings, to which he was entitled:

> He owned his wife's and children's services, and had the sole right to collect wages for their work outside the home. He owned his wife's personal property outright, and had the right to manage and control all of his wife's real property during marriage, which included the right to use or lease property, and to keep any rents and profits from it. (Babcock, Freedman, Norton, & Ross, 1975, p. 561)

So even when she was the actual provider, the legal recognition was granted the husband. Therefore, whatever the husband's legal responsibilities for support may have been, he was not necessarily a good provider in the way the term came to be understood. The wife may have been performing that role.

In our country in Colonial times women were still viewed as performing a providing role, and they pursued a variety of occupations. Abigail Adams managed the family estate, which provided the wherewithal for John to spend so much time in Philadelphia. In the 18th century "many women were active in business and professional pursuits. They ran inns and taverns; they managed a wide variety of stores and shops; and, at least occasionally, they worked in careers like publishing, journalism and medicine" (Demos, 1974, p. 430). Women sometimes even "joined the menfolk for work in the fields" (p. 430). Like the household of the proverbial virtuous woman, the Colonial household was a little factory that produced clothing, furniture, bedding, candles, and other accessories, and again, as in the case of the virtuous woman, the female role was central. It was taken for granted that women provided for the family along with men.

The good provider as a specialized male role seems to have arisen in the transition from subsistence to market—especially money—economies that accelerated with the industrial revolution. The good-provider role for males emerged in this country roughly, say, from the 1830s, when de Tocqueville was observing it, to the late 1970s, when the 1980 census declared that a male was not automatically to be assumed to be head of the household. This gives the role a life span of about a century and a half. Although relatively short-lived, while it lasted the role was a seemingly rock-like feature of the national landscape.

As a psychological and sociological phenomenon, the good-provider role had wide ramifications for all of our thinking about families. It marked a new kind of marriage. It did not have good effects on women: The role deprived them of many chips by placing them in a peculiarly vulnerable position. Because she was not reimbursed for her contribution to the family in either products or services, a wife was stripped to a considerable extent of her access to cash-mediated markets. By discouraging labor force participation, it deprived many women, especially affluent ones, of opportunities to achieve strength and competence. It deterred young women from acquiring productive skills. They dedicated themselves instead to winning a good provider who would "take care of" them. The wife of a more successful provider became for all intents and purposes a parasite, with little to do except indulge or pamper herself. The psychology of such dependence could become all but crippling. There were other concomitants of the good-provider role.

Expressivity and the Good-Provider Role

The new industrial order that produced the good provider changed not so much the division of labor between the sexes as it did the site of the work they engaged in. Only two of the concomitants of this change in work site are selected for comment here, namely, (a) the identification of gender with work site as well as with work itself and (b) the reduction of time for personal interaction and intimacy within the family.

It is not so much the specific kinds of work men and women do—they have always varied from time to time and place to place—but the simple fact that the sexes do different kinds of work, whatever it is, which is in and of itself important. The division of labor by sex means that the work group becomes also a sex group. The very nature of maleness and femaleness becomes embedded in the sexual division of labor. One's sex and one's work are part of one another. One's work defines one's gender.

Any division of labor implies that people doing different kinds of work will occupy different work sites. When the division is based on sex, men and women will necessarily have different work sites. Even within the home itself, men and women had different work spaces. The woman's spinning wheel occupied a different area from the man's anvil. When the factory took over much of the work formerly done in the house, the separation of work space became especially marked. Not only did the separation of the sexes become spatially extended, but it came to relate work and gender in a special way. The work site as well as the work itself became associated with gender; each sex had its own turf. This sexual "territoriality" has had complicating effects on efforts to change any sexual division of labor. The good provider worked primarily in the outside male world of business and industry. The homemaker worked primarily in the home.

Spatial separation of the sexes not only identifies gender with work site and work but also reduces the amount of time available for spontaneous emotional give-and-take between husbands and wives. When men and women work in an economy based in the home, there are frequent occasions for interaction. (Consider, for example, the suggestive allusions made today to the rise in the birth rate nine months after a blackout.) When men and women are in close proximity, there is always the possiblity of reassuring glances, the comfort of simple physical presence. But when the division of labor removes the man from the family dwelling for most of the day, intimate relationships become less feasible. De Tocqueville was one of the first to call our attention to this. In 1840 he noted that

> almost all men in democracies are engaged in public or professional life; and . . . the limited extent of common income obliges a wife to confine herself to the house, in order to watch in person and very closely over the details of domestic economy. All these distinct and compulsory occupations are so many natural barriers, which, by keeping the two sexes asunder, render the solicitations of the one less frequent and less ardent—the resistance of the other more easy. (de Tocqueville, 1840, p. 212)

Not directly related to the spatial constraints on emotional expression by men, but nevertheless a concomitant of the new industrial order with the same effect, was the enormous drive for achievement, for success, for "making it" that escalated the provider role into the good-provider role. De Tocqueville (1840) is again our source:

> The tumultuous and constantly harassed life which equality makes men lead [becoming good providers] not only distracts them from the passions of love, by denying them time to indulge in it, but it diverts them from it by another more secret but more certain road. All men who live in democratic ages more or less contract ways of thinking of the manufacturing and trading classes. (p. 221)

As a result of this male concentration on jobs and careers, much abnegation and "a constant sacrifice of her pleasures to her duties" (de Tocqueville, 1840, p. 212) were demanded of the American woman. The good-provider role, as it came to be shaped by this ambience, was thus restricted in what it was called upon to provide. Emotional expressivity was not included in the role. One of the things a parent might say about a man to persuade a daughter to marry him, or a daughter might say to explain to her parents why she wanted to, was not that he was a gentle, loving, or tender man but that he was a good provider. He might have many other qualities, good or bad, but if a man was a good provider, everything else was either gravy or the price one had to pay for a good provider.

Lack of expressivity did not imply neglect of the family. The good provider was a "family man." He set a good table, provided a decent home, paid the mortgage, bought the shoes, and kept his children warmly clothed. He might, with the help of the children's part-time jobs, have been able to finance their educations through high school and, sometimes, even college. There might even have been a little left over for an occasional celebration in most families. The good provider made a decent contribution to the church. His work might have been demanding, but he expected it to be. If in addition to being a good provider, a man was kind, gentle, generous, and not a heavy drinker or gambler, that was all frosting on the cake. Loving attention and emotional involvement in the family were not part of a woman's implicit bargain with the good provider.

By the time de Tocqueville published his observations in 1840, the general outlines of the good-provider role had taken shape. It called for a hard-working man who spent most of his time at his work. In the traditional conception of the role, a man's chief responsibility is his job, so that "by definition any family behaviors must be subordinate to it in terms of significance and [the job]has priority in the event of a clash" (Scanzoni, 1975, p. 38). This was the classic form of the good-provider role, which remained a powerful component of our societal structure until well into the present century.

Costs and Rewards of the Good-Provider Role for Men

There were both costs and rewards for those men attached to the good-provider role. The most serious cost was perhaps the identification of maleness not only with the work site but especially with success in the role. "The American male looks to his breadwinning role to confirm his manliness" (Brenton, 1966, p. 194).[1] To be a man one had to be not only a provider but a *good* provider. Success in the good-provider role came in time to define masculinity itself. The good provider had to achieve, to win, to succeed, to dominate. He was a bread*winner.* He had to show "strength, cunning, inventiveness, endurance—a whole range of traits henceforth defined as exclusively 'masculine' " (Demos, 1974, p. 436). Men were judged as men by the level of living they provided. They were judged by the myth "that endows a money-making man with sexiness and virility, and is based on man's dominance, strength, and ability to provide for and care for 'his' woman" (Gould, 1974, p. 97). The good provider became a player in the male competitive macho game. What one man provided for his family in the way of luxury and display had to be equaled or topped by what another could pro-

---

[1]Rainwater and Yancey (1967), critiquing current welfare policies, note that they "have robbed men of their manhood, women of their husbands, and children of their fathers. To create a stable monogamous family we need to provide men with the opportunity to be men, and that involves enabling them to perform occupationally" (p. 235).

vide. Families became display cases for the success of the good provider. The psychic costs could be high:

> By depending so heavily on his breadwinning role to validate his sense of himself as a man, instead of also letting his roles as husband, father, and citizen of the community count as validating sources, the American male treads on psychically dangerous ground. It's always dangerous to put all of one's psychic eggs into one basket. (Brenton, 1966, p. 194)

The good-provider role not only put all of a man's gender-identifying eggs into one psychic basket, but it also put all the family-providing eggs into one basket. One individual became responsible for the support of the whole family. Countless stories portrayed the humiliation families underwent to keep wives and especially mothers out of the labor force, a circumstance that would admit to the world the male head's failure in the good-provider role. If a married woman had to enter the labor force at all, that was bad enough. If she made a good salary, however, she was "co-opting the man's passport to masculinity" (Gould, 1974, p. 98) and he was effectively castrated. A wife's earning capacity diminished a man's position as head of the household (Gould, 1974, p. 99).

Failure in the role of good provider, which employment of wives evidenced, could produce deep frustration. As Komarovsky (1940, p. 20) explains, this is "because in his own estimation he is failing to fulfill what is the central duty of his life, the very touchstone of his manhood—the role of family provider."

But just as there was punishment for failure in the good-provider role, so also were there rewards for successful performance. A man "derived strength from his role as provider" (Komarovsky, 1940, p. 205). He achieved a good deal of satisfaction from his ability to support his family. It won kudos. Being a good provider led to status in both the family and the community. Within the family it gave him the power of the purse and the right to decide about expenditures, standards of living, and what constituted good providing. "Every purchase of the family—the radio, his wife's new hat, the children's skates, the meals set before him—all were symbols of their dependence upon him" (Komarovsky, 1940, pp. 74–75. Such dependence gave him a "profound sense of stability" (p. 74). It was a strong counterpoise vis-à-vis a wife with a stronger personality. "Whether he had considerable authority within the family and was recognized as its head, or whether the wife's stronger personality ... dominated the family, he nevertheless derived strength from his role as a provider" (Komarovsky, 1940, p. 75). As recently as 1975, in a sample of 3,100 husbands and wives in 10 cities, Scanzoni found that despite increasing egalitarian norms, the good provider still had "considerable power in ultimate decision-making" and as "unique provider" had the right "to organize his life and the lives of other family members around his occupation" (p. 38).

A man who was successful in the good-provider role might be freed from other obligations to the family. But the flip side of this dispensation was that he could not make up for poor performance by excellence in other family roles. Since everything depended on his success as provider, everything was at stake. The good provider played an all-or-nothing game.

Different Ways of Performing the Good-Provider Role

Although the legal specifications for the role were laid out in the common law, in legislation, in legal precedents, in court decisions, and, most importantly, in custom and convention, in real-life situations the social and social-psychological specifications were set by the husband or, perhaps more accurately, by the community, alias the Joneses, and there were many ways to perform it.

Some men resented the burdens the role forced them to bear. A man could easily vent such resentment toward his family be keeping complete control over all expenditures, dispensing the money for household maintenance, and complaining about bills as though it were his wife's fault that shoes cost so much. He could, in effect, punish his family for his having to perform the role. Since the money he earned belonged to him—was "his"—he could do with it what he pleased. Through extreme parsimony he could dole out his money in a mean, humiliating way, forcing his wife to come begging for pennies. By his reluctance and resentment he could make his family pay emotionally for the provisioning he supplied.

At the other extreme were the highly competitive men who were so involved in outdoing the Jones that the fur coat became more important than the affectionate hug. They "bought off" their families. They sometimes succeeded so well in their extravagance that they sacrificed the family they were presumably providing for to the achievements that made it possible (Keniston, 1965).[2]

The Depression of the 1930s revealed in harsh detail what the loss of the role could mean both to the good provider and to his family, not only in the loss of income itself—which could be supplied by welfare agencies or even by other family members, including wives—but also and especially in the loss of face.

The Great Depression did not mark the demise of the good-provider role. But it did teach us what a slender thread the family hung on. It stimulated a

[2]Several years ago I presented a critique of what I called "extreme sex role specialization," including "work-intoxicated fathers." I noted that making success in the provider role the only test for real manliness was putting a lot of eggs into one basket. At both the blue-collar and the managerial levels, it was dysfunctional for families. I referred to the several attempts being made even then to correct the excesses of extreme sex role specialization: rural and urban communes, leaving jobs to take up small-scale enterprises that allowed more contact with families, and a rebellion against overtime in industry (Bernard, 1975, pp. 217–239).

whole array of programs designed to strengthen that thread, to ensure that it would never again be similarly threatened. Unemployment insurance was incorporated into the Social Security Act of 1935, for example, and a Full Employment Act was passed in 1946. But there proved to be many other ways in which the good-provider role could be subverted.

Role Rejectors and Role Overperformers

Recent research in psychology, anthropology, and sociology has familiarized us with the tremendous power of roles. But we also know that one of the fundamental principles of role behavior is that conformity to role norms is not universal. Not everyone lives up to the specifications of roles, either in the psychological or in the sociological definition of the concept. Two extremes have attracted research attention: (a) the men who could not live up to the norms of the good-provider role or did not want to, at one extreme, and (b) the men who overperformed the role, at the other. For the wide range in between, from blue-collar workers to professionals, there was fairly consistent acceptance of the role, however well or poorly, however grumblingly or willingly, performed.

First the nonconformists. Even in Colonial times, desertion and divorce occurred:

> Women may have deserted because, say, their husbands beat them; husbands, on the other hand, may have deserted because they were unable or unwilling to provide for their usually large families in the face of the wives' demands to do so. These demands were, of course, backed by community norms making the husband's financial support a sacred duty. (Scanzoni, 1979, pp. 24–25)

Fiedler (1962) has traced the theme of male escape from domestic responsibilities in the American novel from the time of Rip Van Winkle to the present:

> The figure of Rip Van Winkle presides over the birth of the American imagination; and it is fitting that our first successful home-grown legend should memorialize, however playfully, the flight of the dreamer from the shrew—into the mountains and out of time, away from the drab duties of home . . . anywhere to avoid . . . marriage and responsibility. One of the factors that determine theme and form in our great books is this strategy of evasion, this retreat to nature and childhood which makes our literature (and life) so charmingly and infuriatingly "boyish." (pp. xx–xxi)

Among the men who pulled up stakes and departed for the West or went down to the sea in ships, there must have been a certain proportion who, like their mythic prototype, were simply fleeing the good-provider role.

The work of Demos (1974), a historian, offers considerable support for Fiedler's thesis. He tells us that the burdens thrust on men in the 19th century by the new patterns of work began to show their effects in the family.

When "the [spatial] separation of the work lives of husbands and wives made communication so problematic," he asks, "what was the likelihood of meaningful communication?" (Demos, 1974, p. 438). The answer is, relatively little. Divorce and separation increased, either formally or by tacit consent—or simply by default, as in the case of a variety of defaulters—tramps, bums, hoboes—among them.

In this connection, "the development of the notorious 'tramp' phenomenon is worth noticing," Demos (1974, p. 438) tells us. The tramp was a man who just gave up, who dropped out of the role entirely. He preferred not to work, but he would do small chores or other small-scale work for a handout if he had to. He was not above begging the housewife for a meal, hoping she would not find work for him to do in repayment. Demos (1974) describes the type:

> Demoralized and destitute wanderers, their numbers mounting into the hundreds of thousands, tramps can be fairly characterized as men who had run away from their wives. . . . Their presence was mute testimony to the strains that tugged at the very core of American family life. . . . Many observers noted that the tramps had created a virtual society of their own [a kind of counterculture] based on a principle of single-sex companionship. (p. 438)

A considerable number of them came to be described as "homeless men" and, as the country became more urbanized, landed ultimately on skid row. A large part of the task of social workers for almost a century was the care of the "evaded" women they left behind.[3] When the tramp became wholly demoralized, a chronic alcoholic, almost unreachable, he fell into a category of his own—he was a bum.

Quite a different kettle of fish was the hobo, the migratory worker who spent several months harvesting wheat and other large crops and the rest of the year in cities. Many were the so-called Wobblies, or Industrial Workers of the World, who repudiated the good-provider role on principle. They had contempt for the men who accepted it and could be called conscientious objectors to the role. "In some IWW circles, wives were regarded as the 'ball and chain.' In the West, IWW literature proclaimed that the migratory

---

[3]In one department of a South Carolina cotton mill early in the century, "every worker was a grass widow" (Smuts, 1959, p. 54). Many women worked "because their husbands refused to provide for their families. There is no reason to think that husbands abandoned their duties more often than today, but the woman who was burdened by an irresponsible husband in 1890 usually had no recourse save taking on his responsibilities herself. If he deserted, the law-enforcement agencies of the time afforded little chance of finding and compelling him to provide support" (Smuts, 1959, p. 54). The situation is not greatly improved today. In divorce child support is allotted in only a small number of cases and enforced in even fewer. "Roughly half of all families with an absent parent don't have awards at all. . . . Where awards do exist they are usually for small amounts, typically ranging from $7 to $18 per week per child" (Jones, 1976, abstract). A summary of all the studies available concludes that "approximately 20 percent of all divorced and separated mothers receive child support regularly, with an additional 7 percent receiving it 'sometimes'; 8 percent of all divorced and separated women receive alimony regularly or sometimes" (Jones, 1976, p. 23).

worker, usually a young, unmarried male, was 'the finest specimen of American manhood . . . the leaven of the revolutionary labor movement' " (Foner, 1979, p. 400). Exemplars of the Wobblies were the nomadic workers of the West. They were free men. The migratory worker, "unlike the factory slave of the Atlantic seaboard and the central states, . . . was most emphatically 'not afraid of losing his job.' No wife and family cumbered him. The worker of the East, oppressed by the fear of want for wife and babies, dared not venture much" (Foner, 1979, p. 400). The reference to fear of loss of job was well taken; employers preferred married men, disciplined into the good-provider role, who had given hostages to fortune and were therefore more tractable.

Just on the verge between the area of conformity to the good-provider role—at whatever level—and the area of complete nonconformity to it was the non-good provider, the marginal group of workers usually made up of "the under-educated, the under-trained, the under-employed, or part-time employed, as well as the under-paid, and of course the unemployed" (Snyder, 1979, p. 597). These included men who wanted—sometimes desperately—to perform the good-provider role but who for one reason or another were unable to do so. Liebow (1966) has discussed the ramifications of failure among the black men of Tally's corner: The black man is

> under legal and social constraints to provide for them [their families], to be a husband to his wife and a father to his children. The chances are, however, that he is failing to provide for them, and failure in this primary function contaminates his performance as father in other respects as well. (p. 86).

In some cases, leaving the family entirely was the best substitute a man could supply. The community was left to take over.[4]

At the other extreme was the overperformer. De Tocqueville, quoted earlier, was already describing him as he manifested in the 1830s. And as late as 1955 Warner and Ablegglen were adding to the considerable literature on industrial leaders and tycoons, referring to their "driving concentration" on their careers and their "intense focusing" of interests, energies, and skills on these careers, "even limiting their sexual activity" (pp. 48–49). They came to be known as workaholics or work-intoxicated men. Their preoccupation with their work even at the expense of their families was, as I have already noted, quite acceptable in our society.

Poorly or well performed, the good-provider role lingered on. World War II initiated a challenge, this time in the form of attracting more and more married women into the labor force, but the challenge was papered over in the 1950s with an "age of togetherness" that all but apotheosized the good pro-

---

[4]Even though the annals of social work agencies are filled with cases of runaway husbands, in 1976 only 12.6% of all women were in the status of divorce and separation, and at least some of them were still being "provided for." Most men were at least trying to fulfill the good-provider role.

vider, his house in the suburbs, his homebody wife, and his third, fourth, even fifth, child. As late as the 1960s most housewives (87%) still saw bread-winning as their husband's primary role (Lopata, 1971, p. 91).[5]

Intrinsic Conflict in the Good-Provider Role

Since the good-provider role involved both family and work roles, most people believed that there was no incompatibility between them or at least that there should not be. But in the 1960s and 1970s evidence began to mount that maybe something was amiss.

De Tocqueville had documented the implicit conflict in the American businessman's devotion to his work at the expense of his family in the early years of the 19th century; the Industrial Workers of the World had pro-claimed that the good-provider role which tied a man to his family was an impediment to the great revolution at the beginning of the 20th century; Fiedler (1962) had noted that throughout our history, in the male fantasy world, there was freedom from the responsibilities of this role; about 50 years ago Freud (1930/1958) had analyzed the intrinsic conflict between the demands of women and the family on one side and the demands of men's work on the other:

> Women represent the interests of the family and sexual life, the work of civilization has become more and more men's business; it confronts them with ever harder tasks, compels them to sublimations of instinct which women are not easily able to achieve. Since man has not an unlimited amount of mental energy at his disposal, he must accomplish his tasks by distributing his libido to the best advantage. What he employs for cultural [occupational] purposes he withdraws to a great extent from women, and his sexual life; his constant association with men and his dependence on his relations with them even estrange him from his duties as husband and fa-ther. Woman finds herself thus forced into the background by the claims of culture [work] and she adapts an inimical attitude towards it. (pp. 50–51)

In the last two decades, researchers have been raising questions relevant to Freud's statement of the problem. They have been asking people about the relative satisfactions they derive from these conflicting values—family and work. Among the earliest studies comparing family–work values was a Gal-lup poll in 1940 in which both men and women chose a happy home over an interesting job or wealth as a major life value. Since then there have been a number of such polls, and a considerable body of results has now accumu-lated. Pleck and Lang (1979) and Hesselbart (Note 1) have summarized the findings of these surveys. All agree that there is a clear bias in the direction of the family. Pleck and Lang conclude that "men's family role is far more

---

[5]Although all the women in Lopata's (1971) sample saw breadwinning as important, fewer employed women (54%) than either nonemployed urban (63%) or suburban (64%) women as-signed it first place (p. 91).

psychologically significant to them than is their work role" (p. 29), and Hesselbart—however critical she is of the studies she summarizes—believes they should not be dismissed lightly and concludes that they certainly "challenge the idea that family is a 'secondary' valued role" (p. 14).[6] Douvan (Note 2) also found in a 1976 replication of a 1957 survey that family values retained priority over work: "Family roles almost uniformly rate higher in value production than the job role does" (p. 16).[7]

The very fact that researchers have asked such questions is itself interesting. Somehow or other both the researchers and the informants seem to be saying that all this complaining about the male neglect of the family, about the lack of family involvement by men, just is not warranted. Neither de Tocqueville nor Freud was right. Men do value family life more than they value their work. They do derive their major life satisfactions from their families rather than from their work.

It may well be true that men derive the greatest satisfaction from their family roles, but this does not necessarily mean they are willing to pay for this benefit. In any event, great attitudinal changes took place in the 1960s and 1970s.

Douvan (Note 2), on the basis of surveys in 1957 and 1976, found, for example, a considerable increase in the proportion of both men and women who found marriage and parenthood burdensome and restrictive. Almost three fifths (57%) of both married men and married women in 1976 saw marriage as "all burdens and restrictions," as compared with only 42% and 47%, respectively, in 1957. And almost half (45%) also viewed children as "all burdens and restrictions" in 1976, as compared with only 28% and 33% for married men and married women, respectively, in 1957. The proportion of working men with a positive attitude toward marriage dropped drastically over this period, from 68% to 39%. Working women, who made up a fairly small number of all married women in 1957, hardly changed attitudes at all, dropping only from 43% to 42%. The proportion of working men who found marriage and children burdensome and restrictive more than doubled, from

[6]Pleck and Lang (1979) found only one serious study contradicting their own conclusions: "Using data from the 1973 NORC [National Opinion Research Center] General Social Survey, Harry analyzed the bivariate relationship of job and family satisfaction to life happiness in men classified by family life cycle stage. In three of the five groups of husbands . . . job satisfaction had a stronger association than family satisfaction to life happiness" (pp. 5–6).

[7]In 1978, a Yankelovich survey on "The New Work Psychology" suggested that leisure is now becoming a strict competitor for both family and work as a source of life satisfactions: "Family and work have grown less important than leisure; a majority of 60 percent say that although they enjoy their work, it is not their major source of satisfaction" (p. 46). A 1977 survey of Swedish men aged 18 to 35 found that the proportion saying the family was the main source of meaning in their lives declined from 45% in 1955 to 41% in 1977; the proportion indicating work as the main source of satisfaction dropped from 33% to 17%. The earlier tendency for men to identify themselves through their work is less marked these days. In the new value system, the individual says, in effect, "I am more than my role. I am myself" (Yankelovich, 1978). Is the increasing concern with leisure a way to escape the dissatisfaction with both the alienating relations found on the work site and the demands for increased involvement with the family?

25% to 56% and from 25% to 58%, respectively. Although some of these changes reflected greater willingness in 1976 than in 1957 to admit negative attitudes toward marriage and parenthood—itself significant—profound changes were clearly in process. More and more men and women were experiencing disaffection with family life.[8]

"All Burdens and Restrictions"

Apparently, the benefits of the good-provider role were greater than the costs for most men. Despite the legend of the flight of the American male (Fiedler, 1962), despite the defectors and dropouts, despite the tavern habitué's "ball and chain" cliché, men seemed to know that the good-provider role, if they could succeed in it, was good for them. But Douvan's (Note 2) findings suggest that recently their complaints have become serious, bone-deep. The family they have been providing for is not the same family it was in the past.

Smith (1979) calls the great trek of married women into the labor force a subtle revolution—revolutionary not in the sense of one class overthrowing a status quo and substituting its own regime, but revolutionary in its impact on both the family and the work roles of men and women. It diluted the prerogatives of the good-provider role. It increased the demands made on the good provider, especially in the form of more emotional investment in the family, more sharing of household responsibilities. The role became even more burdensome.

However men may now feel about the burdens and restrictions imposed on them by the good-provider role, most have, at least ostensibly, accepted them. The tramp and the bum had "voted with their feet" against the role; the hobo or Wobbly had rejected it on the basis of a revolutionary ideology that saw it as enslaving men to the corporation; tavern humor had glossed the resentment habitués felt against its demands. Now the "burdens-and-restrictions" motif has surfaced both in research reports and, more blatantly, in the male liberation movement. From time to time it has also appeared in the clinicians' notes.

Sometimes the resentment of the good provider takes the form of simply wanting more appreciation for the life-style he provides. All he does for his family seems to be taken for granted. Thus, for example, Goldberg (1976), a psychiatrist, recounts the case of a successful businessman:

> He's feeling a deepening sense of bitterness and frustration about his wife and family. He doesn't feel appreciated. It angers him the way they seem to

[8]Men seem to be having problems with both work and family roles. Veroff (Note 3), for example, reports an increased "sense of dissatisfaction with the social relations in the work setting" and a "dissatisfaction with the affiliative nature of work" (p. 47). This dissatisfaction may be one of the factors that leads men to seek affiliative-need satisfaction in marriage, just as in the 19th century they looked to the home as shelter from the jungle of the outside world.

> take the things his earnings purchase for granted. They've come to expect it
> as their due. It particularly enrages him when his children put him down for
> his "materialistic middle-class trip." He'd like to tell them to get someone
> else to support them but he holds himself back. (p. 124)

Brenton (1966) quotes a social worker who describes an upper-middle-class
woman: She has "gotten hold of a man who'll drive himself like mad to get
money, and [is] denigrating him for being too interested in money, and not
interested in music, or the arts, or in spending time with the children. But at
the same time she's subtly driving him—and doesn't know it" (p. 226). What
seems significant about such cases is not that men feel resentful about the
lack of appreciation but that they are willing to justify their resentment.
They are no longer willing to grin and bear it.

Sometimes there is even more than expressed resentment; there is an actual repudiation of the role. In the past, only a few men like the hobo or
Wobbly were likely to give up. Today, Goldberg (1976) believes, more are
ready to renounce the role, not on theoretical revolutionary grounds, however, but on purely selfish ones:

> Male growth will stem from openly avowed, unashamed, self-oriented moti-
> vations. . . . Guilt-oriented "should" behavior will be rejected because it is
> always at the price of a hidden build-up of resentment and frustration and
> alienation from others and is, therefore, counterproductive. (p. 184)

The disaffection of the good provider is directed to both sides of his role.
With respect to work, Lefkowitz (1979) has described men among whom the
good-provider role is neither being completely rejected nor repudiated, but
diluted. These men began their working lives in the conventional style, hopeful and ambitious. They found a job, married, raised a family, and "achieved
a measure of economic security and earned the respect of . . . colleagues and
neighbors" (Lefkowitz, 1979, p. 31). In brief, they successfully performed
the good-provider role. But unlike their historical predecessors, they in time
became disillusioned with their jobs—not jobs on assembly lines, not jobs
usually characterized as alienating, but fairly prestigious jobs such as aero-
nautics engineer and government economist. They daydreamed about other
interests. "The common theme which surfaced again and again in their histories, was the need to find a new social connection—to reassert control over
their lives, to gain some sense of freedom" (Lefkowitz, 1979, p. 31). These
men felt "entitled to freedom and independence." Middle-class, educated,
self-assured, articulate, and for the most part white, they knew they could
talk themselves into a job if they had to. Most of them did not want to desert
their families. Indeed, most of them "wanted to rejoin the intimate circle
they felt they had neglected in their years of work" (p. 31).

Though some of the men Lefkowitz studied sought closer ties with their
families, in the case of those studied by Sarason (1977), a psychologist, career changes involved lower income and had a negative impact on families.

Sarason's subjects were also men in high-level professions, the very men least likely to find marriage and parenthood burdensome and restrictive. Still, since career change often involved a reduction in pay, some wives were unwilling to accept it, with the result that the marriage deteriorated (p. 178). Sometimes it looked like a no-win game. The husband's earlier career brought him feelings of emptiness and alienation, but it also brought financial rewards for the family. Greater work satisfaction for him in lower paying work meant reduced satisfaction with life-style. These findings lead Sarason to raise a number of points with respect the the good-provider role. "How much," he asks, "does an individual or a family need in order to maintain a satisfactory existence? Is an individual being responsible to himself or his family if he provides them with little more than the bare essentials of living?" (p. 178). These are questions about the good-provider role that few men raised in the past.

Lefkowitz (1979) wonders how his downwardly mobile men lived when they left their jobs. "They put together a basic economic package which consisted of government assistance, contributions from family members who had not worked before and some bartering of goods and services" (p. 31). Especially interesting in this list of income sources are the "contributions from family members who had not worked before" (p. 31). Surely not mothers and sisters. Who, of course, but wives?

Women and the Provider Role

The present discussion began with the woman's part in the provider role. We saw how as more and more of the provisioning of the family came to be by way of monetary exchange, the woman's part shrank. A woman could still provide services, but could furnish little in the way of food, clothing, and shelter. But now that she is entering the labor force in large numbers, she can once more resume her ancient role, this time, like her male counterpart the provider, by way of a monetary contribution. More and more women are doing just this.

The assault on the good-provider role in the Depression was traumatic. But a modified version began to appear in the 1970s as a single income became inadequate for more and more families. Husbands have remained the major providers, but in an increasing number of cases the wife has begun to share this role. Thus, the proportion of married women aged 15 to 54 (living with their husbands) in the labor force more than doubled between 1950 and 1978, from 25.2% to 55.4%. The proportion for 1990 is estimated to reach 66.7% (Smith, 1979, p. 14). Fewer women are now full-time housewives.

For some men the relief from the strain of sole responsibility for the provider role has been welcome. But for others the feeling of degradation resembles the feelings reported 40 years earlier in the Great Depression. It is not that they are no longer providing for the family but that the role-sharing wife now feels justified in making demands on them. The good-provider role with all its prerogatives and perquisites has undergone profound changes. It will never be the same again.[9] Its death knell was sounded when, as noted above, the 1980 census no longer automatically assumed that the male member of the household was its head.

The Current Scene

Among the new demands being made on the good-provider role, two deserve special consideration, namely, (1) more intimacy, expressivity, and nurturance—specifications never included in it as it originally took shape—and (b) more sharing of household responsibility and child care.

As the pampered wife in an affluent household came often to be an economic parasite, so also the good provider was often, in a way, a kind of emotional parasite. Implicit in the definition of the role was that he provided goods and material things. Tender loving care was not one of the requirements. Emotional ministrations from the family were his right; providing them was not a corresponding obligation. Therefore, as de Tocqueville had already noted by 1840, women suffered a kind of emotional deprivation labeled by Robert Weiss "relational deficit" (cited in Bernard, 1976). Only recently has this male rejection of emotional expression come to be challenged. Today, even blue-collar women are imposing "a host of new role expectations upon their husbands or lovers. . . . A new role set asks the blue-collar male to strive for . . . deep-coursing intimacy" (Shostak, Note 4, p. 75). It was not only vis-à-vis his family that the good provider was lacking in expressivity. This lack was built into the whole male role script. Today not only women but also men are beginning to protest the repudiation of expressivity prescribed in male roles (David & Brannon, 1976; Farrell, 1974; Fasteau, 1974; Pleck & Sawyer, 1974).

Is there any relationship between the "imposing" on men of "deep-coursing intimacy" by women on one side and the increasing proportion of men who find marriage burdensome and restrictive on the other? Are men seeing the new emotional involvements being asked of them as "all burdens and restrictions"? Are they responding to the new involvements under duress? Are they feeling oppressed by them? Fearful of them?

From the standpoint of high-level pure-science research there may be something bizarre, if not even slightly absurd, in the growing corpus of serious research on how much or how little husbands of employed wives contribute to household chores and child care. Yet it is serious enough that all

[9]Among the indices of the waning of the good-provider role are the increasing number of married women in the labor force; the growth in the number of female-headed families; the growing trend toward egalitarian norms in marriage; the need for two earners in so many middle-class families; and the recognition of these trends in the abandonment of the identification of head of household as a male.

over the industrialized world such research is going on. Time studies in a dozen countries—communist as well as capitalist—trace the slow and bungling process by which marriage accommodates to changing conditions and by which women struggle to mold the changing conditions in their behalf. For everywhere the same picture shows up in the research: an image of women sharing the provider role and at the same time retaining responsibility for the household. Until recently such a topic would have been judged unworthy of serious attention. It was a subject that might be worth a good laugh, for instance, as when an all-thumbs man in a cartoon burns the potatoes or finds himself bumbling awkwardly over a diaper, demonstrating his—proud—male ineptness at such female work. But it is no longer funny.

The "politics of housework" (Mainardi, 1970) proves to be more profound than originally believed. It has to do not only with tasks but also with gender—and perhaps more with the site of the tasks than with their intrinsic nature. A man can cook magnificently if he does it on a hunting or fishing trip; he can wield a skillful needle if he does it mending a tent or a fishing net; he can even feed and clean a toddler on a camping trip. Few of the skills of the homemaker are beyond his reach so long as they are practiced in a suitably male environment. It is not only women's work in and of itself that is degrading but any work on female turf. It may be true, as Brenton (1966) says, that "the secure man can wash a dish, diaper a baby, and throw the dirty clothes into the washing machine—or do anything else women used to do exclusively—without thinking twice about it" (p. 211), but not all men are that secure. To a great many men such chores are demasculinizing. The apron is shameful on a man in the kitchen; it is all right at the carpenter's bench.

The male world may look upon the man who shares household responsibilities as, in effect, a scab. One informant tells the interviewer about a conversation on the job: "What, are you crazy?" his hard-hat fellow workers ask him when he speaks of helping his wife. "The guys want to kill me. 'You son of a bitch! You are getting us in trouble.' . . . The men get really mad" (Lein, 1979, p. 492). Something more than persiflage is involved here. We are fairly familiar with the trauma associated with the invasion by women of the male work turf, the hazing women can be subjected to, and the male resentment of admitting them except into their own segregated areas. The corresponding entrance of men into the traditional turf of women—the kitchen or the nursery—has analogous but not identical concomitants.

Pleck and Lang (1979) tell us that men are now beginning to change in the direction of greater involvement in family life. "Men's family behavior is beginning to change, becoming increasingly congruent with the long-standing psychological significance of the family in their lives"(p. 1). They measure this greater involvement by way of the help they offer with homemaking chores. Scanzoni (1975), on the basis of a survey of over 3,000 husbands and wives, concludes that at least in households in which wives are in the labor force, there is the "possibility of a different pattern in which responsibility for households would unequivocally fall equally on husbands as well as wives" (p. 38). A brave new world indeed. Still, when we look at the reality around us, the pace seems intolerably slow. The responsibilities of the old good-provider role have attenuated far faster than have its prerogatives and privileges.

A considerable amount of thought has been devoted to studying the effects of the large influx of women into the work force. An equally interesting question is what the effect will be if a large number of men actually do increase their participation in the family and the household. Will men find the apron shameful? What if we were to ask fathers to alternate with mothers in being in the home when youngsters come home from school? Would fighting adolescent drug abuse be more successful if fathers and mothers were equally engaged in it? If the school could confer with fathers as often as with mothers? If the father accompanied children when they went shopping for clothes? If fathers spent as much time with children as do mothers?

Even as husbands, let alone as fathers, the new pattern is not without trauma. Hall and Hall (1979), in their study of two-career couples, report that the most serious fights among such couples occur not in the bedroom, but in the kitchen, between couples who profess a commitment to equality but who find actually implementing it difficult. A young professional reports that he is philosophically committed to egalitarianism in marriage and tries hard to practice it, but it does not work. He even feels guilty about this. The stresses involved in reworking roles may have an impact on health. A study of engineers and accountants finds poorer health among those with employed wives than among those with nonemployed wives (Burke & Wier, 1976). The processes involved in role change have been compared with those involved in deprogramming a cult member. Are they part of the increasing sense of marriage and parenthood as "all burdens and restrictions"?

The demise of the good-provider role also calls for consideration of other questions: What does the demotion of the good provider to the status of senior provider or even mere coprovider do to him? To marriage? To gender identity? What does expanding the role of housewife to that of junior provider or even coprovider do to her? To marriage? To gender identity? Much will of course depend on the social and psychological ambience in which changes take place.

A Parable

I began this essay with a proverbial woman. I close it with a modern parable by William H. Chafe (Note 5), a historian who also keeps his eye on the current scene. Jack and Jill, both planning professional careers, he as doctor, she as lawyer, marry at age 24. She works to put him through medical school in the expectation that he will then finance her through law school. A child is born during the husband's internship, as planned. But in order for him to support her through professional training as planned, he will have to take time out from his career. After two years, they decide that both will continue their training on a part-time basis, sharing household responsibilities and using day-care services. Both find part-time positions and work out flexible work schedules that leave both of them time for child care and companionship with one another. They live happily ever after.

That's the end? you ask incredulously. Well, not exactly. For, as Chafe (Note 5) points out, as usual the personal is also political:

> Obviously such a scenario presumes a radical transformation of the personal values that today's young people bring to their relationships as well as a readiness on the part of social and economic institutions to encourage, or at least make possible, the development of equality between men and women. (p. 28)

The good-provider role may be on its way out, but its legitimate successor has not yet appeared on the scene.

Reference Notes

1. Hesselbart, S. *Some underemphasized issues about men, women, and work.* Unpublished manuscript, 1978.
2. Douvan, E. *Family roles in a twenty-year perspective.* Paper presented at the Radcliffe Pre-Centennial Conference, Cambridge, Massachusetts, April 2–4, 1978.
3. Veroff, J. *Psychological orientations to the work role: 1957–1976.* Unpublished manuscript, 1978.
4. Shostak, A. *Working class Americans at home: Changing expectations of manhood.* Unpublished manuscript, 1973.
5. Chafe, W. *The challenge of sex equality: A new culture or old values revisited?* Paper presented at the Radcliffe Pre-Centennial Conference, Cambridge, Massachusetts, April 2–4, 1978.

References

Babcock, B., Freedman, A. E., Norton, E. H., & Ross, S. C. *Sex discrimination and the law: Causes and remedies.* Boston: Little, Brown, 1975.

Bernard, J. *Women, wives, mothers.* Chicago: Aldine, 1975.

Bernard, J. Homosociality and female depression. *Journal of Social Issues,* 1976, *32,* 207–224.

Boulding, E. Familial constraints on women's work roles. *SIGNS: Journal of Women in Culture and Society,* 1976, *1,* 95–118.

Brenton, M. *The American male.* New York: Coward-McCann, 1966.

Burke, R. & Weir, T. Relationship of wives' employment status to husband, wife and pair satisfaction and performance. *Journal of Marriage and the Family,* 1976, *38,* 279–287.

David, D. S. & Brannon, R. (Eds). *The forty-nine percent majority: The male sex role.* Reading, Mass: Addison-Wesley, 1976.

Demos, J. The American family in past time. *American Scholar,* 1974, *43,* 422–446.

Farrell, W. *The liberated man.* New York: Random House, 1974.

Fasteau, M. F. *The male machine.* New York: McGraw-Hill, 1974.

Fiedler, L. *Love and death in the American novel.* New York: Meredith, 1962.

Foner, P. S. *Women and the American labor movement.* New York: Free Press, 1979.

Freud, S. *Civilization and its discontents.* New York: Doubleday-Anchor, 1958. (Originally published, 1930.)

Goldberg, H. *The hazards of being male*. New York: New American Library, 1976.

Gould, R. E. Measuring masculinity by the size of a paycheck. In J. E. Pleck & J. Sawyer (Eds.), *Men and masculinity*. Englewood Cliffs, N.J.: Prentice-Hall, 1974. (Also published in *Ms.*, June 1973, pp. 18ff.)

Hall, D. & Hall, F. *The two-career couple*. Reading, Mass.: Addison-Wesley, 1979.

Jones, C. A. *A review of child support payment performance*. Washington, D.C.: Urban Institute, 1976.

Keniston, K. *The uncommitted: Alienated youth in American society*. New York: Harcourt, Brace & World, 1965.

Komarovsky, M. *The unemployed man and his family*. New York: Dryden Press, 1940.

Lefkowitz, B. Life without work. *Newsweek*, May 14, 1979, p. 31.

Lein, L. Responsibility in the allocation of tasks. *Family Coordinator*, 1979, *28*, 489–496.

Liebow, E. *Tally's corner*. Boston: Little, Brown, 1966.

Lopata, H. *Occupation housewife*. New York: Oxford University Press, 1971.

Mainardi, P. The politics of housework. In R. Morgan (Ed.), *Sisterhood is powerful*. New York: Vintage Books, 1970.

Pleck, J. H., & Lang, L. Men's family work: Three perspectives and some new data. *Family Coordinator*, 1979, *28*, 481–488.

Pleck, J. H., & Sawyer, J. (Eds.) *Men and masculinity*. Englewood Cliffs, N.J.: Prentice-Hall, 1974.

Rainwater, L., & Yancey, W. L. *The Moynihan report and the politics of controversy*. Cambridge, Mass.: M.I.T. Press, 1967.

Sarason, S. B. *Work, aging, and social change*. New York: Free Press, 1977.

Scanzoni, J. H. *Sex roles, life styles, and childbearing: Changing patterns in marriage and the family*. New York: Free Press, 1975.

Scanzoni, J. H. An historical perspective on husband-wife bargaining power and marital dissolution. In G. Levinger & O. Moles (Eds.), *Divorce and separation in America*. New York: Basic Books, 1979.

Smith, R. E.(Ed.), *The subtle revolution*. Washington, D.C.: Urban Institute, 1979.

Smuts, R. W. *Women and work in America*. New York: Columbia University Press, 1959.

Snyder, L. The deserting, non-supporting father: Scapegoat of family non-policy. *Family Coordinator*, 1979, *38*, 594–598.

Tocqueville, A. de. *Democracy in America*. New York: J. & H. G. Langley, 1840.

Warner, W. L., & Ablegglen, J. O. *Big business leaders in America*. New York: Harper, 1955.

Yankelovich, D. The new psychological contracts at work. *Psychology Today*, May 1978, pp. 46–47; 49–50.

Zborowski, M., & Herzog, E. *Life is with people*. New York: Schocken Books, 1952.

Household Work, Wage Work, and Sexual Equality

Joann Vanek

In a recent Supreme Court decision which struck down the gender qualification in a program providing benefits for children of unemployed fathers but not unemployed mothers, Justice Blackmun, using language from a Court decision earlier in the term, argued that the presumption that the father has the primary responsibility to provide a home and its essentials while the mother is the center of home and family life is part of "the baggage of sexual stereotypes" that no longer reflects the realities of family life and work behavior (Califano v. Westcott, 1979). Evidence supporting Justice Blackmun's assertion can be gathered easily. The large number of married women in the labor force, the particularly sharp increases in the employment of mothers, the decline in fertility, the drop in men's retirement age, the sharp increase in the number of families in which women have the main economic responsibility—all suggest that men's and women's roles in the market and in the home are changing in fundamental ways.

Direct evidence on what is happening to work roles in the home has been difficult to come by, and consequently supposition rather than fact has shaped interpretations of changes in this domain. With the proliferation of labor-saving goods and services and the decrease in family size, there are compelling reasons to believe that the workload in housework is not large today. Moreover, the sharing between husbands and wives in wage earning *ought* to be accompanied by sharing in housework. Women do leave the labor force to bear and rear children, and this reduces their market productivity and wages relative to men's. Having lower productivity in the market, wives then continue to spend more time in housework, even when employed.

These altogether plausible assumptions about the allocation of work in families are reflected in certain scholarly models. This includes the economic approach developed by Gary Becker and his colleagues. . . . It also includes what came to be known in sociological treatments of the family as "resource theory."[1] What unites these approaches to family and work roles is the emphasis on economic or pragmatic concerns and the neglect of the norms and values which continue to distinguish the duties and responsibilities of the sexes. The economic model ignores completely the cultural factors affecting the allocation of work; and "resource theory," which assumes that equalitarian beliefs

Author's Note: This chapter is a revised version of a paper presented at the annual meetings of the American Sociological Association in Chicago, September 1977. The views expressed here are those of the author and do not represent those of the National Science Foundation.

Reprinted from Joann Vanek, "Household Work, Wage Work, and Sexual Equality," pp. 275–291 in *Women and Household Labor*, Sarah Fenstermaker Berk, ed., © 1980 Sage Publications, Inc., with permission.

are replacing the traditional ideology of sex differences, minimizes the influence of culture.

Now that data on household labor are available, the error in these widely held assumptions can be seen. As it turns out, housework is still divided along traditional lines and is not reallocated when wives enter the labor force. In other words, the allocation of work in the home continues to be shaped by deeply ingrained ideas about the roles of the sexes. In fact, this is also true of market work. Women's lower earnings are not entirely explained by their shorter and more intermittent participation, but are also due to a complex set of underlying structural and cultural forces which place and maintain men and women in different spheres of work.[2]

The study of household labor reveals new and more precise insights on the changes now occurring in family and work roles. This chapter uses national survey data to provide an overview of recent trends.[3] It examines the division of household work, the links between women's responsibilities in the home and their position in the labor force, and the dynamics of change in family and work roles. Finally, it treats policy issues raised by the shifts occurring in family life and work behavior.

Dividing Household Work

Even in modern society a substantial amount of productive activity takes place in the home. Goods must be procured, processed, and maintained for family use. People also need servicing and care. In particular a wide range of tasks is connected with the training of children and with preserving their physical health and safety. Studies show that all these household tasks continue to be time consuming and that they remain primarily "women's work." In the 1960s most married women were spending over 35 hours a week in household labor. If that referred to employment, it would constitute full-time work (Walker & Woods, 1976; Vanek, 1979). By contrast, married men were spending about 11.5 hours a week in housework. In hours alone, these figures might be regarded as evidence that some sharing occurs in household labor. However, a detailed examination of what is done reveals that household tasks are sharply divided by sex. Men's work clusters in only a few activities: yard work, home repairs, shopping, travel on household errands, and to a limited degree child care. The wife is still responsible for routine home and family care, which includes such tasks as meal preparation and clean-up, home care, laundry, mending, and care of children. Only shopping and travel on household errands are divided at all equally. Even child care duties, shared to some degree, are typed by sex. The detailed time budget figures show that wives perform almost all the physical care activities such as diapering, bathing, and feeding.

The sex-typing of housework is so deeply ingrained that the basic household tasks are *not* redivided when a wife enters the labor force. As a result, there are significant differences in the total workweek of husbands and wives. Married women who are not employed spend the least amount of time in work (about 56 hours a week); employed married men, about 6.5 additional hours a week (a total of 62.5 hours); while employed wives work about 8.5 hours longer than married men (71 hours). For employed mothers of young children, work expands to an 80-hour week, but for husbands in such families it increases by a mere 2 or 3 hours to 65 hours (Vanek, 1979: ch.6).

Essentially the same picture emerges from recent data. For example, in a comparison of 1965 and 1975 national time-use surveys conducted by the Survey Research Center at the University of Michigan, John Robinson (1977) shows an overall drop of 20 percent in the time women spend in housework and family care. However, in analyzing this difference, Robinson also shows that the reduction in housework can be almost entirely explained by demographic changes occurring in employment and fertility rather than by more far-reaching shifts in attitudes about men's and women's roles. . . . Robinson's calculations show that once adjustments are made for differences between the two samples in employment status, marital status, family composition, age, and socioeconomic status, women in 1975 spent only about 2.5 hours less time per week doing housework. Nor did Robinson find that the differences were due to any greater help in housework by men, for when the 1965 and 1975 studies were adjusted for compositional differences in the samples, it turned out that in 1975 men were spending less time in housework.

Economists Frank Stafford and Greg Duncan (1977) analyzed the same 1975 data to see whether current patterns in the division of housework can be explained by standard economic models which emphasize the role of market and nonmarket productivity of each spouse, or whether current patterns are also influenced by the deeply embedded attitudes about men's and women's roles. They found that the division of housework was shaped by the market productivity or wage rate of wives as well as husbands. For example, both married men and married women were less likely to be responsible for any routine household task as their own wage (or shadow wage in the case of women) increased, but more likely as their spouse's wage increased.[4] The significance of this pattern is questionable, since only 16 percent of married men are primarily responsible for any routine household chore.

The data provided by Stafford and Duncan show the deep imprint of the sexual patterning of household labor. Women bear primary responsibility for almost all household chores. There is only a small degree of substitution of husbands' work in the home for wives'. This is true even for wives with high earnings. Nor does having preschool children, which significantly alters the workload in housework, result in any clear reallocation of household work.

New insights on the dynamics of allocating family work are revealed in the research of Richard Berk and Sarah Berk (1979). In a 1975 national survey of 750 wives, the Berks collected records which listed the starting and ending times for each activity over a 24-hour period. Information was also collected for 350 husbands—although for men the type of record keeping was somewhat different from and less detailed than for women. This method provided data which permitted the content and the organization of the husband's daily schedule to be compared with the wife's.

The Berk's data, like the 1975 national time-use survey, revealed that housework was still divided along traditional lines. It revealed in addition that the major reason husbands spent time doing routine household tasks was that practical circumstances prevented their wives from doing them. For example, examination of the morning routine showed that wives and husbands reacted somewhat differently to the demands of employment. Wives got up earlier to get a head start on their chores. Husbands, however, did not alter their morning routine when their wives were employed. In the evening routine there was some readjustment in husbands' schedules when their wives were employed, particularly in families with young children. In these families men were more likely to wash dishes and do other after-dinner chores and also to spend time in child care. Insight into why this occurred was provided by comparing the schedules of husbands and wives at this time of day. As it turned out, men took on additional household tasks when their wives left for work just after dinner. Whether this is merely a passive response to women's employment or whether it represents a strategy that families devise to divide work more equally cannot be determined from the data. However these more equalitarian households remain a minority. In as many as two-thirds of the families with employed wives, husbands made virtually no additional contribution to after-dinner chores.

Nor do the Berks see the child care activities fathers engage in during the evening as any great alteration of the traditional division of housework. They interpret these as "backup labor" for a series of tasks which remain primarily women's responsibility. They point out that at this time of day child care typically consists of playing and talking with children, which is not particularly burdensome. Moreover while husbands are occupied with these fairly pleasant tasks, their wives are tied up with the drudgery of after-dinner chores.

In view of all the changes in the technology of housework and in the women's roles outside the home, the persistence of traditional ways in the allocation of housework is altogether unexpected. Although employment reduces the time women spend in housework and thereby increases men's share of labor, the responsibility for housework is still women's, and tasks are not reallocated in any significant way to men.

What determines the division of housework, and why is it so resistant to change? Economic and practical factors have some role in this. As Lein (forthcoming) and her colleagues show through in-depth interviews with employed couples, wives' longer hours of housework are interpreted as their compensation for lower wages in the marketplace. Because their earnings are less, they contribute more work inside the home. But by itself this interpretation explains neither why nonemployed wives work as long as they do nor why the sex-typing of jobs remains so deeply ingrained even when wives are employed.

Perhaps a wife feels she must spend a great deal of time working in the home to equalize her role in the marriage partnership. In her eyes the investment may be threatened if her husband takes on anything but a narrow range of tasks in the home. Furthermore, men typically have little experience or interest in the "feminine tasks," so they perform them grudgingly or ineptly, which of course reinforces the traditional pattern. It may simply be easier for wives to do things themselves. Indeed, Lein and her colleagues found that women were reluctant to relinquish primary responsibility for the household. This reasoning is also supported by national survey data, reported in a later section, which show that wives do not want their husbands to share housework.

Married Women and Wage Earning

That so little has changed in the division of housework becomes all the more striking in view of the important role wives now have in wage earning. With nearly half of all married women in the labor force, it appears that employment rather than full-time housework is becoming the norm. The growth in labor force participation has been most striking among younger wives. Over the past 20 years the rate of employment of wives ages 24–35, now at nearly 50 percent, has almost doubled (U.S. Department of Labor, 1976a). Statistics also show that married women are highly committed to employment. Nearly three-fourths of the employed wives and as many as two-thirds of the employed mothers with preschool children hold full-time jobs (U.S. Department of Labor, 1975a: A-15-18). Most employed wives (63 percent) also worked a full year in 1975, and among those who worked only part of the year, 43 percent would prefer full-time employment, but due to responsibilities in the home were unable to take it (U.S. Department of Labor, 1976a: 24).

The importance of married women's role in the labor force is also measured by earnings. In 1975 the median proportion of income contributed by the wife was a sizable 26 percent (U.S. Department of Labor 1975b: A-30). However, as Carolyn Shaw Bell (1974) points out, an average conceals the full impact of the wife's contribution. First, some familes depend substantially on the wife's earnings. While it is true that the proportion of wives who contribute over half of family income is only 12 percent, in numbers this reflects nearly three million women. To the families of these women, usually at the lower income levels, the earnings are vital. Second, the earnings of wives make an important contribution to raising the family's standard of living: "Between 1950 and 1974, median annual income (adjusted for inflation) of families more than doubled when the wife was in the paid labor force and rose by four-fifths when she was not" (Hayghe, 1976: 15). Third, when wives are employed full time and full year, they contribute considerably more than one-quarter of family income. In 1975, 41 percent of the wives in the labor force were fully and steadily employed, and they provided 39 percent of family income (U.S. Department of Labor, 1975b: A-30, 1976b: 21).

The contribution married women make to family income becomes more impressive when it is recognized that their earnings are lower than married men's. A detailed breakdown of earnings revealed that 55 percent of employed wives earn less than $5500 a year while only 15 percent of husbands earn so little (U.S. Bureau of Census, 1977: 116). At the other end of the income hierarchy, as few as 2 percent of wives have a yearly income over $15,000 in comparison to 32 percent of employed husbands.

Are wives' earnings lower than husbands' because they are not fully or steadily employed? According to measures of differential participation and the wage-earning role of wives, to some degree, this is ture. More detailed analysis reveals, however, that other factors are also important. To begin with, wives' lesser attachment to the labor force is not rooted in family responsibilities alone. For example, data from the Bureau of Labor Statistics tell us that a substantial number of wives who are usually employed part time would prefer full-time work. In 1974, 27 percent of all wives were employed part time because of layoffs, short workweeks, and an inability to find full-time jobs (U.S. Department of Labor, 1976a: 81). The comparable figure for husbands was 14 percent.

Nor is part-year work entirely a matter of preference or family responsibilities. Generally turnover rates are higher in low-level occupations. With little pay, interest, or opportunity for advancement, there is less incentive to stay on a job. Specifically, in 1971, full-year employment was true of 77 percent of professionally employed wives, 65 percent of wives in clerical and sales occupations, and a little over 50 percent of the wives who worked in crafts, as operatives and in service jobs (U.S. Bureau of Census, 1972: Table 68). On the average, low-level occupations figure more heavily in the work experience of women than of men. Thus, when turnover rates are compared for men and women in similar jobs, the differentials are greatly reduced (U.S. Department of Labor, 1972: 269; Bergmann and Adelman, 1973: 511; Sawhill, 1973: 393).

Furthermore, differences in income between husbands and wives are not entirely due to the lesser participation of wives. Single women tend to work longer hours and more continuously than married women, but their earnings are still lower than men's. Although adjustments for participation, experience, and marital status reduce the earnings differential between men and women, a wide gap remains unexplained (compare Suter and Miller, 1973; Fuchs, 1971, 1974).

Other data suggest that structural and cultural factors underlie the differential earnings of husbands and wives. One important cause of women's lower earnings is the kinds of jobs they hold. The jobs held by men and women are so different that they essentially participate in two different labor markets. When earnings are adjusted for occupational differences, the gap between the sexes is almost removed (Bergmann and Adelman, 1973; Fuchs, 1971; Kohen, 1975; Sanborn, 1964; Sawhill, 1973). As recently as 1970, 73 percent of all female workers were in occupations where women were grossly overrepresented—that is, they accounted for 45 to 100 percent of the workers in the particular jobs. The figure was virtually identical ten years earlier—72 percent (Bergmann and Adelman, 1973: 511). Although some women entered male occupations in the 1960s, these gains were neutralized, for the largest employment gains for women were in occupations which were predominantly female. Nevertheless, between 1962 and 1974, women did make slight gains in employment in certain predominantly male professional and service occupations (Garfinkle, 1975: 27).

Women's jobs in the labor force are an extension of the tasks they perform in the home. Jobs with a high proportion of female workers typically require charm, sociability, nurturance, or other characteristics which are believed to be sex linked. They are seldom supervisory positions, least of all over men. They include the lower-level professions, such as nursing and teaching, clerical occupations, private household work, operative work in the clothing and textile industries, and certain kinds of service occupations, such as waitresses, practical nurses, and attendants (Oppenheimer, 1975). Furthermore, as Oppenheimer (1975) and Sawhill (1973) have shown, female jobs require little on-the-job training and in turn provide little opportunity for advancement. In other words, the meaning of job experience is very different for men and for women. Even with continuous employment, women have considerably less opportunity for advancement than does the average male worker.

Thus, occupational segregation is a primary factor in the earnings gap between husbands and wives, although differential participation and wage discrimination (unequal pay for equal work) are also important. As Isabel Sawhill (1973: 394) observes, factors such as these make the "crucial difference larger than it otherwise would be." But important questions about occupational segregation still remain unexplained. Its roots include such diverse phenomena as early socialization and discrimination by employers, but the exact contribution of each factor is not fully understood.

In summary, the patterning of women's work in the labor force complements the division of work in the home. In both domains we have seen the operation of deeply ingrained beliefs about the distinct roles of the sexes. The role of women in the labor force is limited not only by their real burdens in the home but also by the expectation they and others hold that their primary role is in the home. Higher wages are not the sole reason husbands spend relatively little time working in the home, as this too is tied to beliefs that housework is primarily women's work.

The in-depth studies of families made by Lein and her colleagues provide insights on the dynamics of these pressures and counter pressures. They find that although women are spending more time in paid work, in their eyes and in their husbands' they are not undertaking the primary breadwinner function. Men, in turn, see wage earning as their primary role in the family and higher earnings reinforce their own sense of financial responsibility. Thus, any wage earning on the part of the wife and any housework on the part of the husband are interpreted as helping each other in fulfilling their respective role-assigned responsibilities (Lein, forthcoming).

Attitudes on Family and Work Roles

In their second study of Middletown, the Lynds (1937) were impressed by how little change had occurred in attitudes about women's role in the home. Although the employment of wives increased in the decade since their first study, people still believed that women should be at home. According to the Lynds, wives entered the labor force in response to the pressures of a rising standard of living rather than out of disinterest in the family. Changes in family roles were proceeding, as they put it, in a "devious way," as merely an incidental response to the quest for more income rather than by an underlying shift in beliefs about family life (Lynd and Lynd, 1937: 181). The Lynds' description of the way family roles change remains surprisingly accurate. Although there is every appearance of change today, the patterning of work in the home and in the labor force continues to reflect deep cultural beliefs about the duties and responsibilities of the sexes. As the Lynds observed, change in employment and family roles has not proceeded from diminished support for traditional values. Rather, cultural support for the employment of wives had lagged behind actual participation in the labor force. Still slower to change are attitudes about equality of roles in the home.

Today scarcely a majority of the American public sees the sharing of work in marriage as an ideal. Recent Roper poll data show that 50 percent of women and 48 percent of men feel that the most satisfying and interesting way of life is "traditional marriage with the husband assuming the responsibility for providing for the family and the wife running the house and taking care of children" (Roper Organization, Inc. 1974: 31). Women's responses are only slightly more equalitarian than men's. Although the young are less traditional than others, they are more conservative than one might expect given the wave of media publicity, for their preferences refer to sharing "more" than in traditional marriage, not to an equal sharing of home and wage-earning responsibilities. Only 61 percent of women aged 18 to 20 and 51 percent of young men approved of this limited equality in marriage.

To disentangle beliefs about the various components of the new equality in marriage, consider attitudes concerning married women's work in the labor force. The Gallup poll shows that 70 percent of the population now approves of a "married woman earning money in business or industry if she has a husband capable of supporting her" (Greene, 1976: 35). There is little difference between the sexes, and approval increases to 80 percent of both men and women who are younger than 30. Yet when questions about employment refer to mothers, attitudes become overwhelmingly conservative, even among the young. When respondents in a 1968 Department of Labor survey, commonly called the Parnes Study, were asked how they felt about mothers with children between six and twelve years of age taking a full-time job outside the home, only 22 percent of the sample expressed a permissive view (U.S. Department of Labor, 1970: 46). That these responses were not correlated to age or to presence of children suggests how fundamental this belief is. Although many of the respondents were employed mothers they had not rationalized their work outside the home. Nonetheless, support for employed mothers will probably increase as more of them enter the labor force. A finding of Mason et al. (1976) justifies this expectation. Their analysis shows a sharp drop between 1964 and 1974 in the belief that children suffer by a mother's employment.

Nonetheless, most wives still see housework and family care as their responsibility, not as tasks to be shared with their husbands. My analysis of national survey data for 1965–1966 found that as many as 84 percent of nonemployed and 70 percent of employed wives wanted no additional "help" from their husbands even though they reported receiving only two or three hours of assistance. This intriguing finding testifies to the depth of traditional beliefs. Even the conventional phrasing of the question, referring to the amount of "help," reflects the belief that housework is women's responsibility. Beliefs do now appear to be changing. A comparison of a 1970 and a 1974 study reveals a sharp increase in the number of wives who endorsed a sharing of cooking, cleaning and other household tasks with their husbands (Mason et al., 1976). Furthermore, a 1976 Gallup survey found that half the males interviewed believed that husbands should do as much housework and child care as their wives, if wives were employed (Hunt, 1976).

The current decline in traditional beliefs about sex equality parallels the rise of the so-called "women's liberation movement." This movement may not in itself be a cause of change, but rather a reflection of women's rising status. Whatever role the women's liberation movement might have in changing attitudes is not a simple one. For example, Mason and her colleagues suggest that if the movement had a "unique influence" on sex role ideology, attitudinal change would be much greater after 1970, when women's liberation attracted more attention and publicity than before. However, their data do not show a sharp increase in support for sex equality after 1970; attitudinal change proceeded at a steady pace between 1964 and 1974.

What then explains the recent change in attitudes? Mason and colleagues (1976) and the Parnes Study (U.S. Department of Labor, 1970) found that attitudes were much less traditional among women with higher education and recent experience in employment. Age itself was not significantly correlated with attitudes. Instead, the expression of more liberated attitudes among the young was found to be a reflection of their higher rates of employment and education. More generally, attitude change is no doubt tied to the changing composition of the population with respect to education and employment. The women's liberation movement may then provide ideological justification for this change.

Coupled with other factors, the increased education and employment of women should encourage more support for sexual equality in the future. One cannot rule out the possibility of a backlash, a sense that things have already gone too far, or even that trends may reverse. Any such change, however, would require a shift in a wide range of social and economic trends. As families increasingly depend on women's wages and women's own commitment to work increases, it is difficult to believe that this would happen.

Conclusions and Policy Implications

The sharp differences in the work roles of men and women discussed in this chapter raise a wide set of policy issues connected with equalizing the economic position of the sexes and with the organization of housework, especially child care. Considerable controversy surrounds any proposals for change in these areas because the belief is widespread that it will damage the already fragile family. When Richard Nixon, for example, vetoed the Child Development Bill of 1969, he warned that federal provision of services will lead to "collectivization" of child rearing and the demise of the family (Bane, 1976: 115). In the Supreme Court case which introduced this chapter, Secretary Califano argued that the gender qualification in the program providing benefits to children of unemployed fathers but not unemployed mothers is "substantially related to the achievement of an important governmental objective: the need to deter real or pretended desertion by the father" (Califano v. Westcott, 1979).

In view of present conditions, however, such nostalgic notions about what the family should be are not defensible. As the Carnegie Council on Children concluded in its 1977 report, "We may yearn for the story book picture of untroubled families in charge of their own destinies, but we now live with a reality very different from this. It is time . . . to face up to the many new shapes that are emerging for the old family and to bring our ideas and policies into line with reality" (Keniston et al., 1977: 213).

Women's lower salaries and limited career opportunities are often justified by the belief that they do not need to support a family. If this assumption were ever valid, it certainly is not today. With divorce rates at 30 to 40 percent and rising (Glick and Norton, 1977), women can no longer depend on the salaries and benefits earned by their husbands. The number of female-headed families is growing tremendously, and these families are a great deal more likely than are husband-wife families to have low incomes. In 1976, one out of every three such families was living below the officially defined poverty level, compared with only one of 18 husband-wife families. By contrast, the families headed by men rarely face the economic difficulties of families headed by women. Only one of nine families headed by a man without a wife present was living below the poverty level and a much smaller proportion of these families had children under eighteen (Johnson, 1977: 32).

Currently women and children bear a disproportionate cost of divorce. Reviewing evidence from a national survey over the period 1967 to 1975, Mary Jo Bane provides data on this problem (1976: 132–133):

> The women who did not remarry had an average real income drop of 29.3 percent, while the income of men who did not remarry dropped 19.2 percent. Since the women's incomes usually had to support more people than the men's, the differences in the ratio of income to needs dropped 6.7 percent after the separation, while that of the men *rose* 30 percent.

Many of the nation's children are now economically deprived. In 1974, 51 percent of children under eighteen in female-headed families were living in poverty (Bane, 1976: 118).

Although the reform of alimony, child support, and social security is a beginning, it would not fully solve the problems created by women's present economic position. A man with a yearly income of $12,500 may be at the national average, but these earnings cannot be stretched to adequately support two households.[5] A comprehensive restructuring of employment is also required. This would involve, as the Carneigie Commission on Children recommends, full employment—bringing the general unemployment rate down to between 3.5 and 5 percent (numbers which some would say are still too high); fair employment—reducing job barriers and job ceilings for racial minorities and women; and more flexible working conditions—flexitime, the upgrading and structuring of part-time jobs with full benefits, pregnancy leave, and parental leave for child rearing (Keniston et al., 1977: 216–218).

Present conditions also call for a reorganization of housework both to reduce what now can be an inordinately long working day and to enable women to participate more fully in the labor force. The possibilities here range from a reallocation of tasks to husbands, the adoption of simpler living styles less oriented to consumption, and increased public involvement in financing and the provision of services, particularly in child care.

Given the record of the past, the prospect for husbands taking on more housework is not good. However, if, as recent data suggests, attitudes about men's and women's responsibilities in the home change, then husbands may increasingly come to share home responsibilities with employed wives. But taking the past as a guide, it will be some time before these deeply ingrained attitudes and behaviors change in any substantial ways.

The high standards of consumption in this society have been a fundamental factor in the long hours women spend in housework (see Vanek, 1979). While a multitude of goods have been labor saving, these same products, as well as all the other items owned by families today, require service and care. Consuming more is so deeply ingrained in modern society that it is difficult to imagine people will voluntarily lower aspirations and acquire less. Yet rising inflation, energy shortages, and women's growing commitment to market work may cause families to shift living patterns away from the goods-intensive styles of the past. Even if dramatic shifts in living patterns do not occur, families may make greater use of commercial services such as eating out, commercial laundries, and child care.

Although public involvement in certain family functions, in particular child rearing and care, is a matter of great controversy and even fear, the government has been underwriting a greater share of the costs of raising children. For example, Bane (1978) presents data which show a dramatic growth in government funding and provision for child care. This includes support for nursery schools and kindergartens, Head Start, and federally funded day care for the poor. It also includes tax credits for the costs of child care. Since the responsibility for the costs of caring for children is already shared between parents and society, Bane (1978: 2) points out that the "policy question is not whether government should begin to 'interfere' in child rearing, but whether government should extend or change its participation." In an era of budget austerity, she suggests that the major policy issue will not focus on the expansion of day care centers, but on the expansion of preschool education and on tax-transfer policies.

Finally, greater recognition should be given to the socially and economically productive work that takes place in the home. Recently, for example, the Carter Administration proposed plans for welfare reform excluding single parents responsible for preschool children from the work requirement. Since married women will be doing more work in the home than married men for some years to come, programs are needed to improve the economic status of the housewife. Legislation now provides funds to retrain "displaced homemakers." Divorce insurance has been proposed. And reform might also extend to providing social security payments and health and retirement insurance— the basic benefits which normally accrue to workers—to housewives.

The persistence of traditional attitudes and behavior in the face of changes in the family and in the world of work has created strains and discontinuities which have damaging effects on the economic and social well-being of individuals and families. Policies outlined here will provide more options than are now available and will allow husbands and wives to choose more realistically about employment, family demands, or ending an intolerable marriage. In particular, the improvement in the economic position of women will probably result in a further reduction in marriage and in child bearing. However, the result of any such programs should also be improvements in the quality of life of children and in the day-to-day living of husbands and wives.

Notes

1. The approach was developed by Blood and Wolfe (1960), who argued that husbands and wives have different roles in the family because they vary in the time and skills required to perform these roles. Blood and Wolfe have been widely criticized not only for the assumptions their

theory was based on, but also because their own data were inadequate to prove the theory. However, traces of "resource theory" are incorporated in more recent treatments of family roles, for example, in Young and Willmott (1973).

2. This approach (compare Coser and Coser, 1974; Epstein, 1971; Glazer, 1976; Sawhill, 1973) argues that cultural conditioning, beginning very early in life and continuing through the life cycle, makes the interests and training of men and women so distinct that the job preparation and career interests of the sexes are very different. Additionally, employers perceive women as a risk and exclude them from high-level jobs. That this perception is often erroneous does not matter; the effect is the same as if it were true. In turn women, limited in their participation in the labor force, then invest their time and energies in the family. By doing so, they complete, as the Cosers put it, the self-fulfilling prophecy that women have a higher emotional involvement in the family.

3. Unless otherwise specified, the statistics introduced throughout this chapter refer only to married women whose husbands are present, to married men whose wives are present, or to families with both a husband and a wife.

4. Stafford and Duncan examined not only the effect of wages on own time, but also the effect of spouse's wages on own time. Since not all married women earn wages, they took women's shadow wage (as measured by education) in determining how married men's time in housework was affected by wives' wages. However, when looking at the time patterns of married employed women, they took the acutal wage rate and husbands' education as the comparable measures.

5. Census figures for 1977 report median income for families and unrelated individuals as $12,700.

References

Bane, M. J. (1976) Here To Stay. New York: Basic Books.
———— (1978) "Child care in the United States." (unpublished)
Bell, C. S. (1974) "Working women's contribution to family income." Eastern Economic Journal 1: 185–201.
Bergmann, B. and I. Adelman (1973) "The 1973 report of the President's Council of Economic Advisors: the economic role of women." American Economic Review 63: 509–514.
Berk, R. and S. F. Berk (1979) Labor and Leisure at Home: Content and Organization of the Household Day. Beverly Hills, CA: Sage Publications.
Blood, R. and D. Wolfe (1960) Husbands and Wives. New York: Free Press.
Califano, Secretary of Health, Education and Welfare v. Westcott et al. (1979) U.S. Code, 99 S. Ct.
Coser, L. and R. L. Coser (1974) "The housewife and her 'greedy family,' " pp. 89–100 in L. Coser, Greedy Institutions. New York: Free Press.
Epstein, C. (1971) Women's Place. Berkeley: University of California Press.
Fuchs, V. (1971) "Differences in hourly earnings between men and women." Monthly Labor Review 94: 9–15.
———— (1974) "Recent trends and long-run prospects for female earnings." American Economic Review 64: 236–242.
Garfinkle, S. (1975) "Occupations of women and black workers, 1962–74." Monthly Labor Review 9l: 25–35.
Glazer N. (1976) "The caste position of women: housewifery." Presented at the annual meeting of the American Sociological Association, New York City, September.
Glick, P. and A. Norton (1977) "Marrying, divorcing and living together in the U.S. today." Population Bulletin 32: 1–41.
Greene, S. (1976) "Attitudes toward working women have 'long way to go.' " Gallup Opinion Index—Political, Social and Economic Trends, 128.
Hayghe, H. (1976) "Families and the rise of working wives—an overview." Monthly Labor Review 92: 12–19
Hunt, M. (1976) "Today's man: Redbook's exclusive Gallup survey on the emerging male." Redbook (October): 112 ff.
Johnson, B. (1977) "Women who head families, 1970–77: their numbers rose, income lagged." Monthly Labor Review 101, 2: 32–37.

Keniston, K. and Carnegie Council on Children (1977) All Our Children. New York: Harcourt Brace Jovanovich.

Kohen, A. (1975) "Differences in the market," pp. 1256–1262 in H. Kahne (ed.) Special Issue on Economic Perspectives on the Roles of Women in the American Economy, Journal of Economic Literature 13: 1249–1292.

Lein, L. (forthcoming) "Male participation in home life: impact of work, social networks and family dynamics on the allocation of tasks." Family Coordinator.

Lynd, R. and H. M. Lynd (1937) Middletown in Transition. New York: Harcourt Brace Jovanovich.

Mason, K., J. Cazijka, and S. Arber (1976) "Change in U.S. women's sex-role attitudes, 1964–1974." American Sociological Review 41: 573–596.

Oppenheimer, V. (1975) "The sex-labeling of jobs," pp. 307–25 in M. Mednick et al. (eds.) Women and Achievement. New York: John Wiley.

Robinson, J. (1977) Changes in Americans' Use of Time: 1965–1975. Cleveland: Communications Center of Cleveland State University.

Roper Organization, Inc. (1974) The Virginia Slims American Women's Opinion Poll, Volume 3: A Survey of Attitudes of Women on Marriage, Divorce, the Family and American's Changing Sexual Morality. New York: Author.

Sanborn, H. (1964) "Pay differences between men and women." Industrial and Labor Relations Review 17: 534–550.

Sawhill, I. (1973) "The economics of discrimination against women: some new findings." Journal of Human Resources 8: 383–396.

Suter L. and H. Miller (1973) "Income differences between men and career women." American Journal of Sociology 78: 962–974.

Stafford, F. and G. Duncan (1977) "The use of time and technology by households in the United States." (unpublished)

U.S. Bureau of Census (1972) Money Income in 1971 of Families and Persons in the United States. Washington, DC: Government Printing Office.

——— (1977) Money Income in 1975 of Families and Persons in the United States. Washington, DC: Government Printing Office.

U.S. Department of Labor (1970) "Dual careers: a longitudinal study of labor market experience of women." Manpower Research Monograph 21.

——— (1972) "Facts about women's absenteeism and labor turnover," pp. 265–271 in N. Glazer-Malbin and Y. Wuehrer (eds.) Women in Man-Made World. Chicago: Rand McNally.

——— (1975a) Marital and Family Characteristics of the Labor Force, March 1974. Washington, DC: Government Printing Office.

——— (1975b) Marital and Family Characteristics of the Labor Force, March 1975. Washington, DC: Government Printing Office.

——— (1976a) Handbook of Labor Statistics 1975—Reference Edition. Washington, DC: Government Printing Office.

——— (1976b) Work Experience of the Population in 1975. Washington, DC: Government Printing Office.

Vanek, J. (1979) "Time and women's work." (unpublished)

Walker, K. and M. Woods (1976) Time Use: A Measure of Household Production of Family Goods and Services. Washington, DC: American Home Economics Association.

Young, M. and P. Willmott (1973) The Symmetrical Family. New York: Pantheon.

Cultural Contradictions and Sex Roles:
The Masculine Case

Mirra Komarovsky

In a rapidly changing society, normative malintegration is commonly assumed to lead to an experience of strain. Earlier research (Komarovsky, 1946) on cultural contradictions and the feminine sex role showed that women at an eastern college suffered uncertainty and insecurity because the norms for occupational and academic success conflicted with norms for the traditional feminine role. A replication (Wallin, 1950) at a western university reported agreement in the questionnaire data, but the interview material led the investigator to conclude that the problem was less important to the women than the earlier study had suggested. However, Wallin pointed out that, in his replication, the respondents were oriented to marriage, while the Komarovsky study had included an appreciable number of women oriented to careers. This finding tended to support the view that women who were satisfied with the traditional female role would show less strain when confronted with contrary expectations than women who hoped to have both a rewarding career and a rewarding marriage.

Men are also confronted with contradictory expectations. For example, the traditional norm of male intellectual superiority conflicts with a newer norm of intellectual companionship between the sexes. This research investigated the extent of masculine strain experienced by 62 college males randomly from the senior class of an Ivy League male college. The study included a variety of status relationships, but the results reported here deal with intellectual relationships with female friends and attitudes toward working wives.

Methods

Each of the 62 respondents contributed a minimum of three two-hour interviews and also completed a set of five schedules and two psychological tests, the California Personality Inventory and the Gough Adjective Check List. The psychological tests were interpreted by a clinical psychologist. The 13-page interview guide probed for data on actual role performance, ideal role expectations and limits of tolerance, personal preferences, perception of role partner's ideal expectations, and relevant attitudes of significant others. Direct

Reprinted from the *American Journal of Sociology* (January 1973), pp. 873–884, by permission of the University of Chicago Press. Copyright © 1973 by The University of Chicago. All rights reserved. For an expanded version, see Chapter 1 in Mirra Komarovsky's, *Dilemmas of Masculinity: A Study of College Youth*, W. W. Norton & Co., paper, 1976.

questions on strains came only at the end of this sequence. Extensive use was made of quasi-projective tests in the form of brief episodes. The total response rate of the original sample ($N = 79$) was 78%.

Intellectual Relationships with Female Friends

When fewer women attended college, the norm of male intellectual superiority might have had some validation in experience. But today college women are more rigorously selected than men in terms of high school academic performance (*Princeton Alumni Weekly*, 1971). Nevertheless, social norms internalized in early childhood are resistant to change. The first question for this research was, How many men would show insecurity or strain in their intellectual relationships with women when confronted with both bright women and the traditional norm of male superiority?

The Troubled Third

Of the 53 men for whom the data were available (six did not date, three could not be classified reliably), 30% reported that intellectual insecurity or strain with dates was a past or current problem. This number included men who, having experienced stress, sought to avoid it by finding dates who posed no intellectual threat. The following excerpts from interviews illustrate the views of this troubled third:

> I enjoy talking to more intelligent girls, but I have no desire for a deep relationship with them. I guess I still believe that the man should be more intelligent.
>
> * * *
>
> I may be a little frightened of a man who is superior to me in some field of knowledge, but if a girl knows more than I do, I resent her.
>
> * * *
>
> Once I was seeing a philosophy major, and we got along quite well. We shared a similar outlook on life, and while we had some divergent opinions, I seemed better able to document my position. One day, by chance, I heard her discussing with another girl an aspect of Kant that just the night before she described to me as obscure and confusing. But now she was explaining it to a girl so clearly and matter-of-factly that I felt sort of hurt and foolish. Perhaps it was immature of me to react this way.

The mode of strain exemplified by these men might be termed "a socially structured scarcity of resources for role fulfillment." Apart from the ever-present problem of lack of time and energy, some social roles are intrinsically more difficult to fulfill, given the state of technical skills, the inherent risks, or other scarcities of facilities. The strain of a doctor called upon to treat a disease for which modern medicine has no cure is another case in point.

Selective dating and avoidance of superior women solved the problem for some troubled youths, but this offered no solution for six respondents who yearned for intellectual companionship with women but dreaded the risk of invidious comparisons. The newly emerging norm of intellectual companionship with women creates a mode of strain akin to one Merton and Barber (1963) termed "sociological ambivalence." Universalistic values tend to replace sex-linked desiderata among some male undergraduates who now value originality and intelligence in female as well as in male associates. The conflict arises when, at the same time, the norm of masculine intellectual superiority has not been relinquished, as exemplified in the following case: "I am beginning to feel," remarked one senior about his current girl friend, "that she is not bright enough. She never says anything that would make me sit up and say, 'Ah, that's interesting!' I want a girl who has some defined crystal of her own personality and does not merely echo my thoughts." He recently met a girl who fascinated him with her quick and perceptive intelligence, but this new girl made him feel "nervous and humble."

The problem of this youth is to seek the rewards of valued attributes in a woman without arousing in himself feelings of inferiority. It may be argued that in a competitive society this conflict tends to characterize encounters with males as well. Nonetheless, if similar problems exist between two males, the utility curve is shaped distinctively by the norm of male intellectual superiority because mere equality with a woman may be defined as a defeat or a violation of a role prescription.

The Adjusted Majority

The 37 students who said that intellectual relationships with dates were not a problem represented a variety of types. Eleven men felt superior to their female friends. In two or three cases, the relationships were judged equalitarian with strong emphasis on the rewards of intellectual companionship. In contrast, several men—and their dates—had little interest in intellectual concerns. In a few instances the severity of other problems overwhelmed this one. Finally, some eight men were happily adjusted despite the acknowledged intellectual superiority of their women friends. What makes for accommodation to this still deviant pattern?

In seven of the eight cases, the female friend had some weakness which offset her intellectual competence, such as emotional dependence, instability, or a plain appearance, giving the man a compensating advantage. A bright, studious, but relatively unattractive girl may be acceptable to a man who is not as certain of his ability to win a sexually desirable female as he is of his mental ability. In only one of the eight cases the respondent admitted that his steady girl was "more independent and less emotional, actually a little smarter than I. But she doesn't make me feel like a dunce." Her superiority was tolerable because she provided a supportive relationship which he needed and could accept with only mild, if any, emotional discomfort.

Another factor which may account for the finding that 70% of the sample reported no strain is the fact that intellectual qualities are no longer considered unfeminine and that the imperative of male superiority is giving way to the ideal of companionship between equals. This interpretation is supported by responses to two standard questions and by the qualitative materials of the interviews. A schedule testing beliefs on 16 psychological sex differences asked whether the reasoning ability of men is greater than that of women. Only 34% of the respondents "agreed" or "agreed somewhat," while 20% were "uncertain"; almost half "disagreed" or "disagreed somewhat."

Another question was put to all 62 respondents: what are for you personally the three or four most desirable characteristics in a woman (man) who is to be close to you? Of all the traits men desired in a woman, 33% were in the "intellectual" cluster, in contrast with 44% of such traits if the friend were male. The fact that the sex difference was not larger seems significant. The major difference in traits desired in male and female intimates (apart from sexual attractiveness and love) was the relative importance of "social amenities and appearance" for women.

The qualitative data amply document the fact that the majority of the respondents ideally hoped to share their intellectual interests with their female as well as their male friends. To be sure, what men occasionally meant by intellectual rapport with women was having an appreciative listener: "I wouldn't go out," declared one senior, "with any girl who wasn't sharp and perceptive enough to catch an intellectual subtlety." But for the majority a "meaningful relationship" with a woman included also a true intellectual interchange and sharing. As one senior put it, "A guy leaving a movie with his date expects her to make a stimulating comment of her own and not merely echo his ideas." Another man wanted a date with whom he could "discuss things that guys talk about," and still a third man exclaimed: "What I love about this girl is that she is on my level, that I can never speak over her head."

It is this ideal of intellectual companionship with women, we suggest, that may explain the relative adjustment of the men in this sphere. As long as the expectation of male superiority persisted, anything near equality on the part of the woman carried the threatening message to the men: "I am not the intellectually *superior* male I am expected to be." But when the ideal of intellectual companionship between equals replaces the expectation of male superiority, the pressure upon the man eases and changes. Now he need only reassure himself that he is not inferior to his date, rather than that he is markedly superior to her. Once the expectation of clear superiority is relinquished, varieties of relationships may be accommodated. Given a generally similar intellectual level, comparative evaluations are blurred by different interests, by complementary strengths and weaknesses, and occasionally by rationalizations ("she studies harder") and other devices.

One final explanation remains to be considered. May the intellectual self-confidence of the majority be attributed in part to women's readiness to play down their intellectual abilities? That such behavior occurs is attested by a number of studies (Komarovsky, 1946; Wallin, 1950).

When respondents were asked to comment upon a projective story about a girl "playing dumb" on dates, the great majority expressed indignation at such "dishonest, condescending" behavior. But some three or four found the behavior praiseworthy. As one senior put it, "Her intentions were good; she wanted to make the guy feel important."

Although we did not interview the female friends of our respondents, a few studies indicate that such playing down of intellectual ability by women is less common today than in the 1940s. Questionnaires filled out at an eastern women's college duplicated earlier studies by Wallin (1950) and Komarovsky (1946). The 1970 class was a course on the family, and the 1971 class probably recruited a relatively high proportion of feminists. Table 1 indicates that the occasional muting of intellectual competence by women may have played some role in the adjustment of the men, but it would appear to be a minor and decreasing role.

The hypothesis that the emerging ideal of intellectual companionship serves as a buffer against male strain needs a test which includes (as our study did not) some index of intellectual ability as well as indices of norms and of strain. Of the 27 men who disagreed with the proposition that the reasoning ability of men is greater than that of women, only five reported intellectual insecurity with women, whereas of the 34 men who believed in masculine superiority or were uncertain, nine experienced strain. Most troubled were the 12 men who were "uncertain"; four of them were insecure with women. Case analyses suggest that the interplay between a man's experience, personality, and beliefs is complex. For example, one traditional man, having confessed feelings of intellectual insecurity on dates, clung all the more tenaciously to the belief in superior male reasoning ability.

Some men took the "liberal" position on sex differences as a matter of principle. Of the nine black students, eight rejected the belief in male superiority, perhaps because they opposed group comparisons in intelligence. Again, in some cases, the direction of the causal relation was the reverse of the one we posited: men who felt in fact intellectually superior were hospitable to the "liberal" ideology. In view of these complexities, our suggestive results as to the positive association between egalitarian norms and the absence of strain remain to be tested in larger samples.

Attitudes Toward Future Wives' Occupational Roles

The ethos on the campus of this study clearly demanded that men pay at least lip service to liberal attitudes toward working wives. If the initial responses to structured questions were accepted as final, the majority would have been described as quite feminist in ideology. But further probing revealed qualifications which occasionally almost negated the original response. For

Table 1. Readiness of Women to Play Down Intellectual Abilities (%)

	Wallin 1950 (N = 1963)	Sociology class 1970* (N = 33)	Advanced sociology class 1971* (N = 55)
When on dates how often have you pretended to be intellectually inferior to the man?			
Very often, often, or several times.	32	21	15
Once or twice	26	36	30
Never.	42	43	55
In general, do you have any hesitation about revealing your equality or superiority to men in intellectual competence?			
Have considerable or some hesitation. . .	35	21	13
Very little hesitation.	39	33	32
None at all . . . . '.	26	46	55

*Mirra Komarovsky, unpublished study.

example, an affirmative answer to a proposition, "It is appropriate for a mother of a preschool child to take a fulltime job," was, upon further questioning, conditioned by such restrictions as "provided, of course, that the home was run smoothly, the children did not suffer, and the wife's job did not interfere with her husband's career." The interview provided an opportunity to get an assessment of normative expectations, ideal and operative, as well as of actual preferences. The classification of attitudes to be presented in this report is based on the total interview. Preferences reported here assume that a wife's paycheck will not be an economic necessity. The overwhelming majority were confident that their own earnings would be adequate to support the family. Throughout the discussion of working, only two or three men mentioned the temptation of a second paycheck.

Four types of response to the question of wives' working may be identified. The "traditionalists," 24% of the men, said outright that they intended to marry women who would find sufficient fulfillment in domestic, civic, and cultural pursuits without ever seeking outside jobs. "Pseudo-feminists," 16% of the men, favored having their wives work, at least when the question was at a high level of abstraction, but their approval was hedged with qualifications that no woman could meet.

The third and dominant response included almost half (48%) of the respondents. These men took a "modified traditionalist" position which favored a sequential pattern: work, withdrawal from work for child rearing, and eventual return to work. They varied as to the timing of these stages and as to the aid they were prepared to give their wives with domestic and child-rearing functions. The majority saw no substitute for the mother during her child's preschool years. Even the mother of school-age children, were she to work, should preferably be at home when the children return from school. Though they were willing to aid their wives in varying degrees, they frequently excluded specific tasks, for instance, "not the laundry," "not the cleaning," "not the diapers," and so on. Many hoped that they would be "able to assist" their wives by hiring maids. The greater the importance of the wife's work, the more willing they were to help her. (One senior, however, would help only if his wife's work were "peripheral," that is, not as important to her as her home.)

The last the "feminist" type, was the smallest, only 7% of the total. These men were willing to modify their own roles significantly to facilitate their future wives' careers. Some recommended a symmetrical allocation of tasks— "as long as it is not a complete reversal of roles." In the remaining 5% of the cases, marriage was so remote that the respondents were reluctant to venture any views on this matter.

The foregoing summary of types of male attitudes toward working wives fails to reveal the tangled web of contradictory values and sentiments associated with these attitudes. We shall presently illustrate a variety of inconsistencies. But underlying them is one basic problem. The ideological support for the belief in sharp sex role differentiation in marriage has weakened, but the belief itself has not been relinquished. Increasing skepticism about the innate character of psychological sex differences and some convergence in the ideas of masculinity and femininity (see McKee and Sherriffs, 1957, 1959) have created a strain toward consistency. The more similar the perceptions of male and female personalities (see Kammeyer, 1964), the more universalistic must be the principles of evaluation applied to both sexes. "If you could make three changes in the personality of the girl friend who is currently closest to you, what would they be?" we asked the seniors. Universalistic values were reflected in the following, as in many other responses: "I would like her to be able to set a goal for herself and strive to achieve it. I don't like to see people slacking off." Earlier cross-sex association in childhood and early adolescence (see Udry, 1966) has raised male expectation of enjoying an emotional and intellectual companionship with women. These expectations, however, coexist with the deeply rooted norm that the husband should be the superior achiever in the occupational world and the wife, the primary child rearer. One manifestation of this basic dilemma is the familiar conflict between a value and a preference. "It is only fair," declared one senior, "to let a woman do her own thing, if she wants a career. Personally, though, I would want my wife at home."

More interesting are the ambivalent attitudes manifested toward both the full-time homemaker and the career wife. The image of each contained both attractive and repellent traits. Deprecating remarks about housewifery were not uncommon, even among men with traditional views of women's roles. A conservative senior declared, "A woman who works is more interesting than a housewife." "If I were a woman," remarked another senior, "I would want a career. It must be boring sitting around the house doing the same thing day in, day out. I don't have much respect for the type of woman whom I see doing the detergent commercials on TV."

But the low esteem attached by some of the men to full-time homemaking coexisted with other sentiments and convictions which required just such a pattern for one's wife. For example, asked about the disadvantages of being a woman, one senior replied, "Life ends at 40. The woman raised her children and all that remains is garden clubs and that sort of thing—unless, of course, she has a profession." In another part of the interview, this young man explained that he enjoyed shyness in a girl and detested aggressive and ambitious women. He could never be attracted to a career woman. It is no exaggeration to conclude that this man could not countenance in a woman who was to be his wife the qualities that he himself felt necessary for a fulfilled middle age.

A similar mode of contradiction, incidentally, was also disclosed by some seniors with regard to women's majors in college. "There are no 'unfeminine' majors," declared one senior. I admire a girl who is premed or prelaw." But the universalistic yardstick which led this senior to sanction and admire professional goals for women did not extend to the means for their attainment, as he unwittingly revealed in another part of the interview. Questioned about examples of "unfeminine" behavior, this senior answered: "Excessive grade consciousness." If a premed man, anxious about admission to a good medical school, should go to see a professor about a C in chemistry, this senior would understand although he would disapprove of such preoccupation with grades. But in a woman premed he would find such behavior "positively obnoxious."

If the image of the full-time homemaker contained some alienating features, the main threat of a career wife was that of occupational rivalry, as illustrated in the following excerpt from the interviews. A senior speaks:

> I believe that it is good for mothers to return to fulltime work when the children are grown, provided the work is important and worthwhile. Otherwise, housewives get hung up with tranquilizers, because they have no outlet for their abilities. . . . Of course, it may be difficult if a wife becomes successful in her own right. A woman should want her husband's success more than he should want hers. Her work shouldn't interfere with or hurt his career in any way. He should not sacrifice his career to hers. For example, if he is transferred, his wife should follow—and not vice versa.

In sum, work for married women with grown children is approved by this young man, provided that the occupation is of some importance. But such an occupation is precisely one which carries a threat to the husband's pride.

The expectation that the husband should be the superior achiever appears still to be deeply rooted. Even equality in achievement of husband and wife is interpreted as a defeat for the man. The prospect of occupational rivalry with one's wife seems intolerable to contemplate. "My girl friend often beats me in tennis," explained one senior. "Now, losing the game doesn't worry me. It in no way reduces my manhood. But being in a lower position than a woman in a job would hurt my self-esteem."

Another student, having declared his full support for equal opportunities for women in the occupational world, added a qualification: "A woman should not be in a position of firing an employee. It is an unpleasant thing to do. Besides, it is unfair to the man who is to be fired. He may be a very poor employee, but he is still a human being and it may be just compounding his unhappiness to be fired by a woman."

In sum, the right of an able woman to a career of her choice, the admiration for women who measure up in terms of the dominant values of our society, the lure but also the threat that such women present, the low status attached to housewifery but the conviction that there is no substitute for the mother's care of young children, the deeply internalized norm of male occupational superiority pitted against the principle of equal opportunity irrespective of sex —these are some of the revealed inconsistencies.

Such ambivalences on the part of college men are bound to exacerbate role conflicts in women. The latter must sense that even the men who pay lip service to the creativity of child rearing and domesticity reserve their admiration (if occasionally tinged with ambivalence) for women achievers who measure up in terms of the dominant values of our society. It is becoming increasingly difficult to maintain a system of values for women only (Komarovsky, 1953).

Nevertheless, to infer from this account of male inconsistencies that this is an area of great stress for them would be a mistake. It is not. By and large, the respondents assumed that the women's "career and marriage" issue was solved by the sequential pattern of withdrawal and return to work. If this doomed women to second-class citizenship in the occupational world, the outcome was consistent with the conviction that the husband should be the superior achiever.

Men who momentarily worried about the fate of able women found moral anchorage in their conviction that today no satisfactory alternative to the mother's care of young children can be found. Many respondents expressed their willingness to help with child care and household duties. Similarly, many hoped to spend more time with their own children than their fathers had spent with them. But such domestic participation was defined as assistance to the wife who was to carry the major responsibility. Only two or three of the men approved a symmetrical, rather than a complementary, allocation of domestic and occupational roles. An articulate senior sums up the dominant view:

> I would not want to marry a woman whose only goal is to become a housewife. This type of woman would not have enough bounce and zest in her. I don't think a girl has much imagination if she just wants to settle down and raise a family from the very beginning. Moreover, I want an independent girl, one who has her own interests and does not always have to depend on

me for stimulation and diversion. However, when we both agree to have children, my wife must be the one to raise them. She'll have to forfeit her freedom for the children. I believe that, when a woman wants a child, she must also accept the full responsibility of child care.

When he was asked why it was necessarily the woman who had to be fully responsible for the children, he replied:

> Biology makes equality impossible. Besides, the person I'll marry will want the child and will want to care for the child. Ideally, I would hope I'm not forcing her to assume responsibility for raising the children. I would hope that this is her desire and that it is the happiest thing she can do. After we have children, it will be her career that will end, while mine will support us. I believe that women should have equal opportunities in business and the professions, but I still insist that a woman who is a mother should devote herself entirely to her children.

The low emotional salience of the issue of working wives may also be attributed to another factor. The female partners of our respondents, at this particular stage of life, did not, with a few exceptions, force the men to confront their inconsistencies. Apparently enough women will freely make the traditional-for-women adjustments—whether scaling down their own ambitions or in other ways acknowledging the prior claims of the man's career. This judgment is supported by the results of two studies of female undergraduates done on the same campus in 1943 and 1971 (Table 2). The big shift in postcollege preferences since 1943 was in the decline of women undergradutes who opted for full-time homemaking and volunteer activities. In 1971, the majority chose the sequential pattern, involving withdrawal from employment for child rearing. The proportion of committed career women who hope to return to work soon after childbirth has remained constant among freshmen and sophomores.

If women's attitudes have not changed more radically in the past 30 years it is no doubt because society has failed to provide effective supports for the woman who wishes to integrate family life, parenthood, and work on much the same terms as men. Such an option will not become available so long as the care of young children is regarded as the responsibility solely of the mother. In the absence of adequate child care centers, an acceptance of a symmetrical division of domestic and work responsibilities, or other facilitating social arrangements, the attitudes of the majority of undergraduates reflect their decision to make some kind of workable adjustments to the status quo, if not a heroic struggle to change it.

Summary

Role conflicts in women have been amply documented in numerous studies. The problem underlying this study was to ascertain whether recent social changes and consequent malintegration with regard to sex roles have created

Table 2. College Women's Attitudes toward Work and Family Patterns (%)

	Random sample of sophomore class at women's liberal college, 1943 (N = 78)	Class in introductory sociology, same college, 1971 (N = 44)
Assume that you will marry and that your husband will make enough money so that you will not have to work unless you want to. Under these circumstances, would you prefer:		
1. Not to work at all, or stop after childbirth and decide later whether to go back	50	18
2. To quit working after the birth of a child but definitely to go back to work. . . .	30	62
3. To continue working with a minimum of interruption for childbearing.	20	20

Source: Mirra Komarovsky, unpublished studies.

stressful repercussions for men as well as for women. In a randomly selected sample of 62 male seniors in an Ivy League college, nearly one-third experienced some anxiety over their perceived failure to live up to the norm of masculine intellectual superiority. This stressful minority suffered from two modes of role strain: scarcity of resources for role performance and ambivalence. The absence of strain in the majority may be explained by a changed role definition. Specifically, the normative expectation of male intellectual superiority appears to be giving way on the campus of our study to the ideal of intellectual companionship between equals. Attitudes toward working wives abounded in ambivalences and inconsistencies. The ideological supports for the traditional sex role differentiation in marriage are weakened, but the emotional allegiance to the modified traditional pattern is still strong. These inconsistencies did not generate a high degree of stress, partly, no doubt, because future roles do not require an immediate realistic confrontation. In addition, there is no gainsaying the conclusion that human beings can tolerate a high degree of inconsistency so long as it does not conflict with their self-interest.

References

Kammeyer, Kenneth. "The Feminine Role: An Analysis of Attitude Consistency." *Journal of Marriage and the Family,* 26 (August 1964): 295–305.
Komarovsky, Mirra, "Cultural Contradictions and Sex Roles." *American Journal of Sociology,* 52 (November 1946): 182–189.

Komarovsky, Mirra, *Women in the Modern World, Their Education and Their Dilemmas.* Boston: Little, Brown, 1953.
McKee, John P., and Alex C. Sherriffs, "The Differential Evaluation of Males and Females." *Journal of Personality,* 25 (March 1957): 356–363.
McKee, John P., and Alex C. Sherriffs, "Men's and Women's Beliefs, Ideals, and Self-Concepts." *American Journal of Sociology,* 64 (1959), no. 4: 456–363.
Merton, Robert K., and Elinor Barber. "Sociological Ambivalence." In *Sociological Theory, Values and Socio-cultural Change,* edited by E. A. Tiryakian. Glencoe, Ill.: Free Press, 1963.
Princeton Alumni Weekly, February 23, 1971, p. 7.
Udry, J. Richard. *The Social Context of Marriage.* Philadelphia: Lippincott, 1966.
Wallin, Paul. "Cultural Contradictions and Sex Roles: A Repeat Study." *American Sociological Review,* 15 (April 1950): 288–293.

Why Men Resist

William J. Goode

Although few if any men in the United States remain entirely untouched by the women's movement, to most men what is happening seems to be "out there" and has little direct effect on their own roles. To them, the movement is a dialogue mainly among women, conferences of women about women, a mixture of just or exaggerated complaints and shrill and foolish demands to which men need not even respond, except now and then. When men see that a woman resents a common male act of condescension, such as making fun of women in sports or management, most males are still as surprised as corporation heads are when told to stop polluting a river.

For the time being, men are correct in this perception if one focuses on the short run only. It is not often that social behavior deeply rooted in tradition alters rapidly. Over the long run, they are not likely to be correct, and indeed I believe they are vaguely uneasy when they consider their present situation. As against numerous popular commentators, I do not think we are now witnessing a return to the old ways, a politically reactionary trend, and I do not think the contemporary attack on male privilege will ultimately fail.

The worldwide demand for equality is voiced not only by women; many groups have pressed for it, with more persistence, strength, and success over the past generation than in any prior epoch of world history. It has also been pressed by more kinds of people than ever before: ethnic and racial groups, castes, subnational groups such as the Scots or Basques, classes, colonies, and political regimes. An ideal so profoundly moving will ultimately prevail, in some measure, where the structural bases for traditional dominance are weak-

From *Rethinking the Family: Some Feminist Questions* edited by Barrie Thorne and Marilyn Yalom. Copyright © 1982 by Longman Inc. Reprinted by permission of Longman Inc., New York.

ened. The ancient bases for male dominance are no longer as secure as they once were, and male resistance to these pressures will weaken.

Males will stubbornly resist, but reluctantly adjust, because women will continue to want more equality than they now enjoy and will be unhappy if they do not get it; because men on average will prefer that their women be happy; because a majority of either sex will not find an adequate substitute for the other sex; and because neither will be able to build an alternative social system alone. When dominant classes or groups cannot rig the system as much in their favor as they once did, they will work within it just the same; to revise an old adage, if that is the only roulette wheel in town, they will play it even if it is honest and fair.

To many women, the very title of my essay is an exercise in banality, for there is no puzzle. To analyze the peculiar thoughtways of men seems unnecessary, since ultimately their resistance is that of dominant groups throughout history: They enjoy an exploitive position that yields them an unearned profit in money, power, and prestige. Why should they give it up?

The answer contains of course some part of the truth, but we shall move more effectively toward equality only if we grasp much more of the truth that bitter view reveals. If it were completely true, then the greater power of men would have made all societies male-vanity cultures, in which women are kept behind blank walls and forced to work at productive tasks only with their sisters, while men laze away their hours in parasitic pleasure. In fact, one can observe that the position of women varies a good deal by class, by society, and over time, and no one has succeeded in proving that those variations are the simple result of men's exploitation.

Indeed there are inherent socioeconomic contradictions in any attempt by males to create a fully exploitative set of material advantages for all males. Moreover, there are inherent *emotional* contradictions in any effort to achieve full domination in that intimate sphere.

As to the first contradiction, women—and men in the same situation—who are powerless, slavish, and ignorant are most easily exploitable, and thus there are always some male pressures to place them in that position. Unfortunately, such women do not yield much surplus product. In fact, they do not produce much at all. Women who are freer and are more in command of productive skills, as in hunting and gathering societies and increasingly in modern industrial ones, produce far more, but they are also more resistant to exploitation or domination. Without understanding that powerful relationship, men have moved throughout history toward one or the other of these great choices, with their built-in disadvantages and advantages.

As to emotional ties, men would like to be lords of their castle and to be loved absolutely—if successful, this is the cheapest exploitative system—but in real life this is less likely to happen unless one loves in return. In that case what happens is what happens in real life: Men care about the joys and sorrows of their women. Mutual caring reduces the degree to which men are willing to exploit their wives, mothers, and sisters. More interesting, their caring also takes the form of wanting to prevent *other* men from exploiting these women when they are in the outside world. That is, men as individuals know that *they* are to be trusted, and so should have great power, but other men cannot be trusted, and so the laws should restrain such fellows.

These large sets of contrary tensions have some effect on even those contemporary men who do not believe that the present relations between men and women are unjust. Both sets, moreover, support the present trend toward greater equality. In short, men do resist, but these and other tensions prevent them from resisting as fully as they might otherwise, while not so much as a cynical interpretation of their private attitudes would expect. On the other hand, they do resist somewhat more strenuously than we should predict from their public assertion in favor of, for example, equal pay, or slogans like "liberty and justice for all."

This exposition is necessarily limited. Even to present the latest data on the supposed psychological traits of males would require more space than is available here. I shall try to avoid the temptation of simply describing men's reactions to the women's movement, although I do plan to inform you of men's attitudes toward some aspects of equality. I shall try to avoid defending men, except to the extent that explaining them may be a defense. And, as is already obvious, I shall not assert that we are on the brink of a profound, sudden change in sex-role allocations, in the direction of equality, for we must never underestimate the cunning or the staying power of those in charge. Finally, because all of you are also observers of men, it is unlikely that I can bring forward many findings that are entirely unknown to you. At best, I can suggest some fruitful, perhaps new, ways of looking at male roles. Within these limitations, I shall focus on the following themes:

1. As against the rather narrow definition of men's roles to be found in the current literature on the topic, I want to remind you of a much wider range of traditionally approved roles in this and other cultures.
2. As against the conspiracy theory of the oppression of women, I shall suggest a modest "sociology of the dominant group" to interpret men's behavior and thinking about male roles and thus some modest hypotheses about why they resist.
3. I shall point to two central areas of role behavior, occupations and domestic tasks, where change seems glacial at present and men's resistance strong.
4. As against those who feel that if utopia does not arrive with the next full moon, we should all despair, I shall point to some processes now occurring that are different from any in recorded history and that will continue to press toward more fundamental changes in men's social positions and roles in this as well as other countries of the world.

The Range of Sex Roles

Let me begin by reminding you of the standard sociological view about the allocation of sex roles. Although it is agreed that we can, with only small error, divide the population into males and females, the biological differences between the two that might affect the distribution of sex roles—which sex is supposed to do which social tasks, which should have which rights—are much too small to determine the large differences in sex-role allocation within any given society or to explain the curious doctrines that serve to uphold it. Second, even if some differences would give an advantage to men (or women) in some tasks or achievements, the overlap in talent is so great that a large minority of men (or women) could do any task as well as could members of the other sex. Third, the biological differences are too fixed in anatomy and physiology to account for the wide diversity of sex-role allocation we observe when we compare different societies over time and cultures.

Consequently, most of sex-role allocation must be explained by how we rear children, by the sexual division of labor, by the cultural definitions of what is appropriate to the sexes, and by the social pressures we put on the two sexes. Since human beings created these role assignments, they can also change them. On the other hand, these roles afford large advantages to men (e.g., opportunity, range of choices, mobility, payoffs for what is accomplished, cultivation of skills, authority, and prestige) in this and every other society we know. Consequently, men are likely to resist large alterations in roles. They will do so even though they understand that in exchange for their privileges, they have to pay high costs in morbidity, mortality, and failure.[1] As a consequence of this fact about men's position, it can be supposed that they will resist unless their ability to rig the system in their favor is somehow reduced. It is my belief that this capacity is in fact being undermined somewhat, though not at a rapid rate.

A first glance at descriptions of the male role, especially as described in the literature about mass media, social stereotypes, family roles, and personality attributes, suggests that the male role is definite, narrow, and agreed upon. Males, we are told, are pressed into a specific mold. For example, ". . . the male role prescribes that men be active, aggressive, competitive, . . . while the female role prescribes that women should be nurturant, warm, altruistic . . . and the like."[2] The male role requires the suppression of emotion, or "the male role, as personally and socially defined, requires men to appear tough, objective, striving, achieving, unsentimental. . . . If he weeps, if he shows weakness, he will likely be viewed as unmanly. . . ." Or: "Men are programmed to be strong and 'aggressive.'"[3]

We are so accustomed to reading such descriptions that we almost believe them, unless we stop to ask, first, how many men do we actually know who carry out these social prescriptions (i.e., how many are emotionally anesthetized, aggressive, physically tough and daring, unwilling or unable to give nurturance to a child)? Second, and this is the test of a social role, do they lose their membership cards in the male fraternity if they fail in these respects? If socialization and social pressures are so all-powerful, where are all the John Wayne types in our society? Or, to ask a more searching question, how seriously should we take such sex-role prescriptions if so few men live up to them?

The key fact is not that many men do not live up to such prescriptions; rather, it is that many other qualities and performances are also viewed as acceptable or admirable, and this is true even among boys, who are often thought to be strong supporters of sex stereotypes. The *macho* boy is admired, but so is the one who edits the school newspaper, who draws cartoons, or who is simply a warm friend. There are at least a handful of ways of being an admired professor. Indeed a common feminist complaint against the present system is that women are much more narrowly confined in the ways they are permitted to be professors, or members of any occupation.

But we can go further. A much more profound observation is that oppressed groups are *typically* given narrow ranges of social roles, while dominant groups afford their members a far wider set of behavior patterns, each qualitatively different but each still accepted or esteemed in varying degrees. One of the privileges granted, or simply assumed, by ruling groups, is that they can indulge in a variety of eccentricities while still demanding and getting a fair measure of authority or prestige. Consider in this connection, to cite only one spectacular example, the crotchets and quirks cultivated by the English upper classes over the centuries.

Moreover, if we enlarge our vision to encompass other times and places, the range becomes even greater. We are not surprised to observe Latin American men embrace one another, Arab or Indian boys walk together hand in hand, or seminary students being gentle. The male role prescriptions that commonly appear in the literature do not describe correctly the male ideal in Jewish culture, which embodied a love of music, learning, and literature; an avoidance of physical violence; an acceptance of tears and sentiment, nurturance, and a sensitivity to others' feelings. In the South that I knew half a century ago, young rural boys were expected to nurture their younger siblings, and male-male relations were ideally expected to be tender, supporting, and expressed occasionally by embraces. Among my own kin, some fathers then kissed their school-age sons; among Greek-Americans in New York City, that practice continues many decades later. Or, to consider England once more, let us remember the admired men of Elizabethan England. True enough, one ideal was the violent, daring Francis Drake and the brawling poet Ben Jonson. But men also expressed themselves in kissing and embracing, writing love poems to one another, donning decorative (not to say gaudy and efflorescent) clothing, and studying flowers as well as the fiery heavens.

We assert, then, that men manage to be in charge of things in all societies but that their very control permits them to create a wide range of ideal male roles, with the consequence that large numbers of men, not just a few, can locate rewarding positions in the social structure. Thereby, too, they considerably narrow the options left for feminine sex roles. Feminists especially resent the narrowness of the feminine role in informal interaction, where they feel they are dealt with only as women, however this may be softened by personal warmth or affection.

We can recognize that general relationship in a widespread male view, echoed over the centuries, that males are people, individuals, while women are lumped together as an aggregate. Or, in more modern language: Women have roles, a delimited number of parts to play, but men cannot be described so simply.

Nor is that peculiar male view contradicted by the complaint, again found in all major civilizations, that women are mysterious, unpredictable, moved by forces outside men's understanding, and not controllable. Even that master of psychodynamics Sigmund Freud expressed his bewilderment by asking, "What do women want?" Men have found their women difficult to understand for a simple reason: They have continued to try to think of them as a set of roles (above all else, mothers and wives), but in fact women do not fit these roles, not only not now, but not in the past either. Some women were great fighting machines, not compliant; some were competitive and aggressive, not nurturant; many were incompetent or reluctant mothers. They have been queens and astronomers, moralists and nurturers, leaders of religious orders as well as corporations, and so on. At any point, men could observe that women were ignoring or breaking out of their social molds, and men experienced that discrepancy as puzzling. However, it is only recently that many have faced the blunt fact that there is no feminine riddle at all: Women are as complex as men are, and always will escape the confinements of any narrow set of roles.

The Sociology of Superordinates

That set of relationships is only part of the complex male view, and I want to continue with my sketch of the main elements in what may be called the "sociology of superordinates." That is, I believe there are some general principles or regularities to be found in the view held by superordinates—here, the sex-class called males—about relations with subordinates, in this instance women. These regularities do not justify, but they do explain in some degree, the modern resistance of men to their new social situation.[4] Here are some of them:

1. The observations made by either men or women about members of the other sex are limited and somewhat biased by what they are most interested in and by their lack of opportunity to observe behind the scenes of each others' lives.[5] However, far less of what men do is determined by women; what men do affects women much more. As a consequence, men

are often simply less motivated to observe carefully many aspects of women's behavior and activity because women's behavior does not usually affect what men propose to do. By contrast, almost everything men do will affect what women *have* to do, and thus women are motivated to observe men's behavior as keenly as they can.

2. Since any given cohort of men know they did not create the system that gives them their advantages, they reject any charges that they conspired to dominate women.

3. Since men, like other dominants or superordinates, take for granted the system that gives them their status, they are not aware of how much the social structure, from attitude patterns to laws, pervasively yields small, cumulative, and eventually large advantages in most competitions. As a consequence, they assume that their greater accomplishments are actually the result of inborn superiority.

4. As a corollary to this male view, when men weigh their situation, they are more aware of the burdens and responsibilities they bear than of their unearned advantages.

5. Superiors, and thus men, do not easily notice the talents or accomplishments of subordinates, and men have not in the past seen much wisdom in giving women more opportunities for growth, for women are not capable of much anyway, especially in the areas of men's special skills. Thus, in the past, few women have embarrassed men by becoming superior in those areas. When they did, their superiority was seen, and is often still seen, as an odd exception. As a consequence, men see their superior position as a just one.

6. Men view even small losses of deference, advantages, or opportunities as large threats. Their own gains, or their maintenance of old advantages, are not noticed as much.[6]

Although the male view is similar to that of superordinates generally, as the foregoing principles suggest, one cannot simply equate the two. The structural position of males is different from that of superordinate groups, classes, ethnic populations, or castes, Males are, first, not a group, but a social segment or a statistical aggregate within the society. They share much of a common destiny, but they share few if any *group* or *collective* goals (within small groups they may be buddies, but not with all males). Second, males share with certain women whatever gain or loss they experience as members of high or low castes, ethnic groups, or classes. For example, women in a ruling stratum share with their men a high social rank, deference from the lower orders, and so on; men in a lowly Indian caste share that rank with their women, too. In modern societies, men and women in the same family are on a more or less equal basis with respect to "inheritance, educational opportunity (at least undergraduate), personal consumption of goods, most rights before the law, and the love and responsibility of their children."[7] They are not fully equal, to be sure, but much more equal than are members of very different castes or social classes.

Moreover, from the male view, women also enjoy certain exemptions: "freedom from military conscription, whole or partial exemption from certain kinds of heavy work, preferential courtesies of various kinds." Indeed, men believe, on the whole, that their own lot is the more difficult one.[8]

Most important as a structural fact that prevents the male view from being simply that of a superordinate is that these superordinates, like their women, do not live in set-apart communities, neighborhoods, or families. Of course, other such categories are not sequestered either, such as alcoholics, ex-mental patients, or the physically handicapped; but these are, as Goffman points out, "scattered somewhat haphazardly through the social structure." That is not so for men; like their women, they are allocated to households in a nonrandom way, for "law and custom allow only one to a household, but strongly encourage the presence of that one."[9]

A consequence of this important structural arrangement is that men and women are separated from their own sex by having a stake in the organization that gives each a set of different roles, or a different emphasis to similar roles; women especially come to have a vested interest in the social unit that at the same time imposes inequalities on them. This coalition between the two individuals makes it difficult for members of the same sex to join with large numbers of persons of their own sex for purposes of defense or exploitation. This applies equally to men and women.

One neat consequence may be seen in the hundreds of family law provisions created over the centuries that seem to run at cross-purposes. Some gave more freedom to women in order to protect them from predatory or exploitative males (i.e., in the male view, *other* men), and some took freedom away from women and put it in the hands of supposedly good and kindly men (i.e., heads of families, *themselves*). Or, in more recent times, the growing efforts of some fathers to press their daughters toward career competence so that they will not be helpless when abandoned by their future husbands, against those same fathers' efforts to keep their daughters docile and dutiful toward their protecting fathers.

You will note that male *views* are not contradictory in such instances, even though their *actions* may be. In coalition with their women, they oppose the exploitative efforts of outside men; within the family unit, however, they see little need for such protections against themselves, for they are sure of their own goodheartedness and wisdom.

That men see themselves as bound in a coalition with their families and thus with their daughters and wives is the cause of much common male resistance to the women's movement, while some have instead become angered at the unfair treatment their wives and daughters have experienced. The failure of many women to understand that complex male view has led to much misunderstanding.

Responses of Superordinates to Rebellion[10]

First, men are suprised at the outbreak. They simply had not known the depth of resentment that many women harbored, though of course many women had not known it either. Second, men are also hurt, for they feel betrayed. They discover, or begin to suspect, that the previously contented or pleasant facade their women presented to them was false, that they have been manipulated to believe in that presentation of self. Because males view themselves as giving protection against anyone exploiting or hurting their women, they respond with anger to the hostility they encounter, to the discovery that they were deceived, and to the charge that they have selfishly used the dominant position they feel they have rightfully earned.

A deeper, more complex source of male anger requires a few additional comments, for it relates to a central male role, that of jobholder and breadwinner. Most men, but especially most men outside the privileged stratum of professionals and managers, see their job as not yielding much intrinsic satisfaction, not being fun in itself, but they pride themselves on the hard work and personal sacrifice they make as breadwinners. In the male view, men make a gift of all this to their wives and children.[11]

Now they are told that it was not a gift, and they have not earned any special deference for it. In fact, their wives earned what they received, and indeed nothing is owing. If work was a sacrifice, they are told, so were all the services, comforts, and self-deprivations women provided. Whatever the justice of either claim, clearly if you think you are giving or sacrificing much to make gifts to someone over a period of time, and then you learn he or she feels the gifts were completely deserved, for the countergifts are asserted to have been as great and no gratitude or special debt was incurred, you are likely to be hurt or angry.[12]

I am reasonably certain about the processes I have just described. Let me go a step further and speculate that the male resentment is the greater because many fathers had already come to suspect that their children, especially in adolescence, were indifferent to those sacrifices, as well as to the values that justified them.[13] Thus, when women too begin to assert that men's gifts are not worth as much as men thought, the worth of the male is further denied.

Some Areas of Change and Nonchange

Although I have not heard specific complaints about it, I believe that the most important change in men's position, as they experience it, is a loss of centrality, a decline in the extent to which they are the center of attention. In our time, other superordinates have also suffered this loss: colonial rulers, monarchs and nobles, and U.S. whites both northern and southern, to name a few.

Boys and grown men have always taken for granted that what they were doing was more important than what the other sex was doing, that where they were, was where the action was. Their women accepted that definition. Men occupied the center of the stage, and women's attention was focused on them. Although that position is at times perilous, open to failure, it is also desirable.

Men are still there of course, and will be there throughout our lifetime. Nevertheless, some changes are perceptible. The center of attention shifts to women more now than in the past. I believe that this shift troubles men far more, and creates more of their resistance, than the women's demand for equal opportunity and pay in employment.

The change is especially observable in informal relations, and men who are involved with women in the liberation movement experience it most often. Women find each other more interesting than in the past, and focus more on what each other is doing, for they are in fact doing more interesting things. Even when they are not, their work occupies more of their attention, whether they are professionals or factory workers. Being without a man for a while does not seem to be so bereft a state as it once was. I also believe that this change affects men more now than at the time of the suffragist movement half a century ago, not only because more women now participate in it but also because men were then more solidary and could rely on more all-male organizations and clubs; now, they are more dependent on women for solace and intimacy.

As a side issue, let me note that the loss of centrality has its counterpart among feminist women too, and its subtlety should be noted. Such women now reject a certain type of traditional centrality they used to experience, because its costs are too great. Most women know the experience of being the center of attention: When they enter a male group, conversation changes in tone and subject. They are likely to be the focus of comments, many of them pleasurable: affectionate teasing, compliments, warmth. However, these comments put women into a special mold, the stereotyped female. Their serious comments are not welcomed or applauded, or their ideas are treated as merely amusing. Their sexuality is emphasized. Now, feminist women find that kind of centrality less pleasant—in fact, condescending—and they avoid it when they can. In turn, many men feel awkward in this new situation, for their repertory of social graces is now called boorish.

Although I have noted men's feelings of hurt and anger, I want to emphasize that I believe no backlash of any consequence has been occurring, and no trend toward more reactionary male attitudes exists. Briefly, there is a continuing attitude change on the part of both men and women, in favor of more equality. The frequent expressions of male objection, sometimes labeled "backlash" in the popular press, can be attributed to two main sources: (1) The discovery, by some men who formerly did pay lip service to the principle of equality, that they do not approve of its concrete application; and (2) active resistance by men and women who simply never approved of equality anyway and who have now begun to oppose it openly because it can no longer be seen as a trivial threat. Most of this is incorrectly labeled "backlash," which ought instead to refer only to the case in which people begin to feel negative toward a policy they once thought desirable, because now it has led to undesirable results. Those who oppose women's rights like to label any support they get as backlash because thereby they can claim that "women have gone too far."

It may surprise you to learn that it is not possible to summarize here all the various changes in public opinion about sex roles, as attitudes have shifted over the past generation, simply because pollsters did not bother to record the data. They often did not try to find out about social trends and thus only rarely asked the same questions in successive decades. One unfortunate result is that one of the most fiercely debated events of this period, the women's liberation movement, almost does not appear in the polls.[14]

The single finding that seems solid is that no data show any backward or regressive trend in men's attitudes about women's progress toward equality. The most often repeated question is not a profound one: whether a respondent would vote for a qualified woman for President. Favorable answers rose from about one-fourth of the men in 1937 to two-thirds in 1971, and to four-fifths among men and women combined in 1975. Another repeated question is whether a married woman should work if she has a husband able to support her, and here the answers of men and women combined rose from 18 percent in 1936 to 62 percent in 1975. In contrast to these large changes, a large majority favored equal pay, in principle at least, as early as 1942, and later data report no decrease.

In 1953, 21 percent of men said it made no difference whether they worked for a man or woman, and that figure rose slightly to 32 percent in 1975.[15] Polls in 1978 show that a large majority of the nation, both men and women, was in favor of the enforcement of laws forbidding job discrimination against women or discrimination in education; and most agreed that more women should be elected to public office.[16]

A plurality of only about 40 percent held such favorable opinions in 1970. On such issues, men and women do not differ by much, although, until recently, men's attitudes were somewhat more favorable. Divisions of opinion are sharper along other lines: The young are in favor more than the old, the more educated more favorable than the less educated, city dwellers more than rural people, blacks more than whites. Whatever the differences, clearly no substantial amount of male backlash has appeared. Through men's eyes, at least the *principle* of equality seems more acceptable than in the past. Their resistance is not set against that abstract idea. Modest progress, to be sure, but progress nonetheless.

I cannot forego making reference to a subvariety of the backlash, which has been reported in hundreds of articles, that is, that more men are impotent because of women's increased sexual assertiveness. This impotence, we are told, appears when women discover the delights of their own sexuality, make it clear to their men that they will play coy no more, and indeed look at their men as sexual objects, at least sometimes.

The widespread appearance of male impotence as an answer to, or an escape from, increased female willingness would certainly be news,[17] but it violates the sexual view of most men, and much worse, it runs counter to the only large-scale data we have on the topic.[18] The male view may be deduced, if you will permit the literary reference, from traditional pornography, which was written by men and expressed male fantasies. Briefly, in such stories, but entirely contrary to real life, everything went smoothly: At every phase of the interaction, where women in real male experience are usually indifferent if not hostile, the hero encounters enthusiasm, and in response he himself performs miracles of sexual athleticism and ecstasy.

Nothing so embroidered is found in social science data, but it seems reasonably certain that in the five-year period ending in 1970, the married men of the United States increased the frequency of their lovemaking with their wives. Doubtless, there were pockets of increased impotence, but with equal security we can assert that most husbands did not have that experience.

The reason is clear, I think: The message of permission had finally been received by women, and they put it into action. In millions of how-to-do-it books and articles, they were not only told to enjoy themselves but were urged to do so by seducing their men. Since the most important sex organ is the human mind, these changes in the heads of both men and women caused changes in the body. Without question, the simplest and most effective antidote to male impotence, or even lassitude and nonperformance, is female encouragement and welcome. Even if a few cases of the backlash of impotence have occurred, that has not, I think, been a widespread trend among males in our time, as a psychological response to women's move toward some equality in sexuality itself. To this particular change among women, men have offered little resistance.

Domestic Duties and Jobs

So far, the opinion data give some small cause for optimism. Nevertheless, all announcements of the imminent arrival of utopias are premature. Men's approval of more equality for women has risen, but the record in two major areas of men's roles—the spheres of home and occupation—gives but little reason for optimism. Here we can be brief, for though the voluminous data are very complex, the main conclusions can easily be summarized.[19] The striking fact is that very little has changed, if we consider the society as a whole and focus on changes in behavior.

Let is consider the domestic role of men. They have contributed only slightly more time to their duties in the home than in the past—although "the past" is very short for time budgets of men's child-care and homemaking activities. By contrast, the best record now indicates that homemakers without jobs spend somewhat less time at their domestic tasks then they did ten years ago. Working wives allocate much less time (26–35 hours a week) to the home than do stay-at-home wives (35–55 hours), but *husbands* of working wives do almost as little as husbands of stay-at-home wives (about 10–13 hours weekly). We hear much these days about Russian husbands who expect their wives to hold jobs and also take care of housework and child care, but so do American husbands. Moreover, that is as true of the supposedly egalitarian Swedish or Finnish husbands as it is of the German and French ones.[20]

Of course, there are some differences. If a child two years or younger is in the house, the father does more. Better-educated husbands do a bit more, and so do younger husbands. But the massive fact is that men's domestic contribution does not change much whether or not they work, and whether or not their wives work.[21] Still more striking is the fact that the past decade has shown little change in the percentage of women who want their husbands to take a larger share of domestic work, though once again it is the vanguard of the young, the educated, and the black who exhibit the largest increase. Studies have reported that only about 20 to 25 percent of wives express the wish for more domestic participation by their husbands, and that did not change greatly until the late 1970s.[22]

With reference to the second large area of men's roles, job holding, we observe two further general principles of the relations between superordinates and those at lesser ranks. One is that men do not, in general, feel threatened by competition from women if they believe the competition is fair and women do not have an inside track. Men still feel that they are superior and will do better if given the chance. Without actually trying the radical notion of genuinely fair competition, they have little reason to fear as yet: Compared with women, they were better off in wages and occupational position in the 1970s than in the 1950s.

The second principle is that those who hold advantaged positions in the social structure (men, in this case) can perceive or observe that they are being flooded by people they consider their inferiors—by women, blacks, or the lower classes—while the massive statistical fact is that only a few people are rising by much. There are several causes of this seeming paradox.

First, the new arrivals are so visible, so different from those who have held the jobs up to this time. The second cause is our perception of relative numbers. Since there are far fewer positions at higher job levels, only a few new arrivals constitute a fair-sized minority of the total at that level. Third, the mass media emphasize the hiring of women in jobs that seem not to be traditional for them, for that is considered news. Men's structural position, then, causes them to perceive radical change here, and they resist it.

Nevertheless, the general conclusion does not change much. The amount of sex segregation in jobs is not much different from the past.[23] More important, there is no decrease in the gap between the earnings of men and women; at every job level, it is not very different from the past, and in the period from 1955 to 1971 the gap actually became somewhat larger. That is, a higher percentage of women entered the labor force, and at better wages than in the past, but men rose somewhat faster than they.

Although the mass figures are correct, we need not discount all our daily observation. We see women entering formerly masculine jobs from garbage collecting to corporate management. That helps undermine sex stereotypes and thereby becomes a force against inequality. For example, women bus drivers were hardly to be found in 1940, but they now make up 37 percent of that occupation; women bartenders now form 32 percent of that occupation, but a generation ago made up only 2.5 percent.[24] Although occupational segregation continued strong in the 1970s, it did decline in most professions (e.g., engineering, dentistry, science, law, medicine) between 1960 and 1970. That is, the percentage of women in these professions did rise.[25] Women now constitute over one-fourth of the law school classes in the higher-ranking law schools of the country. In occupations where almost everyone was once male, it is not possible to recruit, train, and hire enough women to achieve equality in a few years, but the trend seems clear.

A secondary effect of these increasing numbers should be noted. Percentages are important, but so are absolute numbers. If women lawyers increase from about seven thousand to forty thousand, they become a much larger social force, even though they may be only about 10 percent of the total occupation. When women medical students, while remaining a small percentage of their classes, increase in number so that they can form committees, petition administrators, or give solidarity to one another against the traditional masculine badgering and disesteem, they greatly increase their impact on discriminatory attitudes and behavior. That is, as their rise in numbers permits the formation of real groups, their power mounts faster than the numbers or even (except at the start) the percentages. Thus, changes occur even when the percentage of the occupation made up of women is not large.

Bases of Present Changes

Most large-scale, objective measures of men's roles show little change over the past decade, but men do feel now and then that their position is in question, their security is somewhat fragile. I believe they are right, for they sense a set of forces that lie deeper and are more powerful than the day-to-day negotiation and renegotiation of advantage among husbands and wives, fathers and children, or bosses and those who work for them. Men are troubled by this new situation.

The conditions we live in are different from those of any prior civilization, and they give less support to men's claims of superiority than perhaps any other historical era. When these conditions weaken that support, men can rely only on previous tradition, or their attempts to socialize their children, to shore up their faltering advantages. Such rhetoric is not likely to be successful against the new objective conditions and the claims of aggrieved women. Thus, men are correct when they feel they are losing some of their privileges, even if many continue to laugh at the women's liberation movement.

The new conditions can be listed concretely, but I shall also give you a theoretical formulation of the process. Concretely, because of the increased use of various mechanical gadgets and devices, fewer tasks require much strength. As to those that still require strength, most men cannot do them either. Women can now do more household tasks that men once felt only they could do, and still more tasks are done by repair specialists called in to do them. With the development of modern warfare, there are few if any important combat activities that only men can do. Women are much better educated than before.

With each passing year, psychological and sociological research reduces the areas in which men are reported to excel over women and discloses far more overlap in talents, so that even when males still seem to have an advantage, it is but a slight one. It is also becoming more widely understood that the top posts in government and business are not best filled by the stereotypical aggressive male but by people, male or female, who are sensitive to others' needs, adept at obtaining cooperation, and skilled in social relations. Finally, in one sphere after another, the number of women who try to achieve rises, and so does the number who succeed.

Although the pressure of new laws has its direct effect on these conditions, the laws themselves arise from an awareness of the foregoing forces. Phrased in more theoretical terms, the underlying shift is toward the decreasing marginal utility of males, and this I suspect is the main source of men's resistance to women's liberation. That is, fewer people believe that what the male does is indispensable, nonsubstitutable, or adds such a special value to any endeavor that it justifies his extra "price" or reward. In past wars, for example, males enjoyed a very high value not only because it was felt that they could do the job better than women but also because they might well make the difference between being conquered and remaining free. In many societies, their marginal utility came from their contribution of animal protein through hunting. As revolutionary heroes, explorers, hunters, warriors, and daring capitalist entrepreneurs, men felt, and doubtless their women did too, that their contribution was beyond anything women could do. This earned men extra privileges of rank, authority, and creature services.

It is not then as individuals, as persons, that males will be deemed less worthy in the future or their contributions less needed. Rather, they will be seen as having no claim to *extra* rewards solely because they are members of the male sex-class. This is part of a still broader trend of our generation, which will also increasingly deny that being white, or an upper-caste or upper-class person, produces a marginally superior result and thus justifies extra privileges.

The relations of individuals are subject to continuous renegotiation as people try to gain or keep advantages or cast off burdens. They fail or succeed in part because one or the other person has special resources or lacks that are unique to those individuals. Over the long run, however, the outcome of these negotiations depends on the deeper social forces we have been describing, which ultimately determine which qualities or performances are more or less valued.

Now, men perceive that they may be losing some of their advantages and that more aspects of their social roles are subject to public challenge and renegotiation than in the past. They resist these changes, and we can suppose they will continue to do so. In all such changes, there are gains and losses. Commonly, when people at lower social ranks gain freedom, those at higher ranks lose some power or centrality. When those at the lower ranks also lose some protection, some support, those at the higher ranks lose some of the burden of responsibility. It is also true that the care or help given by any dominant group in the past was never as much as members believed, and their loss in political power or economic rule was never as great as they feared.

On the other hand, I know of no instance when a group or social stratum gained its freedom or moved toward more respect and then had its members decide that they did not want it. Therefore, although men will not joyfully give up their rank, in spite of its burdens, neither will women decide that they would like to get back the older feminine privileges, accompanied with the lack of respect and material rewards that went with those courtesies.

I believe that men perceive their roles as being under threat in a world that is different from any in the past. No society has yet come even close to equality between the sexes, but the modern social forces described here did not exist before either. At the most cautious, we must concede that the conditions favoring a trend toward more equality are more favorable than at any prior time in history. If we have little reason to conclude that equality is at hand, let us at least rejoice that we are marching in the right direction.

Notes

1. Herbert Goldberg, *The Hazards of Being Male* (New York: Nash, 1976); and Patricia C. Sexton, *The Feminized Male: Classrooms, White Collars, and the Decline of Manliness* (New York: Random House, 1969). On the recognition of disadvantages, see J. S. Chafetz, *Masculine/Feminine or Human?* (Itasca, Ill.: Peacock, 1974), pp. 56 ff.
2. Joseph H. Pleck, "The Psychology of Sex Roles: Traditional and New Views," in *Women and Men: Changing Roles, Relationship and Perceptions*, ed. Libby A. Carter and Anne F. Scott (New York: Aspen Institute for Humanistic Studies, 1976), p. 182. Pleck has carried out the most extensive research on male roles, and I am indebted to him for special help in this inquiry.
3. For these two quotations, see Sidney M. Jourard, "Some Lethal Aspects of the Male Role," p. 22, and Irving London, "Frigidity, Sensitivity and Sexual Roles," p. 42, in *Men and Masculinity*, ed. Joseph H. Pleck and Jack Sawyer (Englewood Cliffs, N.J.: Prentice-Hall, 1974). See also the summary of such traits in I.K. Braverman et al., "Sex-Role Stereotypes: A Current Appraisal," in *Women and Achievement*, ed. Martha T. S. Mednick, S. S. Tangri, and Lois W. Hoffman (New York: Wiley, 1975), pp 32–47.

4. Robert Bierstedt's "The Sociology of the Majority," in his *Power and Progress* (New York: McGraw-Hill, 1974), pp. 199–220, does not state these principles, but I was led to them by thinking about his analysis.

5. Robert K. Merton, in "The Perspectives of Insiders and Outsiders," in his *The Sociology of Science* (Chicago: University of Chicago Press, 1973), pp. 99–136, has analyzed this view in some detail.

6. This general pattern is noted at various points in my monograph *The Celebration of Heroes: Prestige as a Social Control System* (Berkeley: University of California Press, 1979).

7. Erving Goffman, "The Arrangement Between the Sexes," *Theory and Society* 4 (1977): 307.

8. Hazel Erskine, "The Polls: Women's Roles," *Public Opinion Quarterly* 35 (Summer 1971).

9. Goffman, "Arrangement Between the Sexes," p. 308.

10. A simple analysis of these responses is presented in William J. Goode, *Principles of Sociology* (New York: McGraw-Hill, 1977), pp. 359 ff.

11. See Joseph H. Pleck, "The Power of Men," in *Women and Men: The Consequences of Power*, ed. Dana V. Hiller and R. Sheets (Cincinnati: Office of Women's Studies, University of Cincinnati, 1977), p. 20. See also Colin Bell and Howard Newby, "Husbands and Wives: The Dynamic of the Deferential Dialectic," in *Dependence and Exploitation in Work and Marriage*, ed. Diana L. Barker and Sheila Allen (London: Longman, 1976), pp. 162–63; as well as Richard Sennett and Jonathan Cobb, *The Hidden Injuries of Class* (New York: Vintage, 1973), p. 125. On the satisfactions of work, see Daniel Yankelovich, "The Meaning of Work," in *The Worker and the Job*, ed. Jerome Rosow (Englewood Cliffs, N.J.: Prentice-Hall, 1974), pp. 19–49.

12. Whatever other sacrifices women want from men, until recently a large majority did *not* believe men should do more housework. On this matter, see Joseph H. Pleck, "Men's New Roles in the Family: Housework and Child Care," to appear in *Family and Sex Roles*, ed. Constantina Safilios-Rothschild, forthcoming. In the mid-1970s, only about one-fourth to one-fifth of wives agreed to such a proposal.

13. Sennett and Cobb, *The Hidden Injuries of Class*, p. 125.

14. To date, the most complete published summary is that by Erskine, "The Polls: Women's Roles," pp. 275–91.

15. Stephanie Greene, "Attitudes Toward Working Women Have 'A Long Way to Go' " *Gallup Opinion Poll*, March 1976, p. 33.

16. *Harris Survey*, 16 February 1978; see also *Harris Survey*, 11 December 1975.

17. It is, however, in harmony with one view expressed by many women (as well as men), that men in the past were a bit necrophiliac (i.e., they preferred to hop on unresponsive women, take their quick crude pleasure, and hop off). It does not accord much with what we know of people generally (they gain more pleasure when their partner does) or even of bawds and lechers (they brag about the delirium they arouse in the women they seduce).

18. See Charles F. Westoff, "Coital Frequency and Contraception," *Family Planning Perspectives* 6 (Summer 1974): 136–41.

19. The most extensive time budget data on a cross-national basis are found in A. Szalai, ed., *The Use of Time* (The Hague: Mouton, 1972). The most useful summary of the data on the above points is in Joseph H. Pleck, "The Work-Family Role System," *Social Problems* 24 (1977): 417–27. See also his "Developmental Stages in Men's Lives: How Do They Differ From Women's?" (National Guidance Association, Hartland, Michigan, 1977), mimeo.

20. Elina Haavio-Mannila, "Convergences Between East and West: Tradition and Modernity in Sex Roles in Sweden, Finland, and the Soviet Union," in Midnick et al., *Women and Achievement*, pp. 71–84. Further data will appear in J. Robinson, *How Americans Use Time*, forthcoming.

21. Pleck, "Men's New Roles in the Family." For details on men's contribution to child care, see Philip J. Stone, "Child Care in Twelve Countries," in Szalai, *The Use of Time.*

22. These data are to be found in Pleck, "Men's New Roles in the Family." However, 1977 data show that in Detroit this figure has risen to over 60 percent: Arland Thornton and Deborah S. Freedman, "Changes in the Sex Role Attitudes of Women 1962–1977," *American Sociological Review* 44 (October 1979): 833.

23. The expansion of women's jobs has occurred primarily in "female" jobs or through new occupations defined as female or (less frequently) by women taking over formerly male jobs. See Council of Economic Advisers, *Economic Report of the President*, 1973, p. 155; and

Barbara R. Bergman and Irma Adelman, "The 1973 Report of the President's Council of Economic Advisors: The Economic Role of Women," *American Economic Review*, September 1973, pp. 510–11. In 1960, about 24 percent of the labor force was made up of women in occupations where women are predominant; in 1970, the figure was 27 percent according to Myra H. Strober, "Women and Men in the World of Work: Present and Future," in Cater et al., *Women and Men: Changing Roles, Relationships, and Perceptions*, pp. 128–33.

24. Jean Lipman-Blumen, "Implications for Family Structure of Changing Sex Roles," *Social Casework* 57 (February 1976): pp. 67–79.

25. Victor R. Fuchs, "A Note on Sex Segregation in Professional Occupations," *Explorations in Economic Research 2*, no. 1 (Winter 1975): 105–11.

Chapter 4

Sexuality

Marital Sex

Morton Hunt

The Western Tradition Concerning Marital Sexual Pleasure

Every human society has forbidden sex between at least some kinds of partners, and sexual relations in all but one kind of partnership have been forbidden by at least some societies. The one universal exception, the one partnership within which sexual activity is everywhere deemed acceptable, is the husband-wife relationship. But the universal acceptability of marital sex is not at all the same thing as universal freedom for husbands and wives to seek maximum enjoyment from their sexual activities; the social legitimacy of marital coitus does not necessarily signify the emotional legitimacy of pleasure. Accordingly, even though marital coitus has been approved everywhere, there are great variations, from society to society, in the precise sexual activities permitted to husbands and wives, in the inner feelings accompanying those activities and in the kinds of satisfaction they have obtained from their physical relationship.

Western civilization has long had the rare distinction of contaminating and restricting the sexual pleasure of married couples more severely than almost any other. From the beginnings of Christianity, marital sex was viewed not as a positive good, nor as a joy to be made the most of, but as an unavoidable lesser evil, preferable only to the far worse one of sex outside of marriage. Saint Paul formulated the doctrine in his *First Epistle to the Corinthians.* "I would that all men were even as I myself (i.e., celibate)," he wrote. ". . . I say therefore to the unmarried and widows, it is good for them if they abide even as I. But if they cannot contain, let them marry: for it is better to marry than to burn."

Later, various fathers of the church carried this antihedonistic and antisexual philosophy much further: Even marital sex, they said, was sinful if it was thoroughly enjoyable. In the 3rd Century A.D., for instance, Clement of Alexandria warned that married coitus remained sinless only if delight was restrained and confined, and in the 5th Century Saint Jerome asserted that "he who too ardently loves his own wife is an adulterer." By the 7th Century it was established church dogma that married intercourse was so incompatible with spiritual exercises that husbands and wives must abstain from sex for three days before taking communion. The same church that had made marriage a holy act thus characterized the essential sexual part of it as an unholy, even though permissible, lapse from purity.

Such was the view that pervaded Western society and severely restricted the ability of men and women to take pleasure in married sexual relations. Although somewhat mitigated during periods of liberalism or learning, it remained generally dominant until modern times; indeed, in America in the late 18th and the 19th Century, its blighting effect was particularly strong, being intensified by the prudish middle-class view of the "good" woman as ethereal, passive and far above having any lustful or passionate feelings. Women's liberationists often assert that this view was part of the apparatus of male dominance, and that it was deliberately promulgated by men to keep women subordinate and enslaved; but although it may indeed have helped to do so, men did not consciously create it for that purpose. Its roots lay not in male dominance but in middle-class puritanism and the fundamentalist explanation of sin, which dichotomized womanhood into sinner and saint, Eve and Mary, whore and mother, minion of Satan and handmaiden of Christ. Besides, in many a non-Christian society, wives, although thoroughly subjugated, were quite capable of being highly sexual and passionate in marriage, these qualities being highly praised in them by men, as is apparent from even the most casual inspection of such classic Near Eastern marriage and sex manuals as the *Kama Sutra* and *The Perfumed Garden of the Shaykh Nefzawi.* In any case, even if the Christian-bourgeois view of woman helped keep her enslaved, it cost her oppressor dearly; he may have the right to enjoy her favors whenever he wished, but it was the right to relieve himself in a silent, inert, unresponding and unseen receptacle (inky darkness being the rule), who did her "conjugal duty" by allowing him to "take his pleasure."

Some wives, nonetheless, did enjoy sex, particularly (if we may trust playwrights and satirists) those wives of the very highest and the very lowest social levels. But in the 19th Century the majority of middle-class and working-class women found intercourse only tolerable at best; and a substantial minority regarded it as revolting, messy, vulgar, animalistic, shameful and degrading. Dr. William Hammond, an expert on sexual matters and onetime surgeon-general of the United States, asserted in a widely used medical textbook that, aside from prostitution, it was doubtful that women felt the slightest pleasurable sensation in one-tenth of their intercourse. No reliable survey data on the matter exist, but at the end of the century many of the best-informed American and European doctors believed that female frigidity was widespread and perhaps even prevalent, their estimates of its incidence in American and European women running anywhere from 10 to 75 percent.

But during the early part of the 20th century the liberation and legitimation of human sexual enjoyment—even by the female—got under way. Freud opened up to view the hidden interior of human desire; women started struggling out of their bonds of helplessness, subservience and purity; and marital intercourse began to be viewed as a positive and healthful activity rather than a shameful and somewhat debilitating indulgence. Liberal doctors, scholars and feminists—Havelock Ellis, Ellen Key, Marie Stopes and Theodor Van de Velde, among others—argued for long and careful wooing of the wife by the husband, praised the aesthetic aspects of varied techniques of lovemaking and preached the emotional and physical importance of mutual orgasm.

In the 1930s and 1940s, when Kinsey was doing his fieldwork, writers and social critics ranging from Sinclair Lewis to Philip Wylie were still scornfully portraying the typical American marital sex act as a crude, hasty, wordless Saturday-night grappling. But Kinsey's data partially gave them the lie; his figures proved that the early phase of sexual liberation had already had a considerable ameliorating effect. The younger married women in Kinsey's sample, for instance, were having somewhat less marital intercourse, at any given age, than older women had had at that same age, undoubtedly because wives' own wishes were beginning to count; but at the same time the percentage of such intercourse resulting in female orgasm was climbing, with something like a fifth more of the younger women than the older ones having orgasm most or all of the time, in any given year of married life. At almost every age, in almost every stage of marriage and in nearly every detail—the degree of nudity during intercourse, the kinds of foreplay used, the use of positional variations—the difference between the older and the younger generation, though not large, were consistently in the direction of greater freedom, pleasure and mutuality. The beginnings of sexual egalitarianism and the legitimation of pleasure were changing marital sex as nothing else had in nearly two millenia.

Everything we have seen thus far in this survey points to the fact that since Kinsey's time those liberating forces have vastly increased in power. Accordingly, sex within marriage should now be far more sensuous, uninhibited and mutually satisfying; yet today there seems to be more and harsher criticism of married sex than ever. Many of the shriller voices in the women's-liberation movement portray married intercourse as male-chauvinist exploitation of the female body, with husbands being clumsy, hasty, brutal and selfish, and making no effort to delight or satisfy their wives, let alone consider, in the first place, whether their wives wish to be made love to. Many sexologists, moreover, have made sweeping statements about the prevalence of sexual incompetence or inadequacy in contemporary marriage. Masters and Johnson, for instance, have repeatedly said—while admitting it to be only a guess—that perhaps 50 percent of all American marriages suffer from sexual dysfunction of one sort or another. Critics of monogamous marriage, and advocates of extramarital relations, have in increasing numbers scornfully portrayed married intercourse as stereotyped, dull and constricted, and nonmarital intercourse as varied, exciting and free.

But our survey data appear to contradict this picture of contemporary married sex. They do not lead us to deny that there is still male chauvinism in many a marriage bed, or that many married people have sexual problems, or that for many people married sex eventually becomes overfamiliar and unexciting. They do, however, lead us to dispute the charge that these negative aspects of married sex are more prevalent or severe today than formerly (we believe, in fact, that the opposite is true), and to disagree with the assertion that they are the predominant and essential characteristics of contemporary marriage. How, then, is one to explain the widespread criticism of married sex? The answer, we think, is that the progress our society has made toward fuller and freer sexuality has revolutionized our expectations and made many of us so intolerant of our dissatisfactions that we forget the improvement that has taken place in our lives; like all partially liberated people, we are more discontented now than we were before our lot began to improve.

Yet improvement is widespread and real. The present survey, as we are about to see, indicates that since Kinsey's time marital sex in America has become a good deal more egalitarian (with husbands being more considerate of their wives' needs, and wives assuming more responsibility for the success of intercourse); that husbands and wives are much freer in terms of the kinds of foreplay and coital positions they use; that the conscious pursuit of sensuous pleasure in marriage has become much more acceptable to both sexes; and that there is a considerable increase in the percentage of marital sexual experiences that yield genuine satisfaction to both persons.

Contemporary Forces Tending to Liberate Married Sexual Behavior

Indeed, one could argue that the principal effect of sexual liberation upon American life has been to increase the freedom of husbands and, even more so, of wives to explore and enjoy a wide range of gratifying sexual practices within the marital relationship. Most discussions of sexual liberation concentrate upon its meaning for the unmarried, the unfaithful and the unconventional; but by far the largest number of people whose sexual behavior has been influenced by it are faithful (or relatively faithful) husbands and wives. All those social developments which have made male and female expectations of sex more nearly compatible, which have emancipated men and women from the guilt and inhibitions generated by fundamentalist religion, and which have broadened the average person's repertoire of sexual acts have affected sexual behavior within marriage as much as outside it; for marriage is not an enclave, impervious to outside influences, but a porous thing, penetrated through and through by the currents of the social milieu.

The most obvious of the openings through which external influences enter marriage is, of course, the sum total of attitudes and experiences that the partners bring with them at the outset. We have seen that the sexual attitudes of most young unmarried persons have become much more permissive in recent years, that this has brought about an increase in the amount—and an improvement in the caliber—of premarital sexual experience, and that while the overall change has been greater for females, it has been substantial even for males, especially those of the educated middle class. It would seem obvious that for a large proportion of younger married adults the difficulties of achieving sexual adjustment in marriage must have been reduced and that the range of sexual practices acceptable within most marriages must have been broadened.

Some experts have disputed the beneficent influence of premarital experience; in fact, a number of minor studies have shown small positive correlations between premarital sexual conservatism—specifically, virginity in females—and successful marriage, and a few sociologists and marriage researchers, among them Harvey Locke, Paul Popenoe, Ernest Burgess and Paul Wallin, have therefore held that premarital sexual experience does little or nothing to promote marital sexual adjustment or marital happiness. But men and women with generally conservative attitudes are very likely to have different expectations of marriage from men and women with generally liberal attitudes, and marriages that the former rate "successful" or "happy" might not seem so to the latter. Similarly, most of the survey data on sexual adjustment come from self-appraisals, but the severely inhibited man or semifrigid woman is apt to term his or her married sex life satisfactory if it involves minimal demands and yields modest rewards, while the more liberated man or woman would probably view such a sex life as disappointing and perhaps even as a severe deprivation.

If we turn to objective and quantifiable activities rather than subjective self-appraisal, we find impressive evidence that successful premarital sexual experience does, indeed, bear a positive relationship to married sexual satisfaction for the wife and hence, inferentially, for the husband. Terman, Burgess and Wallin, and Kinsey all reported positive correlations between premarital orgastic experience for the woman and her orgastic regularity within marriage. Kinsey, for instance, found that 57 percent of the females who had had 25 or more coital orgasms before marriage were having orgasms nearly all the time even in the first year of marriage, as compared with 29 to 44 percent of the females who had had no premarital coital experience. Such data, alone, do not prove that the prior experience is the cause of the later success, for it could be that innately responsive females are more receptive to premarital experience and, by the same token, more responsive within marriage. But Kinsey, anticipating this argument, pointed out that for most females orgastic capacity develops only with years of experience, so that premarital experience tends to shorten the time necessary to achieve sexual success within marriage—a crucially important point, in view of the fact that more marital breakups occur in the first and second years of marriage than any subsequent ones.

Whether or not women had had premarital coitus, however, Kinsey found their orgastic regularity increasing with the duration of the marriage, and continuing to improve even up to the twentieth year of marriage, a phenomenon most experts attributed to such internal processes in the marriage as the growth of intimacy and trust, growing familiarity of the partners with each other's physical needs, the slow wearing away of inhibitions, and the growing willingness of the wife to learn from the husband and to make little experiments at his suggestion. Today, however, the continuing improvement of the marital sexual relationship, though it still owes much to these internal factors, also owes a good deal to various external ones. For one thing, nowadays it grates on many a female to have her husband appropriate the role of teacher and innovator; she is willing to have him do so sometimes, provided he plays the role of pupil and follower at other times. In an egalitarian relationshp, each partner is a source of suggestions and innovations, and with the society around them having become so permissive about the publishing, portraying and discussing of details of sexual technique, each partner has easy access to information and stimuli. A generation or more ago it was almost always the husband who suggested some novel activity—rear-entry coitus, say, or fellatio, or watching the action in a mirror—often to the alarm of the naïve wife, who feared her mate might be giving voice to some perversion or abnormality. Today the young wife is as likely as her husband to have heard and read about these and even far more fanciful novelties, thanks to the bumper crop of best-selling sex manuals, candid magazine articles and erotic novels, and to the new openness of talk about such things among her peers. Moreover, she is nearly as likely as her husband to regard such things as normal, intriguing and worth trying. What young males, and to a greater extent young females, may not have known at the outset of marriage they no longer must discover for themselves or do without; indeed, they can scarcely avoid learning from the outside much of what was known to the ancient writers on the amorous arts, and a good deal that would have astonished even those venerables.*

All of this tends to liberalize the attitudes of both partners in marriage, to increase their repertoire of physical acts and to bring them closer to each other in their expectations and requirements. The sex manuals of the Van de Velde generation held that marital intercourse should always be "person-centered" (the term is Professor Reiss's)—that is, a primarily communicative and emotional act on the part of both partners—although in fact this was more typi-

*We are unable, for instance, to find in the Hindu, Arabian or Chinese erotic guidebooks or in Japanese erotic art any reference to the use of edible substances applied to and licked off the genitals, the application of crushed ice to the genitals at the moment of orgasm, or analingus, although these are among the variations advocated in some contemporary sex manuals.

cally the female attitude than the male one. Many of today's sex manuals pay only lip service to the communicative and emotional aspects of intercourse, stressing instead its earthy, sensuous, appetitive side—the "body-centered" attitudes that used to be regarded as typically male. Male and female attitudes, as we measured them, still show some differences along this dimension, but our evidence suggests that American husbands and wives are moving toward a middle ground in which each can be both person-centered and body-centered, enjoying intercourse for both reasons at the same time, or, on occasion, for either one alone. This shift, we think, is due in considerable part to the continuing impact upon young married people of external influences and sources of information.

A number of items in our questionnaire survey indirectly indicate the impact of outside influences, but the most direct evidence comes from our interviews. Most of our middle-aged interviewees said that while they had recently become more permissive in their attitudes, their marital sex habits were too well established to be changed—and some of them candidly regretted that this was the case. But other middle-aged persons, and nearly all married persons under 35, said that books, magazines, films, erotic materials and discussions with friends had been important factors in expanding and liberating their married sex life. Here are a few typical comments:

FEMALE, 45, BLUE-COLLAR HOMEMAKER: After we'd been married a while, we felt there was a lot happening that we didn't understand, so I asked my husband if him and I should try to read up on it. So he went out and bought three books, and through them we found all different ways of caressing, and different positions, and it was very nice because we realized that these things weren't dirty. Like I could say to my husband, "Around the world in eighty days!" and he'd laugh and we'd go at it, relaxed and having fun. Also, men talk about sex with each other, you know, and sometimes he'll come home and say, "Here's a thing I just heard about, and let's try it," and I'll say "Fine," and we do.

FEMALE, 28, BUSINESSWOMAN: By now, we have what I'd call a pretty wide range of specialties. We experimented even at the beginning, but we were pretty timid; it was reading and talking to friends that made the difference. We went through the *Kama Sutra,* and Henry Miller, and Frank Harris, and some of De Sade, and some of it was ridiculous, but a lot was eye-opening and stimulating. Even blue movies have sometimes given us an idea or two, although mostly they're just for laughs.

FEMALE, 37, WAITRESS: What changed our sex life was that a bunch of us girls on the same block started reading books and passing them around— everything from how-to-do-it sex books to real porno paperbacks. Some of the men said that that stuff was garbage, but I can tell you that my husband was always ready to try out anything I told him I'd read about. Some of it was great, some was awful—we just about wrecked my back, once, with this hassock bit—and some was just funny, like the honey business.

FEMALE, 34, TEACHER: All of a sudden, I kept hearing and reading about this multiple-orgasm thing, and I'd never realized before that it was normal.

It sounded like the greatest, so my husband and I talked it over and decided to make a special try to see if I could. And I did, and wow!—I was really bowled over. He felt pretty proud of himself, too. We don't try for it as a regular thing, but whenever we do, it's really special.

MALE, 26, GRADUATE STUDENT: My wife was never willing to fool around as much as she now is. Not that we didn't have good, open sex, but in the last year she seems to have learned to *abandon* herself to it. I think this has come about from her exposure to other people's opinions—some of our friends talk quite openly about these things—and from reading things, like the Masters and Johnson studies, and even popular stuff like *The Sensuous Woman,* which is sometimes silly and overstated but makes a good case for itself.

MALE, 26, MECHANIC: My wife works, and at lunchtime she and all the girls talk about things, and she comes home one time and tells me she hears there's nothing like pornography for a turn-on. So I go along with it; I go out and buy an armful of stuff—mostly picture magazines—and bring it home. First, it embarrasses her, but then she gets to see it differently, and to like some of the things she sees. Same way with a stag film I borrowed and brought home to show her. Personally, I think it's good and wholesome; it stimulates and opens the mind.

MALE, 33, COLLEGE INSTRUCTOR: Both my wife and I are terribly old-fashioned, but since being married our ideas about sex have changed a lot, partly from maturity, but largely from the influence of the common culture —all the things one reads and hears about, the common coin, so to speak. Even a film can affect our life. Recently we saw a rerun of *I Am Curious, Yellow,* and came home and promptly tried out a position we had never thought of before—the one on the railing—and frankly, it seemed more trouble than it was worth, but we rather enjoyed making the experiment.

In addition to all the preceding milieu influences, which can be loosely termed didactic, there are three others worth mentioning that fall in somewhat different categories. The first is therapy; to be sure, most forms of therapy are partly informational, but primarily they involve conditioning and training. Clinics specializing in sex therapy, many of them patterned upon that of Masters and Johnson and using similar methods, have proliferated around the country; a survey by the *New York Times* in October 1972 located several dozen sex clinics in 20 cities, and many more must exist in other cities. The Masters-Johnson techniques have, however, had an even wider impact through the avenue of general-practice medicine and through the direct adoption, by readers, of the techniques of sex therapy described in their second book, *Human Sexual Inadequacy.*

The second special influence is that of contraception, which has achieved a new level of effectiveness and simplicity in recent years in three forms: pill, I.U.D. and vasectomy. Many millions of married couples have adopted one or another of these methods, and the simplicity and freedom from worry they provide has often brought new spontaneity and joyousness into married intercourse. Among the couples in our interview sample who were most enthusiastic about their sexual life were some who, desiring no more children, had sought the total security of vasectomy—and were dumbfounded at how much more excitement and delight they got from their sexual relationship as a result.

Finally, women's liberation has altered the sexual relationships of countless married couples—often for the better, sometimes for the worse. The topic is far too complex to be treated adequately here. but we must at least mention it because so many questionnaire responses reveal its influence. The beneficial effects have, in general, been an extention of those changes associated with the gradual emanicipation of woman from her subservient, asexual, passive 19th-Century image. The harmful effects have come about in transferring to the sexual arena antagonisms and power struggles between husband and wife that have been exacerbated by the liberation movement. Even though a revision of the power balance between man and wife is often called for, the sexual relationship of the couple may suffer as a consequence. Many an angry woman gets even by deciding that her husband is a lousy lover and that she'll have no more of him except on her own terms; and many a man with traditional attitudes, alarmed or repelled by the new kind of woman, loses his drive or sexual self-assurance. Four out of five sexologists in a round-table discussion in the journal *Medical Aspects of Human Sexuality* held that impotence was definitely on the rise; and a team of three psychiatrists writing in *Archives of General Psychiatry* recently identified a syndrome they called "the new impotence"—the failure of the male to function as a result of the new assertiveness of women, which some men find so threatening that they cease being able to act as men.

Even a liberated and reasonably secure male, furthermore, might well find at least one by-product of the women's-liberation movement too demanding for his taste. Psychiatrist Mary Jane Sherfey, borrowing loosely from Masters and Johnson and spinning her own version of prehistory, concocted a theory not long ago that all normal women are not only capable of multiple orgasms but that without some intervening force to stop them, they would all, by nature, be sexually insatiable. It was the male, says Dr. Sherfey, who forcibly suppressed female sexuality at the dawn of history to make civilized life possible (ungoverned, woman's sexual drive was too strong, impelling and aggressive to permit a settled family life) and who has kept telling woman ever since that she needs only one orgasm, if any, per coition. As we have already noted, some militant feminists, finding this theory a powerful weapon against men, have written pridefully about the female orgasm potential and urged women to use fingers or vibrators to enjoy themselves without stint, rather than seek their primary gratification in marital coitus. But this can only seem an unhealthy and pathogenic view, except to those women who regard all marital intercourse, and marriage itself, as forms of enslavement by the male enemy.

Frequency of Marital Coitus a Generation Ago and Today

As we saw earlier. the Kinsey data show that the earlier stage of the liberation of women brought about a small but distinct decrease in the average frequency of marital intercourse. One might wonder, therefore, whether the later, and virtually explosive, stage of liberation of women that has taken place in the past decade has not greatly accentuated that trend and brought about something close to a sexual standoff within contemporary marriage. This is, indeed, the impression one gets from the writings of many critics and satirists of modern marriage. But critics and satirists, even if they are portraying something real, may be misled as to how widespread that reality is. To know whether what they see and portray is the general rule, we must turn to statistically representative survey data. Our own data tell a different story, contradicting both what the critics of marriage say and what the extrapolation of Kinsey's data seemed to forecast: We find that, by and large, contemporary marriages involve higher frequencies of marital intercourse than did those of a generation ago. With the smug assurance of hindsight, one can say that this was implicit in the Kinsey data. For although in his time the frequency of marital coitus was declining due to the wife's rising status and her growing right to have a voice in sexual matters, the regularity of her orgasm in marital coitus was rising due to a multitude of sexually liberating factors. This increase in orgastic reliability and overall sexual satisfaction eventually offset the forces that caused the initial drop in coital activity. Such, at least, is our interpretation of the data we are about to present in this and the next two sections of this chapter.

First, then, let us see exactly what has happened to the frequency of marital intercourse. In the past several generations a number of researchers have published estimates or survey data on this matter, but nearly all of the pre-Kinsey studies were based on small or special samples—patients in treatment, volunteer respondents and the like—or on groups covering too wide an age span to yield meaningful frequency data. The more recent studies are, in general, statistically more sophisticated; but because of the difficulty of gathering data in this area, they have often been based on what is most easily available, even when it is manifestly biased. A recent study published in the *Journal of Urology,* for instance, gives data on coital frequency based on information collected from 2801 male patients receiving urological treatment, over half of whom had prostatic hypertrophy or prostatitis. But since it is highly likely that these disorders either made for unusual frequencies in them, or, conversely, were the result of unusual frequencies, these frequency data are a poor guide to normal behavior. Even the respected sociologist Robert Bell, seeking to gather data on the coital frequency of contemporary wives, sent out batches of questionnaires to colleagues in the field of family sociology, who handed them out at their own discretion. The returned sample—60 percent of the distributed questionnaires—is strongly biased in the direction of higher-educated employed women, and further distorted by the silence of the 40 percent who accepted questionnaires but decided not to tell about themselves. Professor Bell's study is useful, within limits, but is hardly a reliable measurement of the changes in behavior of the general population since Kinsey.

For such reasons, the best comparisons we can make are those between our own data and those reported by Kinsey in his 1948 volume on the American male and his 1953 volume on the American female. Like Kinsey, however, we can repeat only what our respondents told us, which means that our data may involve subjective distortion—not outright lies, but underestimates or overestimates caused by the individual's feeling that he or she is having too little, or too much, coitus. Terman, Kinsey, Clark and Wallin, and Levinger have interviewed husband-wife pairs separately and compared their answers as to coital frequency: In some pairs, the spouses give different estimates; and when these estimates are correlated with desired frequency, it turns out that a partner who desires more coitus than he or she is having tends to understate the actual frequency, while one who desires less tends to overstate the actual frequency. All who have researched this matter, prior to the present survey, agree that the bulk of such distortions lies in the direction of husbands wanting more intercourse than they were having, and hence giving lower estimates of actual intercourse than wives, and of wives wanting less than they were having, and hence giving higher estimates than husbands.

How much credence, then, can we put in data gathered in such fashion? Kinsey offered a careful analysis of male-female differences in estimates of frequency, based on interviews with over 700 husband-wife pairs. He found that most of them gave substantially the same estimates, and the differences in the remainder averaged out to be rather small. It was, therefore, Kinsey's opinion that the averages derived from each sex were valid and reliable, even though slightly different. Clark and Wallin disagreed, but most other sex researchers have accepted Kinsey's view and used his data. Recently sociologist J. Richard Udry and pediatrician Naomi M. Morris concocted an ingenious experiment that indicated that most females, at least, tell the truth about coital frequency. Udry and Morris, using a cover story to the effect that they were trying to correlate sexual behavior with hormone levels, obtained daily first-morning urine specimens from 58 female subjects plus reports as to whether or not the women had had coitus in the last 24 hours. They found, by microscopic examination of the urine specimens for spermatozoa, that the reports of coitus or no coitus were generally correct.

All of which gives us good grounds for regarding the coital-frequency estimates of husbands and wives as reasonably trustworthy, even if slightly discrepant. Although the undersatisfied and the oversatisfied may distort their estimates somewhat, these people are in the minority; moreover, part of their distortions cancel each other out. The net result is that such distortions, though individually significant, have only a minor effect on the overall averages for all males and all females. If, therefore, we find that our data show consistent differences from Kinsey's, and of a magnitude considerably larger than the discrepancy between male and female averages, we can take this as evidence that significant change has taken place in the past generation.

And we do find such evidence. The data show that there has been an important, even historic, increase in the typical (median) frequency of marital coitus throughout the population. Convincingly, both husbands and wives report such increases. Moreover, the frequency is higher in every age group of each sex than for comparable groups in Kinsey's time.

It is hardly possible to overstate the importance of this finding and what it tells us about the net effect of the twin (and sometimes opposing) forces of sexual liberation and women's liberation. We present the data in detail in Tables 1 and 2 followed by our comments. The figures given in these tables are, of course, group averages and do not indicate the vast range of individual variation; among our 35-to-44-year-old males, for instance, the median rate of marital coitus is just under 100 per year, but some men in that group had intercourse with their wives only two or three times per year, and others several hundred times. Both of these are obvious extremes, but no one should take our group averages to represent norms to which all should seek to conform. We present both kinds of averages—means and medians—in Tables 1 and 2, since it is meaningful that both measures show increases since Kinsey's time. The means are the better measure of the total coital activity of each group, but tend to exaggerate the coital rate of the typical member of the group. The medians are better indicators of the typical frequency, since they represent the level of activity of the midpoint of a group, above which lie half the cases and below which lie the other half when ranked in the order of the frequency of marital coitus.

In the male table (Table 1) every 1972 mean and median is higher than the corresponding 1938–1946 mean and median, in many cases by anywhere from a quarter to a half—a very substantial and remarkable change in a single generation. In the female table (Table 2) the increases are generally somewhat smaller but consistently in the same direction. The difference between the size of the increases shown in the male table and those shown in the female table is very likely due to an increase in perceptual accuracy by women. If, as we

Table 1. Marital Coitus: Frequency Per Week as Estimated by Husbands, 1938–1946 and 1972*

1938–1946 (Kinsey)			1972 (Present survey)		
Age	Mean	Median	Age	Mean	Median
16–25	3.3	2.3	18–24	3.7	3.5
26–35	2.5	1.9	25–34	2.8	3.0
36–45	1.8	1.4	35–44	2.2	2.0
46–55	1.3	.8	45–54	1.5	1.0
56–60	.8	.6	55 & over	1.0	1.0

Table 2. Marital Coitus: Frequency Per Week as Estimated by Wives, 1938–1949 and 1972*

1938–1949 (Kinsey)			1972 (Present survey)		
Age	Mean	Median	Age	Mean	Median
16–25	3.2	2.6	18–24	3.3	3.0
26–35	2.5	2.0	25–34	2.6	2.1
36–45	1.9	1.4	35–44	2.0	2.0
46–55	1.3	.9	45–54	1.5	1.0
56–60	.8	.4	55 & over	1.0	1.0

*In both tables, Kinsey's data have been adapted by recalculating his five-year cohorts into ten-year cohorts to facilitate comparison with our own. The dates 1938–1946 and 1938–1949 refer to the years during which the interviews were conducted on which Kinsey's data are based; our own fieldwork was done, as indicated, in 1972. Our data are based on our white sample; as usual in making direct comparisons with Kinsey's data, we have omitted our blacks to make the samplers more closely comparable.

have suggested, the social emancipation of women in the past generation has made wives less apt to have marital coitus unwillingly than used to be the case, it would follow that they would be less likely to overestimate its frequency. If this is correct, then the increases shown in the female estimates must understate the change since Kinsey's time, since the 1938–1949 estimates were somewhat higher than reality, and the 1972 estimates closer to it. There is no corresponding reason to suppose that the 1972 estimates by males underestimate coital frequency any more or less than the 1938–1946 estimates. In any event, if we were to make the reasonable and conservative assumption that the actual truth lies about halfway between the averages derived from male estimates and those from female estimates, we would find increases in marital coital frequency of the order of magnitude shown in Table 3.

It thus appears that there has been a dramatic reversal of the decline in marital coital frequency that had taken place in the generation prior to the time of Kinsey's fieldwork. Since, as we have suggested, marital coitus today is very likely to represent the desires of both partners rather than of the husband alone, the rise in coital frequency must mean that, in general, today's wives find marital intercourse more rewarding than did their counterparts of a

Table 3. Marital Coitus: Frequency Per Week, Male and Female Estimates Combined, 1938–1946/9 and 1972

1938–1946/9 (Kinsey)		1972 (Present survey)	
Age	Median	Age	Median
16–25	2.45	18–24	3.25
26–35	1.95	25–34	2.55
36–45	1.40	35–44	2.00
46–55	.85	45–54	1.00
56–60	.50	55 & over	1.00

generation ago. As confirmation, we cite the fact that only about a tenth of our entire married female sample reported finding marital sex either neutral or unpleasant in the past year, and that even within this small minority, only a quarter said they would prefer less frequent intercourse with the spouse. In contrast, of the great majority of women who found their marital coitus mostly pleasurable or very pleasurable nearly three-quarters said the frequency was just about right, and a quarter would like it to be higher.

The general explanation of wives' increased appetite for marital coitus, it seems obvious, is that recent developments in sexual liberation have done much to rid women of those culturally created inhibitions, including the inability to convey their wishes to their husbands, that formerly stifled both desire and responsiveness. In addition, one other aspect of sexual liberation deserves special mention: This is the stimulative effect of printed and visual materials dealing with sex, which are now virtually omnipresent in daily life. Many of these materials not only convey new ideas but are meant to be erotically arousing. They succeed in the latter intent because sexual liberation has made most people more receptive to such stimuli than their counterparts of 20 or 25 years ago. Up to twice as many of the males and up to four times as many of the females in our sample as in Kinsey's say they can be sexually aroused by depictions of the nude body and by literature, pictures or film portraying sexual activities. Interestingly enough, our data show that married females are much more arousable by erotic stimuli of various sorts, including out-and-out pornography, than are single females. This is probably because, despite the liberating developments of the past generation, erotic feelings still arise most freely, for most women, within the security of total interpersonal commitment. In any case, erotic stimuli of one sort or another are encountered anywhere from once a month to several times a week by more than four out of ten husbands and nearly three out of ten wives in the younger half of our sample—and according to studies made for the Commission on Obscenity and Pornography, each such exposure tends to increase the sexual activity between married partners for the ensuing couple of days.*

It is particularly noteworthy that the increases in coital frequency shown in Tables 1, 2, and 3 extend to older groups; sexual liberation, which in many ways seems associated with the young, is evidently having important effects throughout the population, making it possible for husbands and wives to remain somewhat more interested and active in marital coitus even after many years of marriage than used to be the case. The following are some of the factors probably associated with this shift:

*Even those females who deny being aroused by erotic stimuli may well respond with higher coital rates in the day or two after exposure. One study made for the Commission on Obscenity and Pornography found that many of the females who expressed disgust·or annoyance when viewing pornographic films nevertheless had distinct clinical symptoms of arousal. In Freudian terms, the ego disapproved but the id responded.

- Increases in the variety of techniques used in foreplay and of positions used in intercourse . . . are keeping marital coitus more interesting.
- Sexual liberation has begun to counteract the puritan-bourgeois notion that sex is unsuitable and disgraceful for the middle-aged or elderly. Kinsey, Masters and Johnson, Isadore Rubin and others have shown that desire and physical capacity, though they wane with age (more in the male than in the female), do not disappear in physically healthy persons, except for psychological reasons, until late in the eighth decade of life.
- Many older females used to lose interest in coitus because of the discomfort and irritation it caused after postmenopausal hormone deprivation had resulted in tissue inelasticity and in a lack of lubricating secretion. These postmenopausal changes are now easily controlled by estrogen-replacement therapy, and many women who once discouraged coitus are now continuing enjoyable coital activity with their husbands.

Another interesting change revealed by the data is a shift in the nature of the discrepancies between the male and female estimates of frequency. In Kinsey's data, young females gave higher frequency estimates than did young males, while among older persons the opposite was true. The explanation, valid at that time, was that young women wanted less than they were having, while older men were unable to provide as much as their wives wanted. Our own data show a very different picture: In the younger half of the sample it is the males, not the females, who give the higher estimates, though the reason can hardly be waning abilities (more likely, it is that liberated young females perceive their coital frequencies as lower than they would like). In the older half of the sample, desire and ability, on the part of both sexes, seem to be in accord, since there are no discrepancies whatever.

In Kinsey's time, education and occupational status, though they bore important relationships to the frequency of masturbation and premarital coitus, had little or no relationship to the frequency of marital coitus. Nor do they today, according to our own data. Religion, on the other hand, did have an important relationship to marital coital frequency in Kinsey's time, and still does. Kinsey reported that less-devout husbands had 20 to 30 percent more marital intercourse than devout ones because the latter carried over into marriage their premarital moral view of sex. For females, however, devoutness did not affect frequency because, according to Kinsey, the male had more control over the frequency of intercourse than the female. Today, religion is still an inhibiting influence on marital coital frequency, but few husbands—especially among the young—are now wholly or principally in control of coital frequency; devoutness in the wife is now likely to cut down on coital frequency, but paradoxically, devoutness in the husband, is not. Perhaps sexual liberation has affected churchgoing males more than churchgoing females; or perhaps the balance of power has been reversed. In any event, the curious figures are given in Table 4.

In sum, we find a considerable increase in the frequency of marital intercourse at every age level, as compared to the same age levels a generation ago.

Table 4. Marital Coitus: Median Frequency Per Week, by Regularity of Church Attendance, Under 35 Males and Females

	Regular churchgoers	Non-churchgoers
Females' estimates	2.0	3.0
Males' estimates	3.0	3.0

Apparently, it is not just the young and single who are currently having more active sex lives than their counterparts in Kinsey's time, but married Americans of every age. Sexual liberation has had its greatest effect, at least in numerical terms, within the safe confines of the ancient and established institution of monogamous marriage.

Blue-Collar Marriage and the Sexual Revolution

Lillian Breslow Rubin

> Experimental? Oh, he's much more experimental than I am. Once in awhile, I'll say, "Okay, you get a treat; we'll do it with the lights on." And I put the pillow over my head. [Thirty-year-old woman, married twelve years]

> Experimental? Not Ann. I keep trying to get her to loosen up; you know, to be more—What would you call it?—adventurous. I mean, there's lots of different things we could be doing. She just can't see it. Sometimes I mind; but then sometimes I think, "After all, she was brought up in a good family, and she always was a nice, sweet girl." And that's the kind of girl I wanted, so I guess I ain't got no real right to complain. [Twenty-seven-year-old man, married seven years]

These comments, typical of a significant number of the fifty white working-class couples* with whom I spoke, made me wonder: Is *this* the revolution in sexual behavior I had been reading about? And if so, were these the issues of the working class alone? To answer the second question, I also talked with

From Chapter 8 of *Worlds of Pain: Life in the Working-Class Family* by Lillian Breslow Rubin. © 1976 by Lillian Breslow Rubin. By permission of Basic Books, Inc., Publishers, New York.

*For the purpose of this study, class was defined by both education and occupation. All the families were intact, neither husband nor wife had more than a high-school education, and the husband was employed in what is traditionally defined as a blue-collar occupation. In addition, because I was interested in studying relatively young families, the wife was under 40 and at least one child under 12 was still in the home. Median age of the women was 28; of the men, 31.

twenty-five professional middle-class couples whose characteristics matched the working-class group in all but education and occupation.

Not one couple is without stories about adjustment problems in this difficult and delicate area of marital life—problems not just in the past, but in the present as well. Some of the problem areas—such as differences in frequency of sexual desire between men and women—are old ones. Some—such as the men's complaints about their wives' reluctance to engage in variant and esoteric sexual behaviors—are newer. All suggest that there is, in fact, a revolution in sexual behavior in the American society that runs wide and deep—a revolution in which sexual behaviors that formerly were the province of the college-educated upper classes now are practiced widely at all class and education levels.

The evidence is strong that more people are engaging in more varieties of sexual behavior than ever before—more premarital, post-marital, extra-marital sex of all kinds. In 1948, for example, Kinsey found that only 15 percent of high-school- educated married men ever engaged in cunnilingus, compared to 45 percent of college-educated men. But the world changes quickly. Just twenty-five years later, a national survey shows that the proportion of high-school-educated men engaging in cunnilingus jumped to 56 percent.[1] And among the people I met, the figure stands at 70 percent.

But to dwell on these impressive statistics which tell us what people *do* without attention to how they *feel* about what they do is to miss a profoundly important dimension of human experience—that is, the *meaning* that people attribute to their behavior. Nowhere is the disjunction between behavior and attitude seen more sharply than in the area of sexual behavior. For when, in the course of a single lifetime, the forbidden becomes commonplace, when the border between the conceivable and the inconceivable suddenly disappears, people may *do* new things, but they don't necessarily *like* them.

For decades, novelists, filmmakers, and social scientists all have portrayed working-class men as little more than boorish, insensitive studs—men whose sexual performance was, at best, hasty and perfunctory; at worst, brutal—concerned only with meeting their own urgent needs. Consideration for a woman's needs, variety in sexual behaviors, experimentation—these, it is generally said, are to be found largely among men of the upper classes; working-class men allegedly know nothing of such amenities.[2]

If such men ever lived in large numbers, they surely do no longer. Morton Hunt's study, *Sexual Behavior in the 1970's,* which does not control for class but does give data that are controlled for education, provides evidence that men at all educational levels have become more concerned with and more sensitive to women's sexual needs—with the greatest increase reported among high-school-educated men. Comparing his sample with the 1948 Kinsey data on the subject of foreplay, for example, he notes that Kinsey reported that foreplay was "very brief or even perfunctory" among high-school-educated husbands, while college-educated husbands reported about ten minutes.

Twenty-five years later, Hunt found that the median for non-college and college-educated husbands was the same—fifteen minutes. Similar changes were found in the variety of sexual behaviors, the variety of positions used, and the duration of coitus—with especially sharp increases reported among high-school-educated men.

Not surprisingly, it is the men more often than the women who find these changing sexual norms easier to integrate—generally responding more positively to a cultural context that offers the potential for loosening sexual constraints. For historically, it is men, not women, whose sexuality has been thought to be unruly and ungovernable—destined to be restrained by a good (read: asexual) woman. Thus, it is the men who now more often speak of their wish for sex to be freer and with more mutual enjoyment:

> I think sex should be that you enjoy each other's bodies. Judy doesn't care for touching and feeling each other though.

. . . who push their wives to be sexually experimental, to try new things and different ways:

> She thinks there's just one right position and one right way—in the dark with her eyes closed tight. Anything that varies from that makes her upset.

. . . who sometimes are more concerned than their wives for her orgasm:

> It's just not enjoyable if she doesn't have a climax, too. She says she doesn't mind, but I do.

For the women, these attitudes of their men—their newly expressed wish for sexual innovation, their concern for their wives' gratification—are not an unmixed blessing. For in any situation, there is a gap between the ideal statements of a culture and the reality in which people live out their lives—a time lag between the emergence of new cultural forms and their internalization by the individuals who must act upon them. In sexual matters, that gap is felt most keenly by women. Socialized from infancy to experience their sexuality as a negative force to be inhibited and repressed, women can't just switch "on" as the changing culture or their husbands dictate. Nice girls don't! Men *use* bad girls but *marry* good girls! Submit, but don't enjoy—at least not obviously so! These are the injunctions that have dominated their lives—injunctions that are laid aside with difficulty, if at all.

The media tell us that the double standard of sexual morality is dead. But with good reason, women don't believe it. They know from experience that it is alive and well, that it exists side-by-side with the new ideology that heralds their sexual liberation. They know all about who are the "bad girls" in school, in the neighborhood; who are the "good girls." Everybody knows! Nor is this knowledge given only among the working class. The definition of "good girl" and "bad girl" may vary somewhat according to class, but the fundamental ideas those words encompass are not yet gone either from our culture or our consciousness at any class level.

We need only to look at our own responses to two questions to understand how vital the double standard remains. When we are asked, "What kind of woman is she?" we are likely to think about her sexual behavior; is she "easy" or not. But the question, "What kind of man is he?" evokes thoughts about what kind of work he does; is he strong, weak, kind, cruel? His sexual behavior is his private business, no concern of ours.

Whether these issues are especially real for working-class women, or whether women of that class are simply more open in talking about them than their middle-class counterparts, is difficult to say. Most of the middle-class women I spoke with came to their first sexual experiences at college where, during the early-to-middle 1960's, they suddenly entered a world where sexual freedom was the by-word. These were the years when it was said, "Sex is no different than a handshake"; when it was insisted that if women would only "do what comes naturally," they'd have no problems with sexual enjoyment; when the young women who did have such problems experienced themselves as personally inadequate; when it was "uncool" for a girl to ask questions about these issues—even, God forbid, to say no. Thus for well over a decade, these college-educated women have lived in an atmosphere that was at once sexually permissive and coercive—permissive in that it encouraged them to unfetter and experience their sexuality; coercive, in that it gave them little room to experience also the constraints upon that sexuality that their culture and personal history until then had imposed upon them. That combination, then, would make them at once less guilty about their sexuality *and* less ready to speak of the inhibitions that remain.

All that notwithstanding, one thing is clear. Among the people I met, working-class and middle-class couples engage in essentially the same kinds of sexual behaviors in roughly the same proportions. But working-class wives express considerably more discomfort about what they do in the marriage bed than their middle-class sisters.

Take, for example, the conflict that engages many couples around the issue of oral-genital stimulation. Seventy percent of the working-class and 76 percent of the middle-class couples engage in such sexual activity. A word of caution is necessary here, however, because these gross figures can be misleading. For about one-third of each group, engaging in oral-genital stimulation means that they tried it once, or that it happens a few times a year at most. Another 30 percent of the middle-class couples and 40 percent of the working-class couples said they have oral sex only occasionally, meaning something over three times but less than ten times a year. Thus, only about one-fourth of the working-class couples and one-third of the middle-class couples who engage in oral sex use this sexual mode routinely as a standard part of their repertoire of sexual techniques. Still, fewer of the working-class women say they enjoy it unreservedly or without guilt. Listen to this couple, married twelve years. The husband:

> I've always been of the opinion that what two people do in the bedroom is fine; whatever they want to do is okay. But Jane, she doesn't agree. I personally like a lot of foreplay, caressing each other and whatever. For her, no. I

think oral sex is the ultimate in making love; but she says it's revolting. [With a deep sigh of yearning] I wish I could make her understand.

The wife . . .

I sure wish I could make him stop pushing me into that (Ugh, I even hate to talk about it), into that oral stuff. I let him do it, but I hate it. He says I'm old-fashioned about sex and maybe I am. But I was brought up that there's just one way you're supposed to do it. I still believe that way, even though he keeps trying to convince me of his way. How can I change when I wasn't brought up that way? [With a pained sigh] I wish I could make him understand.

Notice her plaintive plea for understanding—"I wasn't brought up that way." In reality, when it comes to sex, she, like most of us, wasn't brought up *any* way. Girls generally learn only that it's "wrong" before marriage. But what that "it" is often is hazy and unclear until after the first sexual experience. As for the varieties of sexual behavior, these are rarely, if ever, mentioned to growing children, let alone discussed in terms of which are right or wrong, good or bad, permissible or impermissible.

Still, the cry for understanding from both men and women is real. Each wishes to make the other "understand," to transform the other into oneself for a brief moment so that the inner experience can be apprehended by the other. Yet, given the widely divergent socialization practices around male and female sexuality, the wish is but another impossible fantasy. The result: he asks; she gives. And neither is satisfied with the resolution. Despairing of finding a solution with which both are comfortable, one husband comments . . .

Either I'm forcing my way on her or she's forcing her way on me. Either way, you can't win. If she gives in, it isn't because she's enjoying it, but because I pushed her. I suppose you could say I get what I want, but it doesn't feel that way.

It's true, on the question of oral sex, most of the time, she "gives in— hesitantly, shyly, uncomfortably, even with revulsion. Sometimes women act from a sense of caring and consideration . . .

We don't do it much because it really makes me uncomfortable, you know [making a face], a little sick. But sometimes, I say okay because I know it means a lot to him and I really want to do it for him.

Sometimes from a sense of duty . . .

Even though I hate it, if he needs it, then I feel I ought to do it. After all, I'm his wife.

Sometimes out of fear of losing their men . . .

He can find someone to give it to him, so I figure I better do it.

Sometimes out of resignation and a sense of powerlessness . . .

I tell him I don't want to do it, but it doesn't do any good. If it's what he wants, that's what we do.

And sometimes it is offered as a bribe or payment for good behavior—not surprising in a culture that teaches a woman that her body is a negotiable instrument:

> He gets different treats at different times, depending on what he deserves. Sometimes I let him do that oral stuff you're talking about to me. Sometimes when he's *very* good, I do it to him.

While most of the working-class women greet both cunnilingus and fellatio with little enthusiasm or pleasure, cunnilingus is practiced with slightly greater frequency and with slightly less resistance than fellatio. Partly, that's because many women are talked into cunnilingus by their husbands' "If-I'm-willing-why-do-you-care?" argument . . .

> I don't like him to do it, but I can't figure out what to say when he says that I shouldn't care if *he* doesn't.

. . . and partly, and perhaps more important, because cunnilingus is something that is done *to* a woman—an act not requiring her active engagement as fellatio does; and one, therefore, not quite so incongruent with her socialization to passivity. In all areas of life, she has been raised to wait upon the initiative of another, to monitor both behavior and response carefully so as not to appear too forward or aggressive. Nowhere are these lessons more thoroughly in-grained than in her sexual behavior; nowhere has she learned better to be a reflector rather than a generator of action. Thus, fellatio, perhaps more than any other sex act, is a difficult one for a woman.

Even those women who do not express distinctly negative feelings about oral sex are often in conflict about it—unsure whether it is really all right for them to engage in, let alone enjoy, such esoteric sexual behavior, worrying about whether these are things "nice girls" do. One twenty-eight-year-old mother of three, married ten years, explained . . .

> I always feel like it's not quite right, no matter what Pete says. I guess it's not the way I was brought up, and it's hard to get over that. He keeps telling me it's okay if it's between us, that anything we do is okay. But I'm not sure about that. How do I know in the end he won't think I'm cheap.

> Sometimes I enjoy it, I guess. But most of the time I'm too worried thinking about whether I ought to be doing it, and worrying what he's *really* thinking to get much pleasure.

"How do I know he won't think I'm cheap?"—a question asked over and over again, an issue that dominates these women and their attitudes toward their own sexuality. Some husbands reassure them . . .

> She says she worries I'll think she's a cheap tramp, and she doesn't really believe me when I keep telling her it's not true.

Such reassurances remain suspect, however, partly because it's so hard for women to move past the fears of their own sexuality with which they have been stamped; and partly because at least some men are not without their

own ambivalence about it, as is evident in this comment from one young
husband . . .

> No, Alice isn't that kind of girl. Jesus, you shouldn't ask questions like that.
> [A long, difficult silence] She wasn't brought up to go for all that [pause] fancy
> stuff. You know, all those different ways and [shifting uncomfortably in his
> chair, lighting a cigarette, and looking down at the floor] that oral stuff. But
> that's okay with me. There's plenty of women out there to do that kind of
> stuff with. You can meet them in any bar any time you want to. You don't
> have to marry those kind.

As long as that distinction remains, as long as men distinguish between the girl
they marry and the girl they use, many women will remain unconvinced by
their reassurances and wary about engaging in sexual behaviors that seem to
threaten their "good girl" status.

Those assurances are doubly hard to hear and to believe when women also
know that their husbands are proud of their naivete in sexual matters—a pride
which many men take little trouble to hide.

> It took a long time for me to convince her that it didn't have to be by the
> books. She was like an innocent babe. I taught her everything she knows.

Even men whose wives were married before will say with pleasure . . .

> It's funny how naive she was when we got married. She was married before,
> you know, but still she was kind of innocent. I taught her just about every-
> thing she knows.

For the women, the message seems clear: he wants to believe in her innocence, to believe in the special quality of their sexual relationship, to believe
that these things she does only for him. She is to be pupil to his teacher. So
she echoes his words—"He taught me everything I know." Repeatedly that
phrase or a close equivalent is used as women discuss their sexual behavior and
their feelings about it. And always it is said with a sure sense that it's what
her husband wants and needs to believe, as these incongruent comments from
a woman now in her second marriage show.

> One thing I know he likes is that he taught me mostly all I know about sex,
> so that makes him feel good. It also means that I haven't any habits that have
> to be readjusted to his way or anything like that.
> *That seems a strange thing to say when you were married for some years
> before.*

Startled, she looked at me, then down at her hands uncomfortably.

> Yeah, I guess you'd think so. Well, you know, he likes to feel that way so why
> shouldn't he, and why shouldn't I let him?

Given that knowledge, even if it were possible to do so on command, most
women would not dare risk unleashing their sexual inhibitions. From where
a woman stands, the implicit injunction in her husband's pride in her innocence is that her sexuality be restrained. And restrain it she does—a feat for

which she is all too well trained. The price for that training in restraint is high for both of them, however. He often complains because she doesn't take the initiative . . .

> She never initiates anything. She'll make no advances at all, not even subtleties.

She often replies . . .

> I just can't. I guess I'm inhibited, I don't know. All I know is it's very hard for me to start things up or to tell him something I want.

On the other hand, not infrequently when women put aside that restraint and take the initiative, they may find themselves accused of not being feminine enough.

> It isn't that I mind her letting me know when she wants it, but she isn't very subtle about it. I mean, she could let me know in a nice, feminine way. Being feminine and, you know, kind of subtle, that's not her strong point.

Sensitive to the possibility of being thought of as "unfeminine" or "aggressive," most women shy away from any behavior that might bring those words down upon their heads. For it is painful for any woman of any class to hear herself described in these ways.

> I don't like to think he might think I was being aggressive, so I don't usually make any suggestions. Most of the time it's okay because he can usually tell when I'm in the mood. But if he can't, I just wait.

These, then, are some of the dilemmas and conflicts people face around the newly required and desired sexual behaviors. Among working-class women, isolation and insulation compound their problems. It is one thing to read about all these strange and exotic sexual behaviors in books and magazines, another to know others like yourself who actually do these things.

> He keeps trying to get me to read those books, but what difference would it make? I don't know who those people are. There's a lot of people do lots of things; it doesn't mean I have to do them.

If the books aren't convincing, and it's not culturally acceptable to discuss the intimate details of one's sex life with neighbors, friends, co-workers, or even family, most women are stuck with their childhood and adolescent fears, fantasies, and prohibitions. Small wonder that over and over again during my visit the atmosphere in the room changed from anxiety to relief when subjects such as oral sex were treated casually, with either the implicit or explicit understanding that it is both common and acceptable sexual practice.

> Jim keeps telling me and telling me it's okay, that it's not dirty. But I always worry about it, not really knowing if that's true or not. I read a couple of books once, but it's different. I never talked to anyone but Jim about it before. [Smiling, as if a weight had been lifted from her shoulders] You're so cool about it; talking to you makes it seem not so bad.

In contrast, discussion of these issues with the middle-class women was considerably more relaxed. Regardless of their own feelings about engaging in oral sex, it was clear that most middle-class women recognize that it is a widely practiced and acceptable behavior. In fact, more often than not, they tended to feel guilty and uncomfortable about their own inhibitions, not because they weren't able to please their husbands but because they believed their constraint relfected some inadequacy in their personal sexual adjustment. It was also from middle-class women that I more often heard complaints when their husbands were unwilling to experiment with oral-genital sex. Of the working-class couples who never engage in oral sex, only one woman complained about her husband's unwillingness to do so. Of the middle-class couples in a similar situation, four women offered that complaint.

But it is also true that, generally, the husbands of these middle-class women send fewer ambiguous and ambivalent messages about their wives' sexuality, tend less to think in good girl-bad girl terms, more often expect and accept that their wives had other sexual experiences before they met. Further, these middle-class women are more often in contact with others like themselves in an environment where discussion of sexual issues is encouraged—a course in human sexuality, a women's group, for example.

Still, the recitation of these differences in experience ought not to be read to suggest that middle-class women are now sexually free and uninhibited. The most that can be said on that score is that more of them live in an atmosphere that more seriously encourages that goal, hence more—especially those under thirty—may be closer to its attainment. Meanwhile, at all class levels, most women probably feel comfortable enough with their own sexual responses to be willing participants in sexual intercourse. But when it comes to oral sex—especially among the working class—generally they submit just as their mothers before them submitted to more traditional sexual behaviors.

Sexual conflicts in marriage are not always constellated around such exotic issues, however; nor, as I have said, are any of them the exclusive problem of a particular class. Thus, although what follows rests on material taken from my discussions with working-class couples, much of it applies to the professional middle class as well. True, the middle-class couples more often are able to discuss some of their issues more openly with each other. But despite the current, almost mystical, belief in communication-as-problem-solving, talk doesn't always help. True, middle-class couples much more often seek professional help with these problems. But sexual conflicts in a marriage are among the most intractable—the recent development and proliferation of sex therapies notwithstanding. Those therapies can be useful in dealing with some specific sexual dysfunction—prematurely ejaculating men or nonorgasmic women. But the kinds of sexual conflicts to be discussed here are so deeply rooted in the socio-cultural mandates of our world that they remain extraordinarily resistant regardless of how able the psychotherapeutic help we can buy. Thus, while there are subtle differences between the two classes in the language and tone with which the problems are dealt, in the amount of discussion about them, and in their ability and willingness to seek professional help, in this instance, those differences are not as important as the similarities that remain.

In fact, the earliest sexual problems rear their heads with the couple's first fight. Regardless of what has gone before, at bedtime, he's ready for sex; she remains cold and aloof. Listen to this couple in their mid-to-late-twenties, married nine years. The wife . . .

> I don't understand him. He's ready to go any time. It's always been a big problem with us right from the beginning. If we've hardly seen each other for two or three days and hardly talked to each other, I can't just jump into bed. If we have a fight, I can't just turn it off. He has a hard time understanding that. I feel like that's all he wants sometimes. I have to know I'm needed and wanted for more than just jumping into bed.

The husband . . .

> She complains that all I want from her is sex, and I try to make her understand that it's an expression of love. I'll want to make up with her by making love, but she's cold as the inside of the refrig. Sure I get mad when that happens. Why shouldn't I? Here I'm trying to make up and make love, and she's holding out for something—I don't know what.

The wife . . .

> He keeps saying he wants to make love, but it just doesn't feel like love to me. Sometimes I feel bad that I feel that way, but I just can't help it.

The husband . . .

> I don't understand. She says it doesn't feel like love. What does that mean, anyway? What does she think love is?

The wife . . .

> I want him to talk to me, to tell me what he's thinking about. If we have a fight, I want to talk about it so we could maybe understand it. I don't want to jump in bed and just pretend it didn't happen.

The husband . . .

> Talk! Talk! What's there to talk about. I want to make love to her and she says she wants to talk. How's talking going to convince her I'm loving her.

In sex, as in other matters, the barriers to communication are high; and the language people use serves to further confuse and mystify. He says, "I want to make love." She says, "It doesn't feel like love." Neither quite knows what the other is talking about; both feel vaguely guilty and uncomfortable—aware only that somehow they're passing each other, not connecting. He believes he already has given her the most profound declaration of love of which a man is capable. He married her; he gives her a home; he works hard each day to support her and the children.

> What does she want? Proof? She's got it, hasn't she? Would I be knocking myself out to get things for her—like to keep up this house—if I didn't love her. Why does a man do things like that if not because he loves his wife and kids? I swear, I can't figure what she wants.

This is one time when *she* knows what she wants.

> I want him to let me know in other ways, too, not just sex. It's not enough that he supports us and takes care of us. I appreciate that, but I want him to share things with me. I need for him to tell me his feelings. He keeps saying no, but to me, there's a difference between making love and sex. Just once, I'd like him to love me without ending up in sex. But when I tell him that, he thinks I'm crazy.

For him, perhaps, it *does* seem crazy. Split off, as he is, from the rest of the expressive-emotional side of himself, sex may be the one place where he can allow himself the expression of deep feelings, the one place where he can experience the depth of that affective side. His wife, on the other hand, closely connected with her feeling side in all areas *but* the sexual, finds it difficult to be comfortable with her feelings in the very area in which he has the greatest—sometimes the only—ease. She keeps asking for something she can understand and is comfortable with—a demonstration of his feelings in non-sexual ways. He keeps giving her the one thing he can understand and is comfortable with—his feelings wrapped up in a blanket of sex. Thus do husbands and wives find themselves in an impossibly difficult bind—another bind not of their own making, but one that stems from the cultural context in which girls and boys grow to adulthood.

I am suggesting, then, that a man's ever-present sexual readiness is not simply an expression of urgent sexual need but also a complex compensatory response to a socialization process that *constricts the development of the emotional side of his personality in all but sexual expression.* Conversely, a woman's insistent plea for an emotional statement of a nonsexual nature is a response to a process that *encourages the development of the affective side of her personality in all but sexual expression.*[3]

Such differences between women and men about the *meaning* of sex make for differences between wives and husbands in frequency of desire as well—differences which lead to a wide discrepancy in their perceptions about the frequency of the sexual encounter.[4] Except for a few cases where the women are inclined to be more sexually active than the men, he wants sex more often than she. To him, therefore, it seems as if they have sex less often than they actually do; to her, it seems more often. But the classical caricature of a wife fending off her husband's advances with a sick headache seems not to apply among working-class women. Once in awhile, a woman says . . .

> I tell him straight. I'm not in the mood, and he understands.

Mostly, however, women say . . .

> I don't use excuses like headaches and things like that. If my husband wants me, I'm his wife, and I do what he wants. It's my responsibility to give it to him when he needs it.

Whether she refuses outright or acquiesces out of a sense of duty or responsibility, the solution is less than satisfactory for both partners. In either case, he feels frustrated and deprived. He wants more than release from his own sexual tension; he wants her active involvement as well. Confronted with his ever-present readiness, she feels guilty . . .

> I feel guilty and uncomfortable when he's always ready and I'm not, like I'm not taking care of him.

. . . coerced . . .

> I feel like it hangs over my head all the time. He always wants it; twice a day wouldn't be too much for him. He says he doesn't want me just to give in to him, but if I didn't he'd be walking around horny all the time. If we waited for me to want it, it would never be enough for him.

. . . and also deprived . . .

> Before I ever get a chance to feel really sexy, he's there and waiting. I'd like to know what it feels like sometimes to really want it that bad. Oh, sometimes I do. But mostly I don't get the chance.

Thus, she rarely has the opportunity to experience the full force of her own sexual rhythm, and with it, the full impact of her sexuality. It is preempted by the urgency and frequency of his desires.

Finally, there is plenty of evidence that the battle between the sexes is still being waged in the marriage bed, and in very traditional ways. Several couples spoke of their early sexual adjustment problems in ways that suggest that the struggle was not over sex but over power and control. Often in the early years, when she wants sex, he's tired; when he wants sex, she's uninterested. For many couples, the pattern still repeats itself once in awhile. For about one-fifth of them, the scenario continues to be played out with great regularity and sometimes with great drama, as this story of one early-thirties couple illustrates.

In six months of premarital and ten years of marital coitus, the woman had never had an orgasm.

> We had sex four or five times a week like clockwork all those years, and I just laid there like a lump. I couldn't figure out what all the noise was about.

Asked how he felt about her passivity during that period, her husband—a taciturn, brooding man, whose silence seemed to cover a wellspring of hostility —replied . . .

> If she couldn't, she couldn't. I didn't like it, but I took what I needed. [After a moment's hesitation] She's always been hard to handle.

A year ago, attracted by ideas about women's sexuality that seemed to her to be "in the air," she began to read some of the women's literature on the subject. From there, she moved on to pornography and one night, as she tells it . . .

> The earth shook. I couldn't believe anything could be so great. I kept wondering how I lived so long without knowing about it. I kept asking Fred why he'd never made me understand before. [Then, angrily] But you'll never believe what happened after that. My husband just lost interest in sex. Now, I can hardly ever get him to do it any more, no matter how much I try or beg him. He says he's too tired, or he doesn't feel well, or else he just falls asleep and I can't wake him up. I can hardly believe it's happening sometimes. Can you imagine such a thing? I even wonder whether maybe I shouldn't have made such a big fuss about it. Maybe it scared him off or something.

Her husband refused my attempts to explore the issue with him, insisting that all is well in their sex life, but adding . . .

> She's always asking for something, or hollering about something. I don't have any control around this house any more. Nobody listens to me.

It would seem, then, that as long as he could "take what I needed," he could feel he was asserting some control over his wife and could remain sexually active and potent. When she unexpectedly became an assertive and active participant in the sex act, the only possibility for retaining control was to move from the active to the passive mode. Thus, he felt impotent. His wife, now acutely aware of her sexual deprivation, is left torn between anger, frustration, and the terrible fear that somehow she is responsible for it.

A dramatic story? Certainly, but one whose outlines are clear in 20 percent of these marriages where three women complained about their husbands' impotence and seven about sexual withholding—not surprisingly, a problem most of the men were unwilling to talk about. In the three cases where the husband did address the issue at all, either he denied its existence, "It's no problem; I'm just tired;" or blamed his wife, "She doesn't appeal to me," or "She's too pushy." The last has been a subject of recent concern expressed publicly by psychologists and widely publicized in the mass media. The performance demands being laid on men are extraordinary, we are told, and women are cautioned that their emergent assertiveness—sexual and otherwise—threatens the sexual performance of their men. The time has come, these experts warn, to take the pressure off.

Nowhere, however, do we hear concern about the effects of the performance demand on women. Yet, never in history have heavier demands for sexual performance been laid on them. Until recently, women were expected to submit passively to sex; now they are told their passivity diminishes their husbands' enjoyment. Until recently, especially among the less educated working class, orgasm was an unexpected gift; now it is a requirement of adequate sexual performance.[5] These new definitions of adequacy leave many women feeling "under the gun"—fearful and anxious if they do not achieve orgasm;

if it does not happen at the "right" moment—that is, at the instant of their husbands' ejaculation; or if they are uncomfortable about engaging in behaviors that feel alien or aberrant to them.[6] If anxiety about one's ability to perform adequately has an untoward effect on the male orgasm, is there any reason to believe it would not inhibit the female's as well?

In fact, the newfound concern with their orgasm is a mixed and costly blessing for many women. For some, it has indeed opened the possibility for pleasures long denied. For others, however, it is experienced as another demand in a life already too full of demands. Listen to this thirty-five-year-old woman who works part time, takes care of a house, a husband, six children, and an aging, sick father . . .

> It feels like somebody's always wanting something from me. Either one of the kids is hanging on to me or pulling at me, or my father needs something. And if it's not them, then Tom's always coming after me with that gleam in his eye. Then, it's not enough if I just let him have it, because if I don't have a climax, he's not happy. I get so tired of everybody wanting something from me all the time. I sometimes think I hate sex.

While it is undoubtedly true that more women have more orgasms more often than ever before—and that most of them enjoy sex more than women in earlier generations—it is also true that there are times when a husband's wish for his wife's orgasm is experienced as oppressive and alienating—when it seems to a woman that her orgasm is more a requirement of his pleasure than her own. We may ask: How rational are these thoughts? And we may wonder: Why should it be a matter of question or criticism if, in the course of pleasuring their wives, men also pleasure themselves? When phrased that way, it should not be questioned! But if we look at the discussion around female orgasm or lack of it a little more closely, we notice that it is almost invariably tied to male pleasure. If a woman doesn't have an orgasm, it is a problem, if not for her, then because both her man's pleasure and his sense of manhood are diminished. Can anyone imagine a discussion of male impotence centering around concern for women? In fact, when we talk about the failure of men to achieve erection or orgasm, the discourse takes place in hushed, serious, regretful tones—always in the context of concern about how those men experience that failure. How many of us have ever thought, "What a shame for his woman that he can't have an erection." Any woman who has shared that experience with a man knows that her concern was largely for him, her own frustration becoming irrelevant in that moment. Any man who has experienced impotence knows that his dominant concern was for the failure of his manhood.

It is not surprising, therefore, that several of the women I talked to were preoccupied with their orgasm, not because it was so important to them, but because their husbands' sense of manhood rested on it. Holding her head, one woman said painfully . . .

> I rarely have climaxes. But if it didn't bother my husband, it wouldn't bother me. I keep trying to tell him that I know it's not his fault, that he's really a

> good lover. I keep telling him it's something the matter with me, not with him. But it scares me because he doesn't believe it, and I worry he might leave me for a woman who will have climaxes for him.

With these final words, she epitomizes the feelings of many women, whether orgasmic or not, at least some of the time: *her orgasm is for him, not for her.* It is his need to validate his manhood that is the primary concern—his need, not hers. For women of the working class, who already have so little autonomy and control over their lives, this may well be experienced as the ultimate violation.

To compound the anxiety, now one orgasm is not enough. One woman, having read that some women have multiple orgasms, worried that her husband would soon find out.

> It's really important for him that I reach a climax, and I try to every time. He says it just doesn't make him feel good if I don't. But it's hard enough to do it once! What'll happen if he finds out about those women who have lots of climaxes?

These, then, are some dimensions of sexual experience in the 1970's that are buried under the sensational reports of changing sexual mores. Undoubtedly, there is a loosening of sexual constraints for both women and men; undoubtedly, more people are enjoying fuller sexual experiences than ever before. Certainly, it is important that these changes are discussed publicly, that the subject of sex has come out of the closet. But that is not enough. For we must also understand that such changes are not without cost to the individuals who try to live them out, who must somehow struggle past powerful early training to a new consciousness. For women especially—women of any class—that training in repressing and inhibiting their sexuality makes this a particularly difficult struggle.

It is both sad and ironic now to hear men complain that their wives are too cautious, too inhibited, or not responsive enough in bed. Sad, because the deprivation men experience is real; ironic, because these are the costs of the sexual limitations that generations of their forebears have imposed on women. Changing such historic patterns of thought and behavior will not be easy for either men or women. For certainly, many men are still not without ambivalence about these sexual issues with reference to their women—a subtlety that is not lost on their wives. But even where men unambivalently mean what they say about wanting their wives to be freer in the marriage bed, it will take time for women to work through centuries of socially mandated denial and repression . . .

> All I know is, I can't just turn on so easy. Maybe we're all paying the price now because men didn't used to want women to enjoy sex.

. . . and probably will require their first being freer in other beds as well.

> I was eighteen when we got married, and I was a very young eighteen. I'd never had any relations with anybody, not even my husband, before we were

married. So we had a lot of problems. I guess I was kind of frigid at first. But you know, after all those years when you're holding back, it's hard to all of a sudden get turned on just because you got married.

Yes, it is "hard to all of a sudden get turned on just because you got married." And as long as women's sexuality continues to be subjected to capricious demands and treated as if regulated by an on-off switch—expected to surge forth fully and vigorously at the flick of the "on" switch and to subside quietly at the flick of the "off"—most women will continue to seek the safest path, in this case, to remain quietly someplace between "on" and "off."

1. Morton Hunt, *Sexual Behavior in the 1970's* (Chicago: Playboy Press, 1974). This study, conducted for *Playboy* magazine, included a representative sample of urban and suburban adults, of whom 982 were men and 1,044 were women. Seventy-one percent of the sample were married (not to each other), 25 percent were never married, and 4 percent had been married.
2. For a good description of this stereotype, see Arthur B. Shostak, "Ethnic Revivalism, Blue-Collarites, and Bunker's Last Stand." In *The Rediscovery of Ethnicity,* edited by Sallie TeSelle (New York: Harper Colophon, 1973). See also Mirra Komarovsky, *Blue Collar Marriage* (New York: Vintage Books, 1962) who, while noting that the stereotype applies to "only a small minority" of the families she studied, found that only 30 percent of the women said they were very satisfied with their sexual relations. And some of the data she presents do indeed validate the stereotype more forcefully and very much more often than among my sample where it is practically nonexistent.
3. Cf. William Simon and John Gagnon, "On Psychosexual Development." In *Handbook of Socialization Theory and Research,* edited by David A. Goslin (Chicago: Rand McNally, 1969) and John Gagnon and William Simon, *Sexual Conduct: The Social Sources of Human Sexuality* (Chicago: Aldine Publishing, 1973) whose work is a major contribution toward understanding the differences in male-female sexuality as an expression of the differential socialization patterns for women and men. These authors also point to the masculine tendency to separate love and sex and the feminine tendency to fuse them. They suggest, in fact, that the male "capacity for detached sexual activity, activity where the only sustaining motive is sexual . . . may actually be the hallmark of male sexuality in our culture." For an exploration of the ways in which social structure and personality intersect from the psychoanalytic perspective, see Nancy Chodorow, *The Reproduction of Mothering: Family Structure and Feminine Personality* (Berkeley: University of California Press, 1977, forthcoming), who argues that the root of the differences in male-female personality and the concomitant differences in the development of psychosexual needs and responses lie in the social structure of the family.

   See also Ben Barker-Benfield, "The Spermatic Economy: A Nineteenth Century View of Sexuality." In *The American Family in Social-Historical Perspective,* edited by Michael Gordon (New York: St. Martin's Press, 1973) for a portrait of nineteenth century definitions of male and female sexuality and the fear and abhorrence with which men viewed female sexuality in that era.
4. It is for this reason that studies relying on the recollection of only one spouse for their data —as most do—risk considerable distortion. Thus, for example, when Morton Hunt reports that almost 26 percent of the married women ages twenty-five to thirty-four report having sexual intercourse between 105 and 156 times a year, we know only that this is the wife's perception, and we can assume that the recollection is filtered through her *feelings* about the frequency of the sexual encounter.
5. Again, Hunt's data, while not controlled for class, are suggestive. Using the 1948 Kinsey data as a comparative base, he reports that marital coitus has increased in frequency at every age and educational level. Comparing the Kinsey sample with his own at the fifteenth year of marriage, Hunt reports "a distinct increase in the number of wives who always or nearly always have orgasm (Kinsey: 45 percent; *Playboy:* 53 percent) and a sharp decrease in the number of wives who seldom or never do (Kinsey: 28 percent; *Playboy:* 15 percent)."

6. For a rebuke of the self-styled male "experts" on women's sexuality that is both wonderfully angry and funny as it highlights the absurdity of their advice to women, see Ellen Frankort, *Vaginal Politics* (New York: Bantam Books, 1973): 172–180. She opens this section of her book, entitled "Carnal Ignorance," by saying:

> For the longest time a woman wasn't supposed to enjoy sex. Then suddenly a woman was neurotic if she didn't achieve orgasm simultaneously with her husband. Proof of a woman's health was her ability to come at the very moment the man ejaculated, in the very place he ejaculated, and at the very rate ordained for him by his physiology. If she couldn't, she went to a male psychiatrist to find out why.

The Herpes Syndrome

Daniel Laskin

Five years ago, a spate of panicky headlines alerted Americans to a new alarming byproduct of the sexual revolution. Genital herpes—incurable, recurrent and highly contagious—was spreading rapidly. What the early reports did not convey, though, was the psychological damage and medical bafflement herpes would bring with it. Today, this viral infection has not only established itself as an uncontrollable epidemic; it has proved to be one of the most exasperating ailments, for patients and doctors alike.

Between five million and 20 million Americans are believed to suffer from herpes, which produces painful, fluid-filled blisters on the genitals. Some of them have such mild bouts that they see the disease as no more than an inconvenience; others are in almost constant pain. Virtually all of them, however, must endure an emotional crisis so distinct in its assault on their sense of worth that psychologists speak of a "herpes syndrome." Across the country, herpes victims find themselves suddenly beset by new vulnerabilities and moral dilemmas. They feel tainted, fearful no one will ever want to love them—and thus torn over the question of whether to tell new friends and prospective sex partners about their affliction. Women who plan to have children face particularly frightening risks. Newborn babies can pick up the virus in the birth canal, with devastating results.

Meanwhile, the medical profession has done little to help herpes victims. Doctors can neither cure nor shorten the course of the disease. The only organization that offers authoritative and up-to-date medical information on herpes on a national scale is a young but dramatically growing nonprofit support group, the Herpes Resource Center (formerly known as HELP), located in Palo Alto, Calif., and its local branches around the country.

Still, scientists are beginning to make major discoveries about the herpes virus, and to make headway in combating it. The Food and Drug Administration (F.D.A.) is expected to license the first drug ever proved effective in killing the external manifestations of the virus. And a major pharmaceutical firm will soon begin testing a herpes vaccine. No cure is imminent, however. For now, victims must learn to live with their malady. Indeed, an entire, "self-help" subculture of victims and their families and lovers has emerged. And society at large is beginning to accommodate the disease, too. Some experts believe that young people in general are becoming more cautious and conservative about sex partly because they fear herpes.

The herpes simplex virus has been with man since ancient times, causing cold sores on the lips (herpes labialis) as well as blisters on the sex organs (herpes genitalis). But health officials say that genital herpes became a growing problem only during the mid-1970's, after sexual codes had loosened in American society. Since then, the disease has spread at an ever-increasing rate, and because it is incurable, the number of carriers never shrinks. Moreover, the average herpes sufferer gets four or five outbreaks of the highly contagious blisters a year, thus multiplying the chances of infecting someone else.

Because the virus cannot survive outside human cells, it spreads only by direct physical contact—usually sexual intercourse. One person's cold sore can also become his partner's case of genital herpes. Although type I of the herpes simplex virus usually causes cold sores and type II causes genital herpes, the two breeds are closely related and attack cells in the same way. Once transmitted, the virus replicates rapidly, using the cells' own genetic machinery to manufacture thousands of identical viruses. Within two to 10 days of the primary infection, painful blisters appear, erupting not only on and occasionally within the genitalia but, in some cases, on the inside of the thighs or on the anus, wherever contact with the virus has occurred.

The blisters heal by themselves, as the virus retreats from the skin via nerve pathways to a nerve cluster, the sacral ganglion, at the base of the spine, where it lies dormant. Periodically, the virus reactivates and reappears on the genitals.

Nobody knows precisely how recurrences are triggered. Women may suffer new bouts just before or after their periods. Fever also seems to provoke the virus, as does the friction of sex or masturbation. Emotional stress often rekindles herpes, and many students report flare-ups before exams.

Patients' experiences with the disease vary greatly. Some have herpes almost continuously, others never suffer anything after their first infection. Some get a "prodrome," a tingling or aching prior to an outbreak. Others simply wake up to find a new set of blisters. Some victims suffer such extreme pain during a recurrence that they can scarcely walk; others feel nothing more than soreness.

Herpes sufferers usually transmit the infection during an outbreak of blisters. The virus is "shed" just before the blisters erupt and while they are present. Thus, the best way to avoid passing on herpes is to abstain from sex from the moment the prodrome signals a recurrence until the lesions are entirely healed. A few get no prodrome, though, and may unknowingly pass on the virus before they realize an episode is under way. Silent carriers, asymptomatic shedders, may not even know they have herpes.

Although precise statistics do not exist, because state governments do not require doctors or clinics to report cases of herpes—as they must report syphilis and gonorrhea—authorities estimate that 500,000 to two million Americans contract herpes each year. Of these people, approximately half may never suffer any symptoms. Others, though, soon discover that their ailment carries a totally unexpected emotional burden.

"I couldn't deal with it alone," says Tom Schroeder, a 32-year-old designer with an architectural firm. "I felt like a victim. It's frustrating to be subject to a little tiny virus that messes things up."

Schroeder's life seems to exclude mess. Taste and deliberation reign in his apartment, a quiet ordered place that reflects his talent. In the living room, an ornate chunk of building facade is neatly bracketed to the wall. A large, bamboo Chinese hat leans in the unused fireplace. Schroeder, dark-haired and slender, displays a sense of care and arrangement in his manner, too. He speaks slowly, seriously, with occasional flashes of a smile.

Although he has accepted his disease and appears at peace with himself, Schroeder still feels uneasy enough about his herpes to insist that his real name not be used. When he contracted herpes more than two years ago, his tidy life instantly unraveled. He felt "impaired, damaged—second-class." For a year, he told nobody about the disease, "I thought people would shrivel away," he says. During that period, he canceled dates if he had a recurrence—even if his evening plans involved only dinner or a movie. "I squirreled myself away. I just didn't want to be around people. I was ashamed."

Schroeder went through what some psychologists call the herpes syndrome, a pattern of anguish and isolation that may play havoc with a person's self-image and social life for years while he comes to terms with his disease. Dr. Oscar Gillespie, assistant professor of psychology at Fordham University and a coordinator of the New York Herpes Resource Center chapter, has written a paper on the syndrome with Dr. Elliott Luby, a Detroit psychiatrist on the center's national medical advisory board. According to their study, herpes sufferers often pass from shock and denial through loneliness, anger, fear, self-imposed isolation and finally, a deepening depression and a sense of entrapment similar to the hopelessness often felt by patients with chronic diseases like multiple sclerosis.

"The biggest emotion is sheer, unadulterated rage," says Dr. Gillespie, who once ran the New York herpes hot line single-handedly out of his apartment. He says many people refuse to believe that their new affliction is incurable. As the knowledge sinks in, they become furious, chiefly at the people they believe gave them herpes. At Columbia University in New York, for example, herpes victims sometimes ask if they have grounds to sue their former sex partners, according to Deborah M. Berkowitz, a nurse practitioner at the university's health service. By squarely placing blame on others, she says, the students deflect their own sense of guilt—the feeling of "being punished for having sex."

Denial and anger are accompanied by desperation. Herpes sufferers so frantically want to believe in a cure that they are willing to try anything. Gimmicks, complicated regimens and home remedies for the disease abound, and herpes victims have been known to buy kelp powder, red seaweed, vitamin E oil and other vitamins and minerals in the false hope that these substances will clear up the disease. Some victims have been known to put cold milk compresses or yogurt on their blisters. One doctor has a patient who bathes his lesions in Scotch in an effort to burn them out. Other sufferers even try acupuncture or hypnosis.

The herpes syndrome, above all, is evidence that the disease deals a terrible blow to the victim's self-image. The Herpes Resource Center and its chapters throughout the country regularly receive calls from sufferers who say they have contemplated suicide. Their letters express such sentiments as "This disease has castrated me psychologically" and "I feel loathsome, worthless and untouchable."

For single people, herpes may shatter relationships or render a formerly fulfilling social life erratic and frustrating. Some victims, like Schroeder, withdraw. Others, like Patricia Farmer (a pseudonym), deliberately avoid serious relationships; they don't let themselves get involved with a lover to the point that they might be rejected because of herpes. Miss Farmer, a 30-year-old management consultant, is successful, articulate, widely traveled and strikingly pretty. She speaks with surprising candor about her sex life—a full and active one, by any definition. Her tone is even, almost dispassionate, constrained perhaps by the place where she has chosen to meet, the hushed lounge of a private club in midtown Manhattan.

She knew about herpes when she fell in love two years ago. But she had no idea she had picked up the disease from a former lover. She was, at the time, a silent carrier. After two weeks of deepening romance, her new love acquired a painful case of herpes, and the affair promptly withered. "He never believed that I didn't know I had it," Miss Farmer says earnestly. "He just couldn't deal with what had happened to him sexually, with what he considered an assault on his body. He was totally rejecting. He claimed that his life had been ruined. For me, it was an utter terror. I didn't know what had happened to me as a woman."

Since then, her sex life has consisted largely of casual encounters with men whom she does not tell about her herpes. Miss Farmer says that she now knows her symptoms well enough to avoid sex during periods of contagion. "Sleeping with people that I don't care about, in a long-term sense, doesn't bother me. But if I meet someone whom I might want to be serious about, I almost want to run the other way."

For couples who are married or living together, herpes may strain the relationship to the breaking point. Last summer, a Herpes Resource Center survey of its membership showed that 18 percent of the more than 3,000 respondents believed herpes had contributed to the dissolution of their marriages or longstanding relationships. In the case of extramarital affairs, herpes's telltale blisters may reveal one partner's infidelity and thus provoke a crisis. Just as common, however, according to doctors and Herpes Resource Center officials, are incidents when inexplicable recurrences of old, premarital herpes stir suspicions.

For many men, herpes poses a threat to their sense of sexual prowess. As Dr. Gillespie puts it, "Men's *machismo* gets hit by this virus." Men occasionally suffer periods of impotence because of anxiety stemming from herpes.

Most experts, though, feel that herpes is more emotionally trying for women. Women suffering from the disease are five to eight times more likely than others to get cervical cancer. Although not clearly understood, the link exists, and doctors recommend that women herpes victims get PAP smears twice a year.

Many women with herpes worry about infecting their newborn babies, who can pick up the virus in the birth canal if the mother is suffering an outbreak at the time of delivery. Doctors stress that neonatal herpes is preventable: During the final weeks of pregnancy, regular tissue cultures can be taken to check for the virus, and if it is found, a Caesarean section can be performed. Nevertheless, about 1,000 babies a year are born with the infection, often to women who never noticed their symptoms. The virus quickly spreads through the infants' bodies, killing more than half of them and leaving most of the survivors permanently brain damaged.

For men and women alike, the most agonizing questions raised by herpes involve telling others about it. This goes to the heart of the herpes victim's pain. To tell or not to tell? Whom to tell? And how? With these questions, the herpes sufferer clutches at his own vulnerability, his sense of isolation in a world capable of consoling or spurning him. Telling is one of the most discussed subjects at Herpes Resource Center meetings, and support-group sessions often turn into impromptu rehearsals, with one person playing himself, others playing lover, friend or parent.

Most Herpes Resource Center officials believe that a prospective sex partner should be told, but they disagree on where and how to tell. They feel that each person must work out his own rules. Schroeder, the New York designer, uses intimacy as his criterion, for lovers and friends as well as members of his family. "My rule of thumb is that if I've told them intimate things in the past, I tell them about this," he says. "It's the same rule as with the rest of my private life."

A lover or friend truly worth keeping will respond with support and understanding, he says. "Herpes is like a test. If you think you have a friend, that friendship is tested if you admit you have herpes."

Michele Krieg, a psychotherapist who specializes in treating herpes sufferers and runs the New York Herpes Resource Center chapter's network of discussion groups, advises people to tell a prospective sex partner "as far away from the bedroom as possible." She warns them to avoid "the catastrophic presentation"—that is, saying in a tragic quaver, "I have an incurable disease." Miss Krieg suggests that the conversation be as private and unpressured as possible. "There's something I'd like to tell you about myself." she begins, assuming the role. And she concludes by saying: "I haven't had it in a year, but it's something I never want anyone to get. You have a choice in this, too. I'm careful. I can tell when I get an outbreak. But I ask for your trust."

"Be prepared to answer a lot of questions," warns Dr. Gillespie. "And remember: If you can deal with it, your partner can." Many partners, however, prefer not to. In last summer's Herpes Resource Center survey, 21 percent of the sufferers said they had been rejected after confiding in a prospective lover.

Will the fear of getting herpes actually diminish the amount of casual sex in American society? Although Dr. Gillespie believes that the habits of sexual freedom are too entrenched to change very much, some doctors and nurses who work with young patients feel that fear of herpes has already reinforced more conservative social trends. "There's more inhibition about jumping into bed," says Miss Berkowitz of Columbia's health service. "There's a little bit more of wanting to get to know somebody."

The Food and Drug Administration is expected to license an ointment soon that some scientists are hailing as a breakthrough in the fight against herpes. Although it is not a cure, acyclovir, the result of seven years of research by the Burroughs Wellcome Company of Research Triangle Park, N.C., is the first antiviral drug ever proved effective against genital herpes. The ointment, to be marketed under the name Zovirax, thoroughly destroys the virus within the lesions, though the blisters do not disappear any faster and the virus in the nervous system is unaffected. However, a potent intravenous form of acyclovir that does speed blister healing is expected to win F.D.A. [approval] sometime this year; an oral form—less powerful than the intravenous kind but stronger than the ointment—may be released by the end of this year.

Acyclovir has caused a great deal of excitement among herpes victims. Unlike many antiviral agents, this drug seems to be safe and highly specific, interfering only with the virus's replicating process and leaving the human cell mechanism alone. Scientists at Burroughs Wellcome and elsewhere are already developing other drugs that work on the same principle.

Dr. Lawrence Corey of the University of Washington in Seattle, one of the most respected herpes experts in the country, believes that intravenous or even oral acyclovir, if administered early enough to a person who has just caught herpes could destroy the virus before it establishes latency. But Dr. Corey and other scientists who have tested acyclovir refuse to make any sweeping claims; according to them, the ointment merely shortens the contagious period by a day or two.

The intravenous drug involves several days of hospitalization, and cancer patients in chemotherapy who have either type I or type II herpes will be its primary users. Anticancer drugs can lower the patients' natural defenses, leaving them vulnerable to herpes infection that may spread quickly throughout their bodies, attacking vital organs and even killing them. This form of the drugs has already shown dramatic results with these patients.

Another treatment that appears to offer some promise involves attacking the herpes lesions with a precisely aimed laser beam. Dr. Michael Truppin, an obstetrician-gynecologist on the staff of Mount Sinai Hospital in New York, says the laser treatment "vaporizes" the infected cells, eradicating the lesions and relieving the pain in a matter of minutes. Moreover, two-thirds of the 120 patients Dr. Truppin has treated with the laser during the last year have found their recurrence rates reduced—in some cases, from as many as 12 outbreaks a year to as few as three. Dr. Truppin stresses, however, that even though the laser eliminates the lesions, it may not kill all the virus. And he has only begun to study the effects of the laser on viral "shedding."

Meanwhile, another drug company has placed its hopes in a herpes vaccine. This year, Merck Sharpe & Dohme Research Laboratories of West Point, Pa., will begin tests on humans of a vaccine that has successfully immunized mice against herpes. The vaccine, made of the herpes virus's protein coating, works by triggering production of antiherpes antibodies. Many scientists are skeptical, noting that herpes victims have already produced their own antibodies, but that these fail to prevent recurrences. In a previously uninfected person, however, high antibody levels—induced by the vaccine—could eradicate newly entering viruses before they could infect and establish latency, according to Dr. Maurice Hilleman, director of virus and cell biology research at Merck. Thus, the vaccine would work only for people never exposed to herpes. Dr. Hilleman will not predict when the vaccine will be available, but he notes that Merck's hepatitis B vaccine, approved last November, took 13 years to develop.

A herpes cure eludes scientists in part because the gaps in their understanding of the virus are still so vast. There is no widely accepted theory to explain the mechanism of latency, and the role of the immune system is also unclear.

Perhaps the most nebulous area in herpes research is the link between recurrences and stress. It is generally believed that emotional stress lowers the body's resistance to disease, perhaps through hormonal changes that affect the immune system. And psychosomatic factors play a role in causing and preventing herpes outbreaks. The "placebo effect" is well documented in herpes research: Utterly benign formulations used as controls often "work" for patients, clearing up blisters and preventing their return, while the experimental drugs fail.

"One of the best things you can do for patients with genital herpes is tell them to stop worrying about it," says Dr. Andre J. Nahmias of Emory University in Atlanta, Ga., a leading herpes expert for the past 20 years.

Some doctors urge patients to exploit the benefits of the placebo effect until something better comes along. The outlandish home remedies, from yogurt to Scotch, may serve a purpose after all. "If you find something that works for you," says a New York dermatologist, "then God bless you and do it. But first, tell me what it is so I know you're not harming yourself."

Despite increased public awareness, herpes patients find that many doctors are ignorant about their disease. In the Herpes Resource Center's survey of its membership, 40 percent of the patients had to see more than one doctor before getting their ailment accurately diagnosed. Some had to see five or more physicians. Doctors have been known to prescribe treatments—from penicillin to snake venom—that are ineffective. Some give their patients smallpox, polio or flu vaccines, even though these vaccines are worthless against herpes and carry some risks. Some physicians have advised their patients to apply ether to their lesions—although this is excruciating, dangerously explosive and futile.

The nation's research institutions have not done much for herpes victims, either. After pencillin became widely available during the 1940's, American scientists all but abandoned the study of venereal disease, believing the problem solved.

Founded in February 1979, the Herpes Resource Center, a program of the American Social Health Association (A.S.H.A.), a nonprofit group that promotes the control and prevention of venereal disease, has attracted more than 30,000 members and spawned more than 40 chapters nationwide. Its quarterly newsletter has become a sophisticated medical journal, with articles and reprints by health experts. The center received about 100,000 letters a year, many of them desperate cries for aid. It runs a special hot line for its members. In addition, the parent group, A.S.H.A., contracts with the Federal Government to operate the toll-free V.D. National Hot Line, which handles approximately 100,000 calls a year—40 percent of them about herpes.

The education and commiseration the organization offers takes some of the emotional sting out of herpes. Dr. Gillespie believes that the small discussion groups run by his chapter, for example, have enabled patients to get through the herpes syndrome in five or six months rather than one or two years.

"When you can talk about a problem, you can begin to talk yourself out of it," says Schroeder, who has been through one of the discussion groups. "The group made me feel less unique. It put things into perspective. It helped make me feel that I'm not a herpie—I'm a Tom."

Herpes outbreaks still complicate Schroeder's social life. But he does not cancel dates anymore. And he says he has never been rejected by a prospective lover whom he has told about his herpes, probably because he tells only those whom he genuinely trusts and who are likely to trust him. Today, he says, the disease is simply a periodic annoyance, not an eternal curse.

Nevertheless, herpes has changed Tom Schroeder's life. He has become "choosier" about his sex partners, placing more value on the quality of commitment and less on the quantity of sex. And he feels that American society is moving in the same direction. "There will be more stress on having fewer and deeper relationships," Schroeder predicts. "This promiscuity thing is just too unhealthy—both physically and emotionally."

3

Couples

Introduction

To many people, the current state of marriage seems to provide the clearest evidence that the family is falling apart. In the past two decades, marriage rates declined, divorce rates went up, and increasing numbers of couples came to live together without being married. Yet these changes do not necessarily mean that people no longer want long-term commitments or that they are psychologically incapable of forming deep attachments. Rather, they reflect the fact that in the modern world marriage is increasingly a personal relationship between two people. Over time there have come to be fewer and fewer reasons for couples to remain in unsatisfactory relationships. And as the standards for emotional fulfillment in marriage have risen, the level of discontent may have increased also.

In the preindustrial past, the emotional relationship between husband and wife was the least important aspect of marriage. A marriage was an exchange between kin groups, a unit of economic production, and a means of replenishing populations with high death rates.

In traditional societies, parents often selected their children's mates. Parents were more interested in the practical consequences of choice than in romantic considerations. By contrast, in our modern society, people are supposed to marry for "love." They may marry for practical reasons or for money; nevertheless they often follow their culture's rules and decide that they are "in love."

People may also decide that they are in love and want to live together but do not care to have their union licensed by the state or blessed by clergy. In her review of the literature on cohabitation, Eleanor Macklin finds that approximately 25 percent of all college students have already lived with a partner of the opposite sex without being married. Overall, this statistic represents a major cultural change over a quarter of a century, but more research needs to be done to see whether college students are in the vanguard or are separate from their population age-mates.

Couple relations are thus influenced by a new fluidity and openness with regard to social norms in general and sexual behavior in particular. At one time, a relationship between a man and a woman could be easily categorized: it was either "honorable" or "dishonorable." An "honorable" relationship went through several distinct stages of commitment: dating, keeping company, going steady, agreeing to be married, announcing the engagement, and finally getting married, presumably for life. Divorce was regarded as a personal tragedy and social stigma. Sexual relations at any point before marriage were also shameful, especially for the woman, although the shamefulness decreased depending on the closeness to marriage.

Today the system of courtship has given way to a new pattern of couple relationships. These are less permanent, more flexible, more experimental. Are they less moral? Ann Swidler interprets the contemporary culture of love as expressive of a new and positive morality, one that affirms the moral significance of love in terms of communication and understanding rather than permanence and commitment. The distinction between the different stages of courtship and marriage has broken down. Couple relationships can be intensely personal and sexually intimate very early, yet marital relationships are less stable because they are not expected to last if one of the partners becomes dissatisfied. Bernard Farber (1964) has argued that, in effect, we have a "permanent availability" system of marriage; every adult remains on the marriage market, available to every other potential partner, whether currently married or not.

The tension arising out of a relationship that is deeply intimate and yet not certain to last adds another strain to an institution that already contains many strains. Thus Constantina Safilios-Rothschild points out that limited commitments, at least for some, seem to ease the strain of relationships, particularly as jobs, careers, and geographical mobility complicate attempts to maintain continuity and permanence. Further, the new symmetry between the sexes in work and sex may increase the tensions as well as the joys in any relationship. The more multifaceted the relationship, the more aspects of two lives that have to mesh, the greater the potential for friction.

Harold Kelley's article on personal relationships attempts to analyze the central and unique psychological dynamics of "the close heterosexual dyad—the intimate relationship between man and woman." Kelley analyzes how interdependence, responsive interaction, and interpretations of interaction events ("attributions") can lead to positive or conflictful outcomes.

In short, Kelley's analysis shows that the very qualities that make intimate relationships uniquely rewarding are also sources of strain and tension. Ordinarily, conflict does not lead to an outcome as dramatic as the killing of one lover or spouse by another, but we do know that there is much violence associated with love and family relationships. Laura Meyer's article on battered wives and dead husbands suggests how deadly marital strains can be.

Of course, the more common outcome of severe marital tension is divorce, rather than physical violence. As Ann Goetting points out in her article here, divorce rates have been rising almost continuously since the U.S. Census Bureau started collecting data. Goetting's central concern is the consequences of divorce: What are the long-term effects of divorce on adults and children? Although it seems clear that divorce is usually a painful experience for all concerned, the data as to lasting effects are contradictory and inconclusive. For example, it seems likely that the family conflicts that lead up to divorce may be a more important source of emotional stress than divorce itself. While it would be ideal for a child to grow up in a happy, intact family, for children of unhappily married parents, divorce may often be the lesser of two evils.

The ultimate cause of divorce, as William Goode once pointed out, is marriage itself—the requirement that two individuals with their own desires and values live with one another. Our cultural ideals of marital happiness and emotional fulfillment are often at odds with the realities of everyday married life. The article by John F. Cuber and Peggy Harroff reveals that marriages that are both enduring and satisfying to the spouses can vary a great deal from one another as well as from the ideals of happy marriage.

Ironically, because of rising divorce rates, the level of marital happiness in America may be higher today than it ever has been. This is one of the conclusions reached by Theodore Caplow and his associates in their study of one midwestern community over the past fifty years. In the 1970s, Caplow organized a team of researchers to revisit Muncie, Indiana, the town that had been immortalized as "Middletown" in the classic 1929 and 1937 studies of Helen and Robert Lynd. The chapter reprinted here provides some revealing glimpses into marriage in the American heartland a half century ago, as well as into the changes in marriage that have occurred since. The Lynds' original observations deal a sharp blow to nostalgic images of the past as a time of strong, happy marriages. As Caplow et al. conclude, marriage in Middletown today may not be the best of all possible worlds, but it compares "very nicely" in happiness with the Middletown of 1890, 1924, or 1935.

Traditional societies do not necessarily have happier marriages or even lower divorce rates—some have higher rates than ours. Still, strong kin groups in traditional societies either keep couples together regardless of how they feel or make it easier for couples to break up without severe disruption. Nevertheless, traditional societies were quite conservative in their view of marriage, which was regarded as a permanent moral commitment that the church, and later the state, was to protect and preserve. Traditional marriage was also based on a division of labor between the sexes. The husband was to be head of the family and its chief provider; the wife was to provide services in the form of child care and housework. Divorce could be granted only through the failure of one of the spouses to live up to his or her role, or the betrayal of a spouse through adultery or cruelty.

The new divorce laws, as Lenore J. Weitzman and Ruth B. Dixon point out, abolish this notion of fault or blame; instead "irreconcilable differences" are grounds for the dissolution of marriage. Further, the new laws attempt to establish more equal rights and obligations between husband and wife, both during the marriage and at the time of divorce. While it is still too early to judge the ultimate effects the new laws will have on marriage as an institution, it is clear that they codify a very different conception of marriage and divorce than existed in the law until recently.

The distinction between tradition and modernity lies behind Andrew Cherlin's article on "Remarriage as an Incomplete Institution." Cherlin attributes the higher divorce rate of remarried persons not to personality defects or to experience with divorce—once you've gone through the separation trauma it may not be so hard another time—but to the fact that traditional marriage does not contemplate divorce. Those who remarry are therefore in an "incomplete" institution, lacking the guidelines and supports of traditional marriage. Whether or not one finds Cherlin's thesis persuasive, it is evident that his subjects found marriage attractive. Despite all its difficulties, marriage is thus not likely to go out of style in the near future. Ultimately we agree with Jessie Bernard (1972), who, after a devastating critique of marriage from the point of view of a sociologist who is also a feminist, has this to say:

> The future of marriage is as assured as any social form can be. . . . For men and women will continue to want intimacy, they will continue to want to celebrate their mutuality, to experience the mystic unity which once led the church to consider marriage a sacrament. . . . There is hardly any probability such commitments will disappear or that all relationships between them will become merely casual or transient. The commitment may not take the form we know today, although that too has a future. (p. 301)

References

Bernard, Jessie. 1972. *The Future of Marriage.* New York: World.
Farber, B. 1964. *Family Organization and Interaction.* San Francisco: Chandler.

Chapter 5

Relationships

Nonmarital Heterosexual Cohabitation

Eleanor D. Macklin

Nonmarital cohabitation is fast becoming a part of the dominant culture in this country and it seems likely that in time to come a majority of persons will experience this lifestyle at some point in their life cycle. The phenomenon of men and women living together unmarried is, of course, not new (Berger, 1971; Rodman, 1966); and trial marriage as a concept has been a topic of debate since the early part of this century (Lindsey & Evans, 1927/1929; Mead, 1966, 1968; Russell, 1929). However, it has only been in the past decade that it has been openly practiced by a large number of middle-class Americans.

It was in college towns that evidence of the increasing incidence of cohabitation first appeared, and it is here that most of the research has occurred. In 1968, the first graduate thesis on the topic was written (Johnson, 1968); in 1972, the first professional articles appeared (Lyness, Lipetz, & Davis, 1972; Macklin, 1972) and the initial issue of the *Cohabitation Research Newsletter* was published (Macklin, 1972*a*). Since then it has become increasingly popular to do research on cohabitation, and at this writing more that 25 graduate theses on the topic are known to have been completed and numerous others are currently in process. What have we learned from all of this research activity?

Prevalence Rates

Estimates of prevalence vary to some extent with the particular definition of cohabitation used by the researcher. There has been to date little consistency in the use of the term. Operational definitions have ranged from the ambiguous

From *Marriage & Family Review*, Vol. 1, No. 2 (Spring 1978), pp. 1–12. Reprinted by permission of The Haworth Press.

"living with someone of the opposite sex to whom one is not married"; to "sharing a bedroom and/or bed for four or more nights a week for three or more consecutive months with someone of the opposite sex to whom one is not married;" to "two adult persons of different sex living together under marriage-like conditions in the same household without having officially confirmed their relationship through marriage (Cole, 1977, p. 65).

Most of the estimates of prevalence based on probability samples have come from research using college students, with the estimates seeming to vary as a function of the nature of the particular institution and the population from which it draws. Rates of "ever having cohabited" range from near zero percent at those institutions which are single-sex, or which have rigid parietals and require that all students live on campus, to about one-third of the student population at some large state universities where housing regulations are more liberal.

Because of the tremendous variation from campus to campus, one is hesitant to give an overall estimate of prevalence. However, when one averages the "percent ever having cohabited" reported in 15 known studies involving campus surveys, including both convenience and random samples, a mean of 24 percent is obtained (Macklin, in press). This is very close to the 25 percent reported by Bower and Christopherson in their survey of convenience samples in 16 state universities in eight regions of the U.S. (Bower & Christopherson, 1977). Therefore, it seems safe to conclude that about one-quarter of present U.S. undergraduate students, taking the country as a whole, have had a cohabitation experience.

At most institutions, a higher percentage of males report having cohabited than of females, although this difference usually disappears when one considers only those who have lived together three or more months. The rate will undoubtedly be much higher by the time of graduation or marriage, for the percentages tend to increase from freshman to senior year.

Statistics from noncollege populations are much harder to obtain since survey research on these groups is negligible. Some suggestion of prevalence can be obtained from Census data. In March 1976, the U.S. Bureau of the Census found that 1.3 million persons were living in two-person households in which the household head shared the living quarters with an unrelated adult of the opposite sex. This number includes resident employees and roomers as well as nonmarital partners. Of these 660,000 two-person households, 23 percent were headed by persons between 14 and 24 years of age, 41 percent between 25 and 44 years, 23 percent between 45 and 64 years, and 13 percent were 65 years and older. An increasing trend toward "unrelated adults sharing two-person households" is indicated by the fact that only 242,000 such households were reported in the 1960 Census and 327,000 in 1970; preliminary analysis of 1977 Census data suggests a continued sharp increase in such couples. In spite of this increase, such persons still represent only about 1 percent of all household heads at any given time (U.S. Bureau of the Census, 1977; Note 1).

During the period 1974–75, interviews were held with a nationwide random sample of 2,510 20–30-year-old men who had registered with the Selective Service in 1962 through 1972. Of these men, 18 percent reported having lived non-maritally with a woman for a period of six months or more. Two-thirds of them had had only one such relationship and only five percent were currently cohabiting, suggesting that most such relationships terminate or end in marriage. Cohabitants were more likely to be men who were not attending college or with less than a high school education, supporting the Census finding that cohabitation is not only a college campus phenomenon (Clayton & Voss, 1977).

Attitudes

As was true of prevalence, most of the research on attitudes toward cohabitation has been done with college students, with available evidence suggesting that students in general approve of cohabitation outside of marriage. At City College of New York in 1973, almost 80 percent said they would live with someone of the opposite sex if given an opportunity to do so (Arafat & Yorburg, 1973). About the same time, almost 60 percent of the men who had not cohabited and 35 percent of such women at Arizona State University answered yes when asked if they would want to (Henze & Hudson, 1974). In the Bower and Christopherson survey of 16 state universities in 1975, more than 50 percent of those who had not cohabited indicated they would consider doing so (Bower & Christopherson, 1977). At the University of Delaware, only 28 percent of an undergraduate sample said they would probably or definitely not cohabit (McCauley, Note 2). At Illinois State University in 1972, only 23 percent of the females and 8 percent of the males said they would definitely no cohabit, even if in love (Huang, Note 3). At Cornell University in 1972, only 7 percent of those who had not cohabited said it was because of moral reasons. The most common reasons given for not having cohabited were: Have not yet found a partner with whom I would like to stay for four or more nights a week, or am geographically separated from partner (Macklin, 1976b, p. 121).

It seems reasonable to estimate that, considering the country as a whole, probably about 25 percent of the undergraduate population have cohabited, 50 percent more would if they were to find themselves in an appropriate relationship or in a situation where they could, and 25 percent, for a variety of religious, moral, and personal reasons, think they probably would not, even if it were possible, more of these being female and underclassmen.

Most students do not believe that a long-term commitment to the partner is necessary before persons live together. When asked what kind of relationship should exist before a person cohabits, most students indicate that cohabitation is acceptable as long as there is a strong, affectionate, preferably monogamous relationship between the two persons. Summarizing data from four institutions where similar questionnaires were administered, roughly 5 percent of the undergraduates indicated a couple should be married before living together; 15 percent, formally or tentatively engaged; 40 percent, strong, affectionate, monogamous relationship; 25 percent, strong affectionate, also dating others, relationship, or good friends; and 15 percent, persons who find it expedient to live together should do so, and no emotional involvement is necessary (Macklin, in press).

As of 1975, the parental generation did not share this acceptance of cohabitation. Three studies have compared attitudes of parent and student generations and each reports a large generation gap. The majority of parents consider cohabitation outside of marriage to be either immoral, emotionally unhealthy, or unwise, and say they will work to prevent or eliminate such behavior in their own offspring (Smith & Kimmel, 1970; Steiner, 1975; Macklin, Note 4).

What has caused young persons today to accept a behavior pattern which was unthinkable a generation ago? A myriad of interacting factors have served to create an atmosphere conducive to the change. The shift toward acceptance of cohabitation must be seen as part of a slow evolution in sexual values and behavior patterns that began in the early part of the century with growing urbanization and its increasing opportunities for privacy and anonymity, and with the changing attitudes regarding freedom for women. One can trace from the early 1920s the gradually increasing nonvirginity rates for women and the simultaneously increasing acceptance of sexual involvement in a love relationship. By the end of the 1960s, sexual intercourse among college students who were going steady was commonly approved practice. The late Dr. Guttmacher, a former president of Planned Parenthood-World Population, said in 1972, "It is rather generally accepted that by the senior year in many colleges seventy percent of the single students of both sexes are engaging in intercourse" (Guttmacher & Vadies, 1972, p. 145). One could argue that a natural extension of this was openly to accept spending the night together, and predict that couples who enjoyed being together would come to increase their number of nights together.

Many social forces associated with the late 1960s served to support the trend. The Women's Movement, dormant for many decades, renewed its challenge of the double standard and its demand that women be granted the same rights and privileges as men. An important by-product was the increasing equalization of parietals and housing regulations for male and female students, making is possible for the first time for large numbers of college students to live off-campus or to reside in dormitories without curfew. The phenomenon of extended adolescence, the earlier entrance into puberty, the radical tenor of the period which encouraged youth to question their continued treatment as children, and the demand by college students that they be granted the same privileges as their noncollege age-mates, led to a slow erosion of "in loco parentis" and a gradual acceptance of a policy of 24-hour visitation in the dormitory.

The change in dormitory regulations and the fact that most lived far from the parental eye made it physically feasible for large numbers of young persons to cohabit. Concurrent social changes made it likely that many would take advantage of the opportunity. The increase in divorce rates and the changing conception of the function of marriage caused many youth, and many divorcees, to move more cautiously into that state. The increased acceptance of sexuality outside of marriage and of sex as an expression of affection rather than as an act of procreation, and the increased availability of effective contraception, made it easier for nonmarried persons to engage openly and comfortably in a sexual relationship. Social Security retirement benefits, which gave an advantage to single persons, caused many older persons to question the economic wisdom of marrying. The increased emphasis on relationship and on personal growth, which came with the human growth movement, called into question the superficiality of the traditional courtship process and a too-early commitment to permanence. The result was a search for styles of relating which allowed a high degree of total intimacy as well as an opportunity for individual growth and change.

Nature of the Relationship

It is impossible to discuss "*the* cohabitation relationship," since the concept covers a wide variety of types of relationships which differ in amount of time the two individuals spend together, the nature of the living arrangement, and the degree of commitment. Several attempts have been made to develop a useful typology of cohabitation relationships (Macklin, 1974a; Petty, 1975; Storm, 1973), primarily using some continuum of dyadic commitment as the basis of classification. There are at least five types:

(1) *temporary casual convenience* (including "contract cohabitation") (Van Deusen, 1974), where two persons share the same living quarters because it is expedient to do so;

(2) the *affectionate dating–going together* type of relationship where the couple stays together because they enjoy being with one another and will continue as long as both prefer to do so;

(3) the *trial marriage* type, which includes the "engaged to be engaged" and partners who are consciously testing the relationship before making a permanent commitment;

(4) the *temporary alternative to marriage,* where the individuals are committed to staying together, but are waiting until it is more convenient to marry; and

(5) the *permanent alternative to marriage,* where couples live together in a

long-term committed relationship similar to marriage, but without the traditional religious or legal sanctions.

As one might expect, there are important differences among these types, causing researchers to agree unanimously that we must no longer treat unmarried cohabitants as one homogeneous group.

When college cohabitants have been asked to identify what their relationship was like at the time they *started* living together, the majority define themselves as having been in a "strong, affectionate, monogamous" relationship. This has caused many writers to declare that cohabitation on the college campus, at least during the first year, is merely an added step in the courtship process, a kind of "living out of going steady" (Bower & Christopherson, 1977; Danziger, 1976; Henze & Hudson, 1974; Johnson, 1968; Macklin, 1974 b). The couple generally shares a deep emotional relationship with one another but has not yet reached the point of long-term commitment. Consistent with this is that most college couples, at least initially, maintain two separate residences and may not spend every night together, and the finding by Rubin in his 2-year follow-up of college couples that cohabiting couples were as likely to break up as dating couples (Rubin, Note 5).

We do not yet know enough to say what proportion of older cohabiting couples fall into each of the above categories. One can predict, however, that length of time together will be a key variable regardless of age. The longer the couple has been together, the more likely they are to have moved up the courtship continuum: from living together simply because they enjoy it and find it convenient to do so, to living together because they want to see if they can really "make it together" to being together because they have decided to build a permanent and committed relationship with one another.

Comparison of Cohabitors and Noncohabitors

Much research to date has been directed to answering the question: Can we predict which individuals are more likely to cohabit? The usual method has been to give a questionnaire to a sample of students and compare the answers of those who have and have not cohabited. One must remember, therefore, when interpreting the findings that it is impossible to tell to what extent the established differences were present before, or developed as a consequence of, the cohabitation.

As so often has been found in other research on sexual behavior, the most significant differentiating variable is the individual's religiosity. Those who cohabit are less likely to indicate an affiliation with some established religion and have lower rates of church attendance (Arafat & Yorburg, 1973; Henze & Hudson, 1974; Macklin, 1976b, p. 119; Peterman, Ridley, & Anderson, 1974; Huang, Note 3). There are also some apparent personality differences. Cohabiting females are likely to describe themselves as more competitive, aggressive, independent, and managerial than do noncohabiting females. Cohabiting males are likely to describe themselves as less managerial and competitive and as warmer and more emotionally supportive than do noncohabiting males (Arafat & Yorburg, 1973; Guittar & Lewis, Note 6). In other words, cohabitants tend to perceive themselves as more androgynous and more liberated from traditional sex-role characteristics than do noncohabitants. They are likely to hold more liberal attitudes; their reference groups include more persons who have also cohabited; they tend to perceive campus norms as being more sexually liberal; and they are more likely to major in the arts and the social sciences than in the physical sciences and engineering. They are *not* more likely to come from unhappy or divorced homes, do not have lower academic averages, and are not significantly less likely to want eventually to marry (Henze & Hudson, 1974; Macklin, 1976 *b*, pp. 118–120; McCauley, 1977, Peterman et al., 1974).

Most researchers have been more impressed by the similarities than by the differences between cohabitants and noncohabitants. On campuses where a large percentage of persons engage in cohabitation at some point in their undergraduate life, persons who cohabit do not appear to be dramatically different from those who do not. As people, cohabiting students seem representative of the general undergraduate population, with their cohabitation more a consequence of the opportunity for such a relationship than a result of any demographic characteristics, although they are likely to be persons whose personal and religious values are congruent with this lifestyle, and they must possess sufficient interpersonal skills to initiate such a relationship (Macklin, 1976b, p. 122).

As nonmarital cohabitation becomes a more common phenomenon in this country and the majority of those who experience a love relationship also cohabit at some time during the courtship process, it may no longer be relevant to ask "Who cohabits?" Instead, the crucial question may be: What are the characteristics of persons who are able to engage in a love relationship? Possession of a basic level of heterosexual attractiveness and interpersonal competence may become more predictive of cohabitation than any of the other variables researched to date.

Comparison of Cohabiting and Noncohabiting Couples

In addition to efforts to determine differences between individuals who do and do not cohabit, research has been directed toward comparing cohabiting and noncohabiting couples. In general, the comparison has been between married couples and couples who were living together unmarried, with a few studies comparing cohabiting, engaged, and going-steady couples. The three most commonly studied phenomena have been degree of commitment, division of labor, and expressed satisfaction, with some attention also given to such variables as sexual exclusivity, territoriality, sources of conflict and conflict management, and attitudes regarding children. In reviewing this research it is important to ascertain whether the investigator matched the couples on such relevant variables as age, length of time together, and level of education, and to determine to what extent the couples studied were randomly selected from a clearly defined population. In most cases, the samples have consisted of self-selected volunteers.

Commitment

Commitment as a variable has probably been discussed more fully and more often in the cohabitation literature than any other variable. The interest appears to stem from an assumption that a degree of commitment is necessary for success in any interpersonal relationship, and the popular belief that cohabitation involves insufficient commitment for such success. Researchers have generally seen commitment as having two distinct components:

(1) *personal commitment,* the extent to which one is dedicated to continuing the relationship; and
(2) *behavioral commitment,* the consequences of having lived with an individual which make it more likely that one will continue to do so (specifically, the degree to which others know of the relationship and would disapprove of its termination, and the changes one would have to make in one's life were one to cease cohabiting) (Budd, 1976; Johnson, 1973).

Using the above criteria, nonmarried cohabitants indicate significantly less commitment than do married couples, with married couples reporting a stronger dedication to continuing the relationship and more external constraints on their separation (Budd, 1976; Johnson, 1973). When compared with engaged couples, unmarried cohabitants as a group tend to be as committed to their partners and to the relationship, but are less committed to the ideas of marrying their partner (Lewis, Spanier, Storm, & Lettecka, Note 7). One interesting and perhaps important finding is the indication that there are different predictors of degree of commitment for engaged and for unmarried cohabiting couples. For the engaged couples, the best predictors were such variables as length of the couple's acquaintance and amount of mother's education, while for the cohabiting couples, the more relevant variable was degree of happiness in the relationship. This suggests that commitment between engaged persons may be built more upon quantitative measures (e.g., the couple's endurance over time), whereas degree of commitment for cohabiting couples may depend more upon the present quality of the relationship (Lewis et al., Note 7).

One of the more frequently voiced concerns is that cohabitation leads to exploitation of the female partner by the male, who is often viewed as less emotionally involved and less personally committed. The evidence on this point is mixed, although there is a tendency for cohabiting females to have higher commitment scores than their male counterparts (Budd, 1976; Johnson, 1973; Kieffer, 1972, pp. 79–83; Lyness et al., 1972; Lewis et al., Note 7). Why this is the case and what effect it has on the relationship is not clear.

Division of Labor

Because cohabitation is an innovative lifestyle and the attitudes of cohabitors tend to be relatively liberal, it has been assumed that nonmarital cohabiting relationships would be more androgynous in nature and the division of labor less traditionally sex-roled. Available data suggest that this is not the case. Most studies indicate that cohabiting couples tend to mirror the society around them and engage in sex-role behavior characteristic of other couples their age. Couples today are in general more egalitarian than previously, and cohabiting couples are no more so than married ones (Bower, 1975; Macklin 1976a, p. 38; Makepeace, 1975; Segrest, 1975; Stafford, Backman, and diBona, 1977; Stevens, 1975; Cole & Bower, Note 8; Olday, Note 9). The many years of subtle socialization and role scripting, and the fact that role adaptation requires constant negotiation and accommodation, serve to maintain more conventional modes of behavior, even in what on the surface would appear to be nontraditional relationships (Whitehurst, Note 10).

Satisfaction

A number of studies have compared the degree of satisfaction experienced by nonmarital cohabitants and other couples, and have consistently found few differences (Budd, 1976; Polansky, 1974; Stevens, 1975; Olday, Note 9; Cole & Bower, Note 11; Cole & Vincent, Note 12). The conclusion reached by Cole and Vincent, after studying the degree of overall satisfaction expressed by a matched sample of 20 married and 20 cohabiting couples, is typical: "Apparently it is not so much the legal nature of the relationship that encourages or discourages satisfaction. Instead, it is more likely a factor of how the partners behave toward each other and define their roles that is predictive of happiness within an individual relationship" (Cole & Vincent, Note 13).

Budd gave a list of 32 potential problem areas to 54 cohabiting couples, 48 married couples who had cohabited before marriage, and 49 who had not. When she asked them to indicate how upset they got about each in their present relationship, she found few significant differences among groups. Feelings of being overinvolved in the relationship was the only area rated as significantly more upsetting by cohabitors than by marrieds. The mean rating given most problems, including overinvolvement, was less than 2.0 on a 5-point scale, indicating that the couples in general experienced little problem in their relationship (Budd, 1976).

Exclusivity

Many have hypothesized that cohabitants would be less monogamous in their relationships than others their age, but again there are no data to support this notion. While philosophically cohabitants are more open to nontraditional ideas (Bower & Christopherson, 1977; Peterman et al., 1974, p. 351), in their own relationships they act much like everyone else (Bower, 1975, p. 76; Huang, Note 3; Clatworthy & Scheid, Note 14). For example, Montgomery, in a study of 31 cohabiting couples, found that the majority of the respondents believed that sexual freedom should be available within the relationship; however, most voluntarily restricted their sexual activity as evidence of their commitment to the relationship (Montgomery, Note 15).

Internal Dynamics

How are cohabitation relationships formed? How do such couples deal with conflict? What causes a cohabitation relationship to end? Are the processes involved any different from those in noncohabital intimate relationships?

Formation

As in most intimate relationships, living together is seldom the result of a considered decision, at least initially, but rather results from a gradual, often unconscious, escalation of emotional and physical involvement. Most cohabitation evolves from a drift into sleeping more and more frequently together and a gradual accumulation of possessions at one residence. If and when a decision with conscious deliberation is made, it is usually precipitated by some external force, such as the end of the term, graduation, a change of job, a need for housing, or reduced income. Until such an event occurs, there is only a mutual, often unspoken, recognition of the desire to be together, with little attention given to planning for the relationship.

Survival

Some writers have suggested that because cohabiting relationships operate with fewer external support systems, and often most endure parental displeasure and societal discrimination, they need more internal unifiers than will a more traditional relationship in order to survive. The cohabiting couple may have to work more conscientiously at maintaining their relationship than does the married couple and, in exchange theory terms, may have to see more evident personal benefit from the relationship to continue the investment. This would imply that there must be more day-to-day behavioral evidence of commitment from one's cohabiting partner than from one's marital partner if the relationship is to last (Montgomery, Note 15). There is as yet little evidence concerning this point.

Hennon, in a discussion of conflict management with the cohabiting relationship, raises the question: Will cohabiting couples, because they cannot take the relationship for granted, be more likely to work at it than married couples, and, hence, be more likely to air their areas of conflict and to work at resolving them? Or, instead, because they are less secure in their relationship, will they hesitate openly to disclose and confront areas of conflict (Hennon, Note 16)? It seems likely that conflict management is more a function of the personality, maturity, and skill of the individuals involved than of the nature of the living situation, and that one might find as much variation among unmarried as among married couples.

At present there is little information on the length of cohabiting relationships or how many result in marriage. To obtain such information would require a longitudinal study and currently there is only one in progress. Cole and Bower have been studying a sample of noncollege cohabiting couples for serveral years and as of 1976 had follow-up data on 40 such dyads. At latest report, available evidence suggests that "of those relationships able to satisfactorily work through initial adjustment problems, there is as good a chance that the relationship will continue, with the same chance of success, as found among the married population." Cole lists four reasons why a cohabiting relationship might fail: emotional immaturity; insufficient or unequal degree of commitment; external crises, such as loss of employment, external interference, or pursuit of goals which necessitate an indefinite physical separation; and different value and behavior patterns, primarily with regard to use of time and money and division of labor (Cole, Note 17, pp. 13–14).

Termination

Ganson studied a sample of persons who had terminated cohabitation relationships, in an effort to identify the sources of dissolution. While the most common reason given was "grew apart," the majority of reasons related to feelings of overdependency and loss of identity, with women more likely to report this than men (Ganson, 1975). Rubin, in his study of 231 college couples, also reported that when relationships dissolved, the women tended to cite more problem in the relationship than did men, with need for independence a key factor (Rubin, Note 5). Women may be more emotionally involved in their relationships than men and, hence, more sensitive to problems. Or, as Rubin suggests, they may be more alert to the quality of the relationship because their future status is so dependent upon finding the right husband. On the other hand, if the relationships are as traditionally sex-roled as has been described, and if women are more interested than men in an egalitarian relationship, as has been suggested (McCauley, Note 18), they may actually experience more frustration than their partners.

One reason given for cohabiting is that the relationship is easier to terminate than if one were married. Is separation in fact any easier for cohabiting couples? The only eivdence to date is anecdotal. It suggests that the interpersonal dynamics involved in the severing of a relationship are the same whether one is married or cohabiting, with the degree of trauma dependent upon the length of time the individuals have been together and the degree of emotional involvement between them. Cohabitants can expect to experience the same process of denial, depression, anger, ambivalence, and reorientation to singlehood associated with the dissolution of any serious relationship. There are probably two important differences between cohabitants and married who separate: the public and relatives are likely to apply less social pressure to maintain the cohabiting relationship, and separation can be completed without litigation. With less social stigma and reduced visibility, there is often less guilt and sense of failure, and a faster readjustment in the postseparation period.

Effects of Cohabitation

The rationale for cohabitation has been that the experience is growth-producing for the participant, improves the quality of later marriage, and serves as a more effective screening device, hence, eventually reducing the present high divorce rate. To what extent are these hopes justified?

Personal Growth

The vast majority of cohabitants in studies to date give high positive ratings to their experience, and assert that it served to foster their personal growth and maturity. They indicate they would elect to cohabit again if they "had their lives to live over," and would not wish to marry without having lived with the partner first (Bower, 1975; Lautenschlager, 1975; Macklin, 1976b, pp. 133–134; Peterman et al., 1974; Shuttlesworth & Thorman, Note 19). Unfortunately, no investigator has attempted to develop or apply any objective measures to test what extent cohabitation does in fact lead to enhanced personal growth or whether it provides for any more growth than any of the more traditional dating relationships.

Ridley, Peterman, and Avery have hypothesized that cohabitation is most likely to provide a positive learning experience and better preparation for marriage when the participants:

(1) have as cohabitation goals, greater self-understanding within a heterosexual context and increased knowledge of the day to day aspects of intimate living;
(2) have realistic and mutually agreed upon expectations for the cohabiting experience;
(3) do not have strong deficiency needs for emotional security, or a residue of past grievances and/or unfinished business;

(4) have a high interpersonal skill level, e.g., the ability to openly and honestly express their feeling, the ability to understand and accept their partner, and the ability to mutually solve problems;

(5) have had a relationship where the present degree of involvement closely approximates that of a cohabitation relationship, for example, steadily dating rather than casual dating;

(6) have a rich dating history resulting in positive self perceptions in terms of their desirability to the opposite sex; and

(7) have a fairly extensive network of like and opposite sex relationships where important needs are being met (Ridley, Peterman, & Avery, in press).

Quality of Marriage

There has been little systematic study to determine whether cohabitation leads to a more successful or a different marriage. Four descriptive studies touch on this theme, yet none involves the necessary longitudinal design. Lyness compared 11 married couples who had cohabited before marriage with 13 who had not, on 16 variables representing concepts from open marriage, and found few differences between the groups (Lyness, Note 20). Olday studied 184 married students who had cohabited before marriage and 524 who had not, and found little significant difference between them. Cohabitation before marriage did not seem related to degree of satisfaction, conflict, egalitarianism, or emotional closeness in the later marriage (Olday, Note 9).

When Budd compared 48 married couples who had cohabited before marriage, and 49 who had not, on problems experienced, amount of self-disclosure, and degree of commitment, she found few significant differences. The one major difference was that the marrieds who had not cohabited premaritally were more likely to report loss of love as a problem area that was upsetting to them. It is not clear the extent to which this is due to differences in actual love loss, marriage expectations, or individual need levels, nor is it clear whether the differences between the groups were due to initial personality differences or to the experience of having lived together before marrying (Budd, 1976).

Clatworthy and Schied (Note 14), in another study of married couples who had and had not cohabited, report that while all the couples who had premaritally cohabited considered the experience to be beneficial to their marriage, there was no evidence that couples who live together before marriage have better marriages or less conventional marriages, or that they select better or more compatible mates. They conclude that premarital cohabitation, in and of itself, cannot be considered a cure-all for the problems of traditional marriage.

Although they found many similarities between the marrieds who had and had not cohabited premaritally, Clatworthy and Schied did note some important differences: couples who had cohabited were less likely to acquiesce in disagreements; more often disagreed on such things as finances, household duties, and recreation; were less dependent on their spouses; considered their marriage a less intrinsic part of their lives; had broken up more often; and a higher percentage had sought marriage counseling. Rather than conclude that cohabitation led to these differences, one might hypothesize that these persons would have exhibited these same marital characteristics whether or not they have cohabited premaritally. It is in fact very possible that the same factors which led them to be attracted to cohabitation before marriage would lead them to practice more independence and less acquiescence in marriage, to be more likely to question the role of marriage in their lives, and to view it as less essential to their well-being.

Related to the above is the question: Does movement from cohabitation to legal marriage with its increased sanctions, rights, and responsibilities, change the nature of the couple's relationship to one another? The issue is not settled. Berger, in a retrospective study of 21 couples who had cohabited premaritally, noted that, in general, marriage did not seem to lead to any dramatic change, and that the quality of the relationship after marriage reflected to large extent the apparent quality of the relationship before marriage (Berger, Note 21). Some couples agree, reporting that being married made no difference in their relationship and served only to make parents happy and to facilitate interaction with the larger society. Others claim that they found themselves falling into stereotyped roles, with a resulting loss of identity (Keaough, 1975).

Based on what evidence we have to date, we can hypothesize that movement into marriage will escalate commitment, increase ease with relatives and social institutions, and, because of socialization, increase the likelihood of traditional sex-role behavior, possessiveness, and reduced autonomy. However, both married and unmarried couples are likely to find themselves relating to one another in these more traditional ways unless they consciously contract against this and make a determined effort to maintain the provisions of that contract.

Marriage Rates

Some writers and social critics fear that cohabitation will lead to erosion of the family, a reduction in the rate of marriage, and an increase in children born without the security of legally committed parents. They point with alarm to Sweden with its decided decrease in marriage and increase in cohabitation rates. In Sweden in 1974, 12 percent of all couples living together under marriage-like conditions were unmarried as opposed to only 6.5 percent in 1970; by 1977, this figure had risen to 15 percent. The increased percentages, however, are partly due to the fact that more couples are living together before marriage; about 99 percent of all Swedes who marry today have cohabited premaritally. It is not yet known what percentage of cohabitors will choose nonmarital cohabitation as a permanent life style. (Trost, 1975; Note 22.)

Although there has been a decrease in marriage rates in this country over the past 15 years, and a fairly dramatic increase in the percentage of singles among women aged 20–24 (Bernard, 1975), there is as yet no evidence that large numbers are permanently substituting nonmarital relationships for marriage. Because the vast majority of young persons continues to indicate they hope someday to marry (Bower & Christopherson, 1977; Macklin, 1976b, p. 128), and because societal supports for first and remarriage are so strong in this country, it is predicted that cohabitation will remain part of the courtship phase for most persons, and that there will not be a substantial decrease in marriage rates for some time.

Childrearing

Eiduson and associates are currently involved in a longitudinal comparison of 200 children reared in cohabiting, communal, single-parent, and two-parent nuclear families. Evidence to date suggests that the needs of the infant are such strong determiners of how children are reared that, during the first year of life caretaking practices in nontraditional and traditional families do not differ significantly. At the end of 1 year, the development of the total sample generally fell within the normal range, with lifestyle not a differentiating variable (Eiduson, Note 23). It will be interesting to see to what extent lifestyle appears to affect the development of these children after the first year.

Divorce

Whether cohabitation before legal marriage will lead to more or less divorce is not clear. Some argue that more effective screening of potential marital partners occurs, while others fear that it promotes a life pattern characterized by lack of commitment.

For a number of reasons, the age of marriage is increasing, and since there is general acceptance that the older a person is before marriage the more permanent the marriage, this may have some effect on the divorce rate. On the other hand, there are many factors currently operating against the permanence of relationships. A longer life span, changing views of marriage, wider range of lifestyle options, growing emphasis on personal growth with the possibility that both partners may not grow at the same rate or in the same direction, increasing opportunity for extramarital relationships coupled with little preparation in how to integrate these successfully into ongoing marriage, and greater opportunities for women to satisfy their economic and sexual needs outside of marriage all serve to increase the likelihood of divorce. The fact that a couple had an opportunity to test their initial compatibility through living together may have little effect on whether they will succeed in spending a lifetime together. Premarital cohabitation is but one factor, and probably not a primary factor, influencing the course of relationships over time.

Implications for Practice and Research

Legal statutes and practices need to be adapted to reflect the changing social realities (Hirsch, 1976; King, 1975; Massey & Warner, 1974). As of July 1976 (Lavori, 1976), cohabitation (living together as if husband and wife) was a crime in 20 states, and fornication (sexual intercourse between an unmarried man and woman) was a crime in 16 states and Washington, D. C. Although rarely enforced, the penalties for cohabitation can be stringent, with many states setting a maximum penalty of a $500 fine and a 6-month jail sentence. It would appear that such laws are unconstitutional and violate one's right to privacy without showing compelling reason for doing so, but the U. S. Supreme Court has yet to rule that this is true.

It is difficult to describe with any certainty the present legal status of cohabitants, for laws vary from state to state, the interpretation of any law waits upon judicial review, and new laws and interpretations can appear at any time. Readers are urged to seek informed legal counsel if they require definitive information regarding the laws and precedents in their own state. With this in mind, what can be said about the legal situation facing cohabitants today?

A child born to a man and woman who are living together but not married is still considered illegitimate and as such may experience discrimination, although the rights of such children have been considerably enlarged in recent years. Depending upon the jurisdiction, the rights of the father of a child born in cohabitation will vary. The U. S. Supreme Court ruled in 1972 that it is a denial of due process and equal protection to presume an unwed father an unfit parent, and to take his children from him without providing a proper hearing on the matter *Stanley v. Illinois,* 405 U.S. 645, 1972). However, there are still states which allow the mother primary right of custody, and where the father must not only establish paternity but prove her unfit before receiving custody himself. Should a couple with children divorce and one parent begin living with someone to whom she/he is not married, a judge may on the basis of such cohabitation find that parent unfit to keep custody of the child. Much of this discrimination will undoubtedly change with ratification of the federal Equal Rights Amendment (Myricks, 1977), and with the gradual trend toward recognition of the legitimacy of nontraditional lifestyles.

Since in most states there is no law prohibiting discrimination on the basis of marital status, an owner may choose not to sell, or a landlord not to rent, to an unmarried couple. Moreover, in states where cohabitation or fornication is illegal, or depending on the terms of the lease, living together can be grounds for eviction. Depending upon locale and the biases of one's employer, it is possible to lose one's job by cohabiting out of wedlock. Although Title VII of the 1964 Civil Rights Act prohibits discrimination in employment, it does not cover discrimination on the basis of marital status or living situation. Firing due to cohabitation is theoretically unconstitutional, but, again, this has not yet been established by the courts.

Because membership in professional associations and licensing may be conditional on demonstration of moral fitness, such privileges may on occasion be denied to someone cohabiting out of wedlock. Although the Equal Credit Opportunity Act prohibits discrimination in the granting of credit on grounds of marital status, there is still some question as to whether marital status will be construed to include living together, and hence, some doubt as to whether credit unions would be violating federal law by refusing to grant credit to couples who are living together unmarried. Although there has been some development in the legal protection of cohabiting couples against discrimination in insurance, there are only a few states which prohibit insurance companies from refusing coverage or charging higher premiums.

In some states, such as New York, family court is available to help persons deal with disputes occurring in the family setting, but persons must be legally related in order to have access to this court. Most nonmarital cohabitants do not have the privilege of confidential communication and, hence, unlike married persons, may be called upon to testify against one another in court. Although a notarized power of attorney may be helpful, couples living together do not have the recognized authority to consent to medical treatment for each other, even in case of emergency.

There are numerous inequities within the present tax structure which result in permitting married couples with one income and a joint return to pay less taxes on the same income than two single persons (who, in turn, pay less than a two-income married couple). Moreover, persons who are cohabiting cannot claim each other as dependents. Should the couple remain unmarried and one partner never work outside the home, they will receive less Social Security benefits upon retirement than if they had married. If a partner is injured or dies on the job, the surviving partner will receive Workman's Compensation only if there was a legal marriage.

Although there is considerable body of law regarding the distribution of property upon the termination of a marital relationship, unmarried couples have had to rely on judicial decision. When the couple has acquired real property together, the judge has usually determined property rights strictly on the basis of who has title to the property, and in the case of personal property, on the basis of receipts showing who paid for it. If one is not married and dies without a will, one's property goes to one's blood relatives rather than to one's partner, and inheritance taxes favor the married couple, for when a married partner dies and leaves property to the spouse, all or a portion of that property is tax-exempt.

In December 1976, the California Supreme Court, building on earlier cases, established a precedent which may have important legal implications for unwed couples. Michelle Marvin, who had cohabited nonmaritally with Lee Marvin for 7 years, sued for an equal share of all property acquired during their relationship, claiming that she had given up her career to property accumulated during their time together.

Rejecting Lee's contention that the agreement was unenforceable because of the immoral nature of the relationship and because he had been legally married to another woman at the time of the agreement, the majority in *Marvin* v. *Marvin* (18 Cal. 3rd 684, 1976) stated that the courts should uphold express (oral or written) agreements between nonmarital partners to pool or share income or property, unless the agreement was explicitly dependent upon illicit sexual relations. It was suggested by way of dictum, which has no precedental value (Weisberg, Note 24), that a partner may recover for the reasonable value of household services rendered less the reasonable value of support received if it can be shown that the services were rendered with the expectation of monetary reward. The court ignored the issue of whether Michelle was entitled to support after separation.

It should be noted that the *Marvin* decision serves only to establish that prior financial agreements between Michelle and Lee are enforceable. It remains for Michelle to demonstrate what agreements were in fact made, and without written contractual evidence, this may be difficult.

Indicative of the changing legal picture is the statement by Justice Tobriner of the California Supreme Court. Speaking for the majority, he wrote, "The mores of the society have indeed changed so radically in regard to cohabitation that we cannot impose a standard based on alleged moral considerations that have apparently been so widely abandoned by so many" (*Marvin* v. *Marvin,* 18 Cal. 3rd 684, 1976).

To what extent other states will be influenced by the *Marvin* case remains to be seen. Since the *Marvin* decision rested on contract principles, which are universally applicable, there is a good possibility that it may be followed by other jurisdictions (Weisberg, Note 24). On the other hand, there are many courts which may hesitate to follow the *Marvin* precedent, arguing that the household services rendered are implicitly based on sexual services and that by reimbursing such services one is essentially validating the institution of concubinage. There are others who argue that with the *Marvin* case the court is conferring legal rights and imposing legal duties on relationships which were deliberately intended to be extralegal (Foster and Freed, 1977; *The Family Law Reporter,* Note 25).

In addition, the decision left many areas of ambiguity. For instance, the Marvin relationship had extended over a period of 7 years, and it is not clear the extent to which duration may affect later decisions. The court indicated that the "reasonable expectations" of the parties should be the basis for the distribution of property acquired during the relationship, but left undefined the criteria to be used in the determination of "reasonable."

It is obvious that by not marrying, cohabitants deny themselves some of the protections provided by the law to married couples and do not necessarily escape all legal obligations, for they may find themselves economically liable in ways they had not initially anticipated. Lavori, a member of the New York State Bar and an attorney in private practice in New York City, concludes her book, *Living Together, Married or Single: Your Legal Rights,* by saying:

> A man and a woman who are both capable of financial independence and who have the foresight to protect their mutual rights through contracts, wills and compliance with legitimation procedures, and who do not mind doing some legal battle once in a while to secure their rights to housing, credit, insurance, and employment can live together permanently or temporarily with no difficulty. But most people are not in that position. Few have the awareness or the desire to take a self-protective, preventive approach to their personal relationships. For these people, marriage is probably a good idea ultimately, although living together may well be a perfectly appropriate interim status. For them, marriage defines their rights regarding each other and anticipates contingencies that they will not or cannot forsee, prevent, or provide for. (Lavori, 1976, p. 247)

Often persons living together are hesitant to go to marriage and family counselors for fear they will be considered deviant or be pressured into marriage. Yet many of the problems facing cohabiting couples are identical to those facing any couple involved in an intimate living relationship. These include differences in spending habits, degree of sexual interest, childrearing practices, division of household labor, amount of personal freedom, appropriate relationships with parents and other relatives, and expectations and hopes for the duration of the relationship. The only problems that seem unique to cohabitation are those which grow out of the lack of general societal support for this lifestyle, and the hassles some cohabitants experience when dealing with our legal, economic, and religious institutions. Although some counselors are not comfortable dealing with cohabiting couples, and many still consider such behavior as indicative of immaturity, such attitudes no longer can be considered acceptable among professionals.

Research needs to move ahead in new directions. Those who wish to continue to deal specifically with the phenomenon of cohabitation would do well to focus on developing longitudinal research with objective behavioral measures on noncollege and older populations, for it is in these areas where knowledge gaps primarily lie. Such studies should go beyond decriptive analyses comparing cohabitation and legal marriage, and test hypotheses founded on theory.

On the other hand, there is some question about the wisdom of continuing to use cohabitation as a central variable. Knowing that an individual is living with someone to whom she/he is not married tells us little about either the relationship or the person. Rather than focus on the specific legal status of a given relationship, investigators should be concerned with how the particular individuals define their own relationship, their degree of commitment to and investment in that relationship, the quality of the interaction, and the emotional maturity and interpersonal skills of the individuals involved. If the focus of research were more on the dynamics of intimate relationships and on the skills needed to function effectively within them, and less on the structural form of such relationships, progress toward understanding and improving the quality of relationships would be more rapid.

Reference Notes

1. Glick, P. C. Personal communication, June 20, 1977.
2. McCauley, B. Personal communication, 1976.
3. Huang, L. J. *Research with unmarried cohabiting couples: Including non-exclusive sexual relations.* Paper presented at the annual meeting of the National Council on Family Relations, St. Louis, Missouri, October 1974.
4. Macklin, F. D. *Comparison of parent and student attitudes toward non-marital cohabitation.* Paper presented at the annual meeting of the National Council on Family Relations, St. Louis, Missouri, October 1974.
5. Rubin, Z. *Dating project research report.* Unpublished manuscript, Harvard University Department of Psychology and Social Relations, April 1975.
6. Guittar, E. C., & Lewis, R. A. *Self concepts among some unmarried cohabitants.* Paper presented at the annual meeting of the National Council on Family Relations, St. Louis, Missouri, October 1974.
7. Lewis, R. A., Spanier, G. B., Storm, V. L., & Lettecka, C. F. *Commitment in married and unmarried cohabitation.* Paper presented at the annual meeting of the American Sociological Association, San Francisco, August 1975.
8. Cole, C. L., & Bower, D. W. *Role disparity in the cohabitation pair-bond.* Paper presented at the meeting of the North Central Sociological Association, Windsor, Canada, May 1974.
9. Olday, D. E. Personal communication, April 1976.
10. Whitehurst, R. N. *Sex role equality and changing meanings in cohabitation.* Paper presented at the annual meeting of the North Central Sociological Association, Windsor, Canada, May 1974.
11. Cole, C. L., & Bower, D. W. *Cohabitation pair-bond intimacy requirements and love-life development differences.* Paper presented at the annual meeting of the National Council on Family Relations, St. Louis, Missouri, October 1974.
12. Cole, C. M., & Vincent, J. P. *Cognitive and behavioral patterns in cohabitive and marital dyads.* Unpublished manuscript, University of Houston, 1975.
13. Cole, C. M., & Vincent, J. P. Personal communication, 1975.
14. Clatworthy, N. M., & Scheid, L. *A comparison of married couples: Premarital cohabitants with non-premarital cohabitants.* Unpublished manuscript, Ohio State University, 1977.
15. Montgomery, J. P. *Commitment and cohabitation cohesion.* Paper presented at the annual meeting of the National Council on Family Relations, Toronto, Canada, October 1973.
16. Hennon, C. B. *Conflict management within pairing relationships: The case of non-marital cohabitation.* Unpublished manuscript, University of Utah, 1975.
17. Cole, C. L. *Living together as an alternative life style.* Unpublished manuscript, Iowa State University, 1976.
18. McCauley, B. *Sex roles in alternative life styles: Egalitarian attitudes in the cohabiting relationship.* Paper presented at the International Workshop on Changing Sex Roles in Family and Society, Dubrovnik, Yugoslavia, June 1975.
19. Shuttlesworth, G. & Thorman, G. *Living together unmarried relationships.* Unpublished manuscript, University of Texas at Austin, 1973.
20. Lyness, J. F. *Open marriage among former cohabitants: We have met the enemy: Is it us?.* Unpublished manuscript, Pennsylvania State University, 1976.
21. Berger, M. E. *Trial marriage followup.* Unpublished manuscript, 140–70 Burden Crescent, Jamaica, N. Y., 1974.
22. Trost, J. *Dissolution of cohabitation and marriage.* Unpublished manuscript, Uppsala University, 1977.

23. Eiduson, B. T. Personal communication, 1977.
24. Weisberg, D. K. *How to divide the wages of living in sin: unmarried couples, property rights and the law.* Paper presented at the annual meeting of the National Council on Family Relations, San Diego, 1977.
25. *The Family Law Reporter,* January 11, 1977, *3,* (10), Sect. 2.

References

Arafat, I., & Yorburg, B. On living together without marriage. *Journal of Sex Research,* 1973, *9,* 97–106.

Berger, M. E. Trial marriage: Harnessing the trend constructively. *The Family Coordinator,* 1971, *20,* 38–43.

Bernard, J. Note on changing life styles, 1970–1974. *Journal of Marriage and the Family,* 1975, *37,* 582–593.

Bower, D. W. *A description and analysis of a cohabiting sample in America.* Unpublished master's thesis, University of Arizona, 1975.

Bower, D. W., & Christopherson, V. A. University student cohabitation: A regional comparison of selected attitudes and behavior. *Journal of Marriage and the Family,* 1977, *39,* 447–453.

Budd, L. S. *Problems disclosure, and commitment of cohabiting and married couples.* Unpublished doctoral dissertation, University of Minnesota, 1976.

Clayton, R. R., & Voss, H. L. Shacking up: Cohabitation in the 1970s. *Journal of Marriage and the Family,* 1977, *39,* 273–283.

Cole, C. L. Cohabitation in social context. In R. W. Libby & R. N. Whitehurst (eds.), *Marriage and alternatives.* Glenview, Ill.: Scott, Foresman and Co., 1977.

Danziger, C. *Unmarried heterosexual cohabitation.* Unpublished doctoral dissertation, Rutgers University, 1976.

Foster, H. H., & Freed, D. J. Law and the family. *New York Law Journal,* February 25, April 22, 1977.

Ganson, H. C. *Cohabitation: The antecedents of dissolution of formerly cohabiting individuals.* Unpublished master's thesis, Ohio State Universtiy, 1975.

Guttmacher, A. F., & Vadies, E. E. Sex on the campus and the college health services. *Journal of the American College Health Association,* 1972, *21,* 145–148.

Henze, L. F., & Hudson, J. W. Personal and family characteristics of non-cohabiting and cohabiting college students. *Journal of Marriage and the Family,* 1974, *36,* 722–726.

Hirsch, B. B. *Living together: A guide to the law for unmarried couples.* Boston: Houghton Mifflin, 1976.

Johnson, M. P. *Courtship and commitment: A study of cohabitation on a university campus.* Unpublished master's thesis, University of Iowa, 1968.

Johnson, M. P. Commitment: A conceptual structure and empirical application. *Sociological Quarterly,* 1973, *14,* 395–406.

Keaough, D. Without knotting the tie. *The American Republic,* July 27, 1975, pp. 8–15.

Kieffer, C. M. *Consensual cohabitation: A descriptive study of the relationships and sociocultural characteristics of eighty couples in settings of two Florida universities.* Unpublished master's thesis, Florida State University, 1972.

King, M. D. *Cohabitation handbook: Living together and the law.* Berkeley, Calif.: Ten Speed Press, 1975.

Lautenschlager, S. Y. *A descriptive study of consensual union among college students.* Unpublished master's thesis, California State University at Northridge, 1972.

Lindsey, B. B., & Evans, W. *The companionate marriage.* Garden City, N. Y.: Garden City Publishing Co., 1927/1929.

Lavori, N. *Living together, married or single: Your legal rights.* New York: Harper and Row, 1976.

Lyness, J. F., Lipetz, M. E., & Davis, K. E. Living together: An alternative to marriage. *Journal of Marriage and the Family,* 1972, *34,* 305–311.

Macklin, E. D. (Ed.). *Cohabitation Research Newsletter,* Ocotober 1972, 1. (a).

Macklin, E. D. Heterosexual cohabitation among unmarried college students. *The Family Coordinator,* 1972, *21,* 463–472. (b)

Macklin, E. D. (Ed.) *Cohabitation Research Newsletter,* June 1974, 2. (a)

Macklin, E. D. Students who live together: Trial marriage or going very steady. *Psychology Today*, November 1974, pp. 53–59. (b)

Macklin, E. D. (Ed.) *Cohabitation Research Newsletter*, April 1976,5. (a)

Macklin, E. D. Unmarried heterosexual cohabitation on the university campus. In J. P. Wiseman (Ed.), *The social psychology of sex*. New York: Harper and Row, 1976. (b)

Macklin, E. D. Review of research on non-marital cohabitation in the United states. In B. I. Murstein (ed.), *Exploring intimate life styles*. New York: Springer Publishing Co., in press.

Makepeace, J. M. *The birth control revolution: Consequences for college student life styles*. Unpublished doctoral dissertation, Washington State University, 1975.

Massey, C., & Warner, R. *Sex, living together and the law: A legal guide for unmarried couples and groups*. Berkeley, Calif.: Nolo Press, 1974.

McCauley, B. *Self esteem in the cohabiting relationship*. Unpublished master's thesis, University of Delaware, 1977.

Mead, M. Marriage in two steps. *Redbook*, July 1966, *127*, 48

Mead, M. A continuing dialogue on marriage: Why just living together won't work. *Redbook*, April 1968, *130*, 44

Myricks, N. The equal rights amendment: Its potential impact on family life. *The Family Coordinator*, 1977, *26*, 321–324.

Peterman, D. J., Ridley, C. A., & Anderson, S. M. A comparison of cohabiting and non-cohabiting college students. *Journal of Marriage and the Family*. 1974, *36*, 344–354.

Petty, J. A. *An investigation of factors which differentiate between types of cohabitation*. Unpublished master's thesis, Indiana University, 1975.

Polansky, L. *A comparison of marriage and cohabitation on three interpersonal variables*. Unpublished master's thesis, Ball State University, 1974.

Ridley, C. A., Peterman, D. J. & Avery, A. W. Cohabitation: Does it make for a better marriage? *The Family Coordinator*, in press.

Rodman, H. Illegitimacy in the Caribbean social structure: A reconsideration. *American Sociological Review*, 1966, *31*, 673–683.

Russell, B. *Marriage and morals*. New York: Liveright, 1929.

Segrest, M. A. *Comparison of the role expectations of married and cohabiting students*. University of Kentucky, 1975.

Smith, P. B., & Kimmel, K. Student-parent reactions to off-campus cohabitation. *Journal of College Student Personnel*, 1970, *11*, 188–193.

Stafford, R., Backman, E., & diBona, P. The division of labor among cohabiting and married couples. *Journal of Marriage and the Family*, 1977, 39, 43–57.

Steiner, D. *Non-marital cohabitation and marriage: Questionnaire responses of college women their mothers*. Unpublished master's thesis, North Dakota State University, 1975.

Stevens, D. J. H. *Cohabitation without marriage*. Unpublished doctoral dissertation, University of Texas, 1975.

Storm, V. *Contemporary cohabitation and the dating-marital continuum*. Unpublished master's thesis, University of Georgia, 1973.

Trost, J. Married and unmarried cohabitation: the case of Sweden with some comparisons. *Journal of Marriage and the Family*, 1975, *37*, 677–682.

Van Deusen, E. L. *Contract cohabitation: An alternative to marriage*. New York: Grove Press, 1974.

U.S. Bureau of the Census. Marital status and living arrangements: March 1976. *Current Population Reports* (Series P-20, no. 306). Washington, D.C.: U.S. Government Printing Office, 1977.

Love and Adulthood in American Culture

Ann Swidler

Adulthood, which once seemed an uneventful, predictable time of life, has more recently come to seem problematic and mysterious. We find ourselves asking whether adulthood is a period of stability or of change, whether adults "develop" or only drift, whether there are patterned "stages" of adult development or only more and less successful responses to external pressures. The answers to these questions depend in large part on emerging shifts in the way our culture patterns adulthood. By examining the ideology of love, one of the central anchors of our culture's view of adult life, I will explore the changing structure of meaning that shapes the contemporary adult life course.

Love in our culture is both an experience and an ideal, richly arrayed in symbol and myth. These myths outline the shape of adulthood, and the rituals of love mark its moments of transition. Like religious experience, the culturally grounded experience of love links the lives of individuals—their private struggles and triumphs—to larger issues, framing the meaning of adult life. Thus Freud's statement that an adult must be able "to love and to work" is a moral as well as a psychological ideal. If this ideal is undermined, if love and work no longer seem to be significant achievements, the integrity and meaning of adult life are undermined as well.

As Erik Erikson's work has made us aware, ideological and religious images provide symbolic resources which structure individual developmental crises and make possible their resolution. Although love in real life is not like love in literature or in the movies, our culture's images of love provide a background, a language, and a set of symbols within which people enact their own lives. In loving and being loved, people give themselves over, at least for brief periods, to intensely moving experiences through which they achieve new awareness of self and others. Love can make possible periods of crystallization or reformulation of the self and the self's relationship to the world. Beliefs about love permeate people's hopes for themselves, their evaluations of experience, and their sense of achievement in the world.[1]

While love is only one part of adulthood, its symbolic richness makes it an ideal place to examine the cultural dilemmas of contemporary adulthood. We may ask both what resources our culture provides for building a satisfactory adulthood, and what new models and images of adulthood are developing to give meaning to emerging challenges in adult life. . . .

Reprinted by permission of the publishers from *Themes of Work and Love in Adulthood*, N. J. Smelser and E. H. Erikson, eds., Cambridge, Mass.: Harvard University Press. Copyright © 1980 by the President and Fellows of Harvard. Portions of the original have been omitted.

American Culture as a Framework for Adulthood

The way adulthood is experienced is shaped by the way a culture organizes and frames adult life. In Western culture love has played a central symbolic role in integrating the issues of individual identity, moral choice, and social commitment. Courtly tradition made love a moral matter, ennobling and disciplining the self; bourgeois culture made love a central symbol of the individual quest for identity, integrity, and fulfillment.

In the traditional love myth, individuals rebelled against society (family, convention, tradition), but in loving they simultaneously sought new commitments and found their own place in the social world. The search for love and the search for a way to deal with society were inextricably linked. But American culture dealt differently with the symbolism of adulthood. What does the love myth tell us about the attitude of our culture toward adulthood, toward the nexus of individual identity with social commitment? How is this attitude changing? By examining the peculiar form the love myth has taken in American culture, and exploring contemporary changes in the ideology of love, we will see how adulthood itself is changing. In doing so we will better understand whether our culture can infuse the tasks of adulthood—the achievement of fidelity, love, care, and wisdom—with richness and meaning.

The traditional American attitude toward adulthood has been one of fear, and along with this fear has gone great uncertainty about love. The power of the love myth has always come from its ability to bind together contradictory elements—ennobling passion and adulterous betrayal in courtly love; individual rebellion and social commitment in bourgeois romantic love. These conflicting images embody the tension between individual and social demands, and the love myth promises their resolution. But in America the relation between the individual and society has been particularly problematic, and thus the attitude toward love peculiarly ambivalent.

While the traditional love myth has always had a strong place in American popular culture, particularly in "women's literature" (romantic novels, women's magazine fiction, and Gothic romances), Leslie Fiedler (1966) noted some time ago that the greatest American novels, from *The Last of the Mohicans, Huckleberry Finn,* and *Moby Dick* to the modern novels of Faulkner or Nathaniel West, avoid passionate love as a central theme, their male heroes seeking self-definition against nature or Gothic terror and seeking intimacy in the companionship of other men. In the American myth, women and love represent the entangling bonds of social obligation, and the only real self-definition comes from a Faustian quest to face inner and outer evil alone (Fiedler, 1966). Even in popular culture, our traditional heroes are the cowboy and the private eye, men pursuing their own self-created image of freedom and justice outside the corrupting ties of social life (Cawelti, 1976).[2]

Americans have also been criticized, by themselves and others, for a sort of premature closing-off of the self. Kenneth Keniston (1968) has written of an adolescence in which inner conflict is submerged in conformity to the peer group and an adult identity achieved by reluctant submission to the demands of work and marriage. The irony of American identity formation, as Erikson (1963, p. 286) has written, is that it "seems to support an individual's ego identity as long as he can preserve a certain element of deliberate tentativeness of autonomous choice. The individual must be able to convince himself that the next step is up to him and that no matter where he is staying or going he always has the choice of leaving or turning in the opposite direction if he chooses to do." In fantasy Americans remain perpetual adolescents, while adult commitments represent the defeat rather than the fulfillment of the quest for identity. People are "trapped" into marriage;[3] work is a loss of freedom, a shameful "settling down."

Americans have, perhaps, a more passionately developed sense of individuality and selfhood than members of most other cultures, but this individuality remains forever locked in a sort of childish wish not to become adult, a cultural rejection of adulthood itself. The love myth has always had a place in American culture, but a degraded one. While it promised individuality, integrity, and independence, these were compromised by the danger of a confining, settled adulthood. What American culture could not do was to make the achievement of adult commitment, fidelity, intimacy, and care themselves seem heroic, meaningful achievements. In the current period the love myth is undergoing a change. The historic oppositions which traditionally gave the love myth its emotional appeal and cultural dynamism are being intensified, while the balance of elements in the myth is shifting. These changes have important consequences for the definition and meaning of adulthood.

The emerging love ethic reemphasizes the rebellious, free, individualistic side of the love myth. In some ways the values of permanence and commitment have been undermined even further, while the adolescent-fantasy core of American culture has strengthened its hold. On the other hand, the emerging love ideology, because it endorses flexibility and eschews permanence, also sees love more as a continuing process than as a once-and-for-all culmination of life, after which people need only live happily ever after. The central elements of the love myth remain; people still seek moral self-definition, fulfilling intimacy, and a meaningful identity. But the framework of expectations about what it means to achieve these things, and thus the cultural definition of adulthood itself, is changing.

Changes in the cultural meaning of love are grounded on the one hand in changing definitions of the self (and thus implicitly of adulthood as a whole) and on the other hand in changing social-structural demands on the life course. There are four distinguishable oppositions within our culture's love mythology, tensions which have given the myth its richness, its seeming power to reconcile divergent needs and opposing parts of the self. Each of these four oppositions links the lives of individuals to aspects of the social world and thus to specific changes in contemporary society. The tension between choice and commitment embodies the problem of moral self-definition and the achievement of identity. Choice of a marriage partner and its implication of permanent commitment have provided the structural foundation of this aspect of the love myth. The second important symbolic tension in the love myth is that between rebellion against social obligation versus attachment to the social world, particularly the world of work. The third opposition is that between self-realization and self-sacrifice. Love traditionally promised self-realization, yet required self-sacrifice, especially when love led to children and the full burdens of family life. Finally, libidinal expression through love is in tension with the libidinal restraint required by the traditional norm of fidelity and the related problem of the sources and grounds of intimacy.

Choice Versus Commitment

The tension between choice and commitment involves the problem of identity. If identity is something that must be won only once, if the self is a stable achievement, remaining constant despite superficial flux, then the choice that symbolically consolidates identity forecloses further possibilities of or needs for choice. But when the fixity of the self cannot be taken for granted, the tensions implicit in the love myth's treatment of choice and commitment become more apparent.

The love myth describes the attempt to define one's self by the free choice of a love partner, fusing the problem of the search for one's true self with the quest for one's right mate. The correlate of such self-definition is identity and, in Erikson's terms, fidelity. Faithfulness to one's choice becomes faithfulness to one's self. The capacity to make a commitment and stick to it is the measure of successful identity formation. Yet the traditional model of choice and commitment implies a relatively static notion of both love and identity. While a process of liberating personal growth culminates in choice of the "right" partner, the choice consolidates that growth while prohibiting further change. One chooses only once, after which commitment closes off alternative choices and alternative identities.

Here we can see a profound shift in the ideology of love—an attempt to preserve its ennobling moral quality and its power of defining identity, while giving up the ideal of commitment which was traditionally the hallmark of both moral achievement and secure identity. Modern moral ideals for the self, in particular the emphasis on self-actualization and the demand for continuing growth and change in adulthood, clash head on with the traditional ideal of love as commitment.

New ideologies of love attempt to preserve the heroic myth of the struggle for identity by giving it a new content. The discovery of self and other through love, the culminating moment of the traditional love myth, is absorbed into a new ideal of continuing mutual revelation. "Struggle" becomes a sign of virtue in a relationship, and loving comes to mean facing one crisis after another in which two autonomous, growing people work to deepen communication, to understand each other, and to rediscover themselves. Here the whole valence of the love myth is changed. And these changes affect our moral perceptions, fantasies, and intuitive feelings about what is a meaningful, satisfying, or profound love relationship. Even the terms of evaluation change. Whereas once we might have spoken of "true love" or of a love one would die for (or die without), now "deep," "meaningful," or "alive" seem more appropriate terms for praising a love relationship. Even where the new ideology seems most flat and without conviction we can see disconnected threads of an emerging mythology of love, not yet woven into a unified fabric. We can also follow the strands of such developing ideologies, listen to the changing language in which ideals of love and selfhood are expressed, and think about what they imply for the course of adulthood in the contemporary period.

The search for self-knowledge and identity is still central, but that search can no longer be defined by a single decisive choice, a struggle against external obstacles to assert the self against the world. Now the obstacles to love are internal to the self and to the relationship (as, for example, in Ingmar Bergman's "Scenes from a Marriage"), and one can love most fully by deepening the honesty and communication in a relationship, even if the relationship ends as a consequence. True love is not a love to which one is committed, so much as a love in which one can have complete communication. And communication is difficult; it requires heroic struggle with the self and the lover. By the same token, a love relationship that does not require painful change no longer performs its function. The value of love, and its challenge, is that it must stimulate and absorb perpetual change.

New images of love do not reject the core elements of the traditional love myth—that love is a moral achievement, capable of defining and transforming the self. But what the self is, and how it is to be defined and enshrined, is differently conceived. Ralph Turner (1976) has argued that there are two fundamentally opposed ways of viewing the self, which he calls "institution" and "impulse." People who locate the "true self" institutionally define themselves by acts of choice and will, in the institutionalized roles to which they commit themselves. People who define their real selves by impulse see as true only what wells up outside institutional roles. "The outburst or desire is recognized—fearfully or enthusiastically—as an indication that the real self is breaking through a deceptive crust of institutional behavior. Institutional motivations are external, artificial constraints and superimpositions that bridle manifestations of the real self" (pp. 991–992). What the traditional ideal of love accomplished was to fuse these two conceptions of self together into one overriding achievement. One could follow his deepest impulses to find his true self, and imbed that self in an institutional commitment. Will and desire could merge in the achievement of identity. In the shifting structure of the love myth, the impulsive sides of the self are given greater emphasis, and the ideal of permanence is undermined. What is good about a relationship is not the commitment it embodies, but how much a person learns about himself from the relationship. Love is not the emblem of a crystallized identity but the mandate for continuing self-exploration.

In the traditional view, a love that ended was a failure, a sign of some terrible mistake in the search for self and identity. But the new love imagery can claim great gains from failed relationships. Each person can grow and learn, even from loss and disappointment. Indeed permanence, which was the hallmark of success in the earlier model of identity formation, becomes almost a sign of failure. After all, is it likely that one can keep growing and changing with the same partner? Doesn't permanence in a relationship necessarily require some compromise of individual possibilities for growth? And even for those who value permanent commitment, its meaning is changed. Enduring relationships mean a deeper challenge and even more profound opportunities for growth than do short-term relationships. So both those who value long-term and short-term relationships increasingly justify relationships by the opportunities they offer for challenge and change. The greatest sin a lover can commit is not betrayal, renegging on a commitment, but obstruction, trying to thwart, hamper, or limit another's freedom to grow.

In recent films—"Annie Hall" and "Scenes from a Marriage," for example—we are asked to feel that the relationship between two lovers must end because staying in the relationship would mean stagnation, while the end of the relationship forces valuable if painful growth. These films also converge in the view that in some ways one can really love—that is, understand, appreciate, communicate with another—only after a love relationship is over, freeing love from the stifling obligations of day-to-day contact. Another easily idealized love relationship is that of *Love Story* or "Harold and Maude," where the loved one gives the hero strength and helps him grow toward a new joy in living, and then, conveniently, dies, so there is no possibility of constraining further growth. A modified version of this new pattern is the found-lost-found relationship among adults where, by leaving each other, two people discover new possibilities, new facets of themselves, new strengths and vulnerabilities, and then come together again to rebuild their relationship on new terms. This story, in *The War between the Tates*, for example, allows incorporation of the new image of love as a perpetual quest for self and identity without completely abandoning the older ideal of a love that lasts a lifetime.

While the new mythology of love and the new ideal of the self have been criticized as examples of the "new narcissism" (Lasch, 1976), the new ideology is also a shift in the direction of adulthood. In keeping alive the image of love as a crucible for identity, but making the quest for identity and the quest for love continuing preoccupations, the emerging love mythology validates adulthood as a period of continuing crisis, challenge, and change. It rejects the notion that life's dilemmas are resolved at one crucial moment of choice and commitment, after which one must only live happily ever after.

Both Robert Lifton (1971) and Kenneth Keniston (1968) have argued that modern society changes the nature of identity, making it more flexible, less fixed, and less permanent than traditional models of personal development allowed. What we see in the contemporary culture of love is an attempt to give moral content, added meaning, to this new model of development. By drawing on the rich symbolic resources of the Western love mythology, contemporary culture redefines the morally significant elements of love, focuses attention on new frontiers of the quest for identity (communication and understanding rather than permanence and commitment), and enshrines a new image of the self. While in some ways it means abandonment of central aspects of the love myth in our culture, it also opens up new possibilities for exploring the meanings of adult life. By reappropriating elements of the love ideology, it offers the possibility of new cultural grounding for the adult life course.

Rebellion Versus Attachment

Love justifies rebellion against family and society; it legitimates the rejection of social demands. In searching for his own destiny, for his own place in the social world, a person "marries for love"—rejecting the claims of family, defying the prejudices of class. Yet love, like religion, has a profoundly dual aspect. It creates an alternative in contrast to "this world," and it justifies conformity to the world and its demands. In the bourgeois tradition, love leads to marriage, and thereby to social attachment and obligation.

One of the great justifications for conformity to the world of work, for acceptance of social limitations, for "settling down" and "toeing the line" is love. Women are told that washing socks, cooking, and cleaning are morally fulfilling because they express love. Men feel that going off to work every day is meaningful because it supports the wives and children they love. Love elevates and transforms the mundane activities of life, but in doing so it also binds people to that life.

The issue of rebellion versus attachment is linked sociologically to the world of work. While the traditional ideology of love justified rebellion against social constraint, it was rebellion in behalf of a sense of meaning which, ultimately, had to be confirmed by the social world. The love myth was concerned with whether individuals could force from the social world recognition of their true selves and of their real worth. Pamela was successful: her virtue was rewarded with a social position equal to her true merits. But even in tragic love stories, love symbolizes the ability of the individual to struggle against the social world, to confront it on even terms. The significance of rebellion is found only in dialectical tension with the aspiration for meaningful social attachment.

As social attachment comes to seem either dangerous or destructive, love loses some of its appeal. Diana Trilling (1964) has noted that in "good" contemporary literature both love and society itself (that is, money, work, class, or concrete social settings) have all but disappeared. "If we think of Hemingway as the last writer to give us love stories, we realize that he was also the last significant novelist to engage in anything like an equal dialogue with society; we begin to realize that where there is no dialogue between society and the individual there can be very little dialogue between individuals" (pp. 61–62). Society becomes, in Trilling's terms, "a giant implacable power" able to overwhelm and destroy the individual. In place of the individual's struggle with society is an obsession with the isolated self, in which self-exploration replaces social purpose, and "proper awareness of self is equated with social morality" (p. 60). Here the hero is the madcap loner, careening along in a disordered social world. The only escape from society is to turn inward into madness or outward in frenzied, hopeless rebellion.

While the theme of a world of men freed of the entangling demands of women has always had great appeal in American culture, there is nonetheless a remarkable change in both high and popular treatments of rebellion and attachment in recent years. In the traditional romantic myth, even in America, the hero, however much of an individualist, might finally settle down if only he found a girl whose individualism of spirit matched his own. In cowboy movies, for example, though the hero had to fight alone, he could ultimately join society, perhaps marrying the town's schoolteacher. Even when the cowboy hero rode off into the sunset alone, he went with the gratitude and acceptance of society (Wright, 1975). But since the 1960s cowboy movies have shifted from the "classical plot," where the hero used his uniqueness to be accepted by society, to the "professional plot," in which a group of heroes remain outside a corrupt and undesirable society. Whether the heroes live or die, they do it together. The only people they respect are the "bad guys" who are also professionals, with their own skills and code of loyalty. The heroes do not wish to enter society, and they do not do so. Finding a place in society is not at issue (Wright, 1975). In this transformed myth, love also becomes possible again. Since the heroes are building a new society and are totally rejecting conventional society, a woman who joins the "outlaws" can be as much a part of the rebellion as men can (Wright, 1975).

But in "higher" culture the scenario is not quite so optimistic. Here heroes refuse to join society, but they cannot quite escape it either. Indeed, even the hero of Vonnegut's *Slaughterhouse Five* escapes his sordid earth life only to find himself a caged pet of beings from another planet. In *One Flew over the Cuckoo's Nest*, while the hero creates a band of buddies who defy the head nurse (now the paradigm of the overwhelming, repressive, female social force), their triumph is ambiguous. The men recover their masculinity and their will to resist, but the hero is destroyed as a person, though his spirit lives on. And in high culture—the novels of Saul Bellow or Thomas Pynchon, for example—unstrung heroes, with no social attachment anywhere, twist and turn through a world which has disintegrated around them. Madness makes the world incomprehensible and real contact with anyone in it impossible. Society, and the world of love and of women, has become positively sinister—a senseless, overpowering juggernaut. The individual must defy society, but he can never hope to overcome it.

Thus contemporary culture has undermined the romance of rebellion, while it has also made attachment inconceivable. But why has this desolate picture of the possibilities for individual expression come into vogue in contemporary fiction? Why is there now such a terror of forces which can bind or strangle the individual? The implicit claim, found in Trilling and other critics of contemporary culture (Lasch, 1976), is that the death of love in modern literature and the rise of narcissism in contemporary culture reflect the power of modern society to overwhelm the isolated individual. Yet I am not at all convinced that modern work or modern institutions allow fewer possibilities for individual expression, freedom, or achievement than did those of a few generations ago. Our literature speaks of the victory of implacable social power. But I think there are other reasons why individuals resist the social commitment that can be expressed in work, and extend this attitude back into a rejection of confining love relationships.

In the modern economy, those occupations with the greatest prestige and interest are also those which require the greatest readiness for continuing change. Innovation in the economy requires flexibility in elite workers; an occupation in which one can "settle down" is an occupation which represents a "dead end." Only the person who is always ready with a new idea, who can move from one organization or role to another, can succeed.[4] We therefore find a new tentativeness about the meaning of work. Finding one's "right place" in the social world—one of the core meanings of the love myth—now becomes a contradiction in terms. The right place is inevitably wrong, a chimera. The only right solution is to have a set of ideas and talents, completely contained within the self, perpetually renewed, continually shifting into original patterns. One's self is one's only resource, but that self cannot look for "proof" of its worth, either in a fixed calling or in a single love relationship. This emphasis on keeping one's options open weakens the mythic appeal of a rebellious struggle to mold a social destiny. Rebellion is still essential, but not in the service of a new social attachment. Keeping one's inner self vibrant and flexible means remaining in a state of perpetual rebellion, rather than using the capacity to rebel, which the imagery of love contains, in the service of finding one's right place in social life.

In this renegotiation of the balance between rebellion and attachment, the meaning of adulthood changes. The need to be continually ready for new demands creates a wary avoidance of entanglement in love and work, an eagerness to keep the self free and unconstrained. This means that adulthood provides no resting place from demands on the self, and perhaps this is why the demanding society and the demanding lover are such ominous forces in contemporary fiction. Yet the fear of binding attachments which may constrain the self is not necessarily a rejection of adulthood so much as a redefinition of it, and a redirection of emotional and moral energy toward new challenges.

These new challenges create a new relationship between work and love in adulthood. Smelser argues that there is an increasing separation between instrumental and affective realms in modern life, between work and love. At the cultural level there does seem to be a growing rejection of the romantic myth that love both transcends and resolves problems of career and livelihood. The worldly young today believe that finding someone to love is no solution to life's difficulties; you still have to decide who you are and what you want to do. And they also see that work commitments may compete with emotional attachments; two conflicting career trajectories, for example, may destroy a relationship. When people follow their own destinies, they may be driven apart.

But in other ways contemporary culture fuses together rather than separates the issues of work and love. Instead of two separate questions—one of internal identity and the other of social destiny—which must be resolved together, both problems become the same problem, that of the restless self. One pattern in the contemporary popular view of love turns love itself into a kind of work. For some people in modern society the continual negotiation and renegotiation of personal relationships becomes the major sphere of accomplishment in daily life. People take on "struggle" in their relationships with a vengeance, "working at" their relationships, putting in the effort to "make them work." Rather than symbolize social commitments through love, they substitute personal relationships for social commitments. There grows up a new moralism in personal relationships—not the old concern with personal virtue but a new passion for honesty, fairness, equality, and communication. Sometimes the intensity of concern with the self-conscious negotiation of terms, rights, and responsibilities in relationships makes their activities sound like those of a workshop or a battlefield rather than a domestic circle.

Work and love also converge in a second pattern marked by fear of emotional engagement and by the effort to create relationships that demand nothing, threaten nothing, and commit nothing of the self (Hendin, 1975). The self is vulnerable, and its integrity must be protected by clear understanding—no expectations, no strings, no demands for involvement. Relationships are required to have an explicit constitution in which nothing is left to chance, no tentacles of unrecognized attachment can reach out to strangle, no illegitimate expectations can develop. This self-protective openness makes the relationship serious business, but it denies the irrationality and dependence that were part of the traditional myth of commitment, in which one bound oneself to another without bargaining for specific terms (Cagle, 1975). Contemporary ideology, with its serious attention to the work of loving, also reflects a fear of dependency, an assertion that people are bound only to what they have agreed to. Good lovers, like good workers, cannot afford unlimited attachments. They may stay on, but only if the terms are right, if the job or the relationship permits them continued development.

If neither rebellion against nor attachment to the social world can adequately define the self, if work on the self has become the essential and most gratifying form of work (expanding one's capital in an era when the self is one's major capital), then love takes on a new and more somber set of meanings. While it may still appear occasionally as the stimulus to a great rebellion ("The Graduate" or *Love Story*), that fantasy seems to have run aground. There is nowhere for rebellion to go without again becoming binding attachment. Hence the pessimism of much contemporary fiction in which the plot seems to die for want of a satisfactory ending. There is no decisive event which can resolve life's difficulties. However, there is also a new respect for the seriousness and significance of living as an ongoing, day-to-day challenge. The crucial question might be seen as how to give life meaning, how to live it with richness and depth, without requiring that the present be given significance by binding the future. While one aspect of this change in ideology is simply an escape from strong feeling or deep involvement which might threaten individual autonomy, there is also a new attention to adult experience, to making it gratifying, stimulating, and meaningful in its own terms.

Self-Realization Versus Self-Sacrifice

How much to give and what one will be allowed to take, the balance between satisfaction and sacrifice, has been a continuing theme in stories of love. In the traditional mythology the lover seeks his own happiness, fights for his own gratification, and yet the highest form of love is selfless giving. In the traditional imagery of love, the ecstasy of possessing another merges with the altruistic wish to sacrifice oneself for the other's well-being.

As long as we believe that a person can fulfill himself only through love of another, the tension between self-realization and self-sacrifice is minimized. One realizes himself *through* self-sacrifice. But with changes in the kinds of self-definition people expect from love goes a change in the norms and language of love. While these shifts may sound like simple cloaks for self-indulgence, they contain deeper meanings. The obligation to sacrifice oneself for another is replaced by the duty to respect the other person's separateness, to recognize the other's needs for growth and change, to give to the other in return for what one receives.

Marcia Millman (1972) in a study of experimental small groups, has written of two contrasting sets of metaphors with which group relationships are described, which she calls "exchange" and "tragic-mythic." Exchange imagery describes what people "get out of a relationship," how much they will "take" from one another, who will "dump" what onto the group. Tragic-mythic imagery, on the other hand, imbeds the relationship in a dramatic structure: "The group member who uses 'tragic-mythic' imagery frequently describes his relationships in the group in terms of his search for identity, of recalling certain things from his past and rediscovering himself, and of his downfall in the group. He is concerned with the issues of free will and destiny, and his attention is on action. He understands the other characters in terms of their origins and culminations, and he views his present relationships as the reenactment of old stories" (p. 9). The traditional love myth is a "tragic-mythic" organization of self and experience, in which life can be given meaning by its "culmination," the climax of the novel's (or of life's) story. The emerging cultural view of love, on the other hand, emphasizes exchange. What is valuable about a relationship is "what one gets out of it." One values what one can learn from another person, what one can take away from the experience. One is valued in turn for what he gives in exchange. Rather than a relationship standing as the culmination of a drama of self-discovery, the partners in a relationship remain autonomous and separate, each concerned about what he will have gained, what he will take away, when the relationship is over.

Exchange metaphors, indeed, imply impermanence. In a successful exchange each person is enhanced so that each is more complete, more autonomous, and more self-aware than before. Rather than becoming part of a whole, a couple, whose meaning is complete only when both are together, each person becomes stronger; each gains the skills he was without and, thus strengthened, is more "whole." If we enter love relationships to complete the missing sides of ourselves, then in some sense when the exchange is successful, we have learned to get along without the capacities the other person had supplied.

Exchange metaphors and the ideal of the autonomous individual are closely linked. We can see the image in changing ideals of male-female relations, for example, where the demand is for two people who can each be "whole people" with a balance of instrumental and affective capacities, rather than two people who are each specialized halves of a couple but inadequate as individual human beings. This imagery is used explicitly by Philip Slater (1970), and it underlies much of the rhetoric of the women's movement. The moral ideal is the person who is complete in himself or herself, who is able to stand alone, whether or not she chooses to do so.

The hidden message in modern treatments of love is, then, not self-sacrifice but self-development. A good relationship is one in which one has learned something and can leave it a stronger or better person. Most profoundly, the emphasis in love stories is on survival, on a person's need to be reassured that he can endure any loss, can get along without anyone. So in one of the most popular love stories of our recent history, *Love Story*, the essential drama was not that Oliver and Jenny won each other, but rather that Jenny gave Oliver a great lesson in survival. She helped him learn to love and to forgive his parents and to win greater control over himself before she died, leaving him unencumbered yet strong. In a similar way, the theme of movies such as "Alice Doesn't Live Here Anymore" or "An Unmarried Woman" is that people can learn to survive alone, and indeed to prefer their hard-won autonomy to renewed ties of dependence.

This anxiety about the wholeness and integrity of the self also shows up as a new concern with self-realization and a denunciation of self-sacrifice. Of course in social-structural terms, the most significant sacrifice to which one can be committed by loving is the sacrifice one makes for one's children. While one marries for love, for the fulfillment of one's own needs, marrying commits one to a life of serving others—one's spouse and especially one's children.

But in contemporary literature even the sacrifice of parents for their children has been brought into question. Several modern novels portray a conflict between sacrifice for anyone else, including children, and the necessary attention to the imperiled self. Novelists can now portray children as predators or enemies who demand without giving, who threaten the necessary self-nurture of their parents. Recent women's literature, of course, takes up this theme, though in most feminist literature the husband-lover is the enemy who robs women of the energy they need for themselves. But in novels such as *The War between the Tates* children are protrayed as sullen strangers, and in Joseph Heller's *Something Happened*, the demanding child is an enemy to be outsmarted, the retarded child a symbol of hopelessness, and the bright, good child an emblem of the father's guilt.

Self-sacrifice, which once seemed the ultimate proof of love, now seems suspect. For people to try to realize themselves through the sacrifices they make for others comes to seem not nobility but parasitism. We fear clinging wives and smothering mothers and we condemn the man or woman who cannot stand up for his or her own needs. The drama in many modern love stories is whether people will be able to resist the temptations of love and surrender in order to perform the more difficult task of finding themselves.

This cultural legitimation of "selfishness" is in many ways a claim on behalf of adulthood. We no longer believe that an adult's life can be meaningfully defined by the sacrifice he or she makes for spouse or children. Current ideologies of child rearing emphasize that parents have rights also, that it is not enough to use up each adult life in nurturing the lives that come after it. Adulthood is viewed as a period with its own tasks and demands. Just as husbands and wives cannot submerge their own needs in those of their partners, so adults cannot sacrifice themselves completely to their children.

We can cite demographic changes that have intensified the problem of how to live as an adult, particularly for women: the reduced period of child rearing and the prolonged period of the "empty nest" when parental roles no longer define the meaning of a couple's relationship; widowhood and divorce which force women, and men as well, to face the question of what to make of their own lives; and delayed marriage which allows adults to be more fully formed before they undertake marriage at all. But accompanying these demographic challenges to old models of adulthood are new cultural values—a new concern with the survival, wholeness, and autonomy of the self that makes self-sacrifice seem weakness, and self-realization seem a moral duty. In this context the very meaning of love changes. In the attempt to legitimate a concern with adult life on its own terms, our culture also holds up a model of human relatedness that makes the sufficiently complete self a precondition for relations with others. Other people can be only a stimulus to our own growth and development, not a source of the meaning of our lives. We are mistrustful of those who seek to find themselves through love, rather than loving from a position of strength, fully in possession of themselves.

Libidinal Expression Versus Restraint

In the traditional love myth the tension between sexual expression and restraint worked to intensify and strengthen commitment. Love offered the fulfillment of libidinal aspirations, but the ideals of virginity before marriage and fidelity afterward demanded sexual restraint. Sexuality sealed the intimacy of lovers; sexual restraint made their bond exclusive and inviolable.

But there is another layer of significance in the symbolism of sexual restraint. Watt points out that Clarissa's defense of her virtue was ultimately a defense of the integrity of the self; "she proves that no individual and no institution can destroy the inner inviolability of the human personality" (Watt, 1957, p. 225). The integrity of the self is demonstrated by its capacity for unified devotion, for fidelity. Just as there is one right choice in marriage, there is one right self which, when correctly bestowed, can remain true forever. This faith in the wholeness and unity of the self gave special depth and resonance to the experience of intimacy.

In the contemporary period the ideal of sexual restraint has weakened, and the possibilities for sexual expression have been broadened. The ideology of individual development has entered the sexual sphere, condeming relationships that limit individual growth or possibilities for exploring new experiences. In this view jealousy is bad, a possessive attempt to own another person and limit that person's freedom to grow. Sexual restraints are rejected as artificial restrictions on experience, and sexual experimentation is valued because it opens the self to new experiences.

Michael McCall (1966) and Randall Collins (1971) have each provided social-structural explanations of these shifts in sexual ethics. Both see a crucial change in the social functions of marriage. McCall argues that as marriages no longer cement broader alliances between families, as women are less dependent economically on marriage, and as marriages become less stable, the older pattern of courtship bargaining no longer makes sense. Now women and men bargain about the terms of an ongoing relationship, rather than maneuvering to make the best possible marriage. There is no single decisive event that is worth "saving oneself" for; and current pleasures become more important than either future rewards or past commitments. Collins draws a similar link between the traditional morality of sexual restraint and courtship bargaining. However, he emphasizes the conflicting interests of women and men and the role of sex in the battle between them. For women in a market economy, sexual restraint can be used to force men into marriage. Then women, having enforced chastity on each other to improve their collective position in marriage bargaining, can use their increased power (further enhanced by restraints on violent domination by men and the female monopoly of intimacy and emotional support in the household) to extend "sexual property norms" to men (Collins, 1971, pp. 13–14.) In the "advanced market economy," with the spread of female employment, "the greater freedom of women from economic dependence on men means that sexual bargains can be less concerned with marriage; dating can go on as a form of short-run bargaining, in which both men and women trade on their own attractiveness or capacity to entertain in return for sexual favors and/or being entertained" (p. 17).

While on a cultural level these structural shifts undermine the unique significance of the marriage tie, in another sense they are part of an attempt to deepen the adult experience of love. As with most of the other issues we have examined here, the resolution of the tension between sexual expression and restraint has traditionally been designed to heighten the initial experience of discovery, choice, and commitment in love, while giving scant attention to the further development of a love relationship. Launching people into commitment was more important than sustaining a continuing capacity for intimacy. Indeed, part of what is reflected in the changed attitude toward sexual expression is a changed understanding of intimacy.

While on the one hand the new ideology encourages a shallow, exploitative approach to human relationships, it can also encourage couples to be more attentive to the gratifications each derives from the relationship. Both men and women make conscious attempts to enhance the enjoyment of their adult sexual lives. While all of this is often criticized as having become a burdensome obsession rather than a source of pleasure, it is once again clear that the needs of adult life are being given greater attention. Sexuality must do more than motivate people to form relationships; it must also sustain satisfaction and closeness within those relationships. Traditionally in American culture adulthood has meant a renunciation of the aspirations of youth, so that sexuality belongs to the young and is abandoned in adulthood. The new "clinical" approach to sexual fulfillment, which seems so lacking in romance, may be seen as an attempt to keep sexual experience gratifying for people who are not in the first blush of romantic involvement.

Here again, structural change and shifting cultural preoccupations are linked. Postponement of marriage, effective contraception, and female independence, which may be seen as the social bases for the "sexual revolution," also give young people enough sexual experience so that sex is no longer an elusive prize and becomes a normal human experience that may be enjoyed, but also improved. This demythologization of sex does not mean the loss of social and moral meaning. If sexual restraint symbolized preservation of the integrity and moral definition of the self, sexual experience has come to symbolize the expansion and fulfillment of the self—the continuing capacity to grow, learn, and appreciate experience.[5]

But sexuality has also been a symbol of intimacy, and sexual exclusivity was a seal of emotional bondedness. In some ways the new ideology, by legitimating a continuing attention to libidinal needs, encourages a deepening of intimacy and mutuality, both sexual and emotional. On the other hand, by undermining the norm of fidelity, the new ethics may also undermine the trust and continuity necessary for real intimacy. But at least these are genuinely adult dilemmas. To want more from adult life may also be to take greater risks.

In Western culture the experience of love is imbedded in a matrix of moral ideas which have given shape, definition, and meaning to the individual life course. Rich in ritual, myth, and symbols, love has provided an element of broader meaning at the core of the life experience. But the love myth contains tensions between opposing elements, oppositions that account in part for the depth and resonance of the myth. By arousing contradictory impulses, by fusing together divergent aspects of individual experience, love acquires great power as an experience and as a symbolic consolidation of life.

Choice versus commitment, rebellion versus attachment, self-realization versus self-sacrifice, and libidinal expression versus restraint—these are contradictions not in the sense that they present people with irreconcilable alternatives in their practical life arrangements, but in the sense that they permeate the cultural meaning of love with contradictory expectations. The great power of the love myth is that it promises to resolve those contradictions, to fulfill both sides of the duality at once: Love provides the opportunity for profound choice, the choice of a life-long commitment; love sanctions rebellion against social ties in the service of attaching oneself to society; love inspires self-realization through sacrifice of oneself for another; and love intensifies and deepens sexual expression by channeling it through sexual restraint. These paradoxical promises are not accidents or cultural "mistakes"—quite the opposite. The reason love can provide a crucible for identity formation, a symbol of achievement of a place in the social world, a capacity for dedication to something outside oneself, and a potent consolidation of one's deepest emotional urges is precisely because it can embody these dual meanings.

But in American culture the balance of these tensions has been unequal, and hence their power diminished, because of the central importance Americans give to individuality and the low value they place on social connectedness. While the romantic myth has upheld the ideals of attachment, commitment, and intimacy, it has been on the defensive against the culture's dominant individualism. Abandoned on the whole by high culture, the love myth was weakened, so that the "conservative" set of meanings it embodied—love as commitment, acceptance of social attachment, self-sacrifice, and libidinal restraint—predominated, no longer complemented by the sense of passionate choice and rebellious assertion of identity that gave depth and power to the English and European forms of the love myth. All women were mothers, not mistresses or lovers, and all love implied being trapped into congealed domesticity.

In the contemporary period, complex changes are occurring in our love ideology, with important implications for adulthood. The traditional oppositions in the love myth fused together aspirations of youth and adulthood; the myth sanctioned youthful rebellion in the service of finding adult commitments. But in this fusion one moment was given moral meaning—the moment of transition from youth to adulthood. The power of the myth came from glorifying and intensifying the period when identity was crystallized, attachment discovered, aspirations for fulfillment realized, and intimacy achieved. But this left the "adult" sides of the love myth without sustaining meaning. Identity, commitment, self-realization, and intimacy, once achieved, were simply supposed to last a lifetime. Moral meaning lay in being able to stick to what one had chosen, to continue to be animated by the commitments one had made. But in the contemporary period, the valence of the love myth is shifting—in ways which often seem regressive. These "youthful" aspirations for rebellion, choice, self-realization, and sexual expression are being idealized all over again. That is, our culture now seeks moral significance in acts of choice, in attempts to discover, clarify, or deepen the self, whether or not these choices lead to or remain within a commitment. The ideology of love is being partially reworked, so that elements of the love myth—that love transforms, that love allows one to know his true self, that love is a crucible for self-development—are being incorporated into a new structure.

The fate of these shifts in cultural emphasis is still obscure. What is clear, however, is that our culture's view of adulthood is changing. What once seemed a secure if difficult accomplishment, a once-and-for-all achievement, has come to seem much less secure. Pressures for flexibility in adult love and work have cut loose the anchors for many of the old definitions of successful, meaningful, morally integrated adulthood. It is hard for us to find metaphors to express the meaning of love that is not forever and work that is not a lifetime commitment. Much of our cultural response to the uncertainties of modern adulthood has been a kind of empty despair in high culture, abandoning hope for meaning, and in popular culture a shallow and somewhat hysterical emphasis on protecting a childish version of the self.

But there are also signs of hope. As moral emphasis shifts from life-long commitments to a lifetime of choices, there is the possibility of rejoining the fractured elements of the love myth, but on new terms. An identity developed through continuing choice may be a fuller and richer achievement than a single, climactic consolidation of the self. Social attachments may also be more gratifying and less terrifying if they do not mean stifling closure in work or love, but can continue to embody a rebellious streak, a search for new constellations in the relationship of self to the social world. Intimacy can certainly be deeper if there is openness to continuing mutual exploration. A commitment to another person may go beyond loyalty, to an understanding of shared responsibility for the quality of a continuing relationship. And even self-sacrifice, or the possibility of generative giving to others, can perhaps be made richer if it is matched by recognition of one's own incompleteness, one's own capacities for continuing growth and change.

In some ways the most crucial shift in our culture is a change in the symbolic and moral grounding of the self in modern society. If the self can no longer find definition in a single set of adult commitments, a set of roles which consolidate identity, what can the self be? If it must be defined, as seems implicit in the modern culture of love, by its ability to resist attachment, by its ability to go through changes without being fundamentally changed, then we have an ideal of the self cut off from meaningful connection to others, from any danger of commitment, attachment, sacrifice, or self-restraint. This is a model of human relationships in which people are not willing to take the risks of disappointment and defeat that inevitably accompany meaningful love or work.

And yet, there is strength in the recognition that "the capacity to love and to work" is not a one-time accomplishment that settles the adult life course once and for all. Further risks, further choices, further efforts are demanded, and further opportunities for self-knowledge, intimacy, and joy await us. In the past our love ideology has dealt largely with the problems of becoming an adult, as if after the adult course was set there was nothing left to worry about—people did not have to keep living together after they won each other, work did not continue to be problematic after one had settled on an identity. Now we have a cultural attempt to deal with adulthood, to develop a set of myths and images that can give moral meaning and purpose to a life that has no fixed end, no dramatic conclusion. In some ways the reaction to this challenge seems to be a culture of narcissism, in which the self and its perpetuation become all, in which the trick is to remain alive and whole without risking attachments or making binding choices. But the other side of these cultural explorations is a search for models of self and models of love that are compatible with continuing growth and change, that permeate with moral significance the ups and downs of daily life, the struggle to live well, rather than giving moral meaning only to the dramatic moment of the shift from youth to adulthood.

Notes

For helpful comments, I would like to thank Fred Block, Patricia Bourne, Claude Fischer, Arlie Hochschild, Anne Peplau, Theda Skocpol, and the editors of this volume. I would also like to thank Melvin M. Webber and the Institute of Urban and Regional Development, University of California, Berkeley, for support during the later phases of the preparation of this paper.

1. Geertz (1965, p. 8) has said that religious symbols provide "models of" and "models for" reality. "Culture patterns ... give meaning, i.e., objective conceptual form, to social and psychological reality both by shaping themselves to it and by shaping it to themselves." While for many people in modern society religious symbols and rituals have lost their vividness and their direct applicability to daily life, love is still an experience to which people give themselves, and which allows at least a partial experience of transcendence. Like religious experience, culturally grounded experiences of love do not dominate every moment of daily life. As Geertz (1968, p. 110) says, "The key to the question of how religion shapes social behavior, is that much of religion's practical effect, like much of dreaming's, comes in terms of a kind of pale, remembered reflection of religious experience proper, in the midst of everyday life." It is in part through moments of heightened experience and its "pale, remembered reflection" in everyday life that our culture's myths about love shape the experience of adulthood.

2. While the mythic structure of American culture is not the exclusive property of either sex, the love myth is, at least symbolically, differently shaped for men and women. In women's literature the happy ending is still marriage, and love still allows people to find themselves as they find each other. High culture, on the whole, is dominated by men and by the male version of the myth, in which the man escapes both women and society in his lonely quest for selfhood. Of course there can be Faustian heroes who are women (Hester Prynne in *The Scarlet Letter*) and men can fight for love and commitment. But in general, the polarization of the sexes around the different sides of the love myth, while it accounts in large part for the tone of aggressive warfare in America's cultural treatment of the "battle of the sexes" (from Blondie and Dagwood or Little Abner and Daisy Mae to the head nurse in *One Flew over the Cuckoo's Nest*, women tie men down, curtailing their quest for freedom and self-definition), both men and women are caught by the conflict about social commitment expressed in America's treatment of love.

3. Lillian Rubin (1976) and Mirra Komarovsky (1962) have both pointed out how unwillingly many working-class men claim to marry. A high proportion of marriages are precipitated by a pregnancy, so that both men and women marry without having fully chosen to do so. The only way to develop social commitments is to be "trapped." This pattern corresponds to the fantasy Martha Wolfenstein and Nathan Leites (1950) found in their study of American movies. Men and women are thrown together on a train, or forced together by some accident, so that their involvement occurs in spite of, not because of, their wishes in the matter.

4. The argument that the economy requires autonomy and flexibility in elite workers has been around for some time. It can be found in Bennis and Slater, 1968; Berkeley, 1971; Hirschhorn, 1976; and Sarason, 1977, as well as implicitly in those who examine various aspects of "post-industrial" society and politics (Bell, 1973; Inglehart, 1977). There is, so far as I know, little hard evidence of the link between technologically advanced employment and personal flexibility, though see Kohn, 1971. For a negative argument, see Braverman, 1974.

5. For an analysis of sexual fulfillment as a central image of moral transcendence in contemporary novels (those of Irving Wallace, Harold Robbins, or Jacqueline Susann, for example), see John Cawelti (1976, pp. 280–295).

References

Bell, Daniel, 1973. *The coming of post-industrial society: a venture in social forecasting.* New York: Basic Books.

Bennis, Warren G., and Philip E. Slater, 1968. *The temporary society.* New York: Harper and Row.

Berkeley, George E. 1971. *The administrative revolution: notes on the passing of organization man.* Englewood Cliffs, N.J.: Prentice-Hall.

Bloch, Marc. 1964. *Feudal society,* tr. L. A. Manyon. Chicago: University of Chicago Press.

Bloch, R. Howard. 1977. *Medieval French literature and law.* Berkeley: University of California Press.

Block, Fred, and Larry Hirschhorn. 1979. New productive forces and the contradictions of contemporary capitalism: a post-industrial perspective. *Theory and Society,* 7:363–395.

Braverman, Harry. 1974. *Labor and monopoly capital.* New York: Monthly Review Press.

Cagle, Laurence T. 1975. Exchange and romantic love norms. Paper presented at the Annual Meeting of the American Sociological Association, San Francisco (August).

Cawelti, John G. 1976. *Adventure, mystery, and romance.* Chicago: University of Chicago Press.

Collins, Randall. 1971. A conflict theory of sexual stratification. *Social Problems,* 19:3–21.

de Rougemont, Denis. 1956. *Love in the western world.* New York: Pantheon.

Erikson, Erik H. 1963. *Childhood and society,* 2nd ed. New York: Norton.

Fiedler, Leslie. 1966. *Love and death in the American novel,* rev. ed. New York: Stein and Day.

Geertz, Clifford. 1968. *Islam observed: religious development in Morocco and Indonesia.* New Haven: Yale University Press.

———. 1965. Religion as a cultural system. In *Anthropological approaches to the study of religion,* ed. Michael Banton. New York: Praeger.

Hendin, Herbert. 1975. *The age of sensation.* New York: McGraw-Hill.

Inglehart, Ronald. 1977. *The silent revolution.* Princeton: Princeton University Press.

Keniston, Kenneth. 1968. *Young radicals: notes on committed youth.* New York: Harcourt, Brace and World.

Kohn, Melvin. 1971. Bureaucratic man: a portrait and an interpretation. *American Sociological Review,* 36:461–474.

Komarovsky, Mirra. 1962. *Blue-collar marriage.* New York: Random House.

Lasch, Christopher. 1976. The narcissist society. *New York Review of Books,* 23 (Sept. 30):5–13.

Lewis, C. S. 1958. *The allegory of love: a study in medieval tradition.* New York: Oxford University Press.

Lifton, Robert Jay. 1971. Protean man. In *History and human survival.* New York: Random House.

McCall, Michael M. 1966. Courtship as social exchange: some historical comparisons. In *Kinship and family organization,* ed. Bernard Farber. New York: Wiley.

Millman, Marcia. 1972. Tragedy and exchange: metaphoric understandings of interpersonal relationships. Ph.d. diss.: Brandeis University.

Rubin, Lillian B. 1976. *Worlds of pain: life in the working-class family.* New York: Basic Books.

Sarason, Seymour. 1977. *Work, aging and social change.* New York: Free Press.

Slater, Philip. 1970. *The pursuit of loneliness: American culture at the breaking point.* Boston: Beacon Press.

Stephens, William N., ed. 1968. *Reflections on marriage.* New York: Thomas Y. Crowell.

Trilling, Diana. 1964. The image of women in contemporary literature. In *The woman in America,* ed. Robert Jay Lifton. Boston: Beacon Press.

Turner, Ralph H. 1976. The real self: from institution to impulse. *American Journal of Sociology,* 81:989–1016.

Watt, Ian. 1957. *The rise of the novel.* Berkeley: University of California Press.

Wolfenstein, Martha, and Nathan Leites. 1950. *Movies: a psychological study.* New York: Free Press.

Wright, Will. 1975. *Sixguns and society: a structural study of the western.* Berkeley: University of California Press.

Toward a Social Psychology of Relationships

Constantina Safilios-Rothschild*

Up to the middle 60's, most Americans had spouses, children and acquaintances made and unmade rather easily and painlessly. The husbands had careers that required them to move frequently with their families and there was no place for close friendships which were considered to be threatening to marital intimacy. In the 1970's, the explosion of relationships and the focus on intimacy are mainly the results of women's increasing liberation, the creation of a sizable "single" population at all age groups as well as the questioning of the validity of rat-race type achievement and the structural difficulties in attaining success.

Women have been able to establish close, intimate relationships with other women and are asking for an intimate relationship in their marriages as well as independence to do what is important to them, including work or a career. Among a number of other reasons, these new heavy demands on marriage and women's increasing psychological and economic independence have led to an even higher rate of divorce and to the reconceptualization of marriage as a nonpermanent relationship.

Men and women postpone marriage, often up to their late 20's and once divorced, they do not always remarry soon after or ever. Having no permanent notion of marital and familiar relationships, the so-called "single life-style" involves the proliferation of a wide range of relationships from same-sex to cross-sex friendships, sexual-affective homosexual or heterosexual relationships, same-sex and cross-sex colleagueships, "roommate" relationships as well as a variety of others including parental relationships.

While in the 60's, occupational success was still within the reach of hardworking middle and upper middle class men, the present social-structural conditions do not guarantee success even for women and men with graduate degrees. This structural change coupled with the ideological questioning of the desirability of even higher achievements have begun to gradually "liberate" men[1] from the exaggerated achievement concerns that constrained them in the past from making the effort to establish close relationships and from taking the time to enjoy them; they also begin to struggle with different types and levels of intimacy. In a sense, intimacy has become as important (if not more important) a goal as success, desired by all. This new "democratization" of intimacy poses to some extent some of the same problemes as success did in the

From *Psychology of Women Quarterly*, Vol. 5, No. 3 (1981), pp. 377–401. Reprinted by permission of Human Sciences Press.
*The Pennsylvania State University
[1] This does not hold equally true for women who, as newcomers to the achievement and success game, tend to imitate men's achievement behaviors of the 50's and 60's.

past: Can everyone reach and enjoy intimacy? What happens to those who cannot reach or do not want intimacy in one or more relationships? Can intimacy-related skills be identified and taught to people? And what happens to intimacy as a concept when it is "mass produced"?

A structural change, namely the increasing employment of women in non-traditional occupations and positions, has been instrumental in creating a new type of relationship: the cross-sex colleagueships. Saleswomen, women foremen, managers and executives, women on the assembly line, women officers, women skilled workers find themselves as colleagues with men in relationships for which there are no set rules. Men and women in these cross-colleagueships try to evolve, try out and experiment with their own sets of norms and rules (Safilios-Rothschild 1977–1978). And it is not easy to formulate these new norms and rules because they must be predictable enough to allow work efficiency and productivity and yet flexible enough to allow the expression of feelings and emotions and possibly the enjoyment of the relationship.

Despite this increasing wealth of relationships enjoyed by people, most studies examine one type of relationship, e.g. same-sex or cross-sex friendships, or compare same-sex and cross-sex friendships for men and women; or compare heterosexual relationships with lesbian and gay male relationships. Lately, some studies have looked into the developmental stages of a relationship such as friendships throughout the lives of women.

An alternative way to study relationships would be to start from individuals and map all the relationships in which they are involved in order to be able to ask different kinds of research questions. Such a methodology would allow the study of interrelations between different types of relationships. That is, in what ways and under what conditions do same and/or cross-sex friendships and colleagueships act in a supportive role vis-a-vis the individual's marital or sexual/affective relationship? And what factors render these friendships and colleagueships the "mainstream" relationships and the marital or sexual/affective relationship the secondary one, so that the nature of exchanges change radically in the latter in view of the alternative relationships? In other words, under what conditions one or more relationships supplement and under what conditions they tend to undermine and replace each other? Of course, friendships and marital or love/sexual relationships have different dimensions and are supposed to fulfill different needs for the individual. But they also have overlapping areas such as, intimacy in terms of self-disclosure, reciprocity, acceptance, support, emotional commitment and continuity. And it is possible that the more friendships are satisfactory in terms of intimacy, reciprocity, acceptance and support, the more the comparisons with one's love/sexual relationships become difficult and more demands are placed on the latter.

This methodology will, furthermore, allow us to study to what extent in fact one type of relationships carries the psychological burden of all others. At present, there are some indications that close intimate friendships between women are the most open, the most comfortable, the most supportive, the most reciprocal, the most "mature," intimate relationships which in turn sustain women's relationships with men as friends, colleagues, lovers and husbands. There are, furthermore, research indications that men's friendships with women may serve for them (but not for the women involved) the same central, crucial, supportive role for all their relationships with men and women. Thus, women still play a supportive, expressive role for men without reciprocation but at least women's new awareness has opened up the road for intimate, reciprocal relationships among women.

The analysis of individual's networks of relationship requires the longitudinal study of the developmental processes that different relationships undergo through time. There is hardly any data as to the processes, the precipitating factors through which one type of relationship changes into another. When and how does a cross-friendship evolve into a love/sexual relationship? And under what conditions does the friendship survive? Under what conditions does it become submerged under the other relationships? When the friendship part of the relationship manages to survive, in what ways is the love/sexual relationship different from similar relationships which began as love/sexual ones? And what happens to the colleague relationship when a cross-sex colleagueship evolves into an intimate friendship or a love/sexual relationship? How well can people keep separate the boundaries of the two sets of relationships and what norms and strategies do they develop in order to manage the overlapping areas of interaction (Safilios-Rothschild, 1977)? Another important "managerial" problem which can be studied through the mapping of people's relationships is the type of strategies through which people handle multiple reltionships. Of course, it is possible that people with multiple sets of relationships differ significantly in terms of social roles and personality characteristics from those with more limited sets of relationships. But even so, there is a number of important questions to be asked and investigated: How does the existence of multiple sets of relationships qualitatively affect each of the relationships? The earlier assumption has been a "zero-sum-love-involvement" according to which, the more one became involved in one relationship, the less he/she would be involved in other relationships. Recently, however, the opposite "additive" assumption has in fact emerged according to which, one's involvement in one relationship tends to be helpful, supportive and enriching for his/her involvement in other relationships. (Bartell, 1971; O'Neil and O'Neil, 1972; and Huang, [1974]). Which of these assumptions hold true for different types of people involved in different types of relationships?

The above "additive" assumption raises questions as to the need or desirability of *exclusivity* as a necessary condition for intimate relationships as well as about the meaning of exclusivity. Once the principle of multiple sets of relationships is accepted, since no two relationships are ever exactly the same, one can always claim that each relationship is unique and that this way exclusivity is preserved. Or, exclusivity may be maintained for each type and level of intimate relationship but not cross levels. Thus, one may have only one love/sexual relationship and one or more sexual relationships which are viewed as "limited" relationships of no consequence and as noncompeting with the significant love/sexual relationship despite the one overlapping dimension (Huang, [1974]; Bartell, 1971). But except in the case of "swingers" we know little about the nature of experienced dilemmas and frustrations and the balance of emotional cost and benefit from such nonexclusivity. The presence of strains is evident in that many of these people are going to different types of therapists and often sex is no different than a tranquillizer. Is this non-exclusive strategy another symptom of emotional turmoil? Or is therapy needed as support in experiencing new states of being and feeling? In most cases, it is easier in addition to the love/sexual relationship to maintain several intimate same-sex friendships and cross-sex colleagueships and one or more intimate cross-sex friendships. Most people continue to perceive less overlap between intimate friendships (even cross-sex ones) and love relationships (or marriages) than between the latter and sexual relationships despite the fact that sex may facilitate little intimacy, closeness or self-disclosure unless other interpersonal and emotional dimensions are present.

Another strategy for managing the appearance of exclusivity in multiple sets of relationships, especially with respect to several sexual or love/sexual relationships is the maintenance of separate circles of interaction in the same or in different towns and the intermittent involvement in each of the relationships. While sometimes the intensity of these relationships may be low and their authenticity poor, some people are able to maintain, at least for some time, such multiple relationships as satisfactory, reciprocal, continuous and intimate relationships with the appearance of exclusivity.

While in the 60's social scientists talked about the dilemma between exclusivity and permanence (Bernard, 1970 pp. 99–126), in the 70's people often have to cope simultaneously with the lack of total exclusivity as well as with the lack of the security of permanence. And while they have to learn to deal with relative exclusivity, they also have to accept a precarious continuity, that is a continuity safeguarded only by the degree to which the intimate relationship continues to be mutually satisfactory and is not overshadowed by other overlapping, evolving or competing intimate relationships. Within this context of tentativeness, is it possible and are people willing and capable of making emotional commitments to each other? Who are the people who make such commitments and how are these commitments sustained? Are these commitments such that the break-up of the relationship entails less pain than the break-up of relationships clearly defined as exclusive and permanent? Are people able to make emotional commitments without tying their self-worth and their self-validation to the continuity and permanence of the relationship but rather to its quality and success as long as it lasts?

Some people claim that because in the past the price paid for committing to relationships was very high, at present they feel more at ease making "limited" commitments to several relationships, some of which may not last long. In fact, some claim that the only conditions which render their commitment possible is the very nonexclusivity and nonpermanence of the relationships. This is an empirical question, since we do not know for what categories of men and women this new trend holds true and for what categories commitment is not meaningful except within the context of an exclusive relationship, permanence being part of the commitment.

The high degree of geographic mobility of Americans, despite a setback caused by a certain degree of occupational freeze, continues to complicate the careers of relationships as increasingly both members involved in the relationship move around pursuing jobs and careers. This structural change has considerably complicated the establishment and management of marriages and love/sexual relationships and has raised more questions about the need for exclusivity and continuous interaction for the maintenance of these relationships. Couples living in different towns, married or not, often discover that their intimate relationship flourishes because they see each other once or twice a month during weekends and learn to enjoy their aloneness and their freedom to see other intimate friends when they need company. Sometimes they are shocked to find that their most intimate relationships in terms of intensity, reciprocity, self-disclosure, support and security are with other than their marital or love/sexual partners, possibly with their friends. This is something new to be coped with since people have been socialized to believe that the greatest intimacy had to occur within their marriage or at least within their significant love/sexual relationship. It seems, therefore, that another set of assumptions is challenged and needs testing: (1) Sexuality does not necessarily increase or facilitate other types of intimacy; it may in fact hinder and complicate it; and (2) legal commitment and/or consensus regarding continuity do not necessarily increase or facilitate the establishment of intimacy.

Hacker (1981) brings out the important issue that self-disclosure between cross-sex friendships still follows sex role stereotypes: men do not like to disclose their weaknesses and women do not like to disclose their strengths. The reason for this may be the fact that men, even when they are close friends or lovers, react "negatively" toward the disclosure of women's strengths and make women feel insecure and almost dejected as they tend to withdraw the "protector" role they have been socialized to extend to women. Similarly, women often react with fear and disappointment to their close friends' or lovers' disclosures of weaknesses, vulnerabilities, and wishes to escape the tyranny of commitment and responsibility. Women's reaction often involves the withdrawal of admiration and the lowering of attachment to these men because they feel that they cannot "count on them" as the strong men to be leaned on and cannot ask them to shoulder difficulties and responsibilities which they cannot shoulder themselves.

We all cry for intimacy and self-disclosure but it seems that despite women's and men's struggles with liberation, we are not yet able to deal with the non-sex stereotyped disclosures of our cross-sex intimates. We have not yet learned how to accept the fact that both men and women have strengths and weaknesses and the admission of the one does not negate the other; that both need togetherness and self-disclosure as much as aloneness and silence; that both need commitment and continuity as much as freedom and escape.

The multiplication of different types of relationships, the overlapping and interaction between them, the diminshed sense of permanence and centrality of marriage as the one salient relationship, the changing roles of women and men and the appearance of cross-sex friendships and colleagueships create a new setting for intimacy and relationships which must be studied within new methodological frameworks. The mapping of individuals' network of relationships and the study of the ways in which different relationships affect each other over time by changing boundaries and by supporting or replacing each other may represent the appropriate methodologies. Within this framework, a detailed examination of the assumptions made is needed as well as the successful and unsuccessful strategies used by different categories of people. And in studying intimacy, the place and importance of aloneness in intimate relations must not be forgotten. Possibly the enjoyment of aloneness may be a condition for the enjoyment of intimacy.

References

Bartell, G. D. *Group sex*. New York: Signet Books, 1971.

Bernard, J. Infidelity: Some moral and social issues. In J. H. Masserman (Ed.), *The psychodynamics of work and marriage* (Vol. 16). New York: Grune and Stratton, Inc., 1970.

Hacker, H. Blabbermouths and clams: Sex difference in self-disclosure in same-sex and cross-sex friendship dyads. *Psychology of Women Quarterly*, 1981, 5(3), pp. 385–401.

Huang, L. J. Research with unmarried cohabiting couples: Including non-exclusive sexual relations, 1974, Illinois State University, unpublished manuscript.

O'Neil, N. O'Neil, G. *Open marriage*. New York: Avon Books, 1972.

Safilios-Rothschild, C. *Love, sex and sex roles*. Englewood Cliffs, New Jersey: Prentice-Hall, 1977.

Safilios-Rothschild, C. Women and work: policy implications and prospects for the future. In S. Harkess and A. Yates (Eds.), *Women working*. Palo Alto, Ca.: Mayfield, 1978.

Personal Relationships

Harold Kelley

My focus is on the close heterosexual dyad—the intimate relationship between man and woman. I believe (but do not attempt to demonstrate) that my concepts are applicable to any relationship we would regard as a personal one. The choice of the heterosexual dyad as the subject of analysis is dictated partly by the fact that it is the basis of most of the current knowledge about personal relationships. Additionally, in its various manifestations in dating, marriage, cohabitation, and romantic liaisons, the heterosexual dyad is probably the single most important type of personal relationship in the life of the individual and in the history of society. It occasions the greatest satisfactions of life and also the greatest disappointments. As the core of the family group, the heterosexual dyad sometimes generates the old-fashioned, warm, and supportive setting protrayed by the Waltons on television but too often creates the type of modern American home that was recently described in the media as being surpassed in violence only by a battlefield or a riot. Most important, especially in the family context, close heterosexual relationships constitute the most significant settings in which social attitudes, values, and skills are acquired and exercised.

In presenting this conceptualization of the close personal relationship I do not mean to suggest that it is the only possible way to view these relationships for scientific purposes. However, what follows does take account of what I believe to be the central and unique phenomena to be observed in such relationships. This can best be illustrated by considering two brief scenarios of important events within close relationships.

Consider first Bill and Jane, a young university couple. They have been going together off and on for almost two years, and Bill is deciding whether or not to ask Jane to marry him. If he does it means making a commitment to her, breaking off with old girlfriends, and giving up some of his current freedoms. He thinks over their times together and the things Jane has done for his sake. He remembers how wonderful she can make things for him. As he recalls these occasions, he realizes that they have often enjoyed the same things. At the same time he recognizes that some of the things she has done for his sake were probably not things she would have chosen to do herself. He also remembers similar occasions on which he has made sacrifices for her. He thinks of what a good person she is and, in view of her apparent joy at seeing him happy, how much she seems to love him. He senses that she has already made some commitment to him and will be receptive to the idea of extending that commitment into an exclusive relationship. He also knows his own pleasure at seeing her happy. So he decides he wants to "take the leap" (make the final commitment) and propose marriage.

In this example, we see evidence of three essential elements of the personal relationship:

(1) *Interdependence in the consequences of specific behaviors, with both commonality and conflict of interest:* Bill thinks of his dependence on Jane, as evidenced by the importance to him of specific things she had done for him and with him. His decision is whether or not to let himself become more dependent. She also seems to be dependent on him. Though they may share many interests, there are also times in their relationship when what one wants is not what the other one prefers.

(2) *Interaction that is responsive to one another's outcomes:* On certain occasions when they have different interests, she has been aware of his desires and has set aside her own preferences and acted out of consideration of his. In lay language, she has "gone out of her way for him" or even perhaps "put up with a lot from him." To use other everyday terms, she has shown sensitivity to and considerateness of his needs.

(3) *Attribution of interaction events to dispositions:* Bill's decision follows his attribution to Jane of certain *stable* and *general* causes—her dispositions. These include stable preferences and interests compatible with his but, more important, attitudes of love toward him. Her love will last (in common parlance) "through thick and thin" and will "govern all"—that is, control her actions in a variety of situations. Bill probably also attributes stable attitudes to himself: for example, he feels he will always love her. Both the attributions to her and those to himself imply that he can accept his dependence on her and even permit it to increase.

The negative side of a personal relationship, shown in a conflict episode, involves the same three elements. The following incident is rather trivial and certainly less significant for the relationship than the preceding example, but it will serve our purpose. It concerns a small part of the lives of Mary and Dan, a young working couple who live together. Specifically, when Dan uses the bathroom he leaves it in a mess, with towels scattered around, a ring in the washbowl and tub, and so forth. Mary asks Dan not to mess up the bathroom in this manner. Two days later he repeats his usual performance as if Mary had said nothing. She becomes very angry. (On his side, he can't understand what she's so upset about. He had merely forgotten to do what she had asked.)

Referring to the three properties listed earlier:

(1) In this example we see Mary's side of the *interdependence*. Dan does something Mary strongly dislikes. Her outcomes are affected by his actions. There is also conflict of interest: Apparently he himself doesn't care about bathrooms being in a state of messiness or at least not enough to expend the effort to clean up after himself.

(2) There is a failure on Dan's part to be *responsive to her outcomes.* Knowing what she wants of him (in fact, having been told), he has failed to override his habits, preferences, or laziness out of consideration for her desires.

(3) The story doesn't say so explicityly, but Mary probably makes *attributions* of Dan's behavior to *stable dispositions.* Her version of the story is probably: "He repeats his usual performance as if I had said nothing." (Dan's version is that he merely forgot.) When subjects are asked to give explanations for the event as *she* describes it, not surprisingly a majority of them attribute it to Dan's stable properties: his traits (lazy, messy) or his attitude toward Mary (doesn't care about her wishes, doesn't like being told what to do). If she entertains any of these beliefs about the person with whom she is living, Mary's anger is understandable.

In short, in this example of conflict we see the same three elements as in the earlier positive example. Here of course the conflict aspects of the interdependence figure prominently in the scenario. They provide the context within which Dan's lack of sensitivity and considerateness is apparent. This instance of failure on his part is interpreted by Mary in relation to past or recent events: his messy behavior and her request that he discontinue it. The attribution she finds appropriate for the event suggests that Dan's stable dispositions are not those of a person with whom an interdependent existence will be easy.

If we examine the three phenomena listed earlier and consider the relations among them, we gain two important insights into the relationship: First, *the participants make a partitioning of the causes for the events in their interaction.* That is, they make a distinction between the anticipated immediate incentives for behavior—its perceived direct consequences—and stable, general causes—what I have referred to as personal dispositions, which include attitudes, traits, and values. Second, *the participants assume that the dispositional causes are manifest in behavior that is responsive to the partner's outcomes and that therefore sometimes departs from the actor's own immediate interests.* These two aspects of the participants' beliefs about the causes of behavior in their relationship are shown schematically in Fig. 1. The partitioning of causes is shown at the left, the behavioral events in the interaction being affected jointly by anticipated direct consequences and by dispositions. The latter are seen to affect or modulate the causal link between the direct consequences and the enacted behavior. For this reason the dispositions are to be inferred from discontinuities between the direct consequences to the actor and the behaviors he enacts. These assumptions about the causes of interpersonal behavior are most clearly apparent when the participants (a) scan behavior for how it departs from the actor's own immediate interests (its direct consequences for him), (b) interpret such departures in terms of the actor's responsiveness to the partner's interests, and (c) explain patterns of this responsiveness in terms of such things as the actor's attitudes toward the partner.

We now come to an important choice point in our analysis. Are we to take the participants' assumptions in Fig. 1 as reflecting merely a subjective reality

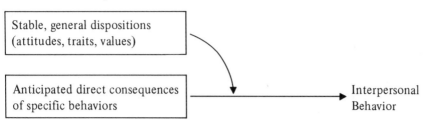

Fig. 1. The participants' assumptions about the causes of interpersonal behavior.

or "story" that they typically develop about their relationships but that has little to do wih the hard realties of their interaction? Or are we to take them as reflecting the real, underlying structure of these relationships and therefore indicative of how *we* should conceptualize it?

The former might be suggested by the comments of Weiss, Hops, and Patterson (1973) about conflictful marital relationships, that in most cases "a considerable amount of mutual training in vagueness has ... taken place and ... assumptions and expectations about the spouse overshadow the data at hand [p. 309]." The partners usually fail to label contingencies governing the mutual behavior, and "rely heavily upon a cognitive—motivational model of behavior. Thus, 'intent,' 'motivation for good or bad,' 'attitude,' etc., are all invoked to 'explain' the behavior of the other [p. 310]." Accordingly, the couple must be helped to set aside these explanations and to pinpoint the specific behavior-consequence-behavior sequences that get them into trouble.

Although admitting that the above view may be appropriate for relationships observed in clinical practice, I am inclined to take a different view of more typical personal relationships. Specifically, I emphasize that the subjective realities—the perceived intentions and attitudes—are of crucial significance in their development and functioning. Inappropriate causal explanations may indeed play a detrimental role in distressed relationships, and attention to specific behaviors and their consequences may be necessary if a battling couple is to break out of a vicious cycle of mutual aggression. However, in more normal relationships and particularly in those that attain high levels of mutual satisfaction, the "cognitive–motivational model of behavior" (as in Fig. 1) provides the basis for both their smooth functioning and the enjoyment of their deepest gratifications.

In short I have chosen to take Fig. 1 as indicating how the personal relationship should be conceptualized. The participants' scanning of behavior for its responsiveness to the partner's versus the actor's interests, and their explanation of this responsiveness in terms of stable dispositions constitute important processes that control behavior and affect in the relationship, are based on objective structures of the relationship, and give rise to other structures.

From this perspective we can review the concepts and evidence regarding the personal relationship under three headings . . . that parallel the three earlier points:

(1) *The structure of outcome interdependence:* This is an analysis of the interdependence between the persons in regard to their immediate concrete outcomes. This is the basic structural foundation of their relationship, defined by how they separately and jointly affect one another's direct outcomes.

(2) *The transformation of motivation: responsiveness to patterns of interdependence.* This is an analysis of the manner in which the person's interaction is responsive to patterned aspects of their interdependence, each one's behavior being governed not only by his/her own outcomes but by the other's outcomes as well. By virtue of its partial independence of the actor's own immediate outcomes, pattern-responsive behavior constitutes in effect a transformation of the interdependence structure defined by those outcomes. Thus we must consider the processes that give rise to and mediate such transformations.

(3) *The attribution and manifestation of interpersonal dispositions:* This analyzes the manifestation in interaction, and particularly in its departures from and transformations of the basic interdependence structure, of relatively stable and general properties of the two persons. These are referred to as interpersonal dispositions because of their unique relevance to interpersonal relations.

In reviewing the evidence under these three headings I present some of the facts that have led to the points emphasized in the foregoing. After examining these three sets of ideas we can finally return . . . to our original problem and attempt to outline a model of the relationship. This constitutes a technical elaboration of Fig. 1 and a suggestion of the interrelations among the structures and processes it implies. At that point we consider how persons are interdependent in regard to their dispositional properties. Thus in our elaboration of Fig. 1 we consider interdependence not only at the specific level but at the general level as well and examine the relations between the two levels. Our model, then, is cast in terms of *levels of interdependence* and the processes linking the levels.

The concepts I employ are found for the most part in prior writings by John Thibaut and myself. . . . To provide a historical context for the analysis, it may be noted that its three key ideas also occur in the writings of earlier social psychologists. The grandfathers for these focal concepts are, respectively, Lewin, Asch, and Heider. In his papers creating the field of group dynamics, Kurt Lewin (1948) emphasized that *interdependence* among its members is the essential, defining property of a group. Lewin specified interdependence in a variety of ways, but particularly appropriate for us is his description of interdependence in satisfying needs, exemplified in his analysis of marriage partners (pp. 84–102). From this notion stemmed Deutsch's conceptualization of interdependence betwen persons in locomotion toward their respective goals. We see later some of the consequences of the important comparison that Deutsch

(1949) made between promotive *versus* contrient interdependence (roughly, a comparison of cooperative and competitive relationships).

The notion of *responsiveness to others' outcomes* is implicit in Solomon Asch's assertion (1959) that "an essential feature of social life [is] the capacity of individuals under some circumstances to transcend their own particular interests and to act in the interest of their group [p. 370]." He remarks that "It is of considerable consequence for any social psychology to establish the grounds of concern for the welfare of other persons or groups, and how these are related to the concern individuals feel for their own welfare [p. 368]." . . . Asch focuses on the concept of "mutually relevant fields," by which he means that each individual represents "to himself the situation that includes himself and others. These individual representations contain, in cases of full-fledged interaction, a reference to the fact that the others also possess a corresponding view of the situation [p. 371]." In the present context, the latter is an essential fact underlying the individual's perception that others take account or fail to take account of his outcomes.

Attribution to dispositions is an idea directly adopted from Fritz Heider (1958). He emphasizes the principle that "man grasps reality, and can predict and control it, by referring transient and variable behavior and events to relatively unchanging underlying conditions, the so-called dispositional properties of his world [p. 79]." Heider notes that in the perception of persons, "the manifold of incoming messages (the proximal stimuli of perception) is encoded in terms of the motives, sentiments, beliefs, and personality traits of other persons. . . . these are dispositional properties, the relatively stable distal features that are relevant to us [p. 53]."

Our initial examples of the close personal relationship suggest that all three of these concepts are necessary in its characterization.

Chapter 6

Marriage

Five Types of Marriage

John F. Cuber and Peggy B. Harroff

The qualitative aspects of enduring marital relationships vary enormously. The variations described to us were by no means random or clearly individualized, however. Five distinct life styles showed up repeatedly and the pairs within each of them were remarkably similar in which they lived together, found sexual expression, reared children, and made their way in the outside world.

The following classification is based on the interview materials of those people whose marriages had already lasted ten years or more and who said that they had never seriously considered divorce or separation. While 360 of the men and women had been married ten or more years to the same spouse, exclusion of those who reported that they had considered divorce reduced the number to 211. The discussion in this chapter is, then, based on 211 interviews: 107 men and 104 women.

The descriptions which our interviewees gave us took into account how they had behaved and also how they felt about their actions past and present. Examination of the important features of their lives revealed five recurring configurations of male-female life, each with a central theme—some prominent distinguishing psychological feature which gave each type its singularity. It is these preeminent characteristics which suggested the names for the relationship; the *Conflict-Habituated,* the *Devitalized,* the *Passive-Congenial,* the *Vital,* and the *Total.*

The Conflict-Habituated

We begin with the conflict-habituated not because it is the most prevalent, but because the overt behavior patterns in it are so readily observed and because it presents some arresting contradictions. In this association there is much tension and conflict—although it is largely controlled. At worst, there is some private quarreling, nagging, and "throwing up the past" of which members of the immediate family, and more rarely close friends and relatives, have some awareness. At best, the couple is discreet and polite, genteel about it in the company of others—but after a few drinks at the cocktail party the verbal barbs begin to fly. The intermittent conflict is rarely concealed from the children, though we were often assured otherwise. "Oh, they're at it again—but they always are," says the high-school son. There is private acknowledgment by both husband and wife as a rule that incompatibility is pervasive, that conflict is ever-potential, and that an atmosphere of tension permeates the togetherness.

An illustrative case concerns a physician of fifty, married for twenty-five years to the same woman, with two college-graduate children promisingly established in their own professions.

> You know, it's funny; we have fought from the time we were in high school together. As I look back at it, I can't remember specific quarrels; it's more like a running guerrilla fight with intermediate periods, sometimes quite long, of pretty good fun and some damn good sex. In fact, if it hadn't been for the sex, we wouldn't have been married so quickly. Well, anyway, this has been going on ever since. . . . It's hard to know what it is we fight about most of the time. You name it and we'll fight about it. It's sometimes something I've said that she remembers differently, sometimes a decision—like what kind of car to buy or what to give the kids for Christmas. With regard to politics, and religion, and morals—oh, boy! You know, outside of the welfare of the kids —too much and that's just abstract—we don't really agree about any-thing. . . . At different times we take opposite sides—not deliberately; it just comes out that way.
>
> Now these fights get pretty damned colorful. You called them arguments a little while ago—I have to correct you—they're brawls. There's never a bit of physical violence—at least not directed to each other—but the verbal gunfire gets pretty thick. Why, we've said things to each other that neither of us would think of saying in the hearing of anybody else. . . .
>
> Of course we don't settle any of the issues. It's sort of a matter of principle *not* to. Because somebody would have to give in then and lose face for the next encounter. . . .
>
> When I tell you this in this way, I feel a little foolish about it. I wouldn't tolerate such a condition in any other relationship in my life—and yet here I do and always have. . . .
>
> No—we never have considered a divorce or separation or anything so clear-cut. I realize that other people do, and I can't say that it has never occurred to either of us, but we've never considered it seriously.
>
> A number of times, there has been a crisis, like the time I was in the automobile accident, and the time she almost died in childbirth, and then I guess we really showed that we do care about each other. But as soon as the crisis is over, it's business as usual.

There is a subtle valence in these conflict-habituated relationships. It is easily missed in casual observation. So central is the necessity for channeling conflict and bridling hostility that these considerations come to preoccupy much of the interaction. Some psychiatrists have gone so far as to suggest that it is precisely the deep need to do psychological battle with one another which constitutes the cohesive factor insuring continuity of the marriage. Possibly so. But even from a surface point of view, the overt and manifest fact of habituated attention to handling tension, keeping it chained, and concealing it, is clearly seen as a dominant life force. And it can, and does for some, last for a whole lifetime.

The Devitalized

The key to the devitalized mode is the clear discrepancy between middle-aged reality and the earlier years. These people usually characterized themselves as having been "deeply in love" during the early years, as having spent a great deal of time together, having enjoyed sex, and, most importantly of all, having had a close identification with one another. The present picture, with some variation from case to case, is in clear contrast—little time is spent together, sexual relationships are far less satisfying qualitatively or quantitatively, and interests and activities are not shared, at least not in the deeper and meaningful way they once were. Most of their time together now is "duty time"—entertaining together, planning and sharing activities with children, and participating in various kinds of required community responsibilities. They do as a rule retain, in addition to a genuine and mutual interest in the welfare of their children, a shared attention to their joint property and the husband's career. But even in the latter case the interest is contrasting. Despite a common dependency on his success and the benefits which flow therefrom, there is typically very little sharing of the intrinsic aspects of career—simply an acknowledgment of their mutual dependency on the fruits.

Two rather distinct subtypes of the devitalized take shape by the middle years. The following reflections of two housewives in their late forties illustrate both the common and the distinguishing features:

> Judging by the way it was when we were first married—say the first five years or so—things are pretty matter-of-fact now—even dull. They're dull between us, I mean. The children are a lot of fun, keep us pretty busy, and there are lots of outside things—you know, like Little League and the P.T.A. and the Swim Club, and even the company parties aren't always so bad. But I mean where Bob and I are concerned—if you followed us around, you'd wonder why we ever got *married*. We take each other for granted. We laugh at the same things sometimes, but we don't really laugh together—the way we used to. But, as he said to me the other night—with one or two under the belt, I think—"You know, you're still a little fun now and then." . . .
>
> Now, I don't say this to complain, not in the least. There's a cycle to life. There are things you do in high school. And different things you do in college. Then you're a young adult. And then you're middle-aged. That's where we are now. . . . I'll admit that I do yearn for the old days when sex was a big thing and going out was fun and I hung on to everything he said about his work and his ideas as if they were coming from a genius or something. But then you get the children and other responsibilities. I have the home and Bob has a tremendous burden of responsibility at the office. . . . He's completely

responsible for setting up the new branch now. . . . You have to adjust to these things and we both try to gracefully. . . . Anniversaries though do remind you kind of hard. . . .

The other kind of hindsight from a woman in a devitalized relationship is much less accepting and quiescent:

> I know I'm fighting it. I ought to accept that it has to be like this, but I don't like it, and I'd do almost anything to bring back the exciting way of living we had at first. Most of my friends think I'm some sort of a sentimental romantic or something—they tell me to act my age—but I do know some people—not very darn many—who are our age and even older, who still have the same kind of excitement about them and each other that we had when we were all in college. I've seen some of them at parties and other places— the way they look at each other, the little touches as they go by. One couple has grandchildren and you'd think they were honeymooners. I don't think it's just sex either—I think they are just part of each other's lives—and then when I think of us and the numb way we sort of stagger through the weekly routine, I could scream. And I've even thought of doing some pretty desperate things to try to build some joy and excitement into my life. I've given up on Phil. He's too content with his balance sheets and the kids' report cards and the new house we're going to build next year. He keeps saying he has everything in life that any man could want. What do you *do?*

Regardless of the gracefulness of the acceptance, or the lack thereof, the common plight prevails: on the subjective, emotional dimension, the relationship has become a void. The original zest is gone. There is typically little overt tension or conflict, but the interplay between the pair has become apathetic, lifeless. No serious threat to the continuity of the marriage is generally acknowledged, however. It is intended, usually by both, that it continue indefinitely despite its numbness. Continuity and relative freedom from open conflict are fostered in part because of the comforts of the "habit cage." Continuity is further insured by the absence of any engaging alternative, "all things considered." It is also reinforced, sometimes rather decisively, by legal and ecclesiastical requirements and expectations. These people quickly explain that "there are other things in life" which are worthy of sustained human effort.

This kind relationship is exceedingly common. Persons in this circumstance frequently make comparisons with other pairs they know, many of whom are similar to themselves. This fosters the comforting judgment that "marriage is like this—except for a few oddballs or pretenders who claim otherwise."

While these relationships lack visible vitality, the participants assure us that there is "something there." There are occasional periods of sharing at least something—if only memory. Even formalities can have meanings. Anniversaries can be celebrated, if a little grimly, for what they once commemorated. As one man said, "Tomorrow we are celebrating the anniversary of our anniversary." Even clearly substandard sexual expression is said by some to be better than nothing, or better than a clandestine substitute. A "good man" or a "good mother for the kids" may "with a little affection and occasional attention now and then, get you by." Many believe that the devitalized mode is the appropri-

ate mode in which a man and woman should be content to live in the middle
years and later.

The Passive-Congenial

The passive-congenial mode has a great deal in common with the devitalized, the essential difference being that the passivity which pervades the association has been there from the start. The devitalized have a more exciting set
of memories; the passive-congenials give little evidence that they had ever
hoped for anything much different from what they are currently experiencing.

There is therefore little suggestion of disillusionment or compulsion to make
believe to anyone. Existing modes of association are comfortably adequate—
no stronger words fit the facts as they related them to us. There is little conflict,
although some admit that they tiptoe rather gingerly over and around a residue
of subtle resentments and frustrations. In their better moods they remind
themselves (and each other) that "there are many common interests" which
they both enjoy. "We both like classical music." "We agree completely on
religious and political matters." "We both love the country and our quaint
exurban neighbors." "We are both lawyers."

The wife of a prominent attorney, who has been living in the passive-
congenial mode for thirty years, put her description this way:

> We have both always tried to be calm and sensible about major life deci-
> sions, to think things out thoroughly and in perspective. Len and I knew each
> other since high school but didn't start to date until college. When he asked
> me to marry him, I took a long time to decide whether he was the right man
> for me and I went into his family background, because I wasn't just marrying
> him; I was choosing a father for my children. We decided together not to get
> married until he was established, so that we would not have to live in dingy
> little apartments like some of our friends who got married right out of college.
> This prudence has stood us in good stead too. Life has moved ahead for us
> with remarkable orderliness and we are deeply grateful for the foresight we
> had. . . .
>
> When the children were little, we scheduled time together with them,
> although since they're grown, the demands of the office are getting pretty
> heavy. Len brings home a bulging briefcase almost every night and more often
> than not the light is still on in his study after I retire. But we've got a lot to
> show for his devoted effort. . . .
>
> I don't like all this discussion about sex—even in the better magazines. I
> hope your study will help to put it in its proper perspective. I expected to
> perform sex in marriage, but both before and since, I'm willing to admit that
> it's a much overrated activity. Now and then, perhaps it's better. I am
> fortunate, I guess, because my husband has never been demanding about it,
> before marriage or since. It's just not that important to either of us. . . .
>
> My time is very full these days, with the chairmanship of the Cancer Drive,
> and the Executive Board of the (state) P.T.A. I feel a little funny about that
> with my children already grown, but there are the grandchildren coming
> along. And besides so many of my friends are in the organizations, and it's
> so much like a home-coming.

People make their way into the passive-congenial mode by two quite different routes—by default and by intention. Perhaps in most instances they arrive at this way of living and feeling by drift. There is so little which they have cared about deeply in each other that a passive-congenial mode is a deliberately intended arrangement for two people whose interests and creative energies are directed elsewhere than toward the pairing—into careers, or in the case of women, into children or community activities. They say they know this and want it this way. These people simply do not wish to invest their total emotional involvement and creative effort in the male-female relationship.

The passive-congenial life style fits societal needs quite well also, and this is an important consideration. The man of practical affairs, in business, government service, or the professions—quite obviously needs "to have things peaceful at home" and to have a minimum of distraction as he pursues his important work. He may feel both love and gratitude toward the wife who fits this mode.

A strong case was made for the passive-congenial by a dedicated physician:

> I don't know why everyone seems to make so much about men and women and marriage. Of course, I'm married and if anything happened to my wife, I'd get married again. I think it's the proper way to live. It's convenient, orderly, and solves a lot of problems. But there are other things in life. I spent nearly ten years preparing for the practice of my profession. The biggest thing to me is the practice of that profession, to be of assistance to my patients and their families. I spend twelve hours a day at it. And I'll bet if you talked with my wife, you wouldn't get any of that "trapped housewife" stuff from her either. Now that the children are grown, she finds a lot of useful and necessary work to do in this community. She works as hard as I do.

The passive-congenial mode facilitates the achievement of other goals too. It enables people who desire a considerable amount of personal independence and freedom to realize it with a minimum of inconvenience from or to the spouse. And it certainly spares the participants in it from the need to give a great deal of personal attention to "adjusting to the spouse's needs." The passive-congenial menage is thus a mood as well as a mode.

Our descriptions of the devitalized and the passive-congenials have been similar because these two modes are much alike in their overt characteristics. The participants' evaluations of their *present situations* are likewise largely the same—the accent on "other things," the emphasis on civic and professional responsibilities; the importance of property, children, and reputation. The essential difference lies in their diverse histories and often in their feelings of contentment with their current lives. The passive-congenials had from the start a life pattern and a set of expectations essentially consistent with what they are now experiencing. When the devitalized reflect, however, when they juxtapose history against present reality, they often see the barren gullies in their lives left by the erosions of earlier satisfactions. Some of the devitalized are resentful and disillusioned; others, calling themselves "mature about it," have emerged with reasonable acceptance of their existing devitalized modes. Still others are clearly ambivalent, "I wish life would be more exciting, but I should have known it couldn't last. In a way, it's calm and quiet and reassuring this way, but there are times when I get very ill at ease—sometimes downright mad. Does it *have* to be like this?"

The passive-congenials do not find it necessary to speculate in this fashion. Their anticipations were realistic and perhaps even causative of their current marital situation. In any event, their passivity is not jarred when teased by memory.

The Vital

In extreme contrast to the three foregoing is the vital relationship. The vital pair can easily be overlooked as they move through their worlds of work, recreation, and family activities. They do the same things, publicly at least; and when talking for public consumption say the same things—they are proud of their homes, love their children, gripe about their jobs, while being quite proud of their career accomplishments. But when the close, intimate, confidential, empathic look is taken, the essence of the vital relationship becomes clear: the mates are intensely bound together psychologically in important life matters. Their sharing and their togetherness is genuine. It provides the life essence for both man and woman.

> The things we do together aren't fun intrinsically—the ecstasy comes from being *together in the doing*. Take her out of the picture and I wouldn't give a damn for the boat, the lake, or any of the fun that goes on out there.

The presence of the mate is indispensable to the feelings of satisfaction which the activity provides. The activities shared by the vital pairs may involve almost anything: hobbies, careers, community service. Anything—so long as it is closely shared.

It is hard to escape the word *vitality*—exciting mutuality of feelings and participation together in important life segments. The clue that the relationship is vital (rather than merely expressing the joint activity) derives from the feeling that it is important. An activity is flat and uninteresting if the spouse is not a part of it.

Other valued things are readily sacrificed in order to enhance life within the vital relationship.

> I cheerfully, and that's putting it mildly, passed up two good promotions, because one of them would have required some traveling and the other would have taken evening and weekend time—and that's when Pat and I *live*. The hours with her (after twenty-two years of marriage) are what I live for. You should meet her. . . .

People in the vital relationship for the most part know that they are a minority and that their life styles are incomprehensible to most of their associates.

Most of our friends think we moved out to the country for the kids; well —the kids *are* crazy about it, but the fact of the matter is, we moved out for ourselves—just to get away from all the annoyances and interferences of other people—our friends actually. We like this kind of life—where we can have almost all of our time together.... We've been married for over twenty years and the most enjoyable thing either of us does—well, outside of the intimate things—is to sit and talk by the hour. That's why we built that imposing fireplace—and the hi-fi here in the corner.... Now that Ed is getting older, that twenty-seven-mile drive morning and night from the office is a real burden, but he does it cheerfully so we can have our long uninterrupted hours together.... The children respect this too. They don't invade our privacy any more than they can help—the same as we vacate the living room when Ellen brings in a date, she tries not to intrude on us.... Being the specialized kind of lawyer he is, I can't share much in his work, but that doesn't bother either of us. The *big* part of our lives is completely mutual....

Her husband's testimony validated hers. And we talked to dozens of other couples like them, too. They find their central satisfaction in the life they live with and through each other. It consumes their interest and dominates their thoughts and actions. All else is subordinate and secondary.

This does not mean that people in vital relationships lose their separate identities, that they may not upon occasion be rivalrous or competitive with one another or that conflict may not occur. They differ fundamentally from the conflict-habituated, however, in that when conflict does occur, it results from matters that are important to them, such as which college a daughter or son is to attend; it is devoid of the trivial "who said what first and when" and I can't forget when you.... " A further difference is that people to whom the relationship is vital tend to settle disagreements quickly and seek to avoid conflict, whereas the conflict-habituated look forward to conflict and appear to operate by a tacit rule that no conflict is ever to be truly terminated and that the spouse must never be considered right. The two kinds of conflict are thus radically different. To confuse them is to miss an important differentiation.

The Total

The total relationship is like the vital relationship with the important addition that it is more multifaceted. The points of vital meshing are more numerous—in some cases all of the important life foci are vitally shared. In one such marriage the husband is an internationally known scientist. For thirty years his wife has been "his friend, mistress, and partner." He still goes home at noon whenever possible, at considerable inconvenience, to have a quiet lunch and spend a conversational hour or so with his wife. They refer to these conversations as "our little seminars." They feel comfortable with each other and with their four grown children. The children (now in their late twenties) say that they enjoy visits with their parents as much as they do with friends of their own age.

There is practically no pretense between persons in the total relationship or between them and the world outside. There are few areas of tension, because the items of difference which have arisen over the years have been settled as they arose. There often *were* serious differences of opinion but they were handled, sometimes by compromise, sometimes by one or the other yielding; but these outcomes were of secondary importance because the primary consideration was not who was right or who was wrong, only how the problem could be resolved without tarnishing the relationship. When faced with differences, they can and do dispose of the difficulties without losing their feeling of unity or their sense of vitality and centrality of their relationship. This is the mainspring.

The various parts of the total relationship are reinforcing, as we learned from this consulting engineer who is frequently sent abroad by his corporation.

> She keeps my files and scrapbooks up to date. . . . I invariably take her with me to conferences around the world. Her femininity, easy charm and wit are invaluable assets to me. I know it's conventional to say that a man's wife is responsible for his success and I also know that it's often not true. But in my case I gladly acknowledge that it's not only true, but she's indispensable to me. But she'd go along with me even if there was nothing for her to do because we just enjoy each other's company—deeply. You know, the best part of a vacation is not *what* we do, but that we do it together. We plan it and reminisce about it and weave it into our work and other play all the time.

The wife's account is substantially the same except that her testimony demonstrates more clearly the genuineness of her "help."

> It seems to me that Bert exaggerates my help. It's not so much that I only want to help him; it's more that I want to do those things anyway. We do them together, even though we may not be in each other's presence at the time. I don't really know what I do for him and what I do for me.

This kind of relationship is rare, in marriage or out, but it does exist and can endure. We occasionally found relationships so total that all aspects of life were mutually shared and enthusiastically participated in. It is as if neither spouse has, or has had, a truly private existence.

The customary purpose of a classification such as this one is to facilitate understanding of similarities and differences among the cases classified. In this instance enduring marriage is the common condition. The differentiating features are the dissimilar forces which make for the integration of the pair within each of the types. It is not necessarily the purpose of a classification to make possible a clear-cut sorting of all cases into one or another of the designated categories. All cannot be so precisely pigeon-holed; there often are borderline cases. Furthermore, two observers with equal access to the facts may sometimes disagree on which side of the line an unclear case should be placed. If the classification is a useful one, however, placement should *as a rule* be clear and relatively easy. The case is only relative because making an accurate classification of a given relationship requires the possession of amounts and kinds of information which one rarely has about persons other than himself. Superficial knowledge of public or professional behavior is not enough. And even in his own case, one may, for reasons of ego, find it difficult to be totally forthright.

A further caution. The typology concerns relationships, not personalities. A clearly vital person may be living in a passive-congenial or devitalized relationship and expressing his vitality in some other aspect of his life—career being an important preoccupation for many. Or, possibly either or both of the spouses may have a vital relationship—sometimes extending over many years —with someone of the opposite sex outside of the marriage.

Nor are the five types to be interpreted as *degrees* of marital happiness or adjustment. Persons in all five are currently adjusted and most say that they are content, if not happy. Rather, the five types represent *different kinds of adjustment* and *different conceptions of marriage*. This is an important concept which must be emphasized if one is to understand the personal meanings which these people attach to the conditions of their marital experience.

Neither are the five types necessarily stages in a cycle of initial bliss and later disillusionment. Many pairings started in the passive-congenial stage; in fact, quite often people intentionally enter into a marriage for the acknowledged purpose of living this kind of relationship. To many the simple amenities of the "habit cage" are not disillusionments or even disappointments, but rather are sensible life expectations which provide an altogether comfortable and rational way of having a "home base" for their lives. And many of the conflict-habituated told of courtship histories essentially like their marriages.

While each of these types tends to persist, there *may* be movement from one type to another as circumstances and life perspectives change. This movement may go in any direction from any point, and a given couple may change categories more than once. Such changes are relatively *in*frequent however, and the important point is that relationship types tend to persist over relatively long periods.

The fundamental nature of these contexts may be illustrated by examining the impact of some common conditions on persons of each type.

Infidelity, for example, occurs in most of the five types, the total relationship being the exception. But it occurs for quite different reasons. In the conflict-habituated it seems frequently to be only another outlet for hostility. The call girl and the woman picked up in a bar are more than just available women; they are symbols of resentment of the wife. This is not always so, but reported to us often enough to be worth noting. Infidelity among the passive-congenial, on the other hand, is typically in line with the stereotype of the middle-aged man who "strays out of sheer boredom with the uneventful, deadly prose" of his private life. And the devitalized man or woman frequently is trying for an hour or a year to recapture the lost mood. But the vital are sometimes adulterous too; some are simply emancipated—almost bohemian. To some of them sexual aggrandizement is an accepted fact of life. Frequently, the infidelity is condoned by the partner and in some instances even provides an indirect (through empathy) kind of gratification. The act of infidelity in such cases is not construed as disloyalty or as a threat to continuity, but rather as a kind of basic human right which the loved one ought to be permitted to have—and which the other perhaps wants also for himself.

Divorce and separation are found in all five of the types, but the reasons, when viewed realistically and outside of the simplitudes of legalistic and ecclesiastical fiction, are highly individual and highly variable. For example, a couple may move from a vital relationship to divorce because for them the alternative of a devitalized relationship is unendurable. They can conceive of marriage only as a vital, meaningful, fulfilling, and preoccupying interaction. The "disvitality" of any other marriage form is abhorrent to them and takes on "the hypocrisy of living a public lie." We have accounts of marriages which were unquestionably vital or total for a period of years but which were dissolved. In some respects relationships of this type are more readily disrupted, because these people have become adjusted to such a rich and deep sharing that evidences of breach, which a person in another type of marriage might consider quite normal, become unbearable.

> I know a lot of close friendships occur between men and women married to someone else, and that they're not always adulterous. But I know Betty —and anyhow, I personally believe they eventually do become so, but I can't be sure about that. Anyway, when Betty found her self-expression was furthered by longer and longer meetings and conversations with Joe, and I detected little insincerities, not serious at first, you understand, creeping into the things we did together, it was like the little leak in the great dike. It didn't take very long. We weren't melodramatic about it, but it was soon clear to both of us that we were no longer the kind of pair we once were, so why pretend. The whole thing can go to hell fast—and after almost twenty years!

Husbands in other types of relationships would probably not even have detected any disloyalty on the part of his wife. And even if they had, they would tend to conclude that "you don't break up a home just because she has a passing interest in some glamorous writer."

The divorce which occurs in the passive-congenial marriage follows a different sequence. One of the couple, typically a person capable of more vitality in his or her married life than the existing relationship provides, comes into contact with a person with whom he gradually (or suddenly) unfolds a new dimension to adult living. What he had considered to be a rational and sensible and "adult" relationship can suddenly appear in contrast to be stultifying, shallow, and an altogether disheartening way to live out the remaining years. He is left with "no conceivable alternative but to move out." Typically, he does not do so impulsively or without a more or less stubborn attempt to stifle his "romanticism" and listen to well-documented advice to the effect that he should act maturely and "leave the romantic yearning to the kids for whom it is intended." Very often he is convinced and turns his back on his "new hope"—but not always.

Whether examining marriages for the satisfactions and fulfillments they have brought or for the frustrations and pain, the overriding influence of life style—or as we have here called it, relationship type—is of the essence. Such a viewpoint helps the observer, and probably the participant, to understand some of the apparent enigmas about men and women in marriage—why infidelities destroy some marriages and not others; why conflict plays so large a role for some couples and is so negligible for others; why some seemingly well-suited and harmoniously adjusted spouses seek divorce while others with provocations galore remain solidly together; why affections, sexual expression, recreation, almost everything observable about men and women is so radically different from pair to pair. All of these are not merely different objectively; they are perceived differently by the pairs, are differently reacted to, and differently attended to.

If nothing else, this chapter has demonstrated that realistic understanding of marital relationships requires use of concepts which are carefully based on perceptive factual knowledge. Unfortunately, the language by which relationships between men and women are conventionally expressed tends to lead toward serious and pervasive deceptions which in turn encourage erroneous inferences. Thus, we tend to assume that enduring marriage is somehow synonymous with happy marriage or at least with something comfortably called adjustment. The deception springs from lumping together such dissimilar modes of thought and action as the conflict-habituated, the passive-congenial, and the vital. To know that a marriage has endured, or for that matter has been dissolved, tells one close to nothing about the kinds of experiences, fulfillments, and frustrations which have made up the lives of the people involved. Even to know, for example, that infidelity has occurred, without knowledge of circumstances, feelings, and other essences, results in an illusion of knowledge which masks far more than it describes.

To understand a given marriage, let alone what is called "marriage in general," is realistically possible only in terms of particular sets of experiences, meanings, hopes, and intentions. This chapter has described in broad outline five manifest and recurring configurations among the Significant Americans.

The Quality of Marriage in Middletown: 1924–1976

Theodore Caplow, Howard M. Bahr, Bruce A. Chadwick, Reuben Hill, and Margaret Williamson

In recent years, considerable media attention has been devoted to claims that the traditional family is losing favor in American society. Some of the more ardent critics have contended that the traditional family has not adapted to the changing society and has become obsolete. It has been argued that the obsolete traditional family stifles, rather than fosters, the happiness of married people. This chapter will assess the validity of such claims by exploring the quality of Middletown marriages in the 1920s, 1930s, and 1970s and by noting changes in levels of marital happiness.

Marriage in the 1920s

The Lynds' portrait of the average marriage in the Middletown of the 1920s was a dreary one, especially for the working class. Marriage for many husbands meant weariness from trying to provide for their families, numerous children, and wives weary from doing other people's washing (Lynd and Lynd 1929, 129). For many wives, marriage meant poverty, cruelty, adultery, and abandonment. The Lynds did observe a few happy marriages. "There are some homes in Middletown among both working and business class families which one cannot enter without being aware of a constant undercurrent of sheer delight of fresh, spontaneous interest between husband and wife" (Lynd and Lynd 1929, 130). But they noted that such marriages stood out because of their rarity and that the majority of Middletown's couples seemed to lead a depressing existence. Though disappointment and depression did not dominate the family's daily life, they lurked in the background, occasionally resulting in a domestic fight or a drinking spree. It appeared to the Lynds that most families, although less than happy, were held together by community values discouraging divorce and by the husband and wife's focusing on "the plans for today and tomorrow," "the pleasures of this half-hour," and their "share in the joint undertaking of children, paying off the mortgage, and generally 'getting on'" (1929, 130). Married life was disappointing, but the prospect of a divorce was even more painful. They forgot their discouragement by focusing on day-to-day living and by ignoring the question of whether it was worth the effort.

Companionship

Observations of husbands and wives revealed that most of them developed a relationship with limited companionship. In the social and recreational activities of the 1920s, the sexes were separated more often than not. At dinners, parties, and other social gatherings, men and women seemed to form separate groups so that the men could talk about business, sports and politics and the women could discuss children, dress styles, and local gossip. Men's leisure activities generally excluded women. Business-class husbands played golf or cards at their clubs without their wives, while no self-respecting working-class wife would join her husband for an evening in the local cigar store. The one recreational activity that husbands and wives shared was card playing with friends in their homes.

Because of the harsh demands of work in the factories, working-class families had less time, energy, and money to spend on family leisure. According to the Lynds, "Not infrequently, husband and wife would meet each other at the end of a day's work too tired or inert to play or go anywhere together" (1929, 119). Compounding the problem was the economic pressure of the times that left few dollars to spend on entertainment.

The time couples did spend at home does not appear to have been filled with pleasant or stimulating conversation. Decisions about the children, the house payment, and the food budget were quickly dealt with in a bickering fashion, and, with those problems disposed of, couples often lapsed into "apathetic silence." The Lynds reported that many times during their survey of wives, the interviewer had a difficult time terminating the interview. The women seemed hungry for someone to talk to.

> "I wish you could come often. I never have anyone to talk to," or "My husband never goes anyplace and never does anything. In the evenings he comes home and sits down and says nothing. I like to talk and be sociable, but I can hardly ever get anything out of him" (Lynd and Lynd 1929, 120).

The limited communication between husbands and wives and the trivial nature of their conversation left many of them isolated in their separate worlds, his pertaining to work and friends and hers to the children and the home. In many marriages, they shared a house, each other's bodies, and little else.

Even their sexual relations seemed troubled. Lack of information about birth control and the prejudice against its use made babies the inevitable consequence of physical intimacy for most working-class couples. The uncertainty of employment often made another child an unwanted burden. The conflict between not wanting more children and needing the physical pleasures of marriage, and the resulting stress placed on the marriage, were evident in the comments of Middletown wives.

> One wife hopes to heaven she'll have no more children. She said that people talked to her about contraceptives sometimes, and she told "him" what they said, but he said it was none of their business. She had never dared ask him what he thought about birth control, but thought he disapproved of it. She would "die" if she had any more children, but is doing nothing to prevent it (Lynd and Lynd 1929, 124).

A wife of twenty-two replied to the question about number of children: "We haven't any. Gracious, no! We mustn't have any till we get steady work. No, we don't use anything to prevent children. I just keep away from my husband. He don't care—only at times. He's discouraged because he's out of work. I went to work but had to quit because I was so nervous" (Lynd and Lynd 1929, 125).

Such comments provide considerable insight into Middletown's working-class marriages of the 1920s. The fact that a wife might not dare ask her husband what he thought about birth control, let alone what he felt about practicing it, shows how shallow some of the relationships were. In some cases, the threat of unwanted children made wives resentful; they felt that their husbands were insensitive and selfish to expose them to the risk of conception. In other cases, the fear of an unwanted pregnancy forced a wife to "keep away" from her husband, which certainly did not strengthen their marital relationship. On the other hand, husbands felt rejected by their wives' avoidance of physical contact.

It may have been that limited marital sex contributed to the flourishing prostitution in Middletown during the 1920s. Husbands whose wives were sexually unresponsive, perhaps because of their fear of pregnancy, may have sought sexual satisfaction outside of marriage. Although a husband's visits to prostitutes probably did not strenthen his marriage, they were not a sure indicator of marital dissatisfaction. Some men sought commercial sex out of consideration for their wives' fear of unwanted pregnancy. And, of course, we do not know what proportion of the clients of Middletown's brothels were unmarried. Moreover, the effects of changing laws and policies on prostitution make its prevalence a very unsure indicator of marital happiness. The number of whorehouses in Middletown fluctuated dramatically over the years, before beginning a permanent decline in the 1940s.

Another glimpse of the shallowness of husband-wife relationships in the 1920s is provided by the responses of 69 working-class wives to the question "What are the thoughts and plans that give you courage to go on when thoroughly discouraged?" Not one of them mentioned her husband as a source of emotional support!

Divorce

The trend in divorce was discussed in detail in *Middletown*. Divorce rates increased significantly in Middletown from 1890 to 1920. Whether there were significantly more unhappy marriages during the 1920s than there had been at the turn of the century is a question neither the Lynds nor we could answer with the available data. The legal grounds for divorce in force at a particular time and contemporary public attitudes toward it greatly influence the likelihood that a marriage will end in divorce. When divorce laws are stringent and public sentiment strongly opposed, unhappy marriages endure. Between 1890 and 1920, Indiana's divorce laws were conspicuously liberalized and prevailing attitudes toward divorce became much less censorious. Nevertheless, the high divorce rate observed during the 1920s does suggest that more marriages were experiencing unresolvable stresses and strains than had been the case 30 years earlier.

Marriage in the 1930s

The Great Depression was thought by Middletown people to have mixed effects on marital happiness. On the one hand, they spoke of how married couples spent more time together and became more dependent on each other, and this enforced togetherness was perceived as strengthening the quality of Middletown's marriages. The Lynds quoted an editorial in a local newspaper in the spring of 1933 that remarked that

> All of us are hoping for a quick return of the prosperity we once knew, or thought we knew, but in the meantime, some millions of Americans already have a kind of prosperity that includes the strengthening of family ties, better health, and the luxury of simple pleasures and quiet surroundings, although of this they may not be aware (Lynd and Lynd 1937, 147).

On the other hand, the economic chaos of the depression created problems in many marriages, including those of the business class. *Middletown in Transition* suggests that the depression did increase the amount of time husbands and wives spent together by making outside activities unaffordable. Although couples spent more time together, they often reacted to economic pressures by mutual recrimination. The wives were quick to reproach their husbands for failing to provide for the family's needs, and the husbands were equally quick to defend their wounded egos by lashing out at wives and children. Despite these mounting tensions, the typical marital relationship during the depression was similar to that of the 1920s. According to the Lynds, in the 1930s Middletown's homes still housed

> somewhat impersonal, tolerant couples, in the same rooms, with the same pictures looking down on them, planning together the big and little immensities of personal living by which people in families in this culture seek to ameliorate the essential loneliness and confusion of life. These homes seem to give the lie to the ricocheting process of social change outside (Lynd and Lynd 1937, 145).

Divorce

The divorce rate decreased in Middletown between 1920 and 1940, a fact that might be taken as evidence for the positive effects of the depression on the quality of marriage. But conversation with divorce lawyers and judges revealed that one very important reason that fewer divorces were being filed in the 1930s was that many couples could not afford the $60 necessary to obtain one. The standard attorney's fee was $50, and court costs were $10. During the depression, the sum was hard to raise, and some bad marriages that would have ended in divorce during more prosperous times seem to have survived for no other reason.

On the other hand, husbands failing to provide for their families, wives entering the labor force, homes being lost by foreclosure, and other adversities placed extreme stress on many marriages, particularly working-class marriages. The Lynds reviewed 90 divorce cases handled by an attorney between 1931 and 1935 and concluded that a large number of them were directly attributable to the depression. The following cases were fairly typical.

> *Case 5.* Husband and wife middle-aged. Married about twenty years. Three children. Husband out of work most of Depression, though willing to work. She grew irritable and quarrelsome and made home life unbearable. He sought other female company (Lynd and Lynd 1937, 159).

> *Case 22.* Both in early thirties, though wife three years older than husband. Married a little more than five years. Three children. Husband has had a streak of hard luck, having been out of work for several years. Her relatives kept them until the relatives tired and urged her to get a divorce. (Lawyer's comment: "This is a real depression case.") (Lynd and Lynd 1937, 160.)

> *Case 49.* Well along in thirties. Married about eight years. One child. Husband had a prosperous business until the Depression hit him. Fine home and family life up to then. Husband began drinking after Depression hit him. Business failed and wife went to work to support the family. (Lawyer's comment: "This is a real Depression case.") (Lynd and Lynd 1937, 160.)

The economic upheaval of the 1930s hit the working class harder than it hit the business class, and this fact was reflected in the divorce rates for the two groups. The majority of the 90 divorces that the Lynds reviewed involved working-class couples, with a smaller group of couples from the lower range of the business class included, as well as a "thin sprinkling of wealthier business class representatives" (Lynd and Lynd 1937, 157).

Marriage in the 1970s

During the years between 1920 and the late 1970s, the family institution faced a great deal of criticism. It has been argued by some that the family has not changed as rapidly as other social institutions and thus it has become obsolete. The death of the nuclear family has also been widely heralded.

> Depending upon whether one regards oneself as an attacker or defender of the institution, the final death scene may be viewed in different terms. The attackers seem to see the family's death as being hastened by natural causes— that is, hardening of the institutional arteries or something akin to inability to make the evolutionary adjustment to a changed social and economic climate. In this latter view, something has caused the family, like some ancient dinosaur, to breathe its last. Some ardent defenders regard the family's demise as having been engineered by a devilish army of debauched sociologists, radical psychiatrists, "Commie perverts," bra-burning feminists, "knee-jerk liberals," and assorted libertines of predictable intent (Pickett 1975, 7).

Those who would celebrate the death of the family feel that, because the family is not in step with modern society, it stifles human potential, creativity, and freedom. Their conclusion is that most people would be happier free of family ties (Crosby 1975, 12). On the other hand, some claim that many of society's current problems—crime, alcoholism, and drug abuse, for instance—stem from the weakening of the family and that a return to the "old-fashioned family" would alleviate such problems.

Some writers (Libby and Whitehurst 1975) contend that, as American society has adjusted to rapid technological development, new forms of the family have emerged even though they have not been accepted by the vast majority of the population. Some of the alternative forms of the family that have appeared are *cohabitation,* in which couples live together without being married; *group marriage,* which involves the marriage of three or more people; *part-time marriage,* in which the couple is married only for certain family activities for a specified time period; *open marriage,* which allows each partner to establish relationships, including sexual relationships, with other people; and *mate swapping,* or *swinging,* which organizes extramarital sexual behavior. The more radical family forms have usually appeared in some type of communal setting, since they require extensive group support to endure.

Except for a few cases of discretely practiced cohabitation and mate swapping, alternative forms of the family are rare in Middletown. This situation is not a function of ignorance about alternative family styles. Middletown people are very much aware of family innovations because of their exposure to the mass media. Middletown's newspapers showed an interest when the members of Synanon began dissolving their marriages and entering into three-year love matches (Middletown's evening newspaper, January 2, 1978). Synanon is an organization of approximately 1,600 individuals that was founded in 1958 to rehabilitate "drug addicts, alcoholics and other social misfits." When the wife of Chuck Dederich, the 65-year-old founder and leader of Synanon, died, he married a much younger woman, and the experience started him thinking about how other people would react to a similar experience. He decided that most would enjoy it as much as he had. Besides, according to Dederich, "Most of these people [members of Synanon] were going to divorce anyway, eventually." He persuaded nearly all the married couples in Synanon to divorce and enter into three-year love matches with other people. Husbands and wives helped each other draw up lists of potential love-match partners, and, within a few weeks, 230 couples had made love matches. Dederich felt that he had demonstrated a viable alternative to the traditional family. He concluded that "what happened is what I thought would happen. People fell madly in love with their new partners." Although the love matches were only for three years, Dederich predicted that many would last much longer. Although this experiment in family style occurred within a mini-society isolated in the mountains of northern California, it was noted and discussed in Middletown. But there was no rush of Middletown couples to involve themselves in love matches.

The consequences, both good and bad, of couples living together before marriage have been continually debated in the mass media. Some social scientists have been reported as favoring cohabitation as a way of determining a couple's compatibility before marriage. This practice, according to them, should reduce the frequency of divorce, ". . . since the subtleties of a marraige relationship are not taught in school and not learned in courtship living together provides the only proving ground" (Snider 1975, 12). Other "behavior experts" take up the opposing position and claim that trail marriages place too much pressure on the partners and make it more difficult to develop a close, stable relationship.

> . . . a truly successful marriage and sexual relationship need time to grow and to mature and must be measured in years rather than weeks or months. To be successful . . . marriage needs the security of an unconditional future. Living together doesn't provide sufficient time for thought about the future. Partners in a trial marriage do not live in a marriage environment while each must be on guard to pass the examinations of the other (Snider 1975, 12).

Contradicting both positions, research has indicated that cohabitation has little effect on the quality of subsequent marriage. A recent study of a sample of college students in a southern state reported that "persons with a history of premarital cohabitation do not describe their marriages differently from persons without a history of cohabitation" (Jacques and Chason 1979, 36). Although living together has received considerable media coverage, very few Middletown couples have adopted this family style. Less than 2 percent of the adult respondents in the various surveys indicated that they were living together.

In spite of the proclamations that the traditional family has not kept pace with modern society and that it is "dead," Americans continue to marry at a very high rate and seem to be happiest and healthiest when married. . . .

Companionship

The last 15 years have witnessed a major change in the style of communication between husbands and wives. Numerous books and magazine articles have appeared, encouraging wives to make their needs and preferences known to their husbands (and vice versa to a lesser degree). Assertiveness-training programs have blossomed across the country. They attempt to teach people, primarily women, to communicate their feelings and opinions to others and, as the term "assertiveness" implies, to do so forcefully. Marriage-enrichment programs, including recorded lessons, weekend training sessions, and month-long retreats, have purported to teach thousands of American couples how to communicate with each other more effectively. The women's rights movement, as well as other forces in American society, have fostered a more equal marriage relationship in which the needs and wishes of the wife are considered to be at least as important as those of the husband.

It is difficult to imagine many contemporary wives who would be afraid to discuss birth control with their husbands, particularly after the couple has had several children. The taboo on discussing financial matters observed in the 1920s has almost disappeared, and today nearly all wives play an active role in the management of family finances, especially when they work and contribute to the family income. The open communication between spouses in most Middletown families today was evident in some of the comments housewives made during our interviews. A typical example from one wife who emphasized the openness between her husband and herself was this: "I feel there is nothing I couldn't go to him and ask. . . . I mostly talk to one of my best friends, but I feel that you should look to your own husband for basic communication."

Free communication between spouses apparently has permitted many contemporary couples to increase the happiness they derive from their marriages; at the same time, it has helped other couples to identify their irreconcilable differences. The process of identifying and solving a marital crisis has occasionally been reported in Middletown newspapers and probably has encouraged couples to improve family communication. An example is an account of a working wife who had been married eight years and who resented the fact that her husband did not do a greater share of the housekeeping chores (Middletown's evening newspaper, January 17, 1978). She attacked the problem by using a communication technique called the "contract method," whereby she negotiated the assignment of household tasks with her husband. She remarked after the initial session that, "for the first time, I could see his side. I didn't agree, but I did [at least] understand how he felt." This couple then drew up a list of housekeeping chores and "listened, negotiated, and compromised" about who would do what. The young wife credited improved communication with resolving a serious marital problem and preserving an otherwise good marriage.

This does not mean that all couples in Middletown communicate openly. Interviews with both husbands and wives about their marriages revealed cases of lack of communication, too. An example was one husband, who admitted, "She tries to tell me what she does all day but I don't like to hear it. . . . We don't really talk a lot. She talks about things at work. But I don't really like to talk about it. . . . We eat together every night, but don't spend much time together." A working class wife said, "I would try to talk to him about the other women he was seeing or money problems we were having, but whatever it was he would refuse to talk about it." She reported that, when she persisted in her complaints, her husband shouted and cursed at her until she stopped. Occasionally, her insistence angered her husband to the point that he "shut her up" with a severe beating. But such cases were relatively uncommon, and the evidence is overwhelming that husband-wife communication has improved during the past 50 years.

Not only are contemporary husbands and wives talking to each other, they are engaging in a great deal of leisure activity together. Shopping; eating out; going for drives and to movies, sporting events, fairs, and musical presentations; and taking part in physical fitness activities are frequently shared by husbands and wives. This conclusion is based on the observations of married couples in the malls, shops, theaters, parks, and playing fields of Middletown made by the research staff over a three-year period. The people we interviewed referred again and again to the voluntary activities and interests they shared with their spouses.

In contemporary American society, television has become an integral part of daily life, a source of news as well as of recreation. The sample of wives interviewed in 1978 was asked how often they watched television with their husbands alone. . . . The majority of both business- and working-class couples spent an average of more than five hours each week watching television together. The time spent watching television may not involve much direct interaction between husband and wife when the attention of both is focused on the screen, but they *are* together and can comment on the program or share a snack. It is interesting that both working- and business-class couples report almost identical patterns of joint television viewing. The pervasive class differences in marital behavior observed during the early part of this century are not apparent in this contemporary behavior.

So that we could assess marital satisfaction, the married respondents in the samples of men and women were asked to describe how they felt about their marital relationships. . . . Our results indicate a high level of satisfaction; 57 percent were "very satisfied" with their relationships, and another 38 percent were "satisfied." Barely 5 percent said they felt "neutral" or were "dissatisfied." Many couples said that their relationships had been satisfactory since their honeymoon, and others reported that they had had to work out an agreeable arrangement. One working-class wife told us that the adjustment was harder than she had expected but that a meaningful relationship eventually developed. "In marriage, there is always an adjustment period. During this time you learn your mate's strengths and weaknesses which you must understand. I expected it would be easier than it was." She said that, although it took them six years to achieve, she and her husband "have a total marriage, . . . [we have] really adjusted to each other."

Although there were some slight differences between the average satisfaction reported by working and business-class couples, none was statistically significant. Working-class couples were as satisfied with their marital relationships as business-class couples. Husbands in both social classes felt somewhat more satisfied with marriage than wives, although the differences were not extreme.

These results do not hinge on the exact wording of the question. When we asked about "happiness" rather than "satisfaction," a similar pattern of response emerged. Again, a majority of the husbands and half of the wives perceived their marriages as "very happy," while very few reported "so-so," "unhappy," or "very unhappy" marriages. . . .

As was the case with satisfaction, the small differences in marital happiness between business- and working-class couples were not significant. Husbands, once again, seemed to find marriage somewhat more pleasant than wives did.

The claims in the mass media that modern marriage is an oppressive yoke borne by many because they do not know how to unburden themselves appear absurd in Middletown, where a happy marriage is the common experience. These findings are consistent with recent studies of other communities and of the nation as a whole (Chadwick, Albrecht, and Kunz, 1976; *The Playboy Report on American Men* 1979).

There is additional evidence suggesting that the quality of the average marital relationship has improved over the past 50 years—the number of wives who mentioned their husbands as a source of strength during difficult times. As noted earlier, when a 1924 sample of Middletown housewives was asked the question "What are the thoughts and plans that give you courage to go on when thoroughly discouraged?" not a single wife mentioned her husband as a source of reassurance. In response to the same question in the 1978 survey, 7 percent of the wives mentioned their husbands as a source of strength and comfort, and another 16 percent referred to their families, which, in most cases, included husbands as well as children. The question was asked in the context of religious beliefs, and most responded in such terms; if it had been set in a different context (in terms of "who" rather than "what"), the number of responses mentioning husbands might have been even higher. The data suggest again that the marital relationship has deepened since the 1920s and that husbands and wives share each other's burdens and provide emotional support to a greater degree now than then. Despair about the family is as fashionable in Middletown as it is elsewhere in the United States, so it comes as something of a surprise to learn that 95 percent of Middletown's husbands and wives are satisfied with their marital relationships.

The influence of the media's portrayal of marital conflict is apparent in people's evaluations of their marriages compared to those of their friends. Almost *all* respondents rated their own marriages as happier than those of their friends ("I wish everyone got along as well as we have"). One business-class woman described her third and current marriage as "incredibly better" than those of her friends. Even those who confessed to having problems were likely to describe their marriages as "better than most." Many couples compare their marriages to what they see of their friends' marriages, what their friends tell them about their marriages, and what they observe of marriages in the media, and they are pleasantly surprised that their own marriages seem so satisfying.

We often heard in the in-depth interviews that a satisfying marriage takes time, even years, to develop. "It took us a long time to kind of get things worked out so that we can work together. . . . We now have things worked out and have a good marriage." "It's lasted four years and gotten better each year." This finding is not inconsistent with studies of marital happiness over the life cycle (Rollins and Feldman 1970; Burr 1970). Such studies have discovered that, on the average, marriages are the happiest during the early years but not necessarily at the very outset.

Divorce

Divorce increased significantly after the turn of the century and peaked during the early 1920s. The divorce rate then declined during the 1930s and early 1940s but shot up in the post–World War II period, when the wartime separations of husbands and wives put millions of marriages under great stress. During the prosperous and placid 1950s, the divorce rate dropped back to the level of the 1930s. In the late 1960s and early 1970s, the number of divorces began to increase again, and it eventually surpassed the level of the 1920s, although it remained well below the post–World War II peak. The divorce rate has increased during the past 15 years, but the popular belief that it has "skyrocketed" is as unfounded in Middletown as it is elsewhere.

Our interviews of housewives revealed considerable ambivalence about divorce. On the one hand, many respondents deplored what they perceived as rampant divorce and blamed it on moral decay, by which they meant sexual freedom and irresponsibility in marriage. They often lamented that the religious and spiritual foundations of marriage have been eroded. One housewife said, "Regardless of how agnostic I am, I feel marriage is a sacrament and it can't be undone. People today don't have any moral aspect to it—it's just legal. I don't think divorce is a solution, you can work out your problems." And another held a similar opinion. "There is a total absence of religion. People focus too much on materialism; it detracts from home life and then it falls apart."

A number of women complained that young people are more selfish, individualistic, and hedonistic than they were in the past. The Vietnam war, the student rebellions, the sexual revolution, and the emergence of a drug culture are variously blamed. Young people dropped out of the "establishment" and insisted on doing "their own thing." The women interviewed think the insistence on personal freedom has carried over into marriage and interfered with the willingness of husbands and wives to make the sacrifices necessary for a successful marriage. There was an undertone of pessimism in these complaints. The prevailing sentiment seemed to be that nothing could be done to remedy the situation.

Some respondents insisted that divorce is contagious. As more couples divorce, their children, relatives, and friends may be induced to do the same. The mass media were blamed by a significant number of respondents for disseminating the idea that marriage is impermanent. Others attributed the same effect to

> the letdown in the moral code. . . . Sure, there are numerous reasons for it. I'm concerned about the answers to it. It's accepted more than it used to be and they're more willing to divorce because of it. It's easy to obtain a divorce. When divorce was difficult to get people stayed together because of that difficulty.

Another housewife said, "It's awfully easy to get a divorce, and I think a lot of young kids go into marriage thinking if it doesn't work out I can always get a divorce."

The major deterrent to divorce for the few unhappy couples we identified was their concern about the effect a divorce would have on their children. This anxiety persists in spite of considerable propaganda to the contrary from various licensed sages. The local newspaper carried a report on research conducted by a university psychologist showing that children are harmed more by living in a family with marital discord than by their parents' divorce. "Parents who hold a troubled marriage together because of their children may do them more psychological harm than if they divorce, according to a research team" (Middletown's morning newspaper, May 22, 1978). Although this finding was based on a very small sample of children and was somewhat speculative, it represents the consensus of at least one school of family counselors. It is resisted by Middletown's parents until, for one reason or another, they decide to divorce and need to be assured that they are not acting irresponsibly. Distress about the contemporary acceptance of divorce and yearning to revert back to the era when divorce was less acceptable and couples worked harder to make a marriage endure were expressed not only by older people who had never been divorced, but also by those who had been married recently and by a fair number of those who had been divorced recently.

In sum, divorce in the abstract is still detested. The erosion of the spiritual foundations of marriage, the emphasis on the right to pursue personal pleasure, and the community's approval of divorce are said to undermine the commitment to marriage and to encourage divorce. And there is widespread nostalgia for the values of an earlier day, when divorce was rare, difficult, and scandalous.

But, even though divorce is condemned in the abstract, there is little disapproval of those who dissolve their marriages. They are excused on various grounds, the gist of which is that it is better to end a bad marriage than to suffer through it. The operative term is "bad marriage." In the words of one respondent, "People are more honest when they end a bad marriage and give themselves the opportunity to find a more satisfying one." A syndicated columnist in Middletown's evening newspaper gave a succinct justification for a divorce as a lesser evil than a bad marriage. "It is true that the divorce rate is rising rapidly, and true that both children and adults suffer when a family breaks up. But the suffering caused by a divorce cannot compare to that of two people trapped in a destructive relationship, one from which escape is impossible" (Middletown's evening newspaper, March 9, 1978).

In relation to particular marriages—a friend's or a daughter's, for example—the ease with which a divorce can now be obtained and the absence of scandal are perceived as social improvements by the same people who condemn divorce in general. It is appropriate, if not virtuous, to end a sincerely unsatisfactory marriage, and this evaluation is not shaken by the presence of children.

Another curious aspect of easy divorce is that it is often perceived as part of a bundle of women's rights associated with economic independence. These quotations are examples of this opinion.

> Women don't have to put up with their [husbands'] crap—they can support themselves. They are free to end an unhappy marriage.

> A lot of it has to do with the freedom women are gaining. Now a woman has rights. A woman is a person, not chattel.

> Girls nowadays are more independent. They can have jobs that provide them with enough money to live alone if they want to. There was a time when a lot of women married to have someone take care of them.

> Women no longer feel they've got to be married to be accepted. Women aren't staying in a miserable situation just to say they have a husband.

As is apparent from these comments, the women's right movement is thought to increase divorce but also, in many cases, to justify it. Middletown's contented wives strongly resent the possibility that a woman might be forced to endure a cruel husband or a miserable marriage because she had no other means of support.

A few women recognized the potentially deleterious effect of a wife's emancipation on her husband. A young policeman's wife remarked thoughtfully:

> I think a lot of it is that women are getting out and working and I think the men feel threatened. They feel threatened that they are no longer the heads of the household and they are worried that while the women are out working they may find a better man. They've become insecure and suspicious.

Middletown housewives are much less likely to perceive the various ways in which women's liberation has also liberated men, especially concerning divorce. Alimony is less frequently awarded today; and, when awarded, it is generally for smaller amounts and for limited periods of time. Current legal doctrine calls for awarding alimony sufficient to allow a wife time to find employment and become self-supporting, not enough to support her indefinitely. The liberation of men is even more apparent in cases in which husbands have sued their wives for alimony. The Supreme Court's ruling that state laws forbidding awards of alimony to men were unconstitutional spurred a flurry of legal activity as men began to ask for support from their former wives.

Not long ago, the custody of children was routinely granted to the mother in cases of divorce. For custody to be granted to the father, the mother had to be proved conspicuously unfit to maintain a home for the children. About the only way a father could gain custody of his children after a divorce was to kidnap them. According to one dubious estimate, some 100,000 children are still kidnapped each year by their desperate fathers (*Marriage and Divorce Today* 1980, 1). But very recently the courts have begun to grant the custody of small children to fathers and to set the two parents on equal footing with respect to the initial determination of custody rights.

Fathers in Middletown appear to be part of this national trend. Divorced Equality for All is an organization in Middletown that is engaged in educating "men presently going through a dissolution of marriage as to their rights in terms of child custody and visitation and payment of child support" (Middletown's morning newspaper, April 26, 1978). Divorced Equality for All urges the courts to consider whether the father or the mother "is the most suitable person to have custody of the children" and assists divorced fathers who have grievances about custody in pursuing legal remedies.

Several other local organizations and programs have offered help for people dealing with the trauma of divorce. Counseling for children and parents, workshops on single-parent family life, and social activities for the recently unmarried are widely advertised. The community mental health association offers psychological counseling on how to cope with feelings of rejection and failure resulting from divorce. Middletown's university sponsored a one-day Creative Divorce Workshop in 1978, in which the social, emotional, legal, and economic effects of divorce on parents and children were discussed and suggestions were offered on how to establish a new life independent of a former spouse. During the summer months, the local chapter of Parents without Partners sponsors weekly volleyball games for single parents and their children. During June of 1978, a three-day workshop with the theme Happy Days '78 was offered by the same organization. The workshop included a seminar on assertiveness training, primarily for divorced women, to help them become more forceful in their interpersonal relationships. Drug and alcohol use was discussed in a session to which both parents and children were invited. There was a skating party, a dance, and an awards banquet on the final evening. The existence of such programs is evidence that the community has managed to normalize the status of divorced persons and their children.

Thus, Middletown both condemns and facilitates divorce. Although such attitudes and actions appear inconsistent at first glance, upon closer inspection, they seem much less so. Middletown people are thoroughly committed to marriage as a way of life, and they consider it essential for the well-being of the individual, the community, and the nation. Most of them are satisfied with their own marriages. On the other hand, they believe that, when partners are mismatched in one way or another, the marriage will be hopelessly and permanently miserable. In such cases, divorce is construed as the removal of a destructive relationship with the expectation that a more satisfactory one will be substituted. Divorce under such conditions is applauded, although there is some anxiety that too many couples use it to escape minor or solvable problems.

Family Violence

During the past four or five years, wife abuse has become a recognized social problem in the United States, complete with all the institutional paraphernalia—government programs, academic experts, journals, conferences, lobbyists—associated with other established social problems, such as drug abuse and water pollution. The attention given to the problem by journalists, officials, police officers, social workers, and activists has been interpreted by the unworldly to mean that the phenomenon is new or increasing and that it represents a further deterioration in the quality of married life. The frequency of wife abuse (or, more rarely, husband abuse) is unknown. Current estimates vary widely and appear to be based on surmise. The residents of Middletown could have found in a column by Jack Anderson an estimate that there were 3 million cases a year (Middletown's evening newspaper, February 15, 1979) or in one of the new books at the public library a more generous estimate that there were 28 million battered wives in the country (Middletown's morning newspaper, August 25, 1977). Whatever the actual number of cases, the number receiving public attention has certainly increased.

The emergence of the battered wife movement, for want of a better name, is probably not symptomatic of a decline in the quality of marriage. It seems to be another step toward the improvement of marital happiness. Conversations with police officers and social workers in Middletown suggest that wife beating has been going on for as long as they can remember but that only recently have wives called it to public attention. The women's rights movement has made women less willing to endure physical abuse from their husbands, and their growing economic independence has made it less necessary for them to do so. In some cases in which the wife obtains outside assistance, the husband accepts psychological help in controlling his emotions, and the problem disappears or is at least reduced. In other cases, abused wives are helped to escape from a physically punishing relationship.

The national trends are evident in Middletown. There are no reasonable estimates of how much wife abuse occurs in Middletown, but there was enough to justify the creation in 1977 of the Middletown County Task Force on Battered Wives, which was to make recommendations to the appropriate city and county social service agencies. A number of public meetings were held, and in 1978 a shelter for battered wives was established. The shelter was named A Better Way to emphasize that there are alternatives to enduring physical abuse from a husband. In 1979 the shelter received approximately 1,900 calls from women with abusive husbands. If the current rate continues through this year, the shelter will receive over 3,500 calls for assistance in 1980.

All things considered, the quality of marriage seems to have improved substantially in Middletown during the past half a century. Such dismal marriages as the Lynds described as typical in the 1920s are now relatively rare.

The overwhelming majority of contemporary husbands and wives say that their marriages are happy and fulfilling.

We do not mean to imply that all marriages in Middletown are happy. The data indicate that most are, but the divorce rate is a reminder that many unhappy marriages occur. Indeed, the high divorce rate is one important reason why contemporary marriages are so happy; most of the unhappy ones have been terminated. Women's employment has freed many wives from economic dependence on their husbands. The public acceptance of divorce, embodied in no-fault divorce statutes, has made divorce a viable option for many people who might formerly have been trapped in unhappy marriages. With respect to divorce, both spouses have been liberated in various ways. Alimony awards have declined; divorced wives are now expected to support themselves eventually. More fathers are claiming the opportunity to raise their children alone or with a new wife.

Divorce not only terminates the unsatisfactory marriage, it allows each unhappy partner to attempt a more satisfying marriage with someone else. The number of happily remarried persons encountered in our various surveys suggests that this procedure often works. It is not the best of all possible worlds, but it compares very nicely with the Middletown of 1935 or 1924 or 1890.

Battered Wives, Dead Husbands

Laura Meyers

Richard J. Daley was the last of the big city bosses. For 21 years he ruled Chicago and its Democratic Party Machine. And during that time supporting The Mayor (as he was known) was never a matter of conscience for most Chicagoans, but a matter of course. In one household, though, it became a matter of life and death as well.

The story is short and sad. And Richard J. Daley brought it to a climax, even if he wasn't its cause. For the husband, the fact that his wife acted contrary to his own political opinions and signed a petition in support of The Mayor was just another excuse that evening for him to beat her—a practice for which he had been finding ample excuse for years. For the wife, however, it was the last straw. Mayor Daley made no little plans, but to hear her tell it, this bruised and desperate woman made no plans at all. "After the beating,

Reprinted by permission from *Student Lawyer* Magazine, Vol. 6, No. 7 (March 1978), pp. 46-51. © 1978 American Bar Association.

he went to bed," recalls William Murphy of the Cook County Public Defender's Office, the man who later became her lawyer. "And then when he was asleep, she snuck up and clunked hell out of him with a Louisville Slugger."

Beating a man to death with a baseball bat is not a very pretty crime, but then neither is domestic violence. And while the short and sad story of husbands beating wives is enacted with horrid regularity in homes everywhere, cases like this are adding endings with bizarre O. Henry twists. "She was a nice lady and had a pattern of being beaten for years," says Murphy. Using a defense of mitigating circumstances he got her off. "The judge gave her probation," he smiles.

Such a decision may seem an affront to civilized values—murder is murder, after all. But the outcome is hardly surprising in light of several well-publicized trials of women accused of killing husbands who beat them, trials from which these women emerged scot-free or with light sentences, trials which seem to say that maybe murder *isn't* murder after all, but rather a justifiable action produced by a confluence of extreme circumstances.

In Lansing, Michigan, Francine Hughes poured gasoline around the double bed and sent her abusive husband up in flames while he slept; the verdict—justifiable homicide. In Rockford, Illinois, an eight-man, four-woman jury acquitted Bernestine Taylor of the stabbing death of her husband after the defense proved she had withstood nine years of serious physical abuse at his hands. And in Chicago over a single weekend, three separate women shot their husbands to death. All claimed that years of merciless beatings "forced" them to do it.

"You have to realize that most of the women who do this are not the feminist type," Murphy quietly cautions, refuting the canard that has made battered women a feminist *cause celebre.* "They're very unsophisticated women. And they're petrified that their husbands would beat them even if they did seek help." Nevertheless, some officials will not surrender their principles to the self-defense argument. Women, they reason, can now take the lethal initiative. And one attorney at Francine Hughes's trial declared the verdict of innocence signified "open season on men."

If so, then it is a goodly number of American males who are in trouble. Estimates of U.S. families harboring wife abuse range from a low of 3 million to a high of 40 million. No one knows how many batteries go unreported; no one knows in how many families violence is chronic. A recent study indicates that in one out of every six marriages, beatings become commonplace. Perhaps this is somewhat exaggerated, but Louis Harris says there may be some validity in that figure; a poll by his organization says 20 percent of all Americans, and 25 percent of those with college educations, condone the use of physical force within marriages.

Wife-beating is not only incredibly widespread, it often escalates into homicide, as the cases mentioned earlier on show. Familial spats result in one-fourth of all American murders, according to the FBI's Uniform Crime Reports, and love triangles account for another seven percent. While these statistics do not break things down by sexes—husbands-killing-wives and wives-killing-husbands—a 1971 California survey indicates that 52 percent of all women killed in that state meet their death at the hands of a husband or lover.

On the other hand, Cook County Deputy State's Attorney Kenneth Gillis claims that the majority of husband-killings by wives are "victim precipitated." That is, the abusers become eventual homicide victims by pushing their women too hard, inevitably forcing them to a homicidal conclusion. Indeed, a survey of Cook County's jail found that 40 percent of all women held for homicide at the facility were accused of killing their husbands or boyfriends after the men battered them.

One of the women held there is Billie Shropshire. Hers is a particularly traumatic case; she feared for her life and her children's. She moved three times to escape the harassment of her ex-boyfriend, but he was determined. He followed them everywhere—slashed her tires, waited for the kids after school, stood below their apartment window at night brandishing what appeared to be a shotgun to her head. Once he held a knife to the woman's throat; another time a gun. Of course, the scenario also included regular beatings.

Billie reported her tormentor to the police, took him to court, but nothing could daunt him. Finally, she took the law into her own hands and shot him.

"It was a classic case of self-defense," says one public defender, "—except for the last minute and a half." Billie Shropshire did not get off like Francine Hughes. Instead she got murder.

There are those who argue that Billie Shropshire did indeed act in self-defense, all the way up to and *through* that last moment. Despite the fact that her life was not in immediate danger, she shot her assailant because she had no alternative. Her comparative physical weakness, her inability to act during the repeated beatings and abuse, her constant terror, all these add up to a new concept of self-defense propounded by some feminist lawyers. "The perspective we have now of self-defense is a law shaped by men and it must now include the experience of women," contends Liz Schneider of New York's Center for Constitutional Rights. "More women are asserting that [killing] was necessary for their survival."

Bunk, says Thomas Tyrell, a former policeman, now a public defender. "The concept of self-defense is so basic to civilized society. It allows for a man to preserve his own life and only to take the life of another when his own life is in imminent danger. To in any way advocate, even tacitly, that someone should use deadly force at any other time than the time when his life is in immediate danger, to allow a time lag, would be to condone murder."

And more than a few female attorneys agree. Prosecutor Marcia Orr asks, "Why are women now claiming more lenient laws in self-defense, when they are claiming equality in every other area? It sets women apart as a weaker sex. If you're going to be equal, you can't take refuge in a status you don't want." Assistant State's Attorney Patricia Bobb agrees and recalls her frustration when a woman was acquitted of murdering her *third* husband. "Being a woman is much more of an advantage. I think women usually get a pass in the system. And what really gets me is women who stick around and get beaten by their husbands, for whatever reason." In Bobb's view, those women acquire "an assumption of risk" which later supersedes any claim of self-defense.

In part, their differences are an attitudinal gap. Independent women, particularly professionally trained, take-charge types like Orr and Bobb, simply cannot imagine themselves caught in an abusive, demeaning relationship. They cannot place themselves in the shoes of a woman who feels her only option is to sneak up on her unsuspecting husband and do him in with a baseball bat. It is outside their probable experience, and so it is outside their capacity for understanding.

But there are women who do feel trapped in situations like these, and worse. And why they stay there goes beyond a question of simple economics—though not many battered women have means of supporting themselves independently. In many cases, these women have no friends or contacts outside their homes. They do not know how to improve their lot, or that the law can help them.

The sort of women who are battered beyond their limits of endurance and ultimately resort to murder are women peculiarly alone. When they succeed at killing their oppressor, their methods are often random and crude: baseball bats, immolation and the like (see sidebar). And when they fail, rarely do they even carry that off with much more finesse. Such a woman is Mary McGuire, currently serving a five-year sentence in the Oregon Women's Correctional Center for soliciting someone to kill her husband. In a way, however, she did succeed. She removed herself from her hostile environment, albeit by throwing herself into another. But most impressive is her ability now to articulate her fears, to give a voice to the mute battered woman:

"I know the horrors of beating; of being shot at and pistol-whipped; of being tied up to watch while my grave was being dug; of having my husband hold a gun to my child's head demanding obedience and threatening to pull the trigger; of trying to prevent my 12-year-old daughter from being raped by my husband, while Father laughs and states, 'I am king of this house and can do as I damn well please.' I and my children have received many beatings. I have cigarette burns on my arms, a broken nose, cracked chest and ribs, a concussion and a cracked pelvic bone. My children were terrorized by their father's attempt to run over my 4-year-old son, and by his act of beheading our pet horse.

"I tried separation but was brought back to the house at gunpoint. He has told me repeatedly that neither my children nor myself would ever be free from him and that he would stop at nothing to destroy us. . . .

"Intolerable isolation, extreme fear and a desperate need for help are the realities of my life."

McGuire notes that law enforcement officials told her that she is the cause of her own problems, and that they could not intervene in domestic conflicts. Small wonder, then, she thinks, that she took the step she did. "What is the difference then whether [a battered woman] goes to the law or takes her and her children's lives into her own hands?"

But in an indirect way, battered women may be a partial cause of their own problems, according to one psychiatrist. Severe psychological dynamics are commonly present in very abused women, says Dr. Anne Seiden of the Illinois Mental Health Department. "A woman who is grossly abused," she says, "generally develops a feeling of herself as a worthless person. The more she takes it, the more worthless she feels."

Seiden describes a pattern of pathological compliance with physical brutality—a pattern that indicates psychological problems making the women compliant to violence in the first place. "These women are pathetically oriented to 'being good.' If someone tells them what to do, they will comply. They have a very unstable sense of self, so they feel good only when they are pleasing someone else. That's partly what makes them appear as 'good girls' to the outside world, and partly why they put up with the beatings."

In Seiden's view, the women strike back finally and only after repeated abuse are the type of persons who could argue innocence under the insanity defense. In all too many cases, she has found, they understand little of their actions, but rather take on the characteristics of a borderline psychotic. (In one instance the doctor recalls, the woman testified she heard voices spurring her on, telling her to "do it, do it, do it." She emerged after the attack from an almost trance-like state, disoriented about the time, place and immediate past.) However, when the situation of stress is relieved—the attack is committed—these women's disordered and unusual behavior disappears. The women return to acting very normally, usually exceptionally agreeable and conforming. (In fact, in the case of the woman who heard voices, the attorney confided to Seiden that he felt guilty pleading the insanity defense when his client behaved so unlike "a crazy person.")

For many of these same reasons, battered women often receive the short shrift in their dealings with police officers and prosecutors. These officials complain that women in domestic-violence situations are seldom "serious" in their charges and are quick not to follow through—a complaint that is disturbingly true.

Couples in abusive relationships can easily fall into a three-stage cycle of love-tension-explosion. By the time a case comes to court, the explosion may be over and the love real. Psychologist Marlene Grossman explains, "Even a man who is abusive is not abusive 100 percent of the time. There are times when the relationship seems very warm and supportive of the woman."

Good experiences are the norm in such relationships, despite recurring violence. During the tension-building stages, the husband becomes irritable and verbally assaults the woman. Her response—harkening back to Seiden's version of these women as "good girls"—is to adopt a peacemaker stance, even at her own expense. The irritation, however, does not subside, and ultimately explodes in a beating.

At this climactic point, Grossman notes, the tension dissipates. The husband becomes tender and loving in a reconciliation effort. He sincerely believes that what he did makes no sense to him, and he doesn't plan to do it again. The woman tends to look at his loving behavior and agree that his badness isn't the "real" him.

As a result, the woman, who may have in a moment of pain reported her mate to the police, now doesn't want to press charges. She doesn't want her lover in jail, so she fails to show in court. She doesn't want to be rid of him, so she doesn't initiate divorce proceedings. "What she really wants," says Grossman, "is to set their marriage right. It sometimes takes five or six beatings for her to be convinced that only counselling and legal remedies can make this relationship right."

Intercepting abused women when they reach this stage—and not after they have crossed the final threshold and murdered their husbands—is the goal of Chicago's Legal Center for Battered Women, the organization that Grossman is affiliated with and one of several newly created legal-service agencies designed to stem this growing problem. It is the Center's goal and that of its many volunteers, two dozen of whom have gathered on a bitterly cold winter morning inside a dreary downtown office to learn what they can do to help.

Sitting in mismatched chairs arranged in a haphazard circle, women aged 18 to 50 clutch legal pads to their breasts and take notes as the learn how to tackle the criminal courts on behalf of battered women. Hardly the least of the pains inflicted upon abused wives is the morass of a "very alienating, very dominated" court system, the Center says. And these women here today are training to help women through it, training to become "victim advocates," lay persons who can counsel and guide confused and hurt women through the courts.

"It's terribly important," Grossman tells the group, "when a woman does decide to take on the courts, that she have a lot of support; that that woman has another woman with her who understands, who doesn't think she's crazy. Women are constantly running into people who tell them it is their fault. A woman who is going to court has not only been abused by her husband; she's been abused by her encounters with the police, and she's had a hard time with some friends or family who tell her, 'You made your bed, now lie in it.'"

"We want women to be able to admit, 'I have been battered,' without shame," says Candace Wayne, director of the Center. In turning to criminal remedies, battered women attempt to put the threat of punishment or the hope of court-ordered counselling before their spouses. But all too often the police refuse to arrest, state's attorneys refuse to prosecute and judges refuse to invoke criminal sanctions. In many ways, it is a process that shames women into submission.

"The legal system has in its own way perpetuated abuse by not responding and not recognizing battered women as an issue," says Wayne. "We're talking about family violence. They're defined in police terms as 'domestic disturbances.' That's a misnomer. These are domestic *violence* cases."

One mission of the Center when it was founded by Chicago's Legal Assistance Foundation and the Chicago Community Trust was to spur recognition of domestic violence as a crime, and not merely silly threats by wives who want to scare their husbands. But since the Center's beginning in October of 1977, the lawyers have had little cooperation toward this end from judges, who, Wayne says, often make rude and stupid remarks to victims of domestic battery. One judge she cites asked a woman if she had been faithful; another queried whether a woman had been beaten by her husband before, and when she answered yes, commented, "Then you must like to get beaten up."

Despite such judicial callousness, the Center is but one example of a national trend toward encouraging enforcement of those domestic-violence laws already on the books. In Chicago specifically, police guidelines allow much less officer discretion in making battery arrests. Any use of a weapon, any intentionally inflicted serious injury, and any prior injury, court appearance or calls to the police—all require immediate arrest, according to that city's *Training Bulletin.*

And among the more creative legal solutions to the wife-beating problem is a court-ordered lawsuit in New York. The suit, which is currently awaiting trial, charges that the police department and Family Court officials violated the rights of battered women in that city by refusing to enforce wife-abuse laws. The plaintiffs represent New York and Kings counties' married women whose husbands commit crimes against them, and who seek police and/or judicial protection that is not forthcoming.

"The violence against [battered women] is not a result of isolated acts," reads the suit, "but rather reflects a societal pattern of male violence against women. As the problem is deep and widespread, so is defendants' failure to respond to it. The legal remedies provided for by the system of justice must be enforced."

A grim tale of judicial and police non-response to wife-battery unfolds in the cases cited in the New York suit. Carmen Bruno alleges that police ran into her apartment while her husband was still hitting her. The officers had to pry his hands from her neck and her face was bleeding from what have since become permanent scars, and still they refused to arrest him.

Susan Borowsky, separated from her husband for two years and paying rent on an apartment leased under her own name, was forced to leave her home after her husband broke in and police refused to arrest or evict him.

Lydia Thomas claims she was punched in the face until she blacked out. On another occasion, her husband hit her and threw her to the floor, but despite facial bruising and swelling, and despite a court order of protection, police officers would not arrest Mr. Thomas. One policeman, according to the suit, said, "You've been taking this for a long time now. You'll get over this."

Justice Abraham J. Gellicoff, the judge who ordered the trial, explained his reasoning: "For too long, Anglo-American law treated a man's physical abuse of his wife as different from any other assault, and indeed as an acceptable practice.... If the allegations of the complaint—buttressed by hundreds of pages of affidavits—are true, only the written law has changed; in reality, wife-beating is still condoned, if not approved, by some of those charged with protecting its victims."

Such tacit approval of wife-beating hangs over all our heads, insists Wayne of Chicago's Center. "It's not just a woman's problem, it's society's problem. We all live in a society plagued by violence." We all remember the horrifying instance of Kitty Genovese, the young New York woman killed in the early 1960s as dozens watched and none sprang to her aid. But how many remember that when bystanders were asked later why they did not help, many responded they thought her attacker was her husband?

"I don't think the legal system can change historical and societal attitudes in a short time," Wayne continues. "But if the legal system says this kind of behavior is criminal, although it does not deter every man in every case, it does set up a standard."

Right now, those values ignore women who have established a conjugal relationship with a man who beats her. Ignores them, that is, until they take matters into their own hands—something that, if matters had been handled properly from the start, they would not have had to do.

"The entire criminal-justice system regards the female victim of abuse as a second-class victim" writes James Bannon, executive deputy chief of the Detroit Police Department. "She is treated more as a 'leper' than anything else.

"She embarrasses the system and, judging from community reactions, the society as well. In fact, she is accorded the same type of treatment reserved for those with some form of social disease who have become ill due to their own vice.

"We turn our heads and close our ears to her screams."

Chapter 7

Divorce and Remarriage

The Transformation of Legal Marriage Through No-Fault Divorce

Lenore J. Weitzman* and Ruth B. Dixon**

Introduction

Divorce and family breakdown constitute one of the major social problems in the United States today. In 1975 alone over 3 million men, women and minor children were involved in a divorce.[1] In the future it is likely that one-third to one-half of all the adults in the United States, and close to one-third of the minor children under 18 will be affected by a divorce or dissolution.[2] These data reflect not only the numerical importance of divorce, but its increased social significance as well. While divorce may have been considered a "deviant family pattern" in the past, it is rapidly becoming accepted as a possible (though not yet a probable) outcome of marriage.

Since 1970 there has been a major reform in divorce law which attempts to institutionalize fundamental social changes in family patterns. Commonly referred to as no-fault divorce, this new legislation seeks to alter the definition of marriage, the relationship between husbands and wives, and the economic and social obligations of former spouses to each other and to their children after divorce.

In 1970, California instituted the first no-fault divorce law in the United States. Since then fourteen other states have adopted "pure" no-fault divorce

Published for the first time in the third edition of *Family in Transition* and reprinted in this edition by permission of the authors. Copyright © 1980 by Lenore J. Weitzman and Ruth B. Dixon.

We are indebted to our co-investigator Professor Herma Hill Kay for her continued advice and collaboration on the California Divorce Law Research Project. We would also like to thank Jerome H. Skolnick and William J. Goode for their valuable comments on an earlier draft of this paper. This research was supported by NIMH grant #MH-27617-02 and National Science Foundation Grant G1-39218

*Department of Sociology and Center for Research on Women, Stanford University, Stanford, CA 94305.

**Department of Sociology, University of California, Davis, CA 95616.

laws[3] and an additional thirteen states have added no-fault grounds to their existing grounds for divorce.[4] No-fault divorce has been praised as the embodiment of "modern" and "enlightened" law, and heralded as the forerunner of future family law in the United States. It has also been strongly attacked for "destroying the family" and for causing irreparable harm to women. This paper aims at analyzing the effects of this new legislation on both marriage and divorce.

The laws governing divorce tell us how a society defines marriage and where it sets the boundaries for appropriate marital behavior. One can generally examine the way a society defines marriage by examining its provisions for divorce, for it is at the point of divorce that a society has the opportunity to reward the marital behavior it approves of, and to punish spouses who have violated its norms.[5] In addition, in virtually all societies which allow divorce, it is assumed that people who were once married continue to have obligations to each other; and these obligations reflect the rights and duties of marriage itself.

This paper is divided into three sections. It begins with a discussion of traditional legal marriage followed by a review of traditional divorce law. The last section examines the aims of the no-fault legislation and its implications for traditional family roles.

Traditional Legal Marriage

The origins of Anglo-American family law[6] may be traced to the tenth or eleventh century, when Christianity became sufficiently influential in Britain to enable the Church to assert its rules effectively. (Clark, 1968: 281). Traditionally legal marriage was firmly grounded in the Christian conception of marriage as a holy union between a man and woman. Marriage was a sacrament, a commitment to join together for life: "to take each other to love and to cherish, in sickness and in health, for better, for worse, until death do us part."

The nature of the marital relationship, and the legal responsibilities of the spouses were specified by law—by statute, case law and common law. While a thorough analysis of legal marriage is obviously beyond the scope of this paper (but see Clark, 1968; Kay, 1974; Weitzman, 1979), five important features may be briefly summarized as follows: First, legal marriage was limited to a single man and a single woman; bigamy, polygamy and homosexual unions were prohibited. Second, legal marriage was monogamous. The spouses were to remain sexually faithful to each other and adultery was explicitly prohibited. Third, marriage was for procreation. One of the major objects of matrimony was the bearing and rearing of (legitimate) children. (Reynolds v. Reynolds, 1862)

Fourth, legal marriage established a hierarchical relationship between the spouses: the husband was the head of the family, with his wife and children subordinate to him. The husband's authority was based on the common-law doctrine of coverture which established the legal fiction that a husband and wife took a single legal identity upon marriage—the identity of the husband. At common law a married woman became a *femme covert*, a legal nonperson, under her husband's arm, protection and cover. (Blackstone, 1765)

Although most of the disabilities of coverture were removed by the Married Women's Property Acts in the nineteenth century—the common-law assumption that the husband was the head of the family remained firmly embodied in statutory and case law in the United States. The married woman's subordination was most clearly reflected in rules governing her domicile and name. In both cases the married woman assumed her husband's identity—taking his name and his domicile as her own. This basic assumption of traditional legal marriage has, of course, been challenged in recent years.

The fifth, and most important feature of traditional legal marriage, was its sex-based division of family roles and responsibilities. The woman was to devote herself to being a wife, homemaker and mother in return for her husband's promise of lifelong support. The husband was given the sole responsibility for the family's financial welfare, while he was assured that his home, his children, and his social-emotional well-being would be cared for by his wife. Professor Homer Clark, a noted authority on family law, summarizes the legal obligations of the two spouses as follows:

> Specifically, the courts say that the husband has a duty to support his wife, that she has a duty to render services in the home, and that these duties are reciprocal. . . . The husband is to provide the family with food, clothing, shelter and as many of the amenities of life as he can manage, either (in earlier days) by the management of his estates, or (more recently) by working for wages or a salary. The wife is to be mistress of the household, maintaining the home with resources furnished by the husband, and caring for children. A reading of contemporary judicial opinions leaves the impression that these roles have not changed over the last two hundred years. (Clark, 1968: 181)

All states, even those with community property systems, placed the burden of the family support on the husband; he was legally responsible for providing necessitites for his wife and his children. Similarly, all states made the wife responsible for domestic and child care services: her legal obligation was to be a companion, housewife and mother. As one court enumerated the services a man could legally expect from his wife:

> (she had a duty) to be his helpmate, to love and care for him in such a role, to afford him her society and her person, to protect and care for him in sickness, and to labor faithfully to advance his interest . . . (she must also perform) her household and domestic duties . . . A husband is entitled to the benefit of his wife's industry and economy. (Rucci v. Rucci, 1962: 127)

The wife was also assigned responsibility for child care, both during marriage and after divorce, as the law viewed her as the "natural and proper" caretaker of the young.

While no one would claim that the law was responsible for the traditional division of labor in the family, it did serve to legitimate, sanction, and reinforce these traditional family roles. For example, the law reinforced the wife's subordinate status—and her economic dependency—by defining the husband as the only person who was responsible for (and capable of) supporting the family. (Kay, 1974).

By promising the housewife lifelong support, the law provided a disincentive for women to develop their economic capacity and to work in the paid labor force. In addition, by making them legally responsible for domestic and child care services, it reinforced the primacy of these activities in their lives, leaving them with neither time nor incentive to develop careers outside of the home.

The law similarly reinforced the traditional male role by directing the husband away from domestic and childcare activities. While the law did legitimate the husband's power and authority in the family, it also encouraged a single-minded dedication to work, and to earning a living, for it made it clear that his sole responsibility was his family's economic welfare.

Traditional Divorce Law

Since marriage was regarded as an indissoluble union, it could be ended only by the death of one of the parties. (Rhinestein, 1972) "Divorce, in the modern sense of a judicial decree dissolving a valid marriage, and allowing one or both partners to remarry during the life of the other, did not exist in England until 1857." (Kay, 1970: 221)[7]

A rare exception, originating in the late 17th century, allowed divorce (on the sole ground of adultery) by special act of Parliament. As a practical matter, however, few of these divorces were granted—and they were available only to the very rich, and to men. (Clark, 1968: 281). The Church also permitted divorce *a mensa et thoro,* literally a divorce from bed and board, which allowed the parties to live apart. But this legal separation did not sever the marital bond.

The Ecclesiastical Courts retained their exclusive jurisdiction over marriage and divorce in England until 1857, when divorce jurisdiction was transferred to the Civil Court System, and divorces were authorized for adultery. But the underlying premise of divorce law remained the same: Marriage was still regarded as a permanent and cherished union which the Church—and then the state—had to protect and preserve. And it was still assumed that the holy bond of matrimony would best be protected by restricting access to divorce. As Clark observed:

> (They believed) that marital happiness is best secured by making marriage indissoluble except for very few causes. When the parties know that they are bound together for life, the argument runs, they will resolve their differences and disagreements and make an effort to get along with each other. If they

are able to separate legally upon less serious grounds, they will make no such effort, and immorality will result. (Clark, 1968: 242–43)

It should also be noted that these early divorce laws established a different standard for men and women: "wives . . . could obtain a divorce only if the husband's adultery was aggravated by bigamy, cruelty or incest, while the husband could get his divorce for adultery alone." (Clark, 1969: 282)[8]

Divorce laws in the United States were heavily influenced by the English tradition. In the middle and southern Colonies, divorces were granted by the legislature, and were rare. However, New England allowed divorce more freely. The Protestant doctrines (and the absence of any system of Ecclesiastical Courts) resulted in statutes which authorized divorce for adultery, desertion, and, in some cases, cruelty—sometimes by the courts and sometimes by acts of the Legislature.

Although some diversity in the divorce laws of the states continued, in nineteenth century most states gave the courts the jurisdiction to dissolve marriages on specified grounds (Kay, 1968: 221), and by 1900 most states had adopted what we shall refer to as the four major elements of traditional divorce laws.

First, *traditional divorce law perpetuated the sex-based division of roles and responsibilities in traditional legal marriage.* As we noted above, in legal marriage the woman presumably agreed to devote herself to being a wife, homemaker and mother in return for her husband's promise of lifelong support. Although traditional family law assumed that the husband's support would be provided in a lifelong marriage, if the marriage did not endure, and if the wife was virtuous, she was nevertheless guaranteed alimony—a means of continued support. Alimony perpetuated the husband's responsibility for economic support, and the wife's right to be supported in return for her domestic services. It thus maintained the reciprocity in the legal marriage contract.

Traditional divorce laws also perpetuated the sex-based division of roles with respect to children: the husband remained responsible for their economic support, the wife for their care. All states, by statute or by case law tradition, gave preference to the wife as the appropriate custodial parent after the divorce; and all states gave the husband the primary responsibility for their economic support.

Second, *traditional divorce law required grounds for divorce.* Divorce could be obtained only if one party committed a marital offense, giving the other a legal basis or ground for the divorce. Since marriage was supposed to be a permanent lifelong union, only serious marital offenses such as adultery, cruelty, or desertion could justify a divorce. As Professor Herma Hill Kay explains:

> The state's interest in marital stability, thus delegated to the courts, was to be guarded by the judge's diligence in requiring that evidence clearly established the ground relied on for a divorce, that the defendant had no valid defense to the plaintiff's suit, and that the parties had not conspired to put on a false case. (Kay, 1970: 221)

The standards for judging appropriate grounds also reflected the sex-typed expectations of traditional legal marriage. While the almost ritualistic "evidence" of misbehavior varied from state to state, husbands charged with cruelty were often alleged to have caused their wives bodily harm, while wives charged with cruelty, were more typically charged with neglecting their husbands (showing lack of affection, belittling him); or their homes (leaving the home in disarray, neglecting dinner), impuning their husband's self-respect or reputation (denigrating or insulting him in front of business associates or friends); or ignoring their wifely duties (what Clark calls the country club syndrome in which the wife "is entirely preoccupied with club and social life, is extravagant, drinks heavily, and wholly disregards the husband's desires for affection and comfort.") (Clark, 1968: 349).

Cruelty was the most commonly used grounds for divorce followed by desertion, which accounted for less than 18% of all divorces (Jacobson, 1959: 124). Adultery was rarely used outside of New York, where it was the only permissible ground for divorce until 1967. While the standards for desertion also varied from state to state, two sex-based standards were common to most: (1) If a wife refused to live in the domicile chosen by her husband, she was held responsible for desertion in the divorce action. In addition, if the husband moved and she refused to accompany him, *she* was considered to have deserted *him*, since he had the legal right to choose the family home. She would then be the guilty party in the divorce, and that had important economic consequences which are discussed below. Second, a spouse's withdrawal from his or her marital roles might be considered desertion, and the standards for these withdrawals were clearly sex-typed. For example, a wife who showed "lack of affection" for the husband, had a relationship with another man (but did not commit adultery), refused to do housework, and nagged the husband, would be guilty of desertion (see, for example, Anton v. Anton, 1955) but a husband who acted in a similar fashion would not—unless he also stopped supporting his wife financially.

Over time, in actual practice many divorcing couples privately agreed to an uncontested divorce where one party, usually the wife, would take the *pro forma* role of plaintiff. Supported by witnesses, she would attest to her husband's cruel conduct and he would not challenge her testimony. But even if these allegations involved collusion and perjury, as many of them did, the type of behavior reported as grounds for divorce nevertheless reflected what the courts considered "appropriate violations" of the marriage contract. The husband, supposed to support and protect his wife, was sanctioned for nonsupport and physical abuse. The wife, obligated to care for her home and husband, was sanctioned for neglecting her domestic responsibilities.

Third, traditional legal divorce *was based on adversary proceedings.* The adversary process required that one party be guilty, or responsible for the divorce, and that the other be innocent. The plaintiff's success in obtaining a divorce depended on his or her ability to prove the defendant's fault for having committed some marital offense. Divorces had to be "won" by the innocent party against the guilty party. As the Tennessee Supreme Court (Brown v. Brown, 1955: 498) stated "divorce is conceived as a remedy for the innocent against the guilty." If a spouse who was found guilty could prove the other was also at fault, or that the other had colluded in or condoned their behavior, the divorce thus might not be granted in order to punish both parties.

Finally, traditional divorce law *linked the financial terms of the divorce to the determination of fault.* Being found "guilty" or "innocent" in the divorce action had important financial consequences.

For example, alimony, or a "suitable allowance for support and maintenance" could be awarded only to the *innocent* spouse "for his or her life, or for such shorter periods as the courts may deem "just" as a judgment *against* the guilty spouse. (California Civil Code 139). Thus a wife found guilty of adultery was typically barred from receiving alimony, while a husband found guilty of adultery or cruelty could be ordered to pay for his transgressions with alimony and property. And many attorneys believed that justice was served by using alimony as a lever against a promiscuous husband, or as a reward for a virtuous wife. As Eli Bronstein, a New York matrimonial lawyer, put it: "If a woman has been a tramp, why reward her? By the same token, if the man is alley-catting around town, shouldn't his wife get all the benefits she had as a married woman?" (Wheeler, 1974: 57)

Property awards were similarly linked to fault. In most states, the court had to award more than half of the property to the "innocent" or "injured" party.[9] This standard easily led to heated accusations and counter–accusations of wrongs in order to obtain a better property settlement. (Hogoboom, 1971: 687) It also allowed a spouse who did not want a divorce to use the property award as a lever in the negotiations. In practice, since the husband was more likely to be the party who wanted the divorce, the wife was more likely to assume the role of the innocent plaintiff (Friedman and Percival, 1976: 77); and she was therefore more likely to be awarded a greater share of the property. Of course, the proportion of her share (and the extent of the inequality) was related to both the amount and type of property involved: significantly unequal awards were most likely to occur in cases in which the only family asset was the house, as the (innocent) wife was typically awarded the family home. (Weitzman, Kay & Dixon, 1979)

Custody awards could also be influenced by findings of fault. A woman found guilty of adultery or cruelty might be deprived of her preference as the custodial parent—especially if her behavior indicated that she was an "unfit" mother.[10]

By linking both the granting of the divorce and the financial settlements to findings of fault, the law gave the "aggrieved" spouse, particularly an "innocent" wife who wanted to stay married, a considerable advantage in the financial negotiations. In return for her agreement to the divorce, her husband was typically willing to be the guilty defendant (in a noncontested divorce) and to give her, as the innocent plaintiff, alimony and more than half of the property.

In summary, traditional divorce law helped sanction the spouses' roles and responsibilities in marriage—by both punishment and reward. On the negative side, if a wife was found guilty of adultery, cruelty or desertion, she would have to pay for her wrongdoings by being denied alimony (and sometimes custody and property as well). And if the husband was at fault, he would be "punished" through awards of property, alimony and child support to his ex-wife.

On the positive side, traditional divorce law promised "justice" for those who fulfilled their marital obligations. It guaranteed support for the wife who devoted herself to her family, thus reinforcing the desirability and legitimacy of the wife's role as homemaker, and the husband's role as supporter. And it assured the husband that he would not have to support a wife who betrayed or failed him. Justice in this system was the assurance that the marriage contract will be honored. If not, the "bad" spouse would be punished, the "good" spouse rewarded, and the husband's obligation to support his wife (if she was good) enforced.

No–Fault Divorce

In 1970 California instituted the first law in the Western world to abolish completely any requirement of fault as the basis for marital dissolution. (Hogoboom, 1971). The no-fault law provided for a divorce upon *one* party's assertion that "irreconcilable differences have caused the irremediable breakdown of the marriage." In establishing the new standards for marital dissolution, the California State Legislature sought to eliminate the adversarial nature of divorce and thereby to reduce the hostility, acrimony and trauma characteristic of fault-oriented divorce.

The California no-fault divorce law marked the beginning of a nationwide trend toward legal recognition of "marital breakdown" as a sufficient justification for divorce. The new law not only eliminated the need for evidence of misconduct; it eliminated the concept of fault itself. And it thereby abolished the notion of interpersonal justice in divorce. With this seemingly simple move, the California legislature dramatically altered the legal definition of the reciprocal rights of husbands and wives during marriage and after its dissolution.

Proponents of the divorce law reform had several aims. They sought to eliminate the hypocrisy, perjury and collusion "required by courtroom practice under the fault system" (Kay, 1968: 1223); to reduce the adversity, acrimony and bitterness surrounding divorce proceedings; to lessen the personal stigma attached to the divorce; and to create conditions for more rational and equitable settlements of property and spousal support. (Hogoboom, 1970; Kay, 1970; Krom, 1970) In brief, the new law attempted to bring divorce legislation into line with the social realities of marital breakdown in contemporary society. It recognized that marital conduct and misconduct no longer fit rigid categories of fault. And it eliminated the punitive element of moral condemnation that had pervaded Western thought for centuries.

The no-fault legislation changed each of the four basic elements in traditional divorce law. First, *it eliminated the fault-based grounds for divorce.* No longer did one spouse have to testify to the other's adultery, cruelty or desertion. And no longer were witnesses necessary to corroborate their testimony.

By replacing the old fault-based grounds for divorce with a single new standard of "irreconcilable differences," the legislature sought to eliminate both the artificial grounds for the breakdown of a marriage, and the artificial conception that one party was "responsible" for the breakdown. Further, the criterion of "irreconcilable differences" recognized that whatever the reasons for marital failure, they were best left out of the proceedings because they were irrelevant to an equitable settlement. Now the divorce procedure could begin with a neutral "petition for dissolution," with no specific acts or grounds needed as a justification.

Second, *the new laws eliminated the adversary process.* Divorce reformers believed that at least some of the trauma of a fault-based divorce resulted from the legal process itself, rather than from the inherent difficulties of dissolving a marriage. (See, for example, Rheinstein, 1972.) They assumed that husbands and wives who were dissolving their marriage were potentially "amicable," but that the *legal process generated hostility and trauma* by forcing them to be antagonists. The reformers assumed that if fault and the adversary process were eliminated from the legal proceedings, "human beings who are entitled to divorces could get them with the least possible amount of damage to themselves and to their families" (Proceedings from the California Assembly Committee on the Judiciary, 1964).

Each aspect of the legal process was therefore changed to reflect the new non-adversary approach to divorce: "Divorce" became "dissolution"; "plaintiffs" and "defendants" became "petitioners" and "respondents"; "alimony" became "spousal support"; and the court records read "*in re* the Marriage of Doe" instead of "Doe vs. Doe."[11] Standard printed forms written in plain English replaced the archaic legalistic pleadings. Residence requirements were reduced from one year to six months in the state before filing, and the minimum period between filing and the final decree was shortened from one year to six months. These revisions were designed in part to smooth the progress of a marital dissolution through the courts and to avoid some of the unnecessary legal wrangling and personal hostilities engendered by the adversarial model.

Third, *the financial aspects of the divorce were to be based on equity, equality, and economic need* rather than on either fault or sex-based role assignments. Proponents of no-fault divorce contended that it was outmoded to grant alimony and property as a reward for virtue, and to withhold them as punishment for wrongdoing. Instead, they advocated more realistic standards for alimony and property awards—standards based on the spouses' economic circumstances and a new principal of equality between the sexes. They argued that justice for both the wife and the husband would be better served by considering their economic situations, rather than by weighing their guilt or innocence. And they believed that men and women should no longer be shackled by the weight of traditional sex roles; new norms were necessary to bring the law into line with modern social reality.

With regard to the new economic criteria for awards, the no-fault law aimed at making the financial aspects of the divorce more equitable to facilitate the post-divorce adjustment of both men and women. Substantively, guidelines for financial settlements were changed to remove evidence of misconduct from consideration. For example, while alimony under the old law could only be awarded to the "injured party," regardless of that person's financial need, under the new law, it was to be based on the financial needs and financial resources of both spouses.

With regard to the new norm of equality between the sexes, the advocates of the divorce law reform pointed to the changing position of women in general, and to their increased participation in the labor force in particular, and urged a reformulation of alimony and property awards which recognized the growing ability of women to be self-supporting. With a reformist zeal they assumed that the employment gains of women had already eliminated the need for alimony as a means of continued support after divorce. Ignoring the fact that even full-time year-round female workers earn less than 60 percent of what men earn, some advocates went so far as to declare that "it does seem somewhat anachronistic, in an era of increasing feminine [sic] equality, that the statutes providing for alimony have remained on the books for as long as they have" (Brody, 1070: 228).

The legislators also challenged the anachronistic assumption that the husband had to continue to support his wife—for life. They pointed to the difficulty that men face in supporting two households if they remarry, and argued that the old law had converted "a host of physically and mentally competent young women into an army of alimony drones who neither toil nor spin and become a drain on society and a menace to themselves." (Hofstadter and Levittan, 1967: 55). Thus while the reformers were willing to consider support for the older housewife, they did not believe that the younger housewife deserved continued support; instead they saw her as a potential "alimony drone" who ought to be self-supporting.

Under the new law, California judges setting alimony are directed to consider "the circumstances of the respective parties, including the duration of the marriage, and the ability of the supported spouse to engage in gainful employment without interfering with the interests of the children of the parties in the custody of each spouse." (Civil Code 4801). California's no-fault divorce law is thus typical of new alimony legislation: It is concerned primarily with financial criteria and, while it specifically mentions the custodial spouse and the wife in a marriage of long duration, the thrust of the law is to encourage the divorced woman to become self-supporting (by engaging in gainful employment.)

The implicit aim of the new alimony was to encourage (some would say force) formerly dependent wives to assume the responsibility for their own support. With the elimination of fault as the basis for alimony, the new standard explicitly excluded the granting of support awards to women just because they had been wives, or just because their husbands had left them, or just because they had spent years as homemakers. The new law recognized, in theory, the need for transitional support, support for the custodial parent, and support for the older housewife who could not become self-supporting.

Property awards under no-fault are also to be based on equity and equality and are no longer limited to findings of fault. For example, in California the community property *must be divided equally.* [12] Underlying the new law is a conception of marriage as a partnership, with each person having made an equal contribution to the community property and therefore deserving an equal share.

The standards for child custody also reflect the new equality between the spouses. The preference for the mother (for children of tender years) has been replaced by a sex-neutral standard which instructs judges to award custody in the "best interests of the child." [13] Finally, the new law makes both husbands and wives responsible for child support.

Fourth, *no-fault divorce re-defined the traditional responsibilities of husbands and wives by instituting a new norm of equality between the sexes.*

Instead of the old sex-typed division of family responsibilities the new law has attempted to institutionalize sex-neutral obligations which fall equally upon the husband and the wife. No longer is the husband the head of the family —both spouses are now presumed to be equal partners in the marriage. Nor is the husband alone responsible for support, or the wife alone obligated to care for the home and children.

Each of the provisions of the new law discussed above reflect these new assumptions about appropriate spousal roles. The new standards for alimony indicate that a woman is no longer supposed to devote herself to her home and family—rather, she now bears an equal responsibility for her own economic support. For the law has clearly established a new norm of economic self-sufficiency for the divorced woman. Similarly, the new standards indicate that men will no longer be held responsible for their wives (and ex-wives) lifelong support.

The criterion for dividing property also reflects the new norm of equality between the sexes. There is no preference or protection for the older housewife —or, even for the custodial mother (although some states do have a preference for the custodial parent to retain the family home while the children are living there). Instead, the two spouses are treated equally—each one receives an equal share of the property.

Finally, the expectations for child support are sex-neutral. Both parents are equally responsible for the financial welfare of their children after divorce. What was previously considered the husband's responsibility is now shared equally by the wife.

In summary, traditional divorce law and no-fault reflect two contrasting visions of "justice." The traditional law sought to deliver a moral justice which rewarded the good spouse and punished the bad spouse. It was a justice based on compensation for *past* behavior, both sin and virtue. The no-fault law ignores both moral character and moral history as a basis for awards. Instead it seeks to deliver a fairness and equity based on the financial *needs* and upon equality of the two parties.

The law is based on the assumption that divorced women can be immediately self-supporting. This assumption stands in contrast to the Uniform Marriage and Divorce Act which specifies that the court should consider the time necessary to acquire sufficient education or training to enable the party seeking temporary maintenance to find appropriate employment. Under this provision, a husband whose wife has supported him during his graduate education or professional training may be required to finance her education or training in order to place her in a position more nearly akin to the one she could have achieved (Kay, 1972). The lack of such provisions in the no-fault divorce laws adopted by most states, such as California, may incur a heavier burden on the wife and make post-divorce adjustment especially difficult for women.

Thus, while the aims of the no-fault laws, i.e. equality and sex-neutrality are laudable, the laws may be instituting equality in a society in which women are not fully prepared (and/or permitted) to assume equal responsibility for their own and their children's support after divorce. Public policy then becomes a choice between temporary protection and safeguards for the transitional woman (and for the older housewife in the transitional generation) to minimize the hardships incurred by the new expectations, versus current enforcement of the new equality, with the hope of speeding the transition, despite the hardships this may cause for current divorcees.

Footnotes

1. In 1975, for the first time in U. S. history, there were over *one million* divorces in a twelve-month period (Carter and Glick, 1976: 394), and the number of divorces is expected to rise.
2. Preston estimates that 44 percent of all current marriages will end in divorce (Preston, 1974: 435), while the more conservative estimate of Carter and Glick (1976: 396) is that at least one-third of all the first marriages of couples under 30 will end in divorce.
3. As of June, 1976, the fourteen states that adopted "pure" no-fault divorce statutes (in which irretrievable breakdown is the only grounds for the dissolution of the marriage) are Arizona, California, Colorado, Delaware, Florida, Iowa, Kentucky, Michigan, Minnesota, Missouri, Montana, Nebraska, Oregon, and Washington.
4. The thirteen states that have added no-fault grounds to their existing fault-based grounds for divorce are Alabama, Connecticut, Georgia, Hawaii, Idaho, Indiana, Maine, Massachusetts, Mississippi, New Hampshire, North Dakota, Rhode Island and Texas. Most of the remaining states have recently added a provision allowing divorce for those "living separate and apart"

for a specified period of time, which is an even more modified version of no-fault. Only three states, Illinois, Pennsylvania, and South Dakota, retain fault as the *only* basis for divorce (Foster and Freed, 1977, Chart B1).

5. Today more citizens come into contact with the legal system in family law cases than in any other type of litigation (with the possible exception of traffic court) as matrimonial actions now comprise over fifty percent of all civil cases at the trial court level in most cities and states. (Friedman and Percival, 1976: 281–83).

6. We are referring explicitly to divorce, or "the legal termination of a valid marriage", (Clark 1968: 280) as distinguished from an annulment, which is a declaration that a purported marriage has been invalid from its beginning.

7. Adultery remained the only grounds for divorce in England until 1937 when the Matrimonial Causes Act added desertion, cruelty and some other offences as appropriate grounds for divorce. (Clark, 1968: 282).

8. In contrast, Maxine Virtue's observations of a Chicago court (1956) indicated identical standards for cruelty among husbands and wives. As she notes (Virtue, 1956: 86–89) "The number of cruel spouses in Chicago, both male and female, who strike their marriage partners in the face exactly twice, without provocation, leaving visible marks, is remarkable."

9. Thirty-six states (twenty-eight common-law jurisdictions and eight community property states) allow the court to divide the property upon divorce. (Krause, 1976: 980). The remaining 14 states all have common law property systems which allow each person to retain the property in his or her name. However, there is a considerable impetus for reforms in these states. Legal scholars, such as Foster and Freed, have called the maintenance of the separate property system at the time of divorce obsolete, archaic and shockingly unfair. The strongest argument against it is that "in its application it ignores the contribution wives make to the family." (Foster and Freed, 1974: 170). This argument has also been the major objection of feminist groups to the common-law property system. For example, the Citizens' Advisory Council on the Status of Women (1974: 6) has advocated the importance of changing the law "to recognize explicitly the contribution of the homemaker . . . and to give courts the authority to divide property (owned by both spouses) upon divorce."

10. Of all the financial aspects of the divorce, only child support was, in theory, unaffected by fault—as it was based on the needs of the children (and the father's financial status.)

11. The new language was not always easy to adopt, however. When filmstar Linda Lovelace was divorced, the newspapers reported that she had "charged her husband with irreconcilable differences."

12. The court may make an unequal award if community property has been deliberately misappropriated, or if immediate equal division will incur an extreme or unnecessary hardship. Property may also be divided unequally in a private agreement between the two parties.

13. In California this was changed in 1972 but was part of the original recommendations from the governor's commission which initiated the no-fault legislation.

References

Anton v. Anton
   1955   49 Del. 431, 118 A.2d 605, (Supp. 1955).
Blackston, William
   1965   Commentaries on the Laws of England
Brody, Stuart
   1970   "California's Divorce Reform: Its Sociological Implication" Pacific Law Journal, 1
Brown v. *Brown*
   1955   198 Tenn. 600, 381 S.W. 2d 492
Carter, Hugh, and Paul C. Glick
   1970   Marriage and Divorce: A social and Economic Study. Cambridge, Mass.: Harvard.
   1976   Marriage and Divorce: A social and Economic Study, Cambridge, Mass.: Harvard (Revised Ed.).

Clark, Homer
  1968   Domestic Relations. St. Paul, Minn.: West.
Citizens' Advisory Council on the Status of Women
  1974   Recognition of Economic Contribution of Homemakers and Protection of Children in
          Divorce and Practice. Washington, D.C.: U.S. Government Printing Office.
Friedman, Lawrence M., and Robert V. Percival
  1976a "Who Sues for Divorce? From Fault Through Fiction to Freedom." Journal of Legal
          Studies 5 (1): 61–82.
  1976b "A Tale of Two Courts: Litigation in Alameda and San Benito Counties." Law and
          Society Review 10 (2); 267–303.
Foster, Henry H. and Doris Jonas Freed.
  1974   "Marital Property Reform in New York; Partnership of Co-Equals?" Family Law
          Quarterly, Vol. 8; pp. 169–205.
  1977   Family Law: Cases and Materials. Boston: Little, Brown (3rd ed.)
Hofstadter, Samuel H., and Shirley R. Levittan
  1967   "Alimony—A Reformulation." Journal of Family Law 7:51–60.
Hogoboom, William P.
  1971   "The California Family Law Act of 1970: 18 Months' Experience." Journal of Missouri
          Bar: 584–589.
Krause, Harry D.
  1976   Family Law: Cases and Materials. St. Paul, Minn.: West.
Kay, Herma Hill
  1970   A Family Court: The California Proposal in Paul Bohannan (ed.) Divorce and After.
          Garden City, New York: Doubleday.
  1974   "Sex-Based Discrimination in Family Law" in Kenneth M. Davidson, Ruth G. Gins-
          burg and Herma Hill Kay, Sex-Based Discrimination Text, Cases and Materials. St.
          Paul, Minn.: West.
Reynolds V. Reynolds
  1862   85 Mass. (3 Allen) 605 (1862)
Rheinstein, Max
  1972   Marriage Stability, Divorce and the Law. Chicago: University of Chicago
Rucci v. Rucci
  1962   23 Conn. Supp. 221, 181 A.2d 125.
Weitzman, Lenore
  1979   The Marriage Contract. Englewood Cliffs, N.J.: Prentice-Hall.
Weitzman, Lenore and Ruth B. Dixon
  1976   "The Alimony Myth." Paper read at the meeting of the American Sociological Associa-
          tion.
  1979   "Child Custody Standards and Awards." Journal of Social Issues, Forthcoming.
Weitzman, Lenore J., Herma Hill Kay, and Ruth B. Dixon
  1979   No Fault Divorce: The Impact of Changes in the Law and the Legal Process. California
          Divorce Law Research Project, Center for the Study of Law and Society. University
          of California, Berkeley.
Wheeler, Michael
  1974   No-Fault Divorce. Boston: Beacon Press.

Divorce Outcome Research: Issues and Perspectives

Ann Goetting *

The divorce rate in the United States has been rising almost continuously since data were first collected by the United States Census Bureau. It is estimated that about 37% of first marriages currently being contracted will end in divorce if present conditions affecting divorce continue (Glick, 1973:71). Also, the number of children involved in divorces and annulments has increased yearly since 1960, exceeding one million per year since 1971 (National Center for Health Statistics, 1976). According to some estimates, over the next few decades perhaps one-third of all children in the United States will be directly affected by divorce (Bane, 1976: 103; Bumpass & Rindfuss, 1978).

Because so many individuals are and probably will continue to be involved in divorce, it is important to understand this phenomenon, including its effects. The purposes of this article are (a) to explore the possible long-term effects of divorce on the adults and children involved and (b) to identify what specifically it is about divorce that may bring on such effects. Although the article provides a review of recent research findings on the effects of divorce on divorcing men and women in the United States and on their children, no attempt is made to present a complete review of relevant research. Methodologically superior studies employing "normal," rather than clinical, subjects and appropriate control groups were selected. Psychoanalytically oriented and qualitative studies are excluded.

The Effects of Divorce on Adults

Practical Problems

In their two-year longitudinal study, Hetherington et al. (1977) studied the impact of divorce on family functioning and the development of children. Utilizing a multimethod, multimeasure approach, they concluded that the main practical problems of everyday life encountered by divorced parents were related to household maintenance and to economic and occupational difficulties. Many divorced men, particularly those from marriages in which conventional sex roles had been maintained and in which the wife had not been employed, initially experienced considerable difficulty and stress in

Reprinted from Ann Goetting, "Divorce Outcome Research: Issues and Perspectives," *Journal of Family Issues*, Vol. 2, No. 3 (September 1981), ©1981 Sage Publications, Inc., with permission.
*Western Kentucky University

maintaining a household routine. Regarding structure in prescribed household roles, problems in coping with routine household tasks and the regulating and scheduling of events, divorced mothers and fathers were more disorganized than parents in intact families, although this disorganization was most marked in the first year following divorce and had significantly decreased by the second year. Members of divorced households were more likely to eat erratically, and divorced mothers and their children (all members of the divorced sample were from homes in which custody had been granted to the mother) were less likely to eat together. Bedtime activity was more irregular; the children were read to less before bedtime. Also, they were more likely to arrive at school late. Divorced men were less likely to eat at home than were married men. They slept less, had more erratic sleep patterns, and had difficulty with shopping, cooking, laundry, and cleaning. Men also reported that they were coping poorly at work.

Financial affairs are often a problem when divorce occurs. Hetherington et al. (1977) observed greater economic stress in divorced couples than in married couples. Although the average income of their divorced families was equal to that of their intact families, they found that economic stress was clearly apparent in their divorced group. Because these couples had been one economic unit before divorce and now had to maintain two households, financial concerns and limitations became apparent. One usual consequence of this was that divorced fathers increased their work load in order to increase their income. These financial concerns also were instigators of conflict and greater stress between the divorced couple.

Divorced women also are affected financially by divorce. Since child custody is usually awarded to the women, and since men commonly fail to contribute to the financial support of their former wives and children (Brandwein et al., 1974), many divorced women who are not accustomed to supporting themselves and their children find themselves strapped with the burden of a family to support. Typically, the woman must sacrifice time usually spent with her children and pay for child care while she is at work. In summary, it is probably safe to say that typically individuals who attempt to maintain their financial responsibilities suffer economically from divorce and consequently their socioeconomic status and standard of living are lowered by it.

Social Life and Intimate Relationships

The loss of old friends together with trying to establish new friendships is often difficult for divorced persons. Bohannan (1970) refers to the loss of old friendships as the "community divorce," one of his six "stations" in the divorce process. Because society tends to organize social life on the basis of couples and two-parent families, divorced persons are often viewed as being ill-suited for participating in social events and, therefore, eventually lose contact with, and support from, friends associated with their earlier married life.

Hetherington et al. (1977) reported that for two months following divorce, married friends remained supportive and spent considerable time with the divorced respondents. However, these contacts rapidly declined. They found that the dissociation from marital friends was greater for women than for men, who were more often included in social activities and sometimes participated in joint family outings on visitation days.

Regarding social life in general, Hetherington et al. (1977) concluded that social activities were less frequent among the divorced than among married couples in the two years following divorce, especially for women. This find is consistent with results of several other studies which suggest that divorced women are likely to have fewer friends, belong to fewer organizations and participate in fewer recreational activities than do married women (Hetherington et al. 1978: 4). The trend suggests a very "slow" social life immediately following divorce and an increase in social involvement over the next two years. These results support those of Raschke (1976: 8–9) who found low social participation for both men and women during the first six months after separation, but over the next two and one-half years participation for both increased, and men's social participation exceeded that of women. Hetherington et al. (1977) reported that divorced women often commented on their sense of being locked into a child's world, though this was less true of working than nonworking mothers. Many nonworking mothers complained that most of their social contacts had been made through professional associates of their husband, and that with divorce these associations terminated. In contrast, the employed mothers had contact with their co-workers and these relations often extended into after-hour social events. In contrast to divorced women who felt trapped, divorced men complained of feeling shut out, rootless and at loose ends, and of a need to engage in social activities even if they often were not pleasurable.

Renne (1971) found in her 1965 questionnaire survey in Alameda County, California where she controlled for age, as did Hetherington et al. (1977) and others, that divorced and separated people were more likely to be socially isolated than married people. But she also found that unhappily married people tended to be even more socially isolated than those who were separated and divorced. Her data suggest that an unhappy marriage may be more socially confining than separation or divorce.

Several research inquiries have been conducted into intimate relationships and sexuality of the divorced. Gebhard (1970) conducted a study on sex behavior of divorced and widowed women between 1939 and 1956 and reported that these women achieved orgasm more often during intercourse than they had during marriage. Then, in 1966, Hunt reported in a study of the middle-class separated and divorced in America that divorced people find their sex life more intense, less inhibited and more satisfying than it had been in marriage. In 1974, Hunt reported the results of his national survey on human sexuality which indicated that divorced men and women had a slightly higher frequency of intercourse than did married men and women. The 1975 *Redbook* study (Levin, 1975) suggested that divorced women were more sexually assertive and more likely to initiate intercourse and to be active partners than were married women. It should be noted here that both the 1974 Hunt study and the *Redbook* study failed to control for such important social variables as socioeconomic status, which, of course, makes interpretation and generalization of their results difficult.

The recent Hetherington et al. (1977) data are at variance with this general impression that divorce brings with it more and better sex. Their addition of the dimensions of length-of-time-divorced contributes new insight into the sexuality of the divorced. They report that, at two months after the divorce, frequency of sexual intercourse was lower for their divorced respondents than for their married respondents at two months after divorce while frequency of intercourse among divorced women rose to about the same frequency as that of married men and women, it becamse significantly higher for divorced men. Then, at two years after divorce the rate was about the same for the divorced and married, both men and women. Divorced men showed a peak of sexual activity and a pattern of dating a variety of women in the first year following divorce. Many men but few women were pleased at the increased opportunity for sexual experiences with a variety of partners immediately following divorce. However, by the end of the first year both divorced men and women were expressing a lack of satisfaction in casual sexual encounters and a desire for intimacy.

Health and Safety

Data are consistent in demonstrating poorer health, higher mortality and more accidents among the divorced than among the married. The marital status of a person is one of the best predictors of health, disease and death (Lynch, 1977: 38–39). But a word of caution is in order in interpreting this fact. Since both poor health and high mortality on the one hand, and divorce on the other, are more common among the lower than the higher socioeconomic classes, the relationship between health and divorce may be at least partly due to factors associated with social class. It follows that social class should be held constant when examining the relationship between divorce and health/mortality. Regrettably, such controls are not made on the available correlational data reviewed in this section. As a result the viability of a causal interpretation relating divorce and health/mortality is weakened.

Mental Health

Landbrook (1976) reports that a national probability study conducted by the National Center for Health Statistics on symptoms of psychological distress revealed that the divorced had more symptoms (such as "nervous breakdown" and "inertia"), and had them more seriously than did persons of other marital statuses. Bloom et al. (1978: 869–871) provide an excellent summary of research relating psychopathy (mental disorder) with marital status. Results consistently indicated that admission rates into psychiatric facilities are lowest among the married, intermediate among the widowed and never married, and highest among the divorced and separated. This relationship holds across different age groups for both sexes and is true for both blacks and whites. Not only are highest admission rates reported for persons with disrupted marriages but the differential between these rates and similarly calculated rates among the married is very substantial. Furthermore, admission rates are substantially higher for males with disrupted marriages than for females with disrupted marriages.

Physical Health and Accidents

Data obtained from the National Center for Health Statistics from 1959 to 1961 demonstrated that, controlling for age, premature death rates (deaths between the ages of 15 and 64) for divorced men and women were significantly higher than for married individuals, with differences being significantly greater for men than for women (Carter and Glick, 1970). Specific causes of death where these relationships held included: cirrhosis of the liver, lung cancer, coronary heart disease, tuberculosis, diabetes, leukemia and aleukemia, suicide, homicide, motor accident deaths, pedestrian deaths, and all other accidental deaths. Consistent with these United States Government data is the fact that terminal cancer strikes divorced individuals, male, female, white and nonwhite, more frequently than it does people who are married (Lynch, 1977: 43). It should be noted that local data have been reported on suicide and on motor accidents as they relate to marital status, and the findings are consistent with the National Center for Health Statistics data. Bloom et al. (1978: 873) review three recent studies on suicide and report that the suicide rate is higher among the divorced than among any other marital status category; and McMurray (1970) demonstrated that the automobile accident rate of persons undergoing divorce in King County, Washington, in 1966 and 1967, doubled during the period of time from six months before until six months after the divorce date.

Once again, as was the case with our earlier analysis of social isolation, the work of Renne (1971) is relevant. Recall that she differentiated her sample of marrieds by marital satisfaction. In general, Renne found that health was associated with marital happiness more strongly than with marital status. In other words, greater differences in health were found between happily and unhappily married persons than between married persons in general on the one hand and divorced and separated persons on the other. Concerning self-reported physical disability, chronic illness, neurosis and depression, then, marriage was associated with better health only when the marital relationship was satisfactory to the respondent. Renne's research suggests that when marriage is unsatisfactory, divorce may be a source of relief from health problems.

The Effects of Parental Divorce on Children

Whereas there is an abundance of research on the effects of father absence on children, there is far too little information on the effects of divorce specifically. Whenever possible, studies employing samples that delineate divorce as a special kind of marital dissolution are described. In some sections, specifically those dealing with the issues of cognitive performance and school success, health, and delinquency, it was necessary to include studies which confound divorce with other types of broken homes because of the paucity of research that isolates divorce, and because the topics were considered too important to ignore.

Cognitive Performance and School Success

Although several methodologically sound and informative studies relating achievement and school behavior to broken homes are available, only two separated out children of divorce from children from other types of broken homes. Those studies were conducted by Crescimbeni (1965) and Levin et al. (1978). The remaining studies reviewed here use confounded samples and therefore need to be interpreted with care.

An old but often cited study which is relevant here was conducted by Nye (1957) on Washington high school students. Nye compared school grades of children from happy intact, unhappy intact and divorced and separated homes. He found when comparing these three categories of adolescents who were similar in terms of other social traits, including socioeconomic status, that there were no significant differences in grade point averages among the members of the three groups.

Other more recent studies have found no significant effects of broken homes on school success. Burchinal (1964) studied and compared Iowa adolescents from intact homes, from homes headed only by the mother, and from reconstituted families—those headed by a natural parent and a stepparent—and found when controlling for socioeconomic status, that no significant differences existed among mean grade points and attitudes toward school. However, he did find that the adolescents from intact homes were absent the fewest number of school days. Bales (1979) studied students enrolled in 23 northern Mississippi public schools, and concluded that when controlling for socioeconomic status there were no significant correlations between home stability and either academic aspiration or grade point average for both black and white males and females.

In their literature review, Walters and Stinnett (1971) concluded that there were no significant differences in achievement between children from one-parent and those from two-parent homes. Also in her more recent review, Bane (1976: 11) notes that studies which adequately control for economic status show few or no differences between children from one-and two-parent families on school achievement, social adjustment, and delinquent behaviors.

Several studies addressing this issue of the effect of marital disruption on cognitive performance and school success have concluded that such disruption does have consequences. For example, Crescimbeni (1965) compared scores on standardized achievement tests for 92 Connecticut children from divorced homes in grades two through six with those of a comparison group from intact homes who were matched for several traits including socioeconomic status. He found that the children from divorced homes scored significantly lower on these achievement tests than did the children from intact homes. This was true in 1962 when the first achievement test was administered and at the end of one year of family disruption for the children from divorced homes, and again in 1963 when the second achievement test was administered and when the children of divorce had been such for two years.

Santrock (1972) observed third and sixth grade I.Q. and achievement test scores for mostly lower-class children, finding that when controlling for socioeconomic status, father-absence due to divorce, desertion, or separation was debilitating when compared with father-presence. The most debilitating age for father-absence onset was the first two years of the boy's life. For girls, onset of father-absence due to divorce, desertion or separation during the first five years of life also was detrimental to achievement when comparisons were made with father-present girls. But for the girls, no such detrimental effects became apparent when the break occurred later on.

Between 1973 and 1976, Conyers (1977) observed the absence rates, grade point averages, and truancy, suspension, expulsion and drop-out records of over 1000 ninth graders in a community of 40,000 people. She compared children from unconventionally structured homes (created by death and divorce, mostly divorce) with children from conventionally structured homes. She found that (a) students from unconventionally structured homes had an average absence rate that was greater than those from conventionally structured homes, (b) students from unconventionally structured homes had an average grade point record that was lower than that associated with students from conventionally structured homes, and (c) students from unconventionally structured homes had higher incidences of truancy, suspension, expulsion, and drop-outs than those from conventionally structured homes. All differences were statistically significant.

Hunt and Hunt (1975; 1977) reanalyzed data collected by Rosenberg and Simmons on 907 junior and senior high school students attending the public school system of Baltimore, Maryland. In the earlier of their two articles (1975), they report the effects of father absence on achievement-related variables for white and black boys. Their data suggest that whereas family structure has marked detrimental consequences on school performance and educational aspirations for white boys, it has no such important effect for black boys. The Hunts explain these findings by suggesting that costs of father-absence are greater in higher status levels (which are dispropor- tionately represented by whites) because in such homes the father (along with other family members) serves as a socialization agent emphasizing achievement and success to his son. But in lower-status homes (which are disproportionately represented by blacks) the father does not typically repre- sent an important resource for achievement and success because he often is not at home and also may not so highly value achievement, and therefore his loss has little effect. Although this "high status" hypothesis is confirmed by the father absence effects by race, its failure to describe class patterns within the two racial groups is problematic. The Hunts suggest that the resolution to this problem may lie in the refinement of the definition and measurement of high and low social status. In the second of their two articles, the Hunts (1977) report the effects of father-absence on academic performance for white and black girls. They found that among white girls father-absence was associated with high grades, whereas among the black girls the presence or absence of a father seemingly had no impact on academic performance. The Hunts reason that in our white society where girls are socialized into a female role which discourages instrumentality in general and achievement specifically, father-absence may leave girls without a key parental resource for normal sex-role adjustment, which may have the effect of disposing them toward greater instrumentality. But in black homes sex role differentiation is less strong; women have historically been expected to perform the key instru- mental role in the family. That fact coupled with the fact that the black father may spend less time as a socializer suggests that father loss to the black girl should be expected to have less effect on achievement than father loss to the white girl.

Levin et al. (1978) analyzed a large national sample of data collected be- tween 1963 and 1970 on the cognitive development (measured by the vocab- ulary and block design subtest of the *Wechsler Intelligence Scale for Children)*, school achievement (measured by the reading and arithmetic sub- tests of the *Wide Range Achievement Test)*, and parental marital status of United States children aged 6 through 17. Having controlled for several so- cial variables including socioeconomic status, they concluded that whereas the children living with divorced mothers showed no significant differences in cognitive development when compared with children from intact homes, they did score significantly lower on the measures of cognitive achievement.

Personality

In their longitudinal research referred to earlier, Hetherington et al. (1977) studied 24 boys and 24 girls from white middle-class Virginia fami- lies in which divorce had occurred. These nursery school age subjects were matched for socioeconomic status with children from intact homes. Based on a checklist of home behavior, the children of divorced parents demonstrated significantly more negative behaviors than did children in intact families, the differences being greater for boys than for girls. At the end of two years the differences had significantly declined among the boys and had largely disappeared among the girls.

Hodges et al. (1979) conducted a study somewhat similar to that of Hetherington et al., but obtained results inconsistent with theirs. They compared 26 preschool children whose parents had divorced and who were living with their mothers with 26 matched preschool children from intact families. Results showed few statistically significant differences on aggression, withdrawal, dependency, and other signs of immaturity and emotional upset. The data suggested that there was no relationship between time since separation (which ranged from 5 to 48 months) and any behavioral differences. Contact with the noncustodial father increased aggression in the child, and pre-separation discord did not predict maladjustment for children of divorce. Finally, they found that limited resources and relative youth of parents did predict negative adjustment for children, as expected.

Santrock (1977) studied the effects of father-absence on sex-typed behavior in 45 predominantly lower class white boys between 10 and 12 years of age; 15 were from divorced homes, 15 from widowed homes and 15 from intact homes. He found that having matched for I.Q., age and school, both categories of father-absent boys were significantly more masculine, physically aggressive, disobedient and likely to "try things out on their own" than boys from father-present homes. Similarly, Patterson et al. (1973) found a high degree of out-of-control behavior in boys from divorced families when compared to boys from intact homes, especially immediately following the divorce. These data do not support the common fear that divorce may lead to masculinity deficiencies in boys.

The work of Raschke and Raschke (1979) and of Zill (1978) are of special importance here because they, as did Renne (1971), considered the variable of marital discord. In their study of 289 third, sixth, and eighth graders who were homogeneous in socioeconomic status, the Raschkes (1979) measured self-concept using the *Piers-Harris Children's Self Concept Scale* and family structure (e.g., divorced, intact, and the like) and presence of home conflict using self-report measures. They found no significant differences in the self-concept of children from intact, single-parent, reconstituted or other types of family structure. They did find, however, that self-concept of children was significantly lower where conflict in the home was high, regardless of family structure.

As did the Raschkes, Zill (1978) found a component of personality to be more highly related to marital discord than to family structure. Using a national level sample of 2,258 children between seven and eleven years of age, he found that when education and income were controlled, the children in divorced, unhappily married and separated groups were significantly more aggressive than were the children of parents who were very happily and fairly happily married.

The studies considered thus far in the area of personality have dealt with young children. Since our interest here is in determining long-term effects of divorce, we will look at the work of Young and Parish (1977), Hetherington (1972), Kulka and Weingarten (1980), and Landis (1962) who studied adolescents, college students, and adults. Young and Parish (1977) administered attitude measures to 98 college women and concluded that father loss due to both divorce and death has detrimental effects on personality development for young women. Both groups of women who had lost fathers thought much more unfavorably of themselves and thought of themselves as being more insecure than the women who had not lost fathers. These statistically significant findings held only for women whose mothers had not remarried. The women whose mothers had remarried tended to check more unfavorable adjectives and indicate more insecurity than the women who had not lost fathers, but the difference was not significant. This suggests that the presence of stepfathers may attenuate and compensate for some effects of father loss.

Hetherington (1972) also researched women in late adolescence, but reported very little difference in personality structure between the daughters of divorce, daughters who had lost their fathers due to death, and the women from intact homes. Exceptions to this general finding were that daughters of divorce and daughters whose fathers had died were lower on internalization on personal control items and were also more anxious.

Kulka and Weingarten (1980), using two national cross-sectional surveys of adults conducted in 1957 and 1976, concluded that long-term negative effects on psychological adjustment (happiness, distress) associated with parental divorce and separation are both minimal and, consistent with the Hetherington et al. nursery school-age subjects, modifiable over time.

Though the Landis (1962) study is quite dated now (the data were collected in the early 1950's), it is worthy of consideration here because of the samples which were used. Comparisons were made among subjects from happy unbroken homes, unhappy unbroken homes, and homes broken by divorce. Landis studied self-concept among college students and found that while there was very little difference between the responses from the two categories of unhappy marriages, the respondents from happy marriages gave a significantly higher self-evaluation on nine of the twelve questionnaire items. These data suggest that while marital stress may lower the self-concept of the children, parental divorce has no effect once severe tension has set in on the marriage.

Interpersonal Relationships

Landis (1962) also explored the reported relationships of college students with their parents at the time of the study and the dating histories of the college students. Regarding relationships with parents, he found that respondents from happy homes reported having closer relationships with their parents than adolescents from both unhappy intact homes and homes where the parents had divorced. Furthermore, he found that both men and women reported that their relationship was more distant with the divorced father than it was with the unhappily married father. Although there were no significant differences for the men concerning their relationships with their mothers, the women from divorced homes reported closer relationships with their mothers than did the women from unhappy nondivorced marriages. Landis' data suggest that happy homes produce the closest relationships, and that since the children usually go with the mother after divorce, relationships with the mother become closer while relationships with the father become more distant.

Regarding dating history, Landis found significant differences between students from happy homes on one hand and students from two categories of unhappy homes on the other hand on 11 of the 12 variables tested. But he found a significant difference on only one variable when he compared students from unhappy intact marriages with students from divorced marriages, and that one difference showed up for men only. Essentially what Landis concluded was that children from unhappy marriages (whether or not the parents divorced) tend to begin dating later, date fewer different people and date less frequently than do children from happy marriages, but they go steady with and have as many private understanding engagements as do those from happy marriages. Landis' study suggests that it is marital conflict, not divorce, that influences dating behavior.

In her study on women in late adolescence cited earlier, Hetherington (1972) examined differences in heterosexual behavior of white lower and lower-middle class women from divorced, widowed and nuclear families. She found that when compared in a number of settings with women from both intact and widowed homes, the women from divorced families exhibited sexually precocious and inappropriately assertive behavior with male but not female peers and adults, and that the effects of early separation were usually greater than those of late separation. Furthermore, this greater receptiveness to men by the women whose fathers were absent due to divorce is supported by their interview reports of earlier and more dating and sexual intercourse. These findings on dating are, of course, in opposition to Landis' findings.

A follow-up study was conducted on Hetherington's women one year following their marriages to determine how long-lasting the effects of father absence were, as reflected in the women's subsequent marital relationships (Hetherington et al. 1978: 22–24). Daughters of the divorced married younger and a greater number were pregnant at the time of marriage than were daughters from intact homes. No differences in frequency of marital intercourse were reported among the three groups of women, but orgasmic satisfaction was lower in women from single-parent families. It is of interest to note that the husbands of daughters of divorcees were less educated, had less stable employment records and were more frequently involved in problems with the law than were the other two groups of husbands. In addition they felt more ambivalent or hostile toward their wives and infants and were less emotionally mature, more impulsive, and self-centered. All of this suggests that the effects of divorce on daughters' interaction with men may be long-lasting and even influence marital choices.

Young and Parish (1977), in their attitude study cited earlier on college women, found that divorcees' daughters showed no differences in stated willingness to associate with the opposite sex when compared with the women from intact homes. All of this suggests that whereas divorce may not affect women's desire to interact with men, it may affect the *manner* in which they do so and this difference in manner can, in turn, affect mate selection and marital success.

There is evidence that children of divorced or separated parents are at somewhat greater risk of having their own first marriages end in divorce or separation than are children from intact homes. Pope and Mueller (1976), using five data sets and controlling for socioeconomic status and rural-urban origin, suggest that the correlation does not appear to be attributable solely to a single-parent upbringing since it is more likely to occur among children who have lived with their mothers than those who have lived with their fathers and in situations where separation has been caused by divorce rather than death. It may be that different child-rearing patterns, stresses, values and lifestyles are associated with living with a single mother than with a single father and with parents having been divorced rather than widowed. Kulka and Weingarten (1980) found similar modest differences between their subjects from voluntarily disrupted and intact homes.

Health

Very little research has been done relating health and parental marital status. In the area of mental health the few data available offer conflicting and, therefore, inconclusive results. Some researchers have investigated the representation of children of divorce in psychiatric clinics. Despert (1962) and Westman (1970) found an underrepresentation of children of divorce in their clinics, while others (McDermott, 1970; Tuckman & Regan, 1966; Kalter, 1977) reported an overrepresentation of children of divorce in their clinics.

Arey (1978) analyzed interview data from a general population of adults residing in four Florida counties. Controlling for race, sex, and age of the respondent at the time of the interview, she found that on three measures of adult mental health (depression, anxiety, and psychosocial dysfunction), children of divorce reflected statistically significant lower scores than children from intact families and from families broken by death of a parent, but that in all cases the differences were attributed to an unhappy childhood rather than to a broken family structure.

Zill (1978), cited in the earlier section on personality, found when using his *Psychological Help Index* that children from "not too happy marriages" scored close to children from divorced households, and that both groups showed signficantly higher average scores than did the children from "very happy" marriages. Furthermore the average score for children from "fairly happy" marriages fell between these extremes, significantly lower than the mean score for children of divorce and from "not too happy" marriages, significantly higher than the mean score for children from "very happy" marriages.

In the area of physical health, only one recent study is reported here. Leatherton located 35 children with insulin-dependent diabetes living in Sacramento, California (Diabetes Via Divorce, 1977). This sample was matched by age, sex, race, and socioeconomic status with a randomly selected control group from the same community. He found that 40% of the children with diabetes had lost a parent through divorce or separation (mostly divorce) prior to the onset of the disease, and only 17% of the control group had lost a parent. Of the 14 children from broken homes who had diabetes 12 had not shown symptoms until 3 to 10 years after the marital breakup. All of this supports the contention of Thomas Willis who believed that diabetes is caused by "prolonged sorrow" (Diabetes Via Divorce, in *Human Behavior,* 1977).

Nye (1957) compared children from happy intact, unhappy intact, and divorced and separated homes. Among his sample of Washington high school students he found less psychosomatic illness for children of divorce and separation than for those in unhappy intact homes. Furthermore, he found the least psychosomatic illness among children from happy intact homes. Nye's data suggest one advantage for children to divorcing or separating when there is marital tension.

Delinquency

The impact of family structure on delinquency rates is a concern which no longer carries the enthusiasm that it did in the early part of this century (Sykes, 1980: 19–22). At that time, when the trend toward industrialization and urbanization in the United States was affecting drastically the lives of the masses, the idea that the broken family was a major source of delinquency was much influenced by the rural and traditional perspective of many sociologists who were inclined to place a high value on kinship bonds, the role of tradition and the need for stability. At that time theories concerning broken homes viewed the child as being prepared for delinquency by defective socialization in a pathological family. Since divorce, along with other anomalies of family structure, was most frequent in the lower class, the correlation between poverty and delinquency was considered to be a function of the more significant relationship between divorce and delinquency. Then in the early 1930s, the influential work of Shaw and McKay at the University of Chicago challenged this pervasive view. At a time when divorce and working mothers were becoming commonplace and more socially acceptable, their work indicated that broken homes were not an important cause of crime. In subsequent decades the work of Thrasher, Merton, Sutherland, Cohen, and the Gluecks deemphasized the role that divorce plays in delinquent behavior. Sykes (1980) points out that while the early sentimental view of "normal" family life may have biased the perception of delinquency causes, it is also possible that the broken family was in fact an important cause of crime and delinquency prior to 1930. In subsequent decades, as public schooling and mass media began to play a larger role in child socialization, the importance of the family as an agency of socialization may have declined sharply.

Since there is a paucity of recent data relating divorce as a specific cause of marital disruption with delinquency in the United States, indirect evidence is reported here to shed light on the issue. Consistent with his results regarding psychosomatic illness, Nye (1957) found that among his sample of high school students, delinquency was most common among the children from unhappy intact homes and least common for the children from happy intact homes, with the proportion of delinquent children from homes broken by divorce and separation falling between the two extremes.

Three recently conducted literature reviews are relevant here. Recall that in her recent review of the effects of marital disruption on children, Bane (1976) concluded that studies which adequately control for economic status show few or no differences between children from one-and two-parent homes in terms of delinquent behaviors. Herzog and Sudia (1971: 19) and Rutter and Madge (1976: 183) reviewed studies of broken homes in the United States and other countries and agreed that the broken home, per se, is less salient among relevant factors associated with delinquency than are the climate and tone of the home.

Summary and Concluding Statements

This article is an attempt to explore the possible long-term effects of divorce on the adults and children involved, and to address the issue of what specifically it is about divorce that may bring on such effects. For selected areas of concern the relevant literature has been reviewed, and the following statements can be made.

1. Problems of household maintenance and of economic and occupational difficulties may accompany divorce.
2. Social participation may decrease when marriage becomes unsatisfactory, and then increase somewhat eventually after divorce.
3. While, at least temporarily, divorce may lead to an enhanced sex life, especially in men, casual sex among the divorced seemingly leaves something to be desired.

4. Both physical and mental health are best among the happily married, worst among the unhappily married, and somewhere between these two extremes among the divorced.
5. Data relating parental divorce with cognitive performance and school success are indirect, inconsistent and, therefore, inconclusive. The only related finding that reflects any consistency is the higher rate of school absence for children from broken homes when compared with children from intact homes.
6. Data are conflicting and, therefore, inconclusive in terms of the relationship between parental marital status and personality structure. However, there may be a relationship between parental marital happiness and personality structure. Children from happy marriages may display more desirable personality traits (particularly in terms of self-esteem and aggression) than either children from unhappy intact marriages or divorced marriages.
7. Adolescents from happy homes appear to have closer relationships with their parents than adolescents from both unhappy intact homes and homes where the parents have divorced. Furthermore, adolescents from divorced homes may have more distant relationships with their fathers, probably due to the father's absence, than do adolescents from unhappy intact homes. Also, adolescent women, but not men, from divorced homes may have closer relationships with their mothers than do adolescent women from unhappy homes.
8. Data are conflicting and, therefore, inconclusive regarding differences between children from intact homes and children from divorced homes in dating behavior and in heterosexual interaction and "presentation-of-self."
9. Women whose parents have divorced may marry younger and are more likely to be pregnant at the time of marriage than women from intact homes. They may have lower orgasmic satisfaction in marriage, their husbands may be less desirable along some dimensions, and they (along with men from divorced homes) may be more likely to end their own marriages in divorce.
10. Mental health and psychosomatic illness appear to be related to parental family structure, but are more likely related to happiness in the family in terms of parental marital happiness and/or childhood happiness.
11. Diabetes may be more common among children of divorce than among children from intact homes.
12. If there is a positive relationship between parental divorce and delinquency, divorce, per se, may be of no greater importance to the incidence of delinquency than family discord.

When considering the research reviewed here and the summary statements listed directly above, two facts are suggested. The first is that little can be concluded about the long-term effects of divorce with any certainty. This is not due simply to lack of research efforts expended in this direction, but to the conceptual and methodological limitations of the work that has been done. Specifically these limitations are:

1. In many studies divorce is not singled out from other types of marital dissolution and other types of father-absence. Divorce represents a unique process to those involved when compared with death and separation. For this reason research is needed which deals specifically with divorced individuals and their children if we are to make statements about the effects of divorce.
2. The demonstration of statistical association between marital status and outcome variables would be more meaningful if studies did not systematically ignore remarried persons. Outcome studies on divorce typically utilize current marital status rather than marital history; in other words, they compare subjects in their first marriage with currently divorced subjects. Since most of the divorced remarry and do so within a very few years after divorce, the sample of the divorced subjects is heavily biased in favor of those select cases who remarry late or fail to remarry at all. Overall (1971), in his study of psychiatric patients, concludes that marital history is a stronger predictor of psychopathology than is current marital status. Those who remarry after divorce have experienced divorce, and should experience the effects of divorce, unless, of course, such effects are nullified by remarriage.
3. There is, in general, inadequate control for important variables. Research has suggested that some factors affect the impact of divorce on parents and children. For example, Santrock's (1972) work suggest that sex and age of onset determine achievement outcomes for children, and Bale's work (1979) suggests that race is an important factor in the relationship between parental divorce and achievement. Considering adults, several studies suggest that sex affects the consequences of divorce. For example, the Hetherington et al. (1977) study suggested different effects of divorce on social life and sexual behavior for men and women. In addition to these variables of sex, age of onset, and race, others should be controlled because they are believed to affect social life in general (i.e., socioeconomic status and religion) or because they logically might affect the consequences of divorce (e.g., severity of marital discord and postdivorce relationships).
4. Most studies utilize samples drawn from local populations. While such studies are useful, we also need studies which are national in scope, whose findings can be generalized to the entire United States population.
5. The research design commonly used to address the issue of divorce effects is less than ideal for that purpose. Since most studies use correlational data, we can never be certain about the reasons for the statistical relationships. In other words, what are often assumed to be effects may

not be effects at all and, in fact, may be causes. For example, data consistently show a strong relationship between psychopathy and marital status; persons who are divorced are overrepresented among psychiatric patients, and persons who are married and living with their spouses are underrepresented. There are several possible explanations for this type of relationship: (a) the psychopathy may have preceded or occurred during the marriage and constituted a selection factor leading to divorce, (b) the lifestyle associated with marriage may be a protective agent from psychopathy, (c) divorce may be a stressor that can precipitate psychopathy, and (d) a third set of variables may predispose persons both to divorce and to psychopathy.

Of course, an alternative research design to be employed to determine the effects of divorce would be longitudinal in nature involving a large national sample the members of which would be observed from birth until death. They would be checked periodically, possibly annually, for marital structure (intact, separated, divorced, dissolved by death and reconstituted after divorce and death) and for factors representing possible effects of marital structure (practical problems of living, social life and intimate behavior, health and safety, cognitive performance and school success, personality, juvenile delinquency). Essentially the sample members would divide themselves into the six categories of marital structure, the intact family serving as the control group. Within these six groups would be subgroups according to selected variables: sex, age at onset of dissolution (where applicable), socioeconomic status, religion and race, and results would be computed in terms of these variables. Such a design would allow observation of the process of change in marital structure as it relates to change in those factors representing possible effects. It could turn out that some factors believed to be effects actually precede divorce. But if they were to follow divorce and to fail to appear in the other categories of marital structure at the same point in time, we could with some certainty attribute a causal relationship to the change.

Such a longitudinal design represents an idealistic approach to the problem at hand. Practical considerations surrounding its implementation include the prohibitive cost involved in conducting research over the span of a human lifetime of subjects in a highly mobile society. Also, inherent in such an extended time frame are problems of discontinuity (continuous replacement) of research personnel, retest biases and subject attrition. Finally, our methodological sophistication is not as yet sufficiently developed to effectively disentangle the confounding effects of the numerous unanticipated and undefined intervening factors or variables which would come into play over the period of a lifetime.

A realistic compromise to this idealistic design would be a correlational study using representative samples of useful populations, appropriate comparison groups and controlling for relevant social variables. Another more practical design would be retrospective in nature, where a sample of married subjects and a sample of divorced subjects, stratified by age, would be compared on self-reported information describing, from their personal perceptions, which factors influenced which outcomes at various stages in their life cycles.

The second major observation which emerges from a review of the research cited here is that family discord may be a more important determinant of the effects with which we are concerned than marital structure. Research conducted by Renne (1971), Raschke and Raschke (1977), Zill (1978), Landis (1962), Nye (1957), Herzog and Sudia (1971: 19) and Rutter and Madge (1976: 183) indicate that the adverse effects sometimes associated with divorce actually may result from the marital discord which preceded the divorce. In general these researchers found that detrimental characteristics were least prevalent for individuals from intact happy homes and most prevalent for those from unhappy intact homes, with the prevalence of those from divorced homes falling somewhere between these two extremes. These findings suggest that divorce may serve to relieve stress and to neutralize the debilitating effects of marital discord.

It is suggested here that future research should explore this possibility that the marital discord associated with divorce is at least partially responsible for the adversity sometimes associated with it. Such research would require a design, ideally longitudinal but realistically correlational or retrospective in nature that would compare a divorced sample with samples of subjects from intact homes with high and low degrees of marital discord.

What current research suggests is that it is the emotional climate of the home that is critical to our well-being rather than actual family structure. A discouraging aspect of this review is the realization that most research on this topic is conducted in an intellectual vacuum. For decades serious writers have unanimously adopted the premise that discord rather than divorce is the critical variable, yet research designs which incorporate this assumption are few. Commenting on this state of affairs Turner (1980) states, "One is led almost to despair over the noncumulative nature of research in this area."

Another discouraging consideration brought to the fore in this review is the seemingly commonplace nature of marital and family discord and the devastating effects it may have on those involved. The information reviewed here suggests the need to be less concerned with divorce prevention than with the compatability of marital partners. But compatability is difficult partly because men and women have been socialized to be different from one another, to have different, and in some cases, opposing interests and life goals. Furthermore, we all learn as we are socialized into dating and mating procedures and norms to view members of the opposite sex as commodities instead of companions and friends. If Lynch (1977) and others are correct in their assertion that the human mind and body thrive on the comfort of a warm accepting intimate human relationship, then in these contemporary times where emphasis is on flexibility and change, competition and achievement and social and geographical mobility rather than on stability and commitment, we must take special care to see that needed intimacy is attainable. It makes sense then to alter our socialization patterns in such a way that the inevitable conflict of interests between husbands and wives, while being recognized, can remain manageable. We need to teach our children social skills in interacting with the opposite sex so that somewhere in the future men and women will be able to enjoy the companionship of one another and consequently be able to provide for one another the needed benefits of human intimacy.

References

Arey, S.S.
  1978 "A Break in the Family Life Cycle: Childhood Loss and Adult Consequences." Paper presented at the Annual meeting of the American Sociological Association, San Francisco.
Bales, K.B.
  1979 "Academic achievement and the broken home." Southern J. of Educ. Research 13 (Fall): 145–160.
Bane, M.J.
  1976 "Marital disruption and the lives of children." J. of Social Issues 32: 103–117.
Bart, P.B.
  1967 "Depression in middle-aged women: Some sociological factors." Dissertation Abstracts. 28/11-B: 4752.
Bloom, B.L., S.J. Asher and S.W. White
  1978 Marital disruption as a stressor: A review and analysis. Psych. B. 85, 867–894
Bohannon, P.
  1970 "The six stations of divorce." Paul Bohannan (ed)., Divorce and After. Garden City: Doubleday.
Brandwein, R.A., C.A. Brown, and E.M. Fox
  1974 "Women and children last: The social situation of divorced mothers and their families." J. of Marriage and the Family 36: 498–514.
Bumpass L. and R. Rindfuss.
  1978 "Children's Experience of Marital Disruption." Institute for Research on Poverty, University of Wisconsin at Madison, DP #512-78
Burchinal, L.G.
  1964 "Characteristics of adolescents from unbroken, broken and reconstituted families," J. of Marriage and the Family 26: 44–51.
Carter, H. and P. Glick.
  1970 Marriage and Divorce: A Social and Economic Study. Cambridge, MA: Harvard University Press.
Conyers, M.G.
  1977 "Comparing School Success of Students from Conventional and Broken Homes," Phi Delta Kappan 58: 647.
Crescimbeni, J.
  1965 "Broken homes do affect academic achievement." Child and Family, 4: 24–28.
Despert, L.
  1962 Children of Divorce. Garden City: Vintage Press.
Gebhard, P.
  1970 "Postmarital Coitus Among Widows and Divorcees." Paul Bohannan (ed.) Divorce and After. Garden City: Doubleday.
Glick, P.C.
  1973 "Dissolution of Marriage by Divorce and Its Demographic Consequences." Interna-

tional Population Conference. 2: 65–69. Liege, Belgium: International Union for the Scientific Study of Population.

Gove, W.R.
1973   "Sex, marital status, and mortality." Amer. J. of Sociology 79: 45–67.

Hetherington, E.M.
1972   "Effects of father absence on personality development in adolescent daughters." Developmental Psychology 7: 313–326.

Hetherington, E.M., M. Cox, and R. Cox
1978   "The development of children in mother headed families," in H. Hoffman and D. Reiss (eds.) The American Family—Dying or Developing. New York: Plenum.
1977   "The aftermath of divorce," J. H. Stevens, Jr. and M. Matthews (eds.). Mother-child, Father-child Relations. Washington, DC: NAEYC.

Herzog, E. and C. Sudia
1971   Boys in Fatherless Families. Washington, D.C.: U.S. Department of HEW, Office of Child Development, Children's Bureau.

Hodges, W.F., R. Wechsler, and C. Ballantine
1979   "Divorce and the pre-school child: Cumulative stress." J. of Divorce 3: 55–67.

Human Behavior
1977   "Diabetes via divorce." May, p. 55.

Hunt, J.G. and L.L. Hunt
1977   Race, daughters, and father-loss. Does absence make the girl grow stronger? *Social Problems* 25: 90–102.
1975   Race and the father-son connection: The conditional relevance of father absence for the orientations and identities of adolescent boys. *Social Problems* 23: 35–52.

Hunt, M. W.
1974   Sexual Behavior in the 1970s. Chicago: Playboy Press.
1966   The World of the Formerly Married. New York: McGraw-Hill.

Kalter, N.
1977   "Children of divorce in an outpatient psychiatric population." Amer. J. of Orthopyschiatry 47 (January).

Kulka, R.A. and H. Weingarten
1980   "The long-term effects of parental divorce in childhood on adult adjustment." J. of Social Issues 35: 50–78.

Landbrook, D.
1976   "The Health and Survival of the Divorced." Conciliation Courts Review 14: 21–33.

Landis, J.T.
1962   "A comparison of children from divorced and nondivorced unhappy marriages." The Family Life Coordinator 2: 61–65.

Levin, M.L., F. Van Loon, and H.D. Spitler
1978   "Marital Disruption and Cognitive Development and Achievement in Children and Youth." Paper delivered at the Annual Meeting of the Southern Sociological Society, New Orleans, LA.

Levin, R.J.
1975   "The Redbook Report on Premarital and Extramarital Sex." Redbook Magazine, October.

Lynch, J. J.
1977   The Broken Heart: The Medical Consequences of Loneliness. New York: Basic Books.

McDermott, J. F.
1970   "Divorce and its psychiatric sequelae in children." Archives of General Psychiatry 23: 421–427.

McMurray, L.
1970   "Emotional stress and driving performance: The effect of divorce." Behavioral Research in Highway Safety 1: 100–114.

National Center for Health Statistics
1976   "Advance Report, Final Divorce Statistics, 1974." Monthly Vital Statistics Report 25: (April 14).

Nye, F.I.
1957   "Child adjustment in broken and in unhappy unbroken homes." Marriage and Family Living (November): 356–361.

Overall, J. E.
  1971   "Association between marital history and the nature of manifest psychopathology," J.
            of Abnormal Psychology 78: 213–221.
Patterson, S. R., J. A., Cobb, and R.S. Ray
  1973   "A social engineering technology for retraining the families of aggressive boys." In
            H. E. Adams and I. P. Unikel (eds.) Issues and Trends in Behavior Therapy, Spring-
            field, IL: Thomas.
Pope, H. and C. Mueller
  1976   "The intergenerational transmission of marital instability." J. of Social Issues 32: 49–
            67.
Raschke, H. J.
  1978   "The role of social participation in postseparation and postdivorce adjustment." J. of
            Divorce 1: 129–40.
Raschke, H. J. and V. J. Raschke
  1979   "Family conflict and children's self concepts: A comparison of intact and single parent
            families." J. of Marriage and the Family, May: 367–374.
Renne, K. S.
  1971   "Health and marital experience in an urban population." J. of Marriage and the Fam-
            ily (May): 338–350.
Rutter, M. and N. Madge
  1976   Cycles of Disadvantage. London: Heinemann.
Santrock, J. W.
  1977   "Effects of father absence on sex-typed behaviors in male children: Reason for the
            absence and the age of onset of the absence." The J. of Genetic Psychology 130: 3–10.
  1972   "Relation of type and onset of father absence to cognitive development." Child Devel-
            opment 43: 455–469.
Sykes, G.
  1980   The Future of Crime: Crime and Delinquency Issues. United States Department of
            Health and Human Services. National Institute of Mental Health, Center for Studies
            of Crime and Delinquency, Rockville, MD.
Tuckman, J. and R. Regan
  1966   "Intactness of the home and behavioral problems of children." J. of Child Clinical
            Psychiatry 7: 225–233.
Turner, R. H.
  1980   Personal communication (October 30).
Walters, J. and N. Stinnett
  1971   "Parent-child relationships: A decade review of research." J. of Marriage and the
            Family 33: 70–111.
Westman, J.
  1970   "The role of child psychiatry in divorce." Archives of General Psychiatry 23: 416–
            420.
Young, E. R. and T. S. Parish
  1977   "Impact of father absence during childhood on the psychological adjustment of col-
            lege females." Sex Roles 3: 217–227.
Zill, N.
  1978   "Divorce, Marital Happiness, and the Mental Health of Children: Findings from the
            Foundation for Child Development National Survey of Children." Paper presented at
            NIMH Workshop on Divorce and Children, Bethesda, Maryland, February 7–8, 1978.

A content analysis of 116 marriage and family texts showed that only one-third devoted at least a sentence or two to death in the family, with widowhood being the most frequently discussed topic. Unlike divorce, death does not seem to be defined as a crisis by family sociologists; yet, death *will* occur in every family. It is suggested that family sociologists include death in the family in future texts.

Remarriage as an Incomplete Institution

Andrew Cherlin

Sociologists believe that social institutions shape people's behavior in important ways. Gerth and Mills (1953, p. 173) wrote that institutions are organizations of social roles which "imprint their stamps upon the individual, modifying his external conduct as well as his inner life." More recently, Berger and Luckmann (1966) argued that institutions define not only acceptable behavior, as Gerth and Mills believed, but also objective reality itself. Social institutions range from political and economic systems to religion and language. And displayed prominently in any sociologist's catalogue of institutions is a fundamental form of social organization, the family.

The institution of the family provides social control of reproduction and child rearing. It also provides family members with guidelines for proper behavior in everyday family life, and, presumably, these guidelines contribute to the unity and stability of families. But in recent years, sociologists have de-emphasized the institutional basis of family unity in the United States. According to many scholars, contemporary families are held together more by consensus and mutual affection than by formal, institutional controls.

The main source of this viewpoint is an influential text by Ernest Burgess and Harvey Locke which appeared in 1945. They wrote:

> The central thesis of this volume is that the family in historical times has been, and at present is, in transition from an institution to a companionship. In the past, the important factors unifying the family have been external, formal, and authoritarian, as the law, the mores, public opinion, tradition, the authority of the family head, rigid discipline, and elaborate ritual. At present, in the new emerging form of the companionship family, its unity inheres less and less in community pressures and more and more in such interpersonal relationships as the mutual affection, the sympathetic understanding, and the comradeship of its members. [P. vii]

In the institutional family, Burgess and Locke stated, unity derived from the unchallenged authority of the patriarch, was was supported by strong social pressure. But, they argued, with urbanization and the decline of patriarchal authority, a democratic family has emerged which creates its own unity from interpersonal relations.

Many subsequent studies have retained the idea of the companionship family in some form, such as the equalitarian family of Blood and Wolfe (1960) or the symmetrical family of Young and Wilmott (1973). Common to all is the notion that patriarchal authority has declined and sex roles have become less segregated. Historical studies of family life demonstrate that the authority of

Reprinted from the *American Journal of Sociology*, Vol. 84, No. 3 (1978), by permission of The University of Chicago Press.

the husband was indeed stronger in the preindustrial West than it is now (see, e.g., Ariès 1962; Shorter 1975). As for today, numerous studies of "family power" have attempted to show that authority and power are shared more equally between spouses (see Blood and Wolfe 1960). Although these studies have been criticized (Safilios-Rothschild 1970), no one has claimed that patriarchal authority is as strong now as the historical record indicates it once was. Even if we believe that husbands still have more authority than wives, we can nevertheless agree that patriarchal authority seems to have declined in the United States in this century.

But it does not follow that institutional sources of family unity have declined also. Burgess and Locke reached this conclusion in part because of their assumption that the patriarch was the transmitter of social norms and values to his family. With the decline of the patriarch, so they believed, a vital institutional link between family and society was broken. This argument is similar to the perspective of Gerth and Mills, who wrote that a set of social roles becomes an institution when it is stabilized by a "head" who wields authority over the members. It follows from this premise that if the head loses his authority, the institutional nature of family life will become problematic.

Yet institutionalized patterns of behavior clearly persist in family life, despite the trend away from patriarchy and segregated sex roles. As others have noted (Dyer and Urban 1958: Nye and Berardo 1973), the equalitarian pattern may be as firmly institutionalized now as the traditional pattern was in the past. In the terms of Berger and Luckmann, most family behavior today is habitualized action which is accepted as typical by all members—that is, it is institutionalized behavior. In most everyday situations, parents and children base their behavior on social norms: parents know how harshly to discipline their children, and children learn from parents and friends which parental rules are fair and which to protest. These sources of institutionalization in the contemporary American family have received little attention from students of family unity, just as family members themselves pay little attention to them.

The presence of these habitualized patterns directly affects family unity. "Habitualization," Berger and Luckmann wrote, "carries with it the important psychological gain that choices are narrowed" (1966, p. 53). With choices narrowed, family members face fewer decisions which will cause disagreements and, correspondingly, have less difficulty maintaining family unity. Thus, institutional support for family unity exists through the routinization of everyday behavior even though the husband is no longer the unchallenged agent of social control.

Nowhere in contemporary family life is the psychological gain from habitualization more evident than in the families of remarried spouses and their children, where, paradoxically, habitualized behavior is often absent. We know that the unity of families of remarriages which follow a divorce is often precarious—as evidenced by the higher divorce rate for these families than for families of first marriages (U.S. Bureau of the Census 1976). And in the last few decades, remarriage after divorce—as opposed to remarriage after widowhood—has become the predominant form of remarriage. In this paper, I will argue that the higher divorce rate for remarriages after divorce is a consequence of the incomplete institutionalization of remarriage after divorce in our society. The institution of the family in the United States has developed in response to the needs of families of first marriages and families of remarriages after widowhood. But because of the complex structure, families of remarriages after divorce that include children from previous marriages must solve problems unknown to other types of families. For many of these problems, such as proper kinship terms, authority to discipline stepchildren, and legal relationships, no institutionalized solutions have emerged. As a result, there is more opportunity for disagreements and divisions among family members and more strain in many remarriages after divorce.

The incomplete institutionalization of remarriage after divorce reveals, by way of contrast, the high degree of institutionalization still present in first marriages. Family members, especially those in first marriages, rely on a wide range of habitualized behaviors to assist them in solving the common problems of family life. We take these behavioral patterns for granted until their absence forces us to create solutions on our own. Only then do we see the continuing importance of institutionalized patterns of family behavior for maintaining family unity.

I cannot provide definitive proof of the hypothesis linking the higher divorce rate for remarriages after divorce to incomplete institutionalization. There is very little quantitative information concerning remarriages. In fact, we do not even know how many stepparents and stepchildren there are in the United States. Nor has there ever been a large, random-sample survey designed with families of remarriages in mind. (Bernard's 1956 book on remarriage, for example, was based on information supplied nonrandomly by third parties.) There are, nevertheless, several studies which do provide valuable information, and there is much indirect evidence bearing on the plausibility of this hypothesis and of alternative explanations. I will review this evidence, and I will also refer occasionally to information I collected through personal interviews with a small, nonrandom sample of remarried couples and family counselors in the northeast. Despite the lack of data, I believe that the problems of families of remarriages are worth examining, especially given the recent increases in divorce and remarriage rates. In the hope that this article will stimulate further investigations, I will also present suggestions for future research.

The Problem of Family Unity

Remarriages have been common in the United States since its beginnings, but until this century almost all remarriages followed widowhood. In the

Plymouth Colony, for instance, about one-third of all men and one-quarter of all women who lived full lifetimes remarried after the death of a spouse, but there was little divorce (Demos 1970). Even as late as the 1920s, more brides and grooms were remarrying after widowhood than after divorce, according to estimates by Jacobson (1959). Since then, however, a continued increase in divorce (Norton and Glick 1976) has altered this pattern. By 1975, 84% of all brides who were remarrying were previously divorced, and 16% were widowed. For grooms who were remarrying in 1975, 86% were previously divorced (U.S. National Center for Health Statistics 1977). Thus, it is only recently that remarriage after divorce has become the predominant form of remarriage.

And since the turn of the century, remarriages after divorce have increased as a proportion of all marriages. In 1900 only 3% of all brides—including both the single and previously married—were divorced (Jacobson 1959). In 1930, 9% of all brides were divorced (Jacobson 1959), and in 1975, 25% of all brides were divorced (U.S. National Center for Health Statistics 1977). As a result, in 7 million families in 1970 one or both spouses had remarried after a divorce (U.S. Bureau of the Census 1973). Most of this increase is due to the rise in the divorce rate, but some part is due to the greater tendency of divorced and widowed adults to remarry. The remarriage rate for divorced and widowed women was about 50% higher in the mid-1970s than in 1940 (Norton and Glick 1976).

At the same time, the percentage of divorces which involved at least one child increased from 46% in 1950 to 60% in 1974 (U.S. National Center for Health Statistics 1953, 1977). The increase in the percentage of divorces which involve children means that more families of remarriages after divorce now have stepchildren. Although it is not possible with available data to calculate the exact number of families with stepchildren, we do know that in 1970 8.9 million children lived in two-parent families where one or both parents had been previously divorced (U.S. Bureau of the Census 1973). Some of these children—who constituted 15% of all children living in two-parent families—were from previous marriages, and others were from the remarriages.

Can these families of remarriages after divorce, many of which include children from previous marriages, maintain unity as well as do families of first marriages? Not according to the divorce rate. A number of studies have shown a greater risk of separation and divorce for remarriages after divorce (Becker, Landes, and Michael 1976; Bumpass and Sweet 1972; Cherlin 1977; Monahan 1958). Remarriages after widowhood appear, in contrast, to have a lower divorce rate than first marriages (Monahan 1958). A recent Bureau of the Census report (U.S. Bureau of the Census 1976) estimated that about 33% of all first marriages among people 25–35 may end in divorce, while about 40% of remarriages after divorce among people this age may end in divorce. The estimates are based on current rates of divorce, which could, of course, change greatly in the future.[1]

Conventional wisdom, however, seems to be that remarriages are more successful than first marriages. In a small, nonrandom sample of family counselors and remarried couples, I found most to be surprised at the news that divorce was more prevalent in remarriages. There are some plausible reasons for this popular misconception. Those who remarry are older, on the average, than those marrying for the first time and are presumably more mature. They have had more time to search the marriage market and to determine their own needs and preferences. In addition, divorced men may be in a better financial position and command greater work skills than younger, never-married men. (Divorced women who are supporting children, however, are often in a worse financial position—see Hoffman [1977].)

But despite these advantages, the divorce rate is higher in remarriages after divorce. The reported differences are often modest, but they appear consistently throughout 20 years of research. And the meaning of marital dissolution for family unity is clear: when a marriage dissolves, unity ends. The converse, though, is not necessarily true: a family may have a low degree of unity but remain nominally intact. Even with this limitation, I submit that the divorce rate is the best objective indicator of differences in family unity between remarriages and first marriages.

There are indicators of family unity other than divorce, but their meaning is less clear and their measurement is more difficult. There is the survey research tradition, for example, of asking people how happy or satisfied they are with their marriages. The invariable result is that almost everyone reports that they are very happy. (See, e.g., Bradburn and Caplovitz 1965; Glenn 1975; Campbell, Converse, and Rodgers 1976). It may be that our high rate of divorce increases the general level of marital satisfaction by dissolving unsatisfactory marriages. But it is also possible that the satisfaction ratings are inflated by the reluctance of some respondents to admit that their marriages are less than fully satisfying. Marriage is an important part of life for most adults— the respondents in the Campbell et al. (1976) national sample rated it second only to health as the most important aspect of their lives—and people may be reluctant to admit publicly that their marriage is troubled.

Several recent studies, nevertheless, have shown that levels of satisfaction and happiness are lower among the remarried, although the differences typically are small. Besides the Campbell et al. study, these include Glenn and Weaver (1977), who found modest differences in marital happiness in the 1973,

---

[1]A study by McCarthy (1977), however, suggests that remarriages may be more stable than first marriages for blacks. Using life-table techniques on data from 10,000 women under age 45 collected in the 1973 Survey of Family Growth, McCarthy reported that the probability of separation and divorce during the first 15 years of marriage is lower for blacks in remarriages than in first marriages, but is about 50% higher for whites in remarriages than for whites in first marriages.

1974, and 1975 General Social Surveys conducted by the National Opinion Research Center. They reported that for women, the difference between those who were remarried and those who were in a first marriage was statistically significant, while for men the difference was smaller and not significant. In addition, Renne (1971) reported that remarried, previously divorced persons were less happy with their marriages than those in first marriages in a probability sample of 4,452 Alameda County, California, households. Again, the differences were modest, but they were consistent within categories of age, sex, and race. No tests of significance were reported.

The higher divorce rate suggests that maintaining family unity is more difficult for families of remarriages after divorce. And the lower levels of marital satisfaction, which must be interpreted cautiously, also support this hypothesis. It is true, nevertheless, that many remarriages work well, and that the majority of remarriages will not end in divorce. And we must remember that the divorce rate is also at an all-time high for first marriages. But there is a difference of degree between remarriages and first marriages which appears consistently in research. We must ask why families of remarriages after divorce seem to have more difficulty maintaining family unity than do families of first marriages. Several explanations have been proposed, and we will now assess the available evidence for each.

Previous Explanations

One explanation, favored until recently by many psychiatrists, is that the problems of remarried people arise from personality disorders which preceded their marriages (see Bergler 1948). People in troubled marriages, according to this view, have unresolved personal conflicts which must be treated before a successful marriage can be achieved. Their problems lead them to marry second spouses who may be superficially quite different from their first spouse but are characterologically quite similar. As a result, this theory states, remarried people repeat the problems of their first marriages.

If this explanation were correct, one would expect that people in remarriages would show higher levels of psychiatric symptomatology than people in first marriages. But there is little evidence of this. On the contrary, Overall (1971) reported that in a sample of 2,000 clients seeking help for psychiatric problems, currently remarried people showed lower levels of psychopathology on a general rating scale than persons in first marriages and currently divorced persons. These findings, of course, apply only to people who sought psychiatric help. And it may be, as Overall noted, that the differences emerged because remarried people are more likely to seek help for less serious problems. The findings, nevertheless, weaken the psychoanalytic interpretation of the problems of remarried life.

On the other hand, Monahan (1958) and Cherlin (1977) reported that the divorce rate was considerably higher for people in their third marriages who had divorced twice than for people in their second marriages. Perhaps personality disorders among some of those who marry several times prevent them from achieving a successful marriage. But even with the currently high rates of divorce and remarriage, only a small proportion of all adults marry more than twice. About 10% of all adults in 1975 had married twice, but less than 2% had married three or more times (U.S. Bureau of the Census 1976).

Most remarried people, then, are in a second marriage. And the large number of people now divorcing and entering a second marriage also undercuts the psychoanalytic interpretation. If current rates hold, about one-third of all young married people will become divorced, and about four-fifths of these will remarry. It is hard to believe that the recent increases in divorce and remarriage are due to the sudden spread of marriage-threatening personality disorders to a large part of the young adult population. I conclude, instead, that the psychoanalytic explanation for the rise in divorce and the difficulties of remarried spouses and their children is at best incomplete.[2]

A second possible explanation is that once a person has divorced he or she is less hesitant to do so again. Having divorced once, a person knows how to get divorced and what to expect from family members, friends, and the courts. This explanation is plausible and probably accounts for some of the difference in divorce rates. But it does not account for all of the research findings on remarriage, such as the finding of Becker et al. (1976) that the presence of children from a previous marriage increased the probability of divorce for women in remarriages, while the presence of children from the new marriage reduced the probability of divorce. I will discuss the implications of this study below, but let me note here that a general decrease in the reluctance of remarried persons to divorce would not explain this finding. Moreover, the previously divorced may be more hesitant to divorce again because of the stigma attached to divorcing twice. Several remarried people I interviewed expressed great reluctance to divorce a second time. They reasoned that friends and relatives excused one divorce but would judge them incompetent at marriage after two divorces.

Yet another explanation for the higher divorce rate is the belief that many remarried men are deficient at fulfilling their economic responsibilities. We know that divorce is more likely in families where the husband has low earnings (Goode 1956). Some remarried men, therefore, may be unable to earn a sufficient amount of money to support a family. It is conceivable that this inability to be a successful breadwinner could account for all of the divorce rate differential, but statistical studies of divorce suggest otherwise. Three

[2]Despite the lack of convincing evidence, I am reluctant to discount this explanation completely. Clinical psychologists and psychiatrists with whom I have talked insist that many troubled married persons they have treated had made the same mistakes twice and were in need of therapy to resolve long-standing problems. Their clinical experience should not be ignored, but this "divorce-proness" syndrome seems inadequate as a complete explanation for the greater problems of remarried people.

recent multivariate analyses of survey data on divorce have shown that remarried persons still had a higher probability of divorce or separation, independent of controls for such socioeconomic variables as husband's earnings (Becker et al. 1976), husband's educational attainment (Bumpass and Sweet 1972), and husband's and wife's earnings, employment status, and savings (Cherlin 1977). These analyses show that controlling for low earnings can reduce the difference in divorce probabilities, but they also show that low earnings cannot fully explain the difference. It is possible, nevertheless, that a given amount of income must be spread thinner in many remarriages, because of child-support or alimony payments (although the remarried couple also may be receiving these payments). But this type of financial strain must be distinguished from the questionable notion that many remarried husbands are inherently unable to provide for a wife and children.

Institutional Support

The unsatisfactory nature of all these explanations leads us to consider one more interpretation. I hypothesize that the difficulties of couples in remarriages after divorce stem from a lack of institutionalized guidelines for solving many common problems of their remarried life. The lack of institutional support is less serious when neither spouse has a child from a previous marriage. In this case, the family of remarriage closely resembles families of first marriages, and most of the norms for first marriages apply. But when at least one spouse has children from a previous marriage, family life often differs sharply from first marriages. Frequently, as I will show, family members face problems quite unlike those in first marriages—problems for which institutionalized solutions do not exist. And without accepted solutions to their problems, families of remarriages must resolve difficult issues by themselves. As a result, solving everyday problems is sometimes impossible without engendering conflict and confusion among family members.

The complex structure of families of remarriages after divorce which include children from a previous marriage has been noted by others (Bernard 1956; Bohannan 1970; Duberman 1975). These families are expanded in the number of social roles and relationships they possess and also are expanded in space over more than one household. The additional social roles include stepparents, stepchildren, stepsiblings, and the new spouses of noncustodial parents, among others. And the links between the households are the children of previous marriages. These children are commonly in the custody of one parent—usually the mother—but they normally visit the noncustodial parent regularly. Thus they promote communication among the divorced parents, the new stepparent, and the noncustodial parent's new spouse.

Family relationships can be quite complex, because the new kin in a remarriage after divorce do not, in general, replace the kin from the first marriage as they do in a remarriage after widowhood. Rather, they add to the existing kin (Fast and Cain 1966). But this complexity alone does not necessarily imply that problems of family unity will develop. While families of remarriages may appear complicated to Americans, there are many societies in which complicated kinship rules and family patterns coexist with a functioning, stable family system (Bohannan 1963, Fox 1967).

In most of these societies, however, familial roles and relationships are well defined. Family life may seem complex to Westerners, but activity is regulated by established patterns of behavior. The central difference, then, between families of remarriages in the United States and complicated family situations in other societies is the lack of institutionalized social regulation of remarried life in this country. Our society, oriented toward first marriages, provides little guidance on problems peculiar to remarriages, especially remarriages after divorce.

In order to illustrate the incomplete institutionalization of remarriage and its consequences for family life, let us examine two of the major institutions in society: language and the law. "Language," Gerth and Mills (1953, p. 305) wrote, "is necessary to the operations of institutions. For the symbols used in institutions coordinate the roles that compose them, and justify the enactment of these roles by the members of the institution." Where no adequate terms exist for an important social role, the institutional support for this role is deficient, and general acceptance of the role as a legitimate pattern of activity is questionable.

Consider English terms for the roles peculiar to remarriage after divorce. The term "stepparent," as Bohannan (1970) has observed, originally meant a person who replaced a dead parent, not a person who was an additional parent. And the negative connotations of the "stepparent," especially the "stepmother," are well known (Bernard 1956; Smith 1953). Yet there are no other terms in use. In some situations, no term exists for a child to use in addressing a stepparent. If the child calls her mother "mom," for example, what should she call her stepmother? This lack of appropriate terms for parents in remarriages after divorce can have negative consequences for family functioning. In one family I interviewed, the wife's children wanted to call their stepfather "dad," but the stepfather's own children, who also lived in the household, refused to allow this usage. To them, sharing the term "dad" represented a threat to their claim on their father's attention and affection. The dispute caused bad feelings, and it impaired the father's ability to act as a parent to all the children in the household.

For more extended relationships, the lack of appropriate terms is even more acute. At least the word "stepparent," however inadequte, has a widely accepted meaning. But there is no term a child living with his mother can use to describe his relationship to the woman his father remarried after he divorced the child's mother. And, not surprisingly, the rights and duties of the child and this woman toward each other are unclear. Nor is the problem limited to kinship terms. Suppose a child's parents both remarry and he alternates between their households under a joint custody arrangement. Where, then, is his "home"? And who are the members of his "family"? These linguistic inadequacies correspond to the absence of widely accepted definitions for many of the roles and relationships in families of remarriage. The absence of proper terms is both a symptom and a cause of some of the problems of remarried life.

As for the law, it is both a means of social control and an indicator of accepted patterns of behavior. It was to the law, for instance, that Durkheim turned for evidence on the forms of social solidarity. When we examine family law, we find a set of traditional guidelines, based on precedent, which define the rights and duties of family members. But as Weitzman (1974) has shown, implicit in the precedents is the assumption that the marriage in question is a first marriage. For example, Weitzman found no provisions for several problems of remarriage, such as balancing the financial obligations of husbands to their spouses and children from current and previous marriages, defining the wife's obligations to husbands and children from the new and the old marriages, and reconciling the competing claims of current and ex-spouses for shares of the estate of a deceased spouse.

Legal regulations concerning incest and consanguineal marriage are also inadequate for families of remarriages. In all states marriage and sexual relations are prohibited between persons closely related by blood, but in many states these restrictions do not cover sexual relations or marriage between other family members in a remarriage—between a stepmother and a stepson, for example, or between two stepchildren (Goldstein and Katz 1965). Mead (1970), among others, has argued that incest taboos serve the important function of allowing children to develop affection for and identification with other family members without the risk of sexual exploitation. She suggested that current beliefs about incest—as embodied in law and social norms—fail to provide adequate security and protection for children in households of remarriage.[3]

The law, then, ignores the special problems of families of remarriages after divorce. It assumes, for the most part, that remarriages are similar to first marriages. Families of remarriages after divorce, consequently, often must deal with problems such as financial obligations or sexual relations without legal regulations or clear legal precedent. The law, like the language, offers incomplete institutional support to families of remarriages.

In addition, other customs and conventions of family life are deficient when applied to remarriages after divorce. Stepparents, for example, have difficulty determining their proper disciplinary relationship to stepchildren. One woman I interviewed, determined not to show favoritism toward her own children, disciplined them more harshly than her stepchildren. Other couples who had

---

[3]Bernard (1956) noted this problem in the preface to the reprinted edition of her book on remarriage. "Institutional patterns," she wrote, "are needed to help remarried parents establish relationships with one another conducive to the protection of their children."

children from the wife's previous marriage reported that the stepfather had difficulty establishing himself as a disciplinarian in the household. Fast and Cain (1966), in a study of about 50 case records from child-guidance settings, noted many uncertainties among stepparents about appropriate role behavior. They theorized that the uncertainties derived from the sharing of the role of parent between the stepparent and the noncustodial, biological parent. Years ago, when most remarriages took place after widowhood, this sharing did not exist. Now, even though most remarriages follow divorce, generally accepted guidelines for sharing parenthood still have not emerged.

There is other evidence consistent with the idea that the incomplete institutionalization of remarriage after divorce may underlie the difficulties of families of remarriages. Becker et al. (1976) analyzed the Survey of Economic Opportunity, a nationwide study of approximately 30,000 households. As I mentioned above, they found that the presence of children from a previous marriage increased the probability of divorce for women in remarriages, while the presence of children from the new marriage reduced the probability of divorce. This is as we would expect, since children from a previous marriage expand the family across households and complicate the structure of family roles and relationships. But children born into the new marriage bring none of these complications. Consequently, only children from a previous marriage should add to the special problems of families of remarriages.[4]

In addition, Goetting (1978a, 1978b) studies the attitudes of remarried people toward relationships among adults who are associated by broken marital ties, such as ex-spouses and the people ex-spouses remarry. Bohannan (1970) has called these people "quasi-kin." Goetting presented hypothetical situations involving the behavior of quasi-kin to 90 remarried men and 90 remarried women who were white, previously divorced, and who had children from previous marriages. The subjects were asked to approve, disapprove, or express indifference about the behavior in each situation. Goetting then arbitrarily decided that the respondents reached "consensus" on a given situation if any of the three possible response categories received more than half of all responses. But even by this lenient definition, consensus was not reached on the proper behavior in most of the hypothetical situations. For example, in situations involving conversations between a person's present spouse and his or her ex-spouse, the only consensus of the respondents was that the pair should say "hello." Beyond that, there was no consensus on whether they should engage in polite conversation in public places or on the telephone or

---

[4]In an earlier paper (Cherlin 1977), I found that children affected the probability that a woman in a first marriage or remarriage would divorce only when the children were of preschool age. But the National Longitudinal Surveys of Mature Women, from which this analysis was drawn, contained no information about whether the children of remarried wives were from the woman's previous or current marriage. Since the Becker et al. (1976) results showed that this distinction is crucial, we cannot draw any relevant inferences about children and remarriage from my earlier study.

whether the ex-spouse should be invited into the new spouse's home while waiting to pick up his or her children. Since meetings of various quasi-kin must occur regularly in the lives of most respondents, their disagreement is indicative of their own confusion about how to act in common family situations.

Still, there are many aspects of remarried life which are similar to life in first marriages, and these are subject to established rules of behavior. Even some of the unique aspects of remarriage may be regulated by social norms—such as the norms concerning the size and nature of wedding ceremonies in remarriages (Hollingshead 1952). Furthermore, as Goode (1956) noted, remarriage is itself an institutional solution to the ambiguous status of the divorced (and not remarried) parent. But the day-to-day life of remarried adults and their children also includes many problems for which there are no institutionalized solutions. And since members of a household of remarriage often have competing or conflicting interests (Bernard 1956), the lack of consensual solutions can make these problems more serious than they otherwise would be. One anthropologist, noting the lack of relevant social norms, wrote, "the present situation approaches chaos, with each individual set of families having to work out its own destiny without any realistic guidelines" (Bohannan 1970, p. 137).

Discussion and Suggestions for Research

The lack of institutionalized support for remarriage after divorce from language, the law, and custom is apparent. But when institutional support for family life exists, we take it for granted. People in first marriages rarely stop to notice that a full set of kinship terms exists, that the law regulates their relationships, or that custom dictates much of their behavior toward spouses and children. Because they pay little attention to it, the institutional nature of everyday life in first marriages can be easily underestimated. But such support contributes to the unity of first marriages despite the decline of the patriarch, who was the agent of social control in past time. Institutional guidelines become manifest not only through the transmission of social pressure by a family head but also through the general acceptance of certain habitual behavior patterns as typical of family life. Since this latter process is an ongoing characteristic of social life, the pure "companionship" family—which, in fairness, Burgess and Locke defined only as an ideal type—will never emerge. We have seen this by examining the contrasting case of remarriage after divorce. In this type of marriage, institutional support is noticeably lacking in several respects, and this deficiency has direct consequences for proper family functioning. I have tried to show how the incomplete institutionalization of remarriage after divorce makes the maintenance of family unity more difficult.

One of the first tasks for future research on remarriage is to establish some basic social demographic facts: what proportion of remarried couples have children present from a previous marriage, what proportion have children present from the remarriage, how many children visit noncustodial parents, how frequent these visits are, and so on. As I mentioned, there is no reliable information on these questions now. The U. S. Bureau of the Census, for example, has not discriminiated in most of its surveys between parents and stepparents or between children and stepchildren. Yet until figures are available, we can only guess at the number of families which face potential difficulties because of complex living arrangements.

And if we reinterviewed families of remarriage some time after obtaining this information from them, we could begin to test the importance of institutional support for family unity. It follows from the argument advanced here that the more complex the family's situation—the more quasi-kin who live nearby, the more frequently adults and children interact with quasi-kin, the more likely each remarried spouse is to have children from a previous marriage—the more serious becomes the lack of institutional guidelines. Thus, adults in remarriages with a more complex structure should be more likely to divorce or separate in the future, other things being equal. Also, a more complex structure might increase the financial strain on family members, so their earnings and financial obligations should be carefully assessed.

But beyond collecting this fundamental information, we need to discover, by a variety of means, what norms are emerging concerning remarriage and how they emerge. Content analyses of literature, for example, or close study of changes in the language and the law may be illuminating. Just in the past few years, discussion groups, adult education courses, newsletters, and self-help books for remarried parents have proliferated. Whether these developments are central to the instutionalization of remarriage remains to be seen, but they represent possible sources of information about institutionalization which should be monitored. In addition, detailed ethnographic studies could allow us to uncover emerging patterns of institutionalization among families of remarriages.

And in all these investigations of the institutionalization of remarried life, we must develop a perspective different from that of traditional family research. In much past research—starting with the work of Burgess and others—family sociologists have been concerned primarily with the interpersonal relations of family members, especially of husbands and wives (Lasch 1977). But sociologists' theories—and their research strategies—have assumed, for the most part, that interpersonal relations in families can be accounted for without many references to social institutions. Thus, Burgess and Locke (1945) popularized the notion of the companionship family, whose stability depended largely on what went on within the household. And Locke (1951) measured marital adjustment through a questionnaire which focused largely on such personal characteristics as adaptability and sociability. Yet in order to understand family life—whether in first marriages or remarriages—we must explicitly consider the influences of social institutions on husbands and wives and on parents and children.

We need to know what the institutional links are between family and society which transmit social norms about everyday behavior. That is, we need to know exactly how patterns of family behavior come to be accepted and how proper solutions for family problems come to be taken for granted. And the recent rise in the number of remarriages after divorce may provide us with a natural laboratory for observing this process of institutionalization. As remarriage after divorce becomes more common, remarried parents and their children probably will generate standards of conduct in conjunction with the larger society. By observing these developments, we can improve our understanding of the sources of unity in married—and remarried—life.

References

Ariès, Philippe. 1962. *Centuries of Childhood.* New York: Knopf.
Becker, G., E. Landes, and R. Michael. 1976 "Economics of Marital Instability." Working Paper no. 153. Stanford, Calif.: National Bureau of Economic Research.
Berger, Peter L., and Thomas Luckmann. 1966. *The Social Construction of Reality.* New York: Doubleday.
Bergler, Edmund. 1948. *Divorce Won't Help.* New York: Harper & Bros.
Bernard, Jessie. 1956. *Remarriage.* New York: Dryden.
Blood, Robert O., and Donald M. Wolfe. 1960. *Husbands and Wives.* New York: Free Press.
Bohannan, Paul. 1963 *Social Anthropology.* New York: Holt, Rinehart & Winston.
———. 1970. "Divorce Chains, Households of Remarriage, and Multiple Divorces." Pp. 127–39 in *Divorce and After,* edited by Paul Bohannan. New York: Doubleday.
Bradburn, Norman, and David Caplovitz. 1965 *Reports on Happiness.* Chicago: Aldine.
Bumpass, L. L., and A. Sweet. 1972. "Differentials in Marital Instability: 1970." *American Sociological Review* 37 (December): 754–66.
Burgess, Ernest W., and Harvey J. Locke. 1945 *The Family: From Institution to Companionship.* New York: American.
Campbell, Angus, Philip E. Converse, and Willard L. Rodgers. 1976 *The Quality of American Life.* New York: Russell Sage.
Cherlin, A. 1977. "The Effects of Children on Marital Dissolution." *Demography* 14 (August): 265–72.
Demos, John. 1970. *A Little Commonwealth: Family Life in Plymouth Colony.* New York: Oxford University Press.
Duberman, Lucile. 1975 *The Reconstructed Family.* Chicago: Nelson-Hall.
Dyer, W. G., and D. Urban. 1958. "The Institutionalization of Equalitarian Family Norms." *Journal of Marriage and Family Living* 20 (February): 53–58.
Fast, I., and A. C. Cain. 1966. "The Stepparent Role: Potential for Disturbances in Family Functioning." *American Journal of Orthopsychiatry* 36 (April): 485–91.
Fox, Robin. 1967. *Kinship and Marriage.* Baltimore: Penguin.
Gerth, Hans, and C. Wright Mills. 1953. *Character and Social Structure.* New York: Harcourt, Brace & Co.
Glenn, N. 1975. "The Contribution of Marriage to the Psychological Well-Being of Males and Females." *Journal of Marriage and the Family* 37 (August): 594–601.
Glenn, N., and C. Weaver. 1977. "The Marital Happiness of Remarried Divorced Persons." *Journal of Marriage and the Family* 39 (May): 331–37.
Goetting, Ann. 1978a. "The Normative Integration of the Former Spouse Relationship." Paper presented at the annual meeting of the American Sociological Association, San Francisco, September 4–8.
———.1978b. "The Normative Integration of Two Divorce Chain Relationships." Paper presented at the annual meeting of the Southwestern Sociological Association, Houston, April 12–15.
Goldstein, Joseph, and Jay Katz. 1965. *The Family and the Law.* New York: Free Press.
Goode, William J. 1956. *Women in Divorce.* New York: Free Press.

Hoffman, S. 1977. "Marital Instability and the Economic Status of Women." *Demography* 14 (February): 67–76.

Hollingshead, A. B. 1952. "Marital Status and Wedding Behavior." *Marriage and Family Living* (November), pp. 308–11.

Jacobson, Paul H. 1959. *American Marriage and Divorce.* New York: Rinehart.

Lasch, Christopher. 1977. *Haven in a Heartless World: The Family Besieged.* New York: Basic.

Locke, Harvey J. 1951 *Predicting Adjustment in Marriage: A comparison of a Divorced and a Happily Married Group.* New York: Holt.

McCarthy, J. F. 1977. "A Comparison of Dissolution of First and Second Marriages." Paper presented at the 1977 annual meeting of the Population Association of America, St. Louis, April 21–23.

Mead, M. 1970. "Anomalies in American Postdivorce Relationships." P. 107–25 in *Divorce and After,* edited by Paul Bohannan. New York: Doubleday.

Monahan, T. P. 1958. "The Changing Nature and Instability of Remarriages." *Eugenics Quarterly* 5:73–85.

Norton, A. J., and P. C. Glick. 1976. "Marital Instability: Past, Present, and Future." *Journal of Social Issues* 32 (Winter): 5–20.

Nye, F. Ivan, and Felix M. Berardo. 1973. *The Family: Its Structure and Interaction.* New York: Macmillan.

Overall, J. E. 1971. "Associations between Marital History and the Nature of Manifest Psychopathology." *Journal of Abnormal Psychology* 78 (2): 213–21.

Renne, K. S. 1971. "Health and Marital Experience in an Urban Population." *Journal of Marriage and the Family* 33 (May): 338–50.

Safilios-Rothschild, Constantina. 1970. "The Study of Family Power Structure: A Review 1960–1969." *Journal of Marriage and the Family* 32 (November): 539–52.

Shorter, Edward. 1975. *The Making of the Modern Family.* New York: Basic.

Smith, William C. 1953. *The Stepchild.* Chicago: University of Chicago Press.

U.S. Bureau of the Census. 1973 *U.S. Census of the Population: 1970. Persons by Family Characteristics.* Final Report PC(2)-4B. Washington, D.C.: Government Printing Office.

———. 1976. *Number, Timing, and Duration of Marriages and Divorces in the United States: June 1975.* Current Population Reports, Series P-20, No. 297. Washington, D.C.: Government Printing Office.

U.S. National Center for Health Statistics. 1953. *Vital Statistics of the United States, 1950.* Vol 2. *Marriage, Divorce, Natality, Fetal Mortality, and Infant Mortality Data.* Washington, D.C.: Government Printing Office.

———. 1977. *Vital Statistic Report. Advance Report. Final Marriage Statistics, 1975.* Washington, D.C.: Government Printing Office.

Weitzman, L. J. 1974. "Legal Regulation of Marriage: Tradition and Change." *California Law Review* 62:1169–1288.

Young, Michael, and Peter Wilmott. 1973. *The Symmetrical Family.* New York: Pantheon.

4

Parents and Children

Introduction

No aspect of childhood seems more natural, universal, and changeless than the relations between parents and children. Yet the historical evidence suggests that there have been profound changes in the conceptions of childhood and adulthood, in the psychological relations between children and parents, and in the stages of the life span. No doubt there have always been emotional bonds between parents and children. But before the eighteenth century, people placed little emphasis on these bonds or on the value of children as unique individuals. In the past, relations between parents and children were based largely on economic necessity; children were a necessary source of labor in the family economy and a source of support in old age. But before reliable contraceptives were invented, children were often born when another mouth to feed threatened the survival of the family. Today, children have been transformed into economic liabilities, and parents can have sex without having children. But children now have profound emotional significance. Parents have children hoping that offspring will provide intimacy, identity, and even genetic immortality.

Social scientists have traditionally looked at parent-child relations under the heading of *socialization*, a process by which new generations replace their elders. Children are born, socialized, and take their place in the social order until they die; new children are born, and the process is repeated. The obedient child, in this conception, is the forerunner of the good citizen. The parents are cast in the role of upholders of social order and civilization itself.

Concepts of socialization also imply images of what children are like. Two images of the child have prevailed in Western culture. One is the child as angel, all sweetness and innocence, to be protected from the sexuality and workaday concerns of the adult world. This image has always coexisted with actual conditions of great brutality and neglect of children. The opposing image is found in both Calvinistic Protestantism and early psychoanalysis: it is the child as devil, imp of darkness, seething cauldron of murderous and sexual impulses, a beast who must be tamed. This image has been forcefully portrayed in fiction and films, such as *Lord of the Flies* and *The Omen*.

Both images of the child share the assumption that socialization is something done to children, that they learn to be reasonable, moral, and competent from the outside as a result of adult guidance. As Jerome Kagan points

404

out in his selection here, these traditional views of child development contain several myths or, as Kagan puts it, prejudices. One of these is the assumption that "each day the child is being seriously influenced by the actions of others, and that the relationship between these social experiences (say, being spanked for stealing money) and his future behavior, motivational, and moral development is absolute, fixed, and knowable." Another questionable assumption is that there is an ideal, best adult, as well as a set of parental practices that will produce this ideal adult.

Such assumptions not only overlook the lack of social consensus concerning what the ideal adult is—business executive, artist, politician, teacher, revolutionary—they also overlook children's role in their own development. The creative side of human growth has been most forcefully stated and experimentally documented in the work of Jean Piaget (1969). According to his view, children are active participants in the attainment of logical and moral competence rather than the passive recipients of rules and rewards from the outside. Infants banging their cups, throwing toys out of their crib, or fitting objects into each other are actually performing experiments in physics, learning about the nature of matter. Later, when they learn to communicate in words, they will also learn the rules of logic and morality. As Roger Brown writes:

> The mature persons with whom a child interacts behave in accordance with such systems of norms or rules as are called logic, mathematics, language, morality, aesthetics... and so on. For the most part these systems have not been explicitly formulated by the adults whose behavior is governed by them and they will not be explicitly formulated by the child who acquires them. This process is not a simple "passing over" of the systems from one generation to another. What each child extracts at a given age is a function of his idiosyncratic experience and of his present intellectual capabilities. The systems governing the child change as he grows older and they need not, in the end, simply reproduce the rules that prevail in his society. The outcome can be unique and sometimes revolutionary (1965, p. 193).

Child Abuse

Another central theme in the traditional view of parent-child relations was harmony between needs of children, parents, and society. The child's need for love and care was assumed to be matched by complementary needs of parents—especially mothers—to nurture them. Society, for its part, supported parental roles because of required further population. But parental love is not a social universal. Neither families nor societies always require or want the children born to them. Indeed, as noted earlier, infanticide has been a traditional means of controlling population, not only in "primitive" societies but in our own Western culture as well until the invention of reliable contraception. Recent historical studies show that in the allocation of scarce resources, European society preferred adults to children.

Recent findings by sociologists and psychiatrists have revealed a greater amount of physical and psychological conflict in families than had been recognized. For example, many researchers in the field of child abuse point out that such incidents are a potential for many parents, given a sufficient degree of environmental strain. Most child abusers are not pathological monsters, and the line between normal punishment and child abuse is sometimes hard to draw. In sum then, the traditional social science view of parenthood has accepted parents too often as nurturers and socializers of children and too rarely as adults whose own needs may come into conflict with those of their children.

In one of the leading studies on the battered child syndrome (Steele & Pollack 1968, p. 104), the sample consisted of parents of infants and children under three who had been significantly abused by their parents, short of direct murder. Although these children had come to the attention of hospitals, doctors, or the police, their parents seemed a cross section of the population. Such attributes as social class, occupation, IQ, or urban-rural residence did not set them apart. Nor did the researchers find any particular psychopathology or character type. What they did find was a pattern of childrearing that exaggerated the normal. They conclude:

> There seems to be an unbroken spectrum of parental action towards children ranging from the breaking of bones and the fracturing of skulls through severe bruising, through severe spanking and on to mild "reminder" pats on the bottom. To be aware of this, one has only to look at the families of one's friends and neighbors, to look and listen to the parent-child interactions at the playground and the supermarket, or even to recall how one raised one's own children or how one was raised oneself. The amount of yelling, scolding, slapping, punching, hitting, and yanking acted out by parents on very small children is almost shocking (p. 104).

Although the idea of the battered child thus suggests a physical phenomenon, child abuse is, as Eli H. Newberger and Richard Bourne point out here, a social phenomenon created and shaped through the definitions applied by clinicians and other professionals—often more to the advantage of their own interests than to the benefit of the clients they are supposed to serve. Children are frequently battered in our society. Reprehensible battering or "abuse" is a label, perhaps well deserved, but one that varies with such factors as social class, ethnicity, and professional intervention.

The problem is not simply that parents are sadistic. The modern family, especially in its more isolated version, gives parents nearly absolute power over children at the same time that it makes parenthood more burdensome. Jules Henry states the problem succinctly as follows:

> Pinched off alone in one's own house, shielded from critical eyes, one can be as irrational as one pleases with one's children as long as severe damage does not attract the attention of the police (1963, pp. 331–332).

The realities of modern parenthood, especially motherhood, are often considerably less idyllic than the myth portrays them. As Alice Rossi points out in her selection here, the transition to the role of parent is usually experienced as a life crisis. Even "good" mothers may be overwhelmed at times by the relentless demands of young children and be horrified by the rage their children are capable of stirring up in them. For battering parents, the myth that children are supposed to be fulfilling and gratifying has dangerous effects; these parents blame their own children for not living up to the mythical standards they suppose other children meet.

Maternal Deprivation

If the sentimental model of the family tends to place child beaters out in the moral limbo reserved for sex fiends and other "degenerates," while denying the danger to children from ordinary parents, it also exaggerated in an opposite but perhaps equal direction another threat to children, that of maternal deprivation.

The first studies of children placed in institutions early in life revealed many cases of irreparable emotional, intellectual, and, in some cases, physical damage. The concept of maternal deprivation passed into the popular lore on childrearing to mean that any separation from the mother must have devastating effects on the child. All separations, regardless of how long they lasted and for what reasons and without regard to what happened to the child in the interim, tended to be lumped together. One of the consequences has been large-scale inattention to the possibilities of enriching children's lives through day-care centers, supervised playgrounds, and similar institutions that relieve the strain of both parenthood and childhood.

Another consequence has been inattention to exploring the notion that men, as well as women, enjoy the capacity to be effective nurturers of their children. Robert A. Fein argues, in his article reprinted here, that social science has been lagging in its understanding of the nurturant possibilities of fatherhood and therefore has failed to make some potentially positive contributions to social policies affecting families in the United States. In the long run, however, we must understand that the power of parents to influence their children's lives is limited in at least two fundamental ways. The first involves interactional limitations. Jane Loevinger (1959) argues, for example, that in spite of the physical power of the parent over the child, no parent can ensure that the child will learn precisely what the parent wants him or her to learn. Even the professional knowledge of the psychiatrist or the child-development expert does not help; the parent-child relationship inevitably involves a conflict of interest and impulse.

Indeed, the vast literature advising parents how to rear their children has generated untold guilt and anxiety. It suggests that the normal state of family life is quiet and harmonious, and any tensions between parents and children or unhappiness in a child are the parents' fault.

Laura Lein and Mary Blehar's study of working couples as parents, reprinted here, reveals the stresses created by overly idealized images of child-rearing. Although the researchers were impressed by the ability of these families to cope with the demands of child care, household work, and jobs outside the home, the family members themselves, especially the women, were burdened by standards of performance they could not live up to. The study presents a realistic picture of family and work life in America today. These families may not resemble the image of the perfect, happy family our culture idealizes, but neither do they portray the narcissistic, disintegrating family described by some of our gloomiest social critics.

References

Piaget, J. 1969. *The Psychology of the Child*. New York: Harper Torchbooks.

Brown, R. 1965. *Social Psychology*. Glencoe, Illinois: Free Press.

Steele, B. F. and C. B. Pollack, 1968. A psychiatric study of parents who abuse infants and small children. In R. E. Helfer and C. H. Kempe (eds.) *The Battered Child*. Chicago: University of Chicago Press.

Henry, J. 1963. *Culture against Man*. New York: Random House.

Loevinger, J. 1959. "Patterns of Child Rearing as Theories of Learning." *Journal of Abnormal and Social Psychology*, Vol. 59, pp. 148–150.

Chapter 8

The Child and the Family

The Psychological Requirements
for Human Development

Jerome Kagan

The Western mind is friendly to four prejudices regarding the development of the child. The first premise is that each day the child is being seriously influenced by the actions of others, and that the relationship between those social experiences (say, being spanked for stealing money) and his future behavioral, motivational and moral development is absolute, fixed and knowable. The second assumption is that development consists of a series of discrete stages, each with its own unique pattern of characteristics, catalyzed by a special alchemy between maturation and experience. "Now you see it, now you don't" captures this metaphor for growth. The third notion, a corollary of the second, is that successful passage through one developmental stage makes passage through the next easier. Contrariwise, failure to master all the necessary tasks of one stage impedes movement to the next higher one, as if development were like rising through successive Boy Scout ranks rather than an intercontinental sea journey. The final premise, which is at once the most profound and most controversial, is that there is an ideal, best adult and, correspondingly, a best collection of experiences that maximizes the probability that the ideal adult will emerge from the cacophony of childhood encounters. In simpler terms, most American parents believe in the existence of a small set of psychological traits that are necessarily correlated with a maximally happy adulthood. If parents and teachers praise, punish and posture at the right time and with the proper enthusiasm—like the conducting of a major symphony—they would create the perfect adult. This essay questions this last idea by suggesting that there are several reasonable answers to the query,

From *Raising Children in Modern America: Problems and Prospective Solutions*, edited by Nathan B. Talbot, M.D. © 1976 by Little, Brown and Company (Inc.). By permission of Little, Brown and Company.

"What are a child's psychological requirements?" The substance of each of the answers depends, first, on one's views concerning the nature of the human child and the mechanisms that mediate his growth and, second, on the subtle messages the larger society communicates to parents regarding the kinds of adult that are needed for the succeeding generation.

The most popular contemporary American conception of the young child is that he is an inherently helpless, dependent organism prepared by nature to establish a strong emotional bond with the adults who care for him. If these adults attend to his drives and desires with consistency and affection, it is assumed that he will gradually learn to trust them, be motivated to adopt their values and develop such a sturdy concept of self that he will possess a vital capacity for love and will be able to deal with conflict, anxiety and frustration effectively. The traditional Japanese mother, prior to the Western accultura-tion of her attitudes, viewed her young infant through different lenses. He was neither helpless nor dependent, but a willful, asocial creature destined to move away from people unless she could tame him and deflect his natural instincts. Hence, she usually soothed and quieted her infant, suppressing the excitement that the American mother tried to arouse. The Indian mother in the highlands of Guatemala believes that infants are born with different dispositions depend-ing upon the day of their birth. She is convinced there is little she can do to change these fixed developmental directions, and her fatalism leads her to stand aside so that her child can grow as nature intended.[1] Most children in all three communities grow up equally well adapted to their societies. More-over, there is such a remarkable similarity among the ten-year-olds in each of these settings that one is forced to question the validity of these local theories.

Most parents are absolutistic in their view of psychological growth, assum-ing that all children should be headed for the same ideal telos and should require a best combination of psychological nourishment to complete the long and difficult journey. Contrast this view of the infant, which is predominant in the United States, with the more relativistic notion that a child's psychologi-cal requirements not only change with his stage of development, but also become, with age, increasingly dependent upon the local culture. Lest this statement sound too general, consider a concrete illustration. In contemporary America, a willingness to defend intrusions into one's space and property and acceptance of the effect of anger and the motive of hostility are regarded as necessary for taming each day. Hence, it is generally acknowledged that the family should not always punish mild displays of anger or aggression in or out of the home. A parent who never permitted the child any expression of hos-tility would be called bad names by the majority of American psychologists, psychiatrists, pediatricians and social workers.

Among the Utku of Hudson Bay, who are restricted for nine months a year to a tight three hundred feet of living space, it is necessary that any sign of anger, hostility and aggression be consistently suppressed. A good mother conscientiously starts to train this inhibition as early as twenty-four months of her child's age by ignoring acts of defiance and, by the time he is nine, the behavioral indexes of anger, so common in American children, are not in evidence.[2] An Eskimo mother who allowed her child easy displays of aggression would be called the same bad names we apply to the American mother who did not permit this behavior. The Eskimo ten-year-old is as well adjusted to his community as his American counterpart. But if the Eskimo and American children exchanged locales, each would quickly develop the symptoms psychiatrists call neurotic. Each would have brought to his new home a set of dispositions inappropriate to the standards of that residential space.

Freda Rebelsky has noted that during the first ten months of life infants in the eastern part of Holland are held only when they are being fed.[3] At other times, they lie tightly bound in bassinets that are placed in small rooms isolated from the more dynamic parts of the house. They have no toys, no mobiles, and minimal stimulation, and the amount and variety of adult contact is far less than that encountered by the average American infant. Yet, by age five, these Dutch children do not seem to be different from five-year-old Americans. Indian infants living in the isolated highlands of Guatemala are held by adults over six hours a day, in contrast to the sixty minutes of maternal carrying characteristic of American Homes. Yet, at age ten, there is no evidence of major differences in fundamental intellectual competence or affective vitality between Indian and American children.

Since these are not uniquely exotic examples of relativism in child development, it is reasonable to repeat the question contained in the title of this paper: namely, "What do children need?" when food and protection from excessive disease and physical discomfort are guaranteed. We wish to take a strong stand on this issue by suggesting that *children do not require any specific actions from adults in order to develop optimally.* There is no good evidence to indicate that children must have a certain amount or schedule of cuddling, kissing, spanking, holding or deprivation of privileges in order to become gratified and productive adults. The child does have some psychological needs, but there is no fixed list of parental behaviors that can be counted on to fill these critical requirements.

Psychologists must develop an appreciation for the message it took biologists so long to learn: namely, that environmental niches are neither good nor bad in any absolute sense. Rather, they are appropriate or inappropriate for a specific species; hence, an organism's requirements can never be separated from the environment in which it grows. Frogs are best situated in a New England forest pond, not in the Mojave Desert; lizards have the opposite profile of ecological requirements. To ask what a child needs is to pose half a question. We must always specify the demands the community will make upon the adolescent and young adult. Since we are primarily concerned with the problems of psychological growth in this society, the remainder of the discussion will take America as the context of development, although it is hoped that some of the presumptious statements to be made have some application beyond North America.

An American child must believe, first of all, that he is valued by his parents and a few special people in his community (usually a teacher or two, but often older peers, uncles, aunts and coaches). Since our society makes personal competence synonymous with virtue, the sculpting of a particular talent, or better yet, talents, is usually necessary but not sufficient requirement for the development of a sense of worth. Obviously it is possible to list the appropriate set of competences to be attained only if one knows the domains of mastery that the community values. In the remote Indian village in western Guatemala in which I worked last year, the ability to care for young children with efficiency and skill produced this feeling of worth in preadolescent girls. In the United States, it is more closely tied to quality of performance in junior high school. Hence, competence in academic subjects is a *sine qua non* for the American child. It is difficult, if not impossible, to fail this requirement completely and still retain a sense of dignity and worth in adulthood.

The American child must also develop autonomy, the belief that he or she is able to and desires to make decisions regarding his conduct and his future, independent of coercive pressures from parents, teachers, and friends. The recent increase in drug use among American youth threatens older Americans not because of an automatic revulsion toward pills or smoking, but because it is believed that marijuana and heroin destroy the desire to be independent and autonomous. In a culture in which the majority of twenty-five-year-olds do not live within visiting distance of the family and friends with whom intense childhood intimacies were shared, it can be argued that it is adaptive for autonomy to be promoted so conscientiously. There is another reason why autonomy has become such a precious characterstic. A society's typical mode of livelihood always exerts some influence on the psychological characteristics it extols. There is greater independence, autonomy and permissiveness toward aggression among African tribes in which pastoralism dominates the economy than among tribal groups in the same country where agriculture is the main source of income.[4] The reasonableness of this correlation derives from the fact that a twelve-year-old boy who is given daily responsibility for fifty head of cattle must make a series of independent decisions that do not arise for a twelve-year-old who helps his father plow a field or plant maize. Moreover, personal disputes are less disruptive in a pastoral setting, where the disputants can easily put miles between them, than in a fixed agricultural village, where actors are totally captive in a small area, and feuds, therefore, must be suppressed.

Most Americans earn and increase their livelihood by perfecting talents that an institution wants. We have an economy in which services and skills are offered for payment. Unlike the situation in modern Japan, where each worker has a primary lifetime loyalty to the company for which he works,[5] the unwritten understanding in the United States is that primary loyalty is not awarded to the institution (be it company, university or governmental agency) but to the self. (I assume it is understood that the writer is not condoning this arrangement, but merely describing it.) If financial gain is to be maximized, young adults must be socialized to make decisions that are best for them. Hence, most parents unconsciously encourage their children to decide conflicts for themselves. The parental admonition to a fifteen-year-old, "You will have to decide whether you want to go to the movies or save your allowance," which is so rare outside the Western community, is part of the daily preparation for adulthood. Parents are probably unaware of the hidden message in these communications, but their effect is measurable, nonetheless.

Finally, and here we are more similar to other cultures, America requires the young adult to be heterosexually successful; to be able to love and be loved and to take pleasure from sexual experience. As a result we promote a permissive attitude toward sexuality.

These attributes comprise the core of America's current ego ideal. There is much to celebrate in this list, but also much to mourn. There is, in our opinion, insufficient emphasis on intimacy and too much on self-interest; insufficient emphasis on cooperation and too much on competitiveness; insufficient emphasis on altruism and too much on narcissism. But we cannot alter this catechism by shaking our heads and pulling at our chins. These values derive, in part, from the form of our economy, our densely crowded, impersonal cities and the fact that our educational institutions function as twelve-to-sixteen-year selection sites for tomorrow's doctors, teachers, laywers, administrators, scientists and business executives. These basic structures will have to change a little if we want our values to reflect more humanism. Put succinctly, the fact that Bobby Fischer's flagrant narcissism was excusable because he beat Boris Spassky for the chess championship last year suggests that the only thing more important to Americans than character is individual success.

Since it is not likely that our economy, our cities and our institutions will change dramatically during the next decade—perhaps they will over a longer period—American parents will probably not alter their tendency to encourage the values and associated competences listed above: namely, academic success, autonomy, independence, and a permissive emotional attitude toward hostility and sexuality. However, at another time, they might easily be persuaded to promote a different creed.

The ego ideal we have been considering is appropriate to the adolescent and adult. There is merit in considering the more specific accomplishments appropriate to each of the developmental stages—infancy, the preschool years, preadolescence, and adolescence—and it is these to which we now turn our attention. Again, these suggestions are to be taken as speculations for discussion and hypotheses for testing in the harsh empirical arena, rather than firm inferences from reliable empirical information.

Infancy

During the first year and a half to two years, the infant needs at least four classes of experience. He must have environmental variety that can be assimilated with moderate effort. An excessively homogeneous environment with little discrepant experience temporarily retards psychological growth and turns the child away from the world around him. My observations in the Indian village in Guatemala suggest that infants who received an abundance of physical contact—they were on their mother's bodies a large part of the day —but insufficient experiential variety were intellectually retarded and affectively depressed in comparison with American children during the first two years of life. These infants, who were nursed on demand and held for hours but rarely spoken to or played with, resembled the marasmic infants Spitz saw in the South American orphanages he visited almost thirty years ago.[6] These Indian infants had sufficient physical affection and love, but insufficient stimulus variety. Most American homes have enough assimilable variety for proper psychological growth. For the few that do not, existing information suggests a mild retardation in cognitive and affective processes.

Experiences that are too discrepant to be understood often frighten the child and provoke withdrawal and inhibition; excessive homogeneity promotes a listless, nonalert attitude. The first task of development is to understand unusual happenings in the outside world.

The infant also needs regularity of experience. Regularity is, of course, a relativistic concept. It does not mean that the mother must put the child on a two-, four- or eight-hour schedule, only on a regular one. The child needs some predictability, for by the time he is six months old he is making predictions and altering his sleeping, activity and eating cycles as a function of the regularities in his day. When his expectations are not realized, anxiety grows and can disturb major aspects of functioning. The child needs caretaking by adults rather than machines because our culture requires the older child to relate to people rather than objects. Finally, the infant needs the opportunity to practice his emerging motor skills. There is cognitive and affective gain derived from banging mobiles, shaking rattles, knocking down block towers and crawling.

Preschool Child, Age Two to Five Years

The child continues to need opportunities to master body and object problems. Additionally, when he has begun to master the symbolic language of his community—anywhere from eighteen to thirty months of age—he needs exposure to language. If he does not live in a sea of speech he will remain mute, even though he possesses the biological competence for talking and understanding. Existing evidence suggests that all the child needs is exposure—no special tutoring, books, television programs or radios. The simple experience of hearing people talking—especially to him—seems sufficient.

Third, the child must encounter actions, gestures and communications that affirm his virtue, value and worth. Families will communicate this message in different ways. Hence, the concept of parental (later on, peer) rejection should not be biased toward an absolute definition. There is no definable set of behaviors that always means rejection and leads inevitably to a particular form of the child's self-concept. There has been a tendency for American psychologists to assume that there are specific parental actions that signify rejection, for there is an enormous degree of commonality in the definition of this concept among investigators who have studied a mother's behavior with her child.[7] These and others decided that harsh physical punishment and absence of social play and affection are the signs of maternal rejection. It would be impossible for an American psychologist to categorize a mother as high on both aloofness and a loving attitude. But that view may be provincial. Alfred Baldwin reports that in rural areas of northern Norway where homes are five to ten miles apart, one sees maternal behavior which an American observer would regard as pathognomonically rejecting in an American mother.[8] The Norwegian mother sees her four-year-old sitting in a doorway blocking the passage to the next room. She does not ask him to move, but bends down, picks him up, and silently moves him away before she passes to the next room. A middle-class observer would be tempted to view this indifference as a sign of dislike. However, most mothers in this Arctic outpost behave this way; and the children do not behave the way rejected children should by our theoretical propositions.

An uneducated black mother from North Carolina slaps her four-year-old across the face when he does not come to the table on time. The intensity of the act tempts our observer to conclude that the mother resents her child. However, during a half-hour conservation, the mother indicates her warm feelings for the boy. She hit him because she does not want him to become a "bad boy," and she believes physical punishment is the most effective socialization procedure. Now her behavior seems to be issued in the service of affection rather than hostility. Evaluation of a parent as rejecting or accepting cannot be answered by noting the parent's behavior, for rejection is not a fixed quality of behavior. Like pleasure, pain or beauty, rejection is in the mind of the rejectee. It is a belief held by the child, not an action by a parent.

We must acknowledge an important discontinuity in the meaning of acceptance-rejection for the child prior to eighteen months of age, before he symbolically evaluates the actions of others, in contrast to the symbolic child of three of four years. We require a concept to deal with the child's belief in his value in the eyes of others. The five-year-old is conceptually mature enough to recognize that certain resources parents possess are difficult for him to obtain. He views these resources as sacrifices and interprets receiving them as signs that the parents value him. The child constructs a tote board of the differential value of parental gifts, be they psychological or material. The value of the gift depends on its scarcity. A ten-dollar toy from an executive father is not a valued resource; the same toy from a father out of work is prized. The value depends on the child's personal weighting. This position would lead to solipsism were it not for the fact that most parents are narcissistic and do not readily give the child long periods of uninterrupted companionship. Hence most children place a high premium on this act. Parents are also reluctant to donate unusually expensive gifts, and such a prize acquires value for many youngsters. Finally, the American child learns through the public media that physical affection means a positive evaluation, and he is persuaded to assign premium worth to this experience. There is, therefore, some uniformity across children in our culture with respect to the evaluation of parental acts of acceptance or rejection. But the anchor point lies within the child, not with particular parental behaviors. It is suggested, therefore, that different concepts are necessary for the following phenomena:

- an attitude on the part of the parent,
- the quality and frequency of acts of parental care and stimulation, and, finally,
- the child's assessment of his values in the eyes of another.

All three categories are currently viewed as of the same cloth.

Fourth, the preschool child needs models to whom he feels similar and who he believes possess competence, power and virtue in the group he takes as his primary reference. This phenomenon of vicarious sharing in the strength and positive emotional states of another to whom one feels similar is called identification. A young man recalls his childhood feelings for his father: "My admiration for him transcended everything. I always wanted to work with my hands on machinery, to drive big trucks, to fix things like he did. I didn't really like spinach, but I never lost the image of his bathtub filled with it, and up until a few years ago I always ate it—it was good for me and would make me strong like him."[9]

The child's self-concept and values derive, in part, from his pattern of identifications with those models with whom he shares basic psychological and physical similarities. Although parents are the primary identification figures for most children, each teacher is a potential model, and the teacher's power to sculpt values and self-esteem is usually underestimated.

Since school success is so important in American society, we should not forget that the teacher has the power to persuade the child of the joy, beauty and potential utility of knowledge, even though the typical second-grader initially rejects that idea. The teacher's most potent weapon of persuasion is herself, for if she is seen as kind, competent and just, the child will award to the school tasks she encourages the same reverence he assigns to her.

Finally, the preschool child needs to experience consistency with respect to the standards being socialized. The content of those standards is less critical than the fact of knowing that what is wrong and what is right remain constant from day to day. A child cannot deal with the dissonance that is produced by being punished for fighting on Monday but jokingly teased for the same violation on Wednesday. It was suggested that during the first two years, the infant was trying to understand unusual experiences in the world. The primary task during the preschool years is to understand the self, and the child needs information that will help him solve that problem.

The School-Age and Preadolescent Years

During preadolescence, the child must successfully master the school's basic requirements, which happen to be at the moment reading, writing and mathematics. These competences are not as central in many parts of the world as they are in our community. Second, the child has to be successful in some minimal number of peer-valued talents. Third, the preadolescent continues to require desirable models for identification. These heroes can be older siblings or friends who seem to have access to resources the ten-year-old values. These resources have a universal quality and usually include strength, power over others, competence at culturally valued skills and a belief in the moral goodness of the model. The ten-year-old needs exposure to one or two of these figures, as well as information that indicates that he shares some similarity with them so that he can confidently expect eventually to become like them. The preadolescent also needs the opportunity to match his attributes to the standards that society has declared to be the sex role ideal. A Kyoto girl is taught that gentleness is the central feminine quality, a Kipsigis girls believes that bearing many children is central, a Los Angeles girl is told that physical beauty has priority. Each of these adolescents wants to know how feminine she is and each tries to elaborate the attributes that define the ideal female identity.

The Needs of the Adolescent

In most peasant societies, it is not necessary that the adolescent be particularly talented at some special aptitude. But America so finely differentiates its children that they cannot carve identities of their own unless they possess beliefs and proficiencies that are, in some way, unique. The adolescent also has to believe that he is attractive to his peers, members of the opposite as well as of the same sex. Many American upper-middle-class adolescents who have developed strong group bonds that are partly asexual promote the value of being attractive to all of one's peers.

The adolescent continues to need exposure to and interaction with models whom he perceives to be heroic, for they make the difficult task of becoming an adult attractive. Moreover, the adolescent must have the opportunity to practice roles and actions that define adulthood, for he must develop an expectation that he can attain that status. Finally, because possession of an ideology is so critical to the modern American adolescent, he needs freedom from excessive dissonance. The adolescent is generating a consistent set of rules to which he wishes to be loyal, and he requires some peer and family support for the tenets he hopes to use in adult life. While the adolescent is trying to give roots to these ideals—as one would a fragile plant—he must believe that this personal ideology is, in some way, better than other dogmas he might have selected. The daily experience of encountering rival beliefs that are inconsistent with one's own premises and displayed by persons whom one cannot easily disenfranchise often leads to chronic anxiety, which erodes the confidence in principles that comes from believing there is something special about the ideology one has established.

Adolescents of all societies must build a sense of self, and the ingredients used in this construction will vary with time and community. Each society posts the rules by which the adolescent can diagnose the rate at which he is progressing toward maturity. In many locales, the simple roles of wife, father, mother and husband are the only requirements for admission into adult circles. Our own community has placed a special obstacle in the path of the adolescent by requiring that he display an autonomously built belief system—a distinct set of values—in order to gain admission into that identity we call adulthood. Since the fourteen-year-old realizes that his values are borrowed from his family, he experiences a deep conflict between what he must attain and his current state. He strives to alter his beliefs in order to persuade himself that the resulting arrangement is his own personal creation and not a warmed-over version borrowed from his family. The ideational rebellion that has become characteristic of middle-class adolescents in our society does not primarily serve hostility, but rather is a product of the more pressing need to persuade the self that its configuration of wishes, values and behaviors derives from a personally constructed philosophy. If "what one believes" were less central to the integrity of the American adolescent than it is at the present time, the clash of values between child and parent might not occur with such ferocity. The task for the adolescent is to know what he believes.

These are tentative suggestions for the needs of American children. It is a much more difficult task to suggest strategies for gratifying these needs. Since we have argued that development of talent is central, we must make serious changes in our educational systems in order to maximize the child's sense of competence. We must, for example, expand the number of talents that we applaud. The Spartans valued physical fitness, the Athenians music, the Puritans knowledge of the Bible, and we, reading and mathematics. Perhaps we should include all of these areas of expertise in our curriculum. The honest award of praise for art, music, oratory, and physical fitness in the primary school would help many children, who, by reason of historical circumstance, enter the first grade less well prepared than others for reading and mathematics instruction.

Although the school cannot, without cooperation from the larger society, singlehandedly change the community's value system, it can at least begin the work. This is not just a sentimental plea for a softer view of education. The industrial revolution following the Civil War created a strong need for managers and technicians, and our educational institutions responded efficiently and met that need. Historical events during the last decade, the war being only one, have created a new, but equally vital, requirement. Our society temporarily needs to restore its belief in the honesty, sincerity and humanity of its members. It has lost its optimism, temporarily, we hope, and this lacuna is as serious as the absence of engineers at the turn of the century. The school and the family, two of our most central institutions, must arrange conditions so that these qualities are awarded greater value until the psychological repair process has been accomplished.

Summary

Let me try to weave the themes of this essay into a closer fabric so that the design is less hazy. The needs of children vary with their age and their context of growth. In our society, they include varieties of manageable experiences during infancy, the opportunity to practice maturing capacities and to attain locally valued talents, to believe one is valued and to identify with role models who are regarded as powerful, talented and virtuous and, finally, protection from excessive irregularity and dissonance of values. I am assuming that the child is not exposed to regular and severe physical pain, hunger, cold and disease.

The psychological differences between a young Boston lawyer and a young Guatemalan Indian farmer do not depend so much on the specific actions their parents displayed toward them during childhood, but rather on their ability to carry out the messages their reference groups sent them regarding the missions to be accomplished on the journey to adulthood. A healthy society is one that both selects missions that need to be assigned to solve future problems and provides the largest number of its youth with opportunities to carry out the requisite assignments.

References

1. Jerome Kagan, "Cross Cultural Perspectives in Early Development" (paper delivered to the American Association for the Advancement of Science, Washington, D.C., December 26, 1972).
2. Jean Briggs, *Never in Anger* (Cambridge: Harvard University Press, 1970).
3. Freda Rebelsky, "Infancy in Two Cultures," *Nederlands Tijdschrift voor de Psychologie* 22 (1967):379–385.
4. Robert B. Edgerton, *Individual in Cultural Adaptation: A Study of Four East African Peoples* (Berkeley: University of California Press, 1971).
5. Chie Nakane, *Japanese Society* (Berkeley: University of California Press, 1972).
6. René A. Spitz and Katherine M. Wolf, "Anaclitic Depression: An Inquiry into the Genesis of Psychiatric Conditions in Early Childhood," in Anna Freud et al., eds., *The Psychoanalytic Study of the Child* (New York: International Universities, 1946), II, 313–342.

7. Alfred L. Baldwin, Joan Kalhorn, and Faye H. Breese, "Patterns of Parent Behavior," *Psychological Monographs* 58, no. 3 (1945); Wesley Becker, "Consequences of Different Kinds of Parental Discipline," in Martin L. Hoffman and Lois W. Hoffman, eds., *Review of Child Development and Research* (New York: Russell Sage Foundation, 1964), I, 169–208; Jerome Kagan and Howard A. Moss, *Birth to Maturity* (New York: Wiley, 1962); Earl S. Schaefer, "A Circumplex Model for Material Behavior." *Journal of Abnormal and Social Psychology* 59 (1959): 226–235; Earl S. Schaefer and Nancy Bayley, "Maternal Behavior, Child Behavior, and Their Intercorrelations from Infancy through Adolescence," *Monographs of the Society for Research in Child Development.* no. 87 (1963), p. 28; and Robert R. Sears, Eleanor E. Maccoby, and Harry Levin, *Patterns of Child Rearing* (Evanston, Ill: Rowe, Peterson, 1957).
8. Alfred L. Baldwin, personal communication.
9. George W. Goethals and Dennis S. Klos, *Experiencing Youth* (Boston: Little, Brown & Co., 1970), p. 44.

Working Couples as Parents

Laura Lein and Mary C. Blehar

Parenthood is almost never an uncomplicated undertaking even in those increasingly rare traditional families where husband and wife have agreed to devote themselves single-mindedly to the respective roles of breadwinner and emotional nurturer of children. The emergent phenomenon of the working mother compounds the job of raising young children by placing demands on parents to assume new responsibilities and new roles for which no well-defined models exist. Popular literature suggests that a mother's resumption of outside work can be fraught with peril for the family; but her working and the resulting pressures toward change in family structure and functioning may also lead to creative and adaptive innovations. Such is the finding of a Boston-based group of young social scientists who title themselves collectively the *Working Family Project.* Headed by NIMH grantee and social anthropologist Dr. Laura Lein, of Wellesley College, the full Project group (including Kevin Dougherty, Maureen Durham, Gail Howrigan, Laura Lein, Michael Pratt, Michael Schudson, Ronald Thomas, and Heather Weiss) has been studying intensively a small group of 25 middle-income families in which both the husband and wife are employed outside the home and responsible for the care of children, typically of preschool age.

During a preliminary review of field research on families, the Project discovered that the group "in the middle" economically had been neglected, perhaps because the problems they faced were relatively less urgent than

From *Families Today: A Research Sampler on Families and Children*, Eunice Corfman, ed. NIMH Science Monograph #1, Vol. I, pp. 299–321.

those of poverty-stricken families or relatively less glamorous than those of higher income families where both spouses pursued exciting and personally gratifying careers. The middling status of the families obscured the difficulties they had to contend with.

For example, because of their middle-income status, they were usually not eligible for subsidies available to poorer families for such services as formal child care. Nonetheless, most did not have so much money as to be able to pay for the convenience of live-in housekeepers, regular babysitters, or day-care centers affordable by higher income groups. They faced the pressures of having to arrange, within these income limitations, for responsible substitute care of one or more pre-schoolers.

Second, in the absence of many social supports reinforcing their efforts, even in the face of frank social disapproval, spouses in middle-income, dual-worker families had to try to assume new roles and to share tasks around the home. Little money was available to spend on hired help or labor-saving devices that could alleviate some of the strain on working parents. Few realistic models were available of housecleaning husbands and working wives. As it turned out, in the Boston study, although men in some of the families pitched in, and a few consciously tried to assume new domestic roles, women usually bore the major burden of household work. Standards of performance concerning the care of children and home were little lowered by working mothers, however. Rather, most evolved ever more complex schedules to accommodate increased demands in decreased time.

A third problem, although not tied to families' middle-income status, was nonetheless foremost in their minds. Parents saw as their primary responsibility the successful rearing of children, and many perceived the larger social environment to be a hostile, threatening influence that could ruin their offspring despite the parents' best efforts. For some parents, skepticism of formal child care emerged from a fear that outsiders would influence their children in undesirable directions.

The Working Family Project described the families they studied as *dual-worker families*. The term was meant not to minimize the labor contribution of full-time housewives but to distinguish the kind of families they studied from more traditionally structured, two-parent, one-worker families as well as from *dual-career* families in which the wife's position and advancement in her occupation were closely tied to cumulative training and work experience. Only some of the women in the Working Family Project's sample had intended to hold paying jobs while raising preschool children, and relatively few thought of their jobs in terms of a career.

In further contrast to dual-career families, the dual-worker families were of relatively modest means, with family incomes ranging from $6,500 to $20,000 in 1974. The criterion used to include a family in the sample was strictly income rather than occupation or some combination of occupation and income, so that a range of professions and potential professions was represented among both husbands and wives. For instance, a few of the men were students at the time but were engaged in training for lucrative careers that promised to lift their families out of their current tight financial straits into more affluent life-styles. The majority of men, however, worked in occupations that did not lead to high-paid positions and that offered little prospect for change from middle-income status and related difficulties in making ends meet. Although virtually all the families reported themselves as aspiring to own their own homes, only about half actually did so. Of the remainder, few could predict when they might be in a position to achieve this proto-typical American goal. The physical environments in which the families lived—their houses, apartments, and neighborhoods—would be judged by most observers as pleasant, but their financial situation left them with little money to spare for unforeseen contingencies. In many of the families, the financial contribution of the working wife enabled them to maintain a middle-income position.

The attitudes of the dual-worker couples toward the mother's employment outside the home were often complex and contradictory. Husband's appreciation of their wives' contributions was often in conflict with the men's perceived diminution of their masculine role of breadwinner. Perhaps defensively, some men tended to minimize the importance of their wives' jobs to family well-being, even when it was clear to the researchers that the extra money was needed badly.

Both husbands and wives tended to espouse traditional attitudes about the proper roles of men and women in family life. Even though a wife was working full time, she was usually still seen as "helping out" her husband in his primary role as breadwinner. In most instances, a woman's primary role was considered to be that of wife and mother, and the major responsibility for arranging child care and housework still fell to her.

Despite the apparent traditionalism of the families, more subtle secondary motives for a woman's employment emerged. Initially most wives were reluctant to admit to working outside the home for pleasure or personal advancement, especially when their jobs took them away from young children. But such motives existed, and while they may not have been primary when employment began they came to assume importance through a natural evolutionary process. Reasons behind a woman's employment, while most frequently given in terms of economics, were often more complex.

The Working Family Project started the dual-worker study without many preconceived notions of what was to be examined about the families and without specific hypotheses to be tested. The study was viewed as a hypothesis-generating one meant to yield leads that could be followed up more intensively if they seemed worthwhile. It was through initial conversations with the participating families that areas of interest and concern came to be more clearly defined. What emerged as most important to the families were problems in and solutions to such matters as child care, division of housework between spouses, coordination of work with home life, and supports for parenthood in modern urban society.

In the past, it would not have been at all unusual to find a research team composed exclusively of individuals trained in one discipline. The resultant research effort, while it might reflect in depth a psychological or anthropological perspective, would be one-sided. The Working Family Project took another approach to social-science research: a multidisciplinary one. Each team member had a different training orientation and different interests in family life. For instance, Lein, a social anthropologist, tended to view the family as a social system enmeshed in a social network. Other members were trained in developmental psychology, clinical psychology, and sociology. Each saw the families from a slightly different perspective, and each brought this perspective to bear on analyses of problems in adapting to demands of home and outside work. Each team member also exerted a corrective influence on the others so as to ensure that no one aspect of the lives of dual-worker families was emphasized at the expense of others. The research product of the team is one wider in scope than would have emerged from a unidisciplinary effort.

The way information was gathered by the Working Family Project can be distinguished from other methods. The 25 Boston families were studied intensively over a relatively short period of time; some of them were also studied longitudinally. Such an approach to gaining information about attitudes and problems can be contrasted to large-scale survey techniques. In the latter, a substantial number of respondents are polled on attitudes or behaviors usually only once. The generality of findings and their accuracy in reflecting attitudes is thought to be ensured by careful sampling and item selection.

By comparison, the small-scale-intensive method does not yield a basis for ready generalization. Findings must be characterized carefully, particularly in terms of the specific group studied. But the small-scale technique, especially if it is intensive, can surpass the survey technique in the credibility one can place in findings.

Respondents to questionnaires may or may not be reporting accurately on their circumstances. Ambivalent feelings may be suppressed in favor of more one-sided and uncomplicated attitudes. In matters requiring verbal reports, different parties in an emotionally keyed interaction may have different impressions of the same "objective" situation.

In this vein, the Working Family Project noted that initial interviews with family members often led to an impression that was modified after greater rapport had been established and after initially hidden conflicts and disagreements had emerged. For instance, husbands reported somewhat differently on their contribution to the running of the household than did their wives. Both spouses underestimated the other's contribution in what was for many an issue of overt conflict. This discrepancy was often discovered only after a series of interviews had taken place.

In general, the tendency to put on a good face is well noted in social-science research. Even on questionnaires that are anonymous, the social desirability of answers to questions can bias responses. Even in face-to-face interviews, threads of consistency in personal reports of attitudes and behavior on emotionally charged topics can usually be established only after rapport has grown between the observer and the observed.

Because the sort of information that emerges from them has great validity, intensive studies can be viewed as complementary to large-scale survey techniques. Intensive studies can yield hunches that can be subject to further verification in studies that employ larger samples. In the specific case of the dual-worker study, the ability to generalize about a large group of urban families was subordinated to a search for uniqueness. The research group was seeking out the creative, innovative ways in which people dealt with the pressures of family life. The 25 families seen were alike in three ways: all had children (usually preschoolers), all the wives worked, and all were middle income. In other ways they were different. The staff deliberately sought to include examples of people who had confronted unusual situations and had evolved unusual solutions to them. In many ways, however, the Working Family Project does not think that the 25 families they saw are much different from most urban middle-income, dual-worker groups, either in the difficulties they encountered or in the range of solutions they formulated. But it is possible that only certain kinds of families will permit researchers to study them. It is clear that findings from such a study should be tested on a broader basis.

The families were both interviewed and observed as they went about their daily lives. Husband and wife were interviewed twice apart and once together. Family life was observed at least three times: once when the wife was alone with her children, once when the husband was alone with them, and once when both parents and the children were together. Spouses were asked to describe their childhood backgrounds, aspirations in work and family life, the stresses they were experiencing, and their attitudes toward their lives. Sometimes the method of questioning was structured; other times it was open-ended. The resulting data, while impressionistic and not amenable to most statistical tests, are extremely credible because of the repeated verification to which they were subject.

Lein notes some difficulties in conducting intensive research. By its very nature, it is intrusive. The people agreeing to cooperate have essentially opened their personal lives to outside scrutiny for a considerable period of time. Working families in particular are under a kind of added stress in that they must give of a very limited resource—hours of leisure time—in order to fulfill research goals. Of families approached, 40 percent agreed to participate; 60 percent refused. Such a high refusal rate is the rule in intensive research in urban areas of the United States. Lein suspects that refusals in the study may have come disproportionately from families in which conflict over the wife's working was most marked and in which the husband, particularly, objected strongly to the airing of these difficulties to outsiders. The sample was gathered in two waves. The first 14 families were contacted in 1973 under the grant auspices of the National Institute of Education (NIE). This group served as a type of pilot for further work. Areas of concentration were narrowed down, given money and time limitations, and the focus was sharpened. The additional 11 families were gathered under NIMH grant auspices to make a total sample of 25. Papers were written by staff members at regular intervals in the course of data collection and were subject to revision or expansion in light of further investigation. For instance, a paper based on the first 14 families dealt with the division of household labor between husband and wife, and the findings held for the 25. Further analyses of the 25, however, also yielded new aspects of labor splits that were reported on in other contexts. Rich in anecdotes which portray the families vividly and enable the reader to empathize with them readily, each paper can stand alone, yet every aspect of family life is in reality integrated with every other one.

In partial return for their participation, the Working Family Project shared their findings with the families. Both spouses were given papers to read and react to. In many instances, they improved the quality of research by providing alternative interpretations or even by pointing out methodological weaknesses. Hence, their perusal of preliminary manuscripts exerted a very useful corrective influence on the product.

To provide the reader with a more personalized view of the families, Table 1 presents some characteristics of the original 14. It can be seen that, with the exception of Mr. Parks and Mr. Sandle, who were full-time students, all the husbands were working full time. The number of hours wives worked varied from 15 to 40 a week. Most of the men had been at their present jobs for some time. The couples ranged in age from their 20s to their 40s, and all but 3 in the sample of 25 had at least 1 preschool child.

Arranging for Child Care

Once the decision had been made for a mother to work, the first and most pressing practical problem facing couples was the management of satisfactory child care during periods in which the parents were outside the home. Parents resorted to a variety of care arrangements, partly because day care of good quality was costly (around $40 a week in 1974) and difficult to find and partly because the parents differed in what they considered desirable for their children. In each family, the decision to have an outsider take care of a child was an important issue.

Various alternatives were represented among the families: care of children by each spouse in turn while the other was at work, care by hired babysitters, informal child-care arrangements with neighbors, assistance from relatives if

Table 1   Some Characteristics of the First 14 Families

Families	Husband's occupation	Hrs/wk	Wife's occupation	Hrs/wk	No. of children
Deneux	Business manager	40	Typist	35	2
Farlane	Salesman	35	Nurse	24	5
Henry	Maintenance	40	Factory	35	2
Hunt	Business manager	40	Keypunch	25	2
Jackson	Factory	40	Nurse	24	4
Long	Factory	40	Keypunch	15	2
Nelson	Teacher/ salesman	65	Nurse	15	9
Parks	Student	30	Administration	15	1
Raymond	Business manager	55	Saleswoman	20	4
Samuels	Armed forces	40	Day care	25	2
Sandle	Student	40	Nurse	40	1
Sedman	Maintenance work	40	Keypunch	25	2
Tilman	Draftsman	40	Administration	40	1
Wyatt	Policeman/ construction	55	Secretary	40	2

they were nearby, and formal day care or nursery programs. Often, more than one type of care was used. The complexity to be encountered in scheduling child care was frequently remarkable.

In the face of severe limitations on amount of money available, the solutions some families arrived at were ingenious. Although monetary considerations were important in the minds of the couples, their solutions also reflected a deep concern for the quality of the children's family life and their life away from home. Parents were willing to make tremendous sacrifices in order to ensure that their children enjoyed the best possible care that they could provide.

An adage of sociologists is that "attitudes follow behavior," or that people first of all act and then rationalize actions verbally. To a great extent, this situation held in the Boston sample. The demands of the parents' jobs determined and limited child-care options, but the converse was also true. That is, concern for children determined the parents' work schedules as well. The fears that some parents voiced about their inability to retain sufficient control over their children's environment influenced the type of care that they considered acceptable. Anxieties became especially obvious when parents were queried about outside-the-home child care.

When the Working Family Project was first starting out in their efforts to collect a sample, they went to Boston-area day-care centers on the assumption that working parents would be most likely to use this type of care as a solution of choice. To their surprise, they found relatively few middle-income children enrolled in day care, Instead, the typical paying day-care user was more likely to be a child of a professional couple or the child of a single parent.

When the full range of child-care options used by study families was finally understood, the project found that many arrangements tended to be informal and either free or relatively inexpensive in terms of financial cost. For instance, several parents had worked out a type of child care labeled the "split-shift." In the split-shift arrangement, the father was available to take care of the children during time off from outside work while the mother went out of the home to work. Since all but three fathers in the sample held jobs during the core hours of 7 a.m. to 6 p.m., the majority of split shifts involved the mother's working jobs at night or on weekends. Split-shift arrangements imposed severe limitations on the kinds of jobs that women could take. The project members noted the relatively high proportion of women in the dual-worker sample who were nurses or nursing students—seven to be precise—probably because such a career could be left and re-entered with less loss of tenure and because it offered flexibility in arrangements of work schedules.

One apparent advantage of split-shift arrangements was that they obviated the need for outside paid assistance. Child-development advantages were also apparent. The consensus of the Working Family Project is that split shifts lead to good care for young children who can remain in their homes with familiar caregivers and familiar play objects. However, the arrangements exact costs from the parents. In addition to placing real limitations on a woman's advancement in work, the split shift dramatically decreases the amount of time a couple has to spend together. During the work week, couples often saw each other primarily going in and out of the front door of the family home. However, most had decided that the split-shift arrangement was worth the personal sacrifices involved if the child's comfort and happiness were correspondingly enhanced.

A typical example of the schedules split-shift families followed was seen in the case of the Longs. Mr. Long was employed on a shift at a warehouse from 5 p.m. until 1 a.m. He got home around 2 a.m. and slept until 9 or 10. Mrs. Long had a part-time job where she was allowed to vary her hours within certain limits. She usually worked as a typist from 10 a.m. until 2 p.m. but occasionally went to work later if her husband was sleeping in. Each was responsible for the children while the other was away. One result of the arrangement, Mr. Long explained, is that he now understands why his wife likes to get away from the house. After caring for the children alone while she worked, he was really glad when she returned and took over and he could go to work for some peace and quiet.

The split-shift arrangement could create frictions between husband and wife. For instance, a father who participated in the arrangement might think that he was fulfilling his obligation to help his wife by giving the children dinner and putting them to bed while she was at work. The wife who came home at midnight to a kitchen sink full of dirty dinner dishes left over from a meal she had prepared before going off to work might believe otherwise.

A few families in the sample managed to solve their child-care problems by having the wife work in the home or in other places where she could be with the children. Three women provided family day care, and others worked in day-care centers where their children were enrolled. Although there were exceptions, most of them viewed day-care provision as a good way to solve work problems during their children's preschool years rather than as a long-term career.

A few of the families evolved an informal give-and-take child-care arrangement with like-minded families in their neighborhoods. The three families with this arrangement had mothers who worked only part time. The Henrys were a family using this type of care. As Mrs. Henry explained about her relationship with her neighbor: "Leila takes the Marshs' kids and mine. Now I'll watch hers and the Marshs' little boy. It's done for nothing . . . it does get tiring sometimes. I had five the other day, and I was glad to see them go."

Despite the large proportion of families with relatives in the Boston area, only one family reported using a grandparent for child care during the working day. In explaining why she turned to her mother, Mrs. Raymond said, "This isn't a year-in, year-out thing, this is something that happens maybe 2 months out of 6 or 7 years." Relatives were relied on more often to provide occasional care of children while the parents were engaged in leisure-time pursuits.

A total of 11 families in the sample managed to meet their child-care needs without actually paying for them. Families who used out-of-home paid day care usually discussed its benefits to the child in terms of increasing his or her exposure to a variety of experiences and people. The decision to use a paid care arrangement frequently went along with a mother's employment in so-called prime-time working jobs. In addition, these families were more likely to perceive the mother's work as a stepping stone to a career or to long-term advancement and were usually willing to make the financial investment that out-of-home care required. They also prized dependable care.

Many of the families had at least tried out paid group care at one time or another. Most described how they met with some initial resistance from young children in the form of reluctance to be left—which might continue from a few days to a few weeks. Whether or not they persisted in using the care in the face of a child's reluctance depended in part on the family's dedication to the mother's employment. One difference between those couples who stayed with paid day care and those who did not seemed to be that in the former the wife saw her job as more than a respite from housework or a source of a bit of extra income and was willing to wait out the period of the child's discontent with the child-care situation. In the case of families who gave up after a brief try, the parents often saw in the child's discontent confirmation of the mother's primary role as chief nurturer. While all the families in the study demonstrated deep concern for their children, those who persisted with day care despite a child's protest were less focused on the maternal role as the single most important one in the mother's life.

As was mentioned earlier, use of multiple child-care strategies often complicated the family's scheduling. One reason for use of multiple-care strategies was the presence of two or more children in the family, especially if one child was in school and the other a preschooler. The pressures placed on parents (particularly the mother) in accommodating to the demands of multiple-care strategies were great. For instance, Mrs. Wyatt worked full time as a secretary at a nearby real-estate agency, where she was also studying real-estate sales and management. Mr. Wyatt was a fireman and worked part time as a carpenter. Mrs. Wyatt rose at 5:30 each morning of the week to begin readying the children, Christopher, age 6, and Oliver, age 4, for school. She found this easier than getting the children up later and rushing them (in which case they balked and she was later than ever for work). Christopher attended first grade at a neighborhood school. Oliver was in a local nursery-school program from 9 to 12, 3 days a week. A neighbor and friend, whose son attended the same nursery, drove Oliver to school and then picked the boys up at noon. Mrs. Wyatt had to leave by 8 a.m. for work, so Christopher walked to a friend's house nearby and waited there to go to school with him. When Christopher came home from school at 2:30 p.m., he picked up Oliver and the two boys walked to another neighbor's house, where they were cared for until 5 p.m., when Mrs. Wyatt got them on her way home from work. On the days when Oliver did not have school, he usually stayed with the woman all day.

During the evenings and on weekends, the Wyatts took turns watching the boys, since Mr. Wyatt had to work occasionally. In addition there were often errands that needed to be run. The complicated schedule the Wyatts had worked out could be all too easily undone, as happened when the afternoon babysitter's husband became seriously ill. Mrs. Wyatt's mother lived in a nearby town and was able to fill in for a few days until a temporary substitute could be found. Illness and other emergencies were a constant threat to the precarious stability of multiple-care arrangements. When asked what she might change about her own child-care situation, Mrs. Wyatt replied, somewhat poignantly, "I'd like something a little more permanent. Not so many changes."

Integrating the Worlds of Work: Home and Workplace

Who does what around the house? For most of the couples in the Boston study, a wife's return to the work force necessitated at least a few changes in the way that domestic chores were performed. Different couples evolved various strategies for coping with these new demands, and this variety was the subject of intensive investigation by the Working Family Project.

In writing about their findings on division of labor, 25 Project members make the point that housework is not trivial; its performance has a major impact on a family's quality of life. But it is time-consuming, and there are a number of ways to get it done.

In the dual-worker families, reallocation of chores was not the only important issue that couples had to negotiate. Often, underlying new divisions of labor was the need for changes in attitude toward the work that each partner performed or thought most appropriate to perform. Demands for changes in the way housework was carried out usually came from women who were dissatisfied with having to do nearly everything in the home and work outside as well. Husbands tended to resist such pressures. The issue was a sensitive one for many couples, as it involved challenges to long-held and deeply ingrained notions about the proper roles of men and women.

Some men spoke openly of their discomfort at being compelled or even being asked to do "woman's work." They could develop rather elaborate rationalizations for their unwillingness to perform around the house, as was the case with Mr. Sedman, a bricklayer. Both he and his wife worked all day out of the home. At night her discontent was obvious when he would adjourn after dinner to relax in the living room while she cleaned dishes from a meal that she had prepared. He admitted that she never openly confronted him on the issue, but she made remarks that he interpreted as asking him to help. Mr. Sedman thought that this was unfair. As he pointed out, his work was physical and could not be compared in difficulty to the office work that his wife performed during the day. Therefore, it was all right for him to sit down and relax at night.

Women, while demanding more from their husbands in many instances, also shared some ambivalence about changing the domestic status quo. The Working Family Project found a tendency among wives to equate cleanliness with a high level of performance of their role in the home. Since the home rather than the workplace was central to the identity of most women, they were unwilling to part with the homemaker role. Even in instances where husbands did perform household chores, wives tended to be critical of their efforts. One man noted that his wife was much fussier about dirt since he had assumed some responsibility for dusting, and she, on the other hand, noted how he worked only "around the edges." Even when men took on a particular task, they tended to execute it with less thoroughness than their wives would have.

Members of the Working Family Project made a distinction between role-sharing and task-sharing. Role-sharing, they say, involves the assumption of responsibility for the execution of tasks by both partners. Accordingly, in a role-sharing family, the husband considers himself obligated to see that certain things are done, without advice or reminders from his wife. Task-sharing is a second mechanism for dividing labor without actually changing underlying assumptions about proper roles of the marital partners. The task-sharing husband "helps out" his wife as she needs his assistance, either on a short-term or a long-term basis. But the ultimate responsibility for seeing that something gets done remains hers. Likewise, the task-sharing couple see the woman's outside work as a way of "helping out" the husband in his performance of the breadwinner role. He remains, however, chief performer in this domain. The Working Family Project notes that most of the couples in their study were comfortable with the concept of task-sharing. Viewing their spouses' contributions in this way allowed them to preserve traditional notions of the proper structure of the family (homemaker-nurturer vs. breadwinner) while at the same time dividing tasks among themselves. The researchers also note that women were more willing (and in some cases more eager) to assume a breadwinner role than most of the men were to assume a "househusband" role.

In their sample, the Working Family Project found only two couples who had actually negotiated the issue of roles and had decided upon a split of domestic responsibilities. In each case, the wife reported pleasure with the new equitable division but also a residual reluctance to decenter herself from the home. Each wife also demonstrated a high commitment to her outside job. In the other families, helping out remained the mechanism by which a new division of labor was undertaken. Men who "helped out" might perform a great deal of housework, as in one family where there were several children present in the home. The mother had been working for years and the husband helped out extensively throughout this period. He saw himself as continuing to do so on a more or less permanent basis, but he still described his wife as retaining primary responsibility for the role of homemaker, even though for the forseeable future she could not shoulder the entire burden of domestic work because of the conflicting demands of her outside job.

Many of the women in the sample accepted this definition of their responsibilities. Mrs. Henry stayed at home with her children all day and then went to work at night. Despite the tremendous pressures placed on her, she still expected herself to be a good mother and a meticulous housekeeper. Mrs. Sandle was pregnant with her second child at the time of the study and was working 40 hours a week. Nonetheless, she chided herself for being "lazy" because she rested in the mornings. Hence, the working women in the sample were more likely to add new responsibilities to the domestic ones that most saw as primary rather than to rearrange their households so that tasks and roles would be more equally shared or simplified.

Couples in the sample were asked to complete a checklist on allocation of chores in the home. Results corroborated the impressions gained from interviews. Typically, women reported themselves as carrying out time-consuming daily chores such as cooking, cleaning, doing laundry, and making beds.

These are precisely the tasks whose accomplishment is undone daily by the family. Husbands varied in the amount they helped out but men usually performed repairs and outdoor tasks. Most avoided those activities that the culture at large has defined as "woman's work."

To the extent that husbands regularly shared in home-centered tasks, they were almost invariably more involved with child care than with housekeeping. Since husbands were less preoccupied with the endless demands of managing a home than were their wives, they could play with their children, giving them their relatively undivided attention. The wife, in her role as housekeeper and mother, was usually involved in several activities at once. Especially if she worked outside the home during the day, her children could be particularly in need of attention and interaction at just that time when demands were heaviest on her for the preparation of dinner. Perhaps as a result, both husbands and wives tended to see the man as the more patient parent. For example, in the Henry family, Mrs. Henry cared for the children all day and then went to work at night. Before she left she cleaned the house and prepared a meal for the family. Mr. Henry could not understand why she didn't relax more and enjoy the children as he did. Neither seemed to recognize how the allocation of home-centered work affected the time and emotional energy available to her for enjoyable child care.

The Working Family Project also notes that for many women a source of resentment was to be found in their perception of the husband as taking over many of the more pleasurable aspects of child care—for instance, bed-time stories—while they, the women, were left with domestic chores and routine child care. The husband who helps out may remove from the wife's domain one of the most rewarding aspects of her role.

While not minimizing the strain on the father in dual-worker families, the Working Family Project saw the mother as subject to more pressures. The toll women paid in trying to assume new responsibilities along with the old was a sense of being rushed constantly, under pressure, never able to relax or consider a job properly finished. The toll was compounded when a husband was ambivalent over a wife's working.

Most of the women interviewed admitted to feeling tired during the day although several said they were "ashamed" to say so. Others perceived themselves as irritable and edgy with their spouses and children. Trying to live up to the supermother/superwoman ideal as many did, they took on too many tasks at once. The Working Family Project believes that most of the women lacked clear models of working mothers or even a secure and realistic sense of their own role responsibilities and their limitations and instead strained to combine and reconcile competing demands on their time and energy.

About half the women in the sample expressed dissatisfaction with their domestic work situation. What they actually did varied, however. Some tacitly accepted it without engaging their husbands in overt argument or discussion, and two negotiated changes in roles. For others, the issue of housework remained a constant source of overt tension in the marriage.

On the other hand, change, while slow and difficult, could be noted in the families. For instance, many of the women at first emphasized financial reasons for their return to outside employment, saying that they were "helping out" the family. Subsequently, however, several expressed a real determination to work and to pursue a career. It does not seem implausible to suggest that the tentativeness they felt at the beginning about working was gradually overcome by the success of their new arrangements. Over the course of the experience, many came to see outside employment as a regular and normal part of their daily lives. Likewise, many men expressed to the interviewers how they had to rethink their roles as husband, father, and worker. Most began their participation in child care with an uncertainty which seemed to come from inexperience with infants and toddlers, but as their confidence grew they began to see themselves as much better parents than their own fathers and they took pride in their roles. Nonetheless, despite their apparent willingness to expand their participation in child care, and despite the fact that they were usually doing more than before, they were more resistant about doing housework than were women about doing outside work. This circumstance suggests something of an asymmetry in role transitions for men and women. The Working Family Project hypothesizes that in some of the families the initial stages of "helping out" were being transformed into something closer to actual rolesharing. However, the spouses often had different views of this transformation, many women ultimately seeing their participation in the breadwinner role as more than just helping out and most husbands not sharing this perception. Even in the two self-consciously egalitarian families in the sample, there were pressures to retain a more traditional sex-role organization. Where models of a new social form are unavailable, the impulse toward older norms remains strong.

Choice of Jobs, Career Commitment and Family Responsibilities

The choice of jobs and the individual's attitude toward his or her employment reflected further aspects of differences in perceived roles and responsibilities. While the home front remained a major arena of conflict for many couples, and while some of the women were consciously evolving new notions of their function in the paid work force, the provider role remained the most salient one for men and one which all the men in the dual-worker sample took with great seriousness. The importance with which the earning function was regarded by the men was demonstrated by their work histories. Several explained to the interviewers how marriage and children forced a man to become very concerned with job security. Of the 11 men in the sample over 30 years of age, 3 had held their job for 10 years or longer, and 4 had been at the same job between 5 and 7 years. Time and again, the theme of stability and security recurred in reflections. Mr. Neal left a job in a white-collar company when his first child arrived and took a 30 percent cut in pay to become a teacher for the greater job security that teaching provided. Other men reported that they stayed in jobs they found difficult or boring in order to satisfy their family's needs for security. For men, their main role definition was outside the home, but they considered their outside work to be a family-related activity. Men were likely to report greater stress in the performance of their paid jobs than in their home work, whereas for women the opposite was the case. One of the mothers, a registered nurse, held a very taxing emergency-oriented job, but she spoke of it as a respite from the demands of the home. On the other hand, if men complained of stress, they were likely to identify outside work as its source.

Differences in perceived responsibility were also reflected in the types of jobs chosen. Very few women had jobs that had benefits or retirement programs. Most of the men held such jobs. More than the men, women placed importance in job choice on the task—extrinisic criteria such as hours, convenience of commuting, the character of the physical surroundings, and the friendliness and helpfulness of coworkers.

The differences in importance given to criteria probably reflected real differences in demands placed on men as compared with those placed on women. Women were expected to put their home responsibilities above those of paid work and to bear the principal burden of child care and housework. Many chose jobs because of the need for schedules or locations that would allow them to meet family obligations.

Women's greater emphasis on pleasant physical surroundings and friendly coworkers may have reflected the lesser intrinsic rewards of their outside work. If the work itself is boring, then it is important that the interpersonal aspects of the job be pleasant. Mrs. Samuels, a home day-care provider, described an earlier job she had.

> It was full time but a lot of the time, there wasn't enough to keep me busy even half the day. It was a really boring job. The only thing that made the job worthwhile was the people I worked with. They were just wonderful. But the job was very boring.

For many women, work surroundings were important because outside employment was the means by which they escaped from the isolation and tedium of being at home all day. Some said that work provided a means of preventing personal stagnation, offered a source of adult companionship, and furnished a way of keeping well-rounded. They thought that an expansion of their personal horizons was of benefit to their families as well.

Being a Good Parent

Being a good parent, in a confusing and dangerous world and in the absence of clear role guidelines, was perhaps the chief concern of the majority of the couples in the sample. This concern was reflected in choices of substitute child care, in the compromises many of the women had made in their jobs, and in the men's search for job security even at the expense of excitement or advancement opportunities. It was also reflected in opinions articulated during the hours of conversation that the Working Family Project engaged in with them.

Parents of both sexes, but particularly mothers, tended to be obsessed with the issue of maintenance of high standards in the performance of childrearing. Some complained that outside work had caused them to lower their standards although the evidence they could marshall in support of these claims was limited. Lein reports a particularly telling anecdote about one mother in the sample. Upon arriving at the family home for observation, Lein was greeted at the door by an upset woman who proceeded to characterize herself as a "terrible mother." As it turned out, the woman's 4-year-old daughter had gotten out of bed at sunrise and had gone into the kitchen where she cracked eggs and mixed them with detergent. She proceeded to smear the mixture on the walls of a hallway. Upon discovering the child's deed, the mother lost her composure and screamed at her. This behavior she defined in herself as an incident of poor mothering.

Virtually all parents had difficult-to-maintain notions of what a good parent ought to be. If they had experienced a happy childhood, they measured their performance against that of their own parents. If they did not hold pleasant memories, they strove to surpass their parents' performance. However, despite well-defined goals of producing a happy, adjusted child, very few parents had models of the *behavioral means* for achieving the desired ends.

For example, most parents were reluctant to accept advice about childrearing from their older relatives because they, the parents, thought times had changed so dramatically that such counsel would be obsolete. Others noted that the older generation had been far from faultless in childrearing. As Mrs. Henry remarked, "I don't think the way I raise my children is any of my relatives' business. If their kids were perfect, I'd go to them and ask how they did it, but they're far from perfect." Resistance to advice from grandparents was also a way of differentiating the newer family from their families of origin, particularly if they lived in close proximity.

The dual-worker families were likewise ambivalent about expert opinion. Mrs. Long said of the ubiquitous book of Dr. Spock: "When they [the children] were sick or something, I'd look it up ... otherwise, he has a lot of screwy ideas." And Mrs. Hunt remarked, "When I first started out, I lived with Dr. Spock. Then I decided, I'm not going to bring my children up out of a book."

On the other hand, what reading the parents did in popular child development led many of them to believe that the personality of a child was strongly molded, if not determined, by environmental events occurring before the age of 3. Viewing themselves as responsible for providing an optimal environment for their children's development and yet lacking clear guidelines for parental behavior, the couples tended to rely heavily on their own inner resources or on talking things out between themselves. This need to define standards, particularly during the preschool years, added yet another significant stress to their lives.

The theme of parenting in a dangerous world kept recurring in conversations. The source of threats to the child was not always easily identified, although drug pushers were frequently mentioned, perhaps because of media attention to drug problems in the schools. Couples would discuss their anxiety over the prospects of rearing a child responsibly only to lose control later on. One woman noted that her son was a wonderful individual, "a great kid," and would continue that way unless some force "out there" got to him. Underlying the reluctance of some parents to allow outsiders to care for their children was the anticipation that the substitute rearers would hold values different from those of the parents.

Whatever problems they anticipated in the future or had to deal with in the present, the couples in dual-worker families were highly focused on the needs of their children. They hoped to instill in them "good" values and to promote their healthy development. To that end, the worlds of home and work had to be coordinated to make the children's lives secure and pleasant.

Summary

The Working Family Project came to establish rapport with most of the families they studied. Their efforts allow others to share a candid picture of how one group of urban married couples managed to coordinate the worlds of work and home. What emerges is a view of people trying to maintain some tradition within change. The welfare of children and the value of having them is held highest by most parents, although as concessions to economic factors many have limited family size to fewer offspring than they desired in the early years of marriage. In an era reputed to be egocentric, many of the couples arranged split shifts so that youngsters could remain in the home— this at the sacrifice of free time to spend together as a couple.

Economic factors necessitated wives' return to the paid labor force and had some influence on the way that the house was run. Perhaps understandably, women tended to be more stressed by their dual tasks than men, who oftentimes resisted change. But both men and women appeared to be somewhat reluctant to redefine their central roles. Women remained emotionally tied to the nurturer-homemaker role and tended to hold unrealistic expectations for their performance in the worlds of home and outside work.

The abandonment of traditional nuclear family structure was, initially at least, a source of difficulty for many. Men were concerned about threats to their self-image as breadwinner and women about the effects of their employment on their children. However, there were indications, even among this apparently conservative group, that they were adapting successfully to the changes demanded by maternal employment. Women, more readily than men, were enjoying new role responsibilities, but both spouses showed some signs of assuming each other's roles.

It is regrettable that not enough time has elapsed so that the 25 families could be viewed longtitudinally to see if their apparent ability to cope and adapt despite obvious tensions will be maintained over the years. In the meantime, the findings of the Working Family Project can serve to dissipate some of the more common fears of the decline of the American family as more mothers work outside of the home. The findings highlight positive as well as negative aspects of increasing maternal participation in the paid work force and offer a realistic portrait of family and work life as they exist in urban America today.

References

Dougherty, K. Working Family Project. "Interactions Between Work and Family Life." Final unpublished report. U.S. Public Health Service, National Institute of Mental Health, Rockville, Md., 1977

Howrigan, G. Working Family Project. "Child Care Arrangements in Dual-Worker Families." Final unpublished report. U.S. Public Health Service, National Institute of Mental Health, Rockville, Md., 1977.

Lein, L. Working Family Project. "Family and Social Ties." Final unpublished report. U.S. Public Health Service, National Institute of Mental Health, Rockville, Md., 1977.

Weiss, H. Working Family Project. "Adult Roles in Dual-Worker Families." Final unpublished report. U.S. Public Health Service, National Institute of Mental Health, Rockville, Md., 1977.

Working Family Project, Parenting. In: Rapaport and Rapaport, eds. *Working Couples.* New York: Harper & Row, Inc., 1978.

Working Family Project. Work and the American family. *National PTA*, 1977.

Working Family Project. "Tasks and Roles in Dual-Worker Families." Unpublished manuscript, Wellesley College Center for Research on Women, 1976.

The Effects of Parental Divorce: Experiences of the Child in Later Latency

Judith S. Wallerstein and Joan B. Kelly

The child of latency age* has somehow managed to escape the intensive psychological scrutiny with which his younger and older siblings have been regarded. Although no one has disputed the central significance of latency, which Erickson[3] has characterized as "socially, a most decisive stage," much less is known or conceptualized regarding parent-child relationships during these middle years than of those developmental years which immediately precede or follow them. Moreover, relatively little attention has been devoted to the varying effects of disrupted or fixated development during latency. Although many school-age children come into therapy, the central focus is usually on failure to resolve conflicts that stem from earlier developmental periods. Nor do we tend to learn much about latency from the treatment of adults; there is a relative unavailability of transferences and reconstructions pertaining to these years in most adult analyses. Bornstein[2] attributed the fact that "One learns relatively little about latency from the analysis of adults" to the distorted and idealized memories of adult patients who recall "the ideal of latency," namely, the successful warding-off of instinctual impulses during this time.

It is commonly agreed that the confluence of developmental and social forces propel the school-age child outward and away from the family towards peer relationships and new adult figures. Clinicians have stressed[1,2,5,6,8] the special importance of assuring developmental continuity during these years. Bornstein[2] specifically cautioned against environmental interruptions, referring to the importance of "free energies needed for character development," and observing that the latency child "fears nothing more than the upsetting of his precarious equilibrium." Erickson, [3,4] in addressing the fundamental tasks of this period, called attention to the lasting consequences of partial or total failure to successfully master these at their appropriate times. And Sarnoff,[8] more recently, referring to the fragility of the newly-consolidated latency defenses, warned that the drives in latency "may be stirred into activity at any time by seduction or sympathetic stimulation."

It is within this context, stressing the overriding importance of developmental continuity during his life phase, that our understanding of the impact of

From the *American Journal of Orthopsychiatry*, Vol. 46, No. 2 (April 1976), pp. 257–269. Copyright © 1976 the American Orthopsychiatric Association, Inc. Reproduced by permission.
    *[Latency is a psychoanalytic concept referring to school age, around 6–12, when sexuality is considered "latent" compared to the developmental stages immediately preceding or following.]

438

parental divorce upon the child must be set. For divorce necessarily affects the freedom of the child to keep major attention riveted outside the family circle. Moreover, the decision of divorce frequently ushers in an extended several year period marked by uncertainty and sharp discontinuity which has the potential to move the psychological and social functioning of the latency child into profound disequilibrium and painfully altered parent-child relationships. Alternatively, these changes can bear the potential for promoting development and maturation, as well as the possibility of more gratifying relationships within the post-divorce family structure.

Our data for this paper are drawn from the sample already described,[7] of 57 latency aged children from 47 families, here focused on the experiences of the 31 children from 28 families who were between nine and ten years old at the time that they were initially seen by us. As elaborated elsewhere,[7,9,10] these 31 children from 28 families represent part of a cohort of 131 children from 60 divorcing families referred for anticipatory guidance and planning for their children around the separation, and then seen by us again approximately a year later for the first of two planned follow-up studies.

The Initial Responses

How They Looked When They Came

Many of these children had presence, poise, and courage when they came to their initial interviews. They perceived the realities of their families' disruption and the parental turbulence with a soberness and clarity which we at first found startling, particularly when compared with the younger children who so frequently appeared disorganized and immobilized by their worry and grief. These youngsters were, by contrast, actively struggling to master a host of intense conflicting feelings and fears and trying to give coherence and continuity to the baffling disorder which they now experienced in their lives.

> Robert said, "I have to calm myself down. Everything is happening too fast."

> Katherine told us that a long time ago, when she was little, she thought everything was fine, that her parents really loved each other, and that, "Nothing would happen to them until they got real, real old." She added with the fine perceptions of a latency age child, "Mom and Dad married 12½ years ago. They met 17½ years ago. I always thought love would last if they stayed together that long."

Some children came prepared with an agenda.

> Anna, after a few general comments from the interviewer, designed to put her at ease, interrupted with a brisk, "Down to business," and went on immediately to describe the diffuse feelings of anxiety with which she suffered these days and which made her feel "sick to her stomach."

> Mary volunteered that she was "so glad" her mother brought her to talk
> about the divorce because, "If I don't talk about it soon I'll fall apart."

For others the opportunity to be with a concerned adult had considerable
significance seemingly unrelated to specific content. Some of these children
tried in many ways to continue the relationship.

> Janet begged to return the following week. She offered, "I like to talk about
> my troubles," and drew a heart on the blackboard, writing under it, "I like
> Miss X."

> Mary tried to extend her interview time, saying that her mother had not yet
> returned to fetch her, and then confessing that she had just lied.

Still others among these children found these interviews threatening and painful, and barely kept their anxiety controlled by keeping themselves or their
extremities in continual motion, the rhythm of which motion correlated with
the subject discussed.

> Thus, legs moved much faster when Daddy was mentioned to Jim, who was
> bravely trying to maintain his calm and referred with some disdain to "Moth-
> er's divorce problem," adding, "I wonder who she's got now?"

Others maintained their composure by denial and distancing.

> Jack stated, "I keep my cool. It's difficult to know what I'm thinking."

> David said darkly, "I don't try to think about it."

The Layering of Response

These various efforts to manage—by seeking coherence, by denial, by courage, by bravado, by seeking support from others, by keeping in motion, by
conscious avoidance—all emerged as age-available ways of coping with the
profound underlying feelings of loss and rejection, of helplessness and loneliness that pervaded these children and that, in most of them, only gradually
became visible within the context of the several successive interviews. Actually, testament to the resourcefulness of so many of these children is just this
capacity to function simultaneously on these two widely discrepant levels, not
always discernible to the outside observer. At times, only information from
collateral sources revealed their simultaneous involvement in the mastery
efforts of the coping stance and the succumbing to the anguish of their psychic
pain. This at times conscious layering of psychological functioning is a specific
finding in this age group. It is profoundly useful in muting and encapsulating
the suffering, making it tolerable and enabling the child to move developmentally. But it does not overcome the hurt, which is still there and takes
its toll.

> After his father left the home, Bob sat for many hours sobbing in his darkened
> room. The father visited infrequently. When seen by our project, Bob offered

smilingly, "I have a grand time on his visits," and added unsolicited and cheerily, "I see him enough." Only later would he shamefacedly admit that he missed his father intensely and longed to see him daily.

A few children were able to express their suffering more directly to their parents, as well as to us. This is the more poignant if one bears in mind Bornstein's[2] admonition that the latency child is *normally* engaged developmentally in a powerful battle against painful feelings.

> Jane's father left his wife angrily after discovering her infidelity, and ceased visiting the children. He moved in with a woman who had children approximately the age of his own children. Jane cried on the telephone in speaking with her father "I want to see you. I want to see you. I miss you. Alice (referring to the child of the other woman) sees you every day. We only see you once a month. That's not enough."

A very few children succumbed more totally and regressively.

> Paul responded to his father's departure by lying curled up sobbing inside a closet. He alternated this behavior, which lasted intermittently for several weeks, with telephone calls to his father, imploring him to return.

The suffering of these children was governed not only by the immediate pain of the family rupture, but expressed as well their grief over the loss of the family structure they had until then known, as well as their fears for the uncertain future that lay ahead for their newly diminished family. In a sense, as compared with younger children, their more sophisticated and mature grasp of time and reality and history increased their comprehension of the meanings and consequences of divorce—which enabled some of them better to temper the impact.

> Jim, when told by his parents of the plan to divorce, cried, "Why did you have to wait until we were so old?"

Finally, efforts to master inner distress were conjoined at times with efforts to conceal from the outside observer because of an acute sense of shame. Feelings of shame did not appear in the younger children in our study, but emerged specifically with this age group. These children were ashamed of the divorce and disruption in their family, despite their awareness of the commonness of divorce; they were ashamed of their parents and their behaviors, and they lied loyally to cover these up; and they were ashamed of the implied rejection of themselves in the father's departure, marking them, in their own eyes, as unlovable. . . .

Attempted Mastery by Activity and by Play

Unlike the younger latency children, so many of whom were immobilized by the family disruption, the pain which the children in this age group suffered

often galvanized them into organized activity. This was usually a multideter-
mined response geared to overcome their sense of powerlessness in the face of
the divorce, to overcome their humiliation at the rejection which they experienced, and to actively—and as energetically as possible—reverse the passively
suffered family disruption. In some, this was a direct effort to undo the parental
separation.

> Marian, with considerable encouragement at long distance from the paternal
> grandfather, embarked on a frenzied sequence of activities designed to intimi-
> date her mother and force her to return to the marriage. Marian scolded,
> yelled, demanded, and berated her mother, often making to impossible for her
> mother to have dates, and indeed almost succeeding in reversing the divorce
> decision by mobilizing all her mother's guilt in relation to herself and the
> other children. In one such episode, the child screamed in anger for several
> hours and then came quietly and tearfully to her mother, saying softly,
> "Mom, I'm so unhappy," confessing that she felt "all alone in the world."
> Following this, the harassment ceased.

Several children in this older latency group energetically developed a variety
of new, exciting, and intrinsically pleasurable mastery activities which combined play action with reality adaptation. Many of these activities required not
only fantasy production but the enterprise, organization, and skill of the later
latency child.

> Ann, whose father was a successful advertising and public relations man,
> designed and issued a magazine with articles and drawings, announcing the
> impending divorce of her parents, together with other interesting happenings,
> which she distributed and sold in her school and community.

In her role identification with her public media father, Ann not only overcame
the loss of his ongoing presence, at the very same time, through her newspaper
publication, she proclaimed her acceptance of the reality of this loss. But
central to this maneuver is the psychic gratification in it—Ann transformed
pain into the pleasure of achievement, and recaptured the center stage of
interest. . . .

Anger

The single feeling that most clearly distinguished this group from all the
younger children was their conscious intense anger. It had many sources, but
clearly a major determinant was its role in temporarily obliterating or at least
obscuring the other even more painful affective responses we have described.
Although we have reported elsewhere[10] a rise in aggression and irritability in
the pre-school child following parental separation, the anger experienced by
these older latency children was different in being both well organized and
clearly object-directed; indeed, their capacity directly to articulate this anger
was striking.

> John volunteered that most of the families of the kids on his block were getting a divorce. When asked how the children felt, he said, "They're so angry they're almost going crazy."

Approximately half of the children in this group were angry at their mothers, the other half at their fathers, and a goodly number were angry at both. Many of the children were angry at the parent whom they thought initiated the divorce, and their perception of this was usually accurate.

> Amy said she was angry at Mom for kicking Dad out and ruining their lives. "She's acting just like a college student, at age 31—dancing and dating and having to be with her friends."

> Ben accused his mother, saying, "You told me it would be better after the divorce, and it isn't."

> One adopted child screamed at his mother, "If you knew you were going to divorce, why did you adopt us?"

Interestingly, despite detailed and often very personal knowledge of the serious causes underlying the divorce decision, including repeated scenes of violence between the parents, most of these children were unable at the time of the initial counseling to see any justification for the parental decision to divorce. (By follow-up, many had come more soberly to terms with this.) Although one father had held his wife on the floor and put bobbie pins in her nose while their two children cried and begged him to stop, both children initially strongly opposed the mother's decision to divorce.

For some, anger against the parents was wedded to a sense of moral indignation and outrage that the parent who had been correcting their conduct was behaving in what they considered to be an immoral and irresponsible fashion.

> Mark said that "three days before my dad left he was telling me all these things about 'be good.' That hurt the most," he said, to think that his father did that and knew he was going to leave all the time.

This kind of moral stance in judgment upon parents is reminiscent of the attitudes we found frequently in the adolescent group,[9] but not in the younger groups.

The intense anger of these children was variously expressed. Parents reported a rise in temper tantrums, in scolding, in diffuse demandingness, and in dictatorial attitudes. Sometimes the anger was expressed in organized crescendos to provide a calculated nuisance when the mother's dates arrived.

> Shortly after the divorce, Joe's abusive, erratic, and rejecting father disappeared, leaving no address. The mother reported that now she had to ask the boy for permission to go out on dates, was reproached by him if she drank, and had her telephone calls monitored by him; when she bought something for herself, he screamingly demanded that the same amount of money be spent on him. Joe used his sessions with us primarily to express his anger at his mother for not purchasing a gun for him.

Adding to the dictatorial posturing and swaggering expressions that these children enjoyed playing out following the departure of their fathers was the fact that, in many of these households, the father had carried responsibility for a harsh and frightening discipline. His departure thus signaled a new freedom to express impulses that had been carefully held in check during his presence, a freedom to do so with impunity and with pleasure.

> Mary said that she was scared of her father. He had always required that things be spic and span around the house. "In that way I'm glad he's gone," she said.

Many mothers were immoblized by their own conflicts, as well as by their unfamiliarity with the role of disciplinarian. Others indicated in covert ways that they fully expected that one of the children would assume the father's role within the family. For some of these children the taking on of such an aggressive stance clearly reflected an identification with the attributes of the departed father, and thus an undoing of the pain of his departure.

> Anne congratulated her mother warmly on her decision to divorce her tyrannical husband. Shortly thereafter, however, Anne herself began to act out a commanding and screaming role vis-a-vis her mother and the younger children. This culminated in a dramatic episode of screaming for many hours when an uncle attempted to curb her wild behavior. She became very frightened after this, offering that all men were untrustworthy and that nobody would ever love her again.

Other children showed the obverse of all this—namely, an increased compliance and decreased assertiveness following the divorce.

> Janet's behavior shifted in the direction of becoming mother's helper and shadow, and showing unquestioning obedience to her mother's orders. She became known throughout the neighborhood as an excellent and reliable baby-sitter despite her very young age (nine years). She was, however, not able to say anything even mildly critical of her rejecting father, and was one of the few children who openly blamed herself for the divorce. When initially seen by us, she was preoccupied with her feelings of inadequacy and her low self-esteem.

Fears and Phobias

Unlike the pre-school children and the younger latency group, the children of this sample were not worried about actual starvation, and references to hunger in response to the parental separation were rare. Their fears, however, were nonetheless pervasive. Some, while not entirely realistic, were still tied to reality considerations; others approached phobic proportions. In fact, among this group it was often difficult for us to separate out the reality bases, including their sensitivity to the unspoken wishes of their parents, from the phobic elaboration. Thus, approximately one-quarter of these children were worried about being forgotten or abandoned by both parents.

> John, in tears, said that his mother had left him at the doctor's office and didn't return on time. He cried, "She said that she was doing errands, but I know she was with her boyfriend."

> Martha said to her mother, "If you don't love Daddy, maybe I'm next."

Some of their responses related to their accurate perception of parental feelings that children represent an unwelcome burden at this time in their lives.

> Peggy reported that her mother had said to her, "If you're not good I'm going to leave." Although Peggy knew that her mother had said this in anger, she still worried about it.

> Ann opined, "If Daddy marries Mrs. S., she has two daughters of her own, and I'll be Cinderella."

Some expressed the not wholly unrealistic concern that reliance on one rather than two parents was considerably less secure, and therefore the child's position in the world had become more vulnerable.

> Katherine told us, "If my mother smokes and gets cancer, where would I live?" She repeatedly begged her mother to stop smoking, and worried intensely whenever her mother was late in arriving home.

Some worried, not unrealistically, about emotionally ill parents.

> Ann stated about her mother, "I love her very much, but I have feelings. I'm afraid when Mom takes a long time to come home. She once tried to commit suicide. One day she ate a whole bottle of pills. I think of someone dying . . . how I'll be when I'm alone. Mom tried to commit suicide because of my father. It wasn't until after the divorce that she stopped crying. I think of her jumping over the Golden Gate Bridge. Mom thinks no one worries about her, but I do."

Many of these children experienced the additional concern that their specific needs were likely to be overlooked or forgotten.

> Wendy referred several times through her interviews to the fact that her mother insisted on buying Fig Newtons, when she perfectly well knew that Wendy hated them.

Responsibility for the Divorce

Only a few children expressed concern about having caused the divorce, although we endeavored in a variety of ways, including direct observations, play, and drawings, to elicit such material. We may, perhaps, cautiously infer from the fact that their occasional stealing occurred in situations where the child was assured of being caught, that there may exist some need for punishment relating to guilty fantasies. However, our direct evidence on this issue was limited to a few children in this later latency group, and appeared only in those children who showed a variety of other symptomatic behaviors in addition to the guilty thinking.

> Lorraine, whose petty pilfering and lying and school difficulties were greater exacerabated with the parental separation, said, "Whenever I think something is going to happen, it goes and happens. Like the time I thought my great-aunt was going to die, and then she died. And like the time I thought there was going to be a divorce." She wished that she could grow up and become a good witch, like Samantha.

Shaken Sense of Identity

Many of these children experienced a sense of a shaken world in which the usual indicators had changed place or disappeared. For several children, these changed markers were particularly related to their sense of who they were and who they would become in the future. Critical to this new sense of stress is that during latency years the child's normal conception of his own identity is closely tied to the external family structure and developmentally dependent on the physical presence of parental figures—not only for nurture, protection, and control, but also for the consolidation of age appropriate identifications.[3,7] Specifically, the self image and identity which in latency is still organized around, "I am the son of John and Mary Smith," is profoundly shaken by the severance of the parental relationship. Some children expressed this confusion and sense of ruptured identity with anxious questions, comparing physical characteristics of their parents and themselves, as if trying in this manner to reassemble the broken pieces into a whole.

> Jack, unsolicited, volunteered a long discussion of his physical features. "My eyes change colors, just like my Mom's. My hair is going to change to light brown, just like my Dad's. Other people say I'm like my Dad. My Dad says I'm like my Mom. I say I'm like a combination."

Another aspect of this threat to the integrity of self which occurs at the time of divorce is posed more specifically to the socialization process and superego formation. The child feels that his conscience controls have been weakened by the family disruption, as the external supports give way and his anger at the parents moves strongly into consciousness. One manifestation of this may be new behaviors of petty stealing and lying which make their appearance in this age group around the time of family disruption. The threat the child perceives to his sense of being socialized is related, as well, to his concern of having to take care of himself; it was conveyed to us by Bob's moving story of his two rabbits.

> Bob volunteered, "I think I want to talk to you today." He told about the two little rabbits he had bought several years ago and cared for in an elaborate

high-rise hutch he had carefully constructed. One day, despite his protective watchfulness, vicious neighborhood dogs ripped the cage apart, and the rabbits disappeared or were dragged off. The two rabbits, whom he had named Ragged Ear and Grey Face, may have escaped, he thinks, because recently he came upon two rabbits playing in the woods. They were wild rabbits now, but they resembled the two he had lost.

The two rabbits of this rich fantasy may well have referred to the child and his brother, and his story may reflect his fear of the primitive angers (the vicious dogs) let loose at the time of divorce, his fear that he would be destroyed, and the projected rescue solution—via return to a pre-socialized wild state in which the child-equals-rabbit takes responsibility for his own care. Clearly, the little wild rabbits who survived had a different identity and a different superego formation than the rabbits who were cared for so lovingly in the elaborately built hutch.

Loneliness and Loyalty Conflicts

Children in this older latency group described their loneliness, their sense of having been left outside, and their sad recognition of their powerlessness and peripheral role in major family decisions.

Betty said,"We were sitting in the dark with candles. Then they (her parents) told us suddenly about the divorce. We didn't have anything to say, and so then we watched TV."

These feelings of loneliness, not observed in this way in the younger age groups, reflect not only the greater maturational achievement of these children but also their more grown-up expectation of mutuality, as well as reciprocal support, in their relationships with parents and other adults. They thus felt more hurt, humiliated, and pushed aside by the events visited upon them, over which they had so little leverage.

It should be noted that these children, in their wrestling with this loneliness, realistically perceived the very real parental withdrawal of interest in children which so often occurs at the time of divorce. In addition to the departure of one parent, both parents understandably at such times become preoccupied with their own needs; their emotional availability, their attention span, and even the time spent with the children are often sharply reduced. Moreover, the families in our study were, by and large, nuclear families, unconnected to wider extended families or support systems of any enduring significance to the children. In this sense the children's feelings of loneliness and of loss reflected their realization that the central connecting structures they had known were dissolving.

Perhaps, however, the central ingredient in the loneliness and sense of isolation these children reported was related to their perception of the divorce as a battle between the parents, in which the child is called upon to take sides.[7] By this logic, a step in the direction of the one parent was experienced by the child (and, of course, sometimes by the parent) as a betrayal of the other parent, likely to evoke real anger and further rejection, in addition to the intrapsychic conflicts mobilized. Thus, paralyzed by their own conflicting loyalties and the severe psychic or real penalties which attach to choice, many children refrained from choice and felt alone and desolate, with no place to turn for comfort or parenting. In a true sense, their conflict placed them in a solitary position at midpoint in the marital struggle. . . .

Changes in Parent-Child Relationships

We turn now to a necessarily abbreviated discussion of some of the new parent-child configurations that emerged as a response to the marital strife and parental separation. These changed relationships constitute a significant component of the total response of children in this age group. The divorce-triggered changes in the parent-child relationship may propel the child forward into a variety of precocious, adolescent, or, more accurately, pseudoadolescent behaviors. They can, on the other hand, catalyze the development of true empathic responsiveness and increased responsibility in the child. And they can also result, as in the case of alignment with one parent against the other, in a lessening of the age-appropriate distance between parent and child and a retreat by the child along the individuation-separation axis of development.

Alignment

One of the attributes of the parent-child relationship at this particular age is the peculiar interdependence of parent and child, which can become enhanced at the time of the divorce, and which accords the child a significant role in restoring of further diminishing the self-esteem of the parent. Thus the child in late latency, by his attitude, his stance, and his behavior has independent power to hurt, to reject, to confront, to forgive, to comfort, and to affirm. He also has the capacity to be an unswervingly loyal friend, ally, and "team member," exceeding in reliability his sometimes more fickle and capricious adolescent sibling.

Among the 31 children in this cohort, eight (or 26%) formed a relationship with one parent following the separation which was specifically aimed at the exclusion or active rejection of the other. These alignments were usually initiated and always fueled by the embattled parent, most often by the parent who felt aggrieved, deserted, exploited, or betrayed by the divorcing spouse. The angers which the parent and the child shared soon became the basis for complexly organized strategies aimed at hurting and harassing the former spouse, sometimes with the intent of shaming him or her into returning to the marriage. More often the aim was vengeance. For many of these parents, these anger-driven campaigns served additionally to ward off depressions, and their intensity remained undiminished for a long time following parental separation. It should be noted that none of these children who participated, many of them as ingenious and mischievous allies, had previously rejected the parent who, subsequent to the alignment, became the target of their angers. Therefore, their provocative behavior was extremely painful and their rejection bewildering and humiliating to the excluded parent.

Our data indicate that, although the fight for allegiance may be initiated by the embattled parent, these alignments strike a responsive chord in the children within this specific age group. In fact, it is our suggestion that for children in late latency, the alignment with one parent against the other represents a highly complexly organized, over-determined, ego-syntonic coping behavior, which serves a diversity of psychological needs and keeps at bay a number of significant intrapsychic conflicts and their attendant anxieties. A central part of the dynamic of this behavior is the splitting of the ambivalent relationship to the parents into that with the good parent and the bad parent. Moreover, in our findings, these alignments have the hurtful potential for consolidation and perpetuation long past the initial post-separation period, especially in those families where the child is aligned with the custodial parent.

> Paul's father was referred to us informally by the court to which the father had gone to complain of his wife's vindictive blocking of his visits with his three children. The father, a successful chemical engineer, expressed sadness and longing for his children, and concern that his children were being systematically turned against him by their mother's unremitting attacks and falsehoods. For example, the children were told by the mother that they had to give up their dog because the father was refusing to purchase food for it, although at that time the family was receiving well over $16,000 a year in support. Paul's mother expressed astonishment and bitterness at his father for the unilateral divorce decision, describing her many years of devoted love and hard work to support the father's graduate education. She coldly insisted that, as a devout Christian woman, she would never harbor anger. Yet she was convinced that, since the father had rejected both her and their three children, Paul would "never forgive his father, nor forget."
>
> Paul's initial response to the parental separation was his regression to sobbing in a dark closet, which we have earlier described, alternating with telephone pleas to his father to return. Later, in recalling this time, the child said to us, "I felt that I was being torn into two pieces." By the time we saw Paul, several months following the separation, he had consolidated an unshakable alignment with his mother. He extolled her as small and powerful, possessed of ESP, and knowledgeable in six languages. Of his father, he stated, "He'll never find another family like us." He volunteered that he never wanted to visit his father—ever. In response to our efforts to elicit fantasy material, he said that he would like best to live on a desert island with his mother and siblings and have a very, very long telephone cord for speaking with his father, and maybe a speedboat for visiting him.

Among Paul's activities during the year following our initial contact was his continuing reporting to his mother, and eventually to her attorney, about his father's "lurid" social life and presumed delinquencies, and his continued rejections of his father's increasingly desperate overtures, including gifts and wishes to maintain visitation. Paul also maintained a coercive control over his younger sisters, who were eager to see their father, and he made sure by his monitoring of them that they would not respond with affection in his presence. At follow-up he told us, "We are a team now. We used to have an extra guy, and he broke us up into little pieces." His anger and his mother's anger seemed undiminished at this time.

Empathy

Heightened empathic response to one or both distressed parents—and siblings—was catalyzed in several children as a specific consequence of the separation and the ensuing divorce.

With unusual insight, Anne described this process in *status nascendi*. She said, "I know that my mother isn't ready for the divorce, because I can put myself in her place. I can think just like I think my mother thinks."

Some youngsters were able to perceive their parent's needs with great sensitivity, and to respond with compassion and caring.

Mary told us, "My mom cried. She was so tired of being so strong for the children, and she asked us to sleep with her." Mary and her brother complied. "It made Mom feel better. Then we got up in the morning and made her breakfast in bed. Sometimes we just tell her, 'we are here, it's going to be all right.' "

We were interested to find that parents were often profoundly appreciative of this sensitivity and consideration.

Jane's mother told us that Jane was a wonderful child who wordlessly responded to the mother's needs and feelings. "Whenever I feel alone in the evening she cuddles me," her mother said.

Some of these children, especially the little girls, worried about their fathers and were concerned about the particulars of where they were sleeping and eating.

Jane told us how much she worries about her father, that he works late, that he only has a couch to sleep on, and that he seems so "extra tired."

Sometimes the children took on responsibility for the younger children, as well as for themselves, and for important routines in the household. Many parents had no adult relationships to lean on, and they relied heavily on these children for emotional support and advice, as well as for practical help.

Sometimes empathic feelings were stimulated by unequal treatment of siblings by the departing parent.

Jack suddenly began to wheeze as he told us that his father had invited him, but not his sister, to live with him. He added that his father had sent him a

> Christmas card, signing it, "With all my love," but had only sent his sister a signed card. "I guess it made her feel pretty bad," he added sadly.

A few children were particularly sensitive to the changing moods and needs of their emotionally ill parent, and learned early to dissemble and protect what they understood to be the fragility of the parent's adjustment.

> Jane stated as one of her problems that it was hard for her to be honest with her mother. Her mother kept asking questions about the father's relationship with his new girlfriends. She, Jane, could not tell her mother that her father and his girlfriend didn't fight, because "I'm scared that it will make her sad and cry." At follow-up, Jane solemnly told us, "Mom will probably marry, but she is not ready. She just got the divorce and wants to be settled. I think she has gone through a lot of trouble and sadness and needs more time."

Follow-up at One Year

A first follow-up on these youngsters took place a year after the initial consultation. By and large, as with the younger latency children, the turbulent responses to the divorce itself had mostly become muted with the passage of the intervening year. In about half the children (15 of the 29 available at follow-up) the disequilibrium created by the family disruption—the suffering, the sense of shame; the fears of being forgotten, lost, or actively abandoned, and the many intense worries associated with their new sense of vulnerability and dependence on a more fragile family structure—had almost entirely subsided. But even these children with apparent better outcomes, who seemed relatively content with their new family life and circle of friends, including step-parents, were not without backward glances of bitterness and nostalgia. In fact, the anger and hostility aroused around the divorce events lingered longer and more tenaciously than did any of the other affective responses. Of the total group, ten (or one-third) of the children maintained an unremitted anger directed at the non-custodial parent; of these, four did so in alignment with the custodial mother, the other six on their own.

> Edward, who was doing splendidly in school and in new friendship relationships with his mother and with an admired male teacher, nonetheless said bitterly of his father, "I'm not going to speak to him any more. My dad is off my list now." (This was a father who, prior to the divorce, had had a very warm relationship with his son.)

Although some of these children who were doing well continued to harbor reconciliation wishes, most had come to accept the divorce with sad finality. Some seemed to be unconsciously extrapolating from these reconciliation wishes to plan future careers as repairmen, as bridge builders, as architects, as lawyers. Others, like Jane, were perhaps extending their protective attitudes towards their disturbed parents.

> Asked what she might like to do when she grows up, Jane responded, "You might laugh. A child psychiatrist. You're one, aren't you?" She talked mov-

ingly of working someday "with blind children, or mentally retarded children, or children who cannot speak."

By contrast, the other half (14 of the 29 seen at follow-up) gave evidence of consolidation into troubled and conflicted depressive behavior patterns, with, in half of these, *more* open distress and disturbance than at the initial visit. A significant component in this now chronic maladjustment was a continuing depression and low self-esteem, combined with frequent school and peer difficulties. One such child was described by his teacher at follow-up as, "A little old man who worries all the time and rarely laughs." In this group, symptoms that had emerged had generally persisted and even worsened. For instance, phobic reactions had in one instance worsened and spread; delinquent behavior such as truancy and petty thievery remained relatively unchanged; and some who had become isolated and withdrawn were even more so. One new behavior configuration that emerged during the first post-divorce year in these nine-and ten-year-olds was a precocious thrust into adolescent preoccupation with sexuality and assertiveness, with all the detrimental potential of such phase-inappropriate unfoldings. And amongst all the children, both in the groups with better and with poorer outcomes, relatively few were able to maintain good relationships with both parents.

In a future report we shall present a fuller discussion of the many variables which seem to relate to this bimodal spread of outcomes for the post-divorce course of these children. Here we would like to close with the remarks of a ten-year-old sage from our study, whose words capture the salient mood of these children at the first follow-up—their clear-eyed perception of reality, their pragmatism, their courage, and their muted disappointment and sadness. In summarizing the entire scene, she said, "Knowing my parents, no one is going to change his mind. We'll just all have to get used to the situation and to them."

References

1. Becker, T. 1974. On latency, Psychoanal. Study of Child 29:3–11.
2. Bornstein, B. 1951. On latency. Psychoanal. Study of Child, 6:279–285.
3. Erickson, E. 1959. Identity and the life cycle. Psychological Issues vol. 1.
4. Erickson, E. 1963. Childhood and Society. Norton, New York.
5. Harris, I. 1959. Normal Children and Mothers. Free Press, Glencoe, Ill.
6. Kaplan, S. (Reporter). 1957. Panel: the latency period. JAPA 5:525–538.
7. Kelly, J. and Wallerstein, J. 1976. The effects of parental divorce: experiences of the child in early latency. Amer. J. Orthopsychiat. 46(1):20–32.
8. Sarnoff, C. 1971. Ego structure in latency. Psychoanal. Quart. 40:387–414.
9. Wallerstein, J. and Kelly, J. 1974. The effects of parental divorce: the adolescent experience. *In* the Child in His Family: Children at Psychiatric Risk, J. Anthony and C. Koupernik, eds. John Wiley, New York.
10. Wallerstein, J. and Kelly, J. 1975. The effects of parental divorce: experiences of the preschool child. J. Amer. Acad. Child Psychiat. 14(4).

Chapter 9

Parenthood

Transition to Parenthood

Alice S. Rossi

From Child to Parent: An Example

What is unique about this perspective on parenthood is the focus on the adult parent rather than the child. Until quite recent years, concern in the behavioral sciences with the parent-child relationship has been confined almost exclusively to the child. . . .

The very different order of questions which emerge when the parent replaces the child as the primary focus of analytic attention can best be shown with an illustration. Let us take, for our example, the point Benedek makes that the child's need for mothering is *absolute* while the need of an adult woman to mother is *relative.* From a concern for the child, this discrepancy in need leads to an analysis of the impact on the child of separation from the mother or inadequacy of mothering. Family systems that provide numerous adults to care for the young child can make up for this discrepancy in need between mother and child, which may be why ethnographic accounts give little evidence of postpartum depression following childbirth in simpler societies. Yet our family system of isolated households, increasingly distant from kinswomen to assist in mothering, requires that new mothers shoulder total responsibility for the infant precisely for that stage of the child's life when his need for mothering is far in excess of the mother's need for the child.

From the perspective of the mother, the question has therefore become: what does maternity deprive her of? Are the intrinsic gratifications of maternity sufficient to compensate for shelving or reducing a woman's involvement in nonfamily interests and social roles? The literature on maternal deprivation cannot answer such questions, because the concept, even in the careful specification Yarrow has given it, has never meant anything but the effect on the child of various kinds of insufficient mothering. Yet what has been seen as a failure

From the *Journal of Marriage and the Family,* Vol. 30 (February 1968), pp. 26–39.

or inadequacy of individual women may in fact be a failure of the society to provide institutionalized substitutes for the extended kin to assist in the care of infants and young children. It may be that the role requirements of maternity in the American family system extract diversified interests and social expectations concerning adult life. Here, as at several points in the course of this paper, familiar problems take on a new and suggestive research dimension when the focus is on the parent rather than the child. . . .

Parsons' analysis of the experience of parenthood as a step in maturation and personality growth does not allow for negative outcome. In this view either parents show little or no positive impact upon themselves of their parental-role experiences, or they show a new level of maturity. Yet many women, whose interests and values made a congenial combination of wifehood and work role, may find that the addition of maternal responsibilities has the consequence of a fundamental and undesired change in both their relationships to their husbands and their involvements outside the family. Still other women, who might have kept a precarious hold on adequate functioning as adults had they *not* become parents, suffer severe retrogression with pregnancy and childbearing, because the reactivation of older unresolved conflicts with their own mothers is not favorably resolved but in fact leads to personality deterioration and the transmission of pathology to their children.

Where cultural pressure is very great to assume a particular adult role, as it is for American women to bear and rear children, latent desire and psychological readiness for parenthood may often be at odds with manifest desire and actual ability to perform adequately as parents. Clinicians and therapists are aware, as perhaps many sociologists are not, that failure, hostility, and destructiveness are as much a part of the family system and the relationships among family members as success, love, and solidarity are. . . .

Role-Cycle Stages

A discussion of the impact of parenthood upon the parent will be assisted by two analytic devices. One is to follow a comparative approach, by asking in what basic structural ways the parental role differs from other primary adult roles. The marital and occupational roles will be used for this comparison. A second device is to specify the phases in the development of a social role. If the total life span may be said to have a cycle, each stage with its unique tasks, then by analogy a role may be said to have a cycle and each stage in that role cycle to have its unique tasks and problems of adjustment. Four broad stages of a role cycle may be specified:

1. Anticipatory Stage

All major adult roles have a long history of anticipatory training for them, since parental and school socialization of children is dedicated precisely to this task of producing the kind of competent adult valued by the culture. For our present purposes, however, a narrower conception of the marital role, pregnancy in the case of the parental role, and the last stages of highly vocationally oriented schooling or on-the-job apprenticeship in the case of an occupational role.

2. Honeymoon Stage

This is the time period immediately following the full assumption of the adult role. The inception of this stage is more easily defined than its termination. In the case of the marital role, the honeymoon stage extends from the marriage ceremony itself through the literal honeymoon and on through an unspecified and individually varying period of time. Raush has caught this stage of the marital role in his description of the "psychic honeymoon": that extended postmarital period when, through close intimacy and joint activity, the couple can explore each other's capacities and limitations. I shall arbitrarily consider the onset of pregnancy as marking the end of the honeymoon stage of the marital role. This stage of the parental role may involve an equivalent psychic honeymoon, that post-childbirth period during which, through intimacy and prolonged contact, an attachment between parent and child is laid down. There is a crucial difference, however, from the marital role in this stage. A woman knows her husband as a unique real person when she enters the honeymoon stage of marriage. A good deal of preparatory adjustment on a firm reality base is possible during the engagement period which is not possible in the equivalent pregnancy period. Fantasy is not corrected by the reality of a specific individual child until the birth of the child. The "quickening" is psychologically of special significance to women precisely because it marks the first evidence of a real baby rather than a purely fantasized one. On this basis alone there is greater interpersonal adjustment and learning during the honeymoon stage of the parental role than of the marital role.

3. Plateau Stage

This is the protracted middle period of a role cycle during which the role is fully exercised. Depending on the specific problem under analysis, one would obviously subdivide this large plateau stage further. For my present purposes it is not necessary to do so, since my focus is on the earlier anticipatory and honeymoon stages of the parental role and the overall impact of parenthood on adults.

4. Disengagement-Termination Stage

This period immediately precedes and includes the actual termination of the role. Marriage ends with the death of the spouse or, just as definitively, with separation and divorce. A unique characteristic of parental-role termination is the fact that it is not closely marked by any specific act but is an attenuated process of termination with little cultural prescription about when the authority and obligations of a parent end. Many parents, however, experience the marriage of the child as a psychological termination of the active parental role.

Unique Features of Parental Role

With this role-cycle suggestion as a broader framework, we can narrow our focus to what are the unique and most salient features of the parental role. In doing so, special attention will be given to two further questions: (1) the impact of social changes over the past few decades in facilitating or complicating the transition to and experience of parenthood and (2) the new interpretations or new research suggested by the focus on the parent rather than the child.

1. Cultural Pressure to Assume the Role

On the level of cultural values, men have no freedom of choice where work is concerned: They must work to secure their status as adult men.

The equivalent for women has been maternity. There is considerable pressure upon the growing girl and young woman to consider maternity necessary for a woman's fulfillment as an individual and to secure her status an an adult.*

This is not to say there are no fluctuations over time in the intensity of the cultural pressure to parenthood. During the depression years of the 1930s, there was more widespread awareness of the economic hardships parenthood can entail, and many demographic experts believe there was a great increase in illegal abortions during those years. Bird has discussed the dread with which a suspected pregnancy was viewed by many American women in the 1930s. Quite a different set of pressures were at work during the 1950s, when the general societal tendency was toward withdrawal from active engagement with the issues of the larger society and a turning in to the gratifications of the private sphere of home and family life. Important in the background were the general affluence of the period and the expanded room and ease of child rearing that go with suburban living. For the past five years, there has been a drop in the birth rate in general, fourth and higher-order births in particular. During this same period there has been increased concern and debate about women's participation in politics and work, with more women now returning to work rather than conceiving the third or fourth child.**

*The greater the cultural pressure to assume a given adult social role, the greater will be the tendency for individual negative feelings toward that role to be expressed covertly. Men may complain about a given job, not about working per se, and hence their work dissatisfactions are often displaced to the nonwork sphere, as psychosomatic complaints or irritation and dominance at home. An equivalent displacement for women of the ambivalence many may feel toward maternity is to dissatisfactions with the homemaker role.

**When it is realized that a mean family size of 3.5 would double the population in 40 years, while a mean of 2.5 would yield a stable population in the same period, the social importance of withholding praise for procreative prowess is clear. At the same time, a drop in the birth rate may reduce the number of unwanted babies born, for such a drop would mean more efficient contraceptive usage and a closer correspondence between desired and attained family size.

2. Inception of the Parental Role

The decision to marry and the choice of a mate are voluntary acts of individuals in our family system. Engagements are therefore consciously considered, freely entered, and freely terminated if increased familiarity decreases, rather than increases, intimacy and commitment to the choice. The inception of a pregnancy, unlike the engagement, is not always a voluntary decision, for it may be the unintended consequence of a sexual act that was recreative in intent rather than procreative. Secondly, and again unlike the engagement, the termination of a pregnancy is not socially sanctioned, as shown by current resistance to abortion-law reform.

The implication of this difference is a much higher probability of unwanted pregnancies than of unwanted marriages in our family system. Coupled with the ample clinical evidence of parental rejection and sometimes cruelty to children, it is all the more surprising that there has not been more consistent research attention to the problem of *parental satisfaction,* as there has for long been on *marital satisfaction or work satisfaction.* Only the extreme iceberg tip of the parental satisfaction continuum is clearly demarcated and researched, as in the growing concern with "battered babies." Cultural and psychological resistance to the image of a nonnurturant woman may afflict social scientists as well as the American public.

The timing of a first pregnancy is critical to the manner in which parental responsibilities are joined to the marital relationship. The single most important change over the past few decades is extensive and efficient contraceptive usage, since this has meant for a growing proportion of new marriages, the possibility of and increasing preference for some postponement of childbearing after marriage. When pregnancy was likely to follow shortly after marriage, the major transition point in a woman's life was marriage itself. *This transition point is increasingly the first pregnancy rather than marriage.* It is accepted and increasingly expected that women will work after marriage, while household furnishings are acquired and spouses complete their advanced training or gain a foothold in their work. This provides an early marriage period in which the fact of a wife's employment presses for a greater egalitarian relationship between husband and wife in decision-making, commonality of experience, and sharing of household responsibilities.

The balance between individual autonomy and couple mutuality that develops during the honeymoon stage of such a marriage may be important in establishing a pattern that will later affect the quality of the parent-child relationship and the extent of sex-role segregation of duties between the parents. It is only in the context of a growing egalitarian base to the marital relationship that one could find, as Gavron has, a tendency for parents to establish some barriers between themselves and their children, a marital defense against the institution of parenthood as she describes it. This may eventually replace the typical coalition in more traditional families of mother and children against husband-father. . . .

There is one further significant social change that has important implications for the changed relationship between husband and wife: the increasing departure from an old pattern of role-inception phasing in which the young person first completed his schooling, then established himself in the world of work, then married and began his family. Marriage and parenthood are increasingly taking place *before* the schooling of the husband, and often of the wife, has been completed. An important reason for this trend lies in the fact that, during the same decades in which the average age of physical-sexual maturation has dropped, the average amount of education which young people obtain has been on the increase. Particularly for the college and graduate or professional school population, family roles are often assumed before the degrees needed to enter careers have been obtained. . . .

The major implication of this change is that more men and women are achieving full status in family roles while they are still less than fully adult in status terms in the occupational system. Graduate students are, increasingly, men and women with full family responsibilities. Within the family many more husbands and fathers are still students, often quite dependent on the earnings of their wives to see them through their advanced training. No matter what the couple's desires and preferences are, this fact alone presses for more egalitarian relations between husband and wife, just as the adult family status of graduate students presses for more egalitarian relations between students and faculty.

3. Irrevocability

If marriages do not work out, there is now widespread acceptance of divorce and remarriage as a solution. The same point applies to the work world: we are free to leave an unsatisfactory job and seek another. But once a pregnancy occurs, there is little possibility of undoing the commitment to parenthood implicit in conception except in the rare instance of placing children for adoption. We can have ex-spouses and ex-jobs but not ex-children. This being so, it is scarcely surprising to find marked differences between the relationship of a parent and one child and the relationship of the same parent with another child. If the culture does not permit pregnancy termination, the equivalent to giving up a child is psychological withdrawal on the part of the parent.

This taps an important area in which a focus on the parent rather than the child may contribute a new interpretive dimension to an old problem: the long history of interest, in the social sciences, in differences among children associated with their sex-birth-order position in their sibling set. . . .

Some birth-order research stresses the influence of sibs upon other sibs, as in Koch's finding that second-born boys with an older sister are more feminine than second-born boys with an older brother. A similar sib-influence interpretation is offered in the major common finding of birth-order correlates, that sociability is greater among last-borns and achievement among first-borns. It has been suggested that last-borns use social skills to increase acceptance by their older sibs or are more peer-oriented because they receive less adult stimulation from parents. The tendency of first-borns to greater achievement has been interpreted in a corollary way, as a reflection of early assumption of responsibility for younger sibs, greater adult stimulation during the time the oldest was the only child in the family, and the greater significance of the first-born for the larger kinship network of the family.

Sociologists have shown increasing interest in structural family variables in recent years, a primary variable being family size. . . . The question posed is: what is the effect of growing up in a small family, compared with a large family, that is attributable to this group-size variable? Unfortunately, the theoretical point of departure for sociologists' expectations of the effect of the family-size variables is the Durkheim-Simmel tradition of the differential effect of group size or population density upon members or inhabitants. In the case of the family, however, this overlooks the very important fact that family size is determined by the key figures *within* the group, i.e., the parents. To find that children in small families differ from children in large families is not simply due to the impact of group size upon individual members but to the very different involvement of the parent with the children and to relations between the parents themselves in small versus large families.

An important clue to a new interpretation can be gained by examining family size from the perspective of parental motivation toward having children. A small family is small for one of two primary reasons: either the parents wanted a small family and achieved their desired size, or they wanted a large family but were not able to attain it. In either case, there is a low probability of unwanted children. Indeed, in the latter eventuality they may take particularly great interest in the children they do have. Small families are therefore most likely to contain parents with a strong and positive orientation to each of the children they have. A large family, by contrast, is large either because the parents achieved the size they desired or because they have more children than they in fact wanted. Large families therefore have a higher probability than small families of including unwanted unloved children. Consistent with this are Nye's finding that adolescents in small families have better relations with their parents than those in large families, and Sears and Maccoby's finding that mothers of large families are more restrictive toward their children than mothers of small families.

This also means that last-born children are more likely to be unwanted than first- or middle-born children, particularly in large families. This is consistent with what is known of abortion patterns among married women, who typically resort to abortion only when they have achieved the number of children they want or feel they can afford to have. Only a small proportion of women faced with such unwanted pregnancies actually resort to abortion. *This suggests the possibility that the last-born child's reliance on social skills may be his device for securing the attention and loving involvement of a parent less positively predisposed to him than to his older siblings.*

In developing this interpretation, rather extreme cases have been stressed. Closer to the normal range, of families in which even the last-born child was desired and planned for, there is still another element which may contribute to the greater sociability of the last-born child. Most parents are themselves aware of the greater ease with which they face the care of a third fragile newborn than the first; clearly parental skills and confidence are greater with last-born children than with first-born children. But this does not mean that the attitude of the parent is more positive toward the care of the third child than the first. There is no necessary correlation between skills in an area and enjoyment of that area. Searls found that older homemakers are *more* skillful in domestic tasks but experience *less* enjoyment of them than younger home-makers, pointing to a declining euphoria for a particular role with the passage of time. In the same way, older people rate their marriages as "very happy" less often than younger people do. It is perhaps culturally and psychologically more difficult to face the possibility that women may find less enjoyment of the maternal role with the passage of time, though women themselves know the difference between the romantic expectation concerning child care and the incorporation of the first baby into the household and the more realistic expectation and sharper assessment of their own abilities to do an adequate job of mothering as they face a third confinement. Last-born children may experi-ence not only less verbal stimulation from the parents than first-born children but also less prompt and enthusiastic response to their demands—from feeding and diaper change as infants to requests for stories read at three or a college education at eighteen—simply because the parents experience less intense gratification from the parent role with the third child than they did with the first. The child's response to this might well be to cultivate winning, pleasing manners in early childhood that blossom as charm and sociability in later life, showing both a greater need to be loved and greater pressure to seek approval.

One last point may be appropriately developed at this juncture. Mention was made earlier that for many women the personal outcome of experience in the parent role is not a higher level of maturation but the negative outcome of a depressed sense of self-worth, if not actual personality deterioration. There is considerable evidence that this is more prevalent than we recognize. On a qualitative level, a close reading of the portrait of the working-class wife in Rainwater, Newsom, Komarovsky, Gavron, or Zweig gives little suggestion that maternity has provided these women with opportunities for personal growth and development. So, too, Cohen notes with some surprise that in her sample of middle-class educated couples, as in Pavenstadt's study of lower-income women in Boston, there were more emotional difficulties and lower levels of maturation among multiparous women than primiparous women. On a more extensive sample basis, in Gurin's survey of Americans viewing their mental health, as in Bradburn's reports on happiness, single men are less happy and less active than single women, but among the married respondents the women are unhappier, have more problems, feel inadequate as parents, have a more negative and passive outlook on life, and show a more negative self-image. All of these characteristics increase with age among men. While it may be true, as Gurin argues, that women are more introspective and hence more attuned to the psychological facets of experience than men are, this point does not account for the fact that the things which the women report are all on the negative side; few are on the positive side, indicative of euphoric sensitivity and pleasure. The possibility must be faced, and at some point researched, that women lose ground in personal development and self-esteem during the early and middle years of adulthood, whereas men gain ground in these respects during the same years. The retention of a high level of self-esteem may depend upon the adequacy of earlier preparation for major adult roles: men's training adequately prepares them for their primary adult roles in the occupational system, as it does for those women who opt to participate significantly in the work world. Training in the qualities and skills needed for family roles in contemporary society may be inadequate for both sexes, but the lowering of self-esteem occurs only among women because their primary adult roles are within the family system.

4. Preparation for Parenthood

Four factors may be given special attention on the question of what preparation American couples bring to parenthood.

(a) Paucity of preparation. Our educational system is dedicated to the cognitive development of the young, and our primary teaching approach is the pragmatic one of learning by doing. How much one knows and how well he can apply what he knows are the standards by which the child is judged in school, as the employee is judged at work. The child can learn by doing in such subjects as science, mathematics, art work, or shop, but not in the subjects most relevant to successful family life: sex, home maintenance, child care, interpersonal competence, and empathy. If the home is deficient in training in these areas, the child is left with no preparation for a major segment of his adult life. A doctor facing his first patient in private practice has treated numerous patients under close supervision during his internship, but probably a majority of American mothers approach maternity with no previous child-care experience beyond sporadic baby-sitting, perhaps a course in child psychology, or occasional care of younger siblings.

(b) Limited learning during pregnancy. A second important point makes adjustment to parenthood potentially more stressful than marital adjustment. This is the lack of any realistic training for parenthood during the anticipatory stage of pregnancy. By contrast, during the engagement period preceding marriage, an individual has opportunities to develop the skills and make the adjustments which ease the transition to marriage. Through discussions of

values and life goals, through sexual experimentation, shared social experiences as an engaged couple with friends and relatives, and planning and furnishing an apartment, the engaged couple can make considerable progress in developing mutuality in advance of the marriage itself. No such headstart is possible in the case of pregnancy. What preparation exists is confined to reading, consultation with friends and parents, discussions between husband and wife, and a minor nesting phase in which a place and the equipment for a baby are prepared in the household.*

(c) Abruptness of transition. Thirdly, the birth of a child is not followed by any gradual taking on of responsibility, as in the case of a professional work role. It is as if the woman shifted from a graduate student to a full professor with little intervening apprenticeship experience of slowly increasing responsibility. The new mother starts out immediately on 24-hour duty, with responsibility for a fragile and mysterious infant totally dependent on her care.

If marital adjustment is more difficult for very young brides than more mature ones, adjustment to motherhood may be even more difficult. A woman can adapt a passive dependence on a husband and still have a successful marriage, but a young mother with strong dependency needs is in for difficulty in maternal adjustment, because the role precludes such dependency. This situation was well described in Cohen's study in a case of a young wife with a background of coed popularity and a passive dependent relationship to her admired and admiring husband, who collapsed into restricted incapacity when faced with the responsibilities of maintaining a home and caring for a child.

(d) Lack of guidelines to successful parenthood. If the central task of parenthood is the rearing of children to become the kind of competent adults valued by the society, then an important question facing any parent is what he or she specifically can do to create such a competent adult. This is where the parent is left with few or no guidelines from the expert. Parents can readily inform themselves concerning the young infant's nutritional, clothing, and medical needs and follow the general prescription that a child needs loving physical contact and emotional support. Such advice may be sufficient to produce a healthy, happy, and well-adjusted preschooler, but adult competency is quite another matter.

In fact, the adults who do "succeed" in American society show a complex of characteristics as children that current experts in child-care would evaluate as "poor" to "bad." Biographies of leading authors and artists, as well as the more rigorous research inquiries of creativity among architects or scientists, do not portray childhoods with characteristics currently endorsed by mental-

*During the period when marriage was the critical transition in the adult woman's life rather than pregnancy, a good deal of anticipatory "nesting" behavior took place from the time of conception. Now more women work through a considerable portion of the first pregnancy, and such nesting behavior as exists may be confined to a few shopping expeditions or baby showers, thus adding to the abruptness of the transition and the difficulty of adjustment following the birth of a first child.

health and child-care authorities. Indeed, there is often a predominance of tension in childhood family relations and traumatic loss rather than loving parental support, intense channeling of energy in one area of interest rather than an all-round profile of diverse interests, and social withdrawal and preference for loner activities rather than gregarious sociability. Thus, the stress in current child-rearing advice on a high level of loving support but a low level of discipline or restriction on the behavior of the child—the "developmental" family type as Duvall calls it—is a profile consistent with the focus on mental health, sociability, and adjustment. Yet, the combination of both high support and high authority on the part of parents is most strongly related to the child's sense of responsibility, leadership quality, and achievement level, as found in Bronfenbrenner's studies and that of Mussen and Distler.

Brim points out that we are a long way from being able to say just what parent-role prescriptions have what effect on the adult characteristics of the child. We know even less about how such parental prescriptions should be changed to adapt to changed conceptions of competency in adulthood. In such an ambiguous context, the great interest parents take in school reports on their children or the pediatrician's assessment of the child's developmental progress should be seen as among the few indices parents have of how well *they* are doing as parents.

Research on Fathering: Social Policy and an Emergent Perspective

Robert A. Fein

Discussion of fathering is becoming fashionable. Social scientists, family life educators, clinicians, and parents have begun a long-overdue assessment of the problems and possibilities of relationships between fathers and children. Increasingly, dogmas and conventional wisdoms that have guided and defined those relationships are being scrutinized—and found wanting. Rather than sit by the sidelines or serve as mothers' helpers, men are being urged to participate in the lives of their children, from conception on. And apparently increasing numbers of men are reaching out for more sustaining relationships with the young in their lives.

From *Journal of Social Issues*, Vol. 34, No. 1 (1978), pp. 122–135. Reprinted by permission of Plenum Publishing Corporation.

Changes in social norms which foster re-evaluation of fathering and relationships between men and children deserve support. But to affect relations between fathers and children (and family lives in general), examination of fathering should occur within the context of social policy, with an appreciation of the multitude of social forces that impinge on the daily behaviors of children and parents. As Kamerman and Kahn (1976) note, American social policies concerning families, which have been implicit and unexamined for years, are being made explicit, with attention given to government and business programs which affect the lives of men, women, and children.

Research concerning fathers has occurred within the context of social stereotypes and norms of American society. This paper begins with a description of the two major perspectives on fathering of the past 25 years, a *traditional* view and a *modern* view, then charts some recent developments in research on fathering which may be seen as constituting an *emergent* perspective. The paper concludes by suggesting that the time is ripe for social scientists to contribute to the development of policies that support family life.

The Traditional Perspective

The major image of the father role in the traditional perspective is the aloof and distant father. English's (1954) description exemplified how the father role was viewed.

> Traditionally, Father has been looked on as the breadwinner. In times past, so much of his time and energy was used in this role that at home he was thought of as taciturn and stern, albeit kind. He was respected but feared by his children who never learned to know him very well. He accepted the fact that he earned the money and Mother cared for the home and raised the children. (p. 323)

In the traditional perspective, a father cares for his children primarily by succeeding in the occupational arena. At home, father's job is to provide for his family so that mother can devote herself to the care of the children (Bowlby, 1951). In this view, men offer companionship and emotional support to their spouses and have relatively little direct involvement with the children. It is worth observing that Bowlby (and others in the psychoanalytic tradition) saw no direct caring role for fathers with infants and young children. Men, while symbolically important to children as close-to-home models of power and authority, were supposed to have little to do with the actual parenting of the young.

In sociology, Parsons and Bales (1955) presented the traditional perspective on men in the family: the instrumental/expressive dichotomy. Men were seen as responsible for the family's relationships with the outside world (primarily the world of work), whereas women were the primary "givers of love" at home.

The traditional perspective on fathering generally conformed to social ideals and realities of the late 1940s and 1950s. Relatively few women were in the paid labor force more than temporarily, and of these women only a small percentage were mothers with young children. Mothers stayed home and fathers went out to work. The husband-breadwinner/wife-homemaker nuclear family was the norm, both in a statistical sense and in the social values of the time.

But there were occasional commentators in the 1950s who noted that norms of American society might change to permit different patterns of childrearing. One such observer was psychiatrist Irene Josselyn:

> As long as men are seen as animated toys, mothers' little helpers, or powerful ogres who alone mete out rewards and punishment, the role of men in the family structure will be boring and/or depreciating. Being frustrated in their attempt to find gratification of their fatherliness, and dissatisfied with the watered-down expression of themselves in the home, they will continue to seek release by diverting their available free energy into channels in which they feel more adequate, with a resultant overinvestment in the gratification they attain from activities away from the home. . . .For the sake of the child and the father we should learn a great deal more of the deeper, subtler meanings of the potentialities in the father-child relationship. (1956, p. 270)

The Modern Perspective

The 1960s saw a major increase in the attention given to fathers by social scientists. Whereas the traditional view of fathering assumed that if men successfully fulfilled head of household, provider roles and mothers carried out their expressive responsibilities, children would be socialized successfully into adult roles, the modern perspective on fathering assumed that children (especially boys) were vulnerable in their psychosocial development (Biller, 1971).

Some 1950s researchers (such as Aberle & Naegele, 1956) had pointed toward the modern perspective by suggesting that fathers inculcated attitudes and behaviors that their children needed for educational and vocational attainment. In the 1960s, spurred by a concern for child development, a number of researchers turned to fathering. For example, John Nash (1965) published "The Father in Contemporary Culture and Current Psychological Literature," in which he concluded that most psychologists had mistakenly assumed that fathers were unimportant in childrearing. Apparently, questioning dominant assumptions about childrearing was risky, for Nash concluded his paper with a "disclaimer":

> This paper is not to be interpreted as an attack on motherhood, but merely as a suggestion that there are other aspects to parent-child relationships than those included in the widely discussed interaction between mother and child. (p. 292)

It is important to note that research within the modern perspective on fathering saw successful child development as a goal of fathering. Three child development outcomes were emphasized: (a) achievement of socially appropriate sex-role identity (masculinity and femininity), (b) academic performance, and (c) moral development (often measured as the absence of delinquency). Researchers attempted to study these outcomes by attending to families without fathers, so-called "father-absent" families. Studies of father-absent children, particularly boys, (reviewed, for example, in Biller, 1974) suggested that children without fathers had significantly more difficulty in the development of sex-role identity, in academic achievement, and in moral development and behavior. Since achievement in these areas was viewed as essential for interpersonal adjustment and life success, boys in father-absent families were considered to be at risk.

Whereas the traditional perspective was supportive of social policies designed to maintain the instrumental/expressive dichotomy, the modern perspective on fathering paralleled attention to policies that appeared to decrease the opportunities for children to interact with their fathers. For example, the Aid to Families with Dependent Children (AFDC) program in most circumstances provided lower benefits for families with an adult male in the household compared to those without an adult male. Concern about the development of children in fatherless families gradually became coupled with concern that AFDC appeared to provide incentives for families to exclude fathers. Such concern was highlighted in debates over the "Moynihan Report" (Rainwater & Yancy, 1967), which argued that black family structure was predominantly matriarchal and was a significant factor in maintaining high levels of black male unemployment. The implication of this debate was that young black males suffered from the absence of male role models (fathers) which contributed to their having higher unemployment levels than other segments of the population.

Concerned about claims of researchers who compared father-absent and father-present families (researchers who suggested that boys from father-absent families were more prone to fail in sex-role identity and academic attainments and were more likely to engage in antisocial behaviors), Herzog and Sudia (1968, 1972, 1974) reviewed the father-absence literature and argued that researchers had not demonstrated that boys in father-absent families were consistently different from boys in father-present families.

Herzog and Sudia's review of the research suggested:

(a) that father absence in itself is not likely to depress school performance;
(b) that there might be a slightly greater likelihood of a boy in a father-absent family engaging in delinquent behavior, but even if statistically more likely, the difference would be so small that it would not be practically important; and
(c) that there is no solid research support for the thesis that a resident father is the only source of masculine identification or that the absence of a father from the home necessarily affects a boy's masculine identity.

They noted that many studies which had reported differences between boys in father-absent and father-present families had failed to account for the power of social class, which when statistically controlled removed the differences.

To account for possible differences in some areas between father-absent and father-present families, Herzog and Sudia suggested that key factors might be the additional stresses on families attendant on the loss of a father rather than the absence of the father per se. Writing about the use of masculinity-femininity scales, the authors noted that these scales "add up to dubious definitions of adequate masculinity and femininity," and that a study of the items suggested that Stalin or Al Capone would look better on the scales than Abraham Lincoln or Martin Luther King (Herzog & Sudia, 1972, pp. 177–178).

While most researchers in the modern perspective dwelt on father-absent families, some attempted to study families with fathers present. Mussen and his colleagues conducted a number of studies which suggested that father's nurturance as perceived by the child was a key factor in the development of sex-role identity (reviewed in Mussen, 1969). However, Mussen and his colleagues did not actually observe fathers. Radin (1972, 1973) suggested that paternal nurturance is an antecedent of intellectual functioning in 4- and 5-year-old boys. While her research dealt only with child outcomes, the attention to cognitive development and her effort to observe father-child interaction were significant advances over previous studies.

While from the point of view of contemporary values the modern perspective on fathering represented an improvement on the traditional (in that the modern view focused attention on child development and on the idea that fathers' behaviors influenced their children), some of the assumptions of the modern perspective have been criticized recently. For example, the nature and desirability of sex-role identity, as measured by masculinity scales, has come under question and attack (Pleck, 1975). Researchers like Kotelchuck (1976) and Pederson (1976) highlight the fact that there were relatively few studies of actual fathering behavior by researchers in the modern perspective.

The Emergent Perspective

What I am calling the *emergent* perspective on fathering proceeds from the notion that men are psychologically able to participate in a full range of parenting behaviors, and furthermore that it may be good both for parents and children if men take active roles in childcare and childrearing. While some research in the emergent perspective focuses on effects on the child, analysis has begun to examine the impact of father-children relationships on all members of the family. Researchers are exploring the idea that children's lives are enhanced by the opportunity to develop and sustain relationships with adults of both sexes. Issues of adult development are under consideration, including the idea that opportunity to care for others, including and especially children, can be a major factor in adult well-being.

The emergent perspective on fathering is androgynous in assuming that the only parenting behaviors from which men are necessarily excluded by virtue of gender are gestation and lactation. Arguments suggesting that men are inherently limited in child-rearing capacity have drawn on studies of infrahuman animal species which suggested that parenting behaviors by males are rare. Howells (1971), reviewing these data, suggests that "the main lesson to be found from the study of the care given to young animals is that nature is flexible" (p. 128). There are examples of male animal behavior which can be seen as parental and nurturant. For one, the male stickleback builds a nest, receives eggs from females, fertilizes them, cares for them, and brings up the young. The males of some catfish carry eggs in their mouths until they hatch; "when danger threatens, *he* holds his mouth open so that the frightened youngsters can dash into it to safety" (Howells, 1971, p. 130). Data from infrahuman animal species can refute biologically-based arguments of major inherent limitations in human male parenting capabilities.

In psychology, innovative research on fathering is developing in five areas:

(a) fathers' experience before, during, and after the birth of children;
(b) fathers' ties with newborns and infants;
(c) the development and nature of bonds between young children and fathers;
(d) fathers in nontraditional childcare arrangements; and
(e) effects of parenting experiences on fathers.

While there are overlaps in these categories, each contributes an important focus to the development of the emergent perspective.

Entering Parenthood

Several studies in the 1970s have employed models of male parenting that assume that men are able to participate in pregnancy and childbirth. Influenced by media accounts of men who participated in delivery and by the popularity of childbirth education programs (Wapner, 1976), researchers have compared experiences of men who participated in childbirth education courses with men who did not and have described experiences of men who shared labor and delivery experiences with their wives. Cronenwett and Newmark (1974) gave a questionnaire to 152 fathers and found that fathers who attended childbirth preparation classes and/or the birth rated their overall experience during childbirth and the experience of their wives significantly higher than other men. Interestingly, there were no differences on infant-related items reported between fathers who attended classes and/or the birth and men who did not. Fein (1976) found that effective postpartum adjustment in men was related to development of a coherent fathering role. Interviews with 30 middle-income couples suggested that neither the women nor the men were particularly well prepared for the practical realities of parenting, with men's lack of experience in part a result of social attitudes that have assumed that boys and young men have little interest or aptitude to learn about children and childcare. Reiber (1976) studied nine couples before and after the birth of a child and noted that the fathers were interested in being nurturers and the men appeared to be involved in caring for their babies to the extent that their wives allowed them to be. Manion (1977), in a correlational study of 45 first-time fathers several weeks after the birth of their children, found that although fathers were seldom included in postpartum hospital instruction about child-care, men did become involved in providing care for their infants. Men who remembered their parents as nurturant tended to be more active in childcare than other men. Fathers who had a higher degree of involvement in the birth had a higher degree of involvement in childcare activities.

Ties with Newborns and Infants

Parke and Savin (1976) recently summarized the traditional view of fathers' roles in infancy:

1. Fathers are uninterested in and uninvolved with newborn infants.
2. Fathers are less nurturant toward infants than mothers.
3. Fathers prefer noncaretaking roles and leave the caretaking up to mothers.
4. Fathers are less competent than mothers to care for newborn infants. (p. 365)

Research about father-infant relationships is questioning the credibility of these assumptions. Greenberg and Morris (1974) gave a written questionnaire to 30 first-time fathers who had either attended the births of their babies or who had been shown their babies shortly after birth. In addition, a series of interviews was conducted with half the sample. The researchers noted that fathers enjoyed looking at their babies, reported a desire for and pleasure in physical contact with the newborns, and were aware of unique features and characteristics of their babies. Many fathers were surprised at the impact their contact with the baby had on them. Greenberg and Morris suggested that fathers begin developing a bond to their newborns within three days after birth and called this phenomenon "engrossment."

Parke and O'Leary (1976) observed men interacting with their newborns. Fathers were seen to be active with their infants, being more likely to touch and rock their infants when alone than with the mother. In one of their studies, the researchers compared fathers of different social classes and found that "high interaction fathering" occurred across socioeconomic class lines. Parke and O'Leary suggested that early contact with infants may be important for the development of father-child bonds, raising questions about the thresholds of paternal responsivity to infants.

Bonds Between Young Children and Fathers

Given the power and primacy of cultural assumptions about mother-child bonds, only in the last decade have researchers begun to look carefully at the relationships men establish with their young children. Yogman, Dixon, Tronick, Adamson, Als, and Brazelton (Note 1) found that infants responded differentially to their fathers compared to strangers by four weeks of age, even when the fathers were not their primary caretakers. Kotelchuck (Note 2, 1976), in an observational study of 144 children, found that children responded to both fathers and mothers more than to strangers. While the child's parental preferences at 18 months of age were strongly related to parental involvement in the home, Kotelchuck concluded that the overall lack of mother-father differences in terms of children's observed behaviors suggested that neither the quality of parent-child interaction nor specific caretaking practices are critical issues in formation of a relationship. His study strongly suggested that young children form significant relationships with their fathers.

Cohen and Campos (1974), attempting to measure both attachment behaviors of young children and distress indicators, concluded that fathers were more powerful elicitors of attachment behaviors than strangers, but that mothers were superior to fathers as elicitors of these behaviors. There were no differences between fathers and mothers in eliciting distress vocalization. Lamb and Lamb (1976), reviewing the literature on the development of father-child bonds, concluded that fathers are salient figures in the lives of their children from infancy on. These researchers suggested that the family should be seen as a complex system in which all persons (including infants) influence and are affected by all.

Nontraditional Childcare Arrangements

Responding to changes in family and marital patterns in the United States, a number of social scientists have begun to study fathers who parent outside of the context of the husband-provider/wife-homemaker nuclear family. Separated fathers, widowed fathers, divorced fathers, unmarried fathers, adopting fathers, and stepfathers are recent subjects of study.

Hetherington, Cox, and Cox (1976) studied 96 families, comparing relationships in divorced families with those in intact families. Two years after their divorces, fathers in this group were seen as influencing their children significantly less than the fathers in intact families. Noting that divorced fathers in their sample generally left the home, the children remaining with the mother, Hetherington et al. report that divorced men complained of being rootless, with separation inducing great feelings of loss, particularly with regard to feelings about their children.

Finkelstein-Keshet (1977), studying the coping strategies of fathers following marital separation, found that for some men the opportunity to care for their children became the basis of a major life reorganization. Levine (1976), in a book about varieties of fathering, reported on single men who adopt children, men who share childcare on an equal basis with their wives, and men who become primary parents of their children. His study suggested that a wide variety of fathering roles is practiced in the United States. Rallings (1976), noting that step-fathering has been an understudied phenomenon, suggested that since 15% of all children under age 18 were living with a divorced parent (in 1970), and since courts were more likely to give custody to a mother than to a father, and since remarriage rates have been high, it is likely that there are several million children now living with stepfathers.

Effects of Parenting on Fathers

How men respond to and are affected by the children in their lives is a key area of the emergent perspective on fathering. While novels and popular magazines have presented personal accounts, there has been little systematic exploration of the fathering experience. The clinical literature that exists in this area (see Fein, 1976, and Earls, 1976, for reviews) highlights pathological experiences, with titles such as "Pregnancy as a Precipitant of Mental Illness in Men" (Freeman, 1951), "Fatherhood as a Precipitant of Mental Illness" (Wainwright, 1966), and "Paranoid Psychoses Associated with Impending or Newly Established Fatherhood" (Retterstoll, 1968). Researchers in the four other areas discussed above occasionally touch on aspects of male parenting development—noting, for example, that men may be profoundly affected by participating in childbirth, by holding their newborns, by caring regularly for their toddlers, by becoming primary parents for adolescent children—but there is a need for systematic research. These questions gain importance when placed next to survey data that suggest that a large number of men feel that the trait "able to love" is not highly characteristic of themselves (Tavris, 1977).

The Emergent Perspective and Social Policy

The emergent perspective on fathering both proceeds from and leads to different social policy considerations than either traditional or modern ideologies of fathering. For one thing, the emergent perspective seeks to deal with the reality that increasing numbers of women are entering the paid labor force. A perspective on fathering that accepts the possibility that significant numbers of men can be effective nurturers of children may provide some relief from burdensome debates of the "should mothers mother or should mothers work?" variety (Rowe, 1976). If fathers are seen as able to care for their young, from a social policy perspective the question of childcare becomes one of family support: How can families be aided to carry out their childrearing and paid employment responsibilities? For example, an emergent perspective on fathering suggests attention to parental leave rather than maternity leave, to examination of the ways in which personnel and employment practices and policies affect the options of women and men both to care for their children and to provide economically for their families (Levine, 1977).

The idea of equal parenting, consistent with an emergent perspective on fathering, is receiving attention in discussions of family support. Sweden, several years ahead of the United States in these debates, embarked in the 1960s on a policy to support women to have a full range of options in paid employment. Premised on the ideal of equality, the Swedish program to support women in paid employment was concerned also with developing men's opportunities to participate in home life (Palme, 1972). To these ends, Sweden has enacted programs which allow men and women to care for children at home in the months after their birth and to be compensated at 90% of prebirth salaries. Furthermore, men and women have the same right to stay home from work if the children are sick. Data from Sweden indicate that only one to two percent of fathers of newborn children took advantage of the new policy during the first year after it was enacted into law, but the figure rose to six percent the second year (Liljestrom, 1977).

It would be naive to suggest that the emergent perspective on fathering will provide full answers to complicated questions concerning the relationship between family life and work life in the United States. Liljestrom suggests that, for Swedish society, it would be foolhardy to imagine that fathers should seek to emulate the role of yesterday's mothers and points to the need to think about the implications of equal parenting:

> The time is ripe for retesting our notions about the meaning of parenthood. Perhaps future parents will live in more open families, where it is easier for the adults to coordinate parenthood with work and public affairs interests and where the children are surrounded by a network of adult contacts. Otherwise, how will we be able to solve the conflicts between the roles of parents and other adult life roles? (1977, p. 77)

The new perspective calls attention to issues of equal parenting. That there may indeed be a need for such discussion in the United States is highlighted by a front-page *New York Times Book Review* article on Selma Fraiberg's 1977 book, *Every Child's Birthright: In Defense of Mothering*. Describing the debate about family policy in the United States, the reviewer, Kenneth Keniston, comments on widespread concerns that maternal employment has resulted in inadequate care for many children. While noting that research has not supported a linkage between maternal employment and negative child outcomes (such as failure to thrive in infancy or criminality in adulthood), and arguing that children have a right to be nurtured, Keniston, amazingly, does not once mention fathers as a part of the solution to these problems (Keniston, 1977). In ignoring almost one-half of potential childcarers (men), Keniston may be seen as writing from the traditional perspective on fathering. The exclusion of fathers in a consideration of the needs of children and families would appear to underscore the need for a new perspective.

It seems increasingly clear that the next several years will witness considerable discussion and debate about parenting, family life, and work in the United States. I have tried to suggest that social scientists have tended to lag behind or at best run parallel to debates about social values and policies concerning parenting and fathering. Both the traditional and the modern perspectives of fathering have limited usefulness in a society marked by increasing levels of female paid employment and growing concerns about the care of children. Forthcoming debates on family life will provide opportunities for social scientists to contribute to the formation of policies that will affect millions of American parents and children. Given the importance of these issues, attention to an emergent perspective of fathering appears timely and prudent.

Reference Notes

1. Yogman, M. W., Dixon, S., Tronick, E., Adamson, L., Als, H., & Brazelton, T. B. *Development of infant social interaction with fathers.* Paper presented at the meeting of the Eastern Psychological Association, New York, April 1976.
2. Kotelchuck, M. *The nature of the infant's tie to his father.* Paper presented at the meeting of the Society for Research in Child Development, Philadelphia, 1973.

References

Aberle, D., & Naegele, K. Father's occupational role and attitudes toward children. *American Journal of Orthopsychiatry.* 1956. *22,* 366–378.

Biller, H. B. *Father, child, and sex role.* Lexington, MA.: D. C. Heath, 1971.

Biller, H. B. *Paternal deprivation.* Lexington, MA: D. C. Heath, 1974.

Bowlby, J. *Maternal care and mental health.* Geneva: World Health Organization, 1951.

Cohen, J. J., & Campos, J. J. Father, mother, and stranger as elicitors of attachment behaviors in infancy. *Developmental Psychology,* 1974, *10,* 146–154.

Cronenwett, L. R., & Newmark, L. L. Father's responses to childbirth. *Nursing Research,* 1974, *23,* 210–217.

Earls, F. The fathers (not the mothers): Their importance and influence with infants and young children. *Psychiatry,* 1076, *39,* 209–226.

English, O. S. The psychological role of the father in the family. *Social Casework,* 1954, pp. 323–329.

Fein, R. A. Men's entrance to parenthood. *The Family Coordinator,* 1976, *25,* 341–350.

Finkelstein-Keshet, H. *Marital separation and fathering.* Unpublished doctoral dissertation, University of Michigan, 1977.

Freeman, T. Pregnancy as a precipitant of mental illness in men. *British Journal of Medical Psychology,* 1951, *24,* 49–54.

Greenberg, M., & Morris, N. Engrossment: The newborn's impact upon the father. *American Journal of Orthopsychiatry,* 1974, *44,* 520–531.

Herzog, E., & Sudia, C. Fatherless homes. *Children,* 1968, pp. 177–182.

Herzog, E., & Sudia, C. Families without fathers. *Childhood Education,* 1972, pp. 175–181.

Herzog, E., & Sudia, C. Children in fatherless families. In E. M. Hetherington & P. Ricciuti (Eds.), *Review of child development research* (Vol. 3). Chicago: University of Chicago, 1974.

Hetherington, E. M., Cox, M., & Cox, R. Divorced fathers. *The Family Coordinator,* 1976, *25,* 417–428.

Howells, J. G. Fathering. In J. G. Howells (Eds.), *Modern perspectives in child psychiatry.* New York: Bruner-Mazel, 1971.

Josselyn, I. M. Cultural forces, motherliness and fatherliness. *American Journal of Orthopsychiatry,* 1956, *26,* 264–271.

Kamerman, S. B., & Kahn, A. J. Explorations in family policy. *Social Work,* 1976. *21.* 181–186.

Keniston, K. First attachments. (Review of *Every child's birthright: In defense of mothering* by S. Fraiberg.) *The New York Times Book Review,* December 11, 1977, pp. 1; 40–41.

Kotelchuck, M. The infant's relationship to the father: Experimental evidence. In M. E. Lamb (Ed.), *The role of the father in child development.* New York: Wiley, 1976.

Lamb, M. E., & Lamb, J. E. The nature and importance of the father-infant relationship. *The Family Coordinator,* 1976, *25,* 379–386.

Levine, J. *Who will raise the children? New options for fathers (and mothers).* New York: Lippincott, 1976.

Levine, J. Redefining the child care "problem"—Men as child nurturers. *Childhood Education,* November/December 1977, pp. 55–61.

Liljestrom, R. The parent's role in production and reproduction. *Sweden Now,* 1977, *11,* 73–77.

Manion, J. A study of fathers and infant caretaking. *Birth and the Family Journal,* 1977, *4,* 174–179.

Mussen, P. Early sex-role development. In D. Goslin (Ed.), *Handbook of socialization theory and research.* New York: Rand McNally, 1969.

Nash, J. The father in contemporary culture and current psychological literature. *Child Development,* 1965, *36,* 261–297.

Palme, O. The emancipation of man. *Journal of Social Issues,* 1972, *28*(2), 237–246.

Parke, R. D., & O'Leary, S. E. Father-mother-infant interaction in the newborn period. In K. Riegel & J. Meacham (Eds.), *The developing individual in a changing world.* The Hague: Mouton, 1976.

Parke, R. D., Savin, D. B. The father's role in infancy: A re-evaluation. *The Family Coordinator,* 1976, *25,* 365–372.

Parsons, T., & Bales, R. F. *Family, socialization, and interaction process,* Glencoe, IL: The Free Press, 1955.

Pederson, F. Does research on children reared in father-absent families yield information on father influences? *The Family Coordinator,* 1976, *25,* 459–464.

Pleck, J. H. Masculinity-femininity: Current and alternate paradigms. *Sex Roles,* 1975, *1,* 161–178.

Radin, N. Father-child interaction and the intellectual functioning of four-year-old boys. *Developmental Psychology,* 1972, *6,* 353–361.

Radin, N. Observed paternal behaviors as antecedents of intellectual functioning in young boys. *Developmental Psychology,* 1973, *8,* 369–376.

Rainwater, L., & Yancy, W. L. *The Moynihan report and the politics of controversy.* Cambridge, MA: MIT Press, 1967.

Rallings, E. M. The special role of stepfather. *The Family Coordinator,* 1976, *25,* 445–450.

Reiber, V. D. Is the nurturing role natural to fathers? *American Journal of Maternal Child Nursing,* 1976, *1,* 366–371.

Retterstol, N. Paranoid psychoses associated with impending or newly established fatherhood. *Acta Psychiatrica Scandinavica,* 1968, *44,* 51–61.

Rowe, M. O. That parents may work and love and children may thrive. In N. B. Talbot (Ed.), *Raising children in modern America.* Boston: Little, Brown, 1976.

Tavris, C. Men and women report their views on masculinity. *Psychology Today,* 1977, *10,* 34–43.

Wainwright, W. Fatherhood as a precipitant of mental illness. *American Journal of Psychiatry,* 1966, *123,* 40–44.

Wapner, J. The attitudes, feelings and behaviors of expectant fathers attending Lamaze classes. *Birth and the Family Journal,* 1976, *3,* 5–14.

The Medicalization and Legalization of Child Abuse

Eli H. Newberger and Richard Bourne

Child abuse has emerged in the last fifteen years as a visible and important social problem. Although a humane approach to "help" for both victims of child abuse and their families has developed (and is prominently expressed in the title of one of the more influential books on the subject[29]), a theoretical framework to integrate the diverse origins and expressions of violence toward children and to inform a rational clinical practice does not exist. Furthermore, so inadequate are the "helping" services in most communities, so low the standard of professional action, and so distressing the consequences of incompetent intervention for the family that we and others have speculated that punishment is being inflicted in the guise of help.[3, 28]

What factors encourage theoretical confusion and clinical inadequacy? We propose that these consequences result, in part, from medical and legal ambiguity concerning child abuse and from two fundamental, and in some ways irreconcilable, dilemmas about social policy and the human and technical response toward families in crisis. We call these dilemmas *family autonomy versus coercive intervention* and *compassion versus control.*

This paper will consider these dilemmas in the context of a critical sociologic perspective on child abuse management. Through the cognitive lens of social labeling theory, we see symptoms of family crisis, and certain manifestations of childhood injury, "medicalized" and "legalized" and called "child abuse," to be diagnosed, reported, treated, and adjudicated by doctors and lawyers, their constituent institutions, and the professionals who depend on them for their social legitimacy and support.

We are mindful, as practitioners, of the need for prompt, effective, and creative professional responses to child abuse. Our critical analysis of the relationship of professional work to the societal context in which it is embedded is meant to stimulate attention to issues that professionals ignore to their and their clients' ultimate disadvantage. We mean not to disparage necessary efforts to help and protect children and their families.

How children's rights—as opposed to parents' rights—may be defined and protected is currently the subject of vigorous, and occasionally rancorous, debate.

The *family autonomy* vs. *coercive intervention* dilemma defines the conflict central to our ambiguity about *whether* society should intervene in situations of risk to children. The traditional autonomy of the family in rearing its offspring was cited by the majority of the U.S. Supreme Court in its ruling against the severely beaten appellants in the controversial "corporal punish-

From the *American Journal of Orthopsychiatry*, Vol. 48, No. 4 (October 1978), pp. 593–607.

ment" case (*Ingraham* vs. *Wright et al*).[25] The schools, serving *in loco parentis,* are not, in effect, constrained constitutionally from any punishment, however cruel.

Yet in California, a physician seeing buttock bruises of the kind legally inflicted by the teacher in the Miami public schools risks malpractice action if he fails to report his observations as symptoms of child abuse *(Landeros* vs. *Flood).*[32] He and his hospital are potentially liable for the cost of the child's subsequent injury and handicap if they do not initiate protective measures.[7]

This dilemma is highlighted by the recently promulgated draft statute of the American Bar Association's Juvenile Justice Standards Project, which, citing the low prevailing quality of protective child welfare services in the U.S., would sharply *restrict* access to such services.[28] The Commission would, for example, make the reporting of child neglect discretionary rather than mandatory, and would narrowly define the bases for court jurisdiction to situations where there is clear harm to a child.

Our interpretation of this standard is that it would make matters worse, not better, for children and their families.[3] So long as we are deeply conflicted about the relation of children to the state as well as to the family, and whether children have rights independent of their parents', we shall never be able to articulate with clarity *how* to enforce them.

The *compassion* vs. *control* dilemma has been postulated and reviewed in a previous paper,[47] which discussed the conceptual and practical problems implicit in the expansion of the clinical and legal definitions of child abuse to include practically every physical and emotional risk to children. The dilemma addresses a conflict central to the present ambiguity about *how* to protect children from their parents.

Parental behavior that might be characterized as destructive or criminal were it directed towards an adult has come to be seen and interpreted by those involved in its identification and treatment in terms of the psychosocial economy of the family. Embracive definitions reflect a change in the orientation of professional practice. To the extent to which we understand abusing parents as sad, deprived, needy human beings (rather than as cold, cruel murderers) we can sympathize with their plight and compassionately proffer supports and services to aid them in their struggle. Only with dread may we contemplate strong intervention (such as court action) on the child's behalf, for want of alienating our clients.

Notwithstanding the humane philosophy of treatment, society cannot, or will not, commit resources nearly commensurate with the exponentially increasing number of case reports that have followed the promulgation of the expanded definitions. The helping language betrays a deep conflict, and even ill will, toward children and parents in trouble, whom society and professionals might sooner punish and control.

We are forced frequently in practice to identify and choose the "least detrimental alternative" for the child[21] because the family supports that make it safe to keep children in their homes (homemakers, child care, psychiatric and medical services) are never available in sufficient amounts and quality.

That we should guide our work by a management concept named "least detrimental alternative" for children suggests at least a skepticism about the utility of these supports, just as the rational foundation for child welfare work is called into question by the title of the influential book from which the concept comes, *Beyond the Best Interests of the Child.*[21] More profoundly, the concept taps a vein of emotional confusion about our progeny, to whom we express both kindness and love with hurt.

Mounting attention to the developmental sequelae of child abuse[16, 33] stimulates an extra urgency not only to insure the physical safety of the identified victims but also to enable their adequate psychological development. The dangers of child abuse, according to Schmitt and Kempe in the latest edition of the Nelson Textbook of Pediatrics,[53] extend beyond harm to the victim:

> If the child who has been physically abused is returned to his parents without intervention, 5 per cent are killed and 35 per cent are seriously reinjured. Moreover, the untreated families tend to produce children who grow up to be juvenile delinquents and murderers, as well as the batterers of the next generation.

Despite the speculative nature of such conclusions about the developmental sequelae of child abuse,[6, 10, 11] such warnings support a practice of separating children from their natural homes in the interest of their and society's protection. They focus professional concern and public wrath on "the untreated families" and may justify punitive action to save us from their children.

This professional response of control rather than of compassion furthermore generalizes mainly to poor and socially marginal families, for it is they who seem preferentially to attract the labels "abuse" and "neglect" to their problems in the public settings where they go for most health and social services.[36] Affluent families' childhood injuries appear more likely to be termed "accidents" by the private practitioners who offer them their services. The conceptual model of cause and effect implicit in the name "accident" is benign: an isolated, random event rather than a consequence of parental commission or omission.[37, 38]

Table 1 presents a graphic display of the two dilemmas of social policy *(family autonomy* vs. *coercive intervention)* and professional response *(compassion* vs. *control)*. The four-fold table illustrates possible action responses. For purposes of this discussion, it is well to think of "compassion" as signifying responses of support, such as provision of voluntary counseling and child care services, and "control" as signifying such punitive responses as "blaming the victim" for his or her reaction to social realities[49] and as the criminal prosecution of abusing parents.

Table 1. Dilemmas of Social Policy and Professional Response

Response	*Family autonomy*	*Versus*	*Coercive intervention*
Compassion ("support")	1 Voluntary child development services 2 Guaranteed family supports: e.g. income, housing, health services		1 Case reporting of family crisis and mandated family intervention 2 Court-ordered delivery of services
Versus Control ("punishment")	1 "Laissez-faire": No assured services or supports 2 Retributive response to family crisis		1 Court action to separate child from family 2 Criminal prosecution of parents

Child Abuse and the Medical and Legal Professions

The importance of a technical discipline's conceptual structure in defining how it approaches a problem has been clearly stated by Mercer:[34]

> Each discipline is organized around a core of basic concepts and assumptions which form the frame of reference from which persons trained in that discipline view the world and set about solving problems in their field. The concepts and assumptions which make up the perspective of each discipline give each its distinctive character and are the intellectual tools used by its practitioners. These tools are incorporated in action and problem solving and appear self-evident to persons socialized in the discipline. As a result, little consideration is likely to be given to the social consequence of applying a particular conceptual work to problem solving.
>
> When the issues to be resolved are clearly in the area of competence of a single discipline, the automatic application of its conceptual tools is likely to go unchallenged. However, when the problems under consideration lie in the interstices between disciplines, the disciplines concerned are likely to define the situation differently and may arrive at differing conclusions which have dissimilar implications for social action.

What we do when children are injured in family crises is shaped also by how our professions respond to the interstitial area called "child abuse."

"Medicalization"

Though cruelty to children has occurred since documentary records of mankind have been kept,[9] it became a salient social problem in the United States only after the publication by Kempe and his colleagues describing the "battered child syndrome."[30] In the four-year period after this medical article appeared, the legislatures of all 50 states, stimulated partly by a model law developed under the aegis of the Children's Bureau of the U.S. Department of Health, Education, and Welfare, passed statutes mandating the identification and reporting of suspected victims of abuse.

Once the specific diagnostic category "battered child syndrome" was applied to integrate a set of medical symptoms, and laws were passed making the syndrome reportable, the problem was made a proper and legitimate concern for the medical profession. Conrad has discussed cogently how "hyperactivity" came officially to be known and how it became "medicalized."[5] Medicalization is defined in this paper as the perception of behavior as a medical problem or illness and the mandating or licensing of the medical profession to provide some type of treatment for it.

Pfohl[41] associated the publicity surrounding the battered child syndrome report with a phenomenon of "discovery" of child abuse. For radiologists, the potential for increased prestige, role expansion, and coalition formation (with psychodynamic psychiatry and pediatrics) may have encouraged identification and intervention in child abuse. Furthermore,

> ... the discovery of abuse as a new "illness" reduced drastically the intraorganizational constraints on doctors' "seeing" abuse ... Problems associated with perceiving parents as patients whose confidentiality must be protected were reconstructed by typifying them as patients who needed help ... The maintenance of professional autonomy was assured by pairing deviance with sickness ...

In some ways, medicine's "discovery" of abuse has benefited individual physicians and the profession.

> One of the greatest ambitions of the physician is to discover or describe a "new" disease or syndrome.[24]

By such involvement the doctor becomes a moral entrepreneur defining what is normal, proper, or desirable: he becomes charged "with inquisitorial powers to discover certain wrongs to be righted."[24] New opportunities for the application of traditional methods are also found—for example, the systematic screening of suspected victims with a skeletal X-ray survey to detect previous fractures, and the recent report in the neurology literature suggesting the utility of diphenylhydantoin* treatment for child abusing parents.[46]

Pfohl's provocative analysis also took note of some of the normative and structural elements within the medical profession that appear to have reinforced a *reluctance* on the part of some physicians to become involved: the norm of confidentiality between doctor and patient and the goal of professional autonomy.[41] For many physicians, child abuse is a subject to avoid.[50]

First, it is difficult to distinguish, on a theoretical level, corporal punishment that is "acceptable" from that which is "illegitimate." Abuse may be defined variably even by specialists, the definitions ranging from serious physical injury to nonfulfillment of a child's developmental needs.[13, 19, 30]

---

*Dilantin, a commonly-used seizure suppressant.

Second, it is frequently hard to diagnose child abuse clinically. What appears on casual physical examination as bruising, for example, may turn out to be a skin manifestation of an organic blood dysfunction, or what appear to be cigarette burns may in reality be infected mosquito bites. A diagnosis of abuse may require social and psychological information about the family, the acquisition and interpretation of which may be beyond the average clinician's expertise. It may be easier to characterize the clinical complaint in terms of the child's medical symptom rather than in terms of the social, familial, and psychological forces associated with its etiology. We see daily situations where the exclusive choice of medical taxonomy actively obscures the causes of the child's symptom and restricts the range of possible interventions: examples are "subdural hematoma," which frequently occurs with severe trauma to babies' heads (the medical name means collection of blood under the *dura mater* of the brain), and "enuresis" or "encopresis" in child victims of sexual assault (medical names mean incontinence of urine or feces).

Third, child abuse arouses strong emotions. To concentrate on the narrow medical issue (the broken bone) instead of the larger familial problem (the etiology of the injury) not only allows one to avoid facing the limits of one's technical adequacy, but to shield oneself from painful feelings of sadness and anger. One can thus maintain professional detachment and avert unpleasant confrontations. The potentially alienating nature of the physician-patient interaction when the diagnosis of child abuse is made may also have a negative economic impact on the doctor, especially the physician in private practice.

"Legalization"

The legal response to child abuse was triggered by its medicalization. Child abuse reporting statutes codified a medical diagnosis into a legal framework which in many states defined official functions for courts. Immunity from civil liability was given to mandated reporters so long as reports were made in good faith; monetary penalties for failure to report were established; and familial and professional-client confidentiality privileges, except those involving attorneys, were abrogated.

Professional autonomy for lawyers was established, and status and power accrued to legal institutions. For example, the growth in the number of Care and Protection cases* before the Boston Juvenile Court "has been phenomenal in recent years . . . four cases in 1968 and 99 in 1974, involving 175 different children."[44] Though these cases have burdened court dockets and personnel, they have also led to acknowledgement of the important work of the court. The need for this institution is enhanced because of its recognized expertise in handling special matters. Care and Protection cases are cited in response to

---

*Care and Protection cases are those juvenile or family court actions which potentially transfer, on a temporary or permanent basis, legal and/or physical custody of a child from his biological parents to the state.

recommendations by a prestigious commission charged with proposing reform and consolidation of the courts in Massachusetts. Child protection work in our own institution would proceed only with difficulty if access to the court were legally or procedurally constrained. Just as for the medical profession, however, there were normative and structural elements within law which urged restraint. Most important among them were the traditional presumptions and practices favoring family autonomy.

If individual lawyers might financially benefit from representing clients in matters pertaining to child abuse, they—like their physician counterparts— were personally uncertain whether or how to become involved.

> Public concern over the scope and significance of the problem of the battered child is a comparatively new phenomenon. Participation by counsel in any significant numbers in child abuse cases in juvenile or family courts is of even more recent origin. It is small wonder that the lawyer approaches participation in these cases with trepidation.[26]

Lawyers, too, feel handicapped by a need to rely on concepts from social work and psychiatry and on data from outside the traditional domain of legal knowledge and expertise. As counsel to parents, lawyers can be torn between advocacy of their clients' positions and that which advances the "best interest" of their clients' children. As counsel to the petitioner, a lawyer may have to present a case buttressed by little tangible evidence. Risk to a child is often difficult to characterize and impossible to prove.

Further problems for lawyers concerned with child abuse involve the context of intervention: whether courts or legislatures should play the major role in shaping practice and allocating resources; how much formality is desirable in legal proceedings; and the propriety of negotiation as opposed to adversary confrontation when cases come to court.

Conflicts Between Medical and Legal Perspectives

Despite the common reasons for the "medicalization" and the "legalization" of child abuse, there are several areas where the two orientations conflict:

1. *The seriousness of the risk.* To lawyers, intervention might be warranted only when abuse results in serious harm to a child. To clinicians, however, *any* inflicted injury might justify a protective legal response, especially if the child is very young. "The trick is to prevent the abusive case from becoming the terminal case."[14] Early intervention may prevent the abuse from being repeated or from becoming more serious.
2. *The definition of the abuser.* To lawyers, the abuser might be defined as a wrongdoer who has injured a child. To clinicians, both the abuser and child might be perceived as victims influenced by sociological and psychological factors beyond their control.[17, 35]

3. *The importance of the abuser's mental state.* To lawyers, whether the abuser intentionally or accidentally inflicted injury on a child is a necessary condition of reporting or judicial action. So-called "accidents" are less likely to trigger intervention. To clinicians, however, mental state may be less relevant, for it requires a diagnostic formulation frequently difficult or impossible to make on the basis of available data. The family dynamics associated with "accidents" in some children (*e.g.,* stress, marital conflict, and parental inattention) often resemble those linked with inflicted injury in others. They are addressed with variable clinical sensitivity and precision.

4. *The role of law.* Attorneys are proudly unwilling to accept conclusions or impressions lacking empirical corroboration. To lawyers, the law and legal institutions become involved in child abuse when certain facts fit a standard of review. To clinicians, the law may be seen as an instrument to achieve a particular therapeutic or dispositional objective (*e.g.,* the triggering of services or of social welfare involvement) even if, as is very often the case, the data to support such objectives legally are missing or ambiguous. The clinician's approach to the abuse issue is frequently subjective or intuitive (*e.g.,* a *feeling) that a family is under stress or needs help, or that a child is "at risk"),* while the lawyer demands evidence.

Doctoring and Lawyering the Disease

These potential or actual differences in orientation notwithstanding, both medicine and law have accepted in principle the therapeutic approach to child abuse.

To physicians, defining abuse as a disease or medical syndrome makes natural the treatment alternative, since both injured child and abuser are viewed as "sick"—the one, physically, the other psychologically or socially. Therapy may, however, have retributive aspects, as pointed out with characteristic pungency by Illich:[24]

> The medical label may protect the patient from punishment only to submit him to interminable instruction, treatment, and discrimination, which are inflicted on him for his professionally presumed benefit.

Lawyers adopt a therapeutic perspective for several reasons. First, the rehabilitative ideal remains in ascendance in criminal law, especially in the juvenile and family courts which handle most child abuse cases.[1]

Second, the criminal or punitive model may not protect the child. Parents may hesitate to seek help if they are fearful of prosecution. Evidence of abuse is often insufficient to satisfy the standard of conviction "beyond all reasonable doubt" in criminal proceedings. An alleged abuser threatened with punishment and then found not guilty may feel vindicated, reinforcing the pattern of abuse. The abuser may well be legally freed from any scrutiny, and badly needed social services will not be able to be provided. Even if found guilty, the perpetrator of abuse is usually given only mild punishment, such as a short jail term or probation. If the abuser is incarcerated, the other family members may equally suffer as, for example, the relationship between spouses is undercut and child-rearing falls on one parent, or children are placed in foster home care or with relatives. Upon release from jail, the abuser may be no less violent and even more aggressive and vindictive toward the objects of abuse.

Third, the fact that child abuse was "discovered" by physicians influenced the model adopted by other professionals. As Freidson[15] noted:

> Medical definitions of deviance have come to be adopted even where there is no reliable evidence that biophysical variables "cause" the deviance or that medical treatment is any more efficacious than any other kind of management.

Weber, in addition, contended that "status" groups (e.g., physicians) generally determine the content of law.[45]

The Selective Implementation of Treatment

Medical intervention is generally encouraged by the Hippocratic ideology of treatment (the ethic that help, not harm, is given by practitioners), and by what Scheff[52] called the medical decision rule: it is better to wrongly diagnose illness and "miss" health than it is to wrongly diagnose health and "miss" illness.

Physicians, in defining aberrant behavior as a medical problem and in providing treatment, become what sociologists call agents of social control. Though the technical enterprise of the physician claims value-free power, socially marginal individuals are more likely to be defined as deviant than are others.

Characteristics frequently identified with the "battered child syndrome," such as social isolation, alcoholism, unemployment, childhood handicap, large family size, low level of parental educational achievement, and acceptance of severe physical punishment as a childhood socializing technique, are associated with social marginality and poverty.

Physicians in public settings seem, from child abuse reporting statistics, to be more likely to see and report child abuse than are those in private practice. As poor people are more likely to frequent hospital emergency wards and clinics,[36] they have much greater social visibility where child abuse is concerned than do people of means.

The fact that child abuse is neither theoretically nor clinically well defined increases the likelihood of subjective professional evaluation. In labeling theory, it is axiomatic that the greater the social distance between the typer and the person singled out for typing, the broader the type and the more quickly it may be applied.[48]

In the doctor-patient relationship, the physician is always in a superordinate position because of his or her expertise; social distance is inherent to the relationship. This distance necessarily increases once the label of abuser has been applied. Importantly, the label is less likely to be fixed if the diagnostician and possible abuser share similar characteristics, especially socioeconomic status, particularly where the injury is not serious or manifestly a consequence of maltreatment.

Once the label "abuser" is attached, it is very difficult to remove; even innocent behavior of a custodian may then be viewed with suspicion. The tenacity of a label increases in proportion to the official processing. At our own institution, until quite recently, a red star was stamped on the permanent medical record of any child who might have been abused, a process which encouraged professionals to suspect child abuse (and to act on that assumption) at any future time that the child would present with a medical problem.

Professionals thus engage in an intricate process of selection, finding facts that fit the label which has been applied, responding to a few deviant details set within a panoply of entirely acceptable conduct. Schur[55] called this phenomenon "retrospective reinterpretation." In any pathological model, "persons are likely to be studied in terms of what is 'wrong' with them," there being a "decided emphasis on identifying the characteristics of abnormality;" in child abuse, it may be administratively impossible to return to health, as is shown by the extraordinary durability of case reports in state central registers.[58]

The response of the patient to the agent of social control affects the perceptions and behavior of the controller. If, for example, a child has been injured and the alleged perpetrator is repentant, a consensus can develop between abuser and labeler that a norm has been violated. In this situation, the label of "abuser" may be less firmly applied than if the abuser defends the behavior as proper. Support for this formulation is found in studies by Gusfield,[22] who noted different reactions to repentant, sick, and enemy deviants, and by Piliavin and Briar,[42] who showed that juveniles apprehended by the police receive more lenient treatment if they appear contrite and remorseful about their violations.

Consequences of Treatment for the Abuser

Once abuse is defined as a sickness, it becomes a condition construed to be beyond the actor's control.[39] Though treatment, not punishment, is warranted, the *type* of treatment depends on whether or not the abuser is "curable," "improvable," or "incurable," and on the speed with which such a state can be achieved.

To help the abuser is generally seen as a less important goal than is the need to protect the child. If the abusive behavior cannot quickly be altered, and the child remains "at risk," the type of intervention will differ accordingly (*e.g.,* the child may be more likely to be placed in a foster home). The less "curable" is the abuser, the less treatment will be offered and the more punitive will society's response appear. Ironically, even the removal of a child from his parents, a move nearly always perceived as punitive by parents, is often portrayed as helpful by the professionals doing the removing ("It will give you a chance to resolve your own problems," etc.).

Whatever the treatment, there are predictable consequences for those labeled "abusers." Prior to diagnosis, parents may be afraid of "getting caught" because of punishment and social stigma. On being told of clinicians' concerns, they may express hostility because of implicit or explicit criticism made of them and their child-rearing practices yet feel relief because they love their children and want help in stopping their destructive behavior. The fact that they see themselves as "sick" may increase their willingness to seek help. This attitude is due at least in part to the lesser social stigma attached to the "sick," as opposed to the "criminal," label.

Socially marginal individuals are likely to accept whatever definition more powerful labelers apply. This definition, of course, has already been accepted by much of the larger community because of the definers' power. As Davis[8] noted:

> The chance that a group will get community support for its definition of unacceptable deviance depends on its relative power position. The greater the group's size, resources, efficiency, unity, articulateness, prestige, coordination with other groups, and access to the mass media and to decision-makers, the more likely it is to get its preferred norms legitimated.

Acceptance of definition by child abusers, however, is not based solely on the power of the labelers. Though some might consider the process "political castration,"[43] so long as they are defined as "ill" and take on the sick role, abusers are achieving a more satisfactory label. Though afflicted with a stigmatized illness (and thus "gaining few if any privileges and taking on some especially handicapping new obligations"[15]) at least they are merely sick rather than sinful or criminal.

Effective social typing flows down rather than up the social structure. For example, when both parents induct one of their children into the family scapegoat role, this is an effective social typing because the child is forced to take their definition of him into account.[48] Sometimes it is difficult to know whether an abusive parent has actually accepted the definition or is merely "role playing" in order to please the definer. If a person receives conflicting messages from the same control agent (*e.g.* "you are sick and criminal") or from different control agents in the treatment network (from doctors who use the sick label, and lawyers who use the criminal), confusion and upset predictably result.[56]

As an example of how social definitions are accepted by the group being defined, it is interesting to examine the basic tenets of Parents Anonymous, which began as a self-help group for abusive mothers:

> A destructive, *disturbed* mother can, and often does, produce through her actions a physically or emotionally abused, or battered child. Present avail-

able *help* is limited and/or expensive, usually with a long waiting list before the person requesting help can actually receive *treatment* . . . We must understand that a problem as involved as this cannot be *cured* immediately . . . the problem is *within us* as a parent . . . [29] [emphases added]

To Parents Anonymous, child abuse appears to be a medical problem, and abusers are sick persons who must be treated.

Consequences of Treatment for the Social System

The individual and the social system are interrelated; each influences the other. Thus, if society defines abusive parents as sick, there will be few criminal prosecutions for abuse; reports will generally be sent to welfare, as opposed to police, departments.

Since victims of child abuse are frequently treated in hospitals, medical personnel become brokers for adult services and definers of children's rights. Once abuse is defined, that is, people may get services (such as counseling, child care, and homemaker services) that would be otherwise unavailable to them, and children may get care and protection impossible without institutional intervention.

If, as is customary, however, resources are in short supply, the preferred treatment of a case may not be feasible. Under this condition, less adequate treatment stratagems, or even clearly punitive alternatives, may be implemented. If day care and competent counseling are unavailable, court action and foster placement can become the only options. As Stoll[56] observed,

> . . . the best therapeutic intentions may be led astray when opportunities to implement theoretical guidelines are not available.

Treating child abuse as a sickness has, ironically, made it more difficult to "cure." There are not enough therapists to handle all of the diagnosed cases. Nor do most abusive parents have the time, money, or disposition for long-term therapeutic involvement. Many, moreover, lack the introspective and conceptual abilities required for successful psychological therapy.

As Parents Anonymous emphasizes, abuse is the *abuser's* problem. Its causes and solutions are widely understood to reside in individuals rather than in the social system.[5, 17] Indeed, the strong emphasis on child abuse as an individual problem means that other equally severe problems of childhood can be ignored, and the unequal distribution of social and economic resources in society can be masked.[20] The child abuse phenomenon itself may also increase as parents and professionals are obliged to "package" their problems and diagnoses in a competitive market where services are in short supply. As Tannenbaum[57] observed in 1938:

> Societal reactions to deviance can be characterized as a kind of "dramatization of evil" such that a person's deviance is made a public issue. The stronger the reaction to the evil, the more it seems to grow. The reaction itself seems to generate the very thing it sought to eliminate.

Conclusion

Dispelling the Myth of Child Abuse

As clinicians, we are convinced that with intelligence, humanity, and the application of appropriate interventions, we can help families in crisis.

We believe, however, that short of coming to terms with—and changing—certain social, political, and economic aspects of our society, we will never be able adequately to understand and address the origins of child abuse and neglect. Nor will the issues of labeling be adequately resolved unless we deal straightforwardly with the potentially abusive power of the helping professions. If we can bring ourselves to ask such questions as, "Can we legislate child abuse out of existence?" and, "Who benefits from child abuse?", then perhaps we can more rationally choose among the action alternatives displayed in the conceptual model (Table 1).

Although we would prefer to avoid coercion and punishment, and to keep families autonomous and services voluntary, we must acknowledge the realities of family life and posit some state role to assure the well-being of children. In making explicit the assumptions and values underpinning our professional actions, perhaps we can promote a more informed and humane practice.

Because it is likely that clinical interventions will continue to be class and culture-based, we propose the following five guidelines to minimize the abuse of power of the definer.

1. *Give physicians, social workers, lawyers, and other intervention agents social science perspectives and skills.* Critical intellectual tools should help clinicians to understand the implications of their work, and, especially, the functional meaning of the labels they apply in their practices.

   Physicians need to be more aware of the complexity of human life, especially its social and psychological dimensions. The "medical model" is not of itself inappropriate; rather, the conceptual bases of medical practice need to be broadened, and the intellectual and scientific repertory of the practitioner expanded.[12] Diagnostic formulation is an active process that carries implicitly an anticipation of intervention and outcome. The simple elegance of concepts such as "child abuse" and "child neglect" militate for simple and radical treatments.

   Lawyers might be helped to learn that, in child custody cases, they are not merely advocates of a particular position. Only the child should "win" a custody case, where, for example, allegations of "abuse" or "neglect," skillfully marshalled, may support the position of the more effectively represented parent, guardian, or social worker.

2. *Acknowledge and change the prestige hierarchy of helping professions.* The workers who seem best able to conceptualize the familial and social context of problems of violence are social workers and nurses. They are least paid,

most overworked, and as a rule have minimal access to the decision prerogatives of medicine and law. We would add that social work and nursing are
professions largely of and by women, and we believe we must come to terms
with the many realities—including sexual dominance and subservience—
that keep members of these professions from functioning with appropriate
respect and support. (We have made a modest effort in this direction at our
own institution, where our interdisciplinary child abuse consultation program is organized under the aegis of the administration rather than of a
medical clinical department. This is to foster, to the extent possible, peer
status and communication on a coequal footing among the disciplines
involved—social work, nursing, law, medicine, and psychiatry.)

3. *Build theory.* We need urgently a commonly understandable dictionary of
concepts that will guide and inform a rational practice. A more adequate
theory base would include a more etiologic (or causal) classification scheme
for children's injuries, which would acknowledge and integrate diverse
origins and expressions of social, familial, child developmental, and environmental phenomena. It would conceptualize strength in families and
children, as well as pathology. It would orient intervenors to the promotion
of health rather than to the treatment of disease.

A unified theory would permit coming to terms with the universe of need.
At present, socially marginal and poor children are virtually the only ones
susceptible to being diagnosed as victims of abuse and neglect. More affluent families' offspring, whose injuries are called "accidents" and who are
often unprotected, are not included in "risk" populations. We have seen
examples of court defense where it was argued (successfully) that because
the family was not poor, it did not fit the classic archetypes of abuse or
neglect.

The needs and rights of all children need to be spelled out legally in
relation to the responsibilities of parents and the state. This is easier said
than done. It shall require not only a formidable effort at communication
across disciplinary lines but a serious coming to terms with social and
political values and realities.

4. *Change social inequality.* We share Gil's[20] view that inequality is the basic
problem underlying the labeling of "abusive families" and its consequences.
Just as children without defined rights are *ipso facto* vulnerable, so too does
unequal access to the resources and goods of society shape a class hierarchy
that leads to the individualization of social problems. Broadly-focused
efforts for social change should accompany a critical review of the ethical
foundations of professional practice. As part of the individual's formation
as doctor, lawyer, social worker, or police officer, there could be developed
for the professional a notion of public service and responsibility. This would
better enable individuals to see themselves as participants in a social process
and to perceive the problems addressed in their work at the social as well
as the individual level of action.

5. *Assure adequate representation of class and ethnic groups in decision-making forums.* Since judgments about family competency can be affected by class and ethnic biases, they should be made in settings where prejudices can be checked and controlled. Culture-bound value judgments in child protection work are not infrequent, and a sufficient participation in case management conferences of professionals of equal rank and status and diverse ethnicity can assure both a more appropriate context for decision making and better decisions for children and their families.

References

1. Allen, F. 1964. The Borderland of Criminal Justice. University of Chicago Press, Chicago.
2. Becker, H. 1963. Outsiders: Studies in the Sociology of Deviance. Free Press, New York.
3. Bourne, R. and Newberger, E. 1977. 'Family autonomy' or 'coercive intervention?' ambiguity and conflict in a proposed juvenile justice standard on child protection. Boston Univ. Law Rev. 57(4):670–706.
5. Conrad, P. 1975. The discovery of hyperkinesis: notes on the medicalization of deviant behavior. Soc. Prob. 23(10):12–21.
6. Cupoli, J. and Newberger, E. 1977. Optimism or pessimism for the victim of child abuse? Pediatrics 59(2):311–314.
7. Curran, W. 1977. Failure to diagnose battered child syndrome. New England J. Med., 296(14):795–796.
8. Davis, F. 1975. Beliefs, values, power and public definitions of deviance. *In* The Collective Definition of Deviance, F. Davis and R. Stivers, eds. Free Press, New York.
9. Demause, L., *ed.* 1974. The History of Childhood. Free Press, New York.
10. Elmer, E. 1977. A follow-up study of traumatized children. Pediatrics 59(2):273–279.
11. Elmer, E. 1977. Fragile Families, Troubled Children. University of Pittsburgh Press, Pittsburgh.
12. Engel, G. 1977. The need for a new medical model: a challenge for biomedicine. Science 196(14): 129–136.
13. Fontana, V. 1964. The Maltreated Child: The Maltreatment Syndrome in Children. Charles C. Thomas, Springfield, Ill.
14. Fraser, B. 1977. Legislative status of child abuse legislation. *In* Child Abuse and Neglect: the Family and the Community, C. Kempe and R. Helfer, eds. Ballinger, Cambridge, Mass.
15. Freidson, E. 1970. Profession of Medicine: A Study of the Sociology of Applied Knowledge. Dodd, Mead, New York.
16. Galdston, R. 1971. Violence begins at home. J. Amer. Acad. Child Psychiat. 10(2):336–350.
17. Gelles, R. 1973. Child abuse as psychopathology: a sociological critique and reformulation. Amer. J. Orthopsychiat. 43(4):611–621.
18. Gelles, R. 1978. Violence toward children in the United States. Amer. J. Orthopsychiat. 48(4):580–592.
19. Gil, D. 1975. Unraveling child abuse. Amer. J. Orthopsychiat. 45(4): 346–356.
20. Gil, D. 1970. Violence Against Children. Harvard University Press, Cambridge, Mass.
21. Goldstein, J., Freud, A. and Solnit, A. 1973. Beyond the Best Interests of the Child. Free Press, New York.
22. Gusfield, J. 1967. Moral passage: the symbolic process in public designations of deviance. Soc. Prob. 15(2):175–188.
23. Hyde, J. 1974. Uses and abuses of information in protective services contexts. *In* Fifth National Symposium on Child Abuse and Neglect. American Humane Association, Denver.
24. Illich, I. 1976. Medical Nemesis: The Expropriation of Health. Random House, New York.
25. *Ingraham v. Wright.* 1977. 45 LW 4364 U.S. Supreme Court.
26. Isaacs, J. 1972. The role of the lawyer in child abuse cases. *In* Helping the Battered Child and His Family, R. Helfer and C. Kempe, eds. Lippincott, Philadelphia.
27. Joint Commission on the Mental Health of Children. 1970. Crisis in Child Mental Health. Harper and Row, New York.

28. Juvenile Justice Standards Project. 1977. Standards Relating to Abuse and Neglect. Ballinger, Cambridge, Mass.
29. Kempe, C. and Helfer, R., eds. 1972. Helping the Battered Child and His Family. Lippincott, Philadelphia.
30. Kempe, C. et al. 1962. The battered child symdrome. JAMA 181(1):17–24.
31. Kittrie, N. 1971. The Right To Be Different. Johns Hopkins University Press, Baltimore.
32. *Landeros v. Flood.* 1976. 131 Calif. Rptr 69.
33. Martin, H., ed. 1976. The Abused Child: A Multidisciplinary Approach to Developmental Issues and Treatment. Ballinger, Cambridge, Mass.
34. Mercer, J. 1972. Who is normal? two perspectives on mild mental retardation. *In* Patients, Physicians and Illness (2nd ed.), E. Jaco, ed. Free Press, New York.
35. Newberger, E. 1975. The myth of the battered child syndrome. *In* Annual Progress in Child Psychiatry and Child Development 1974, S. Chess and A. Thomas, eds. Brunner Mazel, New York.
36. Newberger, E., Newberger, C. and Richmond, J. 1976. Child health in America: toward a rational public policy. Milbank Memorial Fund Quart./Hlth. and Society 54(3): 249–298.
37. Newberger, E. and Daniel, J. 1976. Knowledge and epidemiology of child abuse: a critical review of concepts. Pediat. Annuals 5(3):15–26.
38. Newberger, E. et al. 1977. Pediatric social illness: toward an etiologic classification. Pediatrics 60(1): 178–185.
39. Parsons, T. 1951. The Social System. Free Press, Glencoe, Ill.
40. Paulsen, M. 1966. Juvenile courts, family courts, and the poor man. Calif. Law Rev. 54(2): 694–716.
41. Pfohl, S. 1977. The 'discovery' of child abuse. Soc. Prob. 24(3):310–323.
42. Piliavin, I. and Briar, S. 1964. Police encounters with juveniles. Amer. J. Sociol. 70(2): 206–214.
43. Pitts, J. 1968. Social control: the concept. *In* The International Encyclopedia of the Social Sciences 14:391. Macmillan, New York.
44. Poitrast, F. 1976. The judicial dilemma in child abuse cases. Psychiat. Opinion 13(1):22–28.
45. Rheinstein, M. 1954. Max Weber on Law in Economy and Society. Harvard University Press, Cambridge, Mass.
46. Rosenblatt, S., Schaeffer, D. and Rosenthal, J. 1976. Effects of diphenylhydantoin on child abusing parents: a preliminary report. Curr. Therapeut. Res. 19(3):332–336.
47. Rosenfeld, A. and Newberger, E. 1977. Compassion versus control: conceptual and practical pitfalls in the broadened definition of child abuse. JAMA 237 (19): 2086–2088.
48. Rubington, E. and Weinberg, M. 1973. Deviance: The Interactionist Perspective (2nd ed.). Macmillan, New York.
49. Ryan, W. 1971. Blaming the Victim. Random House, New York.
50. Sanders, R. 1972. Resistance to dealing with parents of battered children. Pediatrics 50(6): 853–857.
51. Scheff, T. 1966. Being Mentally Ill: A Sociological Theory. Aldine, Chicago.
52. Scheff, T. 1972. Decision rules, types of error, and their consequences in medical diagnosis. *In* Medical Men and Their Work, E. Freidson and J. Lorber, eds. Aldine, Chicago.
53. Schmitt, B. and Kempe, C. 1975. Neglect and abuse of children. *In* Nelson Textbook of Pediatrics (10th ed.), V. Vaughan and R. McKay, eds. W. B. Saunders, Philadelphia.
54. Schrag, P. 1975. The Myth of the Hyperactive Child. Random House, New York.
55. Schur, E. 1971. Labeling Deviant Behavior. Harper and Row, New York.
56. Stoll, C. 1968. Images of man and social control. Soc. Forces 47(2):119–127.
57. Tannenbaum, F. 1938. Crime and the Community. Ginn and Co., Boston.
58. Whiting, L. 1977. The central registry for child abuse cases: rethinking basic assumptions. Child Welfare 56(2):761–767.

5

A Wider Perspective

Introduction

Introduction

During the 1950s and 1960s, family scholars and the mass media presented an image of the typical, normal, or model American family. It included a father, a mother, and two or three children who lived a middle-class existence in a single-family home in an area neither rural nor urban. Father was the breadwinner, and mother was a full-time homemaker. Both were, by implication, white.

No one denied that many families and individuals fell outside the standard nuclear model. Single persons, one-parent families, two-parent families in which both parents worked, three-generation families, and childless couples abounded. Three- or four-parent families were not uncommon, as one or both divorced spouses often remarried. Moreover, many families, neither white nor well-off, varied from the dominant image. White and seemingly middle-class families of particular ethnic, cultural, or sexual styles also differed from the model. The image scarcely reflected the increasing ratio of older people in the postfamily part of the life cycle. But like poverty before its "rediscovery" in the middle 1960s, family complexity and variety existed on some dim fringe of semiawareness.

When noticed, individuals or families departing from the nuclear model were analyzed in a context of pathology, Studies of one-parent families or working mothers, for example, focused on the harmful effects to children of such situations. Couples childless by choice were assumed to possess some basic personality inadequacy. Single persons were similarly interpreted or else thought to be homosexual. Homosexuals symbolized evil, depravity, and degradation.

As Marvin Sussman (1971) has noted, "This preoccupation with the model nuclear family pattern and efforts to preserve it at all costs prevented sociologists from describing what was becoming obvious to non-sociological observers of the American scene: a pluralism in family forms existing side by side with members in each form having different problems to solve and issues to face" (p. 42). Curiously, although social scientists have always emphasized the pluralism of American society in terms of ethnic groups, religion, and geographic region, the concept of pluralism had never been applied to the family.

What we are actually witnessing today is not so much new forms of family living as a new way of looking at alternative family patterns that have been around for a long time. Even the flowering of communal living experiments in America during the late 1960s was not something new under the sun but rather the revival of an old American tradition. But while communes were being developed, nuclear family ideology was challenged on other grounds. Blacks challenged the validity of the white middle-class family as a model for all groups in society; the population explosion made singleness, childlessness, and even homosexuality seem to be adaptive responses to a pressing social problem; the women's movement challenged the traditional roles of wife and mother and argued for the validity of singleness, childlessness, unwed motherhood, homosexuality, and even celibacy.

Our selections here are intended to reflect this diversity and the controversies surrounding it. Robert Staples and Alfredo Mirandé review the literature of the past decade in terms of classical theoretical controversies about the nature of minority families. For example, does research suggest that the black family should be viewed primarily as culturally deviant (pathological), culturally equivalent (middle-class), or culturally variant (unique, legitimate)? What is the history, contemporary evidence for, and future of each of these perspectives? Should the machismo of the Chicano family be mainly interpreted as representing power, control, and violence; or is a more benevolent interpretation, stressing honor, respect and dignity, supported by the research evidence? Staples and Mirandé also review the sparser literature on Asian-American and Native American families.

If racial and cultural differentiation represents one way of analyzing family variation, age differentiation represents another. Many believe that the aged might benefit a return to traditional values, assuming that the three-generational family would solve the problem of the aged. But, as Beth B. Hess and Joan M. Waring point out in their article on aging, "some parents with large families, often the foreign-born with 'extended expectations,' will be disappointed at the unwillingness or inability of children to meet such claims." In reality, the problems of the aging result from the triumph of modernization, which implies the development of new values, plus a major extension of the life span. During the past 100 years, the proportion of the population over sixty-five has tripled, and expectations that might have worked for a much smaller population of the aged will not work for a much larger.

Besides, it would be a mistake to assume that the extended family or the three-generational household was ever the norm in American or western European society. The myth of the large kin group living happily on the grandparents' farm has repeatedly been laid to rest by sociologists and historians. Still, it lives on in the minds of many. Confronted with the different problems raised by a modern aging population, it is easy to yearn for some golden time of the past when the old lived happily in the bosom of the family. Yet there is little evidence that such a golden time ever existed. Even when old people and young people lived together, their lives were not necessarily idyllic (Kent, 1965).

Can There Be An Ideal?

Family life is, if nothing else, marked by diversity. The dominant cultural value brings an expectation that married couples will have children. Not all fulfill that expectation, and J. E. Veevers explores the complex processes by which childless couples define themselves as "different."

Even greater cultural variation is found among singles, whose lifestyles are analyzed by Leonard Cargan, and particularly among gays and lesbians, some of whom are single, some of whom aren't, but all of whom generate social and legal controversy over their sexual identity and lifestyles. There still remains a paucity of nonpolemical social-scientific research literature on homosexuality. And even when quality literature exists, it and its issues seem quickly outdated. We need not here reprint, as we did in the early 1970s, a well-reasoned article by a psychiatrist explaining that homosexuality is not the equivalent of mental illness. By now, that is well understood by educated and intelligent people. We have chosen instead to reprint here a brief non-scientific article from *Newsweek* in the expectation that it will generate discussion of the status of contemporary homosexuality on campus. We are not altogether certain that *Newsweek*'s portrait is accurate. We are, however, confident that the problems of homosexual identity, social organization, and intergenerational conflict it raises do exist on many campuses—and off them as well.

Is there some ideal form of family—or nonfamily organization—that will unfailingly provide love, security, and personality fullfillment throughout the life cycle? The answer seems to be no. We have evidence concerning a variety of family forms: the traditional extended family; the nuclear or conjugal family; the mother-child or matrifocal family; and many varieties of communal family. Each offers benefits as well as liabilities. For example, traditional family systems may provide lifelong security, but they are often experienced as oppressive by the family members locked into them, especially women and young people.

Society and the Family

In part, family life falls short of the ideals ascribed to it because families are not isolated havens set off from the surrounding society. In societies marked by scarcity, insecurity, inequalities of goods and power, anxiety over status, fear, and hatred, family life will bear the impact of these qualities. The family in a malfunctioning society is usually part of the problem.

Chances are family life will still be problematic, even in a relatively untroubled society, because of the special psychology of close relationships. The family, as one writer put it, is where you are dealing with life and death voltages. No matter what form the family takes, the distinctive intimacy and commitment of family life provide the source of both the joy and torment to be found there.

Still, it is important to note that whatever form the family takes, it is not self-sufficient, insulated from society. If the nation goes to war, family lives are disrupted. When a provider—father, mother, brother—is unemployed by the closing of a factory or an airline, everybody in the family is affected. Louis Ferman's study of family adjustment to unemployment (described here by Mary C. Blehar) shows how serious that condition can be to family life. Public policy and the family is an underdeveloped field. Largely, this underdevelopment is traceable to a narrow and confining perspective on the family as an autonomous unit, remote from society, and unaffected by major political decisions. On the contrary, Blehar suggests, in her article on families and public policy, the actions of government might well be judged, at least in some significant part, by their impact on families and family members.

As we move toward the future, public policy requires that full recognition be given to the complexity and variety of forms and life styles the family and other intimate environments can take. This is not to suggest that the nuclear family is going to disappear, nor should it. But as Alvin L. Schorr and Phyllis Moen point out in the selection we reprint here, the traditional family of husband, wife and children of the first marriage of the spouses now accounts for only 45 percent of American families. Even in the suburbs, where the traditional nuclear family still reigns, changes in the ecology and organization of domestic work could ease the strain on that venerable institution as well as on the single person. The trick, of course, is to maintain a philosophy of public policy that seeks to provide facilitative communal arrangements while avoiding the temptation to intrude on private lives. In any case, public policy should be based on the reality of variation, rather than on unrealistic visions of an outmoded orthodoxy.

References

Kent, Donald P. "Aging: Fact or Fancy." *The Gerontologist*, Vol. 5, No. 2 (June 1965), pp. 51–56.

Sussman, Marvin B. 1971. "Family Systems in the 1970s: Analysis, Policies, and Programs." *The Annals of the American Academy of Political and Social Science*, Vol. 396. The American Academy of Political and Social Science.

Chapter 10

Lifestyle Variation

Racial and Cultural Variations Among American Families: A Decennial Review of the Literature on Minority Families

Robert Staples * and Alfredo Mirandé * *

As an institution the family continues to be a subject of intense and controversial public concern. This interest is generated, in part, by the lack of consensus on what its form and function should be. In the case of minority groups, the controversy is heightened by their depiction in the literature and an ongoing debate over how their family lifestyles relate to the larger society. Before examining how this issue was expressed in the family literature of the seventies, it is necessary to place some parameters around our definition of minorities. Too global a definition of "minority" militates against the purpose and scope of this decade review. Hence, those groups of interest are any collectivity whose membership is derived from a shared racial identity, with high visibility in the society and a devalued social status: *i.e.*, Asians, blacks, Chicanos and Native Americans.

Given the American commitment to the concept of a melting pot (*i.e.*, the blending of diverse racial and ethnic groups into a standard prototype), there should be no need to study minority families separately. However, that ideal has never been translated into reality. Instead, we have what Gordon (1964) has described as "Anglo conformity": an assumption of the superiority of

We wish to acknowledge our gratitude to Ken Nakamura, Ralph Gomes, Dorothy Miller, Marvin Proson and Annie Williams for their assistance in writing this article.

From the *Journal of Marriage and the Family*, Vol. 42, No. 4 (November 1980), pp. 157–173. Copyrighted 1980 by the National Council on Family Relations. Reprinted by permission.

*Department of Sociology, University of California, San Francisco, California 94143.

**Departments of Sociology and Chicano Studies, University of California, Riverside, California 92521.

Anglo-Saxon culture and the devaluation of all other forms. This conflict between the melting pot theory and the dictates of Anglo conformity is expressed nowhere better than in the family literature on minorities. Thus, this decade review is more than an assessment of basic theory and research, it is also part of an ongoing debate about ideology and its role in the conceptualization of minority-family lifestyles.

The role of ideology is not unique to the field of the family or racial minorities. Under the rubric of the sociology of knowledge, it has been asserted that the social location of the individual within a given society will influence the knowledge he possesses (Mannheim, 1936). Since the study of minority families has been dominated by white, middle-class males, a debate centering around the "insider-outsider thesis" has arisen (Merton, 1972; Staples, 1976a). One side contends that indigenous minorities possess a special capacity for understanding the behavior of their group, while the other side contends that the use of objective scientific methods nullifies the racial membership of the investigator as a significant factor. Those holding the latter view often choose to conceptualize the whole issue as a conflict between ideology and science (Dennis, 1976).

The argument is compounded by the division of minority family researchers into empiricists and nonempiricists. Many minority researchers have used the essay and qualitative anylysis as their main tool in understanding minority families. In part, this is due to a desire for a broader understanding of the behavioral processes that animate the family life of American minorities. Since white males dominate the quantitative studies of minority families, they have often discredited their minority counterparts with the charge of being polemicists and substituting speculation and ideology for objective data. The white male's claim to a monopoly on objectivity is countered by Myrdal's (1944:104l) contention that "biases in social science cannot be erased simply by 'keeping to the facts' and by refined methods of statistical treatment of the data." Facts, he notes, and the "handling of data sometimes show themselves even more pervious to tendencies toward bias than does pure thought."

Questions of objectivity versus ideology would be beyond cavil were it not for the fact that for a very long time, minority families were treated pejoratively in the family literature. At the end of the sixties, the consensus was that minority families were negatively different from the middle-class Anglo family system. The source and nature of their deviance was never agreed upon beyond the fact that they generally constituted dysfunctional units and represented barriers to their group's mobility (Staples, 1971). Part of the problem in understanding minority families was the failure of researchers to distinguish between factors of class and culture in their family lifestyles. This also represented a methodological flaw. In an analysis of empirical research in the *Journal of Marriage and the Family* during the period of 1959 to 1968, it was found that only 7 percent of the *Journal*'s articles reported on lower-class populations. In contrast, almost all the research on minority families, in the same period, had lower-class groups as the subject population (Lieberman, 1973:18).

While lower-class minority families were often compared to middle-class white families and found wanting, a central question persisted. That question might be best framed as: What is the relationship of the family to the larger society? Does the family simply respond passively to the forces it encounters or is it a unit that acts as a conduit for the mobility of its individual members? In other words, does the family structure determine social achievement or does social achievement influence the form of the family? Belief in the determinancy of family structure on social achievement was the prevalent position in the study of minority families for many years. It was this underlying attitude which gave the study of minority families more than theoretical implications. Since research findings can be and are translated into public policy that, in turn, impacts on the life chances of minority individuals, the study of minority families becomes extremely consequential. Thus, it is imperative that all views be given a fair hearing in the family literature.

The Black Family

At the end of the sixties, controversy was still raging over the Moynihan (1965) report. Moynihan's assertion that "at the root of the deterioration of Black society was the deterioration of the Black family" stimulated a plethora of theory and research. Over 50 books and 500 articles related to the black family were published in the last decade. That 10-year period produced five times more black family literature than had been produced in all the years prior to 1970. In the early stages of the decade, such research was primarily in response to the work of Frazier (1939), Moynihan (1965), and Rainwater (1966), who had uniformly depicted the lower-class black family as pathological. Subsequently, however, the researchers expanded into studies of the black family as an autonomous unit.

Along with the expansion of black family research came the development of new theoretical constructs. Allen (1978) has identified three ideological perspectives in research done on the black family: the *cultural deviant* approach; the *cultural equivalent* approach; and the *cultural variant* approach. The cultural deviant approach viewed black families as pathological. The cultural equivalent perspective conferred a legitimacy upon black families as long as their family lifestyles conformed to middle-class family norms. The cultural variant orientation depicted black families as different, but functional, family forms. In an analysis of the treatment of black families in the research literature between 1965 and 1979, Haynes and Johnson (1980) discovered that, in the seventies, the literature shifted dramatically from the cultural deviant to the cultural equivalent perspective. The cultural variant perspective, which views the black family as a culturally unique, legitimate unit, continues to be underrepresented in mainstream journals. In fact, only in the predominantly black journals and in the special issue of the *Journal of Marriage and the Family* on black families does a cultural variant perspective prevail. These journals account for 74 percent of the articles published on the black family using such a perspective.

Theory

Since research on black families has as its dominant orientation the cultural equivalent approach, it would appear that the assimilation model guides most of the empirical studies. However, it remains the case that much research on the family is atheoretical. In the last decade, two new theoretical constructs were applied to the study of black families. The first and most common one is called the "Africanity" model. The underlying tenets of this model are that African traits were retained and are manifested in black styles of kinship patterns, marriage, sexuality, and childrearing, etc. (Staples, 1974; Nobles, 1978). While it is an axiom of human existence that no group loses all of its cultural heritage, the precise locus of African traits in black family lifestyles remains an empirical question. It is possible that the Africanisms that exist are so fused with American traits that it is impractical to seek specific behavioral patterns, values, and structural features that are uniquely African in origin. At this juncture the model remains on an abstract level, untested by any systematic research.

Another conceptual model applied to the study of black families is the "internal colonialism" approach. It has the advantage of bridging the cultural equivalent and cultural variant perspectives. By using the colonial analogy, it assumes that racial domination by outsiders can create weaknesses in a groups' family structure while acknowledging the existence of functional elements in its family system (Lieberman, 1973; Staples, 1978a). Research using this model has been slow in emerging, partly due to the problem of operationalizing the concept of internal colonialism with the kind of data readily available to social scientists. At this point in time, most of the works using this model have been theoretical essays or research which have used the colonial analogy in a serendipitous manner (Staples, 1976b).

Historical Research

Surprisingly, the most groundbreaking research on black families was conducted by historians. For years, the works of Frazier (1939) and Elkins (1968) had been accepted as the definitive history of black families and posited as a causal explanation of their contemporary condition. Based on traditional historical methods, using plantation records and slaveowner testimony, both men reached the conclusion that the family was destroyed under slavery and the culture of the slaves was decimated. The first historian to challenge that thesis was Blassingame (1972), whose use of slave narratives indicated that in the slave quarters black families did exist as functioning institutions and role models for others. Moreover, strong family ties persisted in face of the frequent breakups deriving from the slave trade. To further counteract the Frazier/Elkins thesis, Fogel and Engerman (1974) used elaborate quantitative methods to document that slaveowners did not separate a majority of the slave families. Their contention, also controversial, was that the capitalistic efficiency of the slave system meant it was more practical to keep slave families intact.

Continuing in the vein of revisionist historical research, Genovese (1974) used a mix of slaveholder's papers and slave testimony. Still, he concluded that black culture, through compromise and negotiation between slaves and slaveowners, did flourish during the era of slavery. Within the context of slavery, there was a variety of socially approved and sanctioned relationships between slave men and women. The alleged female matriarchy that was extant during that era is described by Genovese as a closer approximation to a healthy sexual equality than was possible for whites. It was the landmark study by Gutman (1976), however, that put to rest one of the most common and enduring myths about black families. Using census data for a number of cities between 1880 and 1925, he found that the majority of blacks, of all social classes, lived in nuclear families. Through the use of plantation birth records and marriage application, he concluded that the biparental household was the dominant form during slavery. More important than Gutman's compelling evidence that slavery did not destroy the black family was his contention that their family form in the past era had evolved from family and kinship patterns that had been given birth under slavery, a cultural form that was a fusion of African and American traits.

Social historians and historical demographers also made contributions to our understanding of black family history. Furstenberg and his colleagues (1975) investigated the origin of the female-headed black family and its relationship to the urban experience. Basing their analysis on samples from the decennial federal population manuscript schedules for the period from 1850 to 1880, they found that blacks were only slightly less likely to reside in nuclear households than were native whites and immigrants to Philadelphia. While these historical works have, in combination, challenged the Moynihan view that slavery created the conditions for black family disorganization, the prevalence of marital breakups at the hands of slaveowners means that many marriages were not that stable. Even the use of slave accounts does not eliminate bias in slave history. Many of the slave narratives were edited by Northern abolitionists and they constitute the reports of highly literate slaves.

Macrosociological Studies

The studies which focused on generalized aspects of the black family shared certain commonalities. Most of them were responding to the Moynihan thesis about the instability of black families. Additionally, they attempted to delineate the structure and function of black families. The goals may have been similar, but the perspectives, again, fell into one of Allen's (1978) typologies. Studies by Heiss (1975), Scanzoni (1971), and Willie (1976) would belong in the cultural equivalent category. Both Heiss and Scanzoni used quantitative analysis to illustrate that black families are stable, egalitarian, and functional units. They reached this conclusion by delineating how well black families meet the white, middle-class family ideal. Willie used qualitative analysis and examined a variety of black families. The poor black families were still depicted as less than healthy units. Hill's (1972) study of the strengths of black families would fall somewhere in a middle ground. Through the use of census data he demonstrated that black families, like white families, adhere to such sacrosanct American values as strong work, achievement, and religious orientations. Conversely, he stressed the more unique traits of strong kinship bonds and role flexibility, although he did not link them to an autonomous cultural system.

An ongoing debate in black family studies revolves around the appropriate unit of analysis. A number of scholars have contended that the functions of the black family are carried out by the extended, rather than the nuclear, family unit. A number of studies have used the extended family as the focus of research (Aschenbrenner, 1975; Martin and Martin, 1978; McAdoo, 1978a; Shimkin et al., 1978; Stack, 1974). Basically, they have delineated the use of kinship ties, both genealogical and fictive, as a resource for carrying out the functions of role modeling, socialization, mutual aid, and other support functions. The research by McAdoo (1978a) is especially significant because it illustrated that extended family ties transcend class boundaries. Her study of middle-class black families demonstrated that the kinship-help pattern remains strong after individuals have achieved mobility within the larger society.

Nevertheless, the viability of kinship networks must be questioned. First, there are indications that they are statistically a declining form. The number of blacks in each household decreased in the last decade (Bianchi and Farley, 1979). Young females who bear children out-of-wedlock are more likely to move into their own household rather than become part of an extended family network (Bianchi and Farley, 1979). Moreover, as Stack (1974) has noted, kinship ties can militate against stable marital unions. The woman in a stable conjugal relationship uses her resources for her nuclear family, not her kinsmen. Thus, the kinsmen have vested interest in discouraging the development of stable nuclear families. We might also raise the question of how compatible kinship ties are with an industrialized society for some individuals. While it may facilitate mobility in some cases, it may impede it in others. The Parsonian (Parsons and Bales, 1955) notion that the extended family was supplanted by the nuclear family in order to create a mobile work force may have some validity. Individuals tied to an extended kinship system are also chained to the same geographical locale, which impairs the capacity to respond to different and better job opportunities.

Sex Roles

The burgeoning of the women's liberation movement gave rise to a number of books on black women. In the main, they were nonempirical works which focused on the role of black women in their community and the larger society (Cade, 1970; Staples, 1973; Noble, 1978; Rose, 1980). Among the better books was the study by Ladner (1971) of black teenage females growing up in a low-income urban community. Through the use of systematic open-ended interviews, participatory observation, and her own experiences, she explored how these young women coped with the forces of poverty and maintained a sense of positive identity. Many of the books on black women emphasized that while they were strong, due to the need to face adverse forces in the society, they were not overbearing matriarchs. At the end of the decade, a young black feminist broke ranks with her more conciliatory sisters and issued a broadsided attack on black male chauvinism in the black community (Wallace, 1979). It is possible that her book was the harbinger of the eighties and future literature on black sex roles will contain a feminist ideology.

The Family Life Cycle

Other than fertility behavior and child socialization processes, the black family life cycle remains a largely neglected part of black family studies. The few studies of black dating and sexual behavior suggest a convergence of black and white behavioral modalities (Dickinson, 1975; Christensen and Johnson, 1978: Staples, 1978b; Porter, 1979). Almost all of the studies have used biracial comparisons and there has yet to be developed a systematic analysis of black dating and sexual codes. Mate selection norms and processes are equally ignored in the black family literature, despite the large proportion of unmarried blacks in our midst (Staples, in press). Perhaps it is the fact that the majority of adult blacks are unmarried that accounts for the paucity of research on black marriages and divorces (Chavis and Lyles, 1975; Hampton, 1979). At any rate, all we know is that the divorce rate for blacks increased by 130 percent in the last decade (U.S. Bureau of the Census, 1979). While there were few studies of intraracial marriages, there were an abundance of books and articles on interracial marriages produced in the last decade (Henriques, 1975; Stember, 1976; Porterfield, 1977). Many of them were written in an *ad hominem* fashion and concluded that black/ white marriages were problematic but viable. Heer's (1974) more careful analysis of census data documents the sharp increase in black male/white female pairings and the fairly high rate of dissolution of such unions.

Studies of childbearing and rearing practices in the black community reflect the same convergence of black and white behavior. The fertility rate of married black women declined at a slightly higher rate than did that of white women, with college educated black women continuing to have the lowest fertility rate of all groups (Farley, 1970; Kiser, 1970). The biggest racial difference in fertility rates continued to be in out-of-wedlock births occurring to black females. More than half of all black births now occur out-of-wedlock (Bianchi and Farley, 1979). In part, the increase in out-of-wedlock births is due to the decline in fertility rates among married black women. Many of the unwed mothers are teenagers and we have little in the way of research to inform us as to how their children are being reared. There are indications that the informal adoption practices (Hill, 1977) of black families are no longer prevalent (Bianchi and Farley, 1979). Childrearing practices, in general, tend to be similar for black and white parents as does the level of the child's self-esteem (Halpern, 1973; Silverstein and Krate, 1975).

Summary

The past decade has witnessed a basic transformation in ideology and research on the black family. Prior to the seventies, the common wisdom was that black families, in comparison to middle-class white families, were dysfunctional units which could not carry out the normative functions ascribed to that institution. During the last decade, the research emphasis shifted to the investigation of stable black families and their conformity to middle-class family norms. However, it was in this same decade that the economic gains that blacks accrued were translated into greater family stability for many, again raising the question of the relationship between black family stability and changes in the larger society. Another question concerns the interaction between cultural values and family organization; this has yet to be systematically examined by the proponents of the "Africanity" and "colonial" models. Finally, it would appear that we may need to go back to the drawing board on black family research. Based on the latest census data (U.S. Bureau of the Census, 1979), there has been a dramatic increase in teenage pregnancies, out-of-wedlock births, single-parent households, and marital dissolution among blacks of all social classes. Since these changes parallel changes in white families during the same period, it may presage a need to undergo a revolution in theory and research on the family as a viable institution for all groups in society.

The Chicano Family

The last decade has witnessed a proliferation of research and writing on the Chicano family.[1] Prior to this time, social scientists demonstrated an intense interest in the Chicano family and generalizations concerning it abounded, but such generalizations were typically based on either meager or nonexistent data (Mirandé, 1977:747; Kagan and Valdez, in press). In 1970, Miguel Montiel wrote an excellent critique of Mexican American family studies entitled "Social Science Myth of the Mexican American Family." At the risk of oversimplification, it seems fair to say that the bulk of research at the end of the previous decade could be characterized not only as negative and pejorative, but as lacking in empirical support. Montiel (1970:62) has noted that such studies were based on a pathological model wihich "is inherently incapable of defining normal behavior and thus automatically labels all Mexican and Mexican American people as sick—*only in degree of sickness do they vary.*"

During the late 1960s and early 1970s a number of Chicano scholars sought to refute many of the stereotypes and myths perpetrated by pathological studies and to present a more sympathetic "inside" view of *la familia.* These sympathetic studies served as an important corrective, however, in their eagerness to counter negative perspectives, they tended to present an idealized and romanticized conception of the Chicano family. More recently, a body of research has emerged that is sympathetic to Chicanos and the nuance of Chicano culture, but which is increasingly rejecting of idealized and romantic stereotypes. While these approaches correspond roughly with the three chronological periods, adherents to each perspective are still to be found today.

Pejorative Depictions of the Mexican American Family

The traditional pejorative view of the Mexican American family can be traced to pathological studies of the Mexican family; works which see *machismo* as the key variable in explaining both the dynamics of Mexican family life and the emergence of Mexican national character (Bermudez, 1955; Gilbert, 1959; Paz, 1961; Ramos, 1962; Diaz-Guerrero, 1975). Based on psychoanalytic assumptions, such studies have assumed the Mexican to be driven by feelings of inadequacy, inferiority, and a rejection of authority. *Machismo* is thus a compensation for powerlessness.

The pathological view of *machismo* and the rigid patriarchal family has been uncritically applied to Mexicans on this side of the border. The father is depicted as the unquestioned authority—the omnipotent, omniscient "lord

---

[1]There were only 17 articles on Hispanic families between 1950 and 1959, 57 in the following decade, and 155 in the past decade (Padilla *et al.,* 1978).

and master" of the household who is free to come and go as he pleases and to maintain the same lifestyle that he did before marriage.

This empirically unsupported model of Chicano family life, until recently, has been the most prevalent in the social sciences (*cf.* Humphrey, 1944; Jones, 1948; Heller, 1966; and Peñalosa, 1968). According to this view, a man has complete freedom to drink, fight, and carry on extramarital relationships at will. William Madsen (1973:22) has likened the Chicano male to a rooster: "The better man is the one who can drink more, defend himself best, have more sex relations, and have more sons borne by his wife." A man is seen as overly preoccupied with sex and with proving his masculinity and sexual prowess, and "the most convincing way of proving machismo and financial ability is to keep a mistress in a second household" (Madsen, 1973:51).

Not surprisingly, the woman becomes a quiet, saintly, virginal creature who honors and obeys her husband at any cost. According to Madsen (1973:22), the woman is the perfect counterpart to the man: "Where he is strong, she is weak. Where he is aggressive, she is submissive. While he is condescending toward her, she is respectful toward him." So strong is his control that she is expected to accept his marital transgressions and, if she does not, she is likely to be beaten. Moreover, "some wives assert that they are grateful for punishment at the hands of their husbands for such concern with shortcomings indicates profound love" (Madsen, 1973:22).

This patriarchal family system also has been assumed to adversely affect children. Childrearing was presumed to be rigid and authoritarian. The Chicano family was thus the obverse of the middle-class Anglo familial ideal. Where the Anglo family was egalitarian and democratic, the Chicano family was rigid and authoritarian. While the Anglo family encouraged achievement, independence, and a sense of self-worth, the Chicano family engendered passivity and dependence and adversely affected normal personality development. Celia Heller (1966:34-35) has argued that the Chicano family discouraged advancement "by stressing values that hinder mobility—family ties, honor, masculinity, and living in the present." Alvin Rudoff (1971:236–237) has been even more severe in his condemnation of the Chicano family:

> The family constellation is an unstable one as the father is seen as withdrawn and the mother as a self-sacrificing and saintly figure. The Mexican American has little concern for the future, perceives himself as predestined to be poor and subordinate, is still influenced by magic, is gang-minded, distrusts women, sees authority as arbitrary, tends to be passive and dependent, and is alienated from the Anglo culture.

Another commonly assumed effect of the authoritarian and patriarchal structure is family violence. Carroll (1980) has contended that values and norms which are endemic to Chicanos result in a high level of family violence. The democratic Jewish American family, on the other hand, is believed to generate a very low level of violence. Whereas the Chicano family emphasizes severe discipline and violence as a mechanism for conflict resolution, the Jewish American family emphasizes

> the pursuit of knowledge and the use of the mind rather than the body. The value of intellectuality resulting from these values was proposed to lead to the favoring of articulateness, argumentativeness, and bargaining as a way to solve family disputes (Carroll, 1980:80).

Positive Depictions of the Chicano Family

An important outcome of minority movements of the 1960s was that minority scholars began to question social science depictions, which were generally negative or pejorative, and to offer new "insider" (Merton, 1972) perspectives that were not only sensitive and sympathetic to minority cultures but, possibly more valid and consistent with the realities of the minority experience. Given this thrust, it was perhaps inevitable that Chicanos, like blacks, would begin to seriously reevaluate social science perspectives on the Chicano family. Interestingly, while black scholars faced the task of refuting the myth of the "matriarchy" (Staples, 1971), Chicanos had to deal with *machismo* and the issue of male dominance. There emerged, then, a "sympathetic" or "revisionist" view of the Chicano family.

Miguel Montiel (1970, 1972) who not only rejected pathological formulations but suggested that they be replaced with an "appreciative" framework, has been one of the best and most incisive critics of traditional perspectives. Octavio Romano (1973:52) has been similarly critical of social scientists for suggesting that Chicano parents, in effect, "are their children's own worst enemies" and that *la familia* Chicano is "un-American," potentially threatening our "democratic way of life" (1973:50). Alvirez and Bean (1976:277) have responded to the traditional negative view by noting that "only a person who has never experienced the warmth of the Mexican American family would tend to see it primarily from a negative perspective." Another writer to take issue with the traditional view has been Nathan Murillo (1971), who has characterized the Chicano family as a warm and nurturing institution. According to Murillo, family is the most important unit in life and the individual is likely to put the needs of the family above his own. Rather than being rigid and authoritarian, the family is now seen as a stable structure where the individual's place is clearly established and secure. Cooperation among family members is also emphasized. The family "seems to provide more emotional security and sense of belonging to its members" (Murillo, 1971:99). One's status within the family is determined by age and sex. While the father is the ultimate authority, other adults are also respected and honored as "being old and wise" (Goodman and Berman, 1971:111).

Whereas *machismo* was previously synonymous with power, control, and violence, it is now equated with honor, respect, and dignity. "An important part of [the father's] concept of machismo . . . is that [of] using his authority within the family in a just and fair manner" (Murillo, 1971:103). To misuse one's authority is to risk losing respect within the family and in the community.

Another Look at the Patriarchy: The Myth of Machismo

Although there appear to be both positive and negative perspectives of the Chicano family, a closer examination suggests a conversion of the two perspectives (Mirandé, 1977:751). Both agree, for example, that male dominance is a persistent feature of the Chicano family, but one sees it as benevolent and the other as malevolent. Interestingly, the position is one held by both supporters and detractors of la familia, largely without the benefit of empirical support. When research findings have not supported traditional assumptions, there has been a tendency to resist them, especially by detractors of the Chicano family. "Findings which show that the Chicano family is more egalitarian than was previously assumed have been downplayed or explained away as resulting from increasing acculturation and assimilation" (Mirandé, 1979:475).

A study of California migrant farm families by Hawkes and Taylor (1975) hypothesized that male dominance would prevail. They found instead, that the dominant pattern of decision making and action making among these migrant families was egalitarian. Their response to this unexpected finding was to turn to other factors such as acculturation, urbanization, and the decreasing dependence of women on their husbands in the United States. Only after such attempts proved unsuccessful did the authors begin to question the assumption of male dominance as a prevailing feature of Mexican and Chicano culture (Hawkes and Taylor, 1975:811).

Hawkes and Taylor's findings are significant not so much for what they tell us about migrant farm families, but for suggesting a pattern which may not be anomalous or unique to the population studied but characteristic of Chicano families in general. Virtually every systematic study of conjugal roles in the Chicano family has found egalitarianism to be the predominant pattern across socioeconomic groups, educational levels, urban-rural residence, and region of the country. The Mexican-American Study Project, a pioneering effort and one of the most extensive and widely acclaimed studies of the Chicano people, found that Chicanos in Los Angeles and San Antonio did not fall into the traditional patriarchal pattern. Respondent families, especially younger ones and those with higher incomes, were much less patriarchal than previously assumed. There was egalitarianism with respect to the performance of traditional sex-typed tasks, although traditional male tasks appeared to be breaking down more than traditional female tasks, suggesting that Chicanos are increasingly assuming male roles. They found, nonetheless, that sex, age, and income differences were not significant and concluded that "the most striking finding relates not to internal variations in

the departure from traditional sex specializations, but rather to the conspicuous presence of a basically *egalitarian* division of household tasks" (Grebler
et al., 1970:362–363).

A more recent study of 100 married couples in Fresno, California, also
uncovered a basically egalitarian pattern of decision making (Ybarra, 1977).
While Ybarra found that conjugal role relations ranged from a patriarchal
pattern to a completely egalitarian one, the most prevalent pattern was one
in which the husband and wife shared in decisions (Ybarra, 1977:2):

> A large number of Chicano husbands helped their wives with household
> chores and child care. Also, the Chicanos interviewed were not as obsessed
> with the idea of machismo as has been suggested in the literature. The over-
> whelming majority of Chicano husbands preferred to participate in social
> and recreational activities with their wives and children. Overall, the data
> indicated that the majority of Chicano wives played an important and/or
> equal part in most facets of conjugal role relationships.

Factors such as level of acculturation, income, or education were not significantly related to the type of role relationships prevalent in the family. In
fact, the only factor that significantly affected the role relationships exhibited was female employment outside the home, with families with working
wives demonstrating a more egalitarian pattern relative to decision making,
sharing of household tasks, and the caring of children. While couples who
are already more egalitarian may be more predisposed to have a working
wife, the mere fact of the wife's employment outside the home appears to
require adjustments in marital roles and a shift toward a more egalitarian
pattern. Yet, Chicanos can work and acquire more power in the family without assimilating or rejecting their ethnicity (Baca Zinn, 1980).

A study of self-report perceptions of spousal dominance among Kansas
City Chicanos and blacks similarly failed to support the traditional view of
machismo in the Chicano family. Cromwell and Cromwell, (1978) in studying spousal dominance in decision making and conflict resolution, found that
the most common pattern among Chicanos was egalitarianism, rather than
male dominance.

After undertaking an extensive review of literature on power and control
in the domestic sphere, Maxine Baca Zinn (1975, 1976) has gone a step
beyond studies which suggest an egalitarian pattern by proposing that the
Chicano family is, in fact, mother-centered. While the family may present a
facade of patriarchy because cultural values dictate that the male should be
honored and respected as titular head of the household, the day-to-day functioning of the family revolves around *la mujer.* The male has primary responsibility and power outside of the household, but the domestic sphere is the
woman's domain (Baca Zinn, 1976). Other studies have suggested that the
woman's influence is especially strong relative to children. Mothers not only
perform many domestic tasks, but they have primary responsibility for the
caring of children and for setting limits on their behavior (Tuck, 1946;

Heller, 1966; Rubel, 1966; Goodman and Beman, 1971; Sotomayor, 1972). Ultimately, "as the *madrecita*, entitled to respect and homage, she may actually dominate, in all matters that affect her children" (Tuck, 1946:123).

The questioning of the rigid and authoritarian nature of the Mexican and Chicano family has extended beyond conjugal roles to relations between parents and children. Recent research suggests that parent-child relations may be warm and nurturing rather than cold and rigid. An important assumption that has been challenged is that fathers are necessarily more aloof and authoritarian than mothers. An observational study of Mexican family roles found fathers to be playful and companionable with children (Burrows, 1980). Rubel (1966:66) similarly concluded that "without exception, direct observations note the warmth and affection exhibited by fathers with their young sons and daughters, children under ten years of age." Goodman and Beman (1971:12) were also impressed with the strength and warmth of affection demonstrated in the Chicano family, noting that "the strength of intrafamily affection declared by Barrio children is conspicuous by contrast with responses of the Negro and Anglo children we interviewed." Finally, Bartz and Levine (1978:709) reported that it was black, rather than Chicano parents who were "typified as expecting early autonomy, not allowing wasted time, being both highly supportive and controlling, valuing strictness and encouraging egalitarian family roles." Black fathers were also most controlling. Significantly, of the three groups, Chicano parents were found to be most supportive of increasing permissiveness in parent-child relations (Bartz and Levine, 1978:715).

The Chicano Family: Social and Demographic Characteristics

There are a number of structural and demographic features which distinguish the Chicano family from the dominant American form. One distinctive feature is its high fertility relative not only to white but to black families (Alvirez and Bean, 1976:280–281). Not surprisingly, the Chicano population is a youthful one with a median age of about 21, compared to a median of 30 years for the rest of the population (U.S. Bureau of the Census, 1978:2). Whereas Chicano families average approximately four persons per family, other families average three (1978:11). The vast majority of Chicano children under 18 years of age (81 percent) live with both parents in intact families, 16 percent live with the mother, and only 1 percent live with the father (U.S. Bureau of the Census, 1978:46). Chicano families are about as likely to be maintained by a woman (16 percent) as are other Hispanic or Anglo families, but far less likely to be maintained by a woman than are Puerto Rican families (37 percent). The income of Chicano families is substantially lower than for other families. The median income for Chicano families in 1978 was $12,000, compared to $17,000 for families in the population as a whole (U.S. Department of Commerce, 1978). Twenty-two percent of all Mexican-origin families are below the poverty level, whereas only 9 percent of families not of Spanish origin are classified as poor (U.S. Bureau of the Census, 1978:15).

The marital status of Chicanos does not differ significantly from the general population, with approximately 60 percent of the population in each group classified as married, but Chicanos have a higher proportion of single and a lower proportion of widowed or divorced persons (U.S Bureau of the Census, 1978:3). Thus, while Chicanos are about as likely to be married as other groups, they are less likely to be divorced. The divorce rate shows greater stability for Chicanos, especially Chicano men (Alvirez and Bean, 1976; Eberstein and Frisbie, 1976).

Since intermarriage has been presumed to be an important index of assimilation, there has been much interest in the outmarriage rates of Chicanos. The conclusions of earlier studies that intermarriage rates of Chicanos suggested a "breakdown of ethnic solidarity in an increasingly open system" (Grebler *et al.*, 1970:471) have been called into question by more recent research. While the overall trend during the present century has been toward intermarriage in the Southwest (Bean and Bradshaw, 1970), the trend appears to have stabilized and, perhaps, reversed in recent years. Murguia and Frisbie (1977:387) concluded after examining recent trends in intermarriage that:

> If the level of Spanish-surname intermarriage is conceived as the most conclusive, objective indicator of the degree of assimilation . . . , it seems probable that the Mexican American population will continue to represent a distinct sociocultural entity for some time to come.

Asian American Families

This minority group has largely been neglected in the family literature. Theory on their family life is nonexistent and empirical studies are sparse and clustered in a few areas. This is due, in part, to their small numbers and geographical concentration. There are approximately 1.5 million individuals of Chinese, Japanese, Korean, Filipino, Vietnamese, Cambodian, Thai, and East Indian ancestries living in the United States (Yamauchi, 1979). In total they constitute less than 1 percent of the American population and represent fewer than 10 percent of our minority groups. Most of them are concentrated in Hawaii and the Western part of the United States. In addition, they tend to be underrepresented among social scientists and there are few insiders to develop theory and carry out research on their family lifestyles. Another possible reason is that, as a group, they are not perceived as a "problem" in American society or as very different in their family lifestyles. In the past, Asian men were stereotyped as wily and devious, the women as exotic and mysterious. That image essentially has changed to one of a hardworking, conforming, cohesive family group which is a carrier of a traditional culture similar to that of middle-class Anglo families (Sue and Kitano, 1973). Certainly, they fit better the family ideal of middle-class Americans than do the other minorities. Based on the positive indices of success and family stability, they not only are equal to white Americans, but often fare better in terms of educational achievement, median family income, and marital stability (U.S. Department of Health, Education, and Welfare, 1980).

The new stereotype of Asians as model minorities can be deleterious because it masks the problems they face. While they obviously have different characteristics than other minorities, the variations are not evenly spread across generations in their culture. Asian Americans can be separated chronologically into three groups: pre-1924 immigrants, American-born, and recent immigrants. Many of the pre-1924 immigrants, for instance, were males who came to this country alone and were unable to establish families because of immigration laws that prohibited Asian migration to this country for a long period of time (Lyman, 1968). That group, and the more recent immigrants, have not shared equally in the successes of American-born Asians. Even the American-born Asians are subject to tensions in their family life that remain unexplored by family researchers. Many Asian families contain at least two full-time workers, more than the average American family, and must use their income to support an extended family that is larger than most middle-class nuclear families (Wong, 1976).

Acculturation and assimilation seem to be key concepts in understanding Asian family life. This is particularly true of the younger, American-born group, which has adapted more strongly to American values and traditions (Kuroda *et al.*, 1978). In comparison to the other minorities, Asians have more conservative sexual values, a lower fertility rate, fewer out-of-wedlock births, and more conservative attitudes toward the role of women (Monahan, 1977; Braun and Chao, 1978; Leonetti, 1978). The adoption of American values, however, has proved to be a mixed blessing for young Asian Americans. It has created a schism in the Asian community based on generational differences in language, customs, and values. It makes it difficult to maintain generational continuity and ethnic cohesiveness. Nowhere is this more evident than in the high rates of out-marriages among younger Japanese and Chinese Americans (Weiss, 1970; Kikumura and Kitano, 1973). A majority of third generation Japanese Americans marry non-Japanese mates. The majority of out-marriages have involved Japanese women, although the rate for Japanese males is increasing. While many factors account for this high rate of intermarriage, a primary reason is the more acculturated Asian woman's dissatisfaction with the more traditional Japanese male's limited attitude toward women (Kikumura and Kitano, 1973; Braun and Chao, 1978).

Another index of acculturation is child-rearing practices. Studies generally have shown a congruity between third-generation Japanese socialization techniques and American styles of childrearing. However, differences based on some residue of Japanese culture remain. Caudill and Frost (1973) found that young Japanese mothers do more vocal lulling, more breast and bottle feeding, more carrying and more playing with the baby than do American mothers. Connor (1974) also discovered that the legacy of Japanese culture can still be found in third generation Japanese Americans. When compared with whites of the same age and education, the Japanese Americans were significantly different; they were less aggressive, had a greater need for succor and order, and a markedly lesser need for companionship. Johnson (1977) also reported that the Japanese American kinship system operates on a more obligatory basis than the optional basis found in the American kinship system. Her research revealed an increase in kinship contact and sociability among third-generation Japanese American families, despite their social mobility and high degree of assimilation.

In sum, culture seems to be the key element in Asian family life. Their traditional culture stressed the importance of the family unit at the expense of the individual, and socialization processes in the family created patterns of self-control which facilitated the achievement of societal goals. These cultural values were very consonant with traditional American values and made them adaptable to the American family system. Class membership does not seem as important since many of the Asian immigrants brought with them values associated with the middle class: *i.e.*, an emphasis on education and a capitalist orientation (Kitano, 1969). However, there are indications that many of these middle-class values are declining among the general American population. With their high degree of acculturation, younger Asian Americans face a clash of generations and a lack of ethnic cohesiveness that may entail a high cost.

Native American Families

While all our minority groups have certain commonalities, Native Americans have several problems which are unique to their particular group. The other minorities have a homeland that theoretically provides a symbolic identity with some other nation. Native Americans have no ties to any other geographical entity. As a group, they are more widely dispersed across North America and are more likely to reside in rural and isolated areas. Furthermore, they are more unalterably opposed to assimilation and integration into mainstream society and culture than any other minority group (Price, 1976). Even within the Native American group, there is a vast amount of diversity. They speak more than 252 languages and are organized into 280 different tribal groupings (Wax, 1971). Given the existence of these esoteric traits, they cannot be viewed as a monolithic group whose family lifestyles can be easily studied.

In reviewing the family literature on Native Americans, we are hampered by several factors. There is no such institution as a Native American family. There are only tribes, and family structure and values will differ from tribe to tribe. Despite the attempt to impose Western family models on them, various family forms still exist among the different tribal groupings (Unger, 1977). These forms range from polygamy to monogamy, matrilineality to patrilineality (McAdoo, 1978). Most of literature that is extant can be found in social work and mental health journals. These articles primarily focus upon Native American families as cultural deviants constituting a problem for the larger society. Another body of literature consists of anthropological studies, which again raises the insider-outsider issue. Unlike other minority groups, research done on Native Americans is almost exclusively monopolized by white Americans. Since anthropologists have been outsiders in Native American culture, the few existing Native American social scientists have been very critical of outsider perspectives on Native American family life (Redhorse et al., 1978). Oftentimes the outsiders could neither speak the language, nor even locate the living quarters of many Native Americans. In the words of Dorothy Miller (1975:7), a Native American, "most of us look upon 'surveys' and 'research' as being tools of our suppression and withhold data from white investigators."

In a general sense, Native Americans most closely approximate black American families. Both groups are characterized by a high fertility rate, out-of-wedlock births, a strong role for women, female-headed households, and high rates of unemployment (Witt,1974; Unger, 1977; U. S. Department of Health, Education, and Welfare, 1980). For many Native Americans, the extended family is the basic unit for carrying out family functions. This is often true despite the absence of extended kin in the same household. Children are actually raised by relatives residing in different, noncontiguous households. The existence of multiple households sharing family functions is quite common. Redhorse (1979) discovered one community where 92 percent of the elderly population resided in independent households, but maintained close functional contact with their children, grandchildren, and great grandchildren. They fulfilled traditional family roles on a daily basis. Fictive kin are also incorporated into the extended family system. An individual, for example, may become a namesake for a child through formal ritual and subsequently assume family obligations and responsibilities for childrearing and role modeling (Momaday, 1976).

In the move from tribal reservations to the urban frontiers, Native Americans often become more isolated and must confront certain vicissitudes of city life without their traditional support system. Certainly, the proportion of Native Americans living off reservations has rapidly increased. In 1930, only 10 percent lived in urban areas. By 1970 that number had grown to 45 percent (U.S. Bureau of the Census, 1974). In their study of 120 urban Native American families, Miller (1975) and her Native American researchers discovered that: (1) one third were female-headed; (2) 27 percent were receiving public welfare; (3) they had an average of three children; and (4) only one third had an adequate income. They found that traditional childrearing techniques were still used by most of the parents. Native American children continued to be trained for independence at significantly earlier ages than either white or black urban children. Their findings support a bicultural model which holds that families who are at home in both the Native American and white world have a greater ability to survive and adapt to the city than do families who only are comfortable in one culture or who feel alienated from both worlds.

The status of Native American families remains in a state of transition. High unemployment and a desire for a better life have propelled many from the reservations into the urban centers. Once in the cities, they encounter a clash of cultures between Native American ways and the norms of city life. Moreover, they cannot rely on the extended family system which serves as an anchor of Native American culture and life on the reservations. Hence, there is a constant tension as they seek equilibrium in an alien and hostile environment. In a follow-up study of the urban Native American families, Miller (1980) found that 40 percent had returned to the reservation. Some returned because of a dislike for the city, others went back because they could not cope with its demands. Some, however, made a successful bicultural adaptation and returned to their community with leadership and technical skills and an appreciation and understanding of both worlds.

Summary

Our decade review of research and theory on minority families illustrates the fact that there has been an increase in both the quantity and quality of the family literature. Some problems remain. Research continues to be clustered in specific areas while other areas are neglected. In the case of Asian and Native American families, basic studies need to be conducted. Future research needs to focus on the minority family unit as an autonomous system with its own norms, rather than comparing it to or contrasting it with the majority culture using white, middle-class standards. Only by this means will the insider-outsider dichotomy dissipate as a salient issue. Furthermore, both qualitative and quantitative approaches are necessary in the study of minority families. Since these groups remain outside the mainstream of society, the nuances of their cultures cannot be thoroughly understood through the sole use of one-dimensional empirical research. At the same time, we need the solid grounding of quantitative data. Different populations need to be sampled in order to ascertain class and cultural variation within and between minority groups. There is little we can say about class differences among minority families, since few studies have used class controls or accounted for its effect. Finally, while there is no validity to the idea that the family system of a given minority is pathological, there also is little credibility to a philosophical school that assumes that all aspects of minority family life are strong and healthy and that no weaknesses of any kind exist. What we need is theory and research that can give us a balanced account of both the strengths and weaknesses of minority families. That remains our task for the next decade.

References

Allen, W.
1978 "Black family research in the United States: A review, assessment and extension." Journal of Comparative Family Studies 9 (Summer): 167–189.

Alvirez, D., and F. Bean
1976 "The Mexican American family." Pp. 271–292 in Charles H. Mindel and R. Habenstein (Eds.), Ethnic Families in America. New York: Elsevier.

Aschenbrenner, J.
1975 Lifelines: Black families in Chicago. New York: Holt, Rinehart, and Winston.

Baca Zinn, M.
1975 "Political familism: Toward sex role equality in Chicano families." Aztlán: Chicano Journal of the Social Sciences and the Arts 6 (Winter): 13–26.
1976 "Chicanas: Power and control in the domestic sphere." De Colores 2 (Fall): 19–31.
1980 "Employment and education of Mexican-American women: The interplay of modernity and ethnicity in eight families." Harvard Educational Review 50 (February): 47–62.

Bartz, K., and E. Levine
1978 "Childrearing by black parents: A description and comparison to Anglo and Chicano parents." Journal of Marriage and the Family 40 (November): 709–719.

Bean, F., and B. Bradshaw
1970 "Intermarriage between persons of Spanish and non-Spanish surname: Changes from the mid-nineteenth to the mid-twentieth century." Social Science Quarterly 51 (September): 389–395.

Bermudez, M.
1955 La Vida familar del mexicano, Mexico, D.F.: Antigua Libreria Robredo.

Bianchi, S., and R. Farley
1979 "Racial differences in family living arrangements and economic well-being: An analysis of recent trends." Journal of Marriage and the Family 41 (August): 537–552.

Blassingame, J.
1972 The Slave Community. New York: Oxford University Press.

Braun, J., and H. Chao
1978 "Attitudes toward women: A comparison of Asian-born Chinese and American Caucasians." Psychology of Women Quarterly 2 (Spring): 195–201.

Burrows, P.
1980 "Mexican parental roles: Differences between mother's and father's behavior to children." Paper presented to the annual meeting of the Society for Cross-Cultural Research. Philadelphia (February).

Cade, T.
1970 The Black Woman: An Anthology. New York: Signet Books.

Carroll, J. C.
1980 "A cultural-consistency theory of family violence in Mexican-American and Jewish-ethnic groups." Chapter 5 in M. A. Straus and G. T. Hotaling (Eds.), The Social Causes of Husband-Wife violence. Minneapolis: University of Minnesota Press.

Caudill, W., and L. Frost
1973 "A comparison of maternal care and infant behavior in Japanese-American, American and Japanese families." Unpublished paper, National Institute of Mental Health, Bethesda, Maryland.

Chavis, W., and G. Lyles
1975 "Divorce among educated black women." Journal of the National Medical Association. 67 (March): 128–134.

Christensen, H. and L. Johnson
1978 "Premarital coitus and the southern black: a comparative view." Journal of Marriage and the Family 40 (November): 721–732.

Connor, J.
1974 "Acculturation and family continuities in three generations of Japanese Americans." Journal of Marriage and the Family 36 (February): 159–168.

Cromwell, V., and R. Cromwell
1978 "Perceived dominance in decision making and conflict resolution among black and Chicano couples." Journal of Marriage and the Family 40 (November): 749–759.

Dennis, R.
1976 "Theories of the black family: The weak-family and strong-family schools as competing ideologies." Journal of Afro-American Issues 4 (Summer/Fall): 315–328.

Diaz-Guerrero, R.
1975 Psychology of the Mexican: Culture and Personality. Austin: University of Texas Press.

Dickinson, G.
1975 "Dating behavior of black and white adolescents before and after desegregation." Journal of Marriage and the Family 37 (August): 602–608.

Eberstein, I., and W. P. Frisbie
1976 "Differences in marital stability among Mexican Americans, blacks and Anglos: 1960 and 1970." Social Problems 23 (June): 609–621.

Elkins, S.
1968 Slavery: A problem in American Institutional and Intellectual Life. Chicago: University of Chicago Press.

Farley, R.
1970 Growth of the Black Population. Chicago: Markham.

Fogel, W., and S. Engerman
1974 Time on the Cross. Boston: Little, Brown and Company.

Frazier, E. F.
1939 The Negro Family in the United States. Chicago: University of Chicago Press.

Furstenberg, R., Hershberg, T., and J. Modell
1975 "The origins of the female headed black family: The impact of the urban experience." Journal of Interdisciplinary History 5 (Spring): 211–233.

Genovese, E.
1974 Roll, Jordan, Roll. New York: Pantheon Press.

Gilbert, G. M.
1959 "Sex differences in mental health in a Mexican village." The International Journal of Social Psychiatry 3 (Winter): 208–213.

Goodman, M. E., and A. Beman
1971 "Child's-eye-views of life in an urban barrio." Pp. 109–122 in N. Wagner and M. Haug (Eds.). Chicanos: Social and Psychological Perspectives. St. Louis: C. V. Mosby Company.

Gordon, M.
1964 Assimilation in American Life. New York: Oxford University Press.

Grebler, L., Moore, J. W., and R. C. Guzman
1970 The Mexican American People. New York: The Free Press.

Gutman, H.
1976 The Black Family in Slavery and Freedom: 1750–1925. New York: Pantheon Books.

Halpern, F.
1973 Survival: Black/White. New York: Pergamon Press.

Hampton, R.
1979 "Husband's characteristics and marital disruption in black families." Sociological Quarterly (September): 255–266.

Hawkes, G., and M. Taylor
1975 "Power structure in Mexican and Mexican American farm labor families." Journal of Marriage and the Family 37 (November): 807–811.

Haynes, T., and L. Johnson
1980 "Changing perspectives on black families in empirical research: Selected journals: 1965–1979." Unpublished manuscript, Washington, D.C., The Urban Institute.

Heer, D.
1974   The prevalence of black-white marriage in the United States, 1960 and 1970." Journal of Marriage and the Family 35 (February): 246–258.
Heiss, J.
1975   The Case of the Black Family: A Sociological Inquiry. New York: Columbia University Press.
Heller, C.
1966   Mexican American Youth: Forgotten Youth at the Crossroads, New York: Random House.
Henriques, F.
1975   Children of Conflict: A Study of Interracial Sex and Marriage. New York: E. P. Hutton.
Hill, R.
1972   The Strengths of Black Families. New York: Emerson-Hall Publishers.
1977   Informal Adoption. Washington, D.C.: National Urban League Research Department.
Humphrey, H.
1944   "The changing structure of the Detroit Mexican family: An index of acculturation." American Sociological Review 9 (December): 622–626.
Johnson, C. L.
1977   "Interdependence, reciprocity and indebtedness: An analysis of Japanese American kinship relations." Journal of Marriage and the Family 39 (May): 351–364.
Jones, R. C.
1948   "Ethnic family patterns: The Mexican family in the United States." American Journal of Sociology 53 (May): 450–452.
Kikumura, A., and H. Kitano
1973   "Interracial marriage: A picture of the Japanese Americans." Journal of Social Issues 29 (Spring): 67–81.
Kagan S., and D. Valdez
in press   "Mexican American family research: A critical review and conceptual framework." De Colores.
Kiser, C.
1970   Demographic Aspects of the Black Community. New York: Milbank Memorial Fund.
Kitano, H.
1969   Japanese Americans: The Evolution of a Subculture. Englewood Cliffs, New Jersey: Prentice Hall.
Kuroda, Y., Suzuki, T., and C. Hayashi
1978   "A cross-national analysis of the Japanese character among Japanese-Americans in Honolulu." Ethnicity 5 (March): 45–59.
Ladner, J.
1971   Tomorrow's Tomorrow: The Black Woman. Garden City, New York: Doubleday.
Leonetti, D. L.
1978   "The biocultural pattern of Japanese-American fertility." Social Biology 25 (Spring): 38–5l.
Lieberman, L.
1973   "The emerging model of the black family." International Journal of Sociology of the Family 3 (March): 10–22.
Lyman, S.
1968   "Marriage and the family among Chinese immigrants to America. 1850–1960." Phylon 29 (Winter): 321–330.
Madsen, W.
1973   The Mexican-Americans of South Texas (2nd ed.). New York: Holt, Rinehart and Winston.
Mannheim, K.
1936   Ideology and Utopia. New York: Harcourt, Brace, and World.
Martin, E., and J. Martin
1978   The Black Extended Family. Chicago: University of Chicago Press.
McAdoo, H.
1978a   "Factors related to stability in upwardly mobile black families." Journal of Marriage and the Family 40 (November): 762–778.

1978b "Minority families." Pp. 177–195 in J. Stevens and M. Mathews (Eds.), Mother/Child, Father/Child Relationships. Washington, D.C.: National Association of Young Children.

Merton, R. K.
1972 "Insiders and outsiders: A chapter in the sociology of knowledge." American Journal of Sociology 78 (July): 9–48.

Miller, D.
1975 American Indian Socialization to Urban Life. San Francisco: Institute for Scientific Analysis.
1980 "The Native American family: The urban way." Pp. 441–484 in E. Corfman (Ed.), Families Today. Washington, D.C.: U.S. Government Printing Office.

Mirandé, A.
1977 "The Chicano family: A reanalysis of conflicting views." Journal of Marriage and the Family 39 (November): 747–756.
1979 "Machismo: A reinterpretation of male dominance in the Chicano family." The Family Coordinator 28 (October): 473–479.
in press "Machismo: Rucas, chingasos, y chingaderas." De Colores.

Momaday, N. S.
1976 The Names. New York: Harper and Row, Publishers.

Monahan, T.
1977 "Illegitimacy by race and mixture of race." International Journal of Sociology of the Family 7 (January–June): 45–54.

Montiel, M.
1970 "The social science myth of the Mexican American family." El Grito: A Journal of Contemporary Mexican American Thought 3 (Summer): 56–63.
1973 "The Chicano family: A review of research." Social Work 18 (March): 22–31.

Moynihan, D. P.
1965 The Negro Family: The Case for National Action. Washington, D.C.: U.S. Government Printing Office.

Murguia, E., and W. P. Frisbie
1977 "Trends in Mexican-American intermarriage: Recent findings in perspective." Social Science Quarterly 58 (December): 374–389.

Murillo, N.
1971 "The Mexican American family." Pp. 97–108 in N. Wagner and M. Haug (Eds.). Chicanos: Social and Psychological Perspectives. St. Louis: C. V. Mosby Company.

Myrdal, G.
1944 An American Dilemma. New York: Harper and Row, Publishers.

Noble, J.
1978 Beautiful, Also, Are the Souls of My Black Sisters: A History of the Black Woman in America. Englewood Cliffs, New Jersey: Prentice-Hall.

Nobles, W.
1978 "Toward an empirical and theoretical framework for defining black families." Journal of Marriage and the Family 40 (November): 679–698.

Padilla, A. M., Olmedo, S., and R. Perez
1978 "Hispanic mental health bibliography." Spanish Speaking Mental Health Research Center, University of California, Los Angeles, Monograph No. 6.

Parsons, T., and R. Bales
1955 Family, Socialization and Interaction Process. Glencoe, Illinois: The Free Press.

Paz, O.
1961 The Labyrinth of Solitude. New York: Grove.

Peñalosa, F.
1968 "Mexican family roles." Journal of Marriage and the Family 30 (November): 680–689.

Porter, J.
1979 Dating Habits of Young Black Americans. Dubuque, Iowa: Kendall Hunt.

Porterfield, E.
1977 Black and White Mixed Marriages. Chicago: Nelson-Hall.

Price, J.
  1976 "North American Indian families." Pp. 248–270 in C. Mindel and R. Habenstein (Eds.), Ethnic Families in America. New York: Elsevier.
Rainwater, L.
  1966 "The crucible of identity: The lower class Negro family." Daedalus 95 (Winter): 258–264.
Ramos, S.
  1962 Profile of Man and Culture in Mexico. Austin: University of Texas Press.
Redhorse, J. G., R. Lewis, M. Feit, and J. Decker
  1978 "Family behavior of urban American Indians." Social Casework 59 (Winter): 67–72.
  1979 "American Indian elders: Needs and aspirations in institutional and home health care." Unpublished manuscript, Arizona State University.
Romano, O. I.
  1973 "The anthropology and sociology of the Mexican Americans: The distortion of Mexican American history." Pp. 43–56 in O. Romano, (Ed.), Voices: Readings From El Grito. Berkeley: Quinto Sol Publications.
Rose, L.
  1980 The Black Woman. Beverly Hills: Sage Publications.
Rubel, A. L.
  1966 Across the Tracks: Mexican-Americans in a Texas City. Austin: University of Texas Press.
Rudoff, A.
  1971 "The incarcerated Mexican-American delinquent." Journal of Criminal Law, Criminology and Police Science 62 (June): 224–238.
Scanzoni, J.
  1971 The Black Family in Modern Society. Boston: Allyn and Bacon.
Shimkin, D., E. Shimkin, and D. Frate
  1978 The Extended Family in Black Societies. Chicago: Aldine Publishing Company.
Silverstein, B., and R. Krate
  1975 Children of the Dark Ghetto. New York: Praeger Publishing Company.
Stack, C.
  1974 All Our Kin. New York: Harper and Row, Publishers.
Staples, R.
  1971 "Towards a sociology of the black family: A theoretical and methodological assessment." Journal of Marriage and the Family 33 (February): 119–138.
  1973 "The Black Woman in America." Chicago: Nelson-Hall.
  1974 "The black family revisited: A review and a preview." Journal of Social and Behavioral Sciences 20 (Spring): 65–78.
  1976a Introduction to Black Sociology. New York: McGraw-Hill.
  1976 "Race and colonialism: The domestic case in theory and praxis." The Black Scholar 7 (June): 37–50.
  1978a "Mental health and black family life." Pp. 73–94 in L. Gary (Ed.), Mental Health: A Challenge to the Black Community. Philadelphia: Dorrance.
  1978b "Race, liberalism—conservatism and premarital sexual permissiveness: A biracial comparison." Journal of Marriage and the Family 40 (November): 78–92.
  in press The World of Black Singles: Changing Patterns of Male/Female Relations. Westport, Connecticut: Greenwood.
Stember, C.
  1976 Racial Sexism. New York: Elsevier.
Sotomayor, M.
  1971 "Mexican American interaction with social systems." Social Casework 52 (May): 316–322.
Sue, S., and H. Kitano
  1973 "Asian American stereotypes." Journal of Social Issues 29 (Spring): 83–98.
Tuck, R.
  1946 Not With the Fist. New York: Harcourt, Brace, and World.
U.S. Bureau of the Census

1974   "A study of selected socio-economic characteristics of ethnic minorities based on the 1970 Census. Vol. III. American Indians." Washington, D.C.: U.S. Government Printing Office.
1978   "Persons of Spanish origin in the United States: March, 1977." Series p-20, No. 329. Washington, D.C.: U.S. Government Printing Office.
1979   "The social and economic status of the black population in the United States: An historical view, 1790–1978." Series p-28, No. 80. Washington, D.C.: U.S. Government Printing Office.

U.S. Department of Commerce
1978   "U.S. Spanish origin population now 12 million census survey shows." August 21, Washington, D.C.: Commerce News.

U.S. Department of Health, Education, and Welfare
1980   "Health status of minorities and low-income groups." Washington, D.C.: U.S. Government Printing Office.

Unger, S.
1977   The Destruction of American Indian Families. New York: Association on American Indian Affairs.

Wallace, M.
1979   Black Macho and the Myth of the Super Woman. New York: Dial Publishing.

Wax, M. L.
1971   Indian Americans: Unity and Diversity. Englewood Cliffs, New Jersey: Prentice-Hall.

Weiss, M.
1970   "Selective acculturation and the dating process: The patterning of Chinese-Caucasian interracial dating." Journal of Marriage and the Family 32 (May): 273–278.

Willie, C.V.
1976   A New Look at Black Families. Bayside, New York: General Hall.

Witt, S. W.
1974   "Native women today." Civil Rights Digest 6 (Spring): 30–34.

Wong, L.
1976   "The Chinese experience: From yellow peril to model minority." Journal of Social Issues 9 (Fall): 33–41.

Ybarra, L.
1977   "Conjugal role relationships in the Chicano family." Unpublished doctoral dissertation. University of California.
in press
       "Marital decision-making and the role of machismo in the Chicano family." De Colores.

Yamauchi, J. S.
1979   "Asian American communications: The women's self-concept and cultural accommodations." Paper presented at the conference on the Minority Woman in America. San Francisco (March).

Changing Patterns of Aging and Family Bonds in Later Life

Beth B. Hess and Joan M. Waring

Family sociology has gained in sophistication from developments in related disciplines. For example, research by historians of the family has put to rest, at last, the "classical family of Western nostalgia" (Goode, 1963). Unfortunately, this mythical family does not rest in peace, but inhabits the consciousness of the general public with a wondrous tenacity.

The use of the cohort analysis in the study of social change or continutiy directs attention to the changing characteristics of specific age cohorts or generations not only as they move through their life course but also among successive cohorts in a particular society. Both foci warn us against generalizations regarding parent-child relations as fixed. Intergenerational relationships must be studied in historical context, especially in terms of the linkages between family and other institutional spheres as these undergo continual change.

While we may never disabuse the general public of the notion that there once was a time in which the extended family reigned supreme—and, more importantly, that mutual respect and satisfaction governed adult child/aged parent interaction—we must, as family sociologists and practitioners, take an unromanticized view of intergenerational relations at the distal end of the life course. The question usually asked of this topic is "how can such bonds be strengthened?" The one we propose here is "why have any such bonds persisted?"

The modern family is characterized by choice: whom to marry, where to live, how to earn a living, how many children to bear, and, increasingly, how to conduct interpersonal relations and allocate tasks within the nuclear family. As we move from the family of obligatory ties to one of voluntary bonds, relationships outside the nuclear unit similarly lose whatever normative certainty or consistency governed them at earlier times. For example, sibling relationships today are almost completely voluntary, subject to disruption through occupational and geographic mobility, as, indeed, it might be said of marriage itself. Is this also to be the fate of parent-offspring ties in later life? There are many indicators of growing distance between generations, especially so in later life. Thre are also clues to enduring qualities of the parent/child bond. We shall examine the most important of these forces—centripetal and centrifugal—at both the societal and familial levels.

From *Family Coordinator* (October 1978), pp. 304–314. Copyrighted 1978 by the National Council on Family Relations. Reprinted by permission.

Societal Level Processes

Social-Historical Change

Family studies often have concentrated exclusively on the effects of world-wide social trends for young people. Goode's (1963) influential analysis of the "world revolution" in family systems is, for example, basically concerned with the freedom of younger generations, although he does make note of the potential dysfunctions for older family members. But a change in one part of a system has ramifications for other parts; thus, if respect for parents and the obligation to care for elders once was based upon their control of resources, reinforced by religious tradition and normative sanction, then the increasing ability of younger members to determine their own fates in marriage and in work must necessarily reduce the power of elders to demand filial piety. Nonetheless, filial responsibility is often mandated in the law, if not fully realized in practice (Schorr, Note 1; Brody, 1970, for a decade comparison).

The choices which we consider our birthright and that of our children, today, are at the expense of claims on care from our offspring many decades later. Recognition of this dilemma may be one of the compelling forces behind another trend in modern nation states—toward the public assumption of responsibility for income maintenance and primary health care of the aged. In many developed countries, transportation, housing and recreation have also been provided through allocation of societal rather than familial resources. The trade-off is evident: removing claims from the interpersonal system achieves the same aims which Weber (1958) suggests for bureaucracy over nepotism.

Considerations of kinship give way to impersonal but theoretically fairer mechanisms of allocation, "without fear or favor." Although the politically conservative might perceive a usurpation of family obligations, these trends in no way preclude high levels of kin caring for those families willing and able to do so. Yet public programs do ensure that all old people will be taken care of, albeit minimally in many cases, thus removing a financial (and often emotional) burden from both generations. Intergenerational hostility will most likely be muted by transposing this issue to the societal level, so that family ties are strengthened rather than attenuated: an extremely difficult concept to convey to members of a society which idealizes family life. To the extent that practitioners and educators share the public value orientation that families should take care of their own, the myth of the extended family will continue to generate unnecessary levels of guilt among middle-aged children, and resentment among their parent(s).

Cohort Differences

The model for cohort analysis follows the life course of successive birth aggregates, thus allowing us to distinguish (though never perfectly) historical from biographical from aging effects. Several points are immediately apparent: at any one historical moment, cohorts are of different ages. At the same ages, each is in a different historical epoch. And closer analysis will indicate that cohorts vary in their original composition, in fertility and mortality, in life course experiences such as educational and occupational opportunities, and ultimately in the needs and resources they bring to old age.

Before comparing today's oldest cohorts (those 65 with those of their off-spring, we should note the overriding significance of one *similarity*: aged parents and their children are both adults. This means, first, that they are to be considered status equals; and, second, that each is the product of decades of living outside the daily orbit of the other. Moreover, in our society, primary loyalties in adulthood are to the conjugal rather than the consanguine bond. Parent-child relationships in later life are, for the most part, negotiated from positions of independence vis-à-vis the other, and may, during adulthood, actually resemble those of friendship formation and maintenance, what Goode (1963) refers to as "ascriptive friendships," more than the family model of earlier stages with its imbalance in power and emotional dependencies. In extreme old age or illness, of course, the parent may be placed in a position of dependence upon a caretaking offspring, a "role reversal" often difficult for both parties to accept or enact appropriately (Blau, 1973; Simos, 1970). In this respect, Arling (1976) found that friendships are even more important than contacts with grown children for high morale in old age, and for precisely the reasons we suggest: cohort and life state differences between generations, and intra-cohort similarities.

Age and Life Stage Differences

Differences in age mean differences in life stage concerns and exigencies, which, for example, are reflected in considerations of *life space*. The middle-aged male in our society is often portrayed as overburdened with commitments to family, work and community. Many are caught in a "life cycle squeeze" when earnings have peaked while expenses continue to rise, especially if there are college-age children to be educated (Oppenheimer, 1974).

Goode (1960) has analyzed the "role strain" arising from simultaneous demands placed on status-incumbents by role partners, and Brim (1976) speaks of a male "mid-life crisis" as social, economic and biological stresses accumulate. At this point, to deal also with the needs of an aging parent for time, energy, care or financial assistance can only exacerbate the strain. Typically, the beleaguered male could delegate kinkeeping tasks to his wife, freed of her own child-rearing responsibilities, and considered to be the family specialist in interpersonal relations. But no more may she be thus taken for granted. College enrollment (U.S. Dept. of Labor, Note 2) and labor force participation rates of middle-aged women have risen dramatically in the past decade (U.S. Dept. of Labor, Note 3). It is possible that her plans remain somewhat tentative, however, inhibited by the knowledge that an ailing parent or adult child experiencing some setback may require her attention.

Conversely, the aged parents experience a constriction of life space—a spouse or friends die, work-place contacts are given up, neighborhoods are less hospitable than before, energies flag, the body becomes recalcitrant. Needs increase as resources decline. Schooled in independence and self-sufficiency, it is difficult for many old people to place demands upon adult children, especially if they are aware that such needs will conflict with those of grandchildren. Once again, intergenerational tensions are reduced by shifting the offspring's responsibility from the filial to the citizen role. By the same token, with the state rather than the family as caretaker, the recipient of retirement income and health care can define such entitlements as a right of citizenship. However, as one anonymous referee of this paper noted, we are assuming continuing expansion of the economy. Under conditions of contraction and scarcity, the maintenance of nucleated households becomes problematic, with what we would predict to be very stressful outcomes in many cases (including increased incidence of "parent abuse" [Steinmetz, Note 4]).

Differences in Cohorts as Populations

The two age groups of interest here also vary greatly in original composition. Among those who are older Americans today are large numbers of foreign-born, or individuals who grew up on farms and villages here as well as abroad, with less than high school education and a high probability of relatively low-skill employment. Many may have lingering expectations of intrafamily caretaking (Seelbach & Sauer, Note 5), while others are ill adapted to coping with urban life (Lopata, 1973). But most will have internalized the great American virtues of independence and self-reliance, and consider making a home with an adult child only as last resort (Riley & Foner, 1968; National Council on Aging, Note 6; Sussman, Vanderwyst & Williams, Note 7) yet would call for assistance upon a child rather than a friend or neighbor (Berghorn, Schaefer, Steer & Wisemen, 1977).

Their children, on the other hand, are primarily native-born, at least high school educated, beneficiaries of an expanding economy in the post-war era, and examplars of urban or suburban family life. Where the older generation had experienced uprootedness, the Great Depression and other social instabilities of the 1930's, with a consequent low fertility rate, their offspring knew the Depression only as youngsters, and came to adulthood in time to participate in the Second World War, to enjoy the benefits of the GI Bill for further education, to marry and proceed to produce a bumper crop of infants, and to take advantage of the opportunities for geographic and occupational mobility which characterized their young adulthood.

When these mature adults reach old age in the coming decades they will have greater resources—personal and economic—than do their parents for coping with social change, the bureaucracy, and their own physical decrements. Further, they will have more children for whatever benefits can be derived from intergenerational contact. It would seem from the foregoing that a very large "generation gap" could exist between these cohorts today, potentially wider than that between these middle-aged parents and their own young adult children.

As demographic aggregates, birth cohorts not only vary in the characteristics just noted, but also in terms of original size, fertility and differential mortality. The size of any cohort is determined by three processes: fertility, mortality and migration, and all three of these have changed dramatically throughout this century. The experience of cohort members will vary accordingly—family size, dependency ratios, mobility opportunities, life expectancy and probability of institutionalization in old age are contingencies which ultimately affect individual lives (Waring, 1975).

The relative size of age cohorts exerts one of its most obvious effects on the ratios of wage earners to "dependents," namely children and the aged. As already mentioned, today's middle aged are small in number with many children and surviving parents. Cohorts differ in life expectancy at various ages, and in the sex ratio of these survivors, with female life expectancy continuing to diverge from that of males even as life styles are converging. The probability today is that the "dependent" older population as a whole will remain a constant 10–11% through the remainder of this century. But when the "baby boom" contingent reaches old age in the next century, proportions of old people will rise to 15–17% in the 2020's and 2030's (Seigel, Note 8). These shifting percentages place differential burdens on family members and on the society as a whole, but they also translate into political influence as well as the possibility of intergenerational conflict.

And lastly, the process of aging itself has changed over time—the ages at which roles are assumed or relinquished, health and income status, and self definitions. When is one "old," what is it to be old, how does one behave as an older person? Members of different cohorts will answer these questions differently, largely as a consequence of the cohort's experience and current situation. With respect to family interaction in later life, the primary question is "what are the appropriate modes of relating across generations?" Once the query is posed, the lack of a simple ready answer is striking. It is in this sense that we speak of a shift from obligatory to voluntary bonds, to a set of relationships which depend upon mutual initiative and persistence. The contact must be rewarding in some fashion for both parties to agree to its maintenance over time. Not only is the family context changed, but so are aging and old people. One might well reverse the theme of this volume and discuss "The Family in a Changing Context of Aging."

Family Level Processes

Factors Which Inhibit Generational Contacts

While residential and social mobility have not staunched the flow of help between generations, they have contributed to generating "distance" between adult children and their aged parents (Adams, 1970; but cf. Glasser & Glasser, 1962). It is noteworthy that four-fifths of all old parents live within easy visiting range of one child, but these researchers seldom tell us how many children live near their parents. Opportunities for helping may also decline because there is no need to call upon kin for *basic maintenance* (although socioemotional needs remain). That is, Social Security, Medicare and other programs free the older generation from potential dependency or even intimations of material need. Moreover, large numbers of old people value greatly their independence, preferring to live alone until they can no longer do so. There are no more grounds for assuming that older parents wish to live with their adult children than for believing that the middle aged regularly "dump" unwanted parents into institutions.

If parent-child interaction in later life resembles more the process of friendship than that of earlier intrafamily relations, relying upon similarities of values and attitudes leading to liking and the wish for more contact, i.e., homophily (Lazarsfeld & Merton, 1954; Hess, 1972), then the kinds of age and cohort differences discussed above should operate to reduce agreement and attraction between generations. Nonetheless, many similarities result from family socialization and stability of socio-economic status within the lineage. Extent of value agreement might differentiate those children who maintain contact from those who do not, but much of our data is biased by not having measures from all family members.

Another source of intergenerational tension, rarely mentioned in the gerontological literature, are the residues of those earlier conflicts which dominate studies of childhood and adolescence. Can relationships originally founded on disparities of power easily evolve into those based upon mutual respect? What of the rivalries and hostilities engendered during the oedipal phase? And, as the aged parent experiences the inevitable decrements of old age, how graciously can the adult child assume the "parental" role of caretaking? Injunctions to "filial maturity" (Blenkner, 1965; Troll, 1971) notwithstanding, the barriers are considerable (Simos, 1970; Kent & Matson, 1972; Miller, Bernstein & Sharkey, 1975; Clark & Anderson, 1967). Contrary to public perception, most adult offspring make every effort to maintain a declining parent in the community (and often in the child's home) before seeking institutionalization (Riley & Foner, 1968). Such efforts are at the expense of alternative investments of time and energy and finances, which cannot be entirely void of resentment, although ameliorated by a sense of sacrifice in having "honored thy father and mother,"[1] and, in many cases, thy mother-in-law as well.

These various sources of intergenerational distance probably "explain" the trend toward independent residence and the repeated assertions of old people that they prefer it that way. The percentage of aged parents making a home with an adult offspring has steadily declined, while the proportions living as one-person households has risen commensurately (Kobrin, 1976; Siegel, Note 8). Thus, when an old person does move in with the child, she or he is apt to be quite ancient, frail or disoriented. There is, understandably, some ambivalence on the part of the adult offspring to undertake such a responsibility (Wake & Sporakowski, 1972; Fendetti & Gelfand, 1976; Sussman, Vanderwyst & Williams, Note 7).

A final consideration in this section has to do with transitions. Later life is characterized by a number of status passages, most of a decremental nature: post-parenthood, retirement, widowhood. While presenting opportunities for personal growth, these are also periods of difficult adjustment. Those undergoing transition often look to other family members for support in managing the strains of relinquishing an old role and learning a new one. But often family members are disappointing sources of support, absorbed as they are in their own problems. For example, both generations may be undergoing difficult transitions simultaneously, as when a parent reaches retirement at the same time the offspring faces an empty nest. Or both could be responding to the same loss in different ways, as when the death of a spouse for the parent is also the death of a parent for the child. In addition, an event may require of role partners a "counterpart transition," whereby family members must learn to relate to the other in terms of the new role, not always an easy task (Riley & Waring, 1976). Such complex demands may prevent meeting the needs of the other; but, on the other hand, becoming a source of strength to one another should help both in dealing with personal loss. This is illustrative of Erikson's (1959) discussion of "self-absorption" vs. "generativity," in which reaching out to help the other is defined as the "positive" outcome. It is characteristic of the later years that there are many such challenges and that some of these will strain the bonds between family members (Waring, Note 9). For example, remarriage of the parent often leads to generational strain—from fears of losing an inheritance, inability to perceive the parent as sexually active, or beliefs that he or she is being exploited. Once the remarriage has taken place, however, the offspring typically appreciate its positive aspects (McKain, 1972; Treas & Van Hilst, Note 10).

We have discussed some of the more obvious elements tending to inhibit intergenerational contacts: mobility, declining opportunities for helping, age

---

[1] We are indebted to Mildred Seltzer for pointing out that this injunction itself suggests that people needed to be reminded, under extreme sanction, of their duties—an ideal rather than a reflection of intergenerational relations in the earliest historical societies as well as contemporary ones.

and cohort differences in attitudes and values, psychological barriers to closeness, desires for independence, and difficulties in coping with life-course transitions. In the absence of any pressing need to maintain the relationship, how are these impediments overcome by so many—and why?

Factors Which Enhance Intergenerational Bonds

It has been argued by anthropologists that the giving of a gift or favor obligates the recipient to return something of equal value, generating social ties among individuals and groups (Levi-Strauss, 1964). Gouldner (1960) speaks of the Norm of Reciprocity, and Sussman (1976) of an implicit bargain struck with parents during the years of the infant's dependency. The parental investment in the child's survival does create, at some level, a sense of obligation on the part of the child when grown to care for an ailing parent. Guilt and anxiety over one's performance as a dutiful offspring operate as a form of social control (Simos, 1970). The reactions of others—siblings, social work and medical personnel, neighbors, friends—reinforce the norms of filial piety.

Solidarity within lineages is supported by many aspects of socialization: the transmission of values across the generations, moral and religious upbringing, role modeling, and the continued flow of information among members of different age groups. There are powerful forces toward congruence, if not complete agreement, in value orientation within familes (Troll, 1971; Bengtson, 1975; Jacobsen, Berry & Olsen, 1975; Hill, 1970; Kalish & Johnson, 1972; Bengtson & Acock, Note 11). However, some of this apparent harmony may be an artifact of selective perception or lack of data from offspring not in contact with parents. Bengtson and Kuypers (1971) suggest that some distortion arises from the "developmental stake" which old people have in minimizing value disagreement but which junior members of the family will emphasize in order to preserve their self-image as unique. Yet despite the many real and apparent potentials for value dissonance, most families appear to have developed a "tent of values" (Jacobsen, Berry & Olsen, 1975) under which members can meet, enjoy one another's company, share a consciousness of sameness and sense of responsibility for one another.

Socialization involves both direct transmission of expectations for behavior and the indirect learning which is conveyed through role modeling. For example, middle-aged parents caring for an aged relative can hope their own children will observe, record and repeat this behavior in due time, as protection against abandonment in their old age. As a socializing force, role modeling in later life cuts both ways. The aged parent is often coping with situations which will one day be the lot of the adult child, and the latter is attempting to demonstrate ways of gracious aging for the older parent to emulate (e.g., staying youthful). The role modeling efforts of both are complicated by the fact that there are few appropriate role models from previous generations regarding how to grow old or be old.

The exchange of visits and gifts across generations also serves to connect and reaffirm the viability of a lineage. The two- and three-way transfer of gifts, advice, help in emergencies, goods and services is amply documented (Sussman, 1976; Riley & Foner, 1968; Hill, 1970; Cantor, 1975; National Council on Aging, Note 6; Jackson, 1972). There is a "family network" if not precisely a "modified extended family," and it is based upon *voluntary* exchanges, with the amount and direction of flow affected by the relative resources at the disposal of generations. Among the inner city poor, for example, aged parents receive material support from adult children in return for services such as baby sitting or advice (Cantor, Note 12). In more affluent lineages, money and goods are distributed from the oldest generation downward through gifts and inheritance, while the younger members reciprocate with visits and services (Sussman, Cates & Smith, 1970). Two caveats are in order: (a) most adult children (a majority in a recent Social Security Administration survey [Murray, Note 13] provide no material support to parents, and (b) there is no *necessary* relationship between these expressions of solidarity and positive affect (Arling, 1976; Brown, 1969; Berghorn et al., 1977), although some have found such a link (e.g., Adams, 1975; Medley, 1976). A respect for privacy and tactful assessment of the relationship may well govern visiting patterns (Aldous, 1967; Stinnett, Collins & Montgomery, 1970).

Nor can we assume that those who voluntarily establish multi-generation households do so without strain. To the contrary, when independent households are preferred by old and young (see above), sharing a home is a "last resort"—literally—and those who do so may not be in the best of health or spirits. On the other hand, when undertaken out of genuine affection as a freely chosen and well though-out alternative, multi-generation living can be mutually beneficial (e.g., Lynn, 1976). We would expect that such arrangements in the future will be of this nature, given the characteristics of incoming cohorts of old people already noted. For this cohort, however, practitioners should be aware of the peculiar historical circumstances which have shaped the needs and resources of members of both adult generations.

While some of the tasks which traditionally linked generations have become attenuated or obsolete, Kreps (1977) and others in the volume by Shanas and Sussman (1977) have noted the development of a new set of functions for family members: negotiating the bureaucracy and supervising the terminal phases of life. The adult offspring become the guides and interpreters of the administratively arcane, interceding on behalf of the aged parent, securing entitlements, and ultimately making judgments regarding institutionalization and heroic efforts at preserving life. The impersonal must ultimately be made personal. How ironic if this should be the source of a new-found closeness between parent and child in later life. Yet this may be precisely where educators and practitioners could also intercede effectively, offering support and proffering understanding.

Intergenerational Relations and Later Life Satisfaction

Given these varied sources of strain and solidarity at both the societal and interpersonal levels, our frank conclusion is that few conclusive statements can be made at this time. Not that we lack research but that there are no clear-cut patterns readily discernable yet. There are simply (or not so simply) too many vicissitudes to take into account. It would appear logical to state that elderly parents with many offspring should have greater resources for later life satisfaction than do those with a limited supply of family, but the data are equivocal. Some parents with large families, often the foreign-born with "extended expectations," will be disappointed at the unwillingness or inability of children to meet such claims (Lopata, 1973, 1976). Even when such expectations are met some will remain resentful at having to feel like "guests" in the child's home (Cosneck, 1970).

What, then, do adult children contribute to parental well-being in later life? This whole question is clouded by methodological considerations: studies vary greatly in their sampling techniques, the questions asked, and the measurements utilized. Above all, the problem of selective survival intrudes (Spanier, Lewis & Cole, 1975); the only people able and willing to answer such questions are the survivors of a birth cohort whose poorer, less educated, less healthy and perhaps less happy members have already died off. Studies of life satisfaction among the aged may simply be measuring the qualities which have allowed certain subgroups to survive to answer the questionnaire.

Thus, we find Medley (1976, p. 448) declaring that "satisfaction with family was found to make the greatest single impact on life satisfaction" of old people, while finances had no direct impact. Edwards and Klemmack (1973), on the other hand, found that SES washed out other effects; similarly, Spreitzer and Snyder (1974) pinpoint perceived health status (as well as financial position). Sears and Barbee (1977), studying Terman's sample of gifted women in their middle years, find that children are related to one measure of life satisfaction for some women, but that childfree career women do very well on a variety of aspects of life satisfaction (see also Campbell, Converse & Rodgers, 1976). With incoming cohorts of older women being higher than those now old on *both* fertility and work experience, we might predict that life satisfaction of older females will be enhanced. Since males still typically define themselves in terms of occupation rather than family roles, their life satisfaction in old age should be minimally affected by intergenerational resources, which is the finding of Watson and Kivett (1976).

Whether or not children add much more to life satisfaction than does health or financial status, we do know that the absence of family can often have deleterious effects. Old men without family ties are prime candidates for suicide, accidental death, alcoholism and other socially generated diseases (Gove, 1973; Bock & Webber, 1972). There is evidence that older females are somewhat preserved by their ability to seek out and maintain close friends when family ties have disintegrated (Hess, Note 14).

Regarding the relationship between non-family networks—neighborhood, friendship and voluntary association participation—and family integration the evidence is conflicting and complex (Hess, 1972). Some find integration into community life more related to friendship than to family networks (Spakes, Note 15), and others note that respondents living alone, without strong family ties or opportunity to play traditional family roles, tend to compensate through community activity (Trela & Jackson, Note 16; see also Rutzen, Note 17). This pattern of dependency on family vs. friends or neighbors was also found among old people in Kansas City: where relatives were nearby, especially children, one depended upon these when necessary, but where no children lived in the area, old people were likely to depend upon friends and neighbors when in need (Berghorn et al., 1977). The researchers relate these patterns to a cultural level aversion to dependency of any sort in our society, but when it does become necessary, dependency on children carries the least stigma, and may even be justified by invoking the norms of reciprocity and filial piety which are also part of the value system.

Still other studies show that persons with high levels of kin interaction are also high interactors with non-kin, and those with low rates of contact with relatives have similarly depressed investments in other social networks (Booth, 1972; Biesty, DiComo & Hess, Note 18; Croog, Lipson & Levine, 1972). Clearly, there is no simple relationship between family and other social networks: some people will be high or low interactors with anybody; others compensate for losses in one area with enhanced involvement in different groups. Such substitutability, however, may be governed by considerations of functional alternatives; that is, various networks operate to meet certain kinds of needs, so that there are limits to how these can be mixed and matched (Weiss, 1969; Litwak & Szelenyi, 1969). In some cases, moreover, integration into non-family social systems—friendships, voluntary associations, neighborhood, even senior centers—is preferable to total dependence upon a spouse, for if that one person should die the survivor is, indeed, bereft (Bock & Webber, 1972; Rutzen, Note 17).

Much as children and non-family associations add to the life satisfaction of some old people, there is considerable evidence that for those elderly with surviving spouses the martal relationship not only remains paramount but is enhanced by the children's leaving after adolescence. Possibly, there was nowhere for scores of marital satisfaction to go except up since families with adolescent children do show signs of stress (Burr, 1970; Rollins & Feldman, 1970; Renne, 1970; Smart & Smart, 1975; Gilford & Bengtson, Note 19; Miller, 1976). If the presence of teen-age children strains the resources and emotional energies of mid-life parents, postparenthood offers relief which is reflected in satisfaction scores (e.g., Neugarten, 1976). But an additional benefit of the absence of children is the potential for an increase in couple-companionate activities (Miller, 1976; Rollins & Cannon, 1974). The literature on postparental marriages indicates a turning again toward one another for companionship and psychic satisfaction often described as comparable to that of the honeymoon period. However, it must be noted that selective processes have been operating. These are not static relationships—the marriage and the partners themselves have changed over time; efforts at enrichment have been made, experiences shared, tolerance deepened. Couples unable to adapt or develop in these directions drop out of the data base via divorce, desertion or separation. The very poor, whose marital satisfaction is highly problematic, have lower life expectancy as well, further reducing the probability of their experiencing long-term intact marriages (Spanier, Lewis & Cole, 1975).

Not only will selective survival of certain marriages bias the findings on later life satisfaction, perceptual processes may further distort the data. Spanier, Lewis and Cole (1975) note that the longer a couple has remained together, the greater their investment in believing that the commitment has been worthwhile, the less likely to acknowledge threats, and the more apt to reduce dissonance by denying unhappiness. Whatever the forces at work, the end result seems to be that many marriages are strengthened by the departure of offspring and that the conjugal relationship is enhanced and deepened at this time. For the couples who jointly survive, through middle age and later, there is also evidence of a "coming together" of personality traits among postparental spouses (Livson, Note 20): i.e., a relaxing of rigid sex role expectations and behaviors, and a growing acceptance of previously inappropriate tendencies such as nurturance for men and dominance by women (see also Lowenthal, Thurnher & Chiriboga, 1975; Brim, 1976; Neugarten, 1968; Clausen, 1972). A "mellowing"—in every sense of the word—seems to infuse these relationships as the spouses relax from the rigors of rearing children and striving for occupational success. Of course, many couples grow further apart at this stage if a shared interest in the children has been the only bond, but there is no clear evidence of a surge of divorces (Schoen, 1975).

Unfortunately, the facts of later life are that many older women will not be members of a conjugal unit. While widows seem to cope with loss of a spouse less lethally than do widowers, they do not share the high morale of still married. As with measures of life satisfaction and morale applied to postparental couples, the widowed are also affected by non-family variables such as health, education and income (Lopata, 1973; Chevan & Korson, 1972; Morgan, 1976; Cosneck, 1970; Adams, 1968). The role of children in the life space of a widowed parent can be minimal or all-embracing as in the case of sharing a home, and there will be happy and unhappy old people in both categories. However, the existence of adult children with whom one could make a home *is* a hedge against institutionalization (Soldo & Myers, Note 21). We might speculate, however, that in the future, women who limit fertility or choose to remain childfree will also have high educational attainment, retirement incomes from life-time work, and out-going relationships in a variety of non-family systems, and thus reduce the differences in old-age resources between women with many children and those with few or none. In other words, the preservative value of children may become less marked as the life course of women changes.

Conclusion

We began our exploration of intergenerational relations in later life by asking a basic, if impertinent, question, "why do they persist?" We think that the evidence suggests that the maintenance and sustenance of the parent/child bond will be increasingly based upon the willingness of both parties to engage in supportive behaviors, and that this willingness, in turn, hinges on the quality of the relationship over many preceding decades. While guilt and shame will remain powerful motivators of filial performance, and the injunction to "honor thy father and mother" continues to shape our socialization to obligations toward aged parents, the actual course of contacts and the satisfactions derived from them will be subject to the same type of role negotiation characterizing other interpersonal relationships. As a consequence, such variables as basic trust, respect, shared values and beliefs, and genuine affection—the foundations of homophily—will increasingly determine parent/child relations in later life.

The foundation of such a relationship can, of course, be laid in the early years of infancy and childhood dependency, or fostered by the skill with which the generations negotiate an ultimate release from these dependencies. But it is also possible that parents and offspring who were never deeply affectionate at earlier life stages can develop a mutual respect and liking when both are freed from relations of superordination/subordination. Although much of the literature deals with a "special relationship" between older women and their adult daughters (Neugarten, 1968), we would guess that the adult male child might also find his father easier to talk to and get along with after leaving the parental home and becoming a "man" in his own right, free of the need to compete with the father on the latter's own ground.

Trends at both the societal and familial level support our contention that parent and child relations in later life are moving toward the voluntaristic model. Demographically, compared with those now old, incoming cohorts of old people will be more independent financially, better educated, with higher probabilities of joint survival after completion of parental tasks. In terms of attitudes toward family responsibilities, there is evidence that extended expectations of care from one's children (Espenshade, Note 22; Yankelovich, Skelly & White, 1977).

Family life educators and practitioners, looking ahead, might speculate on what such changes portend. Our guesses are that older women, especially, will be affected by the trends noted above, and although widowhood will remain the fate of most, those qualities that enhance independent living and adaptation to loss will increasingly characterize their lives: education, work experience, financial security and lifelong involvement in non-family associations. As for older men, there is some evidence that family roles and leisure activities are encroaching on the time and energies previously expended in the occupational sphere. In old age, these men will have alternative sources of satisfaction, and, possibly, more companionate relationships with their wives than do men currently retired. Aging parents will not have to make demands upon the material or social resources of offspring, although many may do so. Adult children will be spared excruciating choices between the needs of their own children, themselves, and their parents. And those bonds which do persist will do so because they have been willingly sought and nurtured by adults who are authentically concerned with the well-being of one another. Far from disintegrating, the future of parent-child relations in later life may be characterized by the strongest ties of all: mutual respect.

Reference Notes

1 Schorr, A. Filial responsibility in the modern American family. Social Security Administration, DHEW, USGPO, Washington, D.C. 20402, 1960.

2. U.S. Department of Labor. *Marital and family characteristics of the labor force,* March, 1975. Special Labor Force Report 183, Bureau of Labor Statistics, Washington, D.C., 1975.

3. U.S. Department of Labor. *Going back to school at 35 and over.* Special Labor Force Report 184, Bureau of Labor Statistics, Washington, D.C., 1975.

4. Steinmetz, S. *The politics of selective inattention: The case of parent abuse.* Unpublished working paper, University of Delaware, 1978.

5. Seelbach, W., & Sauer, W. *Filial responsibility expectations and morale among aged parents.* Paper presented at the annual meeting of the Gerontological Society, New York City, October, 1976.

6. National Council on the Aging. *The myth and reality of aging in America.* 1974.

7. Sussman, M. B., Vanderwyst, D., & Williams, G. K. *Will you still need me, will you still feed me when I'm 64?* Paper presented at the annual meeting of the Gerontological Society, New York City, October, 1976.

8. Siegel, J. S. *Demographic aspects of aging and the older population in the United States.* Current Population Reports, Special Studies, Series P-23, No. 59, USGPO, Washington, D.C. 20402: U.S. Department of Commerce, Bureau of the Census, May, 1976.

9. Waring, J. M. *Conflict between the middle aged and old: Why not?* Paper presented at the annual meeting of the American Sociological Association, San Francisco, August, 1975.

10. Treas, J., & Van Hilst, A. *Marriage and remarriage among the older population.* Paper presented at the annual meeting of the Gerontological Society, Louisville, 1975.

11. Bengtson, V. L., & Vcock, A. G. *On the influence of mothers and fathers: A covariance analysis of political and religious socialization.* Paper presented at the annual meeting of the American Sociological Society, New York, August, 1976.

12. Cantor, M. *The configuration and intensity of the informal support system in a New York City elderly population.* Paper presented at the annual meeting of the Gerontological Society, New York, October, 1976.

13. Murray, J. *Family structure in the pre-retirement years.* (Retirement History Study Report #4.) U.S. Dept. HEW, Social Security Administration, Publication No. (SSA) 74-11700 USGPO, Washington, D.C. 20402, 1973.

14. Hess, B. B. *Age, gender role and friendship.* Paper presented at annual meeting of the Gerontological Society, New York, October, 1976.

15. Spakes, P. *Social integration, age, and family participation.* Paper presented at the annual meeting of the Gerontological Society, New York, October, 1976.

16. Trela, J. E., & Jackson, D. *Family life and substitutes in old age.* Paper presented at the annual meeting of the Gerontological Society, New York, 1976.
17. Rutzen, R. *Varieties of social disengagement among the aged: A research report on correlates of primary socialization.* Paper presented at the annual meeting of the Eastern Sociological Society, New York City, March, 1977.
18. Biesty, P., DiComo, W., & Hess, B. B. *The elderly of Morris County, New Jersey: Findings of a senior citizens assessment of needs (SCAN) survey.* Mimeo. Morristown, N.J., Area Agency on Aging, 1977.
19. Gilford, R., & Bengtson, V. L. *Measuring marital satisfaction in three generations: Positive and negative dimensions.* Paper presented at the Gerontological Society, New York, October, 1976.
20. Livson, F. B. *Coming together in the middle years: A longitudinal study of sex role convergence.* Paper presented at the annual meeting of the Gerontological Society, New York, October, 1976.
21. Soldo, B. J., & Myers, G. C. *The effects of total fertility on living arrangements among elderly women.* Paper presented at the annual meeting of the Gerontological Society, New York, October, 1976.
22. Espanshade, T. J. *The value and cost of children.* Bulletin of the Population Reference Bureau, Inc. Washington, D.C., 32, 1977.

References

Adams, B. N. The middle-class adult and his widowed or still-married mother. *Social Problems,* 1968, 16, 50–59.

Adams, B. N. *The family: A sociological interpretation* (2nd ed.). Chicago: Rand McNally, 197

Adams, B. N. Isolation, function and beyond: American kinship in the 1960's. *Journal of Marriage and the Family,* 1970, 32, 575–597.

Aldous, J. Intergenerational visiting patterns: Variations in boundary maintenance as an explanation. *Family Process,* 1967, 6, 235–251.

Arling, G. The elderly widow and her family, neighbors and friends. *Journal of Marriage and the Family,* 1976, 38, 757–768.

Bengtson, V. L., & Kuypers, J. A. Generational differences and the developmental stake. *Aging and Human Development,* 1971, 2, 249–260.

Bergtson, V. L. Generation and family effects in value socialization. *American Sociological Review,* 1975, 40, 358–371.

Berghorn, F. L., Schafer, D. E., Steere, G. H., & Wiseman, R. F. *The urban elderly: A study of life satisfaction.* Montclair, N.J.: Allenheld Osman, 1977.

Blau, Z. S. *Old age in a changing society.* New York: New Viewpoints, 1973.

Blenkner, M. Social work and family relationships in later life, with some thoughts on filial maturity. In E. Shanas & G. Streib (Eds.), *Social structure and the family: Generational relations.* Englewood Cliffs, N.J.: Prentice-Hall, 1965.

Bock, E. W., & Webber, I. L. Suicide among the elderly: Isolating widowhood and mitigating alternatives. *Journal of Marriage and the Family,* 1972, 34, 24–31.

Booth, A. Sex and social participation. *American Sociological Review,* 1972, 37, 183–192.

Brim, O. G., Jr. Mate mid-life crisis: A comparative analysis. In B. B. Hess (Ed.), *Growing old in America.* New Brunswick, N.J.: Transaction, 1976.

Brody, E. M. Congregate care facilities and mental health of the elderly. *Aging and Human Development,* 1970, 1, 279–321.

Brown, R. Family structure and social isolation of older persons. *Journal of Gerontology,* 1969, 15, 170–174.

Burr, W. R. Satisfaction with various aspects of marriage over the life cycle: A random middle class sample. *Journal of Marriage and the Family,* 1970, 32, 29–37.

Campbell, A., Converse, P. E., & Rodgers, W. L. *The quality of American life: Perceptions, evaluations and satisfactions.* New York: Russell Sage, 1976.

Cantor, M. Life space and the social support system of the inner city elderly of New York. *The Gerontologist,* 1975, 15, 23–27.

Chevan, A., & Korson, J. H. The widowed who live alone: An examination of social and demographic factors. *Social Forces,* 1972, 51, 45–52.

Clark, M., & Anderson, B. G. *Culture and aging*. Springfield, Ill.: Thomas, 1967.

Clausen, J. The life course of individuals. In M. W. Riley, M. Johnson, & A. Foner (Eds.), *Aging and society* (Vol. 3): *A sociology of age stratification*. New York: Russell Sage, 1972

Cosneck, B. J. Family patterns of older widowed Jewish people. *The Family Coordinator*, 1970, 19, 368–373.

Croog, S. H., Lipson, A., & Levine, S. Help patterns in severe illness: The roles of kin network, non-family resources and institutions. *Journal of Marriage and the Family*, 1972, 34, 32–41.

Edwards, J. N., & Klemmack, D. L. Correlates of life satisfaction: A re-examination. *Journal of Gerontology*, 1973, 28, 497–502.

Erikson, E. Identity and the life cycle. In G. Klein (Ed.), *Psychological issues*. New York: International, 1959.

Fendetti, D. V., & Gelfand, D. E. Care of the aged: Attitudes of white ethnic families. *The Gerontologist*, 1976, 16, 545–549.

Glasser, P. H., & Glasser, L. N. Role reversal and conflict between aged parents and their children. *Marriage and Family Living*, 1962, 24, 46–51.

Goode, W. J. A theory of role strain. *American Sociological Review*, 1960, 25, 483–496.

Goode, W. J. *World revolution and family patterns*. New York: Free Press, 1963.

Gouldner, A. The norm of reciprocity: A preliminary statement. *American Sociological Review*, 1960, 25, 161–178.

Gove, W. Sex, marital status and mortality. *American Journal of Sociology*, 1973, 79, 45–67.

Hess, B. B. Friendship. In M. W. Riley, M. Johnson, & A. Foner (Eds.), *Aging and society* (Vol. 3): *A sociology of age stratification*. New York: Russell Sage, 1972.

Hill, R. *Family development in three generations*. Cambridge, Mass.: Schenkman, 1970.

Jackson, J. J. Marital life among aging blacks. *The Family Coordinator*, 1972, 21, 21–27.

Jacobson, R. B., Berry, K. J., & Olsen, K. F. An empirical test of the generation gap: A comparative intrafamily study. *Journal of Marriage and the Family*, 1975, 37, 841–852.

Kalish, R. A., & Johnson, A. I. Value similarities and differences in three generations of women. *Journal of Marriage and the Family*, 1972, 34, 49–53.

Kent, D. P., & Matson, M. B. The impact of health on the aged family. *The Family Coordinator*, 1972, 21, 29–36.

Kobrin, F. E. The primary individual and the family: Changes in living arrangements in the United States since 1940. *Journal of Marriage and the Family*, 1976, 38, 233–239.

kreps, J. M. Intergenerational transfers and the bureaucracy. In E. Shanas & M. B. Sussman (Eds.), *Family, bureaucracy and the elderly*. Durham, N.C.: Duke, 1977.

Lazarsfeld, P. F., & Merton, R. K. Friendship as social process: A substantive and methodological inquiry. In M. Berger, T. Abel, & C. H. Page (Eds.), *Freedom and control in modern society*. Princeton, N.J. : Van Nostrand, 1954.

Levi-Strauss, C. Reciprocity, the essence of social life. In R. L. Coser (Ed.), *The family: Its structure and functions*. New York: St. Martin's, 1964.

Litwak, E., & Szelenyi, I. Primary group structures and their functions: Kin, neighbors and friends. *American Sociological Review*, 1969, 34, 64–78.

Lopata, H. Z. *Widowhood in an American city*. Cambridge, Mass.: Schenkman, 1973.

Lopata, H. Z. *Polish Americans*. Englewood Cliffs, N.J.: Prentice-Hill, 1976.

Lowenthal, M. F., Thumher, M., & Chiriboga, D. *Four stages of life*. San Francisco: Jossey-Bass, 1975.

Lynn, I. Three-generation household In the middle-class. In B. B. Hess (Ed.), *Growing old in America*. New Brunswick, N.J.: Transaction, 1976.

McKain, W. C. A new look at older marriages. *The Family Coordinator*, 1972, 21, 61–69.

Medley, M. L. Satisfaction with life among persons sixty-five and over. *Journal of Gerontology*, 1976, 31, 448–455.

Miller, B. C. A multivariate developmental model of marital satisfaction. *Journal of Marriage and the Family*, 1976.

Miller, M. B., Bernstein, H., & Sharkey, H. Family extrusion of the aged patient. *The Gerontologist*, 1975, 15, 291–296.

Morgan, L. A. A re-examination of widowhood and morale. *Journal of Gerontology*, 1976, 31, 687–695.

Neugarten, B. L. The awareness of middle age. In B. L. Neugarten (Ed.), *Middle age and aging*. Chicago, Ill.: University of Chicago, 1968.

Neugarten, B. L. Middle age and aging. In B. B. Hess (Ed.), *Growing Old in America.* New Brunswick, N.J.: Transaction, 1976.

Oppenheimer, V. K. Life cycle squeeze: The interaction of men's occupational and family life cycles. *Demography,* 1974, 11, 227–245.

Renne, K. S. Correlates of dissatisfaction In marriage. *Journal of Marriage and the Family,* 1970, 32, 54–67.

Riley, M. W., & Foner, A. *Aging and society* (Vol. 1): *An inventory of research findings.* New York: Russell Sage, 1968.

Riley, M. W., Johnson, M., & Foner, A. *Aging and society* (Vol. 3): *A sociology of age stratification.* New York: Russell Sage, 1972.

Riley, M. W., & Waring, J. J. Age and aging. In R. K. Merton & R. Nisbet (Eds.), *Contemporary social problems* (4th ed.). New York: Harcourt, 1976.

Rollins, B. C., & Feldman, H. Marital satisfaction over the family life cycle. *Journal of Marriage and the Family,* 1970, 32, 20–28.

Schoen, R. California divorce rates by age at first marriage and duration of first marriage. *Journal of Marriage and the Family,* 1975, 37, 548–555.

Sears, P., & Barbee, A. H. Career and life satisfaction among Terman's gifted women. In J. Stanley, W. George & C. Solano (Eds.), *The gifted and the creative: Fifty year perspective.* Baltimore: Johns-Hopkins, 1977.

Shanas, E., & Sussman, M. B. (Eds.) *Family, bureaucracy and the elderly.* Durham, N.C.: Duke, 1977.

Simos, B. G. Relations of adults with aging parents. *The Gerontologist,* 1970, 10, 135–139.

Smart, M. S., & Smart, R. C. Recalled, present and predicted satisfaction in stages of the family life cycle in New Zealand. *Journal of Marriage and the Family,* 1975, 37, 408–415.

Spanier, G. B., Lewis, R. A., & Cole, C. L. Marital adjustment over the family life cycle: The issue of curvilinearity. *Journal of Marriage and the Family,* 1975, 37, 263–275.

Spreitzer, E., & Snyder, E. Correlates of life satisfaction among the aged. *The Gerontologist,* 1974, 29, 454–458.

Stinnett, N., Collins, J., & Montgomery, J. E. Marital need satisfaction of husbands and wives. *Journal of Marriage and the Family,* 1970, 32, 428–434.

Sussman, M. B., Cates, J. N., & Smith, D. T. *The family and inheritance.* New York: Russell Sage, 1970.

Sussman, M. B. The family life of old people. In R. Binstock & E. Shanas (Eds.), *Handbook of aging and the social sciences.* New York: Van Nostrand, 1976.

Troll, L. E. The family of later life: A decade review. *Journal of Marriage and the Family,* 1971, 33, 263–290.

Wake, S. B., & Sporakowski, M, J. An intergenerational comparison of attitudes toward supporting aged parents. *Journal of Marriage and the Family,* 1972, 34, 42–48.

Waring, J. M. Social replenishment and social change: The problem of disordered cohort flow. *American Behavioral Scientist,* 1975, 19, 237–256.

Watson, J. A., & Kivett, V. R. Influences on the life satisfaction of older fathers. *The Family Coordinator,* 1976, 25, 482–488.

Weber, M. Bureaucracy. In H. H. Gerth & C. W. Mills, *From Max Weber.* New York: Oxford, 1958.

Weiss, R. S. The fund of sociability. *Transaction,* 1969, 6, 36–43.

Yankelovich, Skelly, & White, Inc. *Raising children in a changing society.* Minneapolis, Minn. General Mills, 1977.

Voluntarily Childless Wives: An Exploratory Study

J. E. Veevers

Students of the family have generally tended to accept the dominant cultural values that married couples should have children, and should want to have them. As a result of this value bias, although parenthood (especially voluntary parenthood) has been extensively studied, the phenomenon of childlessness has been virtually ignored (Veevers, 1972a). This selective inattention is unfortunate, for to a large extent the social meanings of parenthood can be comprehensively described and analyzed only in terms of the parallel set of meanings which are assigned to non-parenthood (Veevers, forthcoming). Although sociologists have occasionally discussed the theoretical relevance of voluntary childlessness, and have speculated regarding some empirical aspects of it (Pohlman, 1970), virtually no direct research has been conducted. As a preliminary step towards filling this gap in the sociological study of the family, an exploratory study of voluntarily childless wives was conducted. The present article will not attempt to describe this research in its entirety, but rather will be concerned with brief discussions of four aspects of it: first, the career paths whereby women come to be voluntarily childless; second, the social pressures associated with that decision; third, the symbolic importance attributed to the possibility of adoption; and fourth, the relevance of supportive ideologies relating to concern with feminism, and with population problems.

Selection and Nature of the Sample

Conventional sampling techniques cannot readily be applied to obtain large and representative samples of voluntarily childless couples (Gustavus and Henly, 1971). Only about five percent of all couples voluntarily forego parenthood (Veevers, 1972b), and this small deviant minority is characterized by attitudes and behaviors which are both socially unacceptable and not readily visible. The present research, which is exploratory in nature, is based on depth interviews with a purposive sample of 52 voluntarily childless wives. Although the utilization of non-random samples without control groups is obviously not the ideal approach, and can yield only suggestive rather than definitive conclusions, in examining some kinds of social behaviors it is often the only alternative to abandoning the inquiry.

In the present study, respondents were solicited by three separate articles appearing in newspapers in Toronto and in London, followed up by advertisements explicitly asking for volunteers. Of the 86 individuals who replied, 52 wives were selected. Three criteria were evoked in these selections. First, the

From *Sociology and Social Research* (April 1973), pp. 356–365. Reprinted by permission.

wife must have stated clearly that her childlessness was due to choice rather than to biological accident. Second, she must either have been married for a minimum of five years, or have been of post-menopausal age, or have reported that either she or her husband had been voluntarily sterilized for contraceptive purposes. Third, she must have affirmed that she had never borne a child, and had never assumed the social role of mother.

The interviews, which were unstructured, averaged about four hours in length, and included discussion of the woman's life history, considerable detail concerning her marriage and her husband, and attitudinal and evaluative aspects of her responses to the maternal role. Data are thus available on the characteristics of 104 voluntarily childless husbands and wives, whose demographic and social characteristics may be briefly summarized as follows. The average age of the sample is 29, with a range from 23 to 71 years. All are Caucasian and living in urban areas, most are middle class, and many are upwardly mobile. Although educational experience ranges from grade school to the post doctoral level, most have at least some university experience. With the exception of one housewife, all are either employed full-time or attending univeristy. Most individuals are either atheists or agnostics from Protestant backgrounds, and of the minority who do express some religious preference, almost all are inactive. Most individuals come from stable homes where the mother has been a full-time housewife since her first child was born. The incidence of first born and only children is much higher than would ordinarily be expected.

With the exception of two widowers, all of the subjects in the present research are involved in their first marriage. The average marriage duration is seven years, with a range from three to twenty-five years. Most couples have relatively egalitarian relationships, but still maintain conventional marriages and follow the traditional division of labor. Configurations of marital adjustment cover the entire continuum described by Cuber and Harroff (1966), ranging from conflict-habituated to total relationships, with many wives reporting vital or total relationships with their husbands.

All of the couples agree on the desirability of preventing pregnancy, at least at the present time. Most of the wives had never been pregnant, but about a fifth had had at least one induced abortion, and most indicate they would seek an abortion if pregnant. More than half of the wives are presently on the pill. About a quarter of the husbands have obtained a vasectomy, and another quarter are seriously considering doing so. Many of the women express positive interest in tubal ligation, but only one, a girl of 23, has actually been sterilized.

The Nature of Childless Careers

In reviewing the processes whereby couples come to define themselves as voluntarily childless, two characteristic career paths are apparent. One route to childlessness involves the formulation by the couple, before they are even married, of a definite and explicitly stated intention never to become involved in parental roles; a second and more common route is less obvious, and involves the prolonged postponement of childbearing until such time as it was no longer considered desirable at all. These two alternatives will be elaborated.

Nearly a third of the wives interviewed entered into their marriages with a childlessness clause clearly stated in their marriage "contract." Although none of these women had a formal written contract in the legal sense of the work, the husband and wife explicitly agreed upon childlessness as a firm condition of marriage. The woman deliberately sought a future mate who, regardless of his other desirable qualities, would agree on this one dimension. Generally the negative decisions regarding the value of children were made during early adolescence, before the possibility of marriage had ever been seriously considered. In contrast, a few of the wives had different or even vaguely positive attitudes towards childbearing until they met their future husbands. During their courtship and engagement, they gradually allowed themselves to be converted to the world view of voluntary childlessness, and by the time of their marriage were quite content to agree to never have children.

More than two thirds of the wives studied remained childless as a result of a series of decisions to postpone having children until some future time, a future which never came. Rather than explicitly rejecting motherhood prior to marriage, they repeatedly deferred procreation until a more convenient time. These temporary postponements provided time during which the evaluations of parenthood were gradually reassessed relative to other goals and possibilities. At the time of their marriages, most wives involved in the postponement model had devoted little serious thought to the question of having children, and had no strong feelings either for or against motherhood. Like conventional couples, they simply assumed that they would have one or two children eventually; unlike conventional couples, they practiced birth control conscientiously and continuously during the early years of marriage.*

Most couples involved in the postponement pattern move through four separate stages in their progression from wanting to not wanting children. The first stage involves postponement for a definite period of time. In this stage, the voluntarily childless are indistinguishable from conventional and conforming couples who will eventually become parents. In most groups, it is not necessarily desirable for the bride to conceive during her honeymoon. It is considered understandable that before starting a family a couple might want to achieve certain goals, such as graduating from school, travelling, buying a house, saving a nest egg, or simply getting adjusted to one another. The degree of specificity varies, but there is a clear commitment to have children as soon as conditions are right.

*Whelpton, Campbell, and Patterson report in one study that nearly two out of three newly-weds do not start using contraception before the first conception. See Whelpton, Campbell, and Patterson (1966).

The second stage of this career involves a shift from postponement for a definite period of time to indefinite postponement. The couple remains committed to the idea of parenthood, but becomes increasingly vague about when the blessed event is going to take place. It may be when they can "afford it," or when "things are going better" or when they "feel more ready."

The third stage in the cycle involves another qualitative change in thinking, in that for the first time there is an open acknowledgment of the possibility that in the end the couple may remain permanently childless. The third stage is a critical one, in that the very fact of openly considering the pros and cons of having children may increase the probability of deciding not to. During this time, they have an opportunity to experience directly the many social, personal, and economic advantages associated with being childless, and at the same time to compare their life styles with those of their peers who are raising children. It seems probable that the social-psychological factors involved in the initial decision to postpone having children may be quite disparate from the social-psychological factors involved in the inclination to remain childless, and to continue with the advantages of a life style to which one has become accustomed. At this stage in the career, the only definite decision is to postpone deciding until some vague and usually unspecified time in the future.

Finally, a fourth stage involves the definite conclusion that the couple are never going to have children, and that childlessness is a permanent rather than a transitory state. Occasionally this involves an explicit decision, usually precipitated by some crisis or change in the environment that focuses attention on the question of parenthood. However, for most couples, there is never a direct decision made to have or to avoid children. Rather, after a number of years of postponing pregnancy until some future date, they gradually become aware that an implicit decision has been made to forego parenthood. The process involved is one of recognizing an event which has already occurred, rather than of posing a question and then searching or negotiating for an answer. At first, it was "obvious" that "of course" they would eventually have children; now, it is equally "obvious" that they will not. The couple are at a loss to explain exactly how or when the transition came about, but they both agree on their new implicit decision, and they are both contented with its implications.

Childlessness and Informal Sanctions

All of the wives interviewed feel that they are to some extent stigmatized by their unpopular decision to avoid having children, and that there exists a ubiquitous negative stereotype concerning the characteristics of a voluntarily childless woman, including such unfavorable traits as being abnormal, selfish, immoral, irresponsible, immature, unhappy, unfulfilled, and non-feminine (Veevers, 1972c). In addition, these devaluating opinions are perceived to have behavioral consequences for their interaction with others, and to result in considerable social pressure to become mothers. Some of the sanctions reported are direct and obvious, including explicit and unsolicited comments advocating childbirth and presenting arguments relating to the importance of motherhood. Other pressures are more subtle, and in many cases are perceived to be unintentional. For example, the childless frequently complain that, whereas parents are never required to explain why they chose to have children, they are frequently required to account for their failure to do so.

Childlessness is of course not always a disapproved state. Couples are rewarded, not punished, for remaining childless for the first several months of marriage, and thereby negating the possibility that they were "forced" to get married. After the minimum of nine months has passed, there is a short period of time when the young couple is excused from not assuming all of their responsibilties, or are perceived as having been having intercourse for too short a period of time to guarantee conception. The definition of how long a period of time childbearing may be postponed and still meet with conventional expectations is difficult to determine, and apparently varies considerably from one group to another. In most groups, the first twelve months constitutes an acceptable period of time. After the first year, the pressure gradually but continually increases, reaching a peak during the third and fourth years of marriage. However, once a couple have been married for five or six years there appears to be some diminution of negative responses to them. Several factors are involved in this change: part may be attributable to the increased ability of the childless to avoid those who consistently sanction them; part may be attributable to the increased ability of the childless to cope with negative and hostile responses, making the early years only seem more difficult in restrospect; and part may reflect an actual change in the behavior of others. After five or six years, one's family and friends may give up the possibility of persuading the reluctant couple to procreate or to adopt, and resign themselves to the fact that intervention, at least in this case, is ineffective.

It is noteworthy that although all wives report considerable direct and indirect social pressures to become mothers, most are remarkably well defended against such sanctions. Although on specific occasions they may be either indignant or amused, in most instances they are indifferent to negative responses, and remain inner-directed, drawing constant support and reaffirmation from the consensual validation offered by their husbands. Many strategies are employed which "discredit the discreditors" (Veevers, 1973) and which enable the voluntarily childless to remain relatively impervious to the comments of critics and the wishes of reformers. One such strategy concerns the possibility of adoption.

The Symbolic Importance of Adoption

A recurrent theme in discussions with childless wives is that of adoption. Most wives mention that they have in the past considered adopting a child, and many indicate that they are still considering the possibility at some future date. However, in spite of such positive verbalizations, it is apparent that adoption is not seriously contemplated as a viable alternative, and that their considerations are not likely to result in actually assuming maternal roles. The lack of serious thought about adoption as a real possibility is reflected in the fact that generally they have not considered even such elementary questions as whether they would prefer a boy or girl, or whether they would prefer an infant or an older child. With few exceptions, none of the couples have made even preliminary inquiries regarding the legal processes involved in adoption. Those few that had made some effort to at least contact a child placement agency had failed to follow through on their initial contact. None had investigated the issue thoroughly enough to have considered the possibility that, should they decide to adopt, a suitable child might not be immediately available to them.

For the voluntarily childless, the importance of the recurrent theme of adoption appears to lie in its symbolic value, rather than in the real possiblity of procuring a child by this means and thereby altering one's life style. This symbolic importance is twofold: the reaffirmation of normalcy, and the avoidance of irreversible decisions. A willingness to consider adoption as a possiblity communicates to one's self and to others that in spite of being voluntarily childless, one is still a "normal" and "well-adjusted" person who does like children, and who is willing to assume the responsibilities of parenthood. It is an effective mechanism for denying the possibility of considerable psychological differences between parents and non-parents (Veevers, forthcoming), and legitimates the claim of the childless to be just like parents in a number of important respects.

The possibility of adoption at a later date is of symbolic value, in that it prevents the voluntarily childless from being committed to an irreversible state. One of the problems of opting for a postponement model is that eventually one must confront the fact that childbirth cannot be postponed indefinitely. The solution to this dilemma is to include possibility of adoption as a satisfactory "out" should one be needed. The same strategy is employed by many couples who choose sterilization as a means of birth control, but who are not entirely comfortable with the absolute and irreversible solution. The theoretical possibility of adoption is also comforting when faced with the important but unanswerable question of how one will feel about being childless in one's old age.

The Relevance of Supportive Ideologies

The voluntarily childless appear to be in a state of pluralistic ignorance, in that they are unaware of the numbers of other individuals who share their world view. Although the deliberate decision to avoid parenthood is a relatively rare phenomenon, it is not nearly as rare as the childless themselves perceive it to be, especially among urban and well-educated middle class couples. A large proportion of wives indicated that until they read the article and/or advertisement asking for subjects for the present study, they had never seen the topic of voluntary childlessness discussed in the mass media. Many reported that they did not know any other couple who felt as they did about the prospect of parenthood, and many others reported having met only one or two like-minded people during the course of their marriage.

Feelings of uniqueness and of isolation are somewhat mitigated by the explicit agreement of husbands on the appropriateness of foregoing parental roles. However, regardless of how supportive the husband is in his reaffirmation of the legitimacy of childlessness, and how committed he is personally to avoiding fatherhood, because of cultural differences in sex roles he does not share an entirely comparable situation. He may be totally sympathetic, but he has a limited ability to empathize. The childless wife may be generally comfortable with her decision not to have children, and still express the wish that she could discuss her situation with other like-minded women who might have shared similar experiences within the female subculture, and who migth provide a model for identification.

It is noteworthy that within the psychological world of the voluntarily childless, existing social movements concerned with population or with feminism have surprisingly little relevance, and provide relatively little intellectual or emotional support. The concern with population problems, especially as manifest in the Zero Population Growth movement, does provide a supportive rationale indicating that one is not necessarily being socially irresponsible and neglectful of one's civic obligations if one does not reproduce. However, although there is a clear statement that procreation is not necessary for all, most ZPG advocates are careful to indicate that it is not procreation *per se* they are opposed to, but rather excessive procreation. The slogan "Stop at Two" asserts that one should have no more than two children, but also implies that one perhaps should have at least one or two. Some of the childless wives are superficially involved in ZPG and sympathetic with its goals, but in all cases this identification is an *ex post facto* consideration, rather than a motivating force, and their satisfaction with being childless is related to concerns other than their contributions to the population crisis.

It is sometimes suggested than an inclination to avoid motherhood is a logical extension of the new feminism. It is difficult to generalize about a social phenomenon as amorphous as the women's liberation movement, a rubric which incorporates many diverse and even contradictory attitudes. However, "A significant feature of the women's liberation movement is that, although its demands have been made on the basis of equity for women, it has not usually been anti-marriage or anti-children (Commission on Population Growth, 1972, p. 68).

In many instances, the ideological statements endorsed by the women's liberation movement are implicitly or explicitly pro-natalist. Motherhood is not perceived as an unfulfilling and unrewarding experience; rather, it is perceived as a positive experience which, although desirable, is not sufficient in and of itself for maximum self-actualization. Considerable concern is expressed with the problems involved in combining successful motherhood with comparable success in other careers. Rather than advising women to give up having children, the new feminist literature advised them to consider other careers in addition to motherhood, and advocates changes in society which would make the motherhood role easier. For example, there is considerable stress on the provision of maternity leaves, on increased involvement of fathers in childcare, on accessibility to adequate day care facilities. Although advocates of the new feminism may provide some support for the idea that motherhood is neither necessary nor sufficient for fulfillment, they do still advocate that normally it will be an important part of that fulfillment. Only a few of the voluntarily childless are at all concerned with women's liberation, and these few apparently came into the movement after their decision was made and their life style was established.

Although none of the voluntarily childless are actively seeking group support for their life style, many would welcome the opportunity to become involved in a truly supportive social movement. The first example of such an association is the National Organization for Nonparenthood (NON) which was formed in California in 1971. Because of the state of pluralistic ignorance which surrounds voluntary childlessness, and because of the inadequacy of demographic and feminist movements in expressing the world view of the childless, such attempts to formulate a counter culture might be expected to be very successful.

Summary

The present research on a purposive sample of 52 voluntarily childless wives is exploratory in nature. Although it is not possible to make definitive statements regarding the nature of childless couples, several tentative conclusions are offered. It is suggested that couples come to be voluntarily childless by a number of diverse paths beginning both before and after marriage, and that considerable diversity might be expected between those who enter marriage only on the condition of a clear childlessness clause in the marriage contract, and those who remain childless after a series of postponements of parenthood. Although considerable social pressures are directed towards the childless, most of the individuals involved appear to be very well defended against such sanctions, and the mechanisms of redefining situations and of protecting themselves are worthy of further study. One such mechanism appears to be the use of the possibility of adoption to deny the status of voluntary childlessness while not seriously threatening the accompanying life style. Finally, it is suggested that existing social movements do not provide much relevant support for the voluntarily childless, and that an explicit counter culture, such as the National Organization for Nonparenthood, might be expected to meet with considerable success.

References

Commission on Population Growth and the American Future, *Report.* Washington, D.C.: Commission on Population Growth and the American Future, 1972.

Cuber, John F., and Peggy B. Harroff. *Sex and the Significant Americans: A Study of Sexual Behavior among the Affluent.* Baltimore: Penguin, 1966.

Gustavus, Susan O., and James R. Henly, Jr. "Correlates of Voluntary Childlessness in a Select Population." *Social Biology,* 18 (September 1971): 277–284.

Pohlman, Edward. "Childlessness: Intentional and Unintentional." *The Journal of Nervous and Mental Disease,* 151 (1970), no. 1: 2–12.

Veevers, J. E. "Voluntary Childlessness: A Neglected Area of Family Study." *The Family Coordinator,* 21 (April 1972).

Veevers, J. E. "Factors in the Incidence of Childlessness in Canada: An Analysis of Census Data." *Social Biology.* 19 (December 1972).

Veevers, J. E. "The Violation of Fertility Mores: Voluntary Childlessness as Deviant Behavior." In *Deviant Behavior and Societal Reaction,* edited by Craig L. Boydell, Carl F. Grindstaff, and Paul C. Whitehead, pp. 571–592. Toronto: Holt, Rinehart and Winston, 1972.

Veevers, J. E. "The Moral Career of Voluntarily Childless Wives: Notes on the Construction and Defense of a Deviant World View." In *Marriage and the Family in Canada,* edited by S. Parvez Wakil. Toronto: Longmans Green, 1973.

Veevers, J. E. "The Social Meanings of Parenthood." *Psychiatry: Journal for the Study of Interpersonal Processes,* forthcoming.

Whelpton, Pascal K., Arthur A. Campbell, and J. E. Patterson. *Fertility and Family Planning in the United States.* Princeton: Princeton University Press, 1966.

Singles: An Examination of Two Stereotypes

*Leonard Cargan**

One of the fastest growing population categories in the United States is the unmarried category. In the very short period between 1960 and 1975, the number of adults between the ages of 20 and 34 who have never been married increased by 50% while the divorce rate doubled. In addition, the time interval between divorce and remarriage has increased. This has led to a doubling of those divorced but not remarried in the past 10 years. In short, there has been a slowdown of marriage and remarriage rates plus a pronounced increase in the rate of divorce. The result is that there are now over 53 million single adults in the United States ("The Way 'Singles' Are Changing U.S.," 1977).

From *Family Relations*, Vol. 30, No. 3 (1981), pp. 377–385. Reprinted by permission.
*Associate Professor, Department of Sociology, Wright State University, Dayton, Ohio 45435.

Despite these impressive changes and large numbers, the unmarried represent one of the most under-researched topics in the behavioral sciences. Libby (1978, p. 164) notes that single people have received little attention by social scientists and that "family sociologists have either ignored singles or relegated them to boring, out-of-date discussions of dating." Adding to this claim is the belief by Skolnick and Skolnick (1977, p. 3) that the writers on the family "seemed to deny that change was possible in family structure, the relations between the sexes, and parenthood." The main reasons for this factor lie in the functions that marriage supposedly fulfills for society: marriage is seen as the means by which such societal needs as maintaining life itself, socializing the baby with human qualities, and providing for personal needs of affection and security are met (Nye, 1967).

These beliefs mean that marriage is regarded as the social norm and singleness as a temporary period prior to or in between marriages. In addition, such beliefs have led to the development of other beliefs designed to perpetuate the dominance of pairs, beliefs in which marriage is seen as something good and singleness as a bad state (Deegan, 1969). Thus, Deegan found that women portrayed in literary fiction were unmarried because they are unattractive, handicapped, or incompetent. Men also have not escaped the labels. Singleness for men implies alcoholism, homosexuality, personality inadequacy, psychopathology, or, at best overtones of immaturity, selfishness, lechery, and social irresponsibility (Libby, 1978). These beliefs about singles are incorporated in various stereotypes as the means for describing their behavior, attitudes, and motivations. With serious study of singles only beginning, such negative stereotypes remain dominant with serious and often unrecognized discrimination. For example, if perceived as immature, singles may have more difficulty in obtaining home mortgages or in getting an organizational promotion. Thus, the stereotypes need to be investigated.

Two of the more prominent stereotypes are that singles must be terribly lonely and that they are "swingers," i.e., sexually nonexclusive. Thus, Deegan notes that singleness implies one who is lacking a partner, is not complete, and is alone (1969) whereas the sexually nonexclusive lifestyle image implies casual sexual encounters rather than sex on a romantic love basis (Stein, 1976). These two stereotypes imply that singles are lonelier and more sexually casual than marrieds, i.e., singles, because they have no mates, are lonely and in not being legally restricted to one mate via marriage, have encounters with many sexual partners.

The stereotypes imply behavior which is attributable to singles vis-a-vis marrieds. Thus, it is necessary that this be a comparative study in order to note whether this behavior is indeed particular to singles. Only in comparing singles with marrieds on the same dependent variables of loneliness and sexuality will it be known whether singles really qualify as being different on these variables. Since singles by definition are alone, and in order to meet their sexual needs would be likely to have more sexual partners since one is not reserved for them, it would not be surprising to find that more singles than marrieds claim to be lonely or have sexual partners. But whether such behavior is the hallmark of all singles is important to know, since it denies that singleness can be a viable lifestyle which is not necessarily always lonely and which is as irresponsible as sexual "notches on a belt" implies. In short, it is important to note the degree of difference between singles and marrieds on these behaviors in order to note whether singleness is, indeed, undesirable, lonely, and incomplete.

Procedure

Subjects

This study was made in the Dayton Metropolitan area utilizing a probability proportionate to size sample of 400 households. Since this area is also considered one of the ten typical areas of the country by George Gallup ("Pollster Visits Nation's Barometer," 1976), the study takes on added significance. The sample consisted of 114 never marrieds (53% males), 37 divorced (70% females), 205 persons in a first marriage (55% females), and 44 remarrieds (59% females). The youngest portion of the sample were the never marrieds with 77% of them under 30 as compared to 51% of the divorced, 34% in a first marriage and 11% of the remarried.

The Interviews

The questionnaire consisted of 77 predominantly close-ended items which could be self-administered by the respondent. The presence of the interviewer was to answer questions and to ensure the randomness of the sample. In this manner, the biases of the interviewer and that of a mailed questionnaire were overcome.

As a means of ensuring the probability that all desired segments of the population would be included in the sample, the interviews were conducted in the evening or on weekends.

Results

Loneliness

Before examining this factor, it is necessary to deal with a clarification of what is meant by the concept. According to Webster, loneliness is the state of loneliness, whereas lonely consists of being alone, unhappy at being alone, longing for friends, and giving vent to such feelings (1964). Thus, it is the nonvoluntary aspect of being alone that is being dealt with in this study. That is, some people dread being alone because negative values are attributed to it; others because they do not know how to appreciate being alone. For some then, being alone, doing things alone is loneliness; for others, it is precious and important.

Among the many stereotypes heard about the singles population is that their lack of a partner in a couple-oriented society means that they must be lonely. It is probably the most prevalent belief about singles. An examination of the titles in the *Reader's Guide to Periodical Literature* since 1900 reveals that the problem of loneliness has been continuous for singles throughout the century. This often-repeated belief has led to the picture of singles going to singles' bars with the hope of meeting someone—anyone, even if it only for the evening; even if it means a casual assignation. After all, "it's better to be surrounded by people you don't want to talk to . . . than to drink alone in your apartment . . ." ("Games Singles Play," 1973). The implication is that anything is better than remaining at home alone night after night. The first impression of such beliefs is that it must be greatly exaggerated since most people—single or married— do not go out socially very often per week or go with a member of the opposite sex when they do go out. Thus, it is not necessarily the question of doing things with someone but having someone to turn to, to call, to touch when the mood calls for these needs to be fulfilled.

If, then, the stereotypes have a core of truth, the findings should reveal that far more of the unmarried portion of the sample would note feelings of being lonely in various situations. Further, more of the never married would report such feelings since the divorced may lack adult companionship but they usually, at least, have children for company. The findings reveal that these assumptions are partially true for the first part but not in regard to the difference between the never married and the divorced.

As indicated in Table 1, the most unwelcome experience in regards to being lonely for the entire sample but significantly more so for the singles portion is that of entering a restaurant alone. Although 33% of the married category said they felt conspicuous in this regard, 46% of the single categories made a similar statement. Reflected in this situation is the social norm regarding the expectation of engaging in such social activities as dining out in pairs. Thus, it is not surprising that very few of the sample felt some lonesome apprehensions when doing a nonsocial item such as entering an empty room. However, this question does reveal an interesting facet since twice as many of the divorced category (28%) as the sample in general (14%) had apprehensions about entering an empty room. This attitude of the divorced toward being alone is again reflected by a far higher percentage of them than any other category felt depressed when alone. These feelings of the divorced toward being alone may account for their high remarriage rate. After all, "who wants to be free when it means being alone?" (O'Brien, 1973, p. 62).

Adding the variables of gender and age to the above possible conditions of loneliness provides some interesting nuances to the findings indicated. Although the marrieds were less likely to dislike dining alone, sex differences were found. Three-fourths of the marrieds who felt conspicious dining alone were females. This is consistent with the social norm that it has been more conspicuous when a woman does things alone, e.g., traveling, dining, theater, party. No other category revealed a significant gender difference. In reference

Table 1   Affirmative Responses to First Loneliness Scale by Marital Category

Marital status	Dining alone		Entering empty room		Depressed when alone		Unhappy living alone	
	n	%	n	%	n	%	n	%
Never Married	54	47	17	15	23	20	9	8
Divorced	16	44	10	28	12	33	9	25
Singles (Total)	70	46	27	18	35	23	18	12
In First Marriage	70	34	25	12	29	14	37	18
Remarried	14	33	6	14	8	18	9	21
Marrieds (Total)	84	34	31	13	37	15	46	19

to age, 90% of the never married who disliked dining alone were among the youngest of these respondents (under 30), whereas for the remarried, most of those feeling apprehensive in this situation were the older categories of 40 or above (86%). The final of these three lonesome situations—that of feeling depressed when alone—revealed no significant differences in regard to gender or age.

Perhaps the most telling of the loneliness findings is revealed in the question regarding living alone. As noted, it was believed that the never married would be more likely to equate this condition with being unhappy since the divorced may have children for company. The results reveal, however, that the never married were least likely to associate being alone with unhappiness whereas the category with the highest average was the other singles segment—the divorced. This finding may reflect two situations: many of the never married do not actually live alone (66%) and the divorced, especially those without children, are going through the contrasting situation of living without an adult after having experienced living with someone. Thus, the never married may not be lonely because they have not yet experienced marriage.

Three significant differences among the various marital segments of the sample were revealed by questions that dealt with personal loneliness (Table 2). The first of these findings dealt with the need of having someone with whom to share happy and sad moments. Of the married segments, 67% noted that this was rarely true for them, that is, almost always there was someone with whom to share those moments. On the other hand, 36% of the singles made this same assertion. To put it another way, while 29% of the singles segment were saying that they often had no one with whom to be happy and sad, only 8% of the married segments were making the same statement.

The above idea of having no one with whom to talk was reiterated in a question that asked whether they had anyone with whom to discuss their problems. Again, the singles were more negative on this element of being lonely (38% marrieds vs. 60% singles). On the reverse side of this question, a startling revelation of loneliness for the divorced is revealed. Half of the divorced reported they often had no one with whom to discuss their problems

Table 2 Affirmative Responses to Second Loneliness Scale

Marital status	Rarely true		Mostly true	
	n	*%*	*n*	*%*
	No One To Share			
Never Married	41	36	10	1
Divorced	14	39	5	14
Singles (Total)	55	37	15	10
In First Marriage	136	67	8	4
Remarried	29	66	3	7
Marrieds (Total)	165	67	11	5
	No One To Discuss			
Never Married	48	42	12	11
Divorced	9	26	7	20
Singles (Total)	57	38	19	13
In First Marriage	123	60	9	4
Remarried	26	59	6	14
Marrieds (Total)	149	60	15	6
	Most Are Alone			
Never Married	43	38	2	2
Divorced	9	25	7	19
Singles (Total)	52	35	9	6
In First Marriage	72	36	2	1
Remarried	13	30	1	2
Marrieds (Total)	85	35	3	1

compared to a fourth of the never married, and approximately a fifth of the married.

Another question attempted to determine if being lonely was something that was true specifically for them individually or was it true for most people. Again, it is the divorced who differ. While 11% of the other three segments of the sample reported that most people are often or mostly alone and friendless, 21% of the divorced were making this assertion.

The findings revealing that more of the divorced were troubled by loneliness than any other group lend support to much of the literature on divorce. The divorced also recognized their lonely feelings as being something akin to them personally rather than a malaise characteristic of society as a whole. Almost half of the divorced had no one with whom to discuss problems whereas only a fifth believed this was true for others in society.

An examination of these personal situations in regard to the gender and age variables again revealed few differences. The only significant gender difference found was in the once married category with regard to having no one with whom to share happy and sad moments. Slightly more females than males expressed this idea ($\chi^2 = 25.28$, $p < .05$). The only significant age difference was found with the divorced on this same question; all of the very young divorced (18–24) said that such situations were rarely true for them ($\chi^2 = 22.28$, $p < .03$).

It is not surprising that more of the singles were bothered by or suffered from situations that described aloneness, since marrieds have mates and families. Since it was assumed that most of the divorced would have families and would probably retain friends from the marriage while making new ones, it would be the never-married who were thought to live alone and who would, therefore, be more aware of being alone. However, most never-marrieds do not live alone; they live with their family or share a residence, whereas the divorced are more alone when compared to their former state. In sum, loneliness is not as much a result of being single as it of being divorced.

Sexuality

Given a growing secularism and the development of new, more secure forms of birth control techniques, the scientists, such as Kinsey and Hunt, and magazines such as *Playboy*, *Playgirl*, and *Penthouse* are implying that the sexual mores of monogamous sex are attitudes which are more exposed than enacted. Providing impetus to these claims is the single person. The sexual needs and desires of singles are supposedly in the forefront of a move into a so-called new morality, an image fostered by the motion pictures, television, and condominiums for singles. In short, is it true that the sexual activities of singles are significantly different from that of the marrieds?

The answer to this question appears to be an unequivocal *yes* since significant differences were found in all aspects of sexual behavior questioned. However, there were some surprises.

The first of these aspects dealt with the number of partners with whom the subjects have had sexual intercourse (Table 3). A fourth of the never-marrieds have had no sexual partners despite the fact that all persons in the sample were 18 or above. In fact, two-thirds of the never-marrieds claimed to have had only three partners or less during their sexual history as compared to two-thirds of the remarried. Those in their first marriage had the least number of sexual partners; the majority had restricted their sexual experience to the person they married (55%). Among the divorced, 45% have had three partners or less.

The difference in the number of sexual partners between the never-married and the divorced may be a result of age, since the never-marrieds are somewhat younger than the divorced and/or it could imply that the most difficult sexual period in regard to partners is prior to the first one; i.e., it is easier to find or have more sexual partners once one is experienced. In either case, the fact that a majority of the singles have had three sexual partners or less hardly speaks of the kind of casual sex implied by the stereotype. On the other hand, for a small aggregate, this label can be said to be true.

Table 3 Responses Concerning Number of Sexual Partners

Marital status	3 or Less		4–10		11–20		More than 20	
	n	%	n	%	n	%	n	%
Personally								
Never Married	68	63	24	22	7	7	9	8
Divorced	16	45	9	25	5	14	6	17
In First Marriage	156	81	27	14	3	2	7	4
Remarried	25	63	11	28	1	3	3	8
Singles (Total)	84	58	33	23	12	8	5	10
Marrieds (Total)	181	78	38	16	4	2	10	4
Others of Same Status								
Never Married	54	48	35	21	12	11	12	11
Divorced	14	40	15	43	3	9	3	9
In First Marriage	134	72	34	18	10	5	7	4
Remarried	21	53	11	28	4	10	4	10
Singles (Total)	68	46	50	34	15	10	15	10
Marrieds (Total)	155	69	45	20	14	6	11	5

Almost a third of the divorced have had 11 or more sexual partners, compared to 15% of the never-marrieds and 6% of the marrieds. All of the categories had a higher percentage having more than 20 partners than had 11–19 sexual partners. Overall, 71% of these claiming 11 or more partners have had more than 20 sexual partners.

If a great majority of the sample have had relatively few sexual partners, one wonders why the belief of a sexually liberated society is so prevalent. Such magazines as *Hustler* and *Penthouse* imply a freer discussion and display of sexual matters; however, from the present findings, it would appear that sexual encounters with numerous sexual partners is what is believed "other people" do. In order to verify this view, the respondents were asked what they believed about the sexual life of other people their age, sex, and marital status (Table 3). Interestingly, it was only the divorced who believe others of their own kind have had fewer partners than they have had; all the other categories believe that others of similar marital status have had more sexual partners than they have had. Excluding the divorced, three-fourths of the sample have had three or less sexual partners, but only three-fifths believe that others of the same status have had so few partners. On the other hand, a sixth believe that others have had at least 11 sexual partners, which is 6% more than those who have actually had this many partners. Whereas the divorced believe that other divorced persons have not had as many sexual partners—14% of the divorced believed that other divorced have had fewer partners than they have had. In sum, the divorced when compared to the other categories believe that they are less sexually exclusive.

A total of 70% of the sample had three partners or less, but only 60% of the sample believe others have this few sexual partners. On the other side of the picture, 11% note having personally had at least 11 sexual partners, but 15% believe that others have had at least this number of partners. Thus, not very many people of the sample have had a large number of sexual partners nor do they believe that others have had a large number of sexual partners. It would appear that the belief of a sexual revolution is based more on the openness of sexual discussion than it is on reality.

The prevalent belief is that it is the males who are more likely to participate with numerous sex partners. For the never-married and those in their first marriage, this appears to be true but no such significant differences were found among the divorced or remarried. In sum, among those categories who have few persons noting numerous sex partners, it is usually the males who would be making this assertion (80% of the never married and those in their first marriage having 11 plus partners are males), whereas among those categories in which more of the total have noted numerous sex partners (the remarried and the divorced), there is no gender difference.

Similar results were found with the inclusion of the age variable. That is, the age segment in each marital category that were likely to be nonsexually exclusive were the ones that believed this to be true of others in their own status. Not surprising, it appears that one's belief regarding sexual nonexclusivity depends largely upon one's own experience.

Whether having numerous sexual partners is related to frequency of sexual intercourse is another aspect of the differences which may exist between the unmarried and the marrieds in regard to their lifestyles (Table 4). With the unmarried, the number of sexual partners appears to be related to sexual activity, that is, the more partners, the more often one has sexual intercourse per week. Thus, three-fifths of the unmarried have had few sexual partners and three-fifths also note a limited sexual activity of once per week or less. A similar kind of matching occurs on the other end of the scale. Nineteen percent of the unmarrieds admit to having had 11 or more sexual partners and this figure is almost matched by the 18% who engage in sex three or more times per week. Thus, for the unmarried, there appears to be a relationship between the number of sexual partners and the amount of sexual activity. As might be expected, such is not the situation with the married categories. Whereas very few of them noted having a large number of sexual partners (5%), 27% claimed a sexual activity of three or more times per week. It is seen in these significant differences that the "swinging singles" label in regards to the number of sexual partners applies to a small percentage of mostly the divorced, and that such activity has little to do with the actual amount of sexual participation per week.

The situation described above appears to be little changed by adding the gender and age variables. Only those in their first marriage reveal a gender difference, and this was very slight. Of those first marrieds noting an active

Table 4   Frequency of Intercourse Per Week

Marital status	Once/week or less		Twice/ week		Three times or more	
	n	%	n	%	n	%
Never Married	74	67	23	21	13	12
Divorced	15	42	8	22	13	36
In First Marriage	66	35	69	37	53	28
Remarried	17	43	13	33	10	25
Singles (Total)	89	61	31	21	26	18
Marrieds (Total)	83	36	82	36	63	28

sexual participation of three or more times per week, 52% were males. An interesting difference in regard to age is found with the married aggregates. Among the remarried, the most active are the middle aged (30–49) since they comprise 80% of those asserting such an active sexual life whereas there is a decline in sexual activity among the first marrieds of this age.

The final question in this examination of the sexual lifestyles of the sample deals with the end-all product of such sexual activity—the question of sexual satisfaction (Table 5). Although there is a significant difference between the various categories in regards to sexual satisfaction, it would appear that it has little to do with either the number of sexual partners or the rate of sexual participation. More of the divorced personally had more sexual partners, more of them also had a higher weekly sexual participation rate, but also, more of the divorced than any other category were very dissatisfied with their sex life (14%). The numbers among the married categories being very satisfied with their sex life were significantly higher than the unmarried categories despite their avowed lesser number of sexual partners.

This examination of the sexual lifestyles of the various segments of the sample would show that the "grass is greener" belief about singles and their sexual activity is not true in most cases, and most important, may not be necessarily desirable in regards to sexual satisfaction. The swinging idea may be more of an outcome of today's freer discussion of sexual matters. This idea is reiterated in two questions asked of singles only. The first indicated a willingness among singles to engage in sexual relations without marriage since one-half of the singles do not need love to have sexual relations. The second notes that this is not a sign of a morally abandoned sexuality since three-fourths would not engage in intimate relations as the price of a date.

Discussion

Shifting personal preferences have thrust upon the scene a large singles population and with it a need to know more about this growing aggregate. Prior scientific study of this aggregate was limited due to a rapid rise in the

Table 5   Reported Level of Sexual Satisfaction

Marital status	Very satisfied		Somewhat satisfied		Neutral		Somewhat dissatisfied		Very dissatisfied	
	n	%	n	%	n	%	n	%	n	%
Never Married	26	23	29	26	36	32	13	12	7	6
Divorced	12	33	10	28	8	22	1	3	5	14
In First Marriage	89	44	69	34	32	16	9	5	2	1
Remarried	22	52	13	31	5	12	2	5	0	0
Singles (Total)	38	26	39	27	44	30	14	10	12	8
Marrieds (Total)	111	46	82	34	37	15	11	5	2	1

marriage rates in the fifties and sixties which made it appear that singles were merely in transition to or between marriages. Accompanying this lack of scientific information was the "common sense" ideas of why people were single and what it was like to be single. These common sense thoughts resulted in stereotypes, epitomized in such terms as "old maid," "mamma's boy," the lonely individual, and the "swinger." This study provides information concerning the question, "Are singles lonelier and more sexually active than marrieds?"

The stereotype on loneliness was shown to be mostly true; that is, more singles than marrieds felt conspicuous about entering a restaurant alone and more felt apprehensive in regards to entering an empty room. More of them also had no one with whom to share happy and sad moments and no one with whom to discuss their problems. These findings may be construed by the non-sociologist as trumpeting the obvious. However, the degree of difference between the two married categories was not so obvious, nor was the large contrast in lonely expressions between the never-married and the divorced, nor the fact that relatively large numbers of the married also felt these facets of loneliness. In sum, the loneliness stereotype is not a general feeling for all singles, or even most singles and so it is limited as a description of feelings among singles.

Depending on your point of view, the other stereotype of sexual "swinging" was shown to be upheld if utilizing a public stereotype which indicates that singles have more sexual partners. However, the stereotype as applied to singles is a fantasy stereotype regarding the behavior of singles and not one in which singles are compared to marrieds. In this sense, the stereotype was shown to be limited to less than 20% of the singles and was shown to be more a phenomenon of the divorced rather than a situation of singles versus married behavior. Finally, the very limited number of significant differences found on a gender or age basis, reveals these findings to be a difference based on marital status, especially in regards to the divorced. In sum, if a person is sexually non-exclusive, the person is more likely to be divorced. Also, any given single is unlikely to be a swinger; swingers are a minority and appear in all of the categories examined.

The findings indicate that there are distinct differences on various items among the categories of singles and to a somewhat lesser degree for the married categories as well. Thus, the stereotypes being applied to this population aggregate may, like most stereotypes, have a grain of truth, but their application to the total population of singles is more misleading than revealing and the resulting discrimination may be harmful.

These findings also raise questions as to how to deal with stereotypes of loneliness and sexual swinging. Perhaps it explains why singles are seemingly turning away from the bar scene and turning instead to organizations designed to fill their personal needs by providing closeness and insights into the problems of singles via small group discussions. Through further study, perhaps a seeming paradox can be answered: if singles—whether never married or divorced—are more lonely and do not seemingly enjoy their sexual freedom, then why have they chosen this status, that is, why are there such growing numbers?

References

Deegan, D. *The stereotype of the single woman in American novels*. New York: Octagon, 1969.
Libby, R. W. Creative singlehood as a sexual lifestyle: Beyond marriage as a right of passage. In B. I. Murstein (Ed.), *Exploring intimate life styles*. New York: Springer, 1978.
Games singles play. *Newsweek*, 1973, pp. 52–58.
Nye, F. I. Values, family and a changing society. *Journal of Marriage and the Family*, 1967, 29, 241–248.
Obrien, P. *The woman alone*. New York: Quadrangle, 1973.
Pollster visits nation's barometer. *Dayton Journal Herald*, June 22, 1976.
Skolnick, A. S., & Skolnick, J. H. (Eds.), *Family in transition*. Boston: Little, Brown, 1977.
Stein, P. J. *Single*. Englewood Cliffs, NJ: Prentice-Hall, 1976.
Webster's New World Dictionary of the American Language. Cleveland: World Publishing, 1964.
The ways 'singles' are changing the U.S. *U.S. News and World Reports*, January, 1977, p. 59.

Gays and Lesbians on Campus

Gerald C. Lubenow, Pamela Abramson, and Patricia King

I didn't realize I was a lesbian until I came to Mills. When I looked back, I was never with a man I really liked. I didn't know what to call the crushes I had on women. I didn't know what a lesbian was until I was with a woman who was one. We were spending a lot of time together, and one night she said to me, "I really like you. May I kiss you?" I knew right then what I wanted, and I came out pretty quickly on campus. I cut my hair in a butch. I told one roommate, and she gave me a big hug and told me that her younger sister was gay. My other roommate was not quite so overjoyed. She did not talk to me for three days.

—Woman student, 21, Mills College

I had never admitted my sexuality to myself until Gay and Lesbian Awareness Day, April 13, 1980. That was the first time I had any contact with another person I knew to be gay. I knew what I was. I was attracted to other boys. But gay men were always limp-wristed, lisping swishes who like lavender. That's not what I was. I'm not a caricature. I'm not a cartoon. At GLAD day I met real people who were well mannered, intelligent and interesting. And they were gay. And that's what I am.

—Michael Colantuono, 20, Harvard

Whether exploring the unknown, admitting the obvious or choosing heterosexuality, as the overwhelming majority still do, college students today are confronting the question of sexuality as never before. A growing number are living openly as homosexuals and they have formed a supportive subculture, particularly at large universities. Some lesbians feel so much a part of life at Smith College, the women's college in Northampton, Mass., that one of them says, "It's no longer a question of me being comfortable—it's a question of everyone else." Sometimes not everyone is; sexual tensions have begun to complicate life for straight students who want to let go of prejudice while holding tight to a sexual identity still being formed.

Choosing homosexuality still invites personal scorn and public skirmishes. When John Nowak's fraternity brothers at Michigan State University discovered he was gay, they threw him out of Delta Sigma Phi. His reinstatement battle has become the talk of East Lansing. Last year a superior court judge ruled that Georgetown University was in "unmistakable violation" of the District of Columbia Human Rights Act because it refused to give the same financial support to homosexual student organizations that it gives to other campus groups. (Georgetown's contention that it is exempt from the statute as a religious institution is currently being tested in court.) Recent state Supreme Court decisions also denied efforts by Florida state legislators and University of Oklahoma officials to block recognition of gay campus organizations.

The steady erosion of legal barriers has been accompanied by a more enlightened medical attitude that has discarded the notion of homosexuality as a mental illness. The unsurprising result: gays and lesbians seem to have fewer psychological problems. "Most gay students are clear they are gay and have been since puberty," says Nadja Gould, a clinical social worker at Harvard. "Gay students come in for counseling because they are homesick, or depressed or having romantic problems, not because they are gay." "If you are halfway out and people suspect you of being gay or lesbian, you have problems," adds a Yale lesbian. "But once you come out you have a feeling of community and solidarity."

Commonplace: Hundreds of gay groups operate on campuses around the country, providing everything from housing advice to incoming gay freshmen to an emerging old-boy network to place gay graduates. At the University of Wisconsin at Madison, gay events are as commonplace as the homecoming football game. Perhaps 1,000 gays and lesbians live openly on the 40,000-student campus, and "The United," a four-year-old gay-student organization and social-service agency, has 150 regular volunteers. Earlier this year 200 students from 30 schools gathered in San Francisco for the first Western regional gay-lesbian student conference; a Southwestern conference held its initial meeting in Baton Rouge. Lesbian issues are part of the formal training for every residence counselor in the Wellesley College dorms. Smith lists its lesbian organization alphabetically between junior ushers and life-guards in the college dictionary. A national gay Harvard alumni group held a reception for gay graduates at last year's commencement and plans to invite parents to a similar function this June.

In the apolitical '80s, gay organizations are often the most visible and active groups on campus, and their ability to turn out support makes them valued allies in campus coalitions. Gays and lesbians have set up tables in Harvard dining halls, passing out notices that read, "Why are lesbians and gay men eating in your dining hall? We always are. The only difference this time is that we have a sign." At Yale, lesbians regularly study at two tables in Sterling Library, one for smokers and one for nonsmokers.

On coed campuses, there are often separate organizations representing gay men and women because some lesbians think that gay men aren't sensitive to their concerns. One lesbian attributes the friction to the fact that gay men are "still men"; while they may not enjoy society's heterosexual privileges, they do have male privileges. Perhaps because they believe they have more to struggle for, lesbians tend to be more politically active than gay men, even though there are fewer acknowledged lesbians on campus. They are also more preoccupied with their own culture—women's poetry, music and literature—and they spend considerably more time than gay men discussing and exploring their sexual nature. "Men are taught to have sexualities," says Nancy, a Berkeley lesbian. "With women it's a whole different thing. We go through a long process of retrieving our sexuality."

Lesbians seem to be most comfortable and well organized at a handful of all-women colleges and women's schools that have recently gone coed. At Smith they are leaders in every aspect of campus life. They are head residents, captains of athletic temas, even Gold Key Guides, "those preppy-looking women with barrettes who show your father where the gym is during orientation," says one Smith student. At Mills, a small women's college in Oakland, Calif., several top officers in last year's student government were lesbians. Lesbians at both schools describe a climate of tolerance at the college and in the surrounding community that makes it easier to examine their sexuality. Northampton and Oakland both have thriving colonies of lesbian artists and intellectuals.

For some women, more so than for men, homosexual relations are just an experimental phase. Some lesbians on campus were not homosexual when they came to college and may not be after they leave. "Who knows, I might get married," says a former debutante at Smith who likes to point out that she came out twice. "But he would have to be a god." At Wellesley, where acknowledged lesbians are a tiny—and uneasy—minority, one senior says that even among some of the most outspoken lesbians, homosexuality is "not a real thought-out issue." Another woman, at the University of Massachusetts at Boston, refers to women who take "tourist trips through lesbianism." Even some lesbians complain that their life style has a fair amount of trendiness associated with it. Some lesbians at Smith say that straight women sometimes approach them if they want to "try it."

Few women talk about lesbianism as an exclusively sexual matter. "I get totally weirded out sleeping with a woman," says a lesbian who has had a few affairs. Most simply discover that they feel more comfortable, more natural and happier with women. "For years my women friends cared for me much more than my boyfriend," said a lesbian at Smith. "It took time to figure out what was going on."

Others say that they are lesbians for political as well as personal reasons. The most radical lesbians reject heterosexuality as the oppression of a male-dominated society and maintain that women who are not lesbians cannot be feminists. "You get the feeling that if you need men, you can't be a good feminist," says Ann, a straight student at Mills. Among some straight women at Smith, there is an aversion to describing themselves as feminists for fear of being labeled lesbians. For that reason, many stay away from the Women's Resource Center, a campus group that meets to discuss issues concerning women.

That lesbianism can be defined as whatever one chooses it to be creates understandable conflicts. "It forces you to be introspective, to think about yourself," says a Mills junior. "But if you come to grips with it, aren't you one step closer to it? I don't want to be a lesbian."

Gays and lesbians scoff at the notion that straights can be converted or even drift into homosexuality. But while the unease felt by straight students can hardly be compared to discrimination against gays, it is no less real and is likely to increase in an atmosphere of sexual ambiguity. "I'm tired of people coming up to me and saying, 'Hi, I'm gay'," says Debra, a Mills senior. "If it's so OK, why do they keep harping on it?" One Harvard woman says that "homosexuality is fine intellectually. But then you're confronted by it, and you don't know what your relationship is. You can't tell who's what anymore. It seems like soon it will be weird to be heterosexual."

Dinner

Parents are confronted with no less a problem, the "guess who's coming to dinner" phenomenon. Gay rights in the abstract is one thing, but a son or daughter bringing a homosexual friend home is something else. Parents often react badly, threatening to pull the student out of school or withdrawing support. "The problem with parents is that their intentions are good," says Jennie Rudolph, a self-confident Harvard lesbian. "They think your life will be miserable. But it's much more miserable pretending to be straight.

Whatever anguish parents feel, they are not demanding that college administrators reinstate strict regulation of students' private lives. Some officials worry that nondiscrimination against gays will be misinterpreted as support of homosexuality. "There is a feeling that if you are gay it's better to be out of the closet than in," says Harvard assistant dean Marlyn Lewis. "But if it appeared that the college thought this was a good way to live, we might encourage people to try on a form of behavior they would later abandon but never forget. It's not like dying your hair green to have classmates remember you were gay in your freshman year."

Many gays and lesbians are no longer content to be tolerated as eccentrics. They want to get their sexuality out in the open so they can get it out of the way. The problem, as both straight and gay students see it, is that college may be the closest thing to a perfect world that gays will ever find—prospective employers will not accept open homosexuality as easily as the lab partner in Bio 101 does. A gay professor of public policy at Berkeley is more confident; he argues that the number of gay students at some campuses is so large that "this group may just hold its identity in the larger world." In general gay men seem more confident than lesbians about their ability to succeed in a straight society. But even they acknowledge the concern of a Yale lesbian who says, "The fear we all have is of going out into the real world and back into the closet."

Acutely Personal

Learning to live with the gay revolution on campus inevitably poses a problem for many straight students. But in one unusual case at Harvard, the problem became acutely personal. NEWSWEEK'S *Pamela Abramson reports:*

They had known each other since high school, but it was when Alex and Ben (not their real names) both went off to Harvard in 1979 that their friendship flourished. They shared the same interests—from Third World politics to classical music—and often stayed up talking till dawn. "We were alike in every respect," said Alex, a preppy-looking junior. "Except one." Alex is gay. He has known it since he was 13, although he never had the nerve to tell Ben or anyone else. Eventually he decided he had to come out to his friend (he has not yet told his family). "Beyond a certain point," said the 20-year-old, "you have to share something that important. It's not fair to the other person."

It happened in the spring of their freshman year as a result of Gay and Lesbian Awareness Day on campus. One morning a poster appeared on

Ben's door: "Do you know that someone you care about is gay?" After running down a list of his friends and determining that none was gay, Ben dismissed the poster as propaganda. Meanwhile, Alex had been drafting a list of his own—twenty carefully selected questions and answers that he hoped would help him tell Ben the truth. That night Alex sat Ben down on a bench near the library. "Do you think Harvard has changed you?" he asked his friend. ". . . Do you think I have changed any?" Ben found the conversation confusing and somewhat pointless. Alex found it frustrating and unnerving. "I was really shaking," he recalls. "I choked on the word 'gay.' Finally I wimped out and said I was bisexual." It took another half hour of talk before Alex could tell the truth.

Ben felt betrayed—and foolish for not having figured it out. "I tried not to seem stunned, but it was a huge thing. I thought I knew him so well." He worried that his close friend might be attracted to him. "I didn't know how he saw me," said Ben. "You begin to see sexual overtones that might not really be there." Ben embarked on a "paranoid self-examination. If I like this guy so much, what does it say about me? I had no indication he was gay. Maybe I am, too." He became preoccupied with homosexuality and approached Alex with countless questions. ("How is it done?" "What are gay romances like?" "When did you first know you were gay?")

Alex took the time to explain, in great detail, what it was like to be gay. At first he also worried that Ben might think Alex wanted to be more than a friend. "We never actually talked about that," said Alex, "but it just sort of became clear that I didn't." Although it took about a month, Ben eventually accepted his friend for what he was. "A whole realm of reality opened up to me," he said. "We're really not all that different." Added Alex: "I didn't realize what a barrier it was until it had been lifted."

After the dust settled, the pair became roommates. Ben, who once worried that he would be labeled gay if he befriended Alex, could not care less now. "Once I'd examined myself and felt confident I was not gay," Ben said, "I could show affection for my friend and not have to apologize to anyone." Three more friends have since come out to Ben and, he says, thanks to Alex, "the surprise is getting less and less each time."

Chapter 11

The Family and Public Policy

The Family as a Child-Care Environment

Alison Clarke-Stewart

The following set of policy propositions derived from our review of research on child development is most directly linked to the focus of that review—namely, *the family*. Before going into these propositions, a few words of caution or clarification are necessary. There is a danger that some readers will interpret the propositions as a conservative plea to save the nuclear family at all costs since this is the optimal environment for rearing children. That is *not* the intention of the proposition. In fact, we have not examined literature that could lead to that inference. The research that was reviewed merely identified some characteristics of the most adequate kinds of environment and care for young children. However, it does seem true that *at present in our society* these conditions are most *likely* to occur within families. The "families" may be biological, adoptive, or self-chosen, but are small groups of people committed to the long-term care of their children. We are not claiming anything magical about "the family," but merely noting that in our society it is the most likely environment in which people will be decent and committed to each other and thus provide adequate child care. Research does suggest, however, that when outside pressures and environmental stresses act on the family this has an effect not only on children directly but also on the quality of child care that is provided. Research also shows that the number of families affected by these stressful circumstances—divorce, illegitimacy, urbanization, isolation, fragmentation, working mothers—is increasing from year to year (cf. Bronfenbrenner, 1975). Consequently, our propositions about the family take as their general theme urging, suggesting, and justifying services to provide supports that will help parents raise their children and give them satisfactory care.

A Child Should Be Helped to Develop a Secure Attachment to His or Her Parents, and Then, Increasingly, Be Given Opportunities to Interact with Other Adults and Children

During the infant's first year of life forming a *secure* "attachment" relation with another person—usually the mother—is important for development. The child's need for such a relationship has several implications for policy. First, we know that a necessary condition for the development of such an attachment is adequate positive, active interaction with a caregiver. We cannot yet specify precisely the limits of what is "adequate"— this would vary from baby to baby and caregiver to caregiver—but within the limits observed in normal families, the relation seems to be that the *more* interaction engaged in with *more* affection and *more* responsiveness the better. This suggests that the person who has primary responsibility for the infant's care (typically the parent or foster parent) should be encouraged to interact with the infant warmly and frequently, particularly when the baby expresses a social or physical need.

There is also evidence that attachment develops more easily if there are *few* caregivers and if the same ones *continue* for a substantial period of time. This is a situation that in our society is most often provided by parents in a stable family. Children who have been observed by researchers developed attachments in the first year most successfully in the environment provided by a small family which had enough time for frequent, regular, consistent, and positive interaction among family members. If parents behaved negatively and unresponsively to the child or if they were seldom available for interaction, secure attachments did not develop. Under the latter circumstances, when family care in the first year is not adequate or available, other arrangements for child care should be made. When an alternative child-care arrangement is used at this age, however, parents should be especially sensitive to the quality of their—limited—interaction with the child and to the quality of the care provided by the substitute caregiver. Because the quality of interaction more than the quantity affects the attachment relation, it is possible that even brief, regular, interactions with parents, as long as they are positive and responsive, may be sufficient for the development of the infant's attachment to the parents. This issue requires further research.

Although it is true that having too many different caregivers is detrimental to the development of optimal attachment, this does not mean that a child is best raised by one person alone. In fact, after a primary attachment relation has been established, it is necessary for further development that the child separate from that person and form other social relations. This is best achieved when the child interacts often with a variety of people. Therefore, after the child has developed a primary attachment in the first year, parents should be encouraged to share the child's care with other adults, to offer the child opportunities to interact with other adults and, later, with other children. Supportive services for families that are socially isolated might well include supplementary part-time child care—babysitters, parents' helpers, family day care, center day care, nursery school, or play groups.

As we have noted, when a strong relationship with the mother or other caregiver has developed, children often react negatively to separations from that person or to strangers who approach the child intrusively or when alone. Whenever separation from the mother is necessary (for example, if she has to work or be hospitalized, or if the child needs to be hospitalized), measures should be taken to minimize the painful effect on the child. This is especially important from about seven months to three years, when effects of such separation are most pronounced. Such measures to alleviate separation distress might include providing adequate substitute care, preferably in the child's own home so he or she is in at least familiar surroundings; introducing separation gradually so the child learns that the mother will return; allowing the child to visit the mother in the hospital or vice versa; and not leaving the child alone with a stranger (i.e., the substitute caregiver or babysitter) but having mother stay with them until the child gets to know the other person.

Although most research on the development of attachment has focused on mothers, there is evidence that children also form attachments to their fathers in the first year. There are clear advantages for a child in having two strong social relationships—particularly when circumstances necessitate the mother's absence, as in the reasons listed above. To foster children's attachment to their fathers, therefore, fathers also should be encouraged to participate actively and frequently in positive interaction with their infants.

Policy Should Also Promote the Parents' Attachment to the Baby from the Beginning

Adults, as well as infants, develop strong emotional attachments—one of particular significance being that of a mother to her baby. It is this attachment that allows mothers to tolerate the burdens of child rearing and to provide the loving care essential to children's development. Research suggests that the development of this attachment is associated with the birth, initial contact, and early care of the infant; the reciprocally interactive mother-child system clearly begins at the moment of birth, if not before. This has implications for at least three areas of policy: hospital maternity procedures, day-care arrangements, and employment practices.

To foster mutual mother-infant interaction and attachment, a "rooming-in" arrangement in the hospital, in which the newborn baby stays with the mother and is cared for by her rather than staying in a nursery, is supported by the data and is recommended as hospital policy unless there are prohibiting factors such as ill health or prematurity. The rooming-in arrangement should begin immediately after the birth. To facilitate a strong father-child relationship—and possible to strengthen the mother-father tie at the same time—we might also propose that fathers "room-in" too. If rooming-in for father is unfeasible, hospital visiting hours could provide the father with free access to mother and infant at any time of day or night (family-centered maternity care), whereas visiting by others than those likely to be significantly involved in the child's life would be strictly limited. Not only should mother and father be given free access to the newborn, however, they should also—at least with their first infant—be given some guidance in infant care by the medical staff. Since having mothers care for their infants would relieve nurses of some of their nursery chores, the nursing staff might have more time in a family-centered ward to counsel parents who wanted it.

An alternative to the rooming-in scheme, and one which might have economic advantages for parents, would be to provide supportive services for having babies delivered at home. These deliveries could be performed by professional midwives associated with hospitals. In that way, emergency medical services would be available if needed. Another supportive service might be the provision of inexpensive but trained "mother's helpers" who would aid (but not supplant) mothers during the first few days or weeks postpartum, thus permitting an earlier return home from the hospital and an easier recovery for the mother.

Research on parental attachment has also clear and important implications for parents' use of nonparental day care for their infants. Although the quality and continuity of caregiving in the first three months is not as critical for the *infant's* psychological development as care from then on (i.e., the effects of early deprivation are often reversible), this period may be more critical for the development of the *parent's* attachment to the infant. Consequently, full-time day care in the first three months would not ordinarily be advisable.

Finally, the research on early parent-child attachment has implications for employment practices. In particular, it suggests the value for family relations of maternity and paternity leaves. Leaves from work for both mothers and fathers would, ideally, occur at the same time, following the infant's birth, and last for at least a month for both parents and for a least three months for the parent who was to be the primary caregiver. By this time, the parent would surely be "hooked," and the development of strong bonds between parents and infant well established.

Services Should Be Provided to Help Parents Plan Their Families and Raise Their Children

No one family structure is "ideal" for children's development. But it is possible to discuss the likely pros or cons for children in different family structures. The small, intact nuclear family of two parents and two to four children represents the present modal American family. This structure gives children the opportunity to develop an attachment to one or two adults; it gives parents the opportunity to interact often with each child; it allows each parent some help with child care from another adult; and it provides a buffer for unstable or deviant care from one parent, since there is another parent to take over or to provide a balancing influence. The larger extended family, however, has the advantage of providing parents with additional help and guidance with child care, and of providing children with ready access to a variety of different people. Since most families in the United States today are small and without the support of resident relatives, one policy suggestion is that these nuclear families be provided with the additional services ordinarily offered by larger extended families, for instance, supplementary care and social contacts, and, for poor families, "hand-me-down" toys, books, and clothes.

Another suggestion related to family size and structure is that information about and resources for family planning be made more readily accessible to parents and potential parents. Such information could include not only medical advice about birth control, but also information about the *costs* of having children—monetary, practical, and psychological—as well as about the rewards and joy that children can provide. Guidelines for counseling on family size and composition might be derived from research showing that a small family with spacing of at least 3 or 4 years between children may be most encouraging to children's development, because of possible withdrawal, lack of, or competition for parental attention in a large family of closely spaced siblings; or even from research suggesting the advantages of boy-girl sibling combinations for the development of both children's nonstereotyped sex roles. Such counseling naturally would be done on a individual basis, taking into account the clients' personal and cultural values and goals. It would include examination of the clients' motivation for having children, and provision of information that would let them realistically appraise the costs and benefits of having children, so they could make an intelligent and informed decision about having children, when, and how many. Such a counseling service could be particularly valuable for young adults.

There is also research on the *parental* structure of families, which seems to suggest that for children's development, family functioning and climate are more important than the number of parents *per se*. The *lack* of a father (or mother) is not as bad as *having* a father (or mother) is good. However, in our society, two-parent families generally have advantages over one-parent families in terms of status, monetary resources, and division of labor. Moreover, when a single parent has to be both caretaker and breadwinner, this presents great difficulties that can be alleviated only by services to assist him or her either financially or with child care. In line with the suggestion that we propose multiple solutions to such complex problems, here, we might suggest *both* strategies: income support for single parents in any income redistribution scheme, and "homemaker services" to assist single parents with cleaning, housekeeping, laundry, and cooking, thus relieving the physical burdens of parenting. Many single parents, especially those who are divorced or, until very recently at least, unmarried, also face problems of reduction in social status and activities. They must struggle against resentment of the opposite sex, and ex-spouse, or the child. They must overcome isolation, self-doubt, and overprotection or overpermissiveness toward the child. Supportive services for "parents without partners," therefore, might include: psychological or psychiatric counseling to counteract hurt or rejection, social activities (parties, discussions, group activities, etc.) to alleviate loneliness, consciousness-raising activities with other parents without partners, and counseling or help (parent aides) directly oriented toward child care. If the single parent can share the burden of child care with another adult—who is not necessarily a spouse or even of the opposite sex—it will benefit both parent and child. For the parent, it provides relief from the tedium of child care and consultation about child-related problems; for the child, it may break a too-intense bond with the parent, and it provides another role model—another adult to interact with.

As we have just suggested, there are difficulties for parents and children associated with the single parent family. Raising children is a difficult and consuming task—and more so for one person than for two. Problems are more common in one-parent families and more difficult to overcome; such families need extra support. As well as proposing services to assist single parents, therefore, we should also think of ways of preventing families from breaking up unnecesarily, of supporting families in crisis. More ready access for parents to marital counseling services may be one way. This could be accomplished by making marital counseling a tax-deductible expense, by including it in the coverage of insurance or health plans, or by giving or increasing government subsidies to marital therapy clinics (for example, in Community Mental Health Centers). Another preventive measure would be to revise or avoid welfare regulations that make it more profitable for a family to live apart—or to fake living apart. A third strategy would be to give priority to parents with young children or parents in conflict when measures to relieve environmental stresses are recommended or enacted. These measures might include job training and job satisfaction programs, guaranteed income programs, promotion systems, and housing programs. Finally, we might increase public awareness about birth control, abortion, and adoption options for marrieds as well as unmarried parents.

The intention of the proposition and these suggestions about family counseling and family support, it must be stressed once more, is not to "preserve the institution of marriage" and "save the nuclear family," but rather to provide a variety of services to ease the stresses of parenting, prevent unnecessary family breakups, and allow parents of young children to *choose* whether to rear their children together or apart. Our primary goal, here, and elsewhere, is the provision of the best environments for the care of young children.

In the interests of that goal, other strategies for supporting families so they can better care for children can also be envisioned or devised. These, even more clearly than those already suggested, are beyond the domain of the research on child care that was reviewed. They are offered merely as some tentative suggestions of possible strategies for family support. We have no evidence for their relative effectiveness or feasibility—but would propose that all such possibilities be investigated, and then that those which are successful ultimately be made available to all parents who wish or need them.

Day Care

Although it is often viewed as a threat to family integrity, day care can also be seen as a support service for families. Specific suggestions for day-care policy and practice are discussed in a later section. Here, we would just point out that day care—of a variety of forms—can provide a valuable, indeed, often necessary, resource for families in which parents cannot or will not provide adequate and continuous child care.

Temporary (Crisis) Child Care

Such care often could be used even by normally well-functioning families; for example, when the mother is hospitalized. If adequate substitute care during this period is not available, children may suffer. Agencies might be established to provide trained substitute caregivers (like substitute school teachers) who would go into the child's home or, if necessary, take the child into their own home, on a temporary basis.

Child-Family Screening

Especially for parents who are worried about the progress of their child or the adequacy of their child care, a diagnostic screening service could provide support as well as evaluation. In addition to assessing children's development, and pointing out any problems in their intellectual, physical, or psychological development, the screening could include assessment of the child's social and material environment and identification of any major deficiencies there. Such a service could be made available and encouraged on a regular basis from the time a woman became pregnant until the children were grown.

Child-Development Specialists or Child-Care Counselors

These would be concerned and qualified adults who, at the request of the family or some other agency such as the school or a pediatrician, could observe family dynamics, provide a neutral setting for discussion of child-rearing problems among family members, and offer advice about solutions when asked. They would be neither social workers nor family therapists (although their training might be similar to those professionals), but a resource for normal families with difficulties or problems. Such problems might arise with the birth of a new baby, for example. A good way to introduce the service, therefore, would be in the hospital at the time of birth (or adoption) of the baby. Women suffering a depressive postpartum reaction might very well find the child-care counselor a valuable resource. Such counselors would not regard the family as "ill," would not be evaluating the family or controlling the welfare check; they would attempt to increase rather than undermine parents' confidence and competence.

Homemaker Services

These services would include cleaning, cooking (e.g., "meals on wheels"), laundering, child care, and occasional babysitting to relieve parents of some of the *physical* burdens of parenting. Services now available only for the affluent could be subsidized for middle- and low-income families by providing inexpensive help with such activities. Teenagers and senior citizens might be available to work as such "house-helpers" or "family aides."

Family Resource Center

A particularly interesting, but untested proposal—the family resource center—could be a place in the neighborhood, a telephone "hotline," a series of special public programs, or all of these. Its aim would be to offer a centralized service for all families, not just poor ones. Such a resource center might provide:

—information about local schools and day-care facilities (costs, admission criteria, evaluative descriptions, locations)
—diagnostic screening and testing of children
—access to other community social services, including referrals for therapy or health care, counseling for divorce, marital conflict, child custody, or family-planning
—educational programs for parents or expectant parents in child-care skills, nutrition, homemaking, consumerism, home repairs, etc.
—help in organizing parent groups or cooperative child-care facilities (day care, playgroups, babysitting cooperatives, etc.)
—advice concerning legal rights of parents, children, and families
—adoption and foster care referrals
—information about income supplements, food stamps, housing, etc.
—a welcome service for new neighbors
—organization or provision of temporary crisis care or occasional day care for children

—toy/book/film/curriculum library, particularly for materials for and about children and child care

—a service for child abuse—reporting, treatment, preventive programs

—training programs for child-care workers (family helpers, parent aids, day-care workers)

—organization or provision of homemaker services (laundry, meals-on-wheels, etc.)

Support Services, Work Practices, and Income Maintenance Should Be Provided for Mothers to Choose Whether They Want to Work or to Stay Home

Mothers of young children, in larger and larger numbers, are going to work—and will probably continue to do so. One survey shows, however, that even when mothers are working they still spend about the same amount of time on child care as when they are not employed. The outcome of this practice is probably often less adequate care—as mothers are tired from working all day—and less adequate work—since mothers still have to worry about parental and household responsibilities while one the job. It has also been observed that mothers who work are less able than those who do not work to participate in educational programs with their children. Policies to alleviate mothers' double burden would seem to be in order. These might include (a) provision of adequate services for supplementary child care (day care, etc.); (b) shorter work hours for mothers *and* fathers; (c) more opportunities for part-time employment for those who want it; (d) creative work schedules that permit extended periods off for parenting in the first few years of a child's life—"work now, nurture later" or "nurture now, work later" schemes—and reentry and retraining opportunities for parents who take advantage of such schemes; and (e) income support for mothers who wish to stay at home but cannot afford to. Since empirical data suggest that a mother's satisfaction with her role, whether it be at home or in the work force, is related to her behavior toward her children, giving women the option of staying home or working may be one way of increasing the likelihood of positive parenting. It should be noted, however, that the data for this generalization are merely correlational, and therefore, although it makes intuitive sense, the assumption that maternal role satisfaction necessarily leads to more positive child care is not strictly empirically based.

Fathers Should Be Encouraged to Spend More Time Parenting to Adopt a More Nurturant Role if They Choose to

The literature on families suggests that fathers are an underutilized resource for child care. When given the opportunity, many fathers are willing and able to interact with their infants and young children—but in "real life" apparently they seldom do. As women are entering the work force in greater numbers and, consequently, are less available as full-time caregivers, since children benefit from close relations with fathers who are accepting, nurturant, playful, and stimulating, and because a balance between the roles of mother and father (in which neither parent dominates the affection or discipline of the child) is beneficial for children's development, policies that allow and encourage fathers to take a more active role in caring for their children are indicated. Such policies need to be explored on a number of levels. First, we might explore ways of promoting a change in the attitude and values of American society so that such nurturing care would be perceived as appropriate for men to give as well as women. A public campaign might show how skilled men can be at caring for children in day-care centers, as babysitters, as "big brothers," as single parents, and in two-parent families in which the mothers work, for instance. Such a campaign could also stress the subjective experiences—of fun and frustration—for such male caregivers and the benefits of treating child care as a joint, cooperative venture between parents. A number of TV programs on the subject have already been aired, and some magazines now regularly include articles about fathers' experiences. These may reflect a promising trend toward increased participation of men in child care.

On a different level, classes in high school on child development, family life, or preparation for parenthood, should actively recruit and appeal to boys as well as girls. Similarly, prenatal classes for expectant parents, or postnatal programs for first-time parents, could include more information directed specifically to men—supporting, guiding, instructing, and preparing them for fatherhood. Hospital policies that allow the participation of fathers in the birth and early care of the infant could be encouraged more widely. This does seem to be a current trend, but there are still many hospitals that exclude fathers from the delivery room and impose restricted visiting hours. Finally, and perhaps most important, work schedules that allow fathers more time for their families could be explored (paternity leaves, etc.).

As well as generally spending less time with their children, fathers tend to behave differently from mothers when they do interact with their children. With preschool and school-aged children, mothers, traditionally, have been observed to be more expressive, warm, accepting, nurturant, and positive; fathers, more distant and controlling. To the extent that these different patterns of parental behavior are accurate and are the result of parents' behaving in sex-role stereotyped ways—because they think they're *supposed* to—programs or policies which would counteract such stereotypes and demonstrate increased role options would be valuable. Educational programs for parents might well include suggestions for fathers that encourage them to express their affection for their children and participate more in a non-disciplinary caregiving. It is not necessary, or even desirable, however, that mothers and fathers behave identically toward their children. Observation of some variety in adult roles and behavior—if not vastly unbalanced or inconsistent in intention—is beneficial for children's development. Moreover, families, like small groups, may be more productive or harmonious when they have a "social leader" and a "task leader." What should perhaps be avoided, however, is the parents' assumption of markedly different responsibilities and rigid roles strictly on the basis of sex identity. It is perfectly reasonable that in some families the father might feel more comfortable with and therefore assume the relatively more nurturant role.

One of the critical ways in which mothers and fathers differ in their treatment of children is in the area of sex-role development. It has been observed that fathers tend to differentiate more sharply than mothers in their behavior toward girls and boys and in what they consider appropriate activities for each. If this means, as it often does, that fathers do not encourage boys to be expressive and nurturant or girls to be thoughtful and achieving, then any programs that promote the "liberation" of fathers' attitudes and behavior should be recommended.

Parent Education Programs Should Be Improved and Made Available to All Parents and Prospective Parents Who Want Them

Even if it were possible to relieve all environmental stresses, redistribute income equitably, and provide adequate wages, housing, health care, day care, legal care, consumer protection, schools or non-schools for all families, there would still be intrafamilial and interpersonal conflicts and inadequacies, and consequently a place for educational or therapeutic programs for parents. Here, we discuss various formats such programs might adopt.

Unfortunately, we do not yet know very effective ways of providing educational experiences to enhance parenting skills; we do know that some strategies are relatively less effective (cf. Bronfenbrenner, 1974; Horowitz & Paden, 1973). Group education programs for parents, such as lecture and group discussions—even if their children are involved, but especially if they are not—do not particularly attract parents, particularly less affluent, single, working parents with large families or personal problems. Nor are programs as likely to be attractive if parents are contacted by the school or agency rather than initiating that contact themselves. Moreover, programs which attempt to change parents' attitudes are typically not effective in producing that change. It is not surprising that any program, especially a discussion or lecture-type program, does not cause a radical shift in parents' feeling or attitude toward their children. Such profound changes are likely to evolve only gradually through experiencing repeated, rewarding interaction with the child. Similarly, simply *telling* a mother to change her attitude, feeling, or behavior does not produce marked change. At the very least, *demonstration* of the desired behavior, particularly of a more complex behavior, in *interaction* with a child is necessary.

The possibilites of preparental education courses in child development and family life as part of the high school curriculum have not been explored in depth. Particularly if accompanied by extensive practical experience with real children and real family problems, this would seem to be a promising way of reaching and educating prospective parents before the real burdens of parenting descend and before firm attitudes toward one's own children are established. Field experience could be gained in day-care or babysitting settings, with pupils' own families, or by simulated incidents in the classroom. Similar experiences could also be offered in adult education courses in child care and development, in prenatal programs for expectant parents, or at the "family resource center" described earlier. Another medium for parent education that deserves further exploration is television; creative programming here could effectively inform and advise parents about child-care skills.

Judging by results of past educational attempts to enhance the quality of parental child care, programs with the greatest probability of success in attracting parents and changing their behavior would likely involve:

—neighborhood or, better, home-based instruction
—parents' active involvement and participation in teaching or interacting with their own children
—specific, focused, interactional educational experiences for each child, presented individually, in a one-to-one situation
—goal-specific curricula (to date, curricula aimed specifically at children's cognitive or language skills have been most effectively communicated to parents. Curricula should be extended to include experiences that demonstrate to parents the need for being responsive to children's behavior as well as stimulating their senses)
—projects determined, planned, and carried out by parents themselves
—relatively long-term programs that continue instruction and maintain support
—small, intensive programs with a research/evaluation component

In general, it also seems likely that the optimal timing for such programs would be from the prenatal period through the first two or three years of the child's life. As well as being an important period in the child's development, this is a critical time for parents, a time in which they develop expectations about infants and parenting and find out if they were realistic, form initial attitudes toward the child, and evolve strategies and patterns of caregiving.

References

Bronfenbrenner, U. *Is early intervention effective? A report on longitudinal evaluations of pre-school programs.* [DHEW Publication No. (OHD) 74-25]. Washington: Department of Health, Education and Welfare, 1974.
Bronfenbrenner, U. The challenge of social change to public policy and developmental research. Paper presented at biennial meetings of the Society for Research in Child Development, Denver, April, 1975.

Horowitz, F. D., & Paden, L. Y. The effectiveness of environmental intervention programs. In B. M. Caldwell & H. N. Ricciuti (Eds.), *Review of child development research*. Volume 3. Chicago: University of Chicago Press, 1973. Pp. 331–402.

The Single Parent and Public Policy

Alvin L. Schorr and Phyllis Moen

The divorce rate in the United States is at an all time high; we are commonly said to have the highest divorce rate in the world. One result of this has been a striking increase in female-headed families; the number of divorced women heading families nearly tripled between 1960 and 1975 alone.[1] As a result, the number of children living in one-parent families increased by 60 percent in the last decade.[2] A number of quite different forces have contributed to these changes—the increased propensity of mothers without husbands to form separate families, women's increased labor force participation, and the spread of no-fault divorce.

Despite these changes, somewhere in their minds Americans still tend to hold a conventional view of the family as having two parents and two or three children. This conventional version of the family is so powerful that scholars, like citizens, label other family forms pejoratively—as "deviant," "broken," or "unstable."[3] Indeed, single parents label themselves as unique and "abnormal."[4] Nor are conventional views quite repudiated by minorities and the poor. On the contrary, while in some neighborhoods or subcultures half or more of all children live in single-parent families, their parents regard their single status as demonstrably normal on one hand and as evidence of failure and delinquency on the other.

Meanwhile, the traditional family—husband, wife, and children from the first marriage of the spouses—accounts for only 45 percent of American families.[5] The next most frequent types are the single-parent family (15 percent) and the nuclear-dyad—husband and wife alone without children (15 percent).

By the age of eighteen, nearly one out of two children will have lived a period of time with a single parent.[6] Meanwhile, the number of husband-wife families has begun to decline. At any moment in time, 25 to 30 percent of all children are in one-parent families.[7] The gap between the public image of the single-parent family and reality cannot be laid to a new situation we have not had

From *Social Policy*, Vol. 9, No. 5 (March/April 1979), pp. 15–21. Copyright 1979 by Social Policy Corporation. Reprinted by permission of the publisher, Social Policy Corporation, New York, N.Y. 10036.

time to recognize. It may be stipulated that conditions are changing, but they have been changing for a long time, and there was extensive foreshadowing of current patterns. There have, for hundreds of years, been single-parent families and considerable variation in family form, including the three-generation family, the commune, and the nuclear family. Early death of the father combined with an extended span of child-bearing has made the single-parent family fairly common in the twentieth century.[8]

The view that the single-parent family is unique and deviant has other elements bound up in it. Single parenthood is seen as a transitional state. For example, four out of five divorced and widowed persons remarry. Nevertheless, past the age of 30, a greater proportion remain single,[9] and the tendency to remarry appears now to be declining.[10] A recent longitudinal study of unmarried women who headed households found that fewer than one-fifth had married in a five-year period.[11] Single-parent families may live "as if" in a permanent state, whatever their futures may hold, though policy-makers may see their status as transitional.

Pathology is a prominent element of the public view of single parenthood. Although the term has come to be associated with the "Moynihan controversy" of 1965, in truth professionals and social agencies have long regarded single parenthood as pathological for reasons arising from their own backgrounds.[12] "Trained in the clinical model, [they] are conditioned to recognize pathology. While some attention in professional education may be given to preventive care and normal growth and development, the overriding emphasis is on the successful treatment and reversal of problems."[13] Against the background of this public image of single parenthood, policy has been couched in terms of improving the stability of existing intact families and services have been designed to facilitate the reconstitution of families.

Public discussion of the single-parent family in the last decade or two has come to overlap considerably with a discussion of Black family life and welfare. Consequently, the mainstream reality of single-parent families is hidden. A larger proportion of Black families than white families have single parents, 35 percent compared with 11 percent. For reasons that are all but obvious— single-parent families are usually headed by one wage-earner who is usually a woman and likely to earn less than a man—single-parent families are likely to rely on welfare. Still, a third of the women-headed, single-parent families never receive welfare.[14] The stereotype that recipients have simply resigned themselves to welfare has no relation to fact. Of seven million mothers who received welfare over a ten-year period, the typical woman was assisted for two years, left welfare, and eventually received it for two years more. Only 770,000 received welfare for nine or ten years.[15]

Generalizing inevitably leaves an impression of uniformity but the situation of single-parent families varies considerably. For example, single fathers may be in a markedly different position from single mothers. Though still a small minority, single fatherhood is increasing at a faster rate than families headed by women.[16] In part, this reflects changes in courtroom attitude toward custody, but also changing conceptions of the roles of men and women. As women have sought to define identities apart from that of wife and mother, so too have more men seen themselves in roles other than wage-earner.[17]

The most prominent difference is that single fathers command higher incomes. The average income of single mothers in 1973 was $6,000, compared to $12,000 for single fathers.[18] Though a single father's income may more easily permit him to buy housekeeping services, recent studies show that he too usually performs housekeeping duties—helped by his children.[19] Still, many of the stereotypes that constrain women also confine men. Since child care is not seen as their role, it is difficult for fathers to adjust their working hours to meet the needs of their children.[20] Although they report a need for services— child care in the evening, transportation to day care, and so forth —single fathers express feelings of success and satisfaction about parenting; in this they are like single mothers.[21]

Widows with children are a significantly different group from the divorced and separated. Less than a fifth are under 35 (compared with 55 percent of divorced and separated women with children). Possibly for that reason and because they usually receive Social Security benefits, their total income is substantially higher.[22] On the average, Black single-parent families are different from white. Black single mothers are twice as likely to have three children or more—30 out of 100 compared with 15 out of 100 for white single mothers. Black single parents are less likely than white to be working; they have higher unemployment rates, lower educational levels, and higher rates of poverty.[23]

One may attempt to classify single parents logically—as widowed, divorced, separated, and unmarried.[24] Such a distinction directs attention to the rather different causes and feelings that may be at play for the families. For example, death may be a more sudden and final blow. Separation may be a stage on the road to divorce. The unmarried mother faces more stigma, though possibly this is changing a little. She is likely to be younger than the others, and her financial difficulties even more serious. Unmarried mothers are becoming increasingly consequential, as one birth in seven in the United States is now illegitimate.[25]

In whatever ways they differ, however, all single parents suffer from public images of the ideal family.

Parenthood, Work, and Income

Closely linked to the image of the traditional two-parent family is an ideological stance concerning the proper division of labor within the family. Specifically, the male is thought of as the head of the household—the "breadwinner" of the family. Weitzman speaks of the "hidden contract" of marriage: 1) that the husband is the head of the household and responsible for economic support and 2) that the wife is responsible for child care.[26] Consequences of this role differentiation by sex are profound for women in general and especially painful for single mothers. Because women are viewed as marginal workers, they are given marginal jobs—low paying, low status, and insecure.[27]

Most of the wage differentials between men and women arise either from the smaller amount of labor market experience attained by women or from discrimination against women. The former arises directly from the hidden contract or the sexist assignment of roles. Discrimination arises indirectly and directly from the image of the male as provider.[28]

Because women earn 40 percent less than men, on the average, in every occupational category,[29] it is not surprising that in general the most important single determinant of a change in family economic well-being appears to be a change in family composition.[30] With divorce, the economic status of women relative to need goes down while that of men apparently goes up.[31] Three out of five poor children are in single-parent families.

One cannot explore single parenthood and work for women without becoming aware that work affects marital status and vice versa. More divorced than married women work and more work full time at every educational level.[32] Most divorced and separated mothers work a full year; others work less than a full year only because they have been laid off.[33] Conversely, the better a husband provides, the less likely is divorce.[34] Separation rates are twice as high among families where the husband experiences serious unemployment, suggesting that it is not the amount of income alone but its stability that is part of a decision to remain married or separate.[35] Studies of women's earnings produce quite consistent findings. As more women work, some postpone marriage and fewer get married in total.[36] Other things being equal, the higher a wife's earnings, the more likely that a couple will separate.[37] In short, a man's income tends to cement a marriage and a woman's tends to make dissolution possible.

It is important to remember that the amount of income alone does not equal financial security. For example, a study of women who had been divorced for up to two years found every woman saying that despite reduced income the family was better off financially. The researcher suggests that stability and control may have been more important than amount. Respondents said such things as, "I don't have much money to spend, but at least it's regular," and "Now I can buy things for the children."[38]

In any event, the problems concerning work for women are general and rooted in social arrangements broader than single parenthood. They have special impact for single parents but cannot be dealt with within that framework, nor avoided simply if single parenthood could be avoided.

Structured for time and commitment, jobs leave no more time for domestic activities to the mother than to the father. Hours are inflexible and long; few part-time jobs pay enough to support a family. Unless informal care is at hand, adequate, reliable, and inexpensive child care is rarely available. And institutions and businesses operate on the assumption that there are two parents, one of them free to carry on transactions during the day. As we noted the combined effect of working and mothering at once upon the income of single mothers, we now note the strain working creates for housekeeping and parenting. (The problem is felt by married mothers as well; half of them are employed.) If the parenting of single parents may suffer, part of the reason is that, like many mothers with husbands, they work outside the home.

A critical aspect for single parent and dual-worker families is that children are likely to be cared for by persons other than their parents. Implicit in the public image of poor parenting is the belief that small children spend their time in over-crowded institutional settings.[39] The fact is otherwise: Nine out of ten preschool children with working mothers spend their time in informal settings —with relatives, neighbors, or friends. Nor is that because congregate care is scarce, though to be sure it is. Single parents, poor parents, and welfare parents, like middle-class parents who live together, prefer informal care both because it appears to be better and is more practical.[40] As to congregate care, research reveals no effect on intellectual development but possible difficulty in emotional and social development. Studies have generally failed to distinguish between good and poor congregate care though and it is possible that studies of good care would produce different findings.[41] There is no body of research on the effects of informal care.

A modern view regards substitute care as a supplement to maternal care rather than as a substitute for it.[42] A considerable argument can be made for such a development as moderating the "hothouse" aspect of the mother and child bond and "shifting back towards a more natural *i.e., less confined and intense* way of life for both women and children"[43] Seen in this light, conflict is no longer so sharply drawn between maternal and substitute care. The questions about substitute care are no longer categorical: Is substitute care intrinsically a good or bad idea? What qualities are required in substitute care? What duration optimum? And so forth.

Single parents do, of course, face special circumstances. An asset in the two-parent home is the presence of another adult to provide consultation and support with respect to children.[44] "Parents . . . need to have other voices joined with theirs in transmitting values and maturity demands to their children."[45] Single parents may have no one to provide emotional support. The sense of failure which separation may have provoked may readily lead— without adult company and support—to feelings of isolation.[46] A British study reports these feelings as the main personal problem of single parents.[47] Conversely, children with single parents have access to fewer adults and tend to emphasize peer relationships.[48]

The presence or absence of both parents *per se* makes little difference in the adequacy of child-rearing[49] or the socialization of children.[50] There is no evidence that the absence of a father from the home has an effect on the child's sense of sex identity.[51] Single mothers hold the same values for their children as mothers with husbands.[52] A series of studies over the years has found more delinquency in unhappy intact homes than in single-parent ones.[53] In their famous study, Glueck and Glueck found the quality of maternal supervision more important for delinquency than the presence or absence of a man.[54]

"What scientific evidence there is suggests that divorce is often better (or at least less harmful) for children than an unhappy conflict-ridden marriage."[55]

What can one make of all this? Do strain and the absence of one parent or another not alter child-rearing noticeably and adversely? Perhaps the key point with respect to parenting is that the choice of the parents and children does not lie between a sound marriage and single parenthood. Happy couples rarely separate. The choice for many children lies between an unhappy home and a single parent. Parents themselves—though they commonly worry about the effects of a divorce on their children[56]—with experience come to think they have done well by them.[57]

To be sure, some children from single-parent homes pay a penalty, and curiously they may suffer more from maternal than paternal absence, since a single mother without family, friends or the money to purchase help often must deprive a child of her [58] company and attention; that is the deprivation the child feels most keenly.[58] This is consistent with the British finding that damage to school attainment and social adjustment, when they are observed, result from poverty rather than single parenthood itself.[59]

One final effect of single parenthood is relevant. Today, a higher proportion of children under five are living with only their mothers than ever before.[60] The number of children in institutions and in substitute families is declining. One reason is that children are remaining with single parents.[61] For children, single parenthood is an alternative not only to a two-parent family but to no family at all.

Of a sample of single mothers with preschool children, 72 percent had "a moderate or severe distress problem compared to 46 percent of 'married' mothers."[62] While this study shows the disadvantage of single-parent families, it is surely more important that half of the intact families have the same problem. If one starts with that as the basic issue, one can understand the reason why young mothers may feel exhaustion and depression and how single parenthood may add to the problem.[63] But the problem becomes general and not solely one of single parenthood. It is within that context that one must ask how society is to help single-parent families.

Public Image and Public Policy

The core of the argument here is that single-parent families are misrepresented to the public and to themselves. They have special problems and they may benefit from special institutional supports, but that is true of any number of groups otherwise regarded as normal and acceptable. The unemployed, veterans, and widows are examples at one end of the alphabet while single-parent families are statistically and historically in the American mainstream.

Yet the image is itself a powerful policy. The most moving effect of misrepresentation is that many single parents believe what is said of them and add that belief to the problems they face. Separation and divorce are a troubled if not stormy period and so the people involved are vulnerable. While separation is part of every married person's at least occasional speculation, and the actual event a crystal around which fantasies cling, the people involved usually blame themselves, adding normality to their worries about financial responsibility, judgment, concern about children, sexual responsibility, and self-worth. The stereotypes involved are about as legitimate as most that are involved in discriminatory behavior—and as destructive.

It is apparent that changing the image would imply broad changes in government, employment, and other policies. Conversely, such policies are potent in maintaining or altering the image. Each set of policy issues requires extensive exploration not possible here. An examination of these issues indicates the powerful and pervasive influence of the current image in our social arrangements.

If one sees women as normal and regular wage-earners, issues of sex discrimination in wages and occupational opportunity must be faced. Both work at home with children and at outside occupations must permit more flexibility. On one hand are questions of aids for child-care and homemaking, and also the operating assumption that shopping and transactions with physicians and utilities can be carried on in the middle of the day. The spread of single parenthood creates a demand that has moved some businesses to expanded hours, but professions and public utilities seem less sensitive. On the other hand are questions of the structuring of work and careers, the scheduling of employment, the feasibility of shared work, and the growth of part-time work.

Issues in income maintenance policy are similarly complex. The financial problem of the working poor, much debated in the last few years, is from another perspective an issue of single parenthood and minimum wages. That is, a single year-round minimum wage does not provide enough income to keep four people (a couple and two children, a single parent and three children, a grandmother, her daughter, and two children) out of poverty. Most industrial countries have tried to meet this problem by relatively small payments for all children. Americans have preferred to regard the issue as a welfare policy problem, seeing low-paid working people pitted against separated or unmarried women—though often enough they are the same people. If we see these two groups as sharing a problem rather than competing, the solution of a small subsidy for children to which other Western countries have come may seem appealing. The Earned Income Credit, recently introduced into the federal income tax, would, if improved in level and expanded to all children, serve quite well.

In implementation, policies that favor two-parent families are likely to operate to the disadvantage of single-parent families. For example, a woman with children might receive a higher payment from welfare compared with the family's entitlement if the husband were present. Obviously, the family needs more if the husband is not there. On the other hand, making equivalent payments to two-parent families would present costs that are impossible in the real world of limited resources. The result is commonly a smaller payment to the single-parent family than even the amount thought minimally necessary.

Regarding this issue, Isabel Sawhill has proposed an attempt to "define a neutral policy—that is one which would neither encourage [nor] discourage various kinds of family behavior such as marriage or child-bearing." She concludes that considerations such as equity and need make a quite neutral system unlikely.[64] Nevertheless, seeking a system that neither rewards nor penalizes family structure would open negotiation about program design in a way that might portend progress.* But it would be difficult to work at designing neutral programs while talking the language of a policy partisan to intact families.

Another direction to go in income maintenance, more special to single parenthood, is to recognize separation and divorce as social risks similar to the risk of being widowed. There have been proposals to establish a program of "fatherless child insurance"—or "single-parent insurance"—along lines well understood in Social Security. As single parenthood is voluntary, when compared with being widowed, careful design is required but appears to be feasible.[65] In one conception, such programs may be taken as supplementing income that would otherwise be inadequate. In another conception, one may argue that it is sound and constructive for one of the single parents to remain in the traditional role of homemaker, and not to work. The same programs providing "income by right," with possibly larger payments, would enable them to do this.[66] More conservatively and more limited, it has been argued that even if income is not provided, at least the government should provide credit towards Social Security for the work implicit in homemaking.[67]

The issue of parental support of children when there is marital separation is not, by any means, simply a welfare issue. "The primary purpose of child support laws is the protection of the public purse,"[68] but with respect to non-welfare families, the primary issue is one of family law. Courts and administrative agencies are likely to be more lenient in securing support than the law might seem to require. Each state has a welfare standard, a non-welfare standard or understanding, the understanding that will really be enforced, and the agreements that result from the pressures and evasive tactics that husband and wife can bring to bear. There is no general social contract to which courts, agencies, or couples (if they wish to avoid dispute or exploitation of one another) can refer. In this absence of public agreement, as always, the weakest and poorest suffer most.

A Change in Outlook

In this field, the development of a reasonable set of ideas that might lead to consensus would be a giant step for single "mankind." It is a difficult

---

*As an example of recent confusion, in pressing their welfare reforms Presidents Nixon and Carter both said that welfare encourages family breakup. If the observation is accurate, which is doubtful despite the chorus to the contrary, both sets of proposals would still have provided an incentive to separation. That is, they would have allowed more income in total to a separated husband and mother with children than to the intact family.

problem, for it involves reconciling concepts as old as common law with twentieth century reality; and balancing the rights and needs of a wage earner and, chances are, the wage earner's new family against those of the family that is being left; all in a context in which everyone's standard of living is at risk of declining.

The delivery of social services contains its own complex set of issues. Counsellors, for example, need to approach giving help in terms of managing the transition from a marital to a post-marital way of life.[69] Underlying this is professional acceptance that marital separation is a normal transition, a statement that may sound disarmingly simple but requires a profound change in professional point of view. Similarly, if single parenthood is regarded as a normal way of life, practical aids and supports must assume a degree of importance they have possibly not been accorded by social agencies. Day care for children has received a good deal of public attention; we have noted that the single-parent family seems to prefer and have good practical reason for using informal and neighborhood arrangements rather than the congregate care that has been extensively discussed. Beyond this, service organizations attentive to their clients should help them to secure reasonable aid or arrangements from employers, public schools, hospitals, and other institutions. Once again, a more profound change in posture is implied than may have been indicated at first.

With or without the aid of established organizations, it would be constructive to see self-generated groups of single parents organize. In the nature of single parenthood, individuals tend to move in and out of such groups. Nevertheless, they provide a means for sharing experience, moderating the sense of loneliness from which single parents may suffer, and reinforcing their sense of self-esteem. Under certain circumstances such groups can exercise broad influence in securing the social changes that may be important.[70]

Employment, income maintenance, child support, and social services present relatively self-evident issues, but when we grasp the broad changes that have swept over us, other issues will also appear. For example, it seems possible that single parents are living in housing designed for other times. That is, the basic design of apartments and houses was long since established for large families and other two-parent families. While the basic design has been modified to suit smaller families and new construction methods and to meet exigencies of cost and financing, those modifications have been mechanical, not functional—that is, fewer bedrooms, room sizes scaled down, and rooms devoted to certain functions (the dining room, the kitchen) in some cases made rudimentary. However, housing is not designed for one-parent family living. Preparing food and dining may be a unitary activity and more significant for single parents than for others; it may be that a single larger room would serve them better than the conventional kitchen and dining room. Again, it may be that two combination bedroom-work (or play) rooms would serve a parent and child better than the conventional two bedrooms and a living room.[71] Such issues will not be raised until we think of single parenthood as normal rather than marginal. Then designs may be worked out, money ventured, and the judgment of the market cast.

A good deal more thought is required about the issues related to single parents. This discussion is simply intended to indicate how issues change focus if one views single parenthood as a normal and permanent feature of our social landscape.

Notes

1. Allyson Sherman Grossman, "The Labor Force Patterns of Divorced and Separated Women," *Monthly Labor Review* 16 (1977) p. 50.
2. Isabel Sawhill, Gerald E. Peabody, Carol Jones, and Steven Caldwell, *Income Transfers and Family Structure* (Washington, D.C.: The Urban Institute, 1975).
3. Ruth Brandwein, Carol Brown, and Elizabeth Maury Fox, "Women and Children Last: The Social Situation of Divorced Mothers and Their Families," *Journal of Marriage and the Family* 36 (1974), pp. 488–489.
4. William J. Goode, "Economic Factors and Marital Stability," *American Sociological Review* 16 (1951); Robert S. Weiss, *Marital Separation* (New York: Basic Books, 1975).
5. Marvin B. Sussman, "Family Systems in the 1970s: Analysis, Policies and Programs," *The Annals of the American Academy* 396 (July 1971), p. 38.
6. Martin Rein and Lee Rainwater, *The Welfare Class and Welfare* (Cambridge, Mass.: Joint Center for Urban Studies, 1977); Mary Jo Bane, "Marital Disruption and the lives of Children," *Journal of Social Issues* 32, no. 1 (1976), pp. 103–109.
7. Bane, *ibid.*
8. Tamara Hareven, "Family Time and Historical Time," *Daedalus* (Spring 1977), pp. 57–70.
9. Hugh Carter and Paul C. Glick, *Marriage and Divorce: A Social and Economic Study* (Cambridge: Harvard University Press, 1970); Paul C. Glick, "A Demographer Looks at American Families," *Journal of Marriage and the Family* 15 (1975), p. 26.
10. A. J. Norton and P. C. Glick, "Marital Instability: Past, Present and Future," *Journal of Social Issues* 32, no. 1 (1976), pp. 5–19.
11. Greg J. Duncan, "Unmarried Heads of Households and Marriage," in Greg J. Duncan and James N. Morgan (eds.) *Five Thousand American Families—Patterns of Economic Progress* (Ann Arbor, Mich.: Institute for Social Research, 1977).
12. Daniel P. Moynihan, *The Negro Family: The Case for National Action* (Washington, D.C.: U.S. Department of Labor, 1965).
13. Robert Moroney, *The Family and the State: Considerations for Social Play* (London: Longman, 1976).
14. Lee Rainwater, *Welfare and Working Mothers* (Cambridge, Mass.: Joint Center for Urban Studies, 1977).
15. Rein and Rainwater, *op. cit.*
16. Dennis K. Orthner, Terry Brown, and Dennis Ferguson, "Single-Parent Fatherhood: An Emerging Family Life Style," *The Family Coordinator* (October 1976), pp. 429–437.
17. Danile D. Molinoff, "Life With Father," *New York Times Magazine* (May 22, 1977), p. 13.
18. Isabel V. Sawhill, "Discrimination and Poverty Among Women Who Head Families," *Signs* no. 1–3 (1976), pp. 201–221.
19. Brandwein, *op. cit.*; Orthner et al., *op. cit.*; Gassner and Taylor, *op. cit.*
20. James Levine, *Who Will Raise the Children? New Options for Fathers (and Mothers)* (Philadelphia: J.B. Lippincott, 1976).
21. Orthner, *op. cit.*; Gasser and Taylor, *op. cit.*
22. Lucy B. Mallan, "Young Widows and Their Children: A Comparative Report," *Social Security Bulletin* (May 1975).
23. J. Brubacher and W. Rudy, *Higher Education in Transition: A History of American Colleges and Universities,* 1636–1968 (New York: Harper and Row, 1968), pp. 13–14.
24. Benjamin Schlesinger, *The One-Parent Family: Perspectives and Annotated Bibliography* (Toronto: University of Toronto, 1975).

25. Reynolds Farley and Suzanne Bianchi, "Demographic Aspects of Family Structure Among Blacks: A Look at Data a Decade After the Moynihan Report." Paper presented at the American Sociological Association; Chicago, Illinois; 1971.
26. L. J. Weitzman, "To Love, Honor, and Obey: Traditional Legal Marriage and Alternative Family Forms," *The Family Coordinator* 24 (1975).
27. Edward Gross, "Plus ça Change?: The Sexual Structure of Occupations Over Time," *Social Problems* 16 (1968), pp. 198–208.
28. Erik Gronseth, "The Breadwinner Trap," in *The Future of the Family* (New York: Simon and Schuster, 1972), pp. 175–191; Erik Gronseth, "The Husband-Provider Role: A Critical Appraisal," in Andree Michel (ed.), *Family Issues of Employed Women in Europe and America* (Leiden: E.J. Brill, 1971).
29. U.S. Department of Labor, *The Earnings Gap Between Women and Men* (Washington, D.C.: U.S. Government Printing Office, 1976).
30. Greg J. Duncan and James W. Morgan, *Five Thousand American Families—Patterns of Economic Progress,* vol. V (Ann Arbor: Institute of Social Research, 1977).
31. Saul Hoffman and John Holmes, "Husbands, Wives and Divorce," in Greg J. Duncan and James N. Morgan (eds.), *Five Thousand American Families—Patterns of Economic Progress,* vol. IV (Ann Arbor: Institute for Social Research, 1976).
32. Grossman, *op. cit.*
33. *Ibid* and Beverly Johnson McEaddy, "Women Who Head Families: A Socioeconomic Analysis," *Monthly Labor Review* (June 1976).
34. Carter and Glick, *op. cit.*; Goode, *op. cit.*
35. Heather Ross and Isabel Sawhill, *Time of Transition: The Growth of Families Headed by Women* (Washington, D.C.: The Urban Institute, 1975).
36. S. G. Johnson, "The Impact of Women's Liberation on Marriage, Divorce, and Family Life-Style," In C. B. Lloyd (ed.), *Sex Discrimination and the Division of Labor* (New York: Columbia University Press); F. B. Santos, "The Economics of Marital Status," in C. Lloyd (ed.), *Sex Discrimination and Division of Labor* (New York: Columbia University Press).
37. Sawhill, *op. cit.*
38. Goode, *op. cit.*
39. Alice S. Rossi, "A Biosocial Perspective on Parenting," *Daedalus* (Spring 1977).
40. Suzanne H. Woolsey, "Pied Piper Politics and the Child Care Debate." *Daedalus* (Spring 1977), pp. 127–146; Arthur C. Emlen and Joseph B. Perry, "Child-Care Arrangements," in Hoffman and Nye (eds.), *Working Mothers* (San Francisco: Jossey-Bass, 1974).
41. Urie Bronfenbrenner, "Research on the Effects of Daycare on Child Development," in *Toward a National Policy for Children and Families* (Washington, D.C.: National Academy of Sciences, 1976).
42. B. Caldwell, "Infant Day Care—The Outcasts Gain Respectability," in P. Roby (ed.), *Child Care—Who Cares? Foreign and Domestic Infant and Early Childhood Development Policies* (New York: Basic Books, 1973).
43. Alice S. Rossi, "A Biosocial Perspective on Parenting," *Daedalus* (Spring 1977).
44. Ruth Brandwein, Carol Brown, and Elizabeth Maury Fox "Women and Children Last: The Social Situation of Divorced Mothers and Their Families," *Journal of Marriage and the Family* 36 (1974), pp. 488–489.
45. Eleanor E. Maccoby, "Current Changes in the Family and Their Impact Upon the Socialization of Children." Paper presented at the American Sociological Association Meeting, 1977.
46. Maccoby, *op. cit.*; Weiss, *op. cit.*
47. Benjamin Schlesinger, "One-Parent Families in Great Britain," *The Family Coordinator* 26 (1977), pp. 139–141.
48. John C. Condry and M. A. Simon, "Characteristics of Peer and Adult-Oriented Children," *Journal of Marriage and the Family* 36 (1974), pp. 543–554.
49. Reuben Hill, "Social Stress on the Family," in Marvin Sussman (ed.), *Sourcebook in Marriage and the Family* (Boston: Houghton Mifflin, 1968).
50. Jane K. Burgess. "The Single-Parent Family: A Social and Sociological Problem," *The Family Coordinator* 9 (1970), pp. 137–144.
51. Maccoby, *op. cit.*
52. Louis Kriesberg, *Mothers in Poverty* (Chicago: Aldine, 1970).
53. Lee Burchinal, "Characteristics of Adolescents from Unbroken Homes and Reconstituted

Families," *Journal of Marriage and the Family* 26 (1964), pp. 44–51; Judson Landis, "The Trauma of Children When Parents Divorce," *Marriage and Family Living* 22 (1960), pp. 7–13; F. Ivan Nye, "Child Adjustment in Broken and in Unhappy Unbroken Homes," *Marriage and Family Living* 19 (1957), pp. 356–361.

54. Sheldon Glueck and Eleanor Glueck, *Family Environment and Delinquency* (Boston: Houghton Mifflin, 1962).

55. Kenneth Kenniston, *All Our Children* (Carnegie Council on Children, 1977); and *Toward a National Policy for Children and Families* (Washington, D.C.: National Academy of Sciences, 1976).

56. William J. Goode, *Women in Divorce* (New York: Free Press, 1956); Dennis Marsden, *Mothers Alone: Poverty and the Fatherless Family* (London: Penguin, 1969).

57. C. A. Brown, R. Feldberg, E. M. Fox, and J. Kohen, "Divorce: Chance of a New Lifetime," *Journal of Social Issues* 32 (1976), pp. 119–132.

58. Brandwein et al., *op. cit.*

59. Elsa Ferri, "Growing-Up in a One-Parent Family," *Concern* 20 (1976), pp. 7–10; Schlesinger, *op. cit.*

60. Farley and Bianchi, *op. cit.*

61. Ross and Sawhill, *op. cit.*

62. Peter Moss and Ian Plewis, "Mental Distress in Mothers of Pre-School Children in Inner London." Undated paper from the Tomas Coram Research Unit, University of London.

63. Alison Clarke-Stewart, *Child Care in the Family: A Review of Research and Some Propositions for Policy* (New York: Academic Press, 1977); J. A. Clausen and S. R. Clausen, "The Effect of Family Size on Parents and Children," in J. T. Fawcett (ed.), *Psychological Perspectives on Population* (New York: Key Book Services, 1972); N. Richman, "Depression in Mothers of Pre-School Children," *Journal of Child Psychology and Psychiatry* 17 (1976); Rossi, *op. cit.*

64. Sawhill, 1977, *op. cit.*

65. Irvin Garfinkel, "Testimony on Welfare Reform to State Senate Human Services Committee," in Madison, Wisconsin; August 15 and 16, 1978.

66. Heather Ross, "Poverty: Women and Children Last," in Jane Roberts Chapman and Margaret Gates (eds.), *Economic Independence for Women: The Foundation for Equal Rights* (Beverly Hills: Russell Sage, 1976).

67. "Working America." A report of a special task force to the Secretary of Health, Education, and Welfare (Cambridge: MIT Press, 1973).

68. James Kent, *Commentaries on American Law*, vol. 2 (New York: Da Capo, 1826).

69. Weiss, *op. cit.*

70. Michael J. Smith and Beth Moses, "Social Welfare Agencies and Social Reform Movements: The Case of the Single-Parent Family" (Community Service Society of New York, 1976).

71. Thelma Stackhouse, "Housing for One-Parent Families—Faddism or Favorable Options" (Community Service Society of New York, August 1975).

Family Adjustment to Unemployment

Louis A. Ferman and Mary C. Blehar

Almost any week even a casual reader of the financial section of the daily newspaper can find articles that note the closing of this or that business. Some of the "obituaries" are so brief that they are barely noticed amid the scanning of stock quotes and economic indicators. In bolder print, headlines peg the unemployment rate for the 1970s at around 6 percent for the foreseeable future. But what the articles and statistics fail to convey is the human reality of economic upheaval. For many Americans, job loss is much, much more than a single event in time. Rather it is an occurrence of monumental import. It starts them down a long road, the end of which promises nothing.

While American society is such that unemployment can knock at any door, some people are more at risk than others: minorities, women, and youths among them. Tradition, however, has given special attention to the problem of job loss for male heads of household, on the assumption that they are responsible not just for themselves, but also for dependents. Unemployment for a married man is not usually just a personal crisis. It is a family crisis as well.

Dr. Louis Ferman, Research Director of the Institute of Labor and Industrial Relations at the University of Michigan in Ann Arbor and Wayne State University, has been focusing his research on the plight of the unemployed family man. He is asking what happens when a man loses his job. Just what are his experiences and his reactions to them?

Ferman notes that the Recession of the mid-1970s touched many Americans, directly or indirectly. Because of its pervasive impact, large numbers of the Nation's adults became familiar with the institutional machinery that is called into play when a person ceases to be a member of the work force. Unemployment Insurance provides at least a temporary buffer against major economic setbacks. Employment agencies offer channels through which re-employment can be sought. Unions may provide assistance through special programs for members. Welfare offers relief for the truly destitute.

Psychological reactions to job loss are less clearly understood. In the case of a working man who is accustomed to defining himself in terms of his role as a "breadwinner," loss of this role can lead to profound depression, feelings of isolation from his fellows, and lack of hope for tomorrow.

Differences in reactions to job loss do exist. Some of these probably stem from fundamental differences in personality. Certain individuals are by nature optimists; others are pessimists. However influential they may be, personality variables are very difficult to measure, particularly on a large scale, whereas

From *Families Today: A Research Sampler on Families and Children*, Eunice Corfman, ed. NIMH Science Monograph #1, Vol. I, pp. 413–438.

differences in sheer availability and quality of social supports can be documented more readily by the industrial sociologist. In general, the more institutional aids available, the better the outlook for the worker following unemployment and during readjustment to a new job.

Ferman points out that *informal social systems* can play a supportive role in a man's adjustment to unemployment, a role that is as yet poorly understood but more important than one might suspect. Factors such as the amount of sympathy and help received from family and friends can probably mediate between impersonal institutions and the jobless person and have a considerable influence on personal well-being.

Currently, Ferman, recipient of an NIMH grant, is studying career patterns among unemployed blue collar workers in metropolitan Detroit. He is no novice in the field of industrial sociology. Describing himself as a psychological child of the Great Depression and its economic turmoil, he has been researching the area of unemployment for several years.

. . .

The Detroit Unemployment Study

The present NIMH-funded study Ferman and his colleagues are working on is both an informal hypothesis-testing and an hypothesis-generating one. By means of survey-interview techniques a substantial amount of data has been gathered on a large and heterogeneous group of recently unemployed persons in Detroit, Mich., during the mid-1970s. Preliminary hypotheses concerning the role of economic deprivation and various kinds of social support were foremost in the minds of Ferman and his associates when they planned the design; therefore, survey respondents were polled repeatedly over a 2-year period about their economic position and about the state of their health. What economic setbacks, if any, had they suffered? How far were they from their "ideal" economic status? How did they feel physically? (Blood pressure readings were taken on two occasions.) How much had they been sick since becoming unemployed? Were they taking any medicines? Did they have mood swings or periods of depression? How were families and friends responding to their plight? What specific things were they doing to help or hinder the respondents?

The longitudinal feature of the design permits Ferman to look at changes in behavior and feelings over time. Do people optimistically start out seeking reemployment only to become demoralized if time passes and they haven't found a job or the "right" job? Do they hit emotional peaks and troughs? Is there any predictability to these? Are they related systematically to events happening to the person in the social environment?

The sample is not a random one. Because of protection-of-privacy constraints imposed during the period of data collection, Ferman and his research colleagues could not obtain a master list of Unemployment Insurance recipients from which to draw names of potential participants. With much ingenuity and leg work, they solicited the recently unemployed by various means. They went door to door; they distributed flyers about their project in front of Detroit's Unemployment Office. The resultant group of approximately 500 participants consisted of former wage earners, both black and white, and included married men, women, and secondary wage earners (those living with families and not fulfilling a primary support role). All the participants have been interviewed in person and over the telephone a total of five times in a 24-month period commencing shortly after their job loss. Eventually, data analysis will provide information about each of the subgroups in the larger sample. At present, Ferman's initial analytical efforts have concentrated mainly on the large subgroup of white married men who are primary wage earners for their families. Because the sample is not a random one, it may not be generalizable to national samples of unemployed. However, it provides the opportunity for intensive studies of individuals who have evolved different adaptations to their unemployed status.

For instance, preliminary looks at the survey data indicated that married men could be categorized into groups based on their career patterns following the initial episode of job loss. To confirm or disconfirm the validity and usefulness of such categories and to discover personal and circumstantial correlates, Ferman and a research colleague, social anthropologist Leslie (Buzz) Dow, Jr., undertook intensive field studies of a small group of individuals. Dow identified three married men who fit into each of seven categories and who met certain criteria of race (white) and age (between 35 and 60). He then went into their homes and conducted detailed, repeated interviews. Dow not only asked the men about their economic condition but also about their subjective emotional reactions and about the reactions of their family and friends.

Ferman is using these many hours of recorded conversations to generate more tentative hypotheses about the role of social supports and personal attributes in adjustment to unemployment, and these hypotheses in turn will be tested in analyses in the large sample.

Hence, the study to date can be seen as having two major aspects: (1) survey data collection and analyses, and (2) intensive case studies. The preliminary findings of the survey guided efforts at more intensive work—work which in turn has generated yet more hypotheses about the causes and consequences of job loss. The intensive case studies are of special interest because they provide a detailed picture of the human aspect of unemployment, an aspect sometimes missed in survey research.

During interviews in Ann Arbor, Ferman and Dow talked about their findings. Dow explained his role in the study. Anthropologists, he said, are usually thought of as living in relatively simple social groups for purposes of observing behavior and cultural patterns. We are less accustomed to thinking of the anthropologist as going into our own ethnic niches in big cities and observing people who live there. But that is exactly what Dow did.

As a background to the discussion of Dow's field work, Ferman first described some characteristics of the general sample. Most people polled had economic buffers. If they were auto workers or in auto-related jobs, as many were, they received Supplemental Unemployment Benefits (SUB) as well as Unemployment Insurance (UI). Between the two, income was brought up to about 95 percent of its former level. Unlike the Depression unemployed, today's Detroiter is much less likely to be devastated financially because of job loss. Because economic deprivation was relatively mild for many in the sample, Ferman expects to find only a small percentage of really desperate psychological cases.

He also pointed out that most people started the unemployment episode with the expectation that they would be called back to their former jobs. As time passed, some of these optimistic predictions proved to be unfounded in fact. Then people began to be seriously unhappy, particularly if unemployment benefits were also depleted.

Ferman becomes emphatic on this point. "We began by thinking that the actual episode of job loss was the big trauma, but we were dead wrong. What we're finding is that job loss in many cases is only mildly traumatic compared to what follows—searching for new jobs, dashing of hopes that the old employer will call again, being rebuffed by new prospective employers. These are the events that try the patience and sanity of most workers."

When he took an initial look at the survey findings and at Dow's clinical reports, Ferman found that some social supports apparently were not very important in the overall picture. Neighborhood aid was reported by very few of Dow's men as having impact on thier lives, and workplace supports were negligible. Ferman had in therory placed potential significance on these two systems as sources of support, but empirical results are not confirming the speculations. *The family*—nuclear and extended—comes through in Dow's work as the principal source of sustained emotional and functional support for the unemployed.

Ferman explained the goals set for the clinical interviews. They were: to identify the major factors that affected the experiences of the unemployed man and his family; to find out what personal attributes (i.e., age, previous income, number of dependents, skill level) influenced them; and to see which social support systems mattered.

The Seven Types of Unemployed Men

Type 1. Those Who Remain Unemployed After Job Loss

The first of the seven groups contained those who had remained unemployed since losing their last job. The men interviewed by Dow had been unemployed for 3 years at least. Who were they? Contrary to popular stereotype, they were not the very young and very unskilled. It would be unusual, Ferman stated, to find such young men, if able-bodied, out of work for so long. Even though joblessness among the latter group is high, the statistics are probably a bit inflated. Many young men may actually be working in the irregular economy, but because their earnings go unrecorded, they remain formally on the lists of those seeking jobs.

In Dow's case, it was the middle-aged and sick who didn't go back to work again. All three men Dow interviewed had developed disabilities that prevented them from working efficiently or at least diminished them in their employer's eyes.

The similarities between the three male heads of household who fit career pattern type 1 were striking. One of them, fictitiously called Michael Ronan, had worked for a corporation for 33 years and had planned to continue until the age of 60. Early in 1975, at the age of 56, however, he was laid off with 30-minute notice. He felt that the reasons for his layoff—which was really the equivalent of a permanent firing—were his status as a salaried person instead of a union member, a personality conflict with the plant manager, and most importantly, continuing ill health resulting from a severe ulcer condition. The latter problem was costing the company money since Ronan received pay despite frequent week-long stays in the hospital. Ronan was only briefly entitled to Unemployment Insurance benefits but was able to prove his ulcer condition to be work related. Thus, he has lived on Workman's Compensation and a small pension since 1975.

The other two ex-workers interviewed also suffered from illnesses. One had developed cancer of the larynx and has, since the operation, lived on disability benefits and his wife's salary from a full-time job. The third man suffered a heart attack. After his recovery, he had found it impossible to be rehired either by his former employer or any other.

All the other data available in the study suggest that these three men and the lives they lead are typical of elderly, skilled workers whose poor health conditions rob them of their last several years of potentially productive employment. The pattern indicated that a worker's health record, once questionable, becomes anathema to potential employers. Even those who recover completely from disabling disease seem dogged by it. Old age or illness, taken singly, are not usually sufficient to cause sustained unemployment; but in combination, they are almost insurmountable.

The men all felt keenly the frustration of having to lose years of income and most of all of their pensions because of events beyond their control. Even worse, each felt that his work situation had contributed to the health problem. They were bitter toward their former employers and toward the "system"—a bitterness fueled continually by shrinking incomes in the face of inflation. Even though the men had suffered illnesses that most people would consider catastrophic, Dow got the impression that sickness paled in comparison to the suffering caused by losing their jobs. The men expressed ultimate resignation to their plight, but their voices were filled with bitterness about the blind unfairness of life.

Type 2. Those Who Return to Work for Their Former Employers and Remain on the Job

The second pattern consisted of unemployment followed by return to work at the former job. The three individuals in the case study who fit this pattern were unemployed in 1975. In a 1976 questionnaire, Ferman and Dow learned that they had been subsequently rehired by their former employers. By the time of the interviews in the summer and fall of 1977, all three had been working steadily for more than a year. In each case, the men had done a lot of thinking about the impact of the unemployment period and were eager to communicate their thoughts to someone.

One man, Brian Canter, began working for Ford Motor Company in December 1973 and was laid off in November 1974. A college graduate, he has held a highly skilled job both before and after an 11-month period of unemployment. He worked as an experimental parts director, inspecting parts put into engines used in the development of automotive designs. Since he was relatively new in his job at the time when the layoff came, Canter was not eligible for SUB (Supplemental Unemployment Benefits) and was forced to subsist primarily on Unemployment Compensation and his wife's income.

Like other men in the second group, Canter is a skilled worker, but his skills are not widely marketable. When unemployed, he had little hope of finding a job as good as the one he had had with Ford, so he spent only a nominal amount of time exploring avenues of formal employment. Instead, he and a friend started a very modest and off-the-record janitorial service and thus avoided payment of taxes, while they continued to collect Unemployment Insurance. Despite this small supplemental income, Canter still found it difficult to make payments on all the debts he had incurred while with Ford. He watched his savings disappear and his Unemployment Compensation end. He became increasingly depressed and despondent.

To Canter, being unemployed was without a doubt the worst experience of his life. He felt agony when he realized that his family could not maintain its former lifestyle, in spite of his efforts. Toward the end of the 11-month layoff, the strain on his marriage was, in his opinion, critical. Canter asserted that his health was also affected because of emotional and psychological strains. Since his return to work, however, both his ability to meet financial obligations and his personal life have improved dramatically.

The two other men interviewed experienced many of the same emotions as Canter. One, an older, skilled tool-and-die worker, was also worried about finances. While his physical health was not affected, his marriage was dealt a "mortal blow" by his job loss, and he and his wife divorced. The third man received SUB payments while out of work. With 95 percent of his pay not affected by his unemployed status, he was never subject to severe financial pressures. At first he even found his free time enjoyable, but after 2 months he became restless. His drinking increased, and the amount he spent on alcohol ate into the family's budget. Even though he has returned to work, his alcoholism continues unabated, and his wife is suing for a divorce.

Ferman puts forward some generalizations about this group. First, regardless of how stable income was, the men's personal security was affected by unemployment. Two of the men attributed most of their problems to lack of money but a third had money and still suffered. Personal relationships within the family seemed to deteriorate. In all three cases, there was an increase in marital strife. But, however difficult their situation may have been, the men in this group were better off by far than the men in group 3.

Type 3. Those Who Found a New Job and Remained Working at It

Of all the distinctive career patterns observed in the case histories, the third one has proven to be most fraught with peril for the men who follow it. Without exception, these workers believe that the layoff period has been the most difficult challenge of their lives. Also, without exception, each has adjusted to new employment with a determination never again to suffer the humiliation and defeat of losing both job and income.

The men in type 3 never had hopes of being re-employed at their former jobs. They were victims of firms or businesses that had gone bankrupt or companies whose increased automation made their skills obsolete. Accustomed as they were to steady employment, they found job loss extremely devastating to themselves and to their families.

The experience of Miguel Sanchez is a prototype of other men in the group. Sanchez had worked as a security guard until December 1974, when he began a period of unemployment that continued for 14 months. After searching for work throughout his layoff period, he was hired in February 1976 as a patcher in the heating department of the Great Lakes Steel Company, a job he had maintained for 1½ years at the time of the case interview.

Sanchez, his wife, and their three children lived through a series of crises during those 14 months between jobs. The family's only income was a small support payment Mrs. Sanchez received and the Unemployment Insurance benefits Sanchez was entitled to. After a year, however, these latter benefits expired, leaving the family without means to pay even modest bills. Shortly thereafter, they were "kicked out on the street" when their rent fell overdue. Their car was impounded. Prospects for the future seemed bleak indeed.

In the weeks that followed, Sanchez describes nightmares beyond comprehension as he searched for food and shelter for his family. When he finally was hired at his present position, he was a much relieved man. He still considers himself fortunate to have escaped even greater catastrophes while unemployed.

The second man, a middle-aged carpenter, lost his job "out of the clear blue sky." Because of his wife's new job as a secretary and his own unemployment insurance, however, he suffered relatively little economic deprivation. Nonetheless, he remembers the period out of work as one of profound problems. He drank more, ate more, slept more, and watched more TV, meanwhile enjoying all these activities less than before. He contemplated suicide more than once during his layoff period.

The third worker had experiences closely parallel to those of Miguel Sanchez. Because his wife worked and because they had no children, financial difficulties never were as insurmountable. Nonetheless, he did not escape emotional trauma. Particularly unsettling to him were loss of the "provider" role and having to take "handouts."

With all the men what was most disturbing was the increasing doubt that they would ever work again and the nagging realization that financial security might permanently elude them. Because they knew they would not be rehired by their former employers, they were pessimistic about ever being hired by any employer. This sense of hopelessness distinguished type-3 workers most readily from their type-2 counterparts. Uncertainty about the future for the men took perhaps as great a toll of human misery as did reduced income. Depression and anxiety were common experiences.

The men now report themselves as having recovered markedly from their symptoms, but each agrees that he is less optimistic, more cynical, and more thankful than ever that he is working.

Type 4. Those Who Have Been Periodically In and Out of Work With Their Former Employers

The fourth group of men were those who had been periodically in and out of work with their former employers. For each of the type-4 individuals interviewed, periods of work and joblessness were fairly predictable. They were also accompanied by SUB payments and rarely lasted for more than a few months. Economic deprivation was minimal. Under such conditions, unemployment came to resemble something closer to a vacation than a life crisis. Not every one of the type-4 men interviewed acknowledged unmitigated pleasure in being unemployed, but their reactions were so mild as to present an important alternative view to a usually dark picture.

Steve Zaiglin, a typical type 4, is a 29-year-old employee of Massy-Ferguson, a large Detroit producer of tractors and tractor accessories. His specific job involves spray-painting parts before assembly, labor he described as semi-skilled. Since starting work there in 1974, he has been laid off intermittently, an average of 2 ½ months during each year. For every year the layoffs have been spread over several 3-week intervals, each of which Zaiglin was able to anticipate by 2 months.

During a layoff, he received 95 percent of his normal pay plus the virtual guarantee that he would be called back to work. Not surprisingly, he referred to these periods as "the best of times." Far from presenting a threat to his security, unemployment offered him the opportunity to travel, relax, and spend time with his family, all luxuries that are unavailable to most holders of full-time jobs. The other two type-4 men didn't deviate much from Zaiglin in their patterns. One, when pressed to find an unpleasant aspect of his time out of work, mentioned jealousy directed toward him by friends of his who were working 40-hour weeks, yet earning comparable wages. At times he admitted to feelings of guilt that he was, in essence, "cheating the company," though for the most part these sentiments were overridden by his enthusiasm for his lifestyle, with its consequent reduced responsibilities and increased leisure time. The third worker didn't actually enjoy his periods of unemployment but admitted that economic penalties were few. What he disliked was having to spend so much time at home, since he believed that a man should spend only evenings and weekends with wife and children. However, he suffered no severe traumas in contrast to workers of types 1, 2, and 3.

It was after Dow's interview with the men of type 4 that he and Ferman became quite convinced that the unemployed were not homogeneous. The experiences of these men were very different from the others. Unemployment could be a pleasant interlude, a planned-for respite from the drudgery of 9-to-5 work, if a man was sure that he could work again, at will. It became a harrowing experience for the fellow who found his skills suddenly obsolete in the work force and who wasn't sure that he would meet with success in trying to get back in.

Type 5. Those Who Have Been Periodically In and Out of Work With One New Employer

The career pattern of type-5 workers was superficially similar to those in the fourth category in one way. Both types of men established patterns of employment, unemployment, and re-employment. In the case of type 5s, however, this pattern was established only after initial job loss from a first employer and subsequent re-employment with a new one, and type 5s rarely received SUB. Hence, it was unlikely that they had the financial flexibility necessary to pick and choose their next job.

This basic difference between the two types is illustrated by contrasting reactions to unemployment. Type 4s tended to view it as a slight bother at worst, a welcome vacation at best. Type 5s shared little of this attitude, since they had to struggle to supplement their Unemployment Insurance with some other form of income. While it is true that periods of unemployment for the type-5 worker might have been just as temporary and just as short as those experienced by type 4, the former's lack of SUB created an economic crisis seldom endured by the latter. Hence, unemployment was not a welcome respite. However, neither was it the agony of uncertainty faced by workers in the first three career patterns.

It is interesting to note that all three type-5 men interviewed by Dow were mechanics. This occupational similarity allowed them to engage in activities in the "irregular economy" which eased financial difficulties during periods of formal employment.

Jesse Wiley's career pattern exemplifies that of type-5 workers. Since losing his first job as a tool grinder over 15 years ago, Wiley has worked steadily with only temporary layoffs for a small Detroit tool-and-die company. During three layoffs he received no SUB and is entitled only to hospital insurance in addition to UI benefits.

Because he possesses skills as a mechanic, during periods of unemployment he works in the irregular economy and earns an income approaching 50 percent of his normal wages. This income, coupled with monthly unemployment checks, allows him and his family to continue in a lifestyle not radically different from the one they are used to. In short, adjustment made by the Wileys to unemployment is not as considerable as it would be were it not for the irregular economy. Not surprisingly, Wiley's overall response to his periods out of work is free of the trauma which appears virtually always to accompany a dramatic reduction in income.

Type 6. Those Who Have Been Periodically In and Out of Work With More Than One New Employer

The sixth career pattern illuminated in the larger survey study and examined more intensively in the case study was the most chaotic of all. Workers with this type of career history have not only experienced repeated layoffs, but each layoff followed a job with a different employer. Dow's three type-6 men revealed through their histories a variety of reasons for chronic unemployment, so that he and Ferman were left with little basis for generalization about the type. The following brief portraits of type-6 careers illustrate the extreme variability that exists.

Alan Ali, age 33, has worked for six different employers in a 14-year career. The jobs he has held range from stockman at a grocery store to mine worker in Arizona. In between jobs, Ali has worked sporadically as a handyman in the irregular economy, but with little success. He shows no signs of upward or downward job mobility, but remarkably he professes to be undiscouraged by his consistent failure to find work adequate to provide for his family. Not even qualified for Unemployment Insurance, Ali survives through the help of a welfare check. Although he expresses some concern over the emotional adjustment of his 9-year-old child to his father's unemployment and laments the debilitating effects of unemployment on his physical strength (an asset in many jobs he finds), his own adjustment has not been characterized by personal trauma. He remains hopeful and patient.

Keith Laren, another type-6 worker, has a work history quite similar to Ali's. Laren has been through seven jobs in 7 years. Unlike Ali, he shows little inclination to change this career pattern for one more stable or permanent. Throughout the interviews, Laren repeated his motto that "Responsibility isn't worth the heartache." He has long ago exhausted UI benefits and is content with an income well below the poverty line. A job as a mechanic in the irregular economy and a part-time job held by his wife are the only sources of income the family has. Despite this, Laren boasts of great enjoyment of his lifestyle.

The third type-6 worker, a 61-year-old bricklayer, offers an example of why it is difficult to make any generalizations about this career group. James Sullivan is a specialized laborer who throughout the years chose to move from job to job in order to go after "big money." Consequently, he has often found himself out of work and, lacking entry into the irregular economy, has depended on UI and savings to tide his family over during these periods.

Unlike Ali and Laren, Sullivan has experienced shame and bitterness over his failure to provide for his family as he would have liked. Not only a loser of his gamble for higher earnings, he has also sacrificed the benefits of a company pension, insurance, health care, and perhaps most importantly, has given up the greater steadiness and security of a more conventional career. Though economic security is apparently unimportant to Ali and Laren it is crucial to Sullivan's sense of his own worth.

Because workers in the sixth career pattern are so different, Dow and Ferman have little in the way of generalization to offer. Perhaps the most that can be said is that such a work pattern should itself be divided into several subtypes, each of which warrants further observation. Indeed, in recognizing the oversimplification inherent in establishing any limited set of career patterns, they return to their original proposition: that unemployment is a multifaceted phenomenon and that each of its forms must be understood separately and independently before researchers will ever be able to grasp what it means to an individual when he loses his job.

Type 7. Those Whose Career Patterns Conform to None of the Above

A minority of the larger survey sample, 9.5 percent, had experienced work patterns so idiosyncratic as to defy attempts at classification. In selecting three individuals to interview in this catchall grouping, Ferman and Dow wanted to determine if career histories were really as distinctive as they seemed. The emergent data show that the cases are of importance precisely because they demonstrate the great variety of forms that unemployment and its consequence may take.

To give brief examples, the first type-7 worker, George Sampson, age 35, lost a position as a high school history teacher in 1975. The holder of an M.A. degree, he had hoped to remain employed permanently in teaching. During an otherwise arid year of unemployment, he taught as a substitute. Recently, however, he became so disillusioned about ever teaching again that he has taken up painting in the irregular economy. Currently he is planning to leave Detroit altogether and seek a teaching position with the Peace Corps in Algeria. Sampson's disappointments are not primarily financial, since his wife has worked steadily at a full-time job which has provided enough money for them and ther two children. What bothers him the most is the "humiliation of unemployment." He attributes several physical and emotional disorders he suffers from—overweight, insomnia, depression, and cynicism—to frustration and uncertainty.

Joseph Wininski illustrates another variety of unemployment. Wininski, now 59 and retired, quit his former job of 31 years with Chrysler Corporation because it was becoming increasingly onerous to him. He did so realizing that he was entitled to a modest pension which, together with a veteran's disability allowance, his wife's income, and their savings, allowed him to live comfortably even if he should never find another job. He never did. During the first interviews, Wininski professed to be seeking employment, but it soon became apparent that these efforts were at best halfhearted. At present, he says that he is wholly contented with his situation. Because he has a comfortable income available to him approximately 10 years before a more conventional retirement age of 63, Wininski opted for a work status that conforms officially to the category of unemployed but might more correctly be labeled voluntary early retirement.

The final case history of a worker whose career pattern was difficult to classify is that of Randy Jacobs. Jacobs' career has to some degree followed the type-2 pattern since he now has returned to work with a former employer and his remained on the job. What is unusual about his history is that he has worked for other employers in between. First employed as a machine repairman in 1970 by American Can, he continued there until he was laid off in 1974. Before returning to that company for work in 1977, Jacobs worked variously as a Dairy Queen manager and later as a retail salesman in a discount department store. The later two jobs were not sought merely as interim positions. Jacobs reports thinking about not returning to American Can, and he only took his present job because the offer included a pay raise. Unlike other type-2 workers, he had neither the desire to be rehired by his former employer nor the expectation that he ever would be.

As might be inferred from his attitude toward his former job, being unemployed was never a crisis for Jacobs. Dow found him to be one of those rare workers who genuinely enjoyed unemployment, even when it was accompanied by considerable economic sacrifice. His success in finding new jobs, coupled with savings and his wife's jobs, has enabled him to enjoy his time off as a pleasant, extended vacation. Throughout the interviews with Dow, he exulted that life had never treated him better than when he was unemployed, and he lamented his return to American Can. Like the other workers classified under type 7, Jacobs' case history reaffirms the broad range of responses to unemployment and suggests the need for analyzing other factors which mediate the individual's response to the loss of a job.

In generalizing about the findings of the case studies, Ferman noted that the individual's adjustment to unemployment is mediated in a most critical fashion by the postunemployment career pattern. Career pattern sets the background for being laid off and helps translate that event as quite stressful, relatively benign, or even welcome. This fact may be the study's single most important conclusion, for far too often unemployment is envisioned as a uniform, unicausal experience. On the contrary, from the case histories, it emerges clearly that unemployment's surest constant is its variation.

Within that variation, however, patterns of career histories hold much value for their ability to predict likely responses to unemployment. Where SUB is available, the worker is under little if any increased economic burden during his layoff and stands an excellent chance of weathering unemployment quite easily. Not surprisingly, the converse of the above is also true: The worker without SUB who suffers significant financial losses is most likely to succumb to the more destructive personal consequences of unemployment. Yet the picture is also complicated by the degree of certainty with which the worker is able to view the future. Those former employees who felt assured of re-employment were less prone to negative sentiments than those whose future remained uncertain. The analyses of career patterns suggest avoiding overly simplistic arguments regarding the obvious advantages of a stable income and propose an awareness of the vital influence of the worker's outlook toward his chances of finding another job.

.   .   .

Summing Up

When asked about the project's broad implications, Ferman began by making some generalizations: Today's unemployed are an extremely heterogeneous group to whom unemployment can mean different things. For some people, it is the start of a difficult and tenuous course of readjustment, for others a temporary pause, perhaps frustrating, even pleasurable, but one that is more or less defined as time limited. Those who have to live with uncertainty about tomorrow are those who suffer. Not knowing about the future invariably takes a major toll on the individual and his family.

Especially for workers with good prospects of future employment and those whose economic deprivation is minimal, unemployment is not equivalent in psychological impact to that suffered by millions of Americans during the Great Depression. Where economic deprivation is great, however, it is still at the root of many problems, such as psychological depression, loss of hope, alcoholism, and family disruption.

Compounding the effects of economic deprivation, loss of status as a breadwinner adds to personal shame and humiliation. Such emotions are felt most forcefully by older workers who attach a stigma to the unemployed status.

Despite the availability of transfer payment supports such as SUB and UI and opportunities for work in the irregular economy, the majority of unemployed workers appear to remain attached to the world of steady work. A good job is certainly one that pays well, but other facets are important. Chief among these is predictability of employment with its implicit certainty for the future. Dollars and cents so often appear to dominate economic discussions that we are apt to forget that money may be a means to an end of achieving a lifestyle buffered against economic downturns. Other aspects of regular work that make it appealing are overtime, fringe benefits, and personal challenges. Thus, even when supplemental payments from institutional sources and informal work opportunities are available, regular work is sought for its psychological benefits.

Of all the informal social supports studied by Ferman and his colleagues, the only one to emerge as having real significance is kin support. Blood relationships seem to convey a responsibility to give aid that neighboring and worker relationships do not. While sociologists have been wont to speak glowingly of the importance of neighborhood social networks in assisting the individual, they may have been overly zealous in their estimations, at least as far as the unemployed person is concerned.

If the family system is indeed the most critical informal one in mediating the effects of unemployment, it may also be the most difficult one to influence. Congressional fiat and Presidential orders alone cannot strengthen the quality of the family bonds. The forces affecting family cohesiveness are difficult to isolate. At times they are idosyncratic, often so general as to be intertwined with broad economic and social forces. Notions of what is "good" or "right" for the family are open to interpretation and are, at any rate, difficult to implement through systematic action.

When asked where his research fits in the larger scheme of things, Ferman refers to a book, *Mental Illness and the Economy*, which has served as an intellectual inspiration for much of his work. In it, author M. Harvey Brenner argued that a major source of increased mental disorders and serious diseases in the twentieth century was economic recession and depression. Ferman aspires to fill in Brenner's more general sketch with details. "I hope that my study will provide a picture of the impact of job loss on mental health and some idea of the family's role in influencing economically conditioned outcomes."

References

Aiken, M. T.; Ferman, L. A.; and Sheppard, H. *Economic Failure, Alienation and Extremism*. Ann Arbor, Mich.: The University of Michigan Press, 1968.

Angell, R. C. *The Family Encounters the Depression*. New York: Charles Scribner's Sons, 1936.

Bakke, E. W. *Citizens Without Work*. New Haven, Conn.: Yale University Press, 1940.

Brenner, M. H. *Mental Illness and the Economy*. Cambridge, Mass.: Harvard University Press, 1973.

Ferman, L. A., and Ferman, P. The underpinnings of the irregular economy. *Poverty and Human Resources Abstracts*. Beverly Hills: Sage Publications, March 1973.

Ferman, L. A. Sociological perspectives in unemployment research. In: Shostak, A. B., and Gomberg, W., eds. *Blue Collar World*. Englewood Cliffs, N.J.: Prentice-Hall, Inc., 1964. p. 512.

Ferman, L. A., and Aiken, M. T. The adjustment of older workers to job displacement. In: Shostak, A. B., and Gomberg, W., eds. *Blue Collar World*. Englewood Cliffs, N.J.: Prentice-Hall, Inc., 1964. pp. 493–498.

Ferman, L. A.; Berndt, L.; and Selo, E. "Analysis of the Irregular Economy: Cash Flow in the Informal Sector." A report to the Bureau of Employment and Training. Michigan Department of Labor. March 1978.

Gore, S. L. "The Influence of Social Support and Related Variables in Ameliorating the Consequences of Job Loss." Ph.D. Dissertation, Department of Sociology, University of Michigan, 1973.

Komarovsky, M. *The Unemployed Man and His Family*. New York: Holt, Rinehart and Winston, Inc. 1940.

Warren, Donald I. *Neighborhood and Community Contexts in Help Seeking, Problem Coping and Mental Health: Data Analysis Monograph*. Final unpublished report, U.S. Public Health Service, National Institute of Mental Health, Rockville, Md., August 31, 1976.

Families and Public Policy

*Mary C. Blehar**

Diverse Views of the Family

Different current conclusions concerning the health of the American family reflect a range of prevailing beliefs. In *All Our Children* (1977), Kenneth Keniston describes a popular "myth" about the family, that ideally it should be self-sufficient, insulated, almost autonomous, protecting offspring against the corrupting influences of the outside world. According to this myth, if the family fails, parents are at fault, and if it succeeds, they are to be praised. Keniston believes that this limited focus on individual parents is misplaced,

From *Families Today: A Research Sampler on Families and Children*, Eunice Corfman, ed. NIMH Science Monograph #1, Vol. II, pp. 971–976.
*National Institute of Mental Health.

since the causes of family success or failure are more complex and rooted deeply in economic and social conditions. He sees parents not as abdicating their responsibilities but as dethroned by forces they are hepless to alter.

Another view is provided by U.S. Census Bureau demographer Paul C. Glick who sees the quality of family life as improving. In a report entitled "The Future of the American Family" (1978), he casts recent social changes such as the postponement of marriage, lower birth rates, and the increased number of working mothers (lamented by many as a major reason for family decline) as responsible for *improvement* in the quality of family life. In his judgment, fewer offspring signify more time to appreciate each one, and the employment of women is a change of pace that makes the time that mothers spend with their children more enjoyable.

Differences in value judgments are also reflected in definitions that have been proposed of what a family actually is, a preliminary and apparently simple venture into family analysis. Most definitions make mention of two or more individuals related by blood, marriage, or adoption, as well as of other relationships that are continuing though unformalized. To stress the importance of extended family and kinship networks, and of the relationship between the individual and his or her relatives, most definitions do not require co-residence. While it may be argued that definitions of family have become so all encompassing as to be meaningless, and while ordinary use of the term most often implies a household with children, the care given to formulating definitions underscores the extreme sensitivity of the topic.

Despite disagreement about the state of the family and its definition, a consensus might be reached on three points: (1) the family is currently in a state of flux precipitated by economic and social pressures; (2) imperfect though it may be, it is difficult to imagine substituting an alternative that could perform all its functions as well; and (3) it is more desirable to bolster families than to attempt to supplant them with untried structures.

Views on Family Policy

The heterogeneity of the United States' population and the diversity of its interests have contributed to an historic pluralism and consequent difficulty in formulating comprehensive governmental responses to families and their needs. The very diversity that makes it so difficult to legislate any uniform *family policy* has, on the other hand, led to an appreciation of regional, cultural, and religious values represented by different family structures. Along with this respect for variety has come a call for returning to families the means for participating more directly in making decisions about matters directly affecting them, rather than having solutions generated at a more centralized level where sensitivity to the needs of various factions may be dulled by distance or disinterest. While the means for achieving this goal have been cast into liberal and conservative solutions (e.g., Keniston 1977 versus Berger and Neuhaus 1977), advocates of family "re-empowerment" agree on the desirability of the end.

In an analysis of family policy in 11 Western European countries (1978), and in the U.S., Canada, and Israel, Columbia University researchers Sheila Kamerman and Alfred Kahn point out that historically the very diversity of the United States' population has led to opposition to governmental interference in matters considered to be in the private domain. Foremost among these are family matters. While outsiders might intervene in families defined as deviant or failures, they should leave so-called "normal" familes alone. Governmental intervention was a last option after church and secular agency intervention had failed, and help was limited to the underclasses and the deviant, no matter how extensive the provision might become.

In *Government Structure Versus Family Policy*, Kahn, Kamerman and Dowling (1979) note a more recent trend toward increased societal responsibility for certain risks in life, a trend that has accelerated since the New Deal, along with a growth of governmental roles in protecting the individual against such threats as income loss and the consequences of retirement, old age, death of a wage earner, etc. While such policies may have had their most direct effect on individuals, they also indirectly affected families and tended to encompass a broader range of families than previously.

Hence, including "normal" families as proper subjects of governmental purview and action has been gaining increased respectability. In research and analysis has come a parallel "new" view of the family as one interdependent element in a system of interrelated structures. These structures, such as neighborhoods, churches, places of work, and, of course, Government, are seen as defining the boundary conditions within which personal family life is enacted. Consonant with this view is the notion that all elements in the system influence each other and that the family is a product, not only of the peculiar interactions of members' psyches, but of a social milieu. It has complex relationships with an ever-widening circle of related structures.

One result of this systems approach is a conservatism in the face of change. This caution stems both from an appreciation of how change may lead to a course of action that could bring about unintended and perhaps unwanted side-effects and from a realization that the complex, value-laden human context of change defies consensus about what changes are desirable.

Governmental policies have been cited for their unanticipated influence on the family. For example, when the Social Security program was instituted during the Roosevelt era, the average lifespan of a worker was shorter than today. Now the increased longevity of the population and the greater tax burden needed to fund the expanded program threaten to siphon off income from younger families at a time when they are trying to rear their own children in an inflation-ridden economy. Cash benefits aside, Social Security to the elderly provides them with a degree of independence seen by some as weakening the extended family by making it possible for aged parents to live apart from their children. Others view it as encouraging some older persons to live together rather than to marry, which may encourage the same pattern among younger family members.

A second example of the unanticipated influence of governmental actions on family life can be found in the effects of the so-called "marriage tax" levied on married earners of approximately equivalent amounts of income, who end up paying more in taxes than people earning similar amounts but merely living together. The marriage tax may have discouraged matrimony among young dual workers and allegedly has encouraged at least a few to divorce in order to avoid paying out more money to the Federal Government. This tax situation again underscores the difficulty encountered in legislating in value areas. While couple-based units are penalized, individual-based ones are favored, and arguments about the equity of either situation are difficult to resolve.

Hence, the promotion of value is present, implicitly or explicitly, in almost every institutional action taken by Government, by virtue of discouraging some reactions among citizens and encouraging others.

Because so many institutional actions influence family life, *family policies* can be conceived of existing at all levels of Government and even in the private sector. The Federal Government, because of its size and influence, is the greatest potential and actual effector of change. Tax policies concerned with home-mortgage deductions, credits for child care during periods of parental employment, and personal exemption allowances for dependents directly affect families. Less obviously, so do decisions to build four-lane highways, thereby limiting or increasing families' choices about where to live, work, play, or send their children to school. While Federal actions affect families, they affect some more than others. Legislation concerning aid for dependent children, Head Start programs, and school lunches influence lower-income groups most directly and have relatively less impact on middle- and upper-middle-income families, except insofar as their tax burden is increased to support the programs. Conversely, many aspects of tax policy benefit these latter groups disproportionately.

While a cursory analysis of Federal programs and legislation can uncover actions which have impact—direct or indirect, intended or inadvertent—on families, the issue of what the Federal role in family-policy formulation should be remains unresolved.

In their analysis of family policy in 14 countries, Kamerman and Kahn (1978) contrast two views of it—one as a *field*, and the other as a *perspective*. The first view is derived largely from the European experience, where governments have brought together measures, most often directed at disadvantaged and dependent families, and have assigned them to one or two related agencies, bureaus, or departments. Where family policy is a field, the authors find, it usually becomes a modest one, only attempting what can reasonably be integrated under one umbrella. Since so many aspects of Government affect families, myriad rules and regulations defy compartmentalization in one bureau or agency.

By contrast, the perspectival view of family policy would seek to develop a set of explicit criteria by which institutional actions are evaluated from the point of view of their potential family impact. While such a perspective could conceivably attempt to define specific goals and standards and attempt to shape family motives and behavior in a uniform fashion, the authors believe that this uniformity would meet with opposition from diverse segments of the American population. Rather, they conceive of a successful family perspective as one that avoids institutional acts of commission or omission that could harm families and one which protects individual environments in which children are raised and adults find fulfillment, meanwhile not imposing on families any one model, one mode, one pattern, or one value system (Kahn, Kamerman, and Dowling 1979).